Social Ontology and Modern Economics

T0313333

Economists increasingly recognise that engagement with social ontology – the study of the basic subject matter and constitution of social reality – can facilitate more relevant analysis. This growing recognition amongst economists of the importance of social ontology is due very considerably to the work of members of the *Cambridge Social Ontology Group*. This volume brings together important papers by members of this group, some previously unpublished, in a collection that reveals the breadth and vitality of this Cambridge project. It provides a brilliant introduction to the central themes explored, perspectives sustained, insights achieved and how the project is moving forward.

An initial set of papers examine how ontology is understood and justified within this Cambridge project and consider how it compares with prominent historical and contemporary alternatives. The majority of the included papers involve social ontological analysis being put to work directly in underlabouring for specific types of development in economics. The papers are grouped according to their contribution to clarifying and developing: (i) various competing traditions and projects of modern economics, (ii) history of thought contributions, (iii) methodological concerns, (iv) ethics and (v) conceptions of particular aspects of social reality, including money, gender, technology and institutions. Background to and a brief history of the Cambridge group is provided in the Introduction.

Social Ontology and Modern Economics will be of interest not only to economists but also philosophers of social science, social theorists and those eager to explore the nature of gender, social institutions and technology.

Stephen Pratten is Senior Lecturer, Department of Management, King's College London, UK.

Economics as Social Theory
Series edited by Tony Lawson
University of Cambridge

Social Theory is experiencing something of a revival within economics. Critical analyses of the particular nature of the subject matter of social studies, and of the types of method, categories and modes of explanation that can legitimately be endorsed for the scientific study of social objects, are re-emerging. Economists are again addressing such issues as the relationship between agency and structure, between economy and the rest of society, and between the enquirer and the object of enquiry. There is a renewed interest in elaborating basic categories such as causation, competition, culture, discrimination, evolution, money, need, order, organization, power, probability, process, rationality, technology, time, truth, uncertainty, value, etc.

The objective for this series is to facilitate this revival further. In contemporary economics, the label 'theory' has been appropriated by a group that confines itself to largely asocial, ahistorical, mathematical 'modelling'. *Economics as Social Theory* thus reclaims the 'theory' label, offering a platform for alternative rigorous, but broader and more critical, conceptions of theorizing.

Other titles in this series include:

Endorsements for *Social Ontology and Modern Economics*

'Economics has lost its way. Over many years the Cambridge Realism Workshop and the Social Ontology Group have tried to rectify this through systematic reflection on the basic structures of the social world. The papers in this collection demonstrate the richness and vitality of this approach, and its extraordinary range and interdisciplinary character. The authors offer a way of rethinking not just economics but social science for the twenty-first century.'

Andrew Gamble, University of Cambridge

'This collection of essays offers a profound and important contribution by the Cambridge Social Ontology Group to a deeper understanding of the foundations of economic thinking. They will be seen as exemplars should the economics profession ever think seriously about transcending the closed system view of an economy based on atomism and methodological individualism.'

Roy J. Rotheim, Skidmore College, New York

'This collection of eye-opening essays re-examines many of the basic concepts and standard research methods in economics. It offers essential building blocks and useful springboards for a fundamental reconstruction of economics.'

Ha-Joon Chang, University of Cambridge

'This volume collects significant contributions to the social ontology literature, and aptly illustrates the insights to be derived from taking ontology seriously. It is a fine collection and a perfect introduction to the Cambridge Social Ontology project.'

Bruce Caldwell, Duke University

Social Ontology and Modern Economics

Edited by Stephen Pratten

Routledge
Taylor & Francis Group

LONDON AND NEW YORK

First published 2015
by Routledge
2 Park Square, Milton Park, Abingdon, Oxon OX14 4RN

and by Routledge
711 Third Avenue, New York, NY 10017

Routledge is an imprint of the Taylor & Francis Group, an informa business

© 2015 selection and editorial material, Stephen Pratten; individual chapters, the contributors.

The right of the editor to be identified as the author of the editorial material, and of the authors for their individual chapters, has been asserted in accordance with sections 77 and 78 of the Copyright, Designs and Patents Act 1988.

All rights reserved. No part of this book may be reprinted or reproduced or utilised in any form or by any electronic, mechanical, or other means, now known or hereafter invented, including photocopying and recording, or in any information storage or retrieval system, without permission in writing from the publishers.

Trademark notice: Product or corporate names may be trademarks or registered trademarks, and are used only for identification and explanation without intent to infringe.

British Library Cataloguing in Publication Data
A catalogue record for this book is available from the British Library

Library of Congress Cataloguing in Publication Data
Social ontology and modern economics / edited by Stephen Pratten.
pages cm. -- (Economics as social theory)
1. Economics--Sociological aspects. 2. Ontology. 3. Phenomenological sociology. I. Pratten, Stephen.
HM548.S6145 2014
111--dc23
2014007488

ISBN: 978-0-415-85830-4 (hbk)
ISBN: 978-0-415-85829-8 (pbk)
ISBN: 978-1-315-78090-0 (ebk)

Typeset in Palatino
by GreenGate Publishing Services, Tonbridge, Kent

Printed and bound in the United States of America by Publishers Graphics, LLC on sustainably sourced paper.

Contents

Contributors

Vinca Bigo is an Associate Professor in Gender, Ethics and Leadership at KEDGE Business School in the South of France. She holds a PhD from Cambridge University. Her teaching commitments include Gender, Philosophy and Leadership. Her current research centres on ethics, the philosophy of science, leadership, responsibility, gender and diversity.

Philip Faulkner is a Fellow and Senior College Teaching Officer in Economics at Clare College, Cambridge, and a Fellow of the Cambridge Judge Business School. His research focuses on issues in social ontology, in particular the project of critical realism and the nature of technological objects. He is a co-editor of the *Cambridge Journal of Economics*, and has published on various topics in economics and organisational theory in journals including *Academy of Management Review* and *MIS Quarterly*.

Steve Fleetwood is Professor of Employment Relations and HRM in Bristol Business School, University of the West of England, Bristol. His research focuses on the philosophy of science and methodology as it is applied in social science, especially in organisation and management studies and economics.

Mário Graça Moura completed his undergraduate degree in Economics at Faculdade de Economia, Universidade do Porto, in 1989. He holds an M.Phil in Economics (1993) and a PhD (1998) from the University of Cambridge. He is currently Lecturer in Economics at Faculdade de Economia. His research interests include the history and methodology of economics.

John Latsis is currently Lecturer in Organisational Behaviour at Henley Business School, University of Reading. Before his lectureship, John was a graduate student in Cambridge and subsequently held a Junior Research Fellowship at Oxford and a visiting scholarship at Harvard. His research interests are in social theory and economic philosophy. They cover questions about the nature of conventional behaviour and rule following in social life, the influence of theory on economic action, and the socio-economic dimensions of human need. His recent publications include articles in the *Cambridge Journal of Economics*, the *Journal of Institutional Economics* and the *British Journal of Sociology*. He is also an editor of *Economic Thought*, a journal of the World Economics Association that focuses on the philosophy, methodology and history of economics.

Clive Lawson is a Fellow of Girton College, Cambridge, and Assistant Director of Studies at Gonville and Caius College, Cambridge. He has published on American institutionalist economics and regional economics. His current research is in the philosophy of technology. He is a co-editor of the *Cambridge Journal of Economics*.

Tony Lawson is a Reader in Economics at the University of Cambridge, currently a Professorial Research Fellow of the Independent Social Research Foundation and formerly a Director of the Cambridge Centre for Gender Studies. His books include *Economics and Reality* (1997) and *Reorienting Economics* (2003). He is a co-editor of the *Cambridge Journal of Economics*.

Paul Lewis was educated at Peterhouse, Cambridge, and Christ Church, Oxford. He was a Newton Trust Lecturer in the Faculty of Economics and Politics, and the Faculty of Social and Political Sciences, Cambridge University, and a Fellow of Emmanuel and Selwyn Colleges before becoming a Reader at King's College London. His research interests include the Austrian school of economics and the history and methodology of economics.

Nuno Martins is Lecturer in Economics at the University of the Azores, Portugal. He has published *The Cambridge Revival of Political Economy* (Routledge, 2014) and co-edited with Clive Lawson and John Latsis *Contributions to Social Ontology* (Routledge, 2007). His research interests are in the history and methodology of economics.

Leonidas Montes is Dean of the School of Government at Universidad Adolfo Ibáñez. He is the author of *Adam Smith in Context* (Palgrave, Macmillan, 2004) and several articles on Adam Smith and the Scottish Enlightenment, and is also co-editor, with Eric Schliesser, of *New Voices on Adam Smith* (Routledge, 2006). He was member of the Executive Committee of the History of Economics Society (HES), and currently is member of the Board of the International Adam Smith Society (IASS).

Stephen Pratten is Senior Lecturer in Economics in the Department of Management, King's College London. His current research interests are in social ontology, classical American pragmatism and the history of economic thought. He is Executive Editor of the *Cambridge Journal of Economics*.

Jochen Runde is Professor of Economics and Organisation at Cambridge Judge Business School, and Professorial Fellow at Girton College, Cambridge. His current research interests include social ontology and the ontology of technology, decision making under severe uncertainty, and causal explanation in the social sciences. He has written on various topics in economics and organisational theory, is co-author of the LiveEcon™ series of economics textbooks, and is co-editor of *Cambridge Journal of Economics*.

Acknowledgements

This collection brings together various contributions of members of the *Cambridge Social Ontology Group*. The papers included here reflect one stream of work undertaken by members of the group. The decision to focus on how sustained analysis and elaboration of issues in social ontology can deepen our understanding of modern economics has guided the choice of papers. The Cambridge Social Ontology Group is thoroughly interdisciplinary. Many members of the group are based outside of economics and have backgrounds in areas such as philosophy, anthropology, law, sociology, geography and gender studies. The insights of those within the group whose interests lie primarily outside of economics have been important to the ongoing discussions about social ontology that the weekly meetings of the group have facilitated and have, in turn, informed the arguments developed in the papers included in this volume.

The intellectual vitality of the group has over the years been enhanced not only by scholars from many different disciplines but also by a large number of visitors to Cambridge. Some visitors have come to Cambridge for just a few days to present work at the *Cambridge Realist Workshop* run by the group. Other visitors have engaged with the group over an extended period, sometimes staying in Cambridge for a year or more. However long they have been able to stay, the willingness of visitors to critically engage with the positions developed and defended by members of the group has been extremely valuable and has strengthened the contributions emanating from the group including those collected in this volume.

The input of successive generations of research students to the activities of the group has been significant; indeed the origins of the group can be traced back to the alignment of the interests of a number of research students in the then *Cambridge Faculty of Economics and Politics* with the existing research concerns of Tony Lawson back in the late 1980s and early 1990s. Many of the contributors to this volume joined the group initially as research students. Moreover, research students in economics for many years made up a large part of the audience for the Cambridge Realist Workshop. In more recent times, while research students have continued to join (and help sustain the activities of) the group, they have mostly been located outside economics. The openness and intellectual curiosity with which so many research students have approached the work of the group has from the start been an important part of its success.

For a research group to maintain itself and progress, resources are required. One body that has done much to support the group is the *Cambridge Political Economy Society*. Many of the papers included in this volume were first presented at workshops and conferences generously funded by this society.

I would like to thank Simon Holt, Andy Humphries, Laura Johnson and Lisa Thomson at Routledge for their timely and helpful guidance on all aspects of this project.

The majority of the papers included in this volume have been previously published, in some cases the versions published here incorporate minor changes. Details of the original publication and of the copyright holders are duly listed below:

Bigo, V, 2006, 'Open and Closed Systems and the Cambridge School', *Review of Social Economy*, Vol 64, No 4, 493–514. © Taylor & Francis.

Faulkner, P and Runde, J, 2013, 'Technological Objects, Social Positions, and the Transformational Model of Social Activity', *MIS Quarterly*, Vol 37, No 2, 803–818. © The Management Information Systems Research Center (MISRC) of the University of Minnesota.

Fleetwood, S, 1996, 'Order without Equilibrium: A Critical Realist Interpretation of Hayek's Notion of Spontaneous Order', *Cambridge Journal of Economics*, Vol 20, No 6, 729–747. © Cambridge Political Economy Society.

Graça Moura, M, 2002, 'Metatheory as the Key to Understanding Schumpeter after Shionoya', *Cambridge Journal of Economics*, Vol 26, No 6, 805–821. © Cambridge Political Economy Society.

Latsis, J, 2007, 'Quine and the Ontological Turn in Economics', in C, Lawson, J, Latsis and N, Martins, eds, *Contributions to Social Ontology*, Routledge. © Taylor & Francis.

Lawson, C, 2010, 'Technology and the Extension of Human Capabilities', *Journal for the Theory of Social Behaviour*, Vol 40, No 2, 207–223. © Wiley–Blackwell.

Lawson, T, 2003, 'An Evolutionary Economics? On Borrowing from Evolutionary Biology', chapter 5 in *Reorienting Economics*, Routledge. © Taylor & Francis.

Lawson, T, 2006, 'The Nature of Heterodox Economics', *Cambridge Journal of Economics*, Vol 30, No 6, 483–505. © Cambridge Political Economy Society.

Lawson, T, 2007, 'The Nature of Gender', originally published as 'Gender and Social Change', in J. Browne, ed, *The Future of Gender*, Cambridge University Press. © Cambridge University Press.

Lawson, T, 2009, 'Abstraction and Various Methods of Theoretical Isolation in Modern Economics', extract from reply to Geoffrey Hodgson in E. Fullbrook, ed, *Ontology and Economics*, Routledge. © Taylor & Francis.

Lawson, T, 2009, 'Applied Economics, Contrast Explanation and Asymmetric Information', *Cambridge Journal of Economics*, Vol 33, No 3, 405–419. © Cambridge Political Economy Society.

Lawson, T, 2011, 'Ontology and the Study of Social Reality: Emergence, Organisation, Community, Power, Social Relations, Corporations, Artefacts and Money', *Cambridge Journal of Economics*, Vol 36, No 2, 345–385. © Cambridge Political Economy Society.

Lewis, P, 2005, 'Agency, Structure and Causality in Austrian Economics: Tensions and Resolutions', *Review of Political Economy*, Vol 17, No 2, 291–316. © Taylor & Francis.

Martins, N, 2007, 'Realism, Universalism and Capabilities', *Review of Social Economy*, Vol 65, No 3, 253–278. © Taylor & Francis.

Montes, L, 2003, 'Smith and Newton: Some Methodological Issues Concerning General Economic Equilibrium Theory', *Cambridge Journal of Economics*, Vol 27, No 5, 723–747. © Cambridge Political Economy Society.

Pratten, S, 2005, 'Economics as Progress: The LSE Approach to Econometric Modelling and Critical Realism as Programmes for Research', *Cambridge Journal of Economics*, Vol 29, No 2, 179–205. © Cambridge Political Economy Society.

Pratten, S, 2007, 'The Scope of Ontological Theorising', *Foundations of Science*, Vol 12, No 3, 235–256. © Springer.

Introduction

Stephen Pratten

Not so long ago, explicit and systematic contributions to social ontology – the study of the *nature* of social reality, that is, research into the basic *subject matter and constitution* of social reality – were relatively rare in economics. Indeed, Edward Fullbrook (2009) notes that a paper on social ontology by Tony Lawson that appeared as recently as 1994, and in a volume containing programmatic statements by the leading economic methodologists of the time, 'stands out like someone standing alone at a party' (2009, p. 1); and does so just because of it being the only paper in the volume even to mention ontology.

Twenty years on and matters have improved somewhat. Cambridge indeed, where Lawson is based, hosts a *(Cambridge) Social Ontology Group* that is located in the Faculty of Economics. During the period in question, however, with most economics journals initially unaware that ontology is a matter that is central to all social understanding, publications that emerged have been scattered widely, often in sources that are not easily accessible, or anyway not always well known. Indeed, scholars who now regularly spend a period of time visiting the Cambridge Social Ontology Group frequently express surprise that there are so many papers 'out there', and also that people in Cambridge have been working fairly consistently and systematically on themes in social ontology over a period of time.

So, with signs that economists are becoming increasingly interested in social ontology and aware that engagement with it can facilitate more relevant social analysis including economics, this seems an opportune time for a volume such as this. It is timely to make available in one place a collection of papers that together illustrate the sort of research that can be, and indeed has been, pursued, where social ontology is taken seriously.

The focus of this volume is on the work of this Cambridge group. There are of course some others doing similar work outside Cambridge and encouragingly in increasing numbers. But the concern here is with output by those connected with Cambridge, where individuals have been working on issues in social ontology since the 1980s. This collection provides an introduction to the central themes explored, positions sustained and insights achieved over time as well as an indication of how this project is currently being developed.

Although there is certainly no blanket consensus among participants in the Cambridge group, a good deal is shared at the level of philosophical objectives and broad evaluations. Most especially all participants hold to the view that the by-now-widely-recognised generalised explanatory failures and lack of realisticness of modern economics[1] is directly related to pervasive ontological neglect. Theories and methods of modern economics are continually fashioned in ways that pay no attention to the nature of social material, that ignore the sort of stuff they are dealing with. Rather, economists have been more concerned to be seen to be conforming to their own (often actually erroneous) conceptions of how scientists dealing with non-social phenomena proceed. This neglect and scientistic concern has rendered the widespread failings of modern economics almost inevitable. In any case, the approach of the Cambridge group has been different. Here the view accepted by all is that method and substantive theory can benefit if informed by explicit, systematic and sustained social ontology, and indeed that advances in method, substantive theory and ontology are best produced together with developments in each informing the others.[2]

A brief history of the Cambridge project

How and when did research that is explicitly identified as social–ontological emerge at Cambridge? It all started in the late 1980s when a number of Cambridge research students, many of whom were working with Tony Lawson on methodological and philosophical issues relating to economics, began to meet up regularly to discuss topics of common interest.

It became customary to meet on Monday evenings. Though informal at first, these Monday meetings eventually evolved into the *Cambridge Realist Workshop*. The first official meeting of the latter took place in October 1990. Prior to this first official Workshop Tony Lawson circulated a letter within the Cambridge Faculty of Economics and Politics inviting participation. I reproduce here a passage from it that clearly reveals the hoped-for ontological orientation of the Workshop:

> Although it is anticipated that the workshop will entail some philosophical (as well as History of Thought) orientation, the concern is centrally with the doing of substantive economics. All that is presupposed is a commitment to the view that there exists a knowable (under some description) social reality and that economics should primarily address such matters as identifying and understanding real world economic structures, mechanisms, processes and events, etc. This commitment, though minimal, does entail acknowledging that the nature of economic reality bears upon both the types of theories we can legitimately entertain as well as the methods of theory assessment that can be rationally supported. In philosophical jargon it is a presupposition of the realist programme that questions of ontology

are in some sense prior to, and bear upon, questions of epistemology and methodology as well as substantive economic research.

(Tony Lawson – open letter dated 15 October 1990)

The Workshop quickly obtained a relatively prominent profile and has run continuously since. Initially discussions at the Workshop were focused on a core set of concerns that preoccupied a committed small group of regular participants. Over time this group collaborated closely and each participant developed his or her own view through continuous interaction with those of other participants.

After a decade or so, however, the nature of the Workshop began to change. Many of the original attendees left Cambridge to gain academic employment elsewhere. Meanwhile the number of participants had become very large. Although the Workshop became and remains a more general forum for philosophically inclined economists, and is consistently successful in attracting a range of international speakers (from research students to Nobel prize winners from economics, as well as a host of scholars from other social science disciplines), it was felt that something was by now missing. The sense of organic evolution of the early days had inevitably declined with change in the size and composition of the Workshop.

Many of those who had been involved from its earliest days, as well as newcomers attracted to Cambridge by the prospect of engaging with the emerging project, felt a further forum was required where more sustained discussion and treatment of particular topics in social ontology could be had. This led to the establishment in October 2002 of the Cambridge Social Ontology Group, a forum for ontological discussion that has been in place ever since.[3]

Of course, although use of the term ontology is fairly recent in Cambridge economics, a systematic consideration of the nature of social material is not. It certainly underpins Keynes's methodological reflections. Keynes, for example, worries continuously about the tendency of many to apply the frequency theory of probability in a general way to a wide range of situations. Recognising that probability theorising rests on inductive logic, Keynes investigates the conditions under which this logic is valid. In effect Keynes examines its ontological preconditions. He examines the implicit presuppositions of those scientists and others who use such methods regarding the fundamental nature of the material to which they are applying their methods. Thus, in his *Treatise on Probability* Keynes writes:

> The kind of fundamental assumption about the character of material laws, on which scientists appear commonly to act, seems to me to be much less simple than the bare principle of uniformity. They appear to assume something much more like what mathematicians call the principle of the superposition of small effects, or, as I prefer to call it, in this connection, the *atomic* character of natural law. The system

of the material universe must consist, if this kind of assumption is warranted, of bodies which we may term (without any implication as to their size being conveyed thereby) *legal atoms*, such that each of them exercises its own separate, independent, and invariable effect, a change of the total state being compounded of a number of separate changes each of which is solely due to a separate portion of the preceding state. We do not have an invariable relation between particular bodies, but nevertheless each has on the others its own separate and invariable effect, which does not change with changing circumstances, although, of course, the total effect may be changed to almost any extent if all the other accompanying causes are different. Each atom can, according to this theory, be treated as a separate cause and does not enter into different organic combinations in each of which it is regulated by different laws.

(1973, pp. 276, 277)

Nor is Keynes's analysis especially dated. Compare this extract, for example, with Lawson's more recent assessment of the presuppositions of modern methods of mathematical economic (including econometric) modelling:

But this is not the end to the ontological preconditions of methods of mathematical–deductivist modelling as employed in modern economics. A further important feature, which is less often recognised (or at least rarely explicitly acknowledged), is that the dependency of mathematical–deductivist methods on closed systems in turn more or less necessitates, and certainly encourages, formulations couched in terms of (i) isolated (ii) atoms. The metaphorical reference to atoms here is not intended to convey anything about size. Rather the reference is to items which exercise their own separate, independent and invariable (and so predictable) effects (relative to, or as a function of, initial conditions).

(Lawson, 2003a, pp. 13–14)

Additionally, ontological concerns are clear in Alfred Marshall's reasoning. Marshall often expresses the view that the use of mathematical methods within economics leads to much 'elegant toying' but little constructive work. Marshall also questions the possibility of an evolutionary economics. In considering the limitations of static analysis within economics he notes:

The catastrophes of mechanics are caused by changes in the quantity and not in the character of the forces at work: whereas in life their character changes also. 'Progress' or 'evolution', industrial and social, is not mere increase and decrease. It is organic growth, chastened and confined and occasionally reversed by decay of innumerable factors each of which influences and is influenced by those around it; and every such mutual influence varies with the stages which the respective factors have already reached in their growth.

(Marshall, 1898, pp. 42–43)

Of course the sorts of arguments that are embedded within the methodological writings of Keynes and Marshall are developed significantly by the Cambridge group. But the point is clear that the contemporary Cambridge group is rendering explicit various concerns that have been central to an earlier Cambridge tradition.[4]

The basis for the selection and an outline of the contributions

The contributions included in this volume have been selected with the intention of illustrating the breadth and vitality of the Cambridge project. There is no attempt here to be comprehensive; that would require a number of volumes. The contributions of the Cambridge group are numerous and highly diverse. The motivation that guided the selection of the papers was to produce a volume that would reflect the central themes explored by the group and also provide an illustration of how the project is currently being developed.

The papers included in this volume are authored by individuals who have been closely involved with the project over an extended period. Many of the papers were presented initially at the Cambridge Workshop. In all of the contributions, the discussions and debates engaged in at the Workshop and the meetings of the Cambridge Social Ontology Group substantially inform the arguments developed.

Before considering applications of ontological reasoning it is important to elaborate how ontology is understood and justified by members of the Cambridge group as well as how the Cambridge project compares with prominent alternatives. This is the purpose of Part I, entitled 'The Cambridge approach to social ontology'.

The first paper in Part I, Tony Lawson's 'A conception of social ontology', is essentially a position paper setting out the key features of the approach to social ontology that the group adopt. It is a paper that has gone through numerous transformations over time, with many of the different versions critically discussed at meetings of the Cambridge Social Ontology Group.[5] As one would expect of a position paper, it is wide ranging and addresses a series of important clarifying issues including the why, how and wherefore of social ontology as pursued in Cambridge.

In the second paper in this part, entitled 'Quine and the ontological turn in economics', John Latsis focuses on a comparison between the type of ontological investigation viewed as sustainable by the influential American analytical philosopher W.V.O. Quine and the broader approach that accommodates a focus on social ontology adopted by the Cambridge group. Quine is widely interpreted as recommending that exclusive priority be given to the natural sciences as a source of knowledge and that an adequate description of nature consists only of that to which the natural sciences have access. Latsis carefully draws out the similarities and pinpoints the differences between the two projects.

The final paper in this part is Stephen Pratten's 'The scope of ontological theorising'. Here the Cambridge project is compared with a contemporary alternative – the framework developed by the philosopher of science Nancy Cartwright. Pratten demonstrates that the projects draw on different conceptions of the legitimate scope of ontological theorising and specifically that the Cambridge project is a good deal more ambitious in developing and defending an account of the nature of the social realm.[6]

The remaining parts of this volume illustrate social ontological analysis being put to work in under-labouring for specific types of development in economics. The selection of papers included have been organised and grouped according to their contribution to clarifying and developing respectively: (1) various competing traditions and projects of modern economics (Part II); (2) history of economic thought contributions (Part III); (3) methodological concerns (Part IV); (4) ethics (Part V); and finally (5) conceptions of social reality (Part VI).

Part II of the volume opens with a paper by Tony Lawson. Entitled 'The nature of heterodox economics', Lawson here shows how a focus on ontology can help identify both those features that systematically distinguish heterodox traditions from the contemporary mainstream project and also those that serve to differentiate the various heterodox schools from each other. Lawson's paper stands out from other attempts to so classify the various traditions in providing ontologically informed differentiations that without strain render the picture as a whole coherent.

In the second paper of Part II, 'Economics as progress: the LSE approach to econometric modelling and critical realism as programmes for research', Stephen Pratten argues that a few projects of modern mainstream economics depart from the majority in being somewhat sustained rather than fashion driven, and for this reason especially deserve particularly close scrutiny. One such project is the so-called LSE approach to econometric modelling associated with the work of David Hendry and his colleagues. Pratten examines similarities and differences between the LSE approach and the Cambridge project, highlighting the significant role of their competing ontological commitments.[7]

The third paper of this part, Tony Lawson's 'An evolutionary economics? On borrowing from evolutionary biology', contributes to a specific strand of modern economics. Specifically, Lawson considers the possibility of, and prospects for, evolutionary projects in economics. Indeed, he goes much further and indicates how natural selection translates to the social realm, elaborates the ontology of a sustainable social Darwinian conception, and indicates how evolutionary explanation might reasonably proceed in the social domain.

Participants in the Cambridge group have long sought to engage heterodox traditions in ways that are hoped will be mutually beneficial. One such engagement is provided by the final paper of the part, Paul Lewis's 'Structure, agency and causality in post-revival Austrian economics: tensions and resolutions', which seeks to resolve long-standing tensions associated with certain Austrian contributions.[8]

The Cambridge group have also been active in bringing an explicit ontological orientation to history of thought discussions, the focus of Part III of the book. Explicit ontological analysis is unfortunately often marginalised in history of thought discussion, and three papers are included here to provide an indication of the sort of contribution that ontological reasoning can make.[9]

In the first paper of Part III, 'Smith and Newton: some methodological issues concerning general economic equilibrium theory', Leonidas Montes demonstrates that the often repeated claim made by supporters of recent general equilibrium theorising that their project constitutes a continuation, and even the completion, of Adam Smith's account of the invisible hand cannot be sustained. He shows that these projects are in fact fundamentally opposed and presuppose very different accounts of the nature of social reality.

In the following paper, 'Metatheory as a key to understanding Schumpeter after Shionoya', Mário Graça Moura indicates how the widely observed puzzling inconsistencies and tensions in Schumpeter's contributions are easily explained once an explicit ontological orientation is adopted.

In the third paper of Part III, 'Order without equilibrium: a critical realist interpretation of Hayek's notion of Spontaneous order', Steve Fleetwood considers the significant transformations in Hayek's theorising over time. He pays particularly close attention to the way that Hayek decisively abandons equilibrium as a central theoretical device and explores how he gradually develops in his later work an account of social order where social rules are accorded a central role.

Members of the group have also been concerned to use ontology to contribute to economic methodology. This is the focus of Part IV of the book. Here the point is to indicate the sorts of methods that emerge as appropriate to social economic analysis, in the light of insights gained concerning the nature of social material obtained via ontological elaboration.

In the first paper in this part of the volume, here titled 'Abstraction and various methods of theoretical isolation in modern economics' (an abridged version of a piece originally titled 'On the nature and roles of formalism in economics'[10]), Tony Lawson considers the distinction between abstraction and methods of theoretical isolation, arguing that the former always is, but the latter rarely are, appropriate for social analysis.[11]

In the following paper, 'Applied economics, contrast explanation and asymmetric information', Tony Lawson addresses directly the question of determining methods that are appropriate to the sort of material that social ontological analysis shows to characterise social reality. Lawson explores the nature of dialectical explanatory approaches and considers in some detail the specific and especially important form of contrast explanation, providing an enlightening illustration.[12]

In Part V the focus turns to ethics. This is something that has long been debated within the Cambridge group. Tony Lawson, in his early *Economics and Reality*, was already arguing for a specific form of *moral realism* grounded in the generalised flourishing of especially human being. In a paper that was originally intended as a chapter of *Reorienting Economics*, Lawson developed at length an account of his *critical ethical naturalism* that arises from social ontological thinking more generally. Although the paper has provoked considerable discussion within the Cambridge group, its length and other considerations led Lawson to omit it from *Reorienting Economics*. Although Lawson intended to develop the paper as a book, it has since been left unworked on. Here I am pleased to say that Lawson has been persuaded to provide a much shortened, and very slightly updated, version for the current volume. It thus appears as the first paper in Part V entitled 'Critical ethical naturalism: an orientation to ethics'.

If there is an alternative approach to ethics that is also systematically ontologically informed, the most likely contender is the Capability approach associated with the work of Amartya Sen and Martha Nussbaum. Even here though the reliance on ontological reasoning is downplayed. In the second paper in Section V, entitled 'Realism, universalism and capabilities', Nuno Martins indicates how a more explicit, systematic and sustained approach to ontological reasoning can help significantly clarify certain key features of the Capability approach.

The final part of the book, Part VI, is straightforwardly concerned with illustrating how ontological reasoning has been used to advance conceptions of the constitution of social reality. This is where the contributions of the group are most constructive, and I have included six illustrative examples.

The first of these, by Tony Lawson, is entitled 'Ontology and the study of social reality: emergence, organisation, community, power, social relations, corporations, artefacts and money' and demonstrates the sense in which and how the kind of social ontology Lawson defends is consistent with ontological naturalism. Lawson clarifies a series of issues relating to the notion of emergence[13] and goes on to explore more concrete issues including the nature of community, the corporation and money. The work of John Searle is considered as a useful contrast to the Cambridge project, and Lawson starts here to bring out the similarities and differences between these two projects.[14]

One notable characteristic displayed by all members of the Cambridge group has been a willingness to engage with critics and commentators.[15]

Vinca Bigo, in 'Open and closed systems and the Cambridge school', the second paper in this part of the book, concentrates on an aspect of the conception widely accepted by participants in the Cambridge project that has received a substantial amount of critical commentary. Specifically she considers various criticisms that have been made of the Cambridge treatment of open and closed systems. She clarifies how these categories have in fact been deployed by the Cambridge group, counters the criticisms and demonstrates why the categories are illuminating.

The final four papers in this collection consider particular social categories and develop systematic accounts of them that are consistent with the broader social ontological conception defended by most participants in the group.

Tony Lawson, in 'The nature of gender', clarifies those features that are essential to gender systems, defends his account against alternative influential conceptualisations and explores the implications for emancipatory practice. In 'Technological objects, social positions, and the transformational model of social activity', Philip Faulkner and Jochen Runde consider how the kind of social ontology defended by most participants in the Cambridge group can facilitate the development of an account of technological objects. In 'Technology and the extension of human capabilities', Clive Lawson suggests that appreciating the role that technology plays in extending human capabilities is crucial to any project exploring the nature of technology. Finally, in 'What is an institution?', Tony Lawson answers the question of the title. I might note that this latter paper too has remained available only in draft form for some years awaiting final revisions (it was accepted many years ago by a leading business journal, but on condition it be redrafted in a business journal style; Lawson clearly never found the enthusiasm to carry this through). I might note too that unsurprisingly Lawson's views have moved on a little. However, the only change of note in terms of the substance of this paper is that he currently accepts that Veblen has a more mentalistic notion of an institution (see Lawson, 2013c).[16]

Despite the recent financial crisis and the soul searching it has prompted in certain quarters of the economics discipline, modern economics is still clearly characterised by relative ontological neglect. Specifically, the dominant project prioritises the use of methods of mathematical modelling without any consideration of the relevance of these methods to the material to which they are applied. Those economists that participate in the Cambridge Social Ontology Group argue that an alternative approach is both warranted and that various fruitful approaches have been identified; and in fact that an efficacious and indeed emancipatory discipline of economics remains entirely feasible. For this, though, explicit, systematic and sustained ontological reasoning is likely required. The papers included below provide an illustration of how this might be carried through.

Notes

1 For just one illustration of this trend, see Kay (2012), who also reports on and evaluates the attempted defences offered by certain prominent mainstream contributors.

2 Although social ontology, a form of *study*, has throughout been the common thread of the Cambridge group, several of its participants have at one time or other interpreted their *results* as part of the project of *critical realism in economics* and hence it is useful here to clarify how the Cambridge group relates to projects developed under this banner. Key themes that were later to be developed more thoroughly by the Cambridge group are present in certain papers by Tony Lawson dating from the early 1980s. These contributions were explicitly critical of the prevailing practices of mainstream economists, although their ontological orientation was largely left implicit and philosophical language mostly absent. At around the same time a series of similar related critiques of current social scientific practice in various different disciplines were being developed. Meanwhile Roy Bhaskar, partly drawing on the work of Rom Harré (1970) and Harré and Madden (1975), had recently developed a critique of the then dominant positions in the philosophy of science. These differently situated projects came together picking up especially on Bhaskar's philosophical language and formed a loose federation that placed a high priority on ontological analysis and elaboration and involved regular conferences and considerable interdisciplinary interaction. The label of critical realism was adopted by a number of these related but differently situated projects. For example, projects that adopt the title (or are recognised as being closely aligned with) *critical realism* can be discerned in sociology associated with the contributions of Margaret Archer (1995), Andrew Sayer (2000) and more recently Dave Elder-Vass (2010), in management and organisational studies linked with amongst others Stephen Ackroyd and Steve Fleetwood (2000) and Michael Reed (2001 and 2005), in international relations involving the likes of Colin Wight (2006) and Milja Kurki (2008), and in philosophy associated with such scholars as Andrew Collier (1994), Ruth Groff (2004) and Roy Bhaskar (1975, 1979 and 1986). The contributions of the Cambridge group have often been referred to by its members and others under the title of *critical realism in economics*; see in particular Lawson (1997a), Fleetwood (1999) and Lewis (2004). Indeed, many of the contributions in this volume develop their favoured positions under the heading of *critical realism*. However, the label of *critical realism in economics* was always used to refer to important work from others beyond Cambridge; for one relevant collection see Downward (2003). Just as the project associated with the Cambridge group has developed and been extended over time, this is also true of those other projects associated with critical realism. Bhaskar's own work has gone through a series of phases and he has re-labelled his own evolving project several times – critical realism became *dialectical critical realism*, then *transcendental dialectical critical realism* and so on. As these projects continue to develop in a variety of very different ways so there is a danger that any unqualified use of the term critical realism serves to obscure many important differences among a variety of related positions. This is not to deny substantial commonalities, nor in any way to belittle the significance of the contributions that continue to emerge under the critical realism heading. Rather the point is that, as this increasing variety occurs and as the Cambridge project itself evolves, clarity is most likely to be served by elaborating precisely what it is that this project involves rather than establishing that the results achieved are entirely consistent with, still less emerge immediately from, a broader critical realist framework. Thus, although earlier papers make explicit reference to critical realism, sometimes even in the

titles to contributions, and while there is no particular desire to distance the project from critical realist contributions, for reasons of clarity it is currently more common for papers by Cambridge group participants to be presented simply as contributions to social ontology.

3 For further background on the development of the Cambridge group, see the interviews with Tony Lawson in Hirsch and DesRoches (2009) and Dunn (2009). For details about the Cambridge Realist Workshop and the Cambridge Social Ontology Group, see www.csog.group.cam.ac.uk

4 Nuno Martins (2014), in a treatise entitled *The Cambridge Revival of Political Economy* has recently provided an extended discussion that situates the contributions of the Cambridge group thoroughly in the context of (and argues that this contemporary work effectively defends and extends) the older Cambridge tradition.

5 A sense of the Cambridge Social Ontology Group discussions prompted by the paper and their impact on the current version can be obtained by comparing the paper published in the current volume with an early version titled 'A conception of ontology' available at www.csog.group.cam.ac.uk

6 The focus in Part I is on the nature of the ontological project proposed by the Cambridge group and comparing it with certain other ontologically focused projects. The comparisons provided here could of course be extended. For a discussion of the similarities and differences between the Cambridge project and the contributions of Uskali Mäki, see Pratten (2007a). It is also useful to compare the ontological project developed by the Cambridge group with other prominent interventions in the philosophy and methodology of economics; see Sofianou (1995) and Lewis (2003).

7 The Cambridge group have analysed various specific mainstream projects. For example, see Pratten (1997, 2001 and 2004) for consideration of the New Institutional Economics, and Siakantaris (2000) for reflections on developments in experimental economics.

8 Others within the Cambridge group have focused upon post-Keynesian economics – see T. Lawson (1994), Lewis and Runde (1999) and Pratten (2013b); evolutionary theory – see Northover (1999); Old Institutionalism – see T. Lawson (2005); and feminism – see T. Lawson (2003b).

9 Members of the Cambridge group are not entirely alone in suggesting that a focus on ontology and metaphysics can help resolve prominent questions in the history of economic thought. This kind of emphasis was long ago seen in the work of Veblen and has been central to the work of certain Marx scholars for some considerable time; see for example Meikle (2009). Nevertheless, the Cambridge group have been prominent in bringing an explicit ontological orientation to history of thought discussions. Members of the Cambridge group have examined a variety of different figures in the history of economic thought and issues related to their contributions. For discussions of Hayek, see Fleetwood (1995), T. Lawson (1997b) and Lewis (2012); for Lachmann, see Lewis and Runde (2007) and Lewis (2011a); for Keynes, see T. Lawson (1995); for Marx, see Pratten (1993) and Fleetwood (2001); for Marshall, see Pratten (1998b); for Commons, see C. Lawson (1994); and for Veblen, see T. Lawson (2013b).

10 Originally published in Fullbrook (2009) in response to some comments by Geoffrey Hodgson (2009).

11 For further discussion of abstraction, see Runde (1997) and Pratten (2007b).

12 For further elaboration and evaluation of contrast explanation as a method capable of being fruitfully deployed in the social domain, see T. Lawson (2003a, chapter 4; 2008). For consideration of the connections between contrast explanation and feminist standpoint theory, see T. Lawson (2007), and for illustrations of contrast explanation, see Morgan (2013) and Lewis (2013).

13 For detailed elaborations of the form of emergence that the Cambridge group defend, see T. Lawson (2013a), and for comparisons with relevant alternative formulations, see Pratten (2013a).

14 Within philosophical circles (even within analytic philosophy), general metaphysics and ontology have recently become respectable once more, encouraging some to go so far as to speak there too of an 'ontological turn'; see Heil and Martin (1999). Interestingly, mainstream philosophers working in the areas of metaphysics and philosophy of science have begun to defend positions consistent with the results of the Cambridge group. So, for instance, belief in causal powers is now a respectable position and is often explicitly defended within analytical metaphysics; see, for example, Ellis (2002). Moreover, there is a rapidly growing number of contributions focused on topics in social ontology. These have in part been inspired by the pioneering work of John Searle; see Searle (1995 and 2010) but also Gilbert (1989) and Tuomela (2007). For further discussion of Searle's contributions specifically, see Peacock (2006), Faulkner (2002) and Runde (2001 and 2002). Also, note that as this interest in social ontology has gathered pace amongst contemporary philosophers, the work of situating it within the context of a broader history of philosophy has already begun; see Ikaheimo and Laitinen (2011).

15 For examples of productive engagements with various commentators, see T. Lawson (2004b), Fleetwood (2005) and Lewis (2011b).

16 For discussion of specific categories, in addition to the papers grouped in Part VI, for technology, see C. Lawson (2007) and Faulkner and Runde (2009); on trust, see Lewis (2008) and T. Lawson (2000); on need, see Pratten (1998b); on convention, see Bibow, Lewis and Runde (2003), Latsis (2006) and Latsis et al. (2010); on the region, see C. Lawson (1999); on social rules, see Al-Amoudi (2010); on social order, see Lewis and Runde (2007); and on markets, see Fleetwood (2006, 2007 and 2011).

References

Ackroyd, S and Fleetwood, S, eds, 2000, *Realist Perspectives on Management and Organisations*, Routledge, London.

Al-Amoudi, I, 2010, 'Immanent, Non-Algorithmic Rules: An Ontological Study of Social Rules', *Journal for the Theory of Social Behaviour*, Vol 40, No 3, 289–313.

Archer, M, 1995, *Realist Social Theory: The Morphogenetic Approach*, Cambridge University Press, Cambridge.

Bhaskar, R, 1975, *A Realist Theory of Science,* Harvester, Brighton.

Bhaskar, R, 1979, *The Possibility of Naturalism*, Harvester, Brighton.

Bhaskar, R, 1986, *Scientific Realism and Human Emancipation*, Verso, London.

Bibow, J, Lewis, P and Runde, J, 2003, 'On Convention: Keynes, Lewis and the French School', in J. Runde and S. Mizuhara, eds, *The Philosophy of Keynes's Economics: Probability, Uncertainty and Convention*, Routledge, London.

Collier, A, 1994, *Critical Realism*, Verso, London.

Downward, P, ed, 2003, *Applied Economics and the Critical Realist Critique*, Routledge, London.

Dunn, S, 2009, 'Cambridge Economics, Heterodoxy and Ontology: An Interview with Tony Lawson', *Review of Political Economy*, Vol 21, No 3, 481–496.

Elder-Vass, D, 2010, *The Causal Power of Social Structures: Emergence, Structure and Agency*, Cambridge University Press, Cambridge.

Ellis, B, 2002, *The Philosophy of Nature: A Guide to the New Essentialism*, Acumen Publishing, Chesham.

Faulkner, P, 2002, 'Some Problems with the Conception of the Human Subject in Critical Realism', *Cambridge Journal of Economics*, Vol 26, 739–751.

Faulkner, P and Runde, J, 2009, 'On the Identity of Technological Objects and User Innovations in Function', *Academy of Management Review*, Vol 34, No 3, 442–462.

Fleetwood, S, 1995, *Hayek's Political Economy: The Socio-Economics of Order*, Routledge, London.

Fleetwood, S, ed, 1999, *Critical Realism in Economics: Development and Debate*, Routledge, London.

Fleetwood, S, 2001, 'What Kind of Theory is Marx's Labour Theory of Value? A Critical Realist Inquiry', *Capital and Class*, Vol 25, No 1, 41–77.

Fleetwood, S, 2005, 'A Critical Realist Reply to Walters and Young', *Review of Political Economy*, Vol 11, No 3., 587–600.

Fleetwood, S, 2006, 'Re-Thinking Labour Markets: A Critical Realist–Socioeconomic Perspective', *Capital & Class*, Vol 30, No 2, 59–89.

Fleetwood, S, 2007, 'Austrian Economics and the Analysis of Labour Markets', *Review of Austrian Economics*, Vol 20, No 4, 247–267.

Fleetwood, S, 2011, 'Sketching a Socio-Economic Model of Labour Markets', *Cambridge Journal of Economics*, Vol 35, No 1, 15–38.

Fullbrook, E, ed, 2009, *Ontology and Economics*, Routledge, London.

Gilbert, M, 1989, *On Social Facts*, Routledge, London.

Groff, R, 2004, *Critical Realism, Post-Positivism and the Possibility of Knowledge*, Routledge, London.

Harré, R, 1970, *Principles of Scientific Thinking*, University of Chicago Press, Chicago.

Harré, R, and Madden, E, 1975, *Causal Powers*, Basil Blackwell, Oxford.

Heil, J and Martin, CB, 1999, 'The Ontological Turn', *Midwest Studies in Philosophy*, Vol 23, 34–60.

Hirsch, C and DesRoches, CT, 2009, 'Cambridge Social Ontology: An Interview with Tony Lawson', *Erasmus Journal for Philosophy and Economics*, Vol 2, No 1, 100–122.

Hodgson, G, 2009, 'On the Problem of Formalism in Economics', in E. Fullbrook, ed, *Ontology and Economics,* Routledge, London.

Ikaheimo, H and Laitinen, A, eds, 2011, *Recognition and Social Ontology*, Brill, Boston.

Kay, J, 2012, 'The Map is not the Territory: Models, Scientists and the State of Modern Macroeconomics', *Critical Review*, Vol 24, No 1, 87–99.

Keynes, JM, 1973, *The Collected Writings of John Maynard Keynes, Vol VIII, A Treatise on Probability*, Royal Economic Society, London.

Kurki, M, 2008, *Causation in International Relations: Reclaiming Causal Analysis*, Cambridge University Press, Cambridge.

Latsis, J, 2006, 'Convention and Intersubjectivity: New Developments in French Economics', *Journal for the Theory of Social Behaviour*, Vol 36, No 3, 255–277.

Latsis, J, de Larquier, G and Besis, F, 2010, 'Are Conventions Solutions to Uncertainty? Contrasting Visions of Social Coordination', *Journal of Post-Keynesian Economics*, Vol 32, No 4, 525–558.

Lawson, C, 1994, 'The Transformational Model of Social Activity and Economic Analysis: A Re-Interpretation of the Work of J.R. Commons', *Review of Political Economy*, Vol 6, No 2, 186–204.

Lawson, C, 1999, 'Towards a Competence Theory of the Region', *Cambridge Journal of Economics*, Vol 23, 151–166.

Lawson, C, 2007, 'An Ontology of Technology: Artefacts, Relations and Functions', *Techne: Research in Philosophy and Technology*, Vol 12, No 1, 48–64.

Lawson, T, 1994, 'The Nature of Post-Keynesianism and Its Links to Other Traditions', *Journal of Post-Keynesian Economics*, Vol 16, No 4, 503–538.

Lawson, T, 1995, 'Expectations and Economics', in S. Dow and J. Hillard, eds, *Keynes, Uncertainty and Knowledge*, Edward Elgar, Cheltenham.

Lawson, T, 1997a, *Economics and Reality*, Routledge, London.

Lawson, T, 1997b, 'Development in Hayek's Social Theorising', in S. Frowen, ed, *Hayek: Economist and Social Philosopher. A Critical Retrospect,* Macmillan, Basingstoke.

Lawson, T, 2000, 'Evaluating Trust, Competition and Cooperation', in Y. Shinoya and K. Yagi, eds, *Competition, Trust and Competition: A Comparative Study*, Springer, Berlin.

Lawson, T, 2003a, *Reorienting Economics*, Routledge, London.

Lawson, T, 2003b, 'Ontology and Feminist Theorising', *Feminist Economics*, Vol 9, No 1, 119–150.

Lawson, T, 2004a, 'Modern Economics: The Problem and a Solution', in E. Fullbrook, ed, *A Guide to What's Wrong with Economics*, Anthem Press, London.

Lawson, T, 2004b, 'Reorienting Economics: On Heterodox Economics, Themata and the Use of Mathematics in Economics', *Journal of Economic Methodology*, Vol 11, No 3, 329–340.

Lawson, T, 2005, 'The Nature of Institutional Economics', *Evolutionary and Institutional Economic Review*, Vol 2, No 1, 7–20.

Lawson, T, 2007, 'Methodological Issues in the Study of Gender', *Journal of International Economic Studies*, Vol 21, No 1, 1–16.

Lawson, T, 2008, 'Popper and Social Explanation', in T. Boylan and P. O'Gorman, eds, *Popper and Economic Methodology: Contemporary Challenges*, Routledge, London.

Lawson, T, 2013a, 'Emergence and Morphogenesis, Causal Reduction and Downward Causation', in M. Archer, ed, *Social Morphogenesis*, Springer, New York.

Lawson, T, 2013b, 'What Is This "School" Called Neoclassical Economics?', *Cambridge Journal of Economics*, Vol 37, No 5, 947–983.

Lawson, T, 2013c, 'Process, Order and Stability in Veblen', Cambridge University, Mimeograph.

Lewis, P, 2003, 'Recent Developments in Economic Methodology: Rhetorical and Ontological Turns', *Foundations of Science*, Vol 8, No 1, 51–68.

Lewis, P, ed, 2004, *Transforming Economics: Perspectives on the Critical Realist Project*, Routledge, London.

Lewis, P, 2008, 'Uncertainty, Power and Trust', *The Review of Austrian Economics*, Vol 21, 183–198.

Lewis, P, 2011a, 'Far from a Nihilistic Crowd: Lavoie and Lachmann's Theoretical Contribution', *Review of Austrian Economics*, Vol 24, 185–198.

Lewis, P, 2011b, 'On the Merits of Critical Realism and the "Ontological Turn" in Economics: Reply to Steele', *Critical Review,* Vol 23, No 1–2, 207–230.

Lewis, P, 2012, 'Emergent Properties in the Work of Friedrich Hayek', *Journal of Economic Behaviour and Organisation*, Vol 82, No 2–3, 368–378.

Lewis, P, 2013, 'Hayek, Social Theory, and the Contrastive Explanation of Socio-Economic Order', *Critical Review*, Vol 25, No 3–4, 386–408.

Lewis, P and Runde, J, 1999, 'A Critical Realist Perspective on Paul Davidson's Methodological and Rhetorical Strategy for Post-Keynesian Economics', *Journal of Post Keynesian Economics*, Vol 22, No 1, 35–56.

Lewis, P and Runde, J, 2007, 'Subjectivism, Social Structures and the Possibility of Socio-Economic Order', *Journal of Economic Behaviour and Organisation*, Vol 62, No 2, 167–186.

Marshall, A, 1898, 'Distribution and Exchange', *The Economic Journal*, Vol 8, 37–59.

Martins, N, 2014, *The Cambridge Revival of Political Economy*, Routledge, London.

Meikle, S, 2009, 'Marx, the European Tradition and the Philosophic Radicals', in A. Chitty and M. McIvor, eds, *Karl Marx and Contemporary Philosophy*, Palgrave, Basingstoke.

Morgan, J, 2013, 'Forward-Looking Contrast Explanation, Illustrated Using the Great Moderation', *Cambridge Journal of Economics*, Vol 37, No 4, 737–758.

Northover, P, 1999, 'Evolutionary Growth Theory and Forms of Realism', *Cambridge Journal of Economics*, Vol 23, No 1, 33–63.

Peacock, M, 2006, 'Rationality and the Language of Decision Making: Bringing Language into the Foreground in Economic Theory', *International Journal of Social Economics*, Vol 33, No 9, 604–614.

Pratten, S, 1993, 'Structure, Agency and Marx's Analysis of the Labour Process', *Review of Political Economy*, Vol 5, No 4, 403–426.

Pratten, S, 1997, 'The Nature of Transaction Cost Economics', *Journal of Economics Issues*, Vol 31, No 3, 781–803.

Pratten, S, 1998a, 'Needs and Wants: The Case of Broadcasting Policy', *Media, Culture and Society*, Vol 20, No 3, 381–407.

Pratten, S, 1998b, 'Marshall on Tendencies, Equilibrium and the Statical Method', *History of Political Economy*, Vol 30, No 1, 121–163.

Pratten, S, 2001, 'Coase on Broadcasting, Advertising and Policy', *Cambridge Journal of Economics*, Vol 25, 617–638.

Pratten, S, 2004, 'The Conflict between Formalism and Realisticness in Modern Economics: The Case of the New Institutional Economics', in J. Davis, A. Marciano and J. Runde, eds, *The Elgar Companion to Economics and Philosophy*, Edward Elgar, Cheltenham.

Pratten, S, 2007a, 'Ontological Theorising and the Assumptions Issue in Economics', in C. Lawson, J. Latsis and N. Martins, eds, *Contributions to Social Ontology*, Routledge, London.

Pratten, S, 2007b, 'Realism, Closed Systems and Abstraction', *Journal of Economic Methodology*, Vol 14, No 4, 473–497.

Pratten, S, 2013a, 'Critical Realism and the Process Account of Emergence', *Journal for the Theory of Social Behaviour*, Vol 43, No 3, 251–279.

Pratten, S, 2013b, 'Post-Keynesian Economics, Critical Realism and Social Ontology', in G. Harcourt and P. Kreisler, eds, *The Oxford Handbook of Post-Keynesian Economics*, Oxford University Press, Oxford.

Reed, M, 2001, 'Organization, Trust and Control: A Realist Analysis', *Organization Studies*, Vol 22, No 2, 201–228.

Reed, M, 2005, 'Reflections on the "Realist Turn" in Organisation and Management Studies', *Journal of Management Studies*, Vol 42, No 8, 1621–1644.

Runde, J, 1997, 'Abstraction, Idealization and Economic Theory', in P. Arestis, G. Palma and M. Sawyer, eds, *Markets, Unemployment and Economic Policy: Essays in Honour of Geoff Harcourt, Vol 2*, Routledge, London.

Runde, J, 2001, 'Bringing Social Structure back into Economics', *Review of Austrian Economics*, Vol 14, 5–24.

Runde, J, 2002, 'Filling in the Background', *Journal of Economic Methodology*, Vol 9, 11–30.

Sayer, A, 2000, *Realism and Social Science*, Sage, London.

Searle, J, 1995, *The Constitution of Social Reality*, Free Press, New York.

Searle, J, 2010, *Making the Social World*, Oxford University Press, Oxford.

Siakantaris, N, 2000, 'Laboratory Experimentation in Economics under the Microscope', *Cambridge Journal of Economics*, Vol 24, No 3, 267–281.

Sofianou, E, 1995, 'Post-Modernism and the Notions of Rationality in Economics', *Cambridge Journal of Economics*, Vol 19, No 3, 373–389.

Tuomela, R, 2007, *The Philosophy of Sociality*, Oxford University Press, Oxford.

Wight, C, 2006, *Agents, Structures and International Relations: Politics as Ontology*, Cambridge University Library, Cambridge.

PART I

The Cambridge approach to social ontology

1 A conception of social ontology[1]

Tony Lawson

The purpose here is to describe and defend a programme in social ontology. It is a programme being carried through by a group of researchers in Cambridge.[2] Before turning to indicate how ontology is useful, and indeed how it can be reasonably carried through, an indication is provided as to how certain central categories are interpreted.

Basic categories

Ontology

The term ontology[3] derives from Greek, with 'onto' meaning 'being', and 'logos' usually interpreted as 'science'; so that ontology, as traditionally understood, is the science or study of being.[4]

The word 'being' has at least two senses:

1　Something that *is*, or exists;
2　What it is to be or to exist.

It follows that if ontology is the study of being it includes at least the following:

1　The study of what *is*, or what exists, including the study of the nature of specific existents;
2　The study of how existents exist.

This two-fold conception is adopted here.[5]

Scientific and philosophical ontology

The two forms of study just noted are labelled *scientific ontology* and *philosophical ontology*, respectively.

All features of reality can be viewed under the aspect of their being. Yet actual projects concerned with the study of what exists will necessarily be highly specific or restricted in focus. Features that get singled out for extended study at any point will depend on historical circumstance and, most especially, the situations, biases and interests of researchers. Because features or phenomena so singled out will depend on the interests of current science, and, in the case of non-social phenomena at least, be very often first identified in scientific study, the branch of study concerned with what is or what exists, that investigates the natures of particular existents, is reasonably distinguished as *scientific ontology* (it is easily extended to include significant existents posited within, or presupposed by, *social–scientific* thinking). *Clearly, so understood scientific ontology, if irreducible to, is often carried out within science itself.*

Whilst scientific ontology seeks to elucidate specific existents and their natures, *philosophical ontology* focuses on all other aspects of being, or on the existents in their wider context, including connections between existents, common properties if any, their mode of being, and so forth.

Ontological posits or presuppositions

In some contexts, it is impossible to study the nature of putative existents apart from working with the scientific theories in which they are posited or presupposed. Superstring theory provides an example. Notice that to *identify* the presuppositions of such theories is not *per se* to be committed to them. The latter additional step requires an acceptance of the *plausibility* of those theories. Indeed many natural scientists do not at this point accept superstring theory as a plausible theory.

An ontology

A convention adopted here is to refer to the specific results of ontological study as *an ontology*. The ambiguity involved of having the same word for both a form of study and its results is not uncommon; the same duality arises with such categories as history, geography, literature, science and much else; the appropriate meaning will usually be clear from the context.

Metaphysics

The term 'meta' in Greek means over, but it can also be interpreted as denoting behind or after;[6] whilst 'physis' translates as nature.

It is the interpretation of meta as 'after' that most commentators take as significant in the morphology of metaphysics. For the latter term is usually said to owe its origins to the fact that the relevant part of Aristotle's *Metaphysics* (ta meta ta phusika) (concerned with 'being qua being') was placed immediately *after* the part of the book called 'Physics'.[7] However, it seems just as likely that the term had immediate intuitive appeal (and thereby achieved ready acceptance) as denoting the *purpose* of metaphysics, which is (or includes) reaching above or beyond nature (physis) as we immediately perceive it, to uncover its most basic components or fundamental features.

If the term ontology is sometimes used to study hypothetical worlds whether considered possible or not, as well as the world in which we live, metaphysics is usually reserved for the latter.

Regional and specifically social ontology

A traditional goal of ontology has been to explore the possibility of a system of classification that is exhaustive in the sense that everything (we know about) can be interpreted as a particular instance.[8]

Whatever view might be taken regarding the endeavour of seeking a comprehensive schema for the whole of reality, there may be good reason rooted in the nature of being to demarcate sub-branches of ontology, to instigate projects in *domain-specific* or *regional* ontology.

The view defended here is that there is a domain of phenomena reasonably demarcated as social reality or the social realm that provides a site for a viable regional project in ontology. One seemingly non-arbitrary basis for distinguishing sub-domains for projects in regional ontology is according to shared modes of existence of a set of existents. This indeed is the basis upon which the social realm is delineated by the Cambridge group.

By *social realm* is meant that domain of all phenomena, existents, properties, etc. (if any), whose formation/coming into existence and/or continuing existence *necessarily* depend at least in part upon human beings and their interactions.[9] The predicate 'social' thus signifies membership of that realm or domain.

By *social ontology* is meant the study of the social realm in total. Clearly social ontology, as with all forms of social theorising, is part of its own field of study.

Emergence, system and organisation

The division of reality into separate domains raises the question of the relationship between them, if or where they exist. The definition of the social domain as the set of all phenomena resulting from the interactions of human beings indicates a presumed relationship of a form of dependency in this case.

A central category of domain (inter)dependence is that of *emergence*. Generally put, this category is used to express the appearance of novelty, or something unprecedented or previously absent. Of particular interest in the project of ontology described here are emergent entities or *systems* that are formed through the *relational organisation* of pre-existing elements that (perhaps with modification) become, through their being so organised, components of the emergent entity or system. Emergent entities of this sort are thus dependent upon, in the sense of being formed out of, elements (typically also systems) that pre-exist them.

By a *system* is simply meant a compositional, in some sense coherent, totality, embedded in some context and (in contrast say to a mere collection or aggregate) possessing an organising structure (providing coherence), whereby the pre-existing elements become both interrelated as components as well as bound to features of the environment (see Lawson, 2012, 2013a).

Ontological and causal reducibility and downward causation

An interesting set of questions in any context is whether an emergent entity bears causal powers, and if so what is the nature of the relation of these emergent powers to those of its components. Two doctrines, those of *causal reduction* and of *downward causation*,[10] are prominent in the relevant philosophical literature. The doctrine of causal reduction prioritises the causal powers of the components over those of the emergent totality, either synchronically or diachronically (in the latter case the causal powers of the totality are said to be explicable solely in terms of the causal interactions of the components). The doctrine of downward causation prioritises the causal powers of the emergent totality over those of its components, by having the former somehow act upon the latter. Both of these doctrines are rejected by the Cambridge group (see especially Lawson, 2013b). This rejection, in the context of specifically *social* ontology, amounts to a rejection of prominent versions of both *methodological individualism* and *methodological holism* (see Lawson, 2012, 2013a, 2013b).

Why engage in ontology?

So why bother with ontology as conceived here? In any domain where ontology, whether philosophical or scientific, can be successfully pursued, its value lies in bringing *clarity* and *directionality*, thereby facilitating action that is appropriate to context. For in theorising, as in all forms of human endeavour, it is quite obviously helpful to know something of the nature of whatever it is that one is attempting to express, investigate, affect, address, transform or even produce.

It is difficult to think of an area of life where knowledge of the nature of what is before us is not helpful. Ontological insight allows each of us to act differently in appropriate ways in the face of, say, a timid bird, a fragile antique, a bull, a tree, an expectant audience, a car, a hostile enemy or an earthquake. If examples such as these seem obvious, there is no reason for expecting the benefits of ontological awareness, if feasible, to be any less significant when the phenomena of interest are those encountered or addressed in the process of scientific research.

Of particular interest here is the systematic study of the possibilities of, and for, human flourishing, as a likely essential condition of any meaningful projects of human emancipation.

In addition, the study of the ontological *presuppositions* of theories and practices of different groups and communities can facilitate an understanding of varying cultural systems or even of 'academic tribes' (see below).

The study of the ontological *presuppositions* further allows the identification of inconsistencies and other potential inadequacies in scientific and other forms of reasoning. This is possible just where the ontological presuppositions of different aspects of specific theories or practices remain unexamined by their scientific creators and so are not compared either to each other or to any explicitly expressed worldviews.

Other uses of ontology, particularly as they relate to understanding social phenomena, are postponed to the section on social ontology below, where relevant matters are discussed in a less abstract fashion. Suffice it to say at this stage that ontology (in conjunction very often with the study of ontological presuppositions) serves not as a substitute for science or substantive theorising but as a Lockean under-labourer for such activity.[11] Its essential contribution lies in helping clear the ground a little so that substantive theorising can proceed more fruitfully than would otherwise be the case.

In the Cambridge project it is philosophical ontology, and in particular social–philosophical ontology, that so far has figured most prominently and extensively. However, this emphasis is seemingly uncommon in overtly philosophical circles and consequently appears in need of some defence. Indeed, many contributors, and in particular various twentieth-century philosophers working in the analytic tradition, have insisted that scientific ontology, specifically analysis that centres on the elaboration of the content of scientific theories, is the only defensible way of proceeding. In fact, within this latter group, it is very often held that not only is philosophical ontology as conceptualised here infeasible, but it is only the theories of natural science concerned with non-social phenomena that are usable for gaining ontological insight. Furthermore, various contributors even take the view that any kind of ontology concerned with a world *apart* from our theories is out of the question. According to this group, all that we can sensibly seek to achieve is the identification of ontological posits, a project to which they sometimes, if somewhat misleadingly, give the label of internal metaphysics.

At this point it is insightful to address the arguments of the sceptics. In doing so, defences are provided first of scientific ontology and then philosophical ontology where the focus is on non-social natural phenomena, and eventually of specifically social ontology, both scientific and philosophical.

In defence of scientific ontology

To the extent that twentieth-century analytic philosophy has accepted the project of ontology at all, this is usually associated with the contributions of Quine, particularly his 'On What There Is'. In this paper, Quine (1948/49 [1953]) argues that to be is to be a value of a bound variable. Bound variables are terms like 'thing', 'everything' and 'something'. Quine's contention amounts roughly to the claim that to be is to be in the range of reference of a pronoun.

If (to use Quine's example) a person declares 'some dogs are white' that person is actually saying that some things that are dogs are white; and for this statement to be true the things over which the bound variable 'something' ranges must include some white dogs. So in making the original utterance the person is accepting that white dogs are part of her or his ontological commitments.

When using the phrase 'to be is to be a value of a bound variable', Quine gives the impression that he is talking of what exists. However, it must be accepted that, first and foremost at least, he is indicating only how we determine whether someone (the author of a text) is committed to an existent. Thus, it could be argued that Quine is concerned not expressly with the way the world is, but only with ontological posits. Such an interpretation is feasible, and it has led some interpreters of Quine to argue that he is merely laying out a strategy that scientists and others should follow in order to clarify their ontological commitments.

If this was as far as Quine is prepared to go he would indeed belong to that strand of twentieth-century philosophy, inspired by Immanuel Kant and including the likes of Rudolf Carnap, Hilary Putnam and Peter Strawson, that has conceived all ontology as properly concerned not with any ('external') world in itself but only with human concepts, languages or systems of beliefs.

For this group the objective is simply to elucidate the ontological commitments of selected sets of language users or belief holders. Traditional ontology aimed at the world beyond is considered impossible; it is said to necessitate an 'external metaphysics' resting on a neutral perspective or 'God's eye view' capable of comprehending reality as it exists independently of our knowledge frameworks and language. In rejecting such metaphysics, members of the group in question argue that the most that can be undertaken is a study of the presuppositions or ontological commitments of specific theories or systems of belief, an activity termed 'internal metaphysics'.

Ontology in the sense of the study of any 'external' reality is thus replaced by the study of how a particular community or individual conceptualises a particular domain. The goal is merely to identify the conceptual presuppositions of sets of belief systems, languages and so forth. These proponents of 'internal metaphysics' thus seek to uncover features *not* of the world beyond conceptions, but of the belief systems of their subjects; the goal is an account *not* of the broader reality but of such features as the taxonomic system presupposed by speakers of a particular language or by researchers working within a scientific discipline.

However, Quine does seem to go further than this. Not only does he practise 'internal metaphysics' but, in accepting certain theoretical claims as reliable, he seems to be accepting the posited ontology as reliable as well. Further, Quine suggests that the way in which we accept an ontology is similar to the way we come to accept a scientific theory, that is by seeking to accommodate within a simple conceptual scheme all the relevant facts in the domain, albeit with the proviso that ontologists seek to accommodate not empirical facts but 'science in the broadest sense':

> Our acceptance of an ontology is, I think, similar in principle to our acceptance of a scientific theory, say a system of physics: we adopt, at least, insofar as we are reasonable, the simplest conceptual scheme into which the disordered fragments of raw experience can be fitted and arranged. Our ontology is determined once we have fixed upon the overall conceptual scheme which is to accommodate science in the broadest sense.
> (Quine, 1948/49 [1953], pp. 16, 17, page references to the latter)

Quine, then, at least in his influential 1948/49 [1953] contribution, appears seriously to engage in traditional ontology, the project of investigating the nature of reality. He treats it not as the study of scientific language, or some such, but of the world beyond (i.e. that does not merely reduce to) conceptions.[12]

If this is a reasonable interpretation of Quine, problems arise through his strategy for achieving his (pragmatic) goal of limiting the scope of ontology. Although Quine seemingly does always believe that some posits, some ontological commitments inherent in reasoning, are informative of the way the world is, with the passage of time at least, he is found suggesting that this is so only of some very special forms of reasoning. Thus, by the time of his *Word and Object*, Quine (1960) is suggesting that the entities we quantify over, and certain predicates we use, are indeed indispensable in everyday language, but have no ontological significance.

Rather he distinguishes a top-rate conceptual system (basically non-social natural science 'properly formalised') from a 'second-grade conceptual system' and simply asserts that only our first-grade conceptual system provides a serious or reliable account of what the world contains. Thus, Quine (along with Paul Churchland, Bernard Williams and various others) insists that only our best scientific theories about the world say anything seriously about what there is. Later, describing his position as *naturalism*, Quine writes:

Naturalism looks only to natural science, however fallible, for an account of what there is and what what there is does. Science ventures its tentative answers in man-made concepts, perforce, couched in man-made language, but we can ask no better.

(1992, p. 9)

Putnam (2004) amongst others thinks this signals the death of ontology. He observes that many of us (including apparently Quine) say things like 'Some passages in Kant's writing are difficult to interpret'. According to Quine's earlier reasoning, such assessments commit us to the existence of such things as 'passages that are difficult to interpret' as well as correct and incorrect interpretations of passages. Putnam reasons that, because the interpretation of text is not part of our best scientific theories, the later Quine and sympathisers must conclude that 'passages which are difficult to interpret do not exist' (Putnam, 2004, p. 13). Finding such a conclusion to be absurd, Putnam concludes that ontology has received a blow from which there is no recovery.

There are, though, certain features of the various lines of reasoning in play here that are less than compelling.

First, even if it were acceptable to hold that only theories belonging to a top-rate conceptual system ([non-social] natural science properly formalised) provide serious or reliable accounts of what the world contains, it would not follow that things posited in a 'second-grade conceptual system' need not exist. It is one thing to suggest that only our best theories give us *reliable* access to what there is; it is another to say that nothing exists that are not posited by these theories, and in particular that the posits of other second-grade theories must not exist. After all, some entities posited in first-grade science may also be posited in some 'second-grade' conceptual system or theory as well. Furthermore, where or if ideas originate as a second-grade theory which is later transformed into a first-grade one, the reasoning of our philosophers would seem to imply that the entities so posited did not exist until the acquisition of first-grade status of the theory brought them into existence. This is hardly an implication that these would-be scientific realists would want to endorse. In short, even accepting the dualistic thinking of these philosophers, the mere fact of an entity being posited in some 'second-grade' theory implies nothing of necessity about its existence.

Second, who is to say that the interpretation of texts is not part of our best scientific theories? This presupposes a conception of 'best' and of 'scientific' that is not provided.

Third, who is to say, or by what criteria are we to stipulate, that theories considered (by whom?) to be our 'best scientific' ones are the only ones suitable for the (ontological) task at hand? None of the philosophers in question provide any insight on this. It is widely acknowledged that many theories formulated in the social science academy, particularly economics, are unreliable. But the same is not obviously true of lay theorising. Indeed, when eventually the social realm is examined, it will be observed that it is more often the insights of lay theorising that inform the theories of economists rather than the other way around; it is lay theorising and understanding that constrain economists to posit certain real-world categories/ entities such as markets, money, firms, institutions, technology, etc.

Fourth, what anyway is the problem of allowing that things like 'passages that are difficult to interpret' exist, are real, are a part of being? Why should our accepting their reality signal the death of ontology? Quine clearly does not want to grant existence to too many things. But this is merely an a priori or pragmatic preference. Of course, if we refuse to adopt Quine's (arbitrary) stance, we must accept that ontology so conceived has an enormous field of enquiry. Indeed, it is the whole of being. But this merely means that in order to progress it is necessary, as here, to delimit any particular ontological project pursued. There is no obvious problem of principle with this. It just entails that we need to be clear about our field-delimiting strategies.

So there is no compelling case here to conclude that ontology is dead. At least a version of scientific ontology is found to be viable. As long as we are in possession of theories widely regarded as reliable, whose content can serve as premises for ontological analysis, there is reason to suppose that the presuppositions uncovered can relate to a reality beyond conceptions. Where this is not so then we can accept that, when employing the method of Quine, we are learning only about the presuppositions of scientists.

Scientific ontology, then, at least for the non-social natural realm, seemingly remains feasible. However, it is argued below that it is possible to go significantly further. And it is essential that this is so. For, amongst other things, to the extent that the objects of scientific theories are discipline or even sub-discipline specific, the relations between such entities inevitably fall outside the domain of ontology as Quine so narrowly perceives it. These are matters addressed shortly. To this point, the aim has been merely to establish that scientific ontology is not everywhere ruled out on principle. The objective next is to defend philosophical ontology. And this may seem to be the harder task. For it is widely held that this sort of philosophy, before all others, is necessarily a priori and transcendent. The goal here is to indicate that such a fear is unfounded.

In defence of philosophical ontology

The contention to be defended here, then, is that philosophical ontology need not be dogmatic and transcendent, but rather can be conditional and immanent. Quine allows that the theories of natural science constitute a legitimate entry point for scientific ontology just because, or where, they are taken as reliable. Reliability of entry points is the key here. But in seeking such reliability we are *not* constrained to consider, with Quine, only those claims that express the content of theories. It is just as legitimate, for example, to commence from any feature of experience regarded as adequate or successful to the relevant domain of reality, including most especially those concerning *human practices*.

Of course, once this is recognised, it can be seen that ontology need not be restricted either to scientific (as opposed to philosophical) ontology or indeed to the study of non-social phenomena. Philosophical ontology, at least as conceived here, aims at generalised insights, and reliable conceptions of human practices and so forth can be sought that are also reasonably generalised, including those relating to successful natural scientific practices as well as to everyday social ones.[13]

For example, to start with philosophical ontology regarding the non-social domain, it seems to be a relatively non-contentious, reasonably general assessment that practices of well-controlled laboratory experimentation often produce event regularities that otherwise would not (and do not) occur. Moreover, experimental results are also regularly applied outside of experimental scenarios where event regularities are not in evidence. What are the preconditions of these two generalised features of practical experience? Let a system or scenario in which an event regularity is produced, or occurs, be described as *closed*; a domain of reality that comprises more than one ontological level (e.g., that does not consist only of events) be described as *structured;* and let any components of a system which can be insulated from (the effects of) others be described as *separable*. Making sense of the experimental production of an event regularity seems to presuppose that the experimental activity is concerned with a) manipulating an intrinsically stable, and separable, causal mechanism, and more specifically with b) successfully insulating such a mechanism from countervailing factors, so that its effects are not offset by countervailing mechanisms. Under these conditions, an event regularity is produced correlating the triggering of the mechanism and its effects. Similarly, a recognition that experimental insight relates to a causal mechanism rather than an event regularity explains how experimental results are successfully applied where event regularities are not in evidence.

In other words, reflection on the conditions of experimental control reveals the domain of reality in question to be open (allowing the possibility of experimental closure), structured (constituted in part by causal mechanisms irreducible to events and their patterns) and separable.

Notice, then, that whilst reflection on a specific theory of science can provide insights about specific causal mechanisms (or whatever), reflection upon the ontological preconditions of certain generalised successful practices of science, this being an exercise in philosophical ontology, can provide more general insights, such as that the real world is characterised by such general properties as *structure, causality, separability* and *openness*, and so on.

Transcendental reasoning

In the experimental case just examined, the reasoning moves from generalised observations about experimental practices to inferences concerning
their conditions of possibility. Any argument that moves from certain
generalised features of our experience to their conditions of possibility
can reasonably be termed transcendental. It was mentioned above that
the arguments of Putnam, Carnap and others in favour of internalist
metaphysics are inspired by Kant. And this influence stems in significant
part from his use of the transcendental argument. Indeed, Kant explicitly
employs transcendental reasoning in a project concerned with replacing (what he viewed as misguided) endeavour aimed at disclosing the
nature of being by a set of investigations into the presuppositions of our
knowledge of being. Hence, to acknowledge a reliance on transcendental
arguments here may seem confusing.

But as already noted, these two activities – elaborating the structure
of reality and identifying the presuppositions of our knowledge of being
– need not be different projects, and specifically the latter can serve as a
means to achieving insights into the nature of being. An incompatibility
between the two projects arises for Kant only when, in his doctrine of
transcendental idealism, he identifies the task of uncovering the presuppositions of knowledge with that of elucidating the conceptual structures
in terms of which any knowable being must be thought. In this, Kant
is thus conflating practices that are conceptually distinct. Once we dis-
entangle them[14] we can accept transcendental reasoning just as fallible,
practically conditioned, investigation into some or other feature of our
experience, a practice which in philosophical ontology takes the form of
an investigation into generalised features of our experience, including of
human practices (see Lawson, 1998).

A point that warrants emphasis, perhaps, for it is rarely noted even
by those who accept the case for philosophical ontology, is that transcendental reasoning can be employed even where the practices initiating the
exercise are considered inappropriate in some sense. For such an exercise
can still give insight, albeit into the sort of reality in which the practices
being recommended or adopted would be appropriate. In this case, the
conception of reality in question can be contrasted with any other presupposed by successful practices, and relevant inferences can be drawn.[15]

There is no suggestion, finally, that transcendental reasoning is the only
method of philosophical ontology; no presumption that philosophical
ontology is somehow restricted to that method. However, this consideration of the workings of transcendental argument does serve to indicate
that philosophical ontology can be (and of course the argument here is
that it must be) conditional and immanent.

Social ontology

If the Cambridge concern has been mostly with philosophical ontology, the particular or 'regional' concern is with social ontology. To recall, by *social ontology* is meant the study of the *social realm*, where the latter is taken as comprising those phenomena whose coming into being and/or continuing existence depends necessarily on human beings and their interactions.

The concern of the Cambridge group is with the following two projects in particular:

1   *Social–scientific ontology*: the study of what is, or what exists, in the social realm, including the nature of specific social existents of interest; and
2   *Social–philosophical ontology*: the study of how social phenomena exist, their modes of existence, connections between social existents, common properties, and so on.

Although it has proven to be the case that insights of philosophical ontology have facilitated specific endeavours in scientific ontology, it is useful here to touch upon the latter project first.

Social–scientific ontology, an initial orientation

Whatever the extent to which philosophers have disagreed amongst themselves over the possibilities of ontology with regard to the non-social natural realm, there has tended to be a fair measure of agreement (though it is by no means universal) that social ontology is more or less a non-starter.[16]

There is one obvious reason for this widely shared assessment. Not only do the social sciences appear to be largely explanatorily unsuccessful, even by their own standards, but also they constitute a veritable cauldron of claims and counterclaims devoid of anything approaching consensus, and so are seemingly quite unable to provide potential entry points for ontological reasoning. Nowhere is this more obviously the case than within the discipline of modern economics.

Even so, and whatever the inherent difficulties facing projects in social ontology, there is actually one advantage that social–scientific ontology possesses over its non-social counterpart. This is that whilst the entities of (or posited within) natural science (e.g., super strings, quarks, tanon-neutrinos, black holes) are at first unfamiliar, being the objects of conceptions formulated within scientific work in the course of explaining observed phenomena, resolving theoretical contradictions and the like, and so in principle discoveries, the explanatory categories of social science, including economics, are typically already known (and agreed upon), at least under some description, prior to the work of science. This follows just because the social phenomena, unlike those of the non-social realm, emerge through human interaction and, *qua social phenomena*, depend on us, including our conceptions, for their continuing existence.

There is no suggestion here that lay conceptions are always adequate to their objects, of course. The claim is rather that we will likely already be aware of many, and possibly of most, social objects at some level. Thus, for example, any serious substantive account of aspects of capitalism will likely include categories such as markets, institutions, money, firms and production, all of which are prominent in lay conversation even if they often remain ill-defined and under-elaborated.

The primary problem with academic social–scientific theorising lies not with identifying the categories (although it may yet be that a realistic analysis may reveal hitherto unrecognised forms of phenomena) but in the fact that such categories as appear vital are treated differently in competing theories.

Thus, in some social theoretic contributions, the category *institution* denotes a pattern of behaviour, in others a set of rules, in still others a control system, and so on. Notoriously the category *money* is found to take different meanings in different paradigms, for example as a commodity, a unit of account, a means of exchange, a store of value, an accounting system and a marker of debts; whilst in the recently dominant paradigm of general equilibrium theorising, no place is easily found for any notion of money, a feature recognised within that project as a failing (see e.g., Frank Hahn, 1982[17]).

Indeed, observations of the latter sort bear on the assessment indicated briefly above, that by and large it is the insights of lay theorising that inform the theories of economists and not the other way around; it is lay theorising and understanding that constrain economists to posit certain real-world categories/entities such as markets, money, firms, institutions, technology, etc. (or to interpret their absence as a failing).

So, in summary, if social–scientific ontology has a head start on non-social–scientific ontology in being in possession of knowledge of relevant categories even before turning to scientific theorising, its problem is that much social theorising around these categories is found to be unreliable, and certainly contested. As a result it is difficult to find social–scientific claims or theories that can safely be treated as providing suitable premises for the ontological elaboration.

A recognition of the latter state of affairs may even encourage a belief that social ontology is necessarily restricted to investigating ontological posits in the conceptions of social theorists; that in such circumstances ontological enquiry can at best claim to achieve merely a form of 'internal metaphysics', not an understanding of any 'external' reality beyond theorists' conceptions.

It warrants emphasis that even if the latter sort of investigative endeavour were all that is feasible, it could still be of significant value. For to the extent that social theorists are committed to the content of their theories then such enquiry can be informative of the worldviews of social theorists, in the manner that psychology or anthropology can be informative of the worldviews of their subjects. Thus, it may be feasible to elaborate the worldviews of certain significant contributors, or, where a project is shared (and much modern economics, for example, is shared, encouraging Axel Leijonhufvud [1973] to talk of the 'economics tribe' in his classic 'Life Among the Econ'), of particular groups of social theorists.

For example, an ontologist concerned with the posits of modern economics could seek to tease out and elaborate the nature of the existents and interconnections presupposed in general equilibrium theory, or game theory, modern macro and micro economics, or new institutional economics, and so forth. The aim might be to elaborate how categories such as equilibrium, co-ordination, contract, competition, exchange, money, rationality, knowledge, beliefs, networks, society, etc., pan out in such conceptions. This is a project that may well prove attractive to those of an analytical philosophical bent.

Ontology as history of thought

This form of ontological analysis becomes a useful tool in the history of thought (on this see especially Lawson, 2005b). In particular, by examining a contributor's ontological preconceptions, it is often possible to throw further light on the nature and/or meanings of her or his substantive claims and contributions, especially where the latter are found to be otherwise open to a large number of seemingly ill-grounded interpretations.

Thus, through examining the ontological preconceptions of relevant contributors, it has proven possible, in economics, to give support to (contested) assessments, for example, that John Commons did hold a theoretical perspective (see Clive Lawson, 1994, 1995, 1996, 1999); that Friedrich Hayek's position changed significantly over time (Tony Lawson, 1994; Stephen Fleetwood, 1995, 1996); that Thorstein Veblen did favour an evolutionary economics as a realistic approach and not merely because making economics evolutionary would render it up-to-date (Lawson, 2003, chapter 9); that Karl Marx's theory (of capitalist tendencies) is not a deterministic theory (Fleetwood, 2001); and so on.

Of course, such projects of clarification presuppose that contributors being studied are reasonably internally consistent. But, not all are as internally consistent as they might hope to be. Indeed, it is conceivable that economists will sometimes profess worldviews that are at odds with those presupposed by their theorising. Here, though, is a yet further (or alternative) way in which social ontology of the sort in question can be useful: in revealing such inconsistencies (and possibly stimulating a dialectical process aimed at reconciling them).

Examples of this form of contribution already exist, of course. Thus, Mário Graça Moura (1997, 2002) focuses on the often-noted inconsistencies in Schumpeter's writings and shows that the explanation is that the ontological presuppositions of Schumpeter's equilibrium theorising are quite inconsistent with the worldview expressed in his vision of economic development. Stephen Pratten (1998) similarly shows that the inconsistencies between the ontological presuppositions of Marshall's equilibrium theorising and those of the theories of evolutionary biology explain Marshall's failure to achieve an intended second edition of his *Principles* incorporating insights from biology. Further, it is easy enough to subvert the claim of proponents of general equilibrium theorising that their project is essentially identical to Adam Smith's account of the invisible hand in his *Wealth of Nations* (see e.g., Kenneth Arrow and Frank Hahn, 1971, p. 1, for an example) by revealing the ontological presuppositions of the two to be quite opposed (see Leonides Montes, 2003; Lawson, 2005a, 2005b, 2006).

But still these contributions, and others like them, are not enough. Research endeavours aimed at clarifying how certain contested contributions are best interpreted, or at identifying and explaining inconsistencies in an individual's output, are certainly of value. But it does not provide insight into the basic structure of social reality; it throws little if any light on the world beyond our conceptions. It would be preferable to engage in social–scientific ontology that does. But is the latter possible?

Scientific ontology of this sort is indeed possible. But before indicating (and indeed in part in order to indicate) how it is possible, it is useful first to consider the feasibility of social–philosophical ontology. For the latter proves helpful to the former. Of course, where the latter is possible, it could never be sufficient for social–scientific ontology, not least because extra (fallible and contestable) empirical input will always be required. But, it can be enabling of it, not least by providing an account of the nature of social being with which all specific social existents conform. So at this point it is pertinent to turn to the question of the possibility of social–philosophical ontology.

In defence of social–philosophical ontology

It was earlier suggested that one fruitful approach to philosophical ontology is by way of (transcendental) arguments moving from premises concerning successful generalised human practices to conceptions of their conditions of possibility. Although it cannot be said that most social–scientific theories are reliable, we can accept that all of us successfully engage in various practices found reliably to facilitate our achieving day-to-day goals connected to going-on in life. Our practices are successful in the sense that they allow us to negotiate our way round a complex reality, an outcome intelligible only on the assumption that our individual practices are mostly appropriate to their conditions.

For example, a general feature of experience is that in any given community certain practices, for example driving on a particular side of the road, are repeated over and again by seemingly all community participants.

How can this be explained? The obvious explanation is that individuals base their individual practices on a community-wide shared social structure of some sort. In particular within the Cambridge group it is argued that a necessary condition for the observed behaviour to be possible is the existence of community-wide *collective practices*, that is of *accepted* or acknowledged or recognised or observed ways of doing things (the term 'accepted' is utilised as a generic term – without implying there is necessarily approval), which guide the practices that individuals follow throughout a specific community (see e.g., Lawson, 2003, chapter 2; 2012).

So a basic constituent of social reality is the collective practice. A collective practice is a way of proceeding that (implicitly) bears the status of being (collectively) accepted within a community. Various ways of proceeding might be imagined that could serve any outcome that (whether or not by design) happens to be facilitated through generalised conformity with a specific accepted way, i.e. with a specific collective practice; but for whatever reason, one way has turned out to be the way that is generally observed. Notice that there is always a range of behaviours consistent with any given collective practice.

A conception of social–philosophical ontology

In this manner (of transcendental argument) further constituents of the social realm can be identified and elaborated. That is, by similarly seeking out other seemingly general and relatively incontestable features of human practices (e.g., that many repeated practices are followed by [not all, but] only a subset of members of a relevant community; that any given restricted set of repeated practices is oriented to other repeated practices, etc.), and questioning their conditions of possibility, additional general (human interaction-dependent) conditions of (further) human interaction can be identified (see for example Lawson, 2003, chapter 2).

In this way a conception of the nature of the social realm can be built up. Rather than rehearse here the various arguments used in each case (for this again, see Lawson, 2003, chapter 2), the following sketch includes only a brief description of the social–philosophical ontology in this manner produced by, and currently entertained within, the Cambridge group (a more detailed recent account is found, for example, in Lawson, 2012, 2013a, 2013b).

Norms

Collective practices, however they originate, can be, and very often are (in being so 'accepted'), functional in the sense of serving to co-ordinate social interaction, by indicating to all would-be (and/or permitted-to-be) participants within a specific community how, amongst various conceivable ways of proceeding to a certain end, things are in fact done by other members of a community. In this way they facilitate relative stability, and thereby a degree of predictability. For this reason the idea of acceptance bound up with collective practices not only expresses the done thing (or things), but usually also carries connotations of normativity. Indeed, collective practices are often referred to just as *norms*.

Normativity arises because, or when, the noted indicative aspect of any collective practice is also interpreted as stipulative, as indicating how an individual *ought* to proceed. Collective practices, in order to facilitate co-ordination, etc., need to persist, and this usually *requires* that relevant individuals conform to (various interacting sets of) them.

Rights and obligations

The normative aspect of collective practices thus gives rise to the notion of *obligation* along with the associated category of *right*. Obligations refer to accepted ways in which relevant community members are expected to proceed; rights express accepted ways of going on in which relevant individuals may proceed. We accept the obligation to adhere to a community's norms or collective practices, where appropriate, if we wish to participate within that community. Equally, when we are part of a community, we are permitted to enter into at least some of the community's collective practices, and where this is so these can be seen as rights.

So social interaction is structurally organised, and is so through a generalised reliance upon collective practices involving rights and obligations. Notice that the role of rights and obligations in structuring social life presupposes the human capacities of being able to be both trustworthy and trusting of others, of being willing and able to make and keep to promises and other commitments, and to believe that others can and will also do so. It should be clear that these human capacities are necessary conditions for the interactions involved to occur, for obligations in particular to be efficacious. As such these capacities of trusting and being trustworthy, etc., qualify as much as anything for being categorised as the glue of social reality, as the adhesive that enables the organisational structure to achieve a degree of binding.

Organisation in process

Community life, then, is organised; and is so by way of emergent collective practices and their inherent rights and obligations that structure human interaction. The result is a social totality or set of totalities. And the latter have causal powers. A motorway system, for example, structured by various inter-connecting collective practices, has powers of co-ordinating that are irreducible to any of its various motoring components; and a language system has powers to facilitate communication that are irreducible to those of any individual communicator.

Although providing structure, collective practices are also inescapably processual in nature. The network of collective practices in place at any point is a condition of individual practices, and the sum total of individual practices, each a token of a collective practice, serves to reproduce and/or transform the total network of collective practices. So collective practices are both conditions and consequences of the individual practices they facilitate. They are reproduced and/or transformed through the individual practices or activities that they facilitate; they are inherently processual. The overall conception then is one of organisation-in-process; and any stability provided by a given (set of) collective practice(s) is always *relative* and *contingent*.

Social rules

Collective practices, as noted, possess normative aspects, and these are often linked to *social rules*. The latter are interpreted as expressions of the content of acceptances under their purely indicative aspect, *understood as stipulations*. They are representations of norms, interpreted as *generalised procedures for action* (see Lawson, 1997, 2003, 2012). As such they can always be (though they need not be, and are not always) expressed in a codified form along the lines of:

In C, if X then Y

Here C is the relevant community or context, X is type of activity and Y is the content of a collective practice. For example, if on *the continent of Europe* (C) an individual wishes *to drive on public roads* (X), then he or she should (amongst other things) *keep to the right* (Y).[18]

Rules, of course, are not always a posteriori features of spontaneously evolving collective practices. They may equally be introduced in an a priori fashion via a decision or declaration by a relevant body or sub-grouping of the community, and designed either to facilitate new forms of collective practice or co-ordination, or to transform the manner in which forms of co-ordination have previously been achieved, and so forth.

But whether a rule emerges from unplanned interaction or via authoritative declaration it amounts to an expression or formulation of a normative aspect of a collective practice. Thus, according to the conception here sustained, a rule is something that may be misinterpreted, broken, conformed to unwittingly, never codified and so forth, and so is clearly ontologically distinct from any practices with which it is associated.

Division of practice, process and events

Within any community there is also a division of collective practice; certain practices can be followed by some but not by others. In order to follow particular practices, membership of specific sub-groups within a community is often required.

In addition, practices that are accessible only to some community members are always oriented to, and indeed are constituted in relation to (that is, are *internally related* to), different practices accessible only to specific sets of others. Thus the collective practices followed by students are constituted in relation to those followed by teachers; those followed by employers, landlord/ladies, seminar presenters, sellers, etc., are constituted in relation to those followed, respectively, by employees, tenants, seminar participants, buyers and so on. All collective practices then cohere and interrelate with others, and are constitutively interdependent.

Any internally related combination of practices can be termed a *collective process*. Examples include the numerous interactions on a university campus, in a market place or within the governing system of a country. Distinguishable episodes supported by collective processes we might identify as *collective events*. Examples of the latter include particular lectures or seminars, concerts, weddings, funerals and games of football.

The framework of acceptances remains fundamental. In any community there are accepted ways of proceeding for each group, oriented to the collective practices of other groups. Similarly, there are usually accepted ways of allocating individuals to any particular group, processes of allocation that are themselves each a form of collective practice. Thus, the appointment of a particular individual as a university professor, say in the UK, will proceed according to the university and nationally accepted ways of making such appointments, and so on.

Positions

A category bound up with these different groupings is that of *social position*. A position, or rather position occupancy, is an accepted status that confers a social identity; to be allocated to a specific position is to acquire the social identity of being so positioned. Thus, an individual allocated to the position university professor acquires the social/positional identity of (is accepted within the community as possessing the status of) university professor, and so on.

Rights and obligations are now clearly seen to be associated with positions and thereby group membership. If some positional practices *may* be participated in by a specific set of appropriately positioned individuals, being the content of positioned *rights*, a subset of those same practices *should* be undertaken by these positioned individuals, being the subject of positioned *obligations*.

Thus, in the contemporary UK, an individual positioned as a university professor may have the right to borrow books from several libraries, to work in an office at all hours or to attend seminars in other departments. These rights are not available to all members of the wider UK community. But the individual is typically not only allowed, but additionally required, to give lectures and set and mark examinations, etc., and these are included amongst the employment obligations of the position.

Wherever positioned rights are to be found, there are always *accompanying* and *matching* obligations. Focusing on a given position, any rights from which the occupier benefits are always *accompanied* by obligations. Indeed, a position is essentially a locus of a set of specific rights and obligations, where the accepted position occupants are agents or bearers of these rights and obligations and typically possess a status or identity associated with them.

But any given position is always constituted in relation to others. And the rights of individuals in one group over individuals in another are *matched* by obligations of the latter group members with respect to the former. If university teachers have the right to set exams, students have the obligation to sit them, just as students have the right to expect the exams to be marked, and fairly, and teachers have an obligation to undertake this. Even the rights of university teachers to use offices, libraries, etc., are matched to obligations of other positioned individuals or groups to ensure there are processes in place serving to fund, facilitate and maintain university offices, libraries, lecture halls and so forth.

The internal relationality of sets of collective practices that was observed earlier can thus be seen to be bound up with mutually constituted sets of positions and positional rights and obligations.

Social power and social relations

If positional rights and obligations ultimately relate to ways in which certain positioned individuals can influence the behaviours of others, it follows that rights and obligations are in effect positional *powers*, respectively positive and negative powers. For the agents of rights (positive powers) have the causal capacity intentionally to get others, the subjects of those rights (those with relevant obligations, or negative powers), *to do something whether the latter want to do that something or not.* Obligations give reasons for action, and power exists so long as the 'subjects' in question are willing (and able) to fulfil their obligations.

So modern social reality fundamentally comprises a multitude of interrelating multi-component collective practices, processes and events bound up with an emergent structure of positional powers, comprising rights and obligations, in process.

Social relations

If human individuals are organised through being positioned as components of a system, and if the various positions are interrelated by way of connecting rights and obligations, then it is the latter powers that most qualify as the content of the category *social relation*. In other words a *social relation* just is (or is first and foremost) an accepted set of (matching) rights and obligations holding between, and connecting, two or more positions or occupants of positions. Social interaction can be understood as the contingent actualisations of such social relations. And because rights and obligations are forms of power, there is a sense in which all social relations are power relations.

In all this, if to repeat, the glue that renders these social relations as binding as they are is the human capacity both to be trustworthy and to trust, to enter into and to keep to commitments and to accept that others are able and willing to do so as well.

Artefacts and other non-human social objects

Parenthetically, inanimate objects can also, in effect, acquire social identities through being positioned within a social system. Various objects when suitably positioned take on the identity of cash, passports or identity cards, deeds of ownership, wedding rings and so forth. And once more this all depends on community acceptance. Of course, when inanimate objects are so socially positioned, the capacities or powers most closely associated with their positioning take the form *not* of rights and obligations but of system functions (see Lawson, 2009, 2012 and especially 2014a).

In effect this was noted from the outset in this overview of social–philosophical ontology with the category of collective practice. The latter is essentially a status attached to, or position into which is allocated, certain sets of repeated or routinized practices.

The nature of social kinds

Clearly categories of both social and non-social objects involve human construction or determination. Thus, if we want to refer to objects that are allocated to these sorts of categories as respectively social and non-social natural kinds, any distinction to be drawn between them is not a matter of category determination. However, a significant difference is that once categories are determined, then in the social realm, but not the non-social natural realm, the membership of specific kinds is also often down to human determination.

For example, once a specific community has decided that water is that stuff that is made up of H_2O molecules, it is in a sense nature that decides which of the phenomena around qualify as water. However, once a community (or its representatives) has decided the nature of say a university professor or perhaps a passport or form of money (namely anything appropriately positioned within a community), a relevant body of that community can also decide who or what is to be appropriately positioned as a professor or a passport or a given form of money in that community.

Community

The discussion up until this point has taken the idea of a community as a given. However, the conception of the community defended is *not* foundational (there clearly are no social foundations) but of an equally emergent and contingent component of a human practice-dependent social reality in process.

It has been emphasised throughout that collective practices, positions, rights and obligations are effectively properties of communities. Indeed the collective practices, positions, rights and obligations organise a certain group of individuals as members of, or participants in, a community. So a community is an emergent social totality or system. To the extent that there is a set of rights that apply to all community members, and given that all rights and obligations are attached to a position, it follows that community membership itself means occupancy of a specific social position. A community is precisely a structured totality whose individual components comprise the occupants of a certain specific social position.

Clearly, given that (positioned) rights and obligations structure all (positioned) collective practices, there is a sense in which each community must be seen to be a *moral community*. The nature of the community is elaborated at some length in Lawson (2012).

In short, social reality is found to be comprised of a multitude of inter-relating multi-component collective practices, processes and events that simultaneously both ground and presuppose a complex system of positions, positioned rights and obligations, that is, social relations, which are always in process, and serve, amongst other things, to organise individuals as social systems of community participants. The conception supported is clearly one of complex organisation or systems in process.

Social emergence

The conception of social reality elaborated, turning on the category of collective practice, is thus one of an emergent form of system or organisation; indeed, it is a system of systems, with each involving a relational organisation of component individuals that facilitates forms of co-ordinated interaction, (relative) stability and predictability that would be unavailable to each individual in the absence of any such organisation.

Certain powers of co-ordinated interactions are available to individuals *qua* community members, constituting affordances, involving rights and obligations, that would not have emerged if human individuals were instead mere biological beings that just happened to be situated in close time–space proximity to others but without much, if any, sense of group collective practices. So we have a form of organisation (of human interactions) that is ontologically irreducible, involving powers or affordances that are thereby causally irreducible.

It is just because such collective practices, including associated positions, rights and obligations, etc., as emergent forms of organising structure, are efficacious in facilitating co-ordinated interaction that *their reality is established*. And it is because they are irreducible to the individuals and individual practices which they organise that *their relative autonomy is grounded*, as is that of an appropriately oriented social science.

The category *social structure* is used to cover all the various features so far discussed that result from, and serve to relationally organise, human beings and individual activities, without being reducible to those individuals and their individual actions. Social structure, interpreted in this way, is not something additional to the phenomena so far discussed, nor is it a stuff of which they are composed. Rather, it is a general category that collects together the collective practices, acceptances, positions, rules, rights, obligations and such like that are emergent features of human actions and interactions. So the conception arrived at is one of emergent social structural organisation in process.

Just like social systems or communities as totalities, social structure is (synchronically) emergent in the sense of being dependent upon, but distinct from, and ontologically and causally irreducible to, the individual activities which these structures serve in turn to facilitate and coordinate.

Process once more

Social structure, so conceived, is clearly continually undergoing transformation, whether intended or unintended, understood or hardly recognised. Some transformation is clearly by design. But at least as significantly, position occupants regularly transform their positional rights and obligations, and indeed all forms of social structure, not intentionally, but merely as a by-product of merely carrying on in life.

All aspects of social structure depend on us, and so their continuing existence depends on their being reproduced through our individual practices in total. However, we often change how we behave, whether in response to changes in context, knowledge and technology, or merely due to accidents. When we come to act, the contents of previous acceptances, whether embedded in agreements, precedents or whatever, are given to us; and through our acting we both draw on them (whether or not we are explicitly aware of this), and also (if typically unintentionally) contribute not just to the reproduction of social structures but also to their transformation. Even where reproduction of aspects is the outcome, this is a contingent achievement, warranting as much explanation as change. Social reality is everywhere intrinsically dynamic in nature.

The human individual is also subject to continuous transformation. The ever-changing structural context facing the individual makes a difference not just through constraining and facilitating certain causal powers; it also affects the very nature of human individuals. Human beings develop psychological tendencies and social capabilities in a manner clearly influenced by their socio-cultural and geo-historical contexts, and as a result of experiences through life. Human beings, like social systems, are organisations in process; and the two are linked through processes of co-development, as both human individuals and social structures are continuously reproduced and transformed through the sum total of individual practices.

It can be noted, finally, that this account is thoroughly naturalistic, in the sense of being consistent with our best accounts of natural science, and with social phenomena recognised as both emergent and dependent upon non-social phenomena. All the components of social structure are either: 1) accepted or actual structural patterns or structural features of accepted forms of human practice; or 2) ideational, constituting various representations of the former along with interpretations of various aspects or properties as norms or rules, including positions, rights and obligations, along with the content of other previous and on-going acceptances, including the outcomes of decision-making processes, or the content of official declarations, all bearing on matters such as collective practices or the distribution of rights of access to community positions (and so to accompanying positional rights and obligations), etc.; or 3) both.

Consequences

The conception briefly sketched clearly has numerous implications for many matters including approaches to substantive theorising and ethics. For example, it obviously provides *directionality* to social theorising. In particular, it is suggestive of the sorts of scenarios for which researchers ought to be methodologically prepared. Because the social world is found to be structured (it is irreducible to, say, events and practices), it follows that social research will need to concern itself not only with correlating, or otherwise describing, surface actualities, but also, and seemingly primarily, with identifying the latter's underlying conditions. Indeed, it appears to follow that social–scientific research has, as a proper and compelling object, the explaining of surface phenomena in terms of its underlying conditions.

Alternatively expressed, the ontological conception defended encourages a consideration of how in social theorising, including economics, causal explanatory projects might best be conducted.[19]

For matters of ethics and projects of a practical or policy sort, it is relevant to recall that all human beings are found to be both shaped by the evolving relations (to others) in which they stand, as well as differently (or uniquely) positioned. If generalised flourishing is accepted as the goal of ethics, as the general good (see Lawson, 2014b), it follows that all actions, because they are potentially other-affecting, bear a moral aspect. And any policy programmes formulated without attention to differences, that presume homogeneity within human populations, are likely to be question begging from the outset. Certainly, programmes of action that ignore their likely impact on the wider community are immediately seen as potentially deficient (again see Lawson, 2014b).

Eventually, of course, such considerations point to questions of power, democracy and legitimacy. They raise questions of who should be taking decisions in a world of different identities where most of us are likely in some way to be (differentially) affected by actions taken by others. And indeed they invite a questioning of whether anything less than the whole of humanity (and possibly much more) can constitute a relevant unit of analysis and focus in the shaping of emancipatory projects and actions.

If the foregoing indicates something of the nature of the conception of social–philosophical ontology currently maintained, a remaining task to undertake here is to justify the contention that, with regard to social phenomena in particular, insights gained via philosophical ontology can aid the project of scientific ontology, that the results of philosophical ontology applied to social phenomena can facilitate the elaboration of social entities. It is this issue that is considered next.

Social–scientific ontology: some suggested criteria

The objective here is merely to sketch some (non-sufficient) criteria that phenomena investigated in social–scientific ontology might reasonably be expected to satisfy. Four are usefully elaborated.

There can be, to repeat, no direct inference from the results of philosophical ontology to the sorts of existents or categories investigated in scientific ontology. To reach the latter, additional empirical input is always required. However, in the case of social ontology at least, philosophical ontological findings can be said to be helpful to the task before us, and, in the circumstances that currently prevail, are possibly essential to it.

Amongst the results of the exercise in philosophical ontology described above are the insights that social reality is an emergent, open-ended, structured, transformational process in motion, in which the parts are constituted in and through their (changing) relations to each other. It follows that social entities of interest to, say, economists, such as money, markets, institutions, firms, social and individual identities, etc., ought to cohere with this conception. This, then, is a *first* criterion for any sustainable conception of a particular social entity.

If formulations of specific social entities, say of an institution, money, technology or a firm, can indeed be made to cohere in a satisfactory way with the previously elaborated results of social–philosophical ontology, there are likely to be various ways of achieving this in each case. On what basis, then, might a specific formulation be reasonably adopted?

Needless to say, the (realist) orientation adopted here accepts as an objective that the social category employed also picks out a definite feature of reality, that there is a definite referent. This is a *second* suggested criterion for any sustainable conception of a particular social feature.

Notice that, from the philosophical–ontological picture elaborated, all social phenomena are part of an emergent totality. An obvious question to ask of any conception of any particular social phenomenon is, what distinguishes it from anything/everything else? In virtue of what can it be identified? For if everything is constituted through its relations to everything else, how do we draw boundaries? Are there, for example, many markets or just one? And can we really distinguish, say, markets from money, or economy from society? Certainly we cannot use the tools of controlled experiment to insulate a particular social form from any other.

Furthermore, if change is fundamental to all social phenomena, in what sense can anything be identified as the same phenomenon over time? Are the phenomena we call money, Cambridge University, capitalism or the market place the same phenomena that were ascribed the same labels two centuries ago, or even two decades or two days ago?

These are questions less obviously, or perhaps less frequently, pertinent to the theorising of non-social phenomena, where there is perhaps reason to suppose that what we call hydrogen, quarks, tanon-neutrinos and water are the same (sorts of) things (or stuff) today as they always were, and wherever they are located. But in social theory the need to be everywhere addressing such questions as these seems to be unavoidable.

A seemingly important *third* criterion for a formulation of a category to be accepted is that it be consistent in a sense with historical usage. It would be unhelpful to interpret a term in a way that carries connotations that bear no relation to the manner in which the category has previously been understood. But still, how precisely is a specific interpretation to be determined?

An essential part of the answer, albeit one that will always seem unsatisfactory to some, is that it will depend on the context of analysis. We can see that at some level the conceptions resulting from mainstream formalistic–deductivist modelling will be forced into the separable and separated intrinsically constant mechanisms (or 'social atoms'), so that the formulation of categories in this literature must be treated with due caution. But there are other literatures as well as everyday lay understandings. It may even be that (many of) these are widely found to be realistic but perhaps dismissed on erroneous grounds, perhaps for not being sufficiently formalistic.

For example, some notion of an institution is widely adopted; even a dictionary definition can provide an input to a sustainable conception. Further, before the rise of the mathematical mainstream, the largest tradition in North American economics was that of institutionalism. For this project a conception of an institution was a central category, and indeed remains so. It is not being suggested that all such conceptions of an institution will be identical or perfectly coherent. Nor is there a unique way of proceeding. But a task of synthesising conceptions found in this literature can perhaps be usefully undertaken, employing the criterion that the resulting outcome defended be consistent with the earlier defended (philosophically derived) emergentist ontology. This synthesising process will typically be dialectical (preserving the insights of all conceptions dialectically developed). In any case, an initial conception might be continually revised to fit with relevant considerations. Put differently, the process might usefully involve what Strawson calls revisionary metaphysics in addition to the initial descriptive metaphysics. Unlike Strawson's conception though, the goal here are categories that express aspects of the basic structure of social reality.

If 'revisionary metaphysics' is indeed involved, a likely relevant *fourth* criterion to employ is that any conception defended has some theoretical or practical utility. It seems pointless transforming the meaning of a term in order to express something that, say, is already captured by a further category, or carries no analytical insight.

To repeat, there is no presumption here that these four criteria will be sufficient, or will always lead everyone to the same conclusion. But they do seem necessary to the process of elaborating sustainable social categories. The manner of discriminating amongst an array of competing conceptions consistent with the noted criteria will clearly depend on context-specific issues and considerations, though it may sometimes be a relatively simple matter to do so.

It is essentially through being guided by these criteria (augmented by context-specific alternatives) that members of the Cambridge group have elaborated the various social–scientific categories. These include conceptions of technology (Faulkner and Runde, 2009; Clive Lawson, 2012), gender (Lawson, 2007), money (Ingham, 1999, 2004; Tony Lawson, 2012), the corporation (Deakin, 2012; Tony Lawson, 2012) and the institution (Lawson, 2014c), amongst various others, including even a coherent conception of neoclassical economics (see Lawson, 2013c). It is probably fair to say, however, that it is scientific ontology of this sort (though in the process of being developed, and figuring continuously in the weekly workshops of the Cambridge Social Ontology Group) that constitutes the area of the group's thinking that has appeared less in published form.

It might usefully be re-emphasised, finally, that there is no suggestion here that the sort of approach just outlined constitutes the only possibility for ontological elaboration at the level of social entities. It all depends on context.

For example, where, or if, a social theory is, with reason, accepted as reliable, there is a case for scientific ontological elaboration along the lines suggested by Quine. Many accept the social theories of Marx as realistic, and much time has been spent elaborating Marx's categories of socially necessary labour time, exploitation, exchange and use value, and so forth.

But in modern economics, a widespread acceptance of any set of theories as even plausible remains a rarity, and is seemingly always contentious.

A further strategy is to borrow categories or theories or metaphors from domains other than the social, to render them consistent with the onto-logical conception defended here, and then enquire into their usefulness as a social category. In such endeavour, the analysis is necessarily modal rather than injunctive, that is, it involves investigating the relevance of the borrowed features rather than taking them as given.

An example is the borrowing of (Darwinian) evolutionary conceptions from biology. Obviously, in the light of the social ontology set out above, this evolutionary conception, which is already of an intrinsically dynamic mechanism, needs first to be rendered consistent with the account of human practice-dependent social transformation, before looking at, or as part of addressing, the question as to whether this evolutionary con-ception carries social theoretic relevance. The latter issue of course is an empirical one (for a lengthy analysis see Lawson, 2003, chapters 5 and 10; also see Nuno Martins, 2011), and so on.

Final comments

The aim of this 'position paper' is to set out the rationale for, briefly to describe and in part defend an on-going collective programme/project in social ontology.

The features that differentiate the project described from most others in ontology are that a) its primary concern is with the social domain and b) its ontological orientation has thus far been first and foremost philosophi-cal rather than scientific.

However, in contradistinction to many prominent conceptions of the essential nature of philosophical ontology, the approach adopted here is neither dogmatic nor transcendent but conditional and immanent; indeed it is as situated, fallible and practically conditioned as the more substan-tive contributions upon which it draws, and/or for which it seeks to under-labour. It does not analyse a world apart from that investigated by science and/or experienced in some form in (and navigated through) everyday social practices; rather it addresses that same reality but with different questions, emphases and tools.

To this point in time, the project in question has provided, before all else, a conception of the basic structure of social reality, a set of insights into the nature of social being; it has primarily concerned itself with social–philosophical ontology. Less attention has been paid to elaborating basic social categories or entities, the task many allocate to social–scientific ontology. For reasons laid out above, insights into these categories may actually be best achieved by way of (dialectically) com-bining philosophical ontology and socio-substantive accounts (including lay interpretations) in a programme of revisionary metaphysics. The fulfilment of the latter, though, lies mostly in the future. This paper has been concerned at least to provide any such programme with a rationale, and also to set out some grounds for supposing that a successful realisation of its objectives is entirely feasible.

Notes

1 First formulated December 2004 as 'A conception of ontology'; modified October 2009; modified again October 2010; and again October 2012, this time entitled 'A conception of social ontology'; and again July and finally November 2013. For helpful comments on various earlier drafts of this paper I am very grateful to members of (and visitors to) the Cambridge Social Ontology Group, most especially Ismael Al-Amoudi, Dave Elder-Vass, Phil Faulkner, Clive Lawson, John Latsis and Stephen Pratten. For financial support in producing the later versions I am grateful to the Independent Social Research Foundation.

2 On debates surrounding some of the issues elaborated here see Clive Lawson et al., 2007 and Edward Fullbrook, 2009. For comparisons with aspects of other projects see Pratten, 2007, 2013; Lawson, 2013b.

3 'Ontology', or rather 'ontologia', appears to have been coined in 1613 by two philosophers writing independently of each other: Jacob Lorhard in his *Theatrum Philosophicum* and Rudolf Göckel in his *Lexicon Philosophicum*. Its first occurrence in English seems to be in Bailey's Dictionary of 1721, where ontology is defined as 'an account of being in the abstract'.

4 As such, ontology should be distinguished from both epistemology, which is a concern with knowledge, and methodology proper, a concern with method.

5 In recent years the term ontology has also been widely used in the field of computer and information science. It is used to denote a formal language purposefully designed for a specific set of practical applications and contexts or environments. The aim is usually something like the construction of a formal representation of entities and relations in a given domain that can be shared across different contexts of application. This recent interpretation of ontology is not one I am especially concerned with here (for good discussions of it, see the contributions of Barry Smith, for example Smith, 2003).

6 Apparently this is because when X passes *over* Y it ends up either *behind* or *after* X.

7 Aristotle (384–322 BC) never himself used the term metaphysics (when he wishes to refer to the relevant part of his study he uses such terms as 'wisdom' (*sophia*), 'first philosophy' [*prōtē philosophia*] or 'first science' [*prōtē epistēmē*]). Nor even did he assemble the work we now know as *The Metaphysics*. The latter consists of a series of fourteen books, all or most of the material of which was written by Aristotle, most likely during the later period of his work; but it was not assembled in this way by him. Specifically the material was written after his leaving the Academy, Plato's school in Athens (Aristotle became a pupil of Plato [427–347 BC] at the age of seventeen, and remained for twenty years, first as a pupil and later as a relatively independent researcher, leaving after Plato's death), and following his founding (in 335 BC) his own school of philosophy in Athens: the Lyceum or Peripatos. But only after Aristotle's death, and probably between 200 and 100 BC, were these fourteen books arranged and published in the order with which we are now familiar. In fact the title itself, *The Metaphysics* was probably provided by Adronicus of Rhodes when he assembled the *Collected Works of Aristotle* in the first century BC.

8 Whitehead sets out a version of philosophical ontology which accepts this goal in describing his approach to 'metaphysics' identified explicitly as speculative philosophy:

> Speculative philosophy is the endeavour to frame a coherent, logical, necessary system of general ideas in terms of which every element of our system can be interpreted. By this notion of 'interpretation' I mean that everything of which we are conscious, as enjoyed, perceived, willed or thought, shall have the character of a particular instance of the general scheme.
>
> (Whitehead, 1978 [1929])

A similar position is taken by Mario Bunge, who, as well as distinguishing philosophical (or speculative), from scientific, ontology, also, if somewhat unusually for a philosopher, notes that ontology can (as in social ontology, which I turn to below) be 'domain' or 'region' specific. Thus, Bunge writes of ontology that it is

> The serious secular version of *metaphysics*. The branch of philosophy that studies the most pervasive features of reality, such as real existence, change, time, chance, mind, and life. [...] Ontology can be classed into general and special (or regional). *General* ontology studies all existents, whereas each *special* ontology studies one genus of thing or process – physical, chemical, biological, social, etc. Thus, whereas general ontology studies the concepts of space, time, and event, the ontology of the social investigates such general sociological concepts as those of social system, social structure, and social change. Whether general or special, ontology can be cultivated in either of two manners: speculative or scientific. The ontologies of Leibniz, Wolff, Schelling, Hegel, Lotze, Engels, Mach, W. James, H. Bergson, A. N. Whitehead, S. Alexander, L. Wittgenstein, M. Heidegger, R. Carnap, and N. Goodman are typically speculative and remote from science. So is the contemporary *possible worlds* metaphysics.
>
> (Bunge, 1999, pp. 200–1)

9   The term 'necessarily' serves to exclude factors that in a sense depend on us but only contingently so, for example all the natural structures and life-forms that we could destroy but do not.

10 Sometimes referred to as re-constitutive downward causation.

11 The interpretation of philosophy or methodology as an under-labourer for science can fairly be attributed to Locke. It is a conception provided, albeit almost as an aside, in the 'Epistle to the Reader' of his *Essay Concerning Human Understanding*. Here Locke writes:

> The commonwealth of learning is not at this time without master-builders, whose mighty designs, in advancing the sciences, will leave lasting monuments to the admiration of posterity; but everyone must not hope to be a *Boyle* or a *Sydenham*; and in an age that produces such masters as the great *Huygenius* and the incomparable Mr. *Newton*, with some others of that strain, it is ambition enough to be employed as the under-labourer in clearing the ground a little, and removing some of the rubbish that lies in the way to knowledge.
>
> (Locke, 1690 [1947], pp. xlii, xliii)

12 Of course, if Quine is a realist, his emphasis on the empirical under-determination of theories and of the under-determination of translations means that he is very cautious about allowing that anything can actually be known, as opposed to being capable of being ranked according to pragmatic use.

13 The fact that the approach outlined here differs from that of (I might suggest generalises that of) Quine on such issues has been noted in an interesting paper by John Latsis, 2007.

14 I am not even sure that the conceptual disengagement of transcendental argument from Kant's specific mode of application is particularly contentious. Thus I note that in the *Cambridge Dictionary of Philosophy*, Brueckner opens his entry on *transcendental argument* as follows:

transcendental argument, an argument that elucidates the conditions of possibility of some fundamental phenomenon whose existence is unchallenged or uncontroversial in the philosophical context in which the argument is propounded. Such an argument proceeds deductively, from a premise asserting the existence of some basic phenomenon (such as meaningful discourse, conceptualization of objective states of affairs, or the practice of making promises), to a conclusion asserting the existence of some interesting, substantive enabling conditions for the phenomenon. The term derives from Kant's *Critique of Pure Reason*, which gives several such arguments.

(Brueckner, 1995, p. 808)

Of course, although modern familiarity with transcendental argumentation derives from the manner it was taken up by Kant, its employment is found in philosophy stretching back through the middle ages to the ancient Greeks. Over time its interpretation has developed with new understanding, just as has the concept of an atom and almost any other notion. And the interpretation accepted here is certainly continuous with that running up to the present day through Kant.

15 Indeed, such a procedure has been consequential in modern social ontology, especially in relation to the study of the practices of modern economists (see e.g., Lawson, 2003, chapter 1).

16 There are of course exceptions to this, most notably the various contributions of Roy Bhaskar (e.g., 1989) and John Searle (1995, 2010).

17 As Hahn (1982) starkly concludes, 'The most serious challenge that the existence of money poses to the theorist is this: the best model of the economy cannot find room for it' (p. 1).

18 Needless to say, the category of social rule is also highly contested, not least within the Cambridge group itself. For useful discussions and overviews by members of the Cambridge group see for example Ismael Al-Amoudi, 2010; John Latsis, 2005, 2006, 2009, 2010, 2013; Nuno Martins, 2009.

19 This emphasis, in turn, points to a need to develop modes of inference over and above (the usual forms of) deductive and inductive logic. To pursue causal explanation as interpreted here, we require a mode of inference that takes us behind the surface phenomenon to its causes, or more generally from phenomena lying at one level to causes often lying at a different, deeper one. This is *retroduction*. The specifics of the explanatory context will bear upon how in practice the retroductive process might proceed. But it seems likely that it will often be helped along by a logic of analogy and/or metaphor, and rest usually upon ingenuity as well as luck.

References

Al-Amoudi, Ismael (2010) 'Immanent Non-Algorithmic Rules: An Ontological Study of Social Rules', *Journal for the Theory of Social Behaviour*, 4(3): 289–313.

Arrow, Kenneth J. and Frank H. Hahn (1971) *General Competitive Analysis*, San Francisco: Holden-Day.

Bhaskar, Roy (1989) *The Possibility of Naturalism*, Hemel Hempstead: Harvester Wheatsheaf.

Brueckner, A (1995) 'Transcendental Argument' in R. Audi (ed.) *The Cambridge Dictionary of Philosophy*, Cambridge: Cambridge University Press, pp. 808–809.

Bunge, Mario (1999) *Dictionary of Philosophy*, Amherst: Prometheus Books.

Deakin, Simon (2012) 'The Corporation as Commons: Rethinking Property Rights, Governance and Sustainability in the Business Enterprise', *Queen's Law Journal*, 37(2): 339–381.

Faulkner, Philip and Jochen Runde (2009) 'On the Identity of Technological Objects and User Innovations in Function', *Academy of Management Review*, 34(3): 442–462.

Fleetwood, Stephen (1995) *Hayek's Political Economy: The Socio-Economics of Order*, London: Routledge.

Fleetwood, Stephen (1996) 'Order without Equilibrium: A Critical Realist Interpretation of Hayek's Notion of Spontaneous Order', *Cambridge Journal of Economics*, 20(6): 729–747.

Fleetwood, Stephen (2001) 'Causal Laws, Functional Relations and Tendencies', *Review of Political Economy*, 13(2): 201–220.

Fulbrook, Edward (ed.) (2009) *Ontology and Economics: Tony Lawson and His Critics*, London and New York: Routledge.

Graça Moura, Mário (1997) *Schumpeter's Inconsistencies and Schumpeterian Exegesis: Diagnosing the Theory of Creative Destruction*, PhD dissertation, Cambridge.

Graça Moura, Mário (2002) 'Metatheory as the Key to Understanding: Schumpeter after Shionoya', *Cambridge Journal of Economics*, 26(6): 805–821.

Hahn, Frank (1982) *Money and Inflation*, Oxford: Blackwell.

Ingham, Geoffrey (1999) 'Money is a Social Relation', in Steve Fleetwood (ed.) *Critical Realism in Economics: Development and Debate*, London: Routledge.

Ingham, Geoffrey (2004) *The Nature of Money*, Cambridge: Polity Press.

Latsis, John (2005) 'Is There Redemption for Conventions?', *Cambridge Journal of Economics*, 29(5): 707–727.

Latsis, John (2006) 'Convention and Intersubjectivity: New Developments in French Economics', *Journal for the Theory of Social Behaviour*, 36(3): 255–277.

Latsis, John (2007) 'Quine and the Ontological Turn in Economics', in Clive Lawson, John Latsis and Nuno Martins (eds) *Contributions to Social Ontology*, London and New York: Routledge.

Latsis, John (2009) 'Hume and the Concept of Convention', *Recherches sur la Philosophie et le Langage*, 26: 217–234.

Latsis, John (2010) 'Are Conventions Solutions to Uncertainty? Contrasting Visions of Social Coordination', *Journal of Post Keynesian Economics*, 32(4): 535–558. With Guillemette de Larquier and Franck Bessis.

Latsis, John (2013) 'Conventions (Logic of)' in B. Kaldis (ed.) *Encyclopedia of Philosophy and the Social Sciences*, London: Sage Publications.

Lawson, Clive (1994) 'The Transformational Model of Social Activity and Economic Analysis: A Reinterpretation of the Work of J.R. Commons', *Review of Political Economy*, 6(2): 186–204.

Lawson, Clive (1995) *Realism and Institutionalism: John R. Commons, Carl Menger and Economics with Institutions*, PhD dissertation, Cambridge.

Lawson, Clive (1996) 'Holism and Collectivism in Commons', *Journal of Economic Issues*, 30(4): 967–984.

Lawson, Clive (1999) 'Commons' Contribution to Political Economy', in Philip O'Hara (ed.) *Encyclopedia of Political Economy*, London: Routledge.

Lawson, Clive (2012) 'Technology and Recombination', paper presented at the *Cambridge Realist Workshop*, November 2012; forthcoming as Chapter 8 of Clive Lawson, *Technology and Isolation*.

Lawson, Clive, John Latsis and Nuno Martins (eds) (2007) *Contributions to Social Ontology*, London and New York: Routledge.

Lawson, Tony (1994) 'Hayek and Realism: A Case of Continuous Transformation', in Maria Colonna, Harold Haggemann and Omar F. Hamouda (eds) *Capitalism, Socialism and Knowledge: The Economics of F.A. Hayek*, Cheltenham: Edward Elgar.

Lawson, Tony (1997) *Economics and Reality*, London: Routledge.

Lawson, Tony (1998) 'Critical Issues in Economics as Realist Social Theory', *Ekonomia*, 1(2): 75–117. Reprinted in Fleetwood, S. (ed.) (1999) *Critical Realism in Economics: Development and Debate*, London and New York: Routledge.

Lawson, Tony (2003) *Reorienting Economics*, London and New York: Routledge.

Lawson, Tony (2005a) 'The (Confused) State of Equilibrium Analysis in Modern Economics: An (Ontological) Explanation', *Journal for Post Keynesian Economics*, 27(3): 423–444 (Spring).

Lawson, Tony (2005b) 'Reorienting History (of Economics)', *Journal for Post Keynesian Economics*, 27(3): 455–471 (Spring).

Lawson, Tony (2006) 'Tensions in Modern Economics: The Case of Equilibrium Analysis', in Valeria Mosini (ed.) *Equilibrium in Economics: Scope and Limits*, London and New York: Routledge.

Lawson, Tony (2007) 'Gender and Social Change', in Jude Browne (ed.) *The Future of Gender*, Cambridge: Cambridge University Press.

Lawson, Tony (2009) 'The Current Economic Crisis: Its Nature and the Course of Academic Economics', *Cambridge Journal of Economics*, 33(4): 759–788.

Lawson, Tony (2012) 'Ontology and the Study of Social Reality: Emergence, Organisation, Community, Power, Social Relations, Corporations, Artefacts and Money', *Cambridge Journal of Economics*, 36(2): 345–385.

Lawson, Tony (2013a) 'Emergence and Social Causation', in J. Greco and R. Groff (eds) *Powers and Capacities in Philosophy*, London: Routledge.

Lawson, Tony (2013b) 'Emergence, Morphogenesis, Causal Reduction and Downward Causation', in M. Archer (ed.) *Social Morphogenesis*, New York: Springer.

Lawson, Tony (2013c) 'What is this "School" called Neoclassical Economics?', *Cambridge Journal of Economics*, 37(5): 947–983.

Lawson, Tony (2014a) 'A Speeding up of the Rate of Social Change? Power, Technology, Resistance, Globalisation and the Good Society', in Margaret S. Archer (ed.) *Late Modernity: Where are we Going?*, New York: Springer.

Lawson, Tony (2014b) 'Critical Ethical Naturalism: An Orientation to Ethics', in Stephen Pratten (ed.) (2014).

Lawson, Tony (2014c) 'What is an Institution?', in Stephen Pratten (ed.) (2014).

Leijonhufvud, Axel (1973) 'Life Among the Econ', *Western Economic Journal*, 11(3): 327–337.

Locke, J. (1690 [1947]) *An Essay Concerning Human Understanding: Abridgment Selected and Edited by John W. Yolton*, London and Melbourne: Dent.

Martins, Nuno (2009) 'Rules, Social Ontology and Collective Identity', *Journal for the Theory of Social Behaviour*, 39(3): 323–344.

Martins, Nuno (2011) 'An Evolutionary Approach to Emergence and Social Causation', *Journal of Critical Realism*, 10(2): 192–218.

Montes, Leonides (2003) 'Smith and Newton: Some Methodological Issues Concerning General Equilibrium Theory', *Cambridge Journal of Economics*, 27(5): 723–747.

Pratten, Stephen (1998) 'Marshall on Tendencies, Equilibrium and the Statical Method', *History of Political Economy*, 30(1): 121–162.

Pratten, Stephen (2007) 'The Scope of Ontological Theorising', *Foundations of Science*, 12(3): 235–256.

Pratten, Stephen (2013) 'Critical Realism and the Process Account of Emergence', *Journal for the Theory of Social Behaviour*, 43(3): 251–279.

Pratten, Stephen (ed.) (2014) *Social Ontology and Modern Economics*, London and New York: Routledge.

Putnam, Hilary (2004) *Ethics Without Ontology*, Cambridge, Mass: Harvard University Press (page references to a mimeo version of Lecture IV: 'Ontology: An Obituary').

Quine, Willard Van Orman (1948/49 [1953]) 'On What There Is', *Review of Metaphysics*, 2: 21–38. Reprinted in Quine (1953) *From a Logical Point of View*, Cambridge, Mass: Harvard University Press.

Quine, Willard Van Orman (1960) *Word and Object*, Cambridge, Mass: MIT Press.

Quine, Willard Van Orman (1992) 'Structure and Nature', *The Journal of Philosophy*, 89(1): xx–xxx.

Searle, John R. (1995) *The Construction of Social Reality*, London: Penguin Books.

Searle, John R. (2010) *Making the Social World: The Structure of Human Civilisation*, Oxford: Oxford University Press.

Smith, Barry (2003) 'Ontology', in L. Floridi (ed.) *Blackwell Guide to the Philosophy of Computing and Information*, Oxford: Blackwell.

Whitehead, Alfred North (1978 [1929]) *Process and Reality (Corrected Edition)*, edited by D. Ray Griffin and Donald W. Sherbourne, New York: The Free Press.

2　Quine and the ontological turn in economics[1]

John Latsis

1. Introduction

Contemporary social theory (Archer, 1995; Lawson, 2003; Fleetwood & Ackroyd 2004) and philosophy of social science (Bhaskar, 1979 [1998]; Cartwright, 1989; Mäki, 2001) make frequent reference to ontology, often stressing the central importance of ontic considerations in the construction and criticism of both theory and empirical approaches. This 'ontological turn' within the social sciences is a mixed bag, incorporating a number of different and occasionally conflicting points of view (for more detail on this see Pratten, 2007). This paper will focus on one strand within ontologically-orientated social theorising: critical realism. More specifically, I will focus on Tony Lawson's contributions to the development of critical realism in economics in relation to similar developments in analytic philosophy.

The connections between traditional analytic philosophy and critical realism are limited and their respective literatures seem to evolve in parallel, rarely recognising each other. My aim in this chapter is to contribute to a potential dialogue by showing that critical realism is addressing a series of problems that have only recently been re-opened for debate within philosophy in general. Whilst Bhaskar is responsible for this re-awakening within critical realism and the philosophy of the social sciences more generally, Willard Quine re-introduced the study of ontology within analytic philosophy. Quine's impact was revolutionary and, according to my arguments, he raised many of the fundamental questions that need to be addressed by *any* form of ontological research. This is of particular interest to social scientists and philosophers of social science because much of Quine's extended discussion centred around 'abstract objects', a subject that is crucial to the elaboration of modern socio-ontological systems. Moreover, an investigation of Quine's views on ontology raises another important issue for modern social ontology: the diversity of ontological perspectives. In the case of Quine and Lawson, we can see that two authors with similar motivations and styles of argument come to radically different conclusions about the constitution of the world. Common agreement on the importance of *ontology as a discipline* is not sufficient for the common acceptance of *an ontology* (a worldview).

This chapter will begin with a brief exegesis of Quine's early contributions to ontology. I will then argue that there are significant parallels between Lawson's ontological turn in economics and Quine's seminal arguments set out in his 1953 book *From a Logical Point of View*. Having demonstrated that Quine and contemporary social theorists such as Lawson are grappling with the same problems, I will show where the contrast sets in. A common focus on renewing ontological research does not lead in one pre-ordained direction. The conclusions of ontological research and the methodological advice it may generate can take divergent, even conflicting, forms. In the final part of this essay the full implications of Quine's ontology are drawn out. His approach is found to present a distinct set of challenges to Lawson's social-ontological project.

2. Quine's ontological turn

Ontology, normally understood, is the science of being, the systematic study of the fundamental structure of reality. Philosophers of the early twentieth century had distanced themselves from any ability to partake in such an activity, so discussions of ontology were both uncommon and unfashionable when Quine began writing in the 1930s.[2] The logical positivists and empiricists who dominated analytic philosophy tended to regard it as obscure and outdated and references to ontology or metaphysics were usually pejorative. One of the dominant figures of this early period was Rudolf Carnap, who was both the inspiration for, and the target of, Quine's writings.

Carnap believed that philosophers did not engage in substantive debates. Philosophical arguments were mistakenly carried out in the 'material mode' (the mode used to discuss substantive problems) when they should have been carried out in the 'formal mode' reflecting their status as issues about linguistic expression. Thus, according to Carnap, the traditional philosophical disputes about the existence of objects, properties and universals were actually discussions about language. For example, the philosophical question 'Are there properties?' could be translated as 'Should we adopt a linguistic framework which employs " – is a property" as one of its fundamental general terms?'. Questions of ontology ultimately turned on which linguistic frameworks a given community settled on. Moreover, according to this view, the adoption of linguistic frameworks was the result of pragmatic considerations rather than correspondence to reality, so the ontological import of philosophical debate disappeared completely. Philosophers could safely multiply their usage of abstract categories without having to justify them on traditional empiricist grounds because these categories made no claims about the constitution of the world.

Quine's rejection of the dominant orthodoxy was based on a refusal to truncate philosophy and scientific thought in this manner. In a series of essays published in 1953 as *From a Logical Point of View*, Quine provided the basis for a new research programme in analytic philosophy. Quine believed that the natural sciences were the most successful area of human knowledge production and that philosophy was continuous and interconnected with them. The ideas that he explored were intended to demonstrate this posited continuity. One important argument involved showing that both philosophical and scientific questions, unlike his predecessors had maintained, turn on ontological issues.

However, Quine did acknowledge what he regarded as an obvious reason for the belief that ontology didn't matter. He realised that the existence claims of any theory are so basic to it that they can become virtually transparent to the theorist, allowing philosophers to ignore them. 'One who regards a statement on this subject [ontology] as true at all must regard it as trivially true' (Quine, 1953: 10).

Thus, for Quine, any discussion of being is parasitic on a set of sentences that are implicitly accepted as *true*. These 'observation sentences' are the source of human knowledge and any theory can ultimately be reduced to them.[3] It is only once some such set of sentences have been accepted as truths that questions of existence can be raised. This is why Quine concentrates his attention on the ontological commitments of theories. The objects which any given theory is about must be those objects that are claimed to exist if the theory is to be true.

Quine addressed a number of philosophical disputes using these insights.[4] In so doing, he accentuated the parallels between philosophical problems and scientific ones by likening philosophical ontologies to sets of theoretical entities:

> Our acceptance of an ontology is, I think, similar in principle to our acceptance of a scientific theory, say a system of physics: we adopt at least insofar as we are reasonable, the simplest conceptual scheme into which the disordered fragments of raw experience can be fitted and arranged.
>
> (Quine, 1953: 16)

While he did not associate ontological speculation with an ability to intuit the 'real' structure of the universe, Quine was determined to show that philosophers and scientists alike were committed (through their conceptual schemes) to the existence of the entities they discussed: they could not shy away from ontology. In this sense, different theories were describing different worlds, and those who posited apparently fictitious theoretical entities in order to achieve their theoretical goals would have to admit that they held those entities to *exist* and hence presumably to empirically investigate these existence claims.

But ontology had been neglected in philosophy precisely because the ontic commitments of theories were usually implicit and unstated. In order to draw attention to these commitments, Quine proposed a departure from the dominant Russellian theory of reference.[5] In principle, this would allow him to show the ontological commitments of any given theory. He avoided the pitfalls of the riddle of non-being by insisting that a name does not require objective reference in order for it to have meaning. Instead, the conveyors of meaning are what modern logicians call *bound variables*, these can be expressed as sentences beginning with 'there is'; and variables of quantification such as 'something', 'nothing' and 'everything'. Bound variables do not work like names; they possess a generality and intrinsic ambiguity that allows them to refer to entities broadly, without denoting specific, pre-assigned objects. So, according to Quine, 'To be is to be the value of a variable' (1953: 15). In other words, we commit ourselves to an ontology containing a centaur when we say that *'there is something* that is a centaur', but we can still safely say *'there are not* centaurs' without invoking their existence.

Both scientists and philosophers make ontological commitments in their usage of bound variables and they become committed to entities through linguistic performance. The resort to the canonical notation of first-order logic allowed Quine to determine the ontic commitments of theories.[6] These commitments are made explicit through formalisation and cannot be admitted unless they can be translated as the value of a bound variable.

By introducing the study of ontic commitments, Quine recognised that there is basic ontological inconsistency between competing theories. As we shall see later, he suggested that pragmatic criteria such as simplicity would decide between competing conceptual schemes. His discussions of ontology gave renewed credence to the notion that different theories can indeed propose different accounts of the world, and conflicts between these accounts are important to the development of human knowledge.

3. Lawson's ontological turn

Echoes of Quine's work have recently appeared in the writings of some critical realists interested in the social sciences. A recent example of this is Tony Lawson's critique of economics (1997, 2003). For Lawson the critique of mainstream economics must be ontological: '... for a central aim of my project is to indicate the significance of ontological enquiry, of facing up to ontological issues *explicitly*' (Lawson, 1997: 33).

Accordingly, the widespread disarray in economics is due to a generalised neglect of social ontology. Much like Quine, Lawson claims that economists *do* make ontic commitments in their models, yet these commitments are difficult to uncover. Economists are usually quick to deny that the assumptions of their models are supposed to reflect reality, so Lawson investigates explicit commitments in order to uncover implicit ontological *presuppositions*. This leads him to investigate what he sees as the defining feature of modern mainstream economics: *method*.

Through his research into social ontology, Lawson provides a twist on the Quineian dictum that all theories presuppose an ontology; he argues that all methods presuppose one too: 'Now, all methods have ontological presuppositions or preconditions, that is conditions under which their usage is appropriate. To use any research method is immediately to presuppose a worldview of sorts' (Lawson 2003: 12).

The argument is simple. In order for a particular method to generate explanations and predictions it must presuppose a world with certain features. Few economists state or recognise the type of worldview they rely on in their theories. However, their methods do not lie: they are only appropriate for a certain type of world. The lack of appreciation for this relationship between method and ontology is the leading cause of what Lawson perceives to be a systematic lack of fit between economic theories and the social world.

More precisely, Lawson contends that the methods of economics commit economists to a world with certain key characteristics. For example, one important ontological presupposition is a direct consequence of the attempt to deduce predictions in terms of regularities in events: '... any presumption of the universal relevance of mathematical modelling methods in economics ultimately presupposes a ubiquity of (strict) event regularities' (Lawson 2003: 13).

In the language of critical realism, the presuppositions of mainstream economics include the view that the social world is a closed system.[7] In addition to this, economists rely on a number of other implicit ontic commitments. In modelling the social world as a closed system, they are compelled to treat the units of their analysis (individuals) as social atoms devoid of intrinsic structure and only activated by the impingement of external forces and stimuli. Furthermore, in order to be able to aggregate successfully, individuals must also be conceived of as isolates. Their actions must be unresponsive to all conditions not explicitly set out in the model.

Yet according to Lawson, the lack of observable patterns in events is evidence that social scientists are not dealing with a system with these characteristics. The social system that economists study does not display event-regularities of the sort 'whenever x then y' in the form of a closure of causal sequence. Economic agents are not atomistic or isolated. For Lawson, this realisation is the crucial step in the formulation of an alternative ontology for economics, one that is both explicitly stated and studied in its own right. He elaborates a specific vision of the social world inspired by Bhaskar's transcendental realism: the 'transformational model of social activity' (Lawson, 1997: 157–188; 2003: 3–62). According to this alternative worldview, the social world is an open system populated by active intentional agents with their own aims, plans and goals. These agents are not isolated but evolve in an environment characterised by emergent social structures inherited from prior generations. Individuals live in large networks of internally related social positions, their actions are influenced by rules and conventions. The dynamic and processual nature of social life is recognised by the transformational model. Change is incorporated as new generations of agents adopt, reject or transform the structure inherited from their predecessors.

It is not the purpose of this paper to fully develop or defend the ontological reforms suggested by the Lawsonian critique of economics. Instead I describe it in order to show that, like Quine, Lawson has demonstrated a desire to take ontology seriously. This attitude contrasts with the majority of economists who, licensed by the positivistic disdain for ontology, ignore the implications of their ontic commitments. Theoretical assumptions are widely acknowledged by economists not to be descriptive of the social world and are openly adopted in order to facilitate the construction of axiomatic-deductive models which are the typical output of the profession. Thus, the ontic commitments of economics are disguised by both a complex method and a neo-positivist rhetoric, leaving them obscure and implicit. Like Quine before him, Lawson draws attention to the intrinsic problems of this strategy and demands that economists face up to the ontological commitments that their theories necessarily make.

4. Common ground?

A number of features undeniably figure in both Quine's critique of positivist philosophy and Lawson's critique of neoclassical economics. Both writers were reacting against a dominant mainstream that is disdainful of ontological enquiry by emphasising the fact that their opponents cannot avoid ontic commitments. Indeed the revolution in philosophy that was facilitated by Quine's arguments laid the groundwork for many of the modern developments in social ontology. The criticism of positivist philosophy of science encouraged those who favoured a much more metaphysics-heavy approach, hence the increasing dominance of realist philosophies of science within the academic mainstream. The demise of positivism in economic methodology was also in large part due to the transplantation of these critical arguments. Some commentators have explicitly drawn attention to this, linking the development of realism in the philosophy of the social sciences with the philosophies of the leading critics of positivism, Quine and Thomas Kuhn (Hands, 2001: 116–117).

It is also clear that both Quine and Lawson are interested in what some commentators have referred to as traditional metaphysics or ontology (Lowe, 1998: 2; Smith: 8–9). They are both defending a view of ontology that is directed at the world, not at the arguments or ideas of other philosophers or economists. In emphasising the importance of ontological commitment, Quine was pointing out that any theory had to range over some set of entities, and that scepticism or confirmation of the theories should result in the belief or denial of those entities. As a direct result, many of his arguments were negative, directed against the proliferation of philosophical and logical categories that had followed in the wake of logical positivism. Lawson makes a similar point about the structure of the social world. His criticism of economics is premised on the argument that economists must recognise the world that their models purport to describe. By investigating the ontological presuppositions of economic theory, Lawson teases out economists' ontic commitments and suggests an alternative. Even though one talks of the explicit ontic commitments of theory and the other of the implicit ontic presuppositions of method, both Quine and Lawson defend the view that the existence claims of any scientific approach are crucial to our understanding of it.

In addition, both Quine and Lawson share a radical and revisionist approach to ontological theorising. Historically, one of the important functions of ontology has been to uncover and describe the ontological commitments of theological or scientific doctrines. This taxonomic function persists in the work of modern ontologists and is even seen by some as the primary goal of ontology.[8] It is therefore common to emphasise the importance of a taxonomy of existing theory and remain reticent about pursuing an explicitly revisionist programme. Neither Quine nor Lawson hesitate to use ontological arguments for critical purposes. Quine used his ontological insights to problematise a number of empiricist categories that were widely accepted by his contemporaries. By showing what philosophical theories made existence claims about, Quine was able to propose revisions that were consistent with his preferred physicalistic ontology and naturalised epistemology. In the same vein, Lawson proposes a radical overhaul of economic theory by examining its ontology and contrasting it with the transformational model.

5. The status of 'abstract entities'

There is strong evidence that the arguments of Quine and Lawson bear a family resemblance, but the philosophical background to these arguments is significantly different. While they agree on the importance of recognising and studying ontology they disagree on which ontic commitments one should adopt and why. The locus of the disagreement can be drawn out by investigating the Quinian category of 'abstract entities'.

Quine emphasises simplicity as the guiding principle in the choice of ontological and conceptual frameworks. Conceptual frameworks are at the service of research practices. If they increase the organisation and efficiency of scientific procedure, the entities they assume can be admitted. On this reading not all ontic commitments are equal, they are justified by their utility within a productive scientific enterprise. This Quinian take on ontic commitment is usually referred to as 'pragmatic'.[9]

Quine suggests that, given these pragmatic considerations, physical objects are to be generally preferred to abstract ones. There are two overriding reasons for having such confidence in an ontology of physical objects:

physical objects are accepted as the basis of common linguistic communication; and they are also accepted as the termini for scientific explanations (Quine, 1960: 238). According to Quine, this makes them a good bet for ontic commitment. But there is no grand philosophical argument for this view; Quine rejects philosophical arguments that justify the reification of physical objects in light of their closeness to sense experience.[10] Neither logic nor scientific practice rule out a non-physicalist ontology.

Thus, an ontology containing 'abstract entities' is in principle acceptable to Quine, provided that those entities fulfil an indispensable role in simplifying and expediting scientific enquiry. He gives the example of real numbers and classes as possible candidates for this ontological status on the grounds that they can be successfully employed in mathematical and scientific problem-solving (Quine, 1960: 237).

Nevertheless, though Quine's pragmatism rules out an outright rejection of non-physicalistic ontologies, he tries to minimise their invocation. Speaking of his imaginary opponent Wyman, Quine expresses this desire eloquently: 'Wyman's overpopulated universe is in many ways unlovely. It offends the aesthetic sense of us who have a taste for desert landscapes ...' (Quine, 1953: 4). There is an obvious tension between the recognition of abstract entities and Quine's desire to limit the range of entities and promote the simplicity and efficacy of theory.

A major theme of Quine's early writings was the discussion of ways to control the proliferation of ontic commitments and prevent 'disorderly ontic slums'. Though his discussions tend to focus on the philosophical categories prevalent at the time of his writing, he still gives a good idea of how this control could be achieved. Drawing on contemporary philosophical disputes, Quine suggests a criterion for abstract entities to be recognised: *discernible identity conditions*.[11]

> Still the lack of a standard of identity for attributes and propositions can be viewed as a case of defectiveness on the part of 'attribute' and 'proposition'. Philosophers undertook, however unsuccessfully, to supply this defect by devising a standard of identity, because they were persuaded of the advantages, in systematic utility or whatever, of taking 'attribute' and 'proposition' as full-fledged terms and so admitting attributes and propositions to the universe of discourse.
>
> (Quine, 1960: 244)

So, not only must a prospective abstract entity play some important role in increasing the simplicity and power of our theories about the world, it must also have a clearly defined standard of identity. Quine defends physicalistic ontologies by appeal to the body of scientific research that (allegedly) proposes clear and discernible conditions under which any given entity x persists over space and time.

This means that, for Quine, our common-sense vocabulary of material objects is fundamentally anchored in physical theory which ascribes spatio-temporal continuity to objects. Similarly, the advocates of abstract entities must show that these too have discernable identity conditions. According to Quine these identity conditions would then provide more or less definite standards for individuating one abstract entity from another and could therefore play an important role in the development of theory.

At first glance this might seem a significant challenge to a research programme that has principally concerned itself with the elaboration of abstract categories in social ontology. Critical realists use the transcendental method to infer the existence of abstract categories, however few if any attempts to ascribe clear identity conditions to the elements of the transformational model of social activity have been made so far. It appears that ideas such as emergence, social structure, or macroscopic causal powers might be difficult to accommodate within Quine's framework. It is also questionable whether critical realism would be able to subscribe to the Quinian insistence on strict identity conditions.

6. Reality, identity and physicalism

In the case of the transformational model of social activity ontic commitments tend to proliferate. Abstract entities and categories are essential to the attempt to theorise the social world along Lawsonian critical realist lines. So whilst Quine's parsimonious taste does not rule out social ontology, it presents a challenge to those who would regularly appeal to non-physical entities and processes in their analyses of the social world.[12] But before considering how Quine might challenge the Lawsonian approach to economics, we must address an initial objection that could be raised against any juxtaposition of these two authors whatsoever.

A serious question over the validity of any comparison between Lawson and Quine arises out of the status each confers to theoretical language. For Quine, the study of ontic commitment involves the study of the basic observational statements of a scientific language. Thus, his claim that ontology should be taken seriously can be re-interpreted as a simple plea for linguistic clarity in scientific theory. On this view, the specific content of a set of ontological claims is not central to the Quinian project, whereas the logical structure of arguments and the rigour of existential statements is.

It might be objected that in contrast to this Quinian approach, the project of critical realism in economics has a very different purpose. Critical realist ontology is often understood as the study of being itself and, particularly in the case of the social sciences, this activity is not necessarily mediated by existing theory. The introduction of theory as a wedge between ontological elaboration and experience of the world might be seen as a crucial step in the Quinian argument and one which critical realists are unwilling to take. Thus, it could be objected that Quine commits an epistemic fallacy: he takes the subject of ontology to be talk about the world as opposed to the world itself.

While this objection does help to focus attention onto some of the important distinctions between Quine's and Lawson's projects, it does not undermine our ability to draw significant parallels. At the root of the objection is the argument that Quine's emphasis on theoretical entities removes ontological discourse from the realm of entities and places it in the realm of concepts and ideas. The ontologists' concern is thus deflected from questions of being to questions of meaning and reference. But this interpretation of Quine, at least in his early writings, is simplistic. The insistence on the use of existential quantifiers to articulate clear theoretical entities *does* reflect a concern with the concepts we use in order to make existence claims. However, this is an unremarkable observation: ontological analysis is always mediated through concepts. Studying the thing-in-itself and the concept by which we delineate the thing cannot be neatly separated. This applies to Lawson in the same way as Quine: neither can transcend language, and so conceptual analysis remains a crucial part of ontology for both.

At this point an objector might change tack. The crucial difference between Lawson and Quine is one of motivation; the former is concerned with describing the world while the latter is simply concerned with describing the presuppositions of scientists. But this objection involves a further misunderstanding of Quine's position. He was interested in making more precise the 'internal metaphysics' of the scientific community (particularly physicists), but this was not an arbitrary choice, it reflected an ontological commitment to physicalism.[13] Physicalism amounts to the belief that the ultimate constituents of the universe are described by physical theory and that, given this, the termini of explanations should attempt to reflect or at least be consistent with that theory.[14] This, paired with Quine's advocacy of a holistic understanding of science, lead to a belief that physical theory held a privileged position in the web of human knowledge.[15] By elucidating the ontological presuppositions of physical theory, Quine believed that we could get the best available purchase on the world around us.

It is in this overriding commitment to physicalism that the first serious divergence between Lawson and Quine arises. In his later writings such as *Word and Object* (1960), Quine's position is very specific in limiting the legitimate scope of ontology. He distinguishes 'top rate' and 'second grade' conceptual systems, conferring epistemological priority to the former and refusing to acknowledge that the latter might help us elucidate anything about the world. So while the Quinian focus on the presuppositions of natural scientific theory is perfectly in line with the traditional approach to ontology advocated by Lawson and other critical realists, the substance of his ontological position and his advocacy of physicalism is not.

For Lawson the ontological turn in economics involves a form of transcendental argument from practices to their conditions of possibility:

That is, it is accepted that all actual practices, whether or not scientific, and whether or not successful on their own terms, have explanations. There are conditions which render practices actually carried out (and their results) possible. Let me refer to this supposition as the *intelligibility principle*.

(Lawson, 2003: 33)

'The form of reasoning that takes us from widespread features of experience (including here conceptions of generalised human practices, or aspects of them) to grounds or conditions of possibility, is the *transcendental argument*' (ibid.: 34).

In further characterising his argument as *retroductive*, Lawson shows how the strategy he adopts involves a move from the phenomena of experience to their underlying causes. Herein lies a development characteristic of recent philosophy of social science within the critical realist tradition: underlying causes are not restricted (as they would be by Quine) to the microphysical level and hence physicalism is rejected. For Lawson the ontic commitments of a successful economics might include (amongst other things) social relations, positions, rules and conventions. These aspects of social structure are seen as causally implicated in the conditioning of human behaviour and the production of human practices and Lawson makes no attempt to reduce them to the facts of biology or physics. This critical realist perspective sees the restriction of ontology to the domain of the posits of the natural or experimental sciences as arbitrary and unjustified, a relic of scientism.

This brings us to a second major divergence. Quine tends to restrict discussion to ontic commitments to 'entities' of some sort or other. This, of course, fits with his own emphasis on the natural sciences and with the empiricist tradition of modern analytic philosophy. Even when he discusses abstract categories such as real numbers and logical operators, the discussion is still couched in terms of entities.[16] Yet Lawson and other critical realists appear not to restrict their discussions to entities. More specifically, in the case of social ontology the metaphor of entities seems particularly inappropriate. Social categories do not represent 'things' with the phenomenological characteristics of the medium-sized objects so beloved of philosophers. This bears importantly on the difficult Quinian question of identity conditions. If social phenomena are not characterised as entities at all, then how can they be assigned stable conditions of identity?

There is little in the critical realist literature that can settle this issue. However, the extensive reference to social structure as a central mechanism of the transformational model of social activity shows where the difficulties are likely to arise. Social structures, if they are to exist and persist over time, would have to accommodate the possibility of changing membership. If their temporal continuity is to be preserved, they cannot be reduced to the sum of their physical parts (individuals). Thus one traditional candidate (individuals) for a strict reductionist criterion of identity in the case of social structures is ruled out from the onset. In fact, much of what Lawson writes suggests that the analogy of entities and the accompanying quest for stable conditions of identity might be impossible. For example his discussion of society as an 'ontology of process' appears to rule out a sufficiently strict set of such conditions:

> What about the idea that society is a process? According to the conception sustained, social structures such as households, markets, universities, schools, hospitals and systems of industrial relations do not independently exist (and often endure over significant periods of space–time) and undergo change. Rather, change is essential to what they are, their mode of being. They exist as a process of becoming (and decline).
>
> (Lawson, 2003: 44)

Of course, the discourse of critical realism has not been developed in conjunction with older discussions of ontology within analytic philosophy, and so the import of these two Quinian challenges is difficult to assess. My brief discussion of the difficulties of establishing stable criteria of identity within a critical realist ontology of the social world does not rule out the possibility that they might be discoverable.[17] However, it does point to a fundamental divergence in practice between Quine's ontological turn and the one proposed by Lawson and the project of critical realism in economics. Quine's desert landscape is in stark contrast to Lawson's rich and complex social reality.

7. Concluding note

The task of this chapter has been to develop a critical comparison between new developments in critical realist-inspired social ontology and older debates within analytic philosophy. Quine is the main figure in the re-introduction of ontology as a respectable discipline within twentieth-century analytic philosophy and as such his position provides an interesting contrast case. Both Quine and Lawson undertake self-conscious ontological challenges to the assumptions of their respective disciplines. Both deny the ability of practising theorists to shy away from ontic commitments and demand that those commitments be explicitly stated. We can go further by claiming that Quine and Lawson share a traditional ontological perspective that goes beyond the simple enumeration of scientific presuppositions. The presuppositions of science are relevant to ontology inasmuch as they give us a better purchase on the structure of the world around us.

The real divergences emerge when Quine's ontological prescriptions are put into practice. The physicalist perspective that he defends and his scepticism about abstract entities challenge the content of the critical realist transformational model of social activity. Social phenomena are rarely characterised as entities in the latter framework, and our ability to discover clear and stable identity conditions for them is thrown into doubt. These insights suggest a set of issues that could be developed within the literature on social ontology. Are Quine's demands for strict identity conditions legitimate in the case of social objects? If so, can the processual nature of those social objects be accommodated? Future research in social ontology would benefit from attempting to answer the Quinian challenge and adding greater depth and detail to the transformational model in the process.

Notes

1 I am grateful to Lorenzo Bernasconi, Clive Lawson, Nuno Martins and Catherine Meldrum for comments on an earlier draft of this paper. My thanks also go to the participants in the IACR 2004 conference, where a version of this paper was presented. This chapter first appeared as Chapter 8 in Lawson, C, Latsis, J and Martins, N, eds, 2007, *Contributions to Social Ontology*, Routledge.

2 In discussing Quine's contribution I will concentrate on early publications that were crucial to the reintroduction of ontology into modern philosophical debate. His later work on 'ontological relativity' (Quine, 1969) marks a development of these ideas that has also generated a great deal of discussion. I shall not discuss these later views in this chapter as they represent a departure from his initial position.

3 Observation sentences are uncontroversial statements such as 'it's blue', 'there's a car' and 'it's dark'. These sentences must fulfil three criteria: they must be complete utterances whose truth value changes according to the occasion on which they are uttered; they must be directly tied to the stimulation of the uttering individual's sensory system; there must be general acceptance of the conditions under which these utterances are acceptable from the point of view of the linguistic community.

4 Most famous perhaps was the 'riddle of non-being' (Quine,1953: 1–16). In an early article, he contrasts his position with the views of two fictitious philosophers (McX and Wyman). These philosophers contend that there is something that Quine does not recognise. However, in order to formulate the disagreement between them, Quine cannot admit the disputed entity without contradicting his prior rejection of it. This riddle of non-being stubbornly resists Occam's razor because a non-entity must be 'something' in some sense, otherwise what is it that we claim there is not?

5 Russell's theory of descriptions translates names into singular descriptions that affirm the uniqueness that is implicit in the use of 'the' in a given sentence. This approach implies that the name acts as an incomplete symbol that can be paraphrased out in context to give a meaningful description.

6 Theories were never completely isolated however. Echoing Pierre Duhem, Quine argued that scientific theories were interconnected; theories in the biological sciences, for example, are related to and supplemented by theories in the other sciences as well as the theorems of logic and mathematics.

7 According to Lawson, a closed system is one in which the triggering of real causal mechanisms results in the production of predictable empirical patterns expressed as regularities of the form 'whenever x then y', where x and y are two events in a causal sequence. The latter proviso is intended to cover the possibility of event regularities where x and y are simultaneously caused by

a third variable. Closures of this type are referred to as 'closures of concomittance'. These systems involving closures of causal sequence are rare even in the natural world and critical realists have argued that they only infrequently occur outside the laboratory.

8 See the work of Uskali Mäki for an example of this. His definition of economic ontology highlights the taxonomic character of ontology: 'The study of economic ontology is concerned with what may be called "the economic realm": the economic realm consists of those parts or aspects of the universe which are set apart as constituting the subject matter of economics' (Mäki, 2001: 4).

9 A reference to the American pragmatist tradition of Dewey and James.

10 For a discussion of the possible conflict between the physicalistic and phenomenological conceptual schemes see Quine (1953: 17–19).

11 This is consistent with his discussion of ontic commitment because clearly stated conditions of identity make terms accessible to variables of quantification.

12 The only recent attempt to introduce Quine into the methodology of economics is notable for its quietist attitude towards social ontology and its criticism of 'Lawsonian Realism' (Boylan & O'Gorman, 1995: 171–177).

13 Ironically, Quine's overriding physicalism eventually affected his attitude towards ontology in general. In a later piece he carried out a systematic deconstruction of the very concept of a physical object motivated by his (updated) understanding of contemporary physical theory (Quine, 1976). Quine concluded that, as physicalists, our ontology of the world must reduce to pure set theory, yet he recognised that theories and systems of knowledge cannot be so reduced (ibid.: 502–503). This move permeated his writings in the seventies and eighties, bringing them much closer to the caricature alluded to above. Quine's radical shift towards internal metaphysics is stated unambiguously in the final lines of the 1976 paper:

> We might most naturally react to this state of affairs by attaching less importance to mere ontological considerations than we used to do. We might come to look to pure mathematics as the locus of ontology as a matter of course, and consider rather that the lexicon of natural science, not the ontology, is where the metaphysical action is.
>
> (ibid.: 503–504)

14 In a more recent contribution Quine refers to naturalism as fundamental to his position:

> Naturalism looks only to natural science, however fallible, for an account of what there is and what there is does. Science ventures its own tentative answers in man-made concepts, perforce, couched in man-made language, but we can ask no better.
>
> (Quine, 1992: 9).

This has been recognised as a return to a more explicitly ontological project on his part (Georgalis, 1999).

15 Quine's views on the interlinked nature of human knowledge are discussed in a later publication, *The Web of Belief* (Quine & Ullian, 1970).

16 This position changed in his later writings as the 'entities' physicalist philosophers liked to invoke came to be undermined by physical theory itself (see for example Quine, 1976; and note 13 in this essay).

17 A critical realist response could, of course, take a completely different tack in responding to the demand for identity criteria. Quine's later writings on ontology suggest that stable identity conditions for physical objects are highly problematic themselves (1976: 497–499). With the development of physics through the latter part of the twentieth century, it could be argued that physical objects have begun to take on many of the problematic features of their social counterparts. Thus for example, one potential account of what physical

objects might be views them as spatio-temporally scattered and lacking the neat boundaries that the early Quine required.

References

Archer, M. 1995. *Realist Social Theory: The Morphogenetic Approach*. Cambridge: Cambridge University Press.

Bhaskar, R. 1979 [1998]. *The Possibility of Naturalism: A Philosophical Critique of the Contemporary Human Sciences* (3rd ed.). London: Routledge.

Boylan, T. & O'Gorman, P. 1995. *Beyond Rhetoric and Realism in Economics*. London: Routledge.

Cartwright, N. 1989. *Nature's Capacities and Their Measurement*. Oxford: Oxford University Press.

Fleetwood, S. & Ackroyd, S. 2004. *Critical Realist Applications in Organisation and Management Studies*. London: Routledge.

Georgalis, N. 1999. 'Ontology Downgraded All the Way', *Pacific Philosophical Quarterly*, Vol. 80: 3, pp. 238–256.

Hands, D.W. 2001. *Reflection without Rules*. Cambridge: Cambridge University Press.

Lawson, T. 1997. *Economics and Reality*. London: Routledge.

Lawson, T. 2003. *Reorienting Economics*. London: Routledge.

Lowe, E.J. 1998. *The Possibility of Metaphysics*. Oxford: Clarendon Press.

Mäki, U. (ed.) 2001. *The Economic World View*. Cambridge: Cambridge University Press.

Pratten, S. 2007. 'Ontological Theorising and the Assumptions Issue in Economics', in C. Lawson, J. Latsis and N. Martins (eds), *Contributions to Social Ontology*. London: Routledge.

Quine, W. V. 1992. *Pursuit of Truth*, revised edition. Cambridge, MA: Harvard University Press.

Quine, W.V.O. 1953. *From a Logical Point of View*. Cambridge, MA: Harvard University Press. (2nd ed., 1980.)

Quine, W.V.O. 1960. *Word and Object*. Cambridge, MA: The MIT Press.

Quine, W.V.O. 1969. *Ontological Relativity and Other Essays*. New York: Columbia University Press.

Quine, W.V.O. 1976. 'Wither Physical Objects', in R.S. Cohen *et al.* (eds), *Essays in Memory of Imre Lakatos*. Dordrecht: D. Reidel Publishing Company.

Quine, W.V.O. & Ullian, J. 1970. *The Web of Belief*. New York: Random Nord.

Smith, B. 2003. 'Ontology', in L. Floridi (ed.), *Blackwell Guide to the Philosophy of Computing and Information*. Oxford: Blackwell.

3 The scope of ontological theorising[1]

Stephen Pratten

1. Introduction

A considerable number of explicitly ontological elaborations and assessments have been undertaken within economics in recent years. Evaluations of the ontological commitments of influential authors or schools of thought have become recognised and valued forms of methodological reflection. Examinations of the ontological status of social rules, institutions and the human agent now regularly feature in the economic methodology literature and in heterodox economics journals. However, ontological analysis in economics is far from a single, unitary endeavour. Rather a range of individuals and groups pursue projects of different kinds with varied intellectual ambitions. These projects often deploy quite distinct conceptions of ontology and come to competing conclusions concerning the contribution that ontological theorising can make to the discipline of economics. Some of these projects see the role of ontology as being primarily descriptive, concerned with revealing the ontological commitments of economists. This, it is often emphasised, is a complex affair; within a particular substantive contribution there may be various layers of analysis with each potentially implying rather different, even incompatible, ontological commitments. Others suggest that beyond this ontological theorising can and should set out and defend an account of the basic features of social reality. Once such an account has been provided some argue it can be used to assess the ontological commitments of economists. If we can formulate an abstract account of social reality, one that can be shown to be more sustainable than alternatives available, then we can move to a negative evaluation of those substantive contributions that presuppose a metaphysics of the social realm dramatically at odds with it. Or at least we can do so in circumstances where such substantive contributions cannot offer much in the way of empirical support of their own for their claims.

If one can speak of an ontological turn in economics it is important to acknowledge that it has taken a variety of different forms. These differences are only beginning to be appreciated, but the dividing lines are

starting to emerge and skirmishes between the various camps are breaking out. Those occupying each end of the spectrum of views concerning
the nature and role of ontological analysis regard those located at the other
pole with a degree of suspicion. Those at the more descriptive end view
those at the other end of the spectrum as engaged in rather wild and rash
metaphysical speculations and prone to loose characterisations of economists' ontological commitments. Meanwhile, those who elaborate and
defend a position in social ontology and use it as a measure with which
to critically evaluate the presuppositions of economists see any limiting
of the role of ontological theorising to outlining the metaphysical commitments of others as altogether too timid an option. Indeed, sometimes
impatience is expressed toward those who endlessly defer offering any
ontological commitments of their own. An examination of how these projects relate to one another is likely to help clarify the contributions of each
and the significance of any general shift toward ontological theorising in
economics and economic methodology.

In this paper I compare two projects engaged in ontological theorising in
economics. The first is that of critical realism in economics associated particularly with the work of Tony Lawson and others based in Cambridge.[2]
The critical realist project has a very explicit ontological focus. According
to advocates of critical realism in economics an engagement with ontological issues can provide both a sharper understanding of the problems
associated with mainstream economics and direction for those seeking a
more relevant alternative. Indeed, it is the focus on ontological issues that
distinguishes critical realism in economics from the variety of heterodox
traditions out of which it has grown and to whose development it seeks to
contribute. Lawson argues that the primary role of ontology is the

> elaboration of as complete and encompassing as possible a concep-
> tion of the broad nature and structure (of a relevant domain) of reality
> as appears feasible. The aim is to derive a general conception that
> seems to include all actual developments as special configurations.
> Put differently, a central objective is to provide a categorial grammar
> expressing all the particular types of realization in specific contexts.
>
> (2003a: xvi)

Lawson and his associates have certainly engaged in the analysis of the
ontological commitments of economists but they also seek to provide an
abstract account of social reality.

The second set of contributions I consider are the writings of Nancy
Cartwright on metaphysics, causality and method and more specifically
on the nature of contemporary economic theory. Her project has been
described by some as in part a metaphysical one. Psillos, when reviewing
Cartwright's work in the philosophy of science, suggests that one of her
major contributions has been to show how

metaphysics can be respectable to empiricists. Hence scientific realism cannot be dismissed on the grounds that it ventures into metaphysics. To be sure, the metaphysics that Cartwright is fond of is not of the standard a priori (or armchair) sort. It is tied to scientific practice and aims to recover basic elements of this practice ... But it is metaphysics, nonetheless.

(2002: 1)

Moreover, when Cartwright turns her attention to economics the focus has, at times, been on explicitly ontological issues. Consider the way she expresses her concerns regarding the assumption, standardly adopted in much econometric analysis, that data can be conceived of as being drawn from an underlying probability distribution: 'You shouldn't think that the probabilistic approach [to econometrics] avoids ontology. It just chooses one ontology over another. To my mind it makes the wrong choice' (1995d: 72–3).

The commonalities between these projects extend beyond a shared focus on ontology. There exist similarities in terms of the methods used and arguably the kind of ontology each elaborate. And yet there are differences too; Cartwright admits to ultimately being reluctant to engage in any bold programme of ontological elaboration. When summarising the message of her book *The Dappled World* she writes: 'My overall conclusion is the old fashioned positivistic advice: Do not let metaphysical issues ... intrude into our scientific practices. Where this is not possible, hedge your bets and hedge them heavily' (2003: 1). This would seem to mark a substantial difference with critical realism in economics where there is greater enthusiasm for sustained ontological elaboration including its extension to incorporate the development of a highly abstract account of the social realm. In this paper I reveal what these projects share and identify the differences that mark them out as distinct enterprises.

Certain aspects of the relationship between Cartwright's work and critical realism have been previously explored in the context of the philosophy of physics (see, for example, Chalmers, 1987). However, no extended comparison of these projects has been offered in relation to how they address central themes in economic methodology.[3] It is particularly useful to draw out this comparison at this time when there still remains much uncertainty as to what precisely ontological analysis can contribute to economics. The comparison is especially helpful because both projects, or so I shall argue, represent alternatives to a narrow conception of the potential of ontological analysis in which it is restricted largely to cataloguing the ontological commitments of economists, where setting out and defending a favoured ontological position is seemingly deferred indefinitely and critical evaluations of the practices of economists are studiously avoided. Both Cartwright and advocates of critical realism in economics offer a more ambitious alternative. Both are prepared to forward far-reaching criticisms of the typical methodological strategies adopted by the majority of contemporary economists. In section 2 I highlight the similar concerns regarding dominant current trends in economics and show how the powerful criticisms offered emerge as a consequence of each project engaging in sustained ontological analysis of a particular type. And yet these are not identical projects by any means. The goal of setting out a highly abstract set of social categories that advocates of critical realism pursue is seemingly not shared by Cartwright who is careful to tie any metaphysical speculation to observations concerning successful scientific practice.

I argue, in section 3, that both the similarities and the differences between these projects can be better understood once we recognise that they draw on distinct conceptions of the nature and legitimate scope of ontological theorising. For Lawson generalised features of experience that are not connected to successful scientific practice are legitimate initiating premises for ontological elaboration. This enables him to develop and defend a particular social ontology. In seeking to clarify certain aspects of the account of ontological theorising that Lawson favours I use Peirce's writings on the nature of sustainable metaphysical analysis as a point of reference. These writings help us understand aspects of the approach to ontological theorising critical realists pursue that have previously not been defended or elaborated on at length. I conclude that Lawson's and Cartwright's projects demonstrate in complementary ways how ontological theorising can help promote the development of a more relevant economics.

2. A shared diagnosis of the limitations of mainstream economics

For some who insist that ontological theorising should adopt a largely descriptive orientation to speak of mainstream economics at all already betrays a worrying clumsiness. The suggestion is that in the current context, with a discipline that is so splintered and specialised, it is rather unhelpful to refer to an overarching category of mainstream or orthodox economics to which key characteristics can be attached. The concern is that those who fall into this trap will only provide a caricatured and unsophisticated reading of the field. For some, there simply is not a mainstream economics which we can usefully refer to and seek to characterise, or at least they argue that it is far too early for us to be able to claim that there is with any degree of confidence. The emphasis they suggest should be upon fine-grained accounts of specific contributions or schools of thought. This might allow for careful comparative work but a global characterisation of 'orthodox economics' is at this time a non-starter.[4] While I think both Cartwright and advocates of critical realism would wish to acknowledge the importance of case studies of the work of particular authors and specific traditions, they are each prepared to identify a mainstream economics or at least refer to the nature of contemporary economic theory. Indeed, for advocates of critical realism one substantial gain from a turn to ontological theorising is a better understanding of the characteristics, limitations and scope of mainstream economics. Cartwright too is willing to express concerns about what she sees as certain problematic and central features of contemporary economic theorising.[5] I argue in this section that these critiques offered of contemporary (mainstream) economic theory are in fact pretty much the same, although (as I demonstrate in the next section) since they are situated in rather different frameworks the methodological implications drawn partially diverge.

The nature of modern mainstream economics

Lawson and other proponents of critical realism in economics argue that contemporary mainstream economics is distinguished by its central concern with formalistic modelling of one type or another.[6] It is formalistic modelling that constitutes the very essence of mainstream economics on this reading. While the substantive topics covered by the mainstream journals may vary with changing intellectual fashions, the broad methodological form expected of contributions remains stable. Indeed, the demand that some kind of formalistic modelling orientation be adopted and a growing intolerance of alternative methods has been an often-remarked-upon feature of developments in the discipline over the last thirty years or so. When identifying mainstream economics by its fixation on formalistic approaches Lawson emphasises that such methods in turn rest on a deductivist mode of explanation. That is to say they assume that for results, claims, hypotheses, etc., to be regarded as genuine explanations or as at all scientific they must take the 'whenever event (or state of affairs) x then event (or state of affairs) y' form.[7] Such regularities can of course be highly complex – they may involve numerous variables, and perhaps be associated with non-linear representations – and be either deterministic or stochastic. Proponents of critical realism refer to situations in which regularities such as these occur, or are closely approximated, as *closed systems*. By supposing that deductivism is of universal application to the social realm mainstream economists effectively assume that closed systems are ubiquitous there. The fact that deductivist, typically mathematical, modelling requires the persistence of such event regularities may be reasonably well recognised by some mainstream economists themselves. What mainstream economists fail to reflect upon is whether closed systems of the required sort can safely be assumed to be common features of social reality.

In addressing this issue Lawson draws on the analysis of the nature of the natural realm and its science. In doing so he is quick to qualify and clarify his strategy. Such a discussion is useful in the context of attempting to come to a better understanding of the nature of mainstream economics because while closed systems are far from ubiquitous in the natural realm they do occur there, or at least are closely approximated, and so we can learn by way of examining them something of the conditions of their occurrence. A clearer understanding of such conditions facilitates an evaluation of the likelihood of their being satisfied in the social realm and allows us to anticipate the kind of manoeuvres those locked into a deductivist framework are likely to contemplate as legitimate when encountering problems in pursuing an explanatory project. As we will see in the next section this is not considered a stand in for an independent analysis of the nature of the social realm but can usefully supplement it.

A significant initial feature of the natural realm that Lawson emphasises is precisely how rare closed systems in fact are. Outside astronomy, natural scientific closures are mostly restricted to experimental situations. And yet despite this he notes that experimental results are often successfully applied in *open* (non-experimental) contexts, in situations in which event regularities are not to be found. These observations he points out immediately pose certain problems for the deductivist. First, the confinement of event regularities largely to controlled experiments would seemingly greatly reduce the scope of the application of science. Second, because any laws of nature are thought to depend on event regularities, and given these mostly are located in well-controlled experimental situations, it would seem to follow that laws of nature must be viewed as dependent on us, on our establishment of experimental contexts, a conclusion that is counterintuitive to say the least. Third, the fact that science is regularly successfully applied outside experimental settings, in situations in which event regularities are not at all in evidence, would seem to be quite unintelligible on the deductivist interpretation.

In order to render intelligible both the restriction of event regularities largely to well-controlled experimental set ups and the application of experimental results in open systems where event regularities are not obtained, Lawson argues that it is necessary to accept an alternative ontology and conception of science to that underpinning deductivism. The ontology required is one of structures, powers, mechanisms and tendencies, etc., that are irreducible to, but which underpin, the actual course of events and states of affairs. Once this ontology is established it supports a conception of science as moving from phenomena at one level to their conditions or causes at a different, deeper one.

Only the briefest outline of the kind of ontology that Lawson and other advocates of critical realism developed can be provided here. Central to it though is the idea that reality is structured in the sense of not being exhausted by events and states of affairs. Consider an aspirin. In virtue of its intrinsic chemical structure it has certain powers, such as to relieve pain or thin the blood. Or consider a bicycle. Because of its physical structure it facilitates rides. Now the powers of aspirins, bicycles and anything else can exist unexercised. When powers are exercised they work by way of mechanisms or processes. For example, the aspirin and the human body work together in such a way as to contribute to the relief of a headache. The category of tendency is reserved to capture the idea that something can be continually active even if its effect is not completely actualised in the outcome. If I have a headache the aspirin will have a tendency to make it better even as other tendencies intervene so as to ensure that the headache intensifies. It should be emphasised that the operation of a tendency in an open system, i.e. in the face of countervailing tendencies, licenses claims that are *transfactual* as opposed to being merely counterfactual. They do not inform us of what would happen if things were different but of what is happening in reality whatever the actual outcome. They tell us for instance that the gravitational tendency acts on the cup in my hand whatever I do with it. The gravitational tendency is not merely something that would, counterfactually, have an impact if the cup were dropped in an experimentally constructed vacuum; it is something that is acting on the cup and continues to do so whether I drop it in a vacuum, juggle with it or rest it on a table.

With a structured ontology of this type Lawson can make sense of the confinement of most event regularities to experimental situations and the applications of the results of science outside the laboratory. Science is best understood as not being restricted to or primarily concerned with correlating actualities; rather it aims to uncover the mechanisms that govern surface phenomena. And the experiment can be recognised as an attempt to intervene in reality in order to isolate a stable mechanism or tendency from countervailing ones so that it is more easily empirically identified. None of the problems attached to the deductivist conception arise on this critical realist perspective. First, science is not restricted to the experimental situation; mechanisms are operative and identifiable in many contexts, whether or not event regularities are in evidence. The experiment with its possibility of event regularities is just one contribution to the scientific process. Second, there is no longer anything counterintuitive about the confinement of event regularities to experimental settings. For laws of nature are not considered to express event regularities, but rather the workings of underlying mechanisms and tendencies. From this perspective the well-controlled experiment can be seen not as a situation in which a law of nature is produced, but merely as one wherein it is empirically identified. Third, the fact that the results of experimental research are applied in open systems is also no longer surprising. For the objects of this research are now recognised as being mechanisms or tendencies, etc, many of which if triggered operate transfactually, i.e. inside and outside the experimental situation alike.

By considering the well-controlled experimental situation it has been found that in order systematically to generate an event regularity, a stable mechanism must be isolated and triggered. We can see that certain conditions have to be in place if event regularities are to be guaranteed. Specifically the relevant domain of reality must consist of factors that are intrinsically stable, isolatable and actually acting in a condition of isolation. Thus the objects of analysis must be intrinsically closed, essentially atomistic, guaranteeing that, in the same conditions, the posited objects of analysis will always act in the same way, that x always tends to produce y. Moreover, all factors that can influence the outcome must be internalised within the system, or effectively held at bay. That is the factors focused upon must not only be isolatable but triggered in conditions that allow tendencies to be expressed unimpeded.

With the very particular conditions that are necessary to guarantee event regularities identified, Lawson can pose the question whether it is wise to assume that these conditions prevail everywhere in the social realm. The mathematical modelling methods adopted by mainstream economists do not constitute some neutral language. Rather, for such methods to be relevant, they require the reality to which they are applied to conform to a certain specific structure. Essentially, the standard practices of economic modellers can now be seen as appropriate in conditions where atomistic factors operate in isolation from the effects of countervailing factors. By insisting that deductivist methods are everywhere utilised the implicit presumption is that these conditions are ubiquitous. Now Lawson, as we shall see, offers an abstract account of the social realm that provides us with good reasons for supposing that these conditions are very unlikely to be met in the social realm. That is, he demonstrates that these conditions obtain rather rarely even in the natural realm and may be without much relevance at all in the social realm. For Lawson the various streams of mainstream economics are united by a commitment to generalised closed system modelling which is undermined by an *ex post* recognition that the social world is open and hardly amenable to scientifically interesting closures. In such a context the a priori insistence upon deductivist methods only serves to encourage plainly fictional formulations in which atomistic individuals tend to be treated as part of an assumed-to-be isolated and self-contained system.

More specifically, Lawson argues that typically the most abstract features within mainstream models refer to only the thinnest and broadest of generalisations that hardly begin to identify the nature of real causal mechanisms at all and possess little in the way of explanatory content. In order to get any novel results out of a modelling exercise in such circumstances a battery of additional assumptions, which he suggests would be more appropriately labelled as bogus abstractions[8] or convenient fictions, have to be relied upon. And it is as these further supporting assumptions are supplied that the a priori commitment to deductivist modes of explanation often makes its presence felt: 'In mainstream economics ... such assumptions which may creep in unnoticed are usually designed to achieve mathematical tractability, system closure and completeness, or some such thing, rather than an understanding of the real causal mechanisms at work' (1997: 233). Lawson suggests that a failure to appreciate the thinness of the original generalisations or the role performed by assumptions 'may lead either to an unthinking and erroneous belief that these assumptions can eventually be replaced with accounts of essential aspects of real generative mechanisms without the whole construction collapsing entirely, or to a misguided attempt to extract more meaning from the constructions than can possibly be legitimate' (1997: 233). Now, an important component of Lawson's assessment of mainstream economics is that he evaluates the presuppositions associated with the methods that it insists upon in relation to an explicit, if highly general, account of the nature of the social realm. But this leads us to a difference between Lawson and Cartwright, one that I will elaborate further upon in the next section. Before doing so I wish to draw out the similarities in their respective critiques of mainstream economics up at least to this stage of outlining and defending a particular social ontology.

Regular behaviour, forms of idealisation and the character of contemporary economic theory

Just as Lawson and other proponents of critical realism note that event regularities are typically not spontaneously occurring but rather laboriously produced, Cartwright insists: 'Most situations do not give rise to regular behaviour. But we can make ones that do' (1999a: 89). It is typically within experimental situations that we see the emergence of regularities according to Cartwright. She suggests that in order to appreciate what is most significant about experimental activity we need to recognise that the event regularity achieved within the laboratory set up is a means to an end rather than an end in itself; in a sense regularities are secondary. For Cartwright in order to make sense of experimental activity it is important to acknowledge that we seek through such interventions to isolate a nature or capacity from the influence of countervailing factors in order to better identify its properties. She notes:

> Outside the supervision of a laboratory or the closed casement of a factory made module, what happens in one instance is rarely a guide to what will happen in others. Situations that lend themselves to generalisations are special, and it is these special kinds of situations that we aim to create, both in our experiments and in our technology ... what makes these situations special is that they are situations that permit a stable display of the nature of the process under study or the stable display of the interaction of several different natures.
>
> (1999a: 86)[9]

While Lawson notes that for the deductivist the absence of spontaneously occurring strict event regularities threatens to fence science off from most of the goings on in the world and restrict its applicability predominantly to artificially constructed contexts, Cartwright argues that 'The facts about an experiment that make that experiment generalisable are not facts that exist in a purely Humean world' (1999a: 87). A law of nature according

to Lawson refers us to an underlying tendency not a patterning of actualities. Cartwright is equally dissatisfied with the traditional regularity
treatment of laws.[10] According to Cartwright 'one cannot make sense of
modern experimental method unless one assumes that laws are basically
about natures' (1992: 47). Moreover, in considering the notion of laws and
conceptualising laws as referring us to Aristotelian natures, Cartwright
often deploys the language of tendencies and sees these as signifying the
continuing activity of a power or capacity that is exercised without necessarily being fully manifest (see Cartwright, 1999a: 82).[11]

Cartwright, like Lawson, is also interested in examining the nature of
systems in which event regularities obtain. Cartwright does not systematically deploy the language of closure to identify these cases (but see
1999a: 67); rather she suggests that a situation that generates a regular
series of events in a well-defined region is part of a nomological machine.
Nevertheless, in elaborating on the characteristics of these machines she
covers much of the same ground that critical realists explore when considering the conditions for closure. For Cartwright a nomological machine is
either an experimental set up designed to identify and isolate a capacity
or set of capacities, or is a circumstance created by a fortuitous accident
of nature. Cartwright emphasises explicitly that for a situation to be a
nomological machine, it must shield some process ensuring that it is not
affected by outside disturbances or influences. She not only emphasises
the issues of separability and isolation but also recognises that for repeat-
able regularities to be guaranteed then the capacities identified need to
conform to a certain level of intrinsic stability.[12]

Given the extent of the ground that they share regarding the assessment of the nature and significance of systems where event regularities
actually hold, it is perhaps not surprising that when Cartwright turns her
attention to the state of modern economic theory her analysis also has
substantial similarities with that provided by Lawson. In particular their
views concerning the role of assumptions within the modelling project
of contemporary mainstream economics seem to overlap, albeit with
Cartwright's analysis expressed in the language of Galilean and non-
Galilean idealisations rather than Lawson's harsher references to bogus
abstractions and convenient fictions.

Cartwright's account of idealisation draws on her interpretation of
experimental activity which, as we have seen, has close correspondences with the analysis provided by proponents of critical realism. For
Cartwright 'Galilean idealisation' is a procedure underlying all modern
experimental enquiry. Cartwright suggests: 'The fundamental idea of the
Galilean method is to use what happens in special or ideal cases to explain
very different kinds of things that happen in very non-ideal cases' (1989a:
191). She is concerned to examine what it is that is ideal about these experimental circumstances:

> The key here is the concept ideal. On the one hand we use this term to mark the fact that the circumstances are not real or, at least, that they seldom obtain naturally but require a great deal of contrivance even to approximate. On the other, the 'ideal' circumstances are the 'right' ones – right for inferring what the nature of the behaviour is, in itself.
>
> (1999a: 84)

It is the material isolation of the relevant factor that is 'falsely' ideal within the process of Galilean idealisation exemplified by certain kinds of experimental interventions. Such isolations are not typically immediately available to us but are hard won and laboriously achieved. However, what is not falsely ideal but on the contrary what is real is the nature of the thing, structure or process which is better revealed within the idealised conditions produced. Cartwright writes:

> Galileo's experiments aimed to establish what I have been calling a tendency claim. They were not designed to tell us how any particular falling body will move in the vicinity of the earth; nor to establish a regularity about how bodies of a certain kind will move. Rather, the experiments were designed to find out what contribution the motion due to the pull of the earth will make, with the assumption that that contribution is stable across all the different kinds of situations falling bodies will get into. How did Galileo find out what the stable contribution from the pull of the earth is? He eliminated (as far as possible) all other causes of motion on the bodies in his experiment so that he could see how they move when only the earth affects them. That is the contribution that the earth's pull makes to their motion. Let us call this kind of idealisation that eliminates all other possible causes to learn the effect of one operating on its own, Galilean idealisation.
>
> (1999b: 5)

When examining the characteristic strategies adopted within contemporary economic theory Cartwright questions whether the mass of assumptions adopted can appropriately be labelled Galilean idealisations.

> What I fear is that in general a good number of the false assumptions made with our theoretical models do not have the form of Galilean idealisations. They do not serve first to isolate a single mechanism but are rather far stronger than this. In these cases the behaviours are overconstrained. The model can tell us what will happen in an ideal experiment, but not in every (or any arbitrary) ideal experiment.
>
> (1999b: 6)

If these assumptions are not Galilean idealisations what are they and what purpose do they serve? According to Cartwright: 'The need for these stronger constraints – the ones that go beyond Galilean idealisation – comes ... on account of the nature of economic theory itself' (1999b: 6). Whereas Lawson speaks of the problems associated with broad but thin generalisations, Cartwright emphasises the meagre nature of the key categories of mainstream models and traces how such mundane concepts are supplemented so as to facilitate deductive modelling:

> Contemporary economics uses not abstract or theoretical or newly invented concepts – like force or energy or electromagnetic field – concepts partially defined by their deductive relations to other concepts, but rather very mundane concepts that are unmediated in their attachment to full empirical reality ... . Nevertheless we want our treatments to be rigorous and our conclusions to follow deductively. And the way you get deductivity when you do not have it in the concepts is to put enough of the right kind of structure into the model. That is the trick of building a model in contemporary economics: you have to figure out some circumstances that are constrained in just the right way that results can be derived deductively.
>
> (1999a: 3–4)

Cartwright suggests that the ontological presuppositions implied by the mainstream modelling exercises are likely to be of relevance only in certain very special circumstances. The result she concludes is that

> economics becomes exact – but at the cost of becoming exceedingly narrow. The kind of precise conclusions that are so highly valued in contemporary economics can be rigorously derived only when very special assumptions are made. But the very special assumptions do not fit very much of the contemporary economy around us.
>
> (1999a: 149)

3. An ontological conception of social reality: an essential development or a step too far?

In terms of understanding the nature of contemporary mainstream economics, Cartwright and Lawson seem to develop very similar positions. This common view is grounded in an understanding of the particularity of systems where event regularities obtain, a similar appreciation of the significance of such situations and a shared assessment that the strategies currently adopted by economic theorists in their modelling exercises do not serve to isolate a real mechanism or nature so that its properties can be better understood but are rather driven by a collectively felt need that results must always take a deductive form in a context where only the thinnest/meagrest of general theoretical principles are offered. At times we see Cartwright and Lawson not only providing a similar analysis of the nature of mainstream economics but drawing out much the same implications. For Lawson, once we recognise that mainstream economics is essentially tied to an insistence on the pursuit in all contexts of deductivist forms of explanation and we note that the project has to date been rather less than successful then we can move to the conclusion that a more pluralistic orientation toward economic theorising would be highly desirable. Cartwright also notes that an exclusive focus upon deductive methods may be unwarranted and crowd out other potentially more fruitful approaches:

> The achievement of rigour is costly ... It requires special talents and special training and this closes the discipline to different kinds of thinkers who may provide different kinds of detailed understanding of how economies can and do work. And rigour is bought at the cost of employing general concepts lacking the kind of detailed content that allows them to be directly put to use in concrete situations. What are its compensating gains? Unless we find different answers from the one I offered ... the gains will not include lessons about real economic phenomena, it seems, despite our frequent feeling of increased understanding of them. For we are not generally assured of any way to take results out of our models and into the world.
>
> (1999b: 33)

Despite all these similarities there are differences between Lawson and Cartwright and I wish to argue here that these can be understood as reflecting a rather fundamental disagreement about the nature and legitimate scope of ontological theorising itself. Lawson, in seeking to demonstrate that there exist alternative methods of greater relevance than the mathematical deductivist ones insisted upon by mainstream economists, engages first in a rather extensive discussion of the nature of the social realm. It is only once this ontological conception has been derived that he then considers what kinds of method might prove fruitful in pursuing causal explanations when addressing such material. Cartwright, in contrast, is more cautious. She does not provide a broad outline of the basic features of social reality and may even regard such an exercise as implausibly ambitious. Now, Lawson has understandably prioritised the doing of social ontology over defending his orientation toward it and has as a consequence not always elaborated upon his approach to ontological theorising as fully as would have been desirable (but see Lawson, 2004). In order to understand the differences between Cartwright and Lawson it is important to clarify certain aspects of his approach and in doing so it proves useful to draw out (perhaps some unlikely[13]) connections between his project and the approach to metaphysical analysis defended by Charles Peirce.

Ontological theorising and Peirce's approach to metaphysics

For Lawson a central goal of (philosophical) ontology is to articulate a theory of the nature and structure of reality that is as encompassing as possible of the actual configurations experienced. The objective is to develop a comprehensive framework as a way of more effectively orienting ourselves toward reality. The system of categories derived is so abstract that by itself it contains nothing concrete and yet if the system were entirely adequate then any concrete process or item one might wish to consider would be interpretable as a specification of the categorial system. In a sense the set of categories provided by philosophical ontology is one whose reference to things remains vague, requiring further specification by less abstract studies that themselves may be incommensurate with one another. The goal of developing such an encompassing system is only ever likely to be partially realised but this does not limit the significance of the endeavour. Lawson notes that this objective can be seen as in line with the ambitions of the type of speculative philosophy pursued by Whitehead. Whitehead himself describes his contribution as at root an attempt 'to frame a ... system of general ideas in terms of which every element of our experience can be interpreted' (quoted in Lawson, 2003b: 134). Such an objective can be seen as consistent not only with Whitehead's speculative philosophy but also with Peirce's account of philosophy as the endeavour which seeks 'to form a general conception of the *All*' (CP 7.579). For Peirce nothing short of striving to render the whole of reality intelligible merits the name of philosophy. More specifically Peirce sees metaphysics as being abstract prescinding from inquiries of lesser abstraction by virtue of singling out what is hypothetically most important and abandoning the trivial, not inclusively general.[14]

A point that Lawson and other advocates of critical realism have continually emphasised is that the adoption of an ontological position of some sort is unavoidable. A position that boasts that it is devoid of an explicit ontology, of what it supposes is any ontology, is often one blindly constrained by an unacknowledged and thus unexamined metaphysics. This is a point that is also nicely drawn out by Peirce, who states: 'Some think to avoid the influence of metaphysical errors, by paying no attention to metaphysics; but experience shows that these men [and women] beyond all others are held in an iron vice of metaphysical theory, because by theories that they never called in question' (CP 7.579). Metaphysical or ontological positions can, especially where tacitly assumed, serve to circumscribe our powers of interrogation. According to Peirce, for example, the

> nominalistic metaphysics [is] the most binding of all systems, as metaphysics generally is the most powerful of all causes of mental cecity, because it deprives the mind of the power to ask itself certain

questions, as the habit of wearing a confining dress deprives one's joints of their suppleness.

(CP 5.499)

The conclusion to which such considerations drive both Lawson and Peirce is that, since everyone must frame, if often only tacitly, conceptions of things in general, it is better, and often crucial, that these conceptions should be carefully constructed and periodically re-examined.

In order to derive an ontological conception Lawson suggests that the theorist supposes at the outset that the world is intelligible that what has happened, the actual, must have been possible. In a similar vein Peirce notes: 'Philosophy tries to understand. In doing so, it is committed to the assumption that things are intelligible ...' (CP 6.581); and elsewhere: 'The sole immediate purpose of thinking is to render things intelligible; and to think and yet in that very act to think a thing unintelligible is a self stultification' (CP 1.406). According to Lawson, the ontological framework he defends has been achieved precisely through theorising sets of conditions, in virtue of which certain *generalised features of widespread experience* were possible. In ontology, he suggests that the starting point is the intelligibility of widespread features of experience. Given that certain things are experienced the question posed is, in virtue of what are they possible? What must the world be like that such and such is a generalised feature of experience? What are its conditions of possibility? The answer forms an assessment of the broad nature of reality or features of it, a theory of aspects of ontology. It is the starting from generalised features of experience that I think particularly deserves further elaboration than that which Lawson himself provides, for it is this point of departure that may make some feel uncomfortable[15] and it is here that Peirce's views on what constitutes a sustainable metaphysics are especially useful.

Peirce observes that many inquirers suppose that recondite phenomena are alone valuable and thus that commonplace experiences (or familiar phenomena) are of little or no value. Peirce argues in opposition to this that the 'great facts of nature which familiar experiences embody are not of the number of those things which can have their juices sucked out of them and be cast aside' (CP 6.565). He notes that our everyday world is for the most part unreflexively inhabited; the strange regions into which some of us are privileged enough to be placed by travel or access to (and training in the use of) instruments such as telescopes and microscopes call forth query and reflection. Thus recondite phenomena elicit inquiry, while easily accessible and readily identifiable phenomena ordinarily fail even to claim vivid attention, much less to prompt extended investigation. According to Peirce the manifest phenomena of everyday experience are in fact, because of their ubiquity and familiarity, amongst the most difficult to delineate, describe and explain. More specifically, he claims that in contrast to recondite phenomena, everyday phenomena 'are as hard or harder to see, simply because they surround us on every hand; we are immersed in them and have no background against which to view them' (CP 6.562). Familiarity breeds not so much contempt but blanket inattention. For Peirce, however, familiar phenomena are not so many squeezed lemons. They are resources to which we can return, again and again. He finds it unfortunate that so little attention is paid to the insistent disclosures of familiar experience (CP 6.563). According to Peirce the observations on which metaphysics depends are precisely those which are so ubiquitous that we ordinarily pay them no attention at all. The great facts of nature and culture – their most abstract and general features – embodied in the most familiar experiences of human beings deserve to be carefully scrutinised, so that their importance can be fully appreciated and their implications developed. But we can do so only if we cultivate 'the faculty of seeing what stares one in the face' (CP 5.42).

While the cultivation of this faculty is a demanding task, Peirce maintains that the delineation, description and explanation of everyday phenomena define the proper scope of philosophical inquiry including metaphysics. For Peirce it is the business of philosophy 'to find out all that can be found out from those universal experiences which confront every man in every waking hour of his life' (CP 1.246). What is disclosed here 'must have its application in every other science' (CP 1.246). Philosophy and the special sciences differ not in kind but in their degree of generality. Both rely on empirical observations (albeit of different types) and in each the reasoning needed links abduction, which allows us to develop explanatory/speculative hypotheses, deduction, that enables us to draw out their consequences and induction, which facilitates an evaluation of the evidence (see Haack, 2006, for discussion). Peirce writes:

> That which renders the modes of thought of the students of a special science peculiar is that their experience lies in a special direction. And the cause of this is that they are trained and equipped to make a particular kind of observation, the man who is continually making chemical analyses lives in a different region of nature from other men. The same is true of men who are constantly using a microscope.
>
> (CP 1.100)

The special sciences are united in their dependence on special observations and this distinguishes them in their totality from philosophy as a discipline depending rather on the observations open to anyone, anywhere and at any time.[16]

According to Lawson ontological analysis can provide an account of the conditions necessary for the possibility of some generalised feature of experience, but there may be rival theories to explain the same thing, just as there are rival theories at the frontiers of science. One ontological conception may explain more than others and so be regarded as the best currently available. But in ontological theorising as in science more generally, while there can be justified beliefs and there can be progress, there can be no final theory, unsusceptible to revision and improvement. For Lawson the ontological conceptions achieved are empirically motivated and so grounded speculative hypotheses to be compared with any others so derived in terms of their relative explanatory power, etc. Peirce too argues for the development of a hypothetical non-dogmatic metaphysics. For him even when metaphysics was conducted in an appropriate fashion mistaken conceptions could still be fashioned and the evidence by which competing ontological theories stand or fall relates to their abilities to render intelligible 'the facts of everyday life'.[17]

Once obtained Lawson argues that an ontological framework can have numerous uses. He suggests that such a framework will likely reveal the particularity of the conceptions of reality presupposed by the many specific methods of science, or policy claims. As a result it can make transparent both the error and non-necessity of universalising such scientific approaches or policy stances a priori. He argues that ontology can identify the errors of treating special cases as though they are universal.

Now we are in a position to understand how ontological theorising of the type envisaged by Lawson informs his critique of mainstream economics. A starting point is the generalised feature of experience that, even in the natural realm, indicates interesting event regularities are not ubiquitous but are restricted in their occurrence, being found to be mostly confined to situations of well controlled experiments. According to Lawson the theory of reality that is best able to make sense of this is the structured ontology sketched earlier. According to this conception, the event regularities achieved in experiments are the result of experimental scientists manipulating reality to insulate stable mechanisms from the effects of countervailing mechanisms; the event regularity is the association of triggering conditions and a mechanism's effects. The confinement of event regularities to experimental conditions, in other words, is explained by the hypothesis that reality is structured and open, allowing experimenters to intervene and close the system by insulating a single stable mechanism from the effects of others. The explanation is only a speculative working hypothesis – one that has to be assessed alongside any others available. But, if viewed as the most sustainable currently available account, then it highlights how restricted are the conditions necessary in order to allow for the relevant application of the mathematical deductivist methods that mainstream economists assume to be universally applicable.

It is especially important when distinguishing Lawson's project from Cartwright's to appreciate that successful scientific practice constitutes but one point of departure for his ontological elaborations. According to Lawson generalised features of experience entirely unconnected to successful scientific practice can equally legitimately act as starting points from which to develop speculative hypotheses. Indeed in seeking to develop an abstract account of social reality he suggests there may be advantages to looking elsewhere for one's initial premises since social science remains so chronically contested. The generalised features of experience Lawson has identified and used as initiating premises for his ontological elaborations include the observation that social practices appear highly routinised (and partially predictable), that shared or typical behaviour is often out of phase with behaviour regarded as proper or legitimate and that the practices people follow, including routines, are highly and systematically differentiated, amongst numerous others. In fact Lawson suggests that the possibilities for ontological analysis of the sort he defends appear almost without limit.[18]

The details of the social ontology that Lawson derives are rich and dense, but the briefest summary will suffice here. For Lawson social reality is the domain of phenomena whose existence depends, at least in part, on us. He argues that the social domain is characteristically open in the sense that strict event regularities are but a special and seemingly rare occurrence. For Lawson the social realm like the natural is structured in the sense of being constituted in part by features that cannot be reduced to actualities. In addition there are underlying features including social rules, relations, positions, powers, mechanisms and tendencies. Related to this he sees the social realm as emergent with social structures possessing emergent powers and having causal powers that are irreducible to those of human individuals. For example, social structures such as language systems emerge out of human interaction, but have powers of their own irreducible to human speech acts on which they depend. He further argues that the social domain is intrinsically dynamic or processual; social structures such as language systems both depend on us and are continually being reproduced or transformed as we draw upon them. In other words the social world is a process. The social realm is also found to be highly internally related (or holistic). That is to say numerous aspects of the social domain are what they are and can do what they do, by virtue of the internal relations in which they stand to other aspects. For Lawson the social domain also consists of internally related positions. Individuals essentially slot into a range of different positions where such positions are found to have rights, obligations and prerogatives attached to them and so on (for detailed elaboration see Lawson, 2003a: chapter 2).

With this kind of social ontology developed and defended Lawson presses his critique of mainstream economics further. It is not simply that we can see the particularity of systems where event regularities of the required sort obtain, but now there are good grounds for supposing that such systems are unlikely to be present at all in the social domain. The elaboration of his social ontology also encourages Lawson to consider what methods might most fruitfully be adopted by those prepared to acknowledge the holistically constituted and essentially processual nature of the social realm but who aim to provide causal explanations of social phenomena. One approach he supports is that of contrast explanation. The essence of this contrastive approach is not to explain some *x* but rather to explain why '*x* rather than *y*' in conditions where *y* was expected given that a process thought to be the same as that producing *x* has produced y. For example, the quest is not to explain crop yield (which involves knowing all the factors responsible) but why it is much higher at one end of the field. The point here is that by asking why *x* rather than *y*, that is why at one end crop yield is higher (*x*) rather than the same as elsewhere (*y*), it can with reason be assumed that all factors affecting yield are fairly constant throughout the field over time except the one (set) making the difference to the yield. The application of the method of contrast explanation requires, then, merely that: (i) over some region, referred to as the *contrast space*, good reasons are available to encourage researchers to expect that two outcomes of a certain kind have the same or a similar causal history and (ii) that a posteriori the researchers are surprised by outcomes that diverge from those anticipated. While the controlled experiment can be seen as constituting a special case of the method of contrast explanation, closure is not a necessary condition for the success of projects in contrast causal explanation. According to Lawson the conditions for contrast explanation hold for the social realm even where the latter is conceived of as an open-ended, holistic and evolving system.[19]

The challenge of social ontology declined

In order to understand the differences between Lawson and Cartwright it is important to appreciate that these ultimately revolve around the nature and legitimate scope of ontological theorising. In part Cartwright does seem to be pursuing an ontological project rather similar to that which Lawson conducts. After all Cartwright seems to be prepared to develop an ontological conception very similar to that which Lawson sets out for the natural realm when she starts from observations relating to features of successful experimental scientific practice. From this point of departure she concludes that an ontology that includes reference to Aristotelian natures is essential if we are to make sense of experimental interventions. Specifically she suggests that 'the use of Aristotelian-style natures is central to the modern explanatory programme' (1999a: 830) and maintains that her ontological conception is more adequate than alternatives available: 'Philosophical arguments for the usual empiricist view about what there is and what there is not are not very compelling to begin with. They surely will need to be given up if they land us with a world that makes meaningless much of what we do and say when we use our sciences most successfully' (1999a: 72). Cartwright argues that we find that the image of the world implied by the methods used in our most successful studies of it is very different from the image of the world that we find implied by more conventional views of science and imported as an ideal into economics.

Yet Cartwright, in contrast to Lawson, is reluctant to engage in an extensive project of philosophical ontology and carefully avoids setting out an abstract account of social reality of the type that Lawson delivers. What might account for this reticence? It seems that while she is prepared to develop some speculative hypotheses about the structure of the world where these are motivated by observations about successful scientific practice she is less prepared to start from generalised features of experience unrelated to successful science. As I have already indicated, Lawson is willing (in circumstances where empirical successes in social science seem rather thin on the ground and social scientific theories remain so highly contested) to move outside science altogether in order to find his initiating premises. It seems unlikely that Cartwright would wish to follow that lead:

> How then do we figure out what the world is like? I agree … that we should 'rely upon what our best available science provides for us'. But I do not believe that there is a convenient place called 'theory' where that is encoded. I also presuppose strong empiricism: it is empirical success that determines what our best available science is. So to figure out what we are warranted in believing we need to find just those claims that are genuinely used in deriving the predictions and applications that constitute our empirical successes.
>
> (2003: 4)

In the context of natural science the implication from this seems to be that we should be much more careful when asserting that scientific knowledge is applied outside the experimental context; we should pause and examine carefully what is being applied and how it is successful. Cartwright's preference even with respect to the natural realm then is to start from much more detailed empirically rich studies of scientific practice than the type of broad conceptualisations of such practices which Lawson uses as his point of departure. In the context of social science, if economics is unable to provide robust empirical successes of the type Cartwright seeks as her starting point and if generalised features of experience outside science will not do as initiating premises, then it seems likely that any ontological outline of the social realm must remain faint indeed. To the extent that we can identify some examples of successful application, then, we should, just as with such cases in natural science, carefully unravel what precisely is going on there.[20]

If it is Lawson's willingness to commit to a particular social ontology that encourages him to explore methods more likely to fit with his account of social being than those insisted upon by mainstream economists, then Cartwright's reluctance to develop broad speculative hypotheses about social reality may help us understand better why she leaves her discussion of methods where she does. In fact, Cartwright sometimes seems to suggest that the problem with the strategies that mainstream economists routinely adopt is not that they mimic the Galilean methods pursued in natural science but that they bodge the attempt. She implies that the way forward is to more effectively mirror the Galilean methods shown to be successful in certain natural science contexts. She suggests for example with respect to modelling in economics that 'Galilean idealisation in a model is a good thing' (1999b: 6). But, Cartwright's advocacy of Galilean idealisation or its analogue in models in the context of social science remains ambiguous. At times she seems to suggest that Galilean idealisation is desirable or even indispensable whatever the domain addressed:

> Galilean methods are all we have. In the Galilean method you study features individually, in isolation. You strip away all the impediments, as best you can, in order to see how the feature behaves on its own. But why do you think that this isolated situation is special among all others? The answer must be that you think in this situation you have learned about the feature itself; you have learned what its natural capacities are. That is why you can predict from what it does in this particular situation to what it will contribute when you set it back in far more encumbered situations. What I want to stress is that this is the method we have – this method that presupposes that individually identifiable features carry with them enduring capacities. We have no method for studying nature holistically; so we had better hope that nature has provided enduring capacities which our methods are competent to find.
>
> (1989b: 197)

When Cartwright suggests that Galilean idealisation in a model is a good thing her emphasis may be on the way in which we move through Galilean idealisation to an understanding of capacities/natures. Alternatively she may mean this *and* that the particular procedures, including the strategies of isolation, through which this is accomplished within the context of the experimental set up is desirable, appropriate or even essential.

To the extent that Galilean idealisation is tied to strategies of isolation, to propose it as a method appropriate for social science, is highly problematic for those, such as many proponents of critical realism, who maintain that the social realm is not only open but also holistically constituted. As soon as Galilean idealisation is exported outside the context of the experimental set up then proponents of critical realism would argue that its relevance has to be assessed by reference to the nature of the material under investigation. It is quite feasible to maintain that the identification of underlying causal mechanisms is the primary scientific objective and yet conclude that the kind of stability and separability presupposed by Galilean methods, as described by Cartwright, cannot be safely assumed in the social realm. If we are committed to an account of the social realm that acknowledges its open, holistic and evolving character then Galilean idealisation is likely only to encourage an ultimately irrelevant form of imagined isolationism.

Cartwright does not commit herself to the kind of atomistic social ontology presupposed by such methods. Indeed, she is careful to highlight that others, including Keynes, have argued forcefully against such metaphysical positions. Rather, her argument seems to be that if the social world is not of a nature which facilitates the application of Galilean methods then the prospects for uncovering underlying capacities in the social realm may turn out to be rather limited. From Lawson's perspective this is over-pessimistic, unnecessary and certainly a premature assessment.

4. Concluding remarks

For many the relevance of ontological analysis for economics is that it reveals the buried metaphysical commitments of economists. It identifies presuppositions, points out inconsistencies where they obtain and so on. Some who would wish to limit ontological theorising to this kind of exercise even suggest that it is premature to identify a mainstream economics at all; much further work would be required, they claim, before we could confidently maintain that such a thing exists. Both Cartwright and Lawson, while acknowledging the importance of, and indeed at times providing, detailed investigations of individual contributions and particular schools of thought, have a more ambitious vision of ontological theorising in which it is conceived of as being about the world, not just about conceptual schemes or linguistic frameworks or the world-as-it-appears-to-us. They are also each prepared to characterise and even to criticise mainstream economics.

However, the two projects differ somewhat in the conception of the kind of service that ontological theorising can offer economics. These differences relate ultimately to alternative understandings of the nature and legitimate scope of ontological theorising. For Lawson perhaps the most important role of ontological theorising is to provide a categorial grammar, to generate a system of categories which, were it entirely adequate, would be able to situate any concrete case as a specification of the system. According to Lawson providing a broad account of the social realm is both eminently feasible and of particular significance given the current state of the economics discipline. Economics has been held back by its failure to promote ontological theorising. Outlining and defending a particular social ontology can help inform the debate regarding the kinds of methods that might be most appropriate for social investigations. Cartwright appears to pursue exercises in ontology with regard to the natural realm and use her results from these in tandem with studies of the presuppositions of various economic projects to criticise mainstream economics. In these respects the projects of Lawson and Cartwright, of course, complement one another. However, Cartwright seems less interested in (or less confident of the possibility of) developing an elaborate ontological conception of the social realm. Ultimately it seems that she wishes any metaphysical speculation to be held firmly in check. She is reluctant to go beyond what is required to make sense of our observations of our most successful sciences.

Cartwright perhaps would question whether the kind of ontological elaboration of social reality Lawson aims to provide is after all achievable. By considering Lawson's approach alongside Peirce's we can see that it is just because the observations on which Lawson's ontological theorising rests are so familiar that they do allow him to engage in ontological theorising without in a sense having to leave his armchair. But the reference to Peirce's account of metaphysics also allows us to see that this does not imply that his project is thereby a priori or indeed in any way unsustainable.

Notes

1 A version of this paper was presented at the *Centre for the Philosophy of Natural and Social Science*, London School of Economics in May 2006. I would like to thank the participants in the seminar for their comments. I would also like to acknowledge the very helpful criticisms and suggestions of Nancy Cartwright, Wade Hands, John Latsis and an anonymous referee of *Foundations of Science* on earlier drafts. The usual disclaimer applies. First published in *Foundations of Science*, 2007, Vol 12, No 3, 235–256.
2 For elaborations of the project of critical realism in economics see Lawson (1997 and 2003a), Fleetwood (1999) and Lewis (2004).
3 For interesting partial commentaries see Hoover (2002) and Hands (2001: 321).
4 Guala, for example, notes: 'I find the repeated use of the "mainstream economics" label ... rather tiresome and unhelpful. Is a "mainstream" model in, say, growth theory used exactly in the same way as a "mainstream" model in game theory? I doubt it' (2005: 3). Meanwhile Mäki suggests:

> One takes big risks by maintaining that economics is like this or economics is like that – for the simple reason that there is no one homogenous 'economics' about which one can justifiably make straightforward claims. A more differentiated approach is advisable.
>
> (2002: 8)

5 A minor point worth noting here is that whereas Lawson typically refers to mainstream or orthodox economics, Cartwright simply refers to the nature of contemporary economic theory or some such. From a critical realist point of view, to collapse contemporary economic theory onto economic modelling is to concede far too much ground. While mainstream economics may currently be hugely dominant, those developing the heterodox traditions are also very much engaged in economic theory albeit of a quite different sort.
6 See Lawson (1997 and 2003a) and for useful short summaries Lawson (2001 and 2005).
7 Lawson clarifies his understanding of the term deductivism in the following passage:

> By deductivism I mean a type of explanation in which regularities of the form 'whenever event x then event y' (or stochastic near equivalents) are a necessary condition. Such regularities are held to persist, and are often treated, in effect, as laws, allowing the deductive generation of consequences, or predictions, when accompanied with the specification of initial conditions ... Notice that it is the structure of explanation that fundamentally is at issue here. The possibility either that many of the entities which economists interpret as outcomes, including events or states of affairs, are fictitious, or that claimed correlations do not actually hold, does not undermine the thesis that deductivism is the explanatory mode of this project.
>
> (2003a: 5).

8 These are to be distinguished from 'real abstractions' which Lawson views as essential to science (see Lawson (1989 and 1997, chapter 16).

9 Later she writes:

> What must be true of the experiment if a general law of any form is to be inferred from it?' I claim that the experiment must succeed at revealing the nature of the process (or some stable consequence of the interaction of the natures) and that the design of the experiment requires a robust sense of what will impede and what will facilitate this.
>
> (1999a: 87)

10 Cartwright writes:

> I defend a very different understanding of the concept of Natural Law in modern science from the 'Laws = universal regularities' account ... We aim in science, I urge, to discover the *natures of things*; we try to find out what powers or capacities they have and in what circumstances and in what ways these capacities can be harnessed to produce predictable behaviours. I call this the study of *natures* because I want to recall the Aristotelian idea that science aims to understand what things are, and a large part of understanding what they are is to understand what they *can do*, regularly and as a matter of course. Regularities are secondary.
>
> (1995a: 277)

11 For both Cartwright and proponents of critical realism when a stable capacity is triggered outside the artificial context of the laboratory this may license a subjunctive conditional about what would have happened if the tendency had been acting in relative isolation. However, they agree even where such a consideration is appropriate, the full force and meaning of the statement cannot be captured in this manner. As we have seen the practice of restricting the use of law statements to conditions wherein event regularities would come about is problematic since science is then effectively purely focused on cases that are rare even in the natural realm and may be without counterpart in the social realm. Our understanding of a capacity or mechanism acting in an open system, i.e. one outside the closed environment of the experiment, is captured not by a hypothetical statement about some event regularity that would have occurred if the situation had been different, but by an indicative and categorical statement describing a capacity's way of acting. Compare Cartwright (1999a: 144) with Bhaskar (1986: 31) and Lawson (1997: 294).

12 She writes that

> regularities are generated by something I call a nomological machine, deploying and harnessing capacities, getting them situated in just the right circumstances, in just the right connections with each other, keeping the whole thing stable enough and shielding it and setting it running, and then we can get regularities emerging. Most of these nomological machines are made by us, but some have been made, as it were by God – the planetary system is a nomological machine. We've got an arrangement of parts, the parts have fixed capacities and the arrangement is such that the whole thing has a stable capacity – put the planets in certain positions, and you get out certain motions.
>
> (1995c: 206)

13 At least this is unlikely to those who confuse Rorty's brand of pragmatism with that which was developed by Peirce. For a discussion of the differences between Rorty and Peirce see Haack (1998).

14 For discussion of Peirce's views on metaphysics see Haack (2007) and Colapietro (2002 and 2004).

15 Indeed it is precisely this issue that has been picked up on by amongst others Guala, who states that Lawson's approach

> looks a lot like a search for the most likely explanation of some 'evident features of social reality' ... informed by our commonsensical understanding of the world. A malicious reviewer now would say that a very thin line separates 'ontological analysis' thus conceived from lazy armchair speculation supported by anecdotal, everyday considerations, rather than carefully collected and analysed empirical data.

(2005: 4)

16 For further discussion of Peirce's view of the relationship between metaphysics and the special sciences see Haack (2006).

17 Thus, for Peirce, when wondering whether there are uniformities in nature no elaborate equipment or skilful experiment will help but aspects of our common experience will:

> [I]nquiry must proceed upon the virtual assumption of sundry logical and metaphysical beliefs; and it is rational to settle the validity of those before undertaking an operation that supposes their truth ... [These] beliefs that appear to be indubitable have the same sort of basis as scientific results have. That is to say, they rest on experience – on the total everyday experience of many generations of multitudinous populations. Such experience is worthless for distinctively scientific purposes, because it does not make the minute distinctions with which science is chiefly concerned ... although all science, without being aware of it, virtually supposes the truth and the vague results of uncontrolled thought upon such experiences, cannot help doing so, and would have to shut up shop if she should manage to escape accepting them ... [T]he instinctive result of human experience ought to have so vastly more weight than any scientific result, that to make laboratory experiments to ascertain, for example, whether there are any uniformity in nature or no, would vie with adding a teaspoonful of saccharine to the ocean in order to sweeten it.

(CP 5.521–522)

For discussion see, Hookway (2000: 215).

18 He also notes that they include using as premises not only generalised features of experience tied to successful social practice:

> the question of intelligibility can be applied not only to nonscientific practices but equally to those practices (scientific or otherwise) found to be unsuccessful in some relevant way. Indeed in economics it is precisely the continuing failure of the dominant project that I have sought to render intelligible.

(2003b: 136)

19 For a detailed discussion of contrast explanation see Lawson (2003a: chapter 4); also see Lipton (2004).

20 A good example of the kind of work that such an orientation might sponsor is that provided by Alexandrova (2006).

References

Alexandrova, A, 2006, 'Connecting Economic Models to the Real World: Game Theory and the FCC Spectrum Auctions', *Philosophy of the Social Science*, Vol 36, No 2, 173–192.

Bhaskar, R, 1978, *A Realist Theory of Science*, Harvester Wheatsheaf, London.

Bhaskar, R, 1986, *Scientific Realism and Human Emancipation*, Verso, London.

Cartwright, N, 1989a, *Nature's Capacities and their Measurement*, Clarendon Press, Oxford.

Cartwright, N, 1989b, 'A Case Study in Realism: Why Econometrics is Committed to Capacities', *PSA*, Proceedings of the Biennial Meeting of the Philosophy of Science Association, Vol 2, 190–197.

Cartwright, N, 1991, 'Replicability, Reproducibility, and Robustness: Comments on Harry Collins', *History of Political Economy*, Vol 23, No 1, 143–155.

Cartwright, N, 1992, 'Aristotelian Natures and the Modern Experimental Method', in J. Earman, ed, *Inference, Explanation and Other Frustrations: Essays in the Philosophy of Science*, University of California Press, Berkeley.

Cartwright, N, 1995a, 'Ceteris Paribus Laws and Socio-Economic Machines', *The Monist*, Vol 78, No 3. Reprinted in U. Mäki, ed, *The Economic World View: Studies in the Ontology of Economics*, Cambridge University Press, Cambridge.

Cartwright, N, 1995b, 'False Idealisation: A Philosophical Threat to Scientific Method', *Philosophical Studies*, Vol 77, Nos 2–3, 339–352.

Cartwright, N, 1995c, 'An Interview with Nancy Cartwright', *Cogito*, Vol 19, No 3, 203–215.

Cartwright, N, 1995d, 'Causal Structures in Econometrics', in D. Little, ed, *On the Reliability of Economic Models*, Kluwer, Boston.

Cartwright, N, 1999a, *The Dappled World: A Study of the Boundaries of Science*, Cambridge University Press, Cambridge.

Cartwright, N, 1999b, 'The Vanity of Rigour in Economics: Theoretical Models and Galilean Experiments', LSE Centre for Philosophy of Natural and Social Sciences, Discussion Paper 43.

Cartwright, N, 2002, 'The Dappled World: A Study of the Boundaries of Science, Book Symposium, Summary', *Philosophical Books*, Vol 43, No 4, 241–243.

Cartwright, N, 2003, 'Against the System', mimeograph, LSE.

Chalmers, A, 1987, 'Bhaskar, Cartwright and Realism in Physics', *Methodology and Science*, Vol 20, 77–96.

Colapietro, V, 2002, 'The Seduction of Linguistics and Other Signs of Eros', *Semiotica*, Vol 142, No 1, 225–290.

Colapietro, V, 2004, 'Striving to Speak in a Human Voice: A Peircean Contribution to Metaphysical Discourse', *The Review of Metaphysics*, Vol 58, 367–398.

Fleetwood, S, ed, 1999, *Critical Realism in Economics: Development and Debate*, Routledge, London.

Guala, F, 2005, 'An Ontology of Economics?', mimeograph, University of Exeter.

Haack, S, 1998, *Manifesto of a Passionate Moderate: Unfashionable Essays*, University of Chicago Press, Chicago.

Haack, S, 2006, 'The Legitimacy of Metaphysics: Kant's Legacy to Peirce, and Peirce's to Philosophy Today', in H. Lenk and R. Wiehl, eds, *Kant Today*, Lit Verlag, Berlin.

Hands, W, 2001, *Reflection without Rules: Economic Methodology and Contemporary Science Theory*, Cambridge University Press, Cambridge.

Hookway, C, 2000, *Truth, Rationality and Pragmatism: Themes from Peirce*, Oxford University Press, Oxford.

Hoover, K, 2002, 'Econometrics and Reality', in U. Mäki, ed, *Fact and Fiction in Economics: Models, Realism and Social Construction*, Cambridge University Press, Cambridge.

Lawson, T, 1989, 'Abstraction, Tendencies and Stylised Facts: A Realist Approach to Economic Analysis', *Cambridge Journal of Economics*, Vol 13, No 1, 59–78.

Lawson, T, 1997, *Economics and Reality*, Routledge, London.

Lawson, T, 2001, 'Two Responses to the Failings of Modern Economics', *Review of Population and Social Policy*, No 10, 155–181.

Lawson, T, 2003a, *Reorienting Economics*, Routledge, London.

Lawson, T, 2003b, 'Ontology and Feminist Theorizing', *Feminist Economics*, Vol 9, No 1, 119–150.

Lawson, T, 2004, 'A Conception of Ontology', mimeograph, University of Cambridge.

Lawson, T, 2005, 'Modern Economics: The Problem and a Solution', in E. Fullbrook, ed, *A Guide to What's Wrong with Economics*, Anthem Press, London.

Lewis, P, 2004, *Transforming Economics: Perspectives on the Critical Realist Project*, Routledge, London.

Lipton, P, 2004, *Inference to the Best Explanation*, Second Edition, Routledge, London.

Mäki, U, 2002, 'The Dismal Queen of the Social Sciences', in *Fact and Fiction: Models, Realism and Social Construction*, Cambridge University Press, Cambridge.

Peirce, CS, 1931–58, *Collected Papers of Charles S. Peirce*, 8 vols, C. Hartshorne, P. Weiss and A. Burks, eds, Harvard University Press, Cambridge, Mass. References in text are to volume and paragraph number.

Psillos, S, 2002, 'Cartwright's Realist Toil: From Entities to Capacities', mimeograph, University of Athens.

PART II
Traditions and projects

4 The nature of heterodox economics[1]

Tony Lawson

Introduction

Recent years have seen the emergence of numerous activities in economics identified first and foremost as heterodox. For example, 1999 witnessed the formation of the Association for Heterodox Economics (AHE), an organisation that now sponsors an annual conference, postgraduate training workshops and more.[2] In October 2002, The University of Missouri at Kansas City hosted a conference on 'The History of Heterodox Economics in the 20th Century'. December 2002 saw the inaugural conference of the Australian Society of Heterodox Economists (SHE) at the University of New South Wales. Six months later, in June 2003, back at the University of Missouri at Kansas City, ICAPE (the International Confederation of Associations for Pluralism in Economics) celebrated its ten-year birthday with its 'First World Conference on the Future of Heterodox Economics'. Soon after this, journals started devoting whole issues to the movement or its history. A *Heterodox Economics Newsletter* has since emerged.[3] At the time of writing, the University of Utah sports a Heterodox Economics Student Association (HESA) and, on the Internet, it is possible to find a large number of sites dedicated to promoting specifically 'heterodox economics' and providing significant relevant resources.[4]

So it seems that something called heterodox economics is alive and flourishing. My question here is, what (sort of thing) is it? In asking this question, I do not wish to reify or fix the project. There is no reason at all to suppose that heterodox economics, any less than any other social phenomenon, is other than intrinsically dynamic and indeed ultimately transient. But I do take the view that things in process can still be known, if only as historical (and geographical and cultural) products. And I believe, and hope to show, that there can be gains to critical self-reflection upon the nature of that with which we are dealing or involved, at any point in time.

Among the very few who have questioned the nature of heterodox economics, it is recognised that heterodoxy serves, in the first instance, as an umbrella term to cover the coming together of sometimes long-standing, *separate* heterodox projects or traditions. The latter include post-Keynesianism, (old) institutionalism, and feminist, social, Marxian, Austrian and social economics, among others.

With this in mind, my initial question can be reformulated as an enquiry into whether there exists a (set of) trait(s) or causal condition(s), etc., that these traditions hold in common, over and above their all being projects in academic economics. For if there is a set of characteristics by virtue of which any tradition qualifies as heterodox (and determining whether this is so is my objective here), it is presumably included among the features, if any, that the often very differently oriented traditions share.

It is on this presumption that I shall proceed. The interpretation I defend is indeed one of unity within difference. It will be seen that to conceptualise and so identify heterodox economics is also to distinguish the mainstream against which it stands opposed. And thus to determine both is to distinguish economics from other disciplines, and so on. A process is thus set in train that stretches far beyond my original question. But I here explicitly step beyond a discussion of heterodox economics only to the extent that it is necessary to do so to get a reasonable initial assessment of its specific determinations.

The separate heterodox traditions

When we turn to the separate heterodox traditions, we find that the task of identifying the nature of any one of them is not straightforward. In fact, there is a good deal of debate within most, if not all, of the various traditions as to whether they constitute constructive programmes at all (see Peukert, 2001) or even coherent individual projects (see e.g., Hamouda and Harcourt, 1988). However, there do appear to be some prominent common features of all these separate traditions, even if some work is required in interpreting the implications. These prominent commonalities are, or include, the following:

1   a set of recurring, fairly abstract tradition-specific themes and emphases;
2   a multiplicity of attempts within each tradition to theorise around its tradition-specific themes and to form policy stances, or else to determine tradition-specific main units of analysis or other methodological principles based on them. The results are often presented as the theory/policy stances, basic units of analysis, or methodological principles that constitute the relevant tradition's alternatives to those of the mainstream;
3   an a posteriori recognition that it is usually impossible to generate very large agreement within any given heterodox tradition on specific 'alternative' theories and policies or specific methodological stances, a recognition typically resulting in an (often begrudging) inference that, even within any one tradition, the only definite common ground in terms of achieved position, is an opposition to the mainstream or 'neoclassical' orthodoxy.

Consider, as an illustration, the case of post-Keynesianism. Few would doubt that various themes or emphases are prominent. I refer, for example, to the concern with fundamental uncertainty in the analysis of decision-making, the rejection of the idea that macro outcomes can be provided with micro-foundations, a significant emphasis on methodological analysis, a recognition of the importance of time, institutions and history, a frequent drawing on the writing of Keynes, and so forth (see, for example, Arestis, 1990; Davidson, 1980; Dow, 1992; Sawyer, 1988).

However, attempts to produce substantive theories, policies or methodological stances have usually led to such a degree of variation or competition that post-Keynesians, and their observers, have tended to conclude that indeed the only definite point of agreement among post-Keynesians is that they stand opposed to the mainstream or 'neoclassical' contributions. Consider the following assessments:

> Post-Keynesian economics can be seen as covering a considerable assortment of approaches. It has sometimes been said that the unifying feature of post-Keynesians is the dislike of neoclassical economics.
>
> (Sawyer, 1988, p. 1)
>
> [P]ost-Keynesian economics is often portrayed as being distinguished more by its dislike of neoclassical theory, than by any coherence or agreement on fundamentals by its contributors.
>
> (Hodgson, 1989, p. 96)
>
> It is less controversial to say what post-Keynesian theory is not than to say what it is. Post-Keynesian theory is not neoclassical theory.
>
> (Eichner, 1985, p. 51)
>
> [P]ost-Keynesians tend to define their program in a negative way as a reaction to neo-classical economics.
>
> (Arestis, 1990, p. 222)
>
> Some have argued that what unites post-Keynesians is a negative factor: the rejection of neoclassical economics.
>
> (Dow, 1992, p. 176)
>
> What seems to be striking to outsiders of post-Keynesianism and neo-Ricardianism is that these two schools of thought and their major proponents only seem to have one cementing theme, their rejection of the dominant neoclassical paradigm.
>
> (Lavoie, 1992, p. 45)

I think heterodox economists will recognise that the sorts of commonalities listed above, and illustrated for the case of post-Keynesianism, hold to a degree for all the heterodox traditions.[5] David Colander, Richard Holt and J. Barkley Rosser Jr appear to speak for many when they conclude that '[i]n economics, at least, beyond this rejection of the orthodoxy there is no single unifying element that we can discern that characterises heterodox economics' (Colander *et al.*, 2004, p. 492).

In short, we appear to reach an apparently widely shared assessment of heterodox economics only in terms of what it is not, or rather in terms of that to which it stands opposed; the one widely recognised and accepted feature of all the heterodox traditions is a rejection of the modern mainstream project.

Of course, such an oppositional stance should not altogether surprise us. For employment of the term heterodox entails precisely this. According to the *Shorter Oxford English Dictionary*, for example, the qualification heterodox just means '[n]ot in accordance with established doctrines or opinions, or those generally recognised as orthodox'.

However, this recognition need not imply that heterodoxy is purely reactive. Nor does it follow that there is little more to be said. Indeed, an explicit rejection of orthodoxy in any sphere is presumably undertaken for certain reasons. And a sustained opposition, such as we find in modern economics, leads us to expect that the reasons for resistance are deep ones. Further, in addition to explicitly formalised grounds for an opposition to any orthodoxy, there are often other less-than-clearly-unrecognised presuppositions. I think this is so with heterodox economics, as we shall see.

It is clear, though, that if we are to progress in our quest to understand the nature of heterodox economics, we need first to determine something of the nature of that to which the heterodox traditions stand opposed. Only with this achieved are we likely to be successful in identifying the basis of the heterodox opposition. That is, before we can elaborate the presuppositions of heterodox economics, we need some insight into the nature of the project to which heterodoxy stands so seemingly implacably opposed.

What is modern mainstream or orthodox economics?

Perhaps at this point the argument begins to get somewhat (more) contentious. For although most observers of modern economics do recognise that the discipline is dominated by a mainstream tradition, and is so to a degree that is rather striking, there is remarkably little sustained discussion or analysis of (as opposed to a few quick assertions about) the nature of that mainstream project (even though practising economists usually agree that they know it when they see it). Among the conceptions of the mainstream that are to be found the following two are perhaps the more prominent, though each, I believe, is ultimately unsustainable.

The first such conception of mainstream economics is as a project concerned primarily with defending the workings of the current economic system, a conception often systematised under the heading of 'mainstream economics as ideology'. A recent example is provided by Guerrien (2004). Although the term ideology is rarely defined, it carries the connotation of a theory adhered to irrespective of its method or level of justification (or lack of justification). It is maintained, rather, because of some purpose it serves. Guerrien (2004) writes in this context of a mainstream ungrounded insistence that '"market mechanisms" produce "efficient" results if you abstract from "frictions", "failures", etc.' (Guerrien, 2004, p. 15).

Kanth (1999) provides an insightful contribution that seems to interpret mainstream economics in a similar fashion. According to Kanth, mainstream economics (which he sometimes refers to as neoclassical economics) is deliberately 'rigged' so as to generate results that support the *status quo*:

> To state the moral: *the entire enterprise of neo-classical economics is rigged to show that laissez-faire produces optimal outcomes,* but for the disruptive operation of the odd externality (a belated correction) here and there.
> (Kanth, 1999, pp. 191–2, emphasis in the original)

How is this rigging said to be achieved? One component of the most common strategy is everywhere to stipulate that human beings are rational (meaning optimising) atomistic individuals. A second is the construction of theoretical set-ups or models specified to ensure that (typically unique) optimal outcomes are attainable.

This is not yet enough to 'show' that the overall economic system is itself optimal in any way. If the claim is that mainstream economists seek to defend the economic system *per se*, something more is required to guarantee this result. This, it is usually supposed, is achieved by the commonplace construction of an equilibrium framework, the latter being so specified that the actions of isolated optimising individuals somehow (tend to) work to bring an equilibrium position about. Thus Kanth, for example, refers to the 'economic science of capitalism' as 'simply *irrelevant* for being a fantasy world of an ideal, rational, capitalism where all motions are mutually equilibriating, in a Newtonian co-ordination of the elements' (Kanth, 1999, p. 194).

There is little doubt that some mainstream economists approach their subject in the manner that Guerrien and others suggest. But most do not. And I do worry that portraying mainstream economics as driven by the goal of achieving results in these terms is overly conspiratorial. Nor is the presumption that mainstream results are consistent with an efficient or optimal social order even correct as a generalisation. Even those who have spent their careers studying models of equilibrium typically do not draw the sorts of inferences that can be used to justify the economic system.

Consider the conclusions of Frank Hahn, a major contributor to general equilibrium theory who has also been concerned to comment continually on the nature of the enterprise of equilibrium theorising. In both his Jevons memorial lecture entitled 'In Praise of Economic Theory' and the introduction to his collection of essays entitled *Equilibrium and Macroeconomics* (Hahn, 1984), Hahn explicitly acknowledges that he everywhere adopts (1) an individualistic perspective, a requirement that explanations be couched solely in terms of individuals, and (2) some rationality axiom. But in referencing questions of economic order or equilibrium, Hahn further accepts *at most* (3) a commitment merely to the *study* of equilibrium states. Poignantly, Hahn believes equilibrium outcomes or states are rarely if ever manifest:

> [I]t cannot be denied that there is something scandalous in the specta-
> cle of so many people refining the analyses of economic [equilibrium]
> states which they give no reason to suppose will ever, or have ever,
> come about. It probably is also dangerous. Equilibrium economics ...
> is easily convertible into an apologia for existing economic arrange-
> ments and it is frequently so converted.
>
> (1970, pp. 88–9)

Further, there are groups of economists, seemingly acceptable to the mainstream, who, though adopting the individualist–rationalistic frame-work, seem determined from the outset to demonstrate the *weaknesses* of the current economic system. Those economists who are often described as 'rational-choice Marxists' seem to be so inclined.

Equally to the point if not more so, most economists who accept the individualist and rationalistic framework do not actually concern them-selves with questions of equilibrium at all or, more generally, do not focus on the workings of the economic system as a whole. Most such economists, rather, concern themselves with highly specific or partial analyses of some restricted sectors or forms of behaviour. Moreover, to the extent that it is meaningful for the various results or theorems of these economists to be considered as a whole, or in total, the only clear conclusion to be drawn from them is that they are mostly wildly incon-sistent with each other.

Notoriously, even econometricians using identical, or almost identi-cal, datasets are found to produce quite contrasting conclusions. The systematic result here, as the respected econometrician Edward Leamer (1983) observes, is that 'hardly anyone takes anyone else's data analysis seriously' (p. 37).

If we turn away from econometrics to the mostly non-empirical 'economic theory' project, and look beyond its general equilibrium pro-gramme (which in any case has been in decline for some time now), there seems not even to be any agreement as to the project's purpose or direc-tion. As one of its leading practitioners, Ariel Rubinstein, admits:

> The issue of interpreting economic theory is ... the most serious
> problem now facing economic theorists ... Economic theory lacks a
> consensus as to its purpose and interpretation. Again and again, we
> find ourselves asking the question 'where does it lead?'
>
> (Rubinstein, 1995, p. 12)

Mainstream economics as the study of optimising individual behaviour

So what are we to make of all this? How are we to understand the project of mainstream economics in a manner that can make sense of this more complex situation? An obvious alternative hypothesis to examine in the light of the discussion so far, perhaps, is that, if there is anything essential to the mainstream tradition of modern economics, it is merely a commitment to individualism, coupled with the axiom that individuals are everywhere rational (optimising) in their behaviour. Perhaps the mainstream is just so committed, but without any overall common purpose in terms of the sorts of substantive results that 'should' be generated?

This is the second reasonably widespread interpretation of the mainstream endeavour, and the chief alternative to the view that the mainstream project is one concerned to defend the workings of the economic system. It constitutes an assessment, in particular, that is probably the more dominant among modern historians of economic thought.

Perhaps this characterisation of the mainstream programme is closer to the mark. But in the end, it is not sustainable. There are numerous game theory contributions where rationality is no longer invoked, and seemingly not even meaningful. Mainstream economists are sometimes even prepared to assume that people everywhere follow fixed, highly simple rules whatever the context (see references in Lawson, 1997, ch. 8). Moreover, some mainstream economists are prepared to abandon the individualist framework entirely if this will help make the 'economic theory' framework more productive in some way. As the 'economic theorist' Alan Kirman writes:

> The problem [of mainstream theorising to date] seems to be embodied in what is an essential feature of a centuries-long tradition in economics, that of treating individuals as acting independently of each other.
> (Kirman, 1989, p. 137)

Kirman adds: 'If we are to progress further we may well be forced to theorise in terms of groups who have collectively coherent behaviour' (Kirman, 1989, p. 138).

So it is not obvious that even assumptions of individualism and rationality are ultimately essential to the mainstream position. Indeed, many (e.g., Davis, 2005) find with Colander *et al.* (2004) that '[mainstream] economics is moving away from strict adherence to the holy trinity—rationality, selfishness, and equilibrium—to a more eclectic position of purposeful behaviour, enlightened self-interest and sustainability' (ibid., p. 485).

Do we, then, give up on our search for the essence of the current mainstream project? Some commentators believe so, with many concluding that the current mainstream is just too slippery a project to pin down. But

I do not think that the latter is the case. Rather, I think that an essential distinguishing feature of the mainstream project of the last fifty years or more is identifiable and remaining in place even through the sort of (ongoing) changes recorded by Colander *et al.*, Davis and others, a matter to which I return below. What then do I take the mainstream to be?

The mathematising inclination

As I say, I believe there is a feature of modern mainstream economics that is essential to it. And it is an aspect so taken for granted that it goes largely unquestioned. This is just the formalistic–deductive framework that mainstream economists everywhere adopt, and indeed insist upon.

I am not suggesting that the mathematical framework goes unrecognised. This could hardly be the case. But the mathematical framework is usually only briefly noted at best; it is considered so essential that worries about its usefulness, or dispensability, if they are raised at all, tend to be summarily dismissed rather than seriously addressed. It is because mathematisation is understood as being so obviously desirable, indeed, that the project is rarely defined in such terms. Serious work, it seems to be supposed, could never be otherwise.

Consider just the (mainstream) economists already mentioned. Rubinstein notes in passing that (mainstream) economic theory 'utilises mathematical tools' without questioning the legitimacy of this. Kirman (1989), though acknowledging that 'the mathematical frameworks that we have used made the task of changing or at least modifying our paradigm hard, is undeniable', insists that 'it is difficult to believe that had a clear well-formulated new approach been suggested then we would not have adopted the appropriate mathematical tools' (Kirman, 1989, p. 137). Leamer, on noting a continuing 'wide gap between econometric theory and econometric practice', laments not being able to perceive 'developments on the horizon that will make any mathematical theory of inference fully applicable' (Leamer, 1978, p. vi; the idea that there may be relevant non-mathematical theories of inference is seemingly never contemplated). And Hahn probably most epitomises widespread sentiment when he declares of any suggestion that the typical emphasis on mathematics may be misplaced that it is 'a view surely not worth discussing' (Hahn, 1985, p. 18). In fact, Hahn later counsels that we 'avoid discussions of "mathematics in economics" like the plague' (Hahn, 1992A; see also Hahn, 1992B).[6]

The truth is that modern mainstream economics is just the reliance on certain forms of the mathematical (deductivist) method. This is an enduring feature of that project, and seemingly the only one; for the mainstream tradition it is its unquestioned, and seemingly unquestionable, essential core.

Consider some more observations. The worry of non-economist observers is often that descriptions or overviews by critics of modern mainstream economics are likely to be uncharitable caricatures. So I focus on more impressions of mainstream economists themselves. Richard Lipsey, an author of a best-selling mainstream economic text book, acknowledges:

> ... to get an article published in most of today's top rank economic journals, you must provide a mathematical model, even if it adds nothing to your verbal analysis. I have been at seminars where the presenter was asked after a few minutes, 'Where is your model?'. When he answered 'I have not got one as I do not need one, or cannot yet develop one, to consider my problem' the response was to turn off and figuratively, if not literally, to walk out.
>
> (Lipsey, 2001, p. 184)

Just as tellingly, when William Thomson was recently invited by a leading mainstream journal to provide a piece entitled 'The young person's guide to writing economic theory', the taken-for-granted meaning of 'writing economic theory' is clear in the opening three sentences:

> Here are my recommendations for writing economic theory (and, to some extent, giving seminar presentations). My intended audience is young economists working on their dissertations or preparing first papers for submission to a professional journal. Although I discuss general issues of presentation, this essay is mainly concerned in its details with formal models.
>
> (Thomson, 1999, p. 157)

Or consider assessments of some Nobel Memorial Prize winners in economics. Wassily Leontief observes critically how '[p]age after page of professional economic journals are filled with mathematical formulas ... Year after year economic theorists continue to produce scores of mathematical models and to explore in great detail their formal properties; and the econometricians fit algebraic functions of all possible shapes to essentially the same sets of data' (Leontief, 1982, p. 104). Friedman concludes that 'economics has become increasingly an arcane branch of mathematics rather than dealing with real economic problems' (Friedman, 1999, p. 137). And Coase finds that '[e]xisting economics is a theoretical [meaning mathematical] system which floats in the air and which bears little relation to what happens in the real world' (Coase, 1999, p. 2). And there are many other observers of this situation, too.[7]

The changing face of the mainstream

Perhaps it will be thought that changes in the mainstream project that are currently under way serve to undermine the assessment sustained above? Colander *et al.* (2004) (in their paper explicitly titled 'The changing face of mainstream economics') argue that the mainstream is currently being transformed quite significantly, and criticise heterodox economists for failing to notice such ongoing developments. Specifically, these authors criticise heterodox contributors for adopting an overly 'static view of the profession' (p. 486); for referring to the current mainstream as neoclassical; and for missing the 'diversity that exists within the profession, and the many new ideas that are being tried out' (p. 487). In contrast, Colander *et al.* insist that '[m]ainstream economics is a complex system of evolving ideas' (p. 489), and refer to the 'multiple dimensionalities that we see in the mainstream profession' (p. 489).

Now, as it happens, I mostly agree with each of these critical assessments. In my view, it has always been unhelpful to make reference to a 'neoclassical economics', a category rarely clearly defined, and always misleading. And diversity within the dominant tradition has never been absent. Further, as always in the past, changes in the dominant tradition (as elsewhere) are certainly currently under way. For example, I can acknowledge (with Colander *et al.*) that evolutionary game theory is redefining how (notions of) institutions are integrated into analysis; that ecological economics is redefining how rationality is treated; that econometric work dealing with the limitations of classical statistics is defining how economists think of empirical proof; that complexity theory is providing a new way to conceptualise equilibrium states; that computer simulations offer a new approach to analysis; that experimental economics is changing the way economists think about empirical work, and so on.

But it remains the case that these and all other widely sanctioned examples of ongoing change, diversity, novelty, complexity, evolution and multi-dimensionality, etc., are occurring within the framework of formalistic modelling. The insistence on mathematical–deductive modelling prevails in all cases; the essential feature of the recent and current mainstream remains intact.

In fact, Colander *et al.* have noticed this aspect of 'the changing face of mainstream economics' themselves. I am not sure they fully appreciate the significance of their observation (they give it little emphasis) but in any case they acknowledge that 'modern mainstream economics is open to new approaches, as long as they are done with a careful understanding of the strengths of the recent orthodox approach and with a modelling methodology acceptable to the mainstream' (Colander *et al.*, 2004, p. 492).

Perceiving an 'elite' within the mainstream that determines which new ideas are acceptable, Colander *et al.* also write: 'Our view is that the current elite are relatively open minded when it comes to new ideas, but quite closed minded when it comes to alternative methodologies. If it isn't modelled, it isn't economics, no matter how insightful' (Colander *et al.*, 2004, p. 492).

And they add, with reason: 'Specifically, it is because of their method, not their ideas, that most heterodox find themselves defined outside the field by the elite' (Colander *et al*, 2004, p. 492).

In any case, an examination of ongoing developments soon enough reveals that they too ultimately provide support for my assessment that the mainstream project of modern economics must be characterised in terms neither of substantive results (such as demonstrating the desirability of the current economic order) nor of basic units of analysis (rationalistic or optimising individuals), but of its *orientation* to method. This is my first major contention: the mainstream project of modern economics just is an insistence, as a discipline-wide principle, that economic phenomena be investigated using only certain mathematical–deductive forms of reasoning. This is the mainstream conception of proper economics. It is the one feature or presupposition[8] that remains common to (if not always explicitly formulated in) all contributions regarded as mainstream, remaining in place throughout all the project's theoretical fads and fashions.

The nature of heterodox economics

What follows for our understanding of heterodox economics? If the latter is first and foremost a rejection of modern mainstream economics, and the latter consists in the insistence that forms of the mathematical–deductive method should everywhere be utilised, then heterodox economics, in the first instance, is just a rejection of this emphasis.

Notice that this does not amount to a rejection of all mathematical–deductive modelling. But it is a rejection of the insistence that we all always and everywhere use it.

In other words, heterodox economics, in the first instance, is a rejection of a very specific form of methodological reductionism. It is a rejection of the view that formalistic methods are everywhere and always appropriate.

To say more about the nature of the heterodox traditions of modern economics, I think it is clear that we need to explain this opposition. And, as noted, we are concerned here with explaining an opposition that is sustained and enduring.

One conceivable explanation, I suppose, is that heterodox economists believe that methodological pluralism is desirable *per se* and no more needs to be said. But is that really all there is to it? After all, in some fields of physics, such as super string theory, mathematical methods seem actually to be universally applied, but without any sign of a heterodox opposition. In economics, by contrast, there clearly is a heterodox opposition to the mainstream. And the phenomenon to explain is not just that a heterodox opposition exists, but that it is, as noted, relatively widespread, firm, often highly vocal and enduring.

Accounting for the nature of the heterodox opposition

To make sense of the fact of a sustained and widespread opposition to the mainstream, I think we must acknowledge that it is at least in some part based on an assessment by heterodox economists and others that the mainstream approach is actually very rarely up to the task at hand. And, indeed, the mainstream project is perceived by many as being more or less systematically irrelevant (see especially Fullbrook, 2003, 2004; Howell, 2000).

Even mainstream contributors seem increasingly to be accepting the assessment that their project (albeit typically conceived just as economics) is not doing too well in a general sense, and may actually be not very appropriate in the way it is done. Once more considering only those mainstream spokespeople already noted, Rubinstein (1995, p. 12) notes the explanatory and predictive weaknesses of the mainstream project, while Leamer (1983, p. 37) draws attention to a disparity of mainstream theory and practice. Coase, as we have seen, concludes that '[e]xisting economics is a theoretical system which floats in the air and which bears little relation to what happens in the real world' while, according to Leontief, the mathematical formulae with which economists fill economic journals lead 'the reader from sets of more or less plausible but entirely arbitrary assumptions to precisely stated but irrelevant theoretical conclusions', while econometricians fail 'to advance, in any perceptible way, a systematic understanding of the structure and the operations of a real economic system' (Leontief, 1982, p. 104).

Ontology

Now how could a project in modern economics turn out to be as systematically deficient as these commentators and others appear to find it? I want to suggest that a compelling (and perhaps the only plausible) explanation of it is that the sorts of methods on which the mainstream put so much emphasis are just not appropriate for dealing with social material, given the latter's nature. This is my second central thesis.

Here we get to the topic of ontology. Ontology is the study of, or a theory about, the basic nature and structure of (a domain of) reality. We all adopt ontological stances, and the acceptance of any method of analysis carries with it certain ontological preconceptions. As Marx says somewhere, microscopes and chemical reagents are not appropriate to the analysis of economic forms. I suspect most of us would agree with this assessment. But the point is a general one. All methods of analysis are appropriate to some sorts of material but not others. This is as true of mathematical methods as others. My claim here is that the explanation of the poor showing of much of modern economics is that mathematical methods are being imposed in situations for which they are largely inappropriate.

In due course, I shall argue further that it is an appraisal that mathematical methods are mostly inappropriate to social analysis that ultimately underpins the heterodox opposition. In short, I am contending that *the essence of the heterodox opposition is ontological in nature*. This, indeed, will be my third central thesis.

Although I shall address this third contention below, let me immediately emphasise that, if it does indeed constitute a correct assessment, I do not claim that the ontological orientation of the heterodox opposition has always been, or is always, recognised. To the contrary, I believe that one reason that the heterodox traditions have been less effective than their case appears to warrant is precisely that the ontological nature of their opposition has rarely been made sufficiently clear. Let me elaborate these various contentions.

The preconceptions of modern mainstream economics

I start by examining the implicit ontological presupposition of the modern mainstream project, thereby indicating the worldview that I believe is, in effect, being opposed by heterodox contributors.

We can note, first, that the sorts of formalistic methods that economists wield mostly require, for their application, the existence (or positing) of closed systems, i.e. those in which (deterministic or stochastic) event regularities occur. Mainstream economics is thus a form of *deductivism*. By deductivism I mean any form of explanatory endeavour that relies upon (which seeks or posits) closed systems.

Actually, mainstream economics is slightly more specific than this: it is a version of deductivism that posits functional relations presupposing *closures of causal sequence*. The latter are closed systems in which the events correlated are such that one set (conceptualised as 'independent variables') are considered to stand in the causal history of the remaining events (the 'dependent variable'). Thus a standard formulation of, say, a 'consumption function', which typically involves the correlation of household expenditure with household disposable income, posits the latter as a factor standing in the causal history of the former.[9]

Of course, the fact that formalistic modelling methods require the identification or construction of event regularities of some sort is well recognised by mainstream economists. Allais (1992), taking the association of deductivist modelling and science for granted, expresses the conventional situation well:

> The essential condition of any science is the existence of regularities which can be analysed and forecast. This is the case in celestial mechanics. But it is also true of many economic phenomena. Indeed, their thorough analysis displays the existence of regularities which are just as striking as those found in the physical sciences. This is why economics is a science, and why this science rests on the same general principles and methods of physics.
>
> (Allais, 1992, p. 25)

But if Allais correctly points to the need for modern mainstream economists to identify or formulate social event regularities, his description of the situation of modern economics is actually quite wrong in two of its aspects. Econometricians repeatedly find that correlations of the sort formulated are no sooner reported than found to break down; social event regularities of the requisite kind are hard to come by (see Lawson, 1997, ch. 7). And, it is just not the case that 'striking' event regularities of the sort Allais appears to reference, and which modern mainstream economists pursue, are essential to science. Their prevalence is a precondition for the mathematical–deductivist methods that economists emphasise as having relevance, but the application of these methods cannot be equated to science (see Lawson, 2003, ch. 1). Here, though, I merely note that any presumption of the universal relevance of mathematical-modelling methods in economics ultimately presupposes the ubiquity of (strict) event regularities.

Atomism and isolationism

But this is not the end of the ontological preconditions of methods of mathematical–deductivist modelling as employed in modern economics. A further important feature, which is less often recognised (or at least rarely explicitly acknowledged), is that the dependency of mathematical–deductivist methods on closed systems in turn more or less necessitates, and certainly encourages, formulations couched in terms of (i) isolated (ii) atoms. The metaphorical reference to atoms here is not intended to convey anything about size. Rather the reference is to items which exercise their own separate, independent and invariable (and so predictable) effects (relative to, or as a function of, initial conditions).

Deductivist theorising of the sort pursued in modern economics ultimately has to be couched in terms of such 'atoms' just to ensure that under given conditions x the same (predictable or deducible) outcome y always follows. If any agent in the theory could do other than some given y in specific conditions x – either because the agent is intrinsically structured and can just act differently each time x occurs, or because the agent's action possibilities are affected by whatever else is going on – the desire to pursue deductive inference would be frustrated.

Notice that this assessment is not novel, at least with regard to econometrics. It is in effect that advanced by Keynes over 60 years ago, albeit using a slightly different terminology. Thus, in response to an invitation from the League of Nations to review Tinbergen's early work on business cycles, Keynes writes:

> There is first of all the central question of methodology – the logic of applying the method of multiple correlation to unanalysed economic material, which we know to be non-homogeneous through time. If we

are dealing with the action of numerically measurable, independent forces, adequately analysed so that we were dealing with independent atomic factors and between them completely comprehensive, acting with fluctuating relative strength on material constant and homogeneous through time, we might be able to use the method of multiple correlation with some confidence for disentangling the laws of their action ...

In fact, we know that every one of these conditions is far from being satisfied by the economic material under investigation ...

To proceed to some more detailed comments. The coefficients arrived at are apparently assumed to be constant for 10 years or for a larger period. Yet, surely we know that they are not constant. There is no reason at all why they should not be different every year.

(1973, pp. 285–6)

The point then, however unoriginal, is that the ontological presuppositions of the insistence on mathematical modelling include the restriction that the social domain is everywhere constituted by sets of isolated atoms.[10] Now it is immediately clear, I think, that this latter restriction *need* not characterise the social realm. I want to suggest indeed that the noted conditions for closure (a world of isolated atoms) may actually be rather rare in the social realm. I draw this conclusion on the basis of an (a posteriori derived) theory of social ontology, a conception of the nature of the material of social reality defended elsewhere (especially in Lawson, 1997, 2003). I shall not provide a *defence* of this ontology here but merely give a brief overview of some the central components of it that are relevant to the purpose at hand.

A theory of social ontology

By *social reality* or the social realm, I mean that domain of all phenomena whose existence depends at least in part on us. Thus, it includes items such as social relations which depend on us entirely, but also others like technological objects, where I take technology to be (or anyway to be included within) that domain of phenomena with a material content but social form.

Now if social reality depends on transformative human agency, its state of being must be intrinsically dynamic or *processual*. Think of a language system. Its existence is a condition of our communicating via speech acts, etc. And, through the sum total of these speech acts, the language system is continuously being reproduced and, under some of its aspects at least, transformed. A language system, then, is intrinsically dynamic, its mode of being is a process of transformation. It exists in a continual process of becoming. But this is ultimately true of all aspects of social reality, including many aspects of ourselves, including our personal and social identities. The social world turns on human practice.

The social realm is also highly *interconnected and organic*. Fundamental here is the prevalence of *internal* social relations. Relations are said to be internal when the relata are what they are and/or can do what they do, just in virtue of the relation to each other in which they stand. Obvious examples are relations holding between employer and employee, teacher and student, landlord/lady and tenant or parent and offspring. In each case, you cannot have the one without the other; each is constituted through its relation to the other.

In fact, in the social realm it is found that it is social positions that are significantly internally related. It is the position I hold as a university lecturer that is internally related to the positions of students. Each year, different individuals slot into the positions of students and accept the obligations, privileges and tasks determined by the relation. Ultimately, we all slot into a very large number of different and changing positions, each making a difference to what we can do.

The social realm is also found to be *structured*. By this I mean that it does not consist just in one ontological level. In particular, it does not reduce to human practices and other actualities but includes underlying social structures and processes of the sort just noted and (their) powers and tendencies.

A further fundamental category of the ontological conception I am laying out is that of *emergence*. A stratum of reality can be said to be emergent, or as possessing emergent powers, if there is a sense in which it (1) has arisen out of a lower stratum, being formed by principles operative at the lower level, (2) remains dependent on the lower strata for its existence, but (3) contains causal powers of its own which are both irreducible to those operating at the lower level and (perhaps) capable of acting back on the lower level.

Thus, organic material emerged from inorganic material. And, according to the conception I am defending, the social realm is emergent from human (inter)action, though with properties irreducible to, yet capable of causally affecting, the latter.

Finally, the stuff of the social realm is found, in addition, to include *value* and *meaning* and to be *polyvalent* (for example, absences are real).

This broad perspective, as I say, is elaborated and defended elsewhere. But I doubt that, once reflected upon, the conception is especially contentious. Nor in its basic emphasis on dynamism and organicism or internal-relationality is it especially novel. However, it should be clear that, if the perspective defended is at all correct, it is *prima facie* quite conceivable that the atomistic and isolationist preconceptions of mainstream economics may not hold very often at all.

That said, I emphasise that the possibility of closures of the causal sequence kind, i.e. of the sort pursued by modern mainstream economists, cannot be ruled out a priori. Certainly, there is nothing in the ontological conception sketched above which rules out entirely the possibility of regularities of events standing in causal sequence in the social realm. But the conception sustained does render the practice of universalising a priori the sorts of mathematical–deductivist methods economists wield somewhat risky if not foolhardy, requiring or presupposing, as it does, that social event regularities of the relevant sort are ubiquitous.

Equally to the point, in discussing the nature of modern mainstream economics above, we saw in passing that it is not in an entirely healthy state; indeed, I think it is fair to say that, intellectually, it is in a state of disarray. In particular, it performs badly according to its own explanatory and predictive criteria, and is plagued by theory–practice inconsistencies. In the foregoing discussion we have an explanation. For if the conception of social ontology sketched above does not altogether rule out the possibility of social event regularities of the sort in question occurring here and there, it does provide a compelling explanation of the a posteriori rather generalised lack of (or at best limited) successes with mathematical–deductivist or closed-systems explanatory methods to date.

I do not doubt that mathematical–deductive methods have many desirable features. But the ability of a set of methods to help us understand social reality matters too. The problem with the mainstream stance is that the ontological preconditions of its formalistic methods appear to be not only *not* ubiquitous in the social realm, but actually rather special occurrences. If we knew both that social life was everywhere atomistic, and also that for any type of outcome we could effectively isolate a fixed set of causes (treating all other causal processes as a kind of stable, non-intervening or homogeneous backdrop), we should have grounds for feeling confident in the emphasis that mainstream economists place on the sorts of deductivist methods they use. However, our best ontological analysis suggests that closures are a special case of social ontology, while our a posteriori experience is that this special case seems not to come about very often at all.

Implications for heterodox economics

So how does all this bear on the central topic of this essay? Specifically, how does this help us understand heterodox economics? My claim is that something like the alternative ontology described above (and defended elsewhere: see Lawson, 1997, 2003) systematises the implicit preconceptions of the various heterodox traditions, and ultimately explains their enduring opposition to the mainstream. This was my third basic thesis already noted.

I repeat that I do not claim that such an ontological orientation is always explicit in heterodox contributions.[11] Indeed, the term ontology itself is rarely mentioned. At least this has been so until recently.[12] I contend, though, that the sorts of emphases that are prominent clearly do presuppose something like the ontological position I have described above.

Thus, briefly, the post-Keynesian emphasis on fundamental uncertainty is easily explained if openness is a presupposition, just like the institutionalist emphasis on the evolutionary method and on technology as a dynamic force (and on institutions as a relatively enduring feature of social life – see Lawson, 2003) are explained if it is presupposed that the social system is a process, and the feminist emphasis on caring and interdependence presupposes an ontology of internal relationality, among other things. The dominant emphases of the separate heterodox traditions, in other words, are just manifestations of categories of social reality that conflict with the assumption that social life is everywhere composed of isolated atoms; as I say, they are categories best explained by an implicit attachment to something like the social ontology outlined above.

As I have also already noted, the heterodox ontological presuppositions are rarely rendered explicit. Part of my contention here is that they should be. Mainstream economists have found it all too easy to find closed-system substitutes for heterodox claims or emphases, once it is admitted that heterodox economists have made a point. Thus, uncertainty is mapped onto risk; evolutionary concepts are shorn of their Darwinianism and reinterpreted in terms of the requirements of non-linear or game theory modelling; care for others becomes a variable in a utility function; and so on.

The fact that heterodox economists resist the mainstream reformulation of their concepts of uncertainty, evolutionary developments, care, institutions and history, etc., reveals that heterodoxy is not so much committed to the latter categories *per se*, as that it insists on their possessing the ontological properties of openness, processuality and internal-relationality, etc., that I have elaborated above. Once the heterodox groups make their attachment to this ontology explicit, the mainstream's transformative manoeuvres are pre-empted. The heterodox challenge becomes at once more powerful and less easily by-passed or seemingly accommodated.

I return to these sorts of considerations in due course. But, for the time being, I want to re-emphasise the point that the feature that drives the heterodox opposition to an insistence on mathematical formalism is an implicit worldview at odds with that which the formalistic methods presuppose. Thus I am arguing that, collectively, heterodox economists are primarily motivated, in their opposition to the mainstream, by ontological (not epistemological) considerations. Specifically, I believe we can explain the heterodox resistance to the mainstream incorporation of their key categories (uncertainty, evolutionary change, caring relations, etc.) only by recognising that the latter are really defended as manifestations of, and that heterodox economists carry commitments to, an underlying ontology of openness, process and internal-relationality. The latter is an ontology which mainstream economists simply cannot accommodate as long as they insist on employing only mathematical–deductivist methods.

The nature of heterodoxy

I have suggested, then, that the various heterodox traditions can be identified as heterodox through a recognition of the fact that they advance claims or practices or orientations which are either concrete manifestations of, or presuppose for their legitimacy, a social ontology of the (seemingly coherent) sort set out above. *In short, the set of projects currently collected together and systematised as heterodox economics is, in the first instance, an orientation in ontology.*

Of course, the heterodox projects on which I am focusing present themselves as projects in economics; I suspect many contributors would resist the idea that their traditions are to be understood as first and foremost an acceptance of the orientation in ontology that, I am suggesting, distinguishes them as heterodox. Indeed, this latter orientation has rarely been explicitly acknowledged anyway, at least until recently, as I have pointed out.[13] However, once we start looking at the more substantive orientations of the heterodox groups, we are confronted with issues that begin to distinguish various heterodox contributions from each other.

At this point a new question of interest arises. If an implicit commitment to the ontological conception described above renders heterodoxy coherent as a collective project, is it the case that the included traditions can each claim individual and distinctive coherency, with the latter being achieved at a more substantive level than ontology?[14] It is this question that I now address.

Distinguishing the heterodox traditions

It will be remembered that I earlier noted of each separate heterodox project that except for its basic guiding emphasis there is much internal debate and disagreement over substantive theories and policy stances, as well as over appropriate basic units of analysis and other methodological principles. This situation, indeed, has led some to question whether projects like post-Keynesianism (e.g., Hamouda and Harcourt, 1988) or old institutionalism (see Rutherford, 2000) can be regarded as coherent. I now want to propose a conception or interpretation of these heterodox traditions that can make sense of, and indeed ground, the fact of competing conceptions or theories and methodological claims within any one separate heterodox tradition, while simultaneously rendering the separate heterodox traditions individually coherent.

I have so far argued that the coherence of each separate project *as a form of heterodoxy* is achieved just by recognising each project as being committed broadly to the sort of ontological conception discussed earlier. With regard to distinctions, I contend that the heterodox traditions *can* be coherently identified and distinguished from each other, but *not* according to any specific theories or policy proposals favoured and defended, nor in terms of any features of the economy held to constitute the most basic units of analysis, nor according to any other specific substantive or methodological claim.

Rather, I suggest that the most, and perhaps only, tenable basis for drawing distinctions between the various heterodox projects is *according to substantive questions raised or problems or aspects of the socio-economic world thought sufficiently important or interesting or of concern as to warrant sustained and systematic examination.* That is, I suggest that the separate projects be characterised according to the features of socio-economic life upon which they find reason continually to focus their study.

In other words, if ontology can account for the distinctions between the heterodox traditions and the modern mainstream, i.e. if *ontological commitments identify post-Keynesians, institutionalists, feminist economists and others as heterodox*, it is their particular *substantive orientations, concerns and emphases, not answers or principles,* that *distinguishes the heterodox traditions from each other*. The latter is my fourth and final basic thesis or contention.

Before I elaborate upon it, let me quickly set this contention in the context of the conception of economics I defend in *Reorienting Economics* (Lawson, 2003). For I believe there are parallels to be drawn. Mainstream economics, of course, has implicitly defined the discipline in terms of method. The obvious alternative approach is to identify the different sciences not according to methods they employ but according to the nature of the material(s) or principles with which they are concerned. Thus physicists study certain physical principles, biologists study life processes, and so on.

Now the social ontology described above provides a conception of properties of all social phenomena (of being open, structured, intrinsically dynamic in a manner dependent on social transformation, and highly internally related though social relations); there is no reason to suppose that there exists an economic sphere or any other sub-domain of the social realm with phenomena devoid of such properties. This recognition supports a contention I defend elsewhere (Lawson, 1997, 2003) that the materials and principles of social reality are the same across economics, sociology, politics, anthropology, human geography, and all other disciplines concerned with the study of social life. Hence I think we must accept that there is no legitimate basis for distinguishing a *separate* science of economics. Rather, economics is best viewed as at most a division of labour within a single social science.

What is that division of labour? I think that the answering of this question must start from a cognisance of the history of the discipline, though guided by ethical considerations such as inclusivity. In *Reorienting Economics* (Lawson, 2003), my strategy is to seek to synthesise the main accounts (of Mill, Marshall and Robbins) traditionally regarded as competing contenders. In doing so, the conclusion I reach is that economics is best characterised as the division of social theory or science primarily concerned with studying all social structures and processes bearing upon the material conditions of well-being.[15] This view is easy to sustain, but in its detail it does not concern the present discussion. For whether or not the specifics of the latter suggestion are accepted, the broader point of relevance here is that, if economics is to be distinguished as a strand of social research, it cannot be according to its own ontology, methodological principles or substantive claims, but in terms only of its particular focus of interest (I elaborate on all this in Lawson, 2003, ch. 6).

It is in a similar fashion that I am proposing that the various heterodox economic traditions might also be considered as divisions of labour, albeit as divisions now within economics. It is the mainstream project that has purported to provide general theories at a substantive level, as well as setting down supposedly universal methodological principles. Heterodox economics can, and I believe should, avoid adopting the mainstream criteria of success uncritically. My suggestion is that just as economics (like all other disciplines) is appropriately conceived as a programme of research, not a set of answers or principles, the same holds for the heterodox traditions within economics.

Specifically, I have at several points noted that each separate heterodox tradition has tended to emphasise various features of social reality regarded as fundamental or of significant interest (even if attempts to theorise around these features are highly variable and competitive). I now propose that each individual heterodox tradition be identified precisely with these sorts of general features and emphases, conceived of as constituting topics for research.[16]

Thus, post-Keynesians, given their previous emphases, might be distinguished according to their concern with the fact of fundamental uncertainty stemming from the openness of social reality. Such a focus could take in the implications of uncertainty or openness for the development of certain sorts of institutions, including money, for processes of decision-making, and so forth. At the level of policy, the concern may well include the analysis of contingencies that recognise the fact of pervasive uncertainty, given the openness of the social reality in the present and to the future, etc. For those influenced by Keynes, especially, a likely focus is how these matters give rise to collective or macro outcomes, and how the latter in turn impact back on individual acts and pressures for structural transformation, etc.

By similar reasoning, I believe that it is best to distinguish institutionalism, *not* according to claims along the lines that institutions or evolutionary processes constitute main units of analysis or some such but, given that project's traditional concern with evolutionary issues, in terms of its interest in *examining how* social items change and/or endure over time. From such a perspective, those aspects of social life that are most enduring, such as institutions and habits, are particularly significant. So too are the interactions of factors such as institutions and technology in the process of reproduction and change (see Lawson 2005).

Austrians may perhaps be best identified according to their emphasis on studying the market process and entrepreneurship in particular, or perhaps in line with the attention given by this project to the role of inter-subjective meaning in social life, and so on.

And feminist economics is best distinguished, I believe, in terms of analyses of issues such as care, etc. And indeed, this ties in with how feminist analysis has tended to proceed. To focus on care, of course, is to be concerned with social relations. Very often feminist economists have identified their own project as one that first of all concerns itself with women as subjects (which may include, for example, giving attention to differences among women, as well as between genders) and takes a particular orientation or focus, namely on the position of women (and other marginalised groups) within society and the economy. But this focus, of course, is inherently relational. It includes an attention to the social causes at work in the oppression of, or in discrimination against, women (and others), the opportunities for progressive transformation or emancipation, questions of (relations of) power and strategy, and so forth. And this orientation has inevitably meant a significant attention, within feminist economics, to relational issues that historically have been gender related, such as looking after children, and indeed, the nature of family structures in specific locations.[17]

In any case, the foregoing is mainly suggestive. I should finally perhaps emphasise (though it is hopefully apparent throughout) that, although I am arguing that each heterodox tradition be distinguished according to a traditional set of concerns and emphases (rather than answers or methodological principles), I do not want to suggest that each somehow works with isolated components of society or economy. The object or subject matter of social theory/science, no less than economics, is an interrelated whole (in process). To focus competently on specific aspects requires an understanding of the totality (just as the investigation of any specific aspect of the human body presupposes some prior understanding of its functioning within the whole). There is no part of the social realm that does not have an economic aspect (although social reality does not reduce to its economic aspects). And, similarly, there is no part of social life that cannot be viewed under the aspect of its degree of openness, or its processuality/fixity, or the nature of its social-relationality, etc. In other words, on the conception laid out, each of the various heterodox traditions is viewed as approaching the same totality but with a distinguishing set of concerns, emphases, motivating interests and (so) questions. And, ideally, each will be achieving results that warrant synthesising[18] with the findings of others (again see Lawson, 2003, especially Part III).

Conclusion

In questioning the nature of heterodox economics, I have advanced and defended four basic theses or contentions. These can be summarised as follows.

The nature of the enduring modern mainstream project which the heterodox traditions continue to oppose, and against which they must ultimately identify themselves as heterodox, is set not in terms of its substantive results or basic units of analysis, but according to its *orientation* to method. The mainstream project of modern economics just is an insistence, as a discipline-wide principle, that economic phenomena be investigated using only (or almost only) certain mathematical–deductive forms of reasoning.

The often noted intellectual failings and limitations of this mainstream project arise just because its *emphasis* on mathematical–deductivist reasoning is inappropriate given the nature of social material. In other words, the ontological presuppositions of these methods do not everywhere match the nature of social reality.

The heterodox opposition is based on a (albeit often no more than implicit) grasping of the situation expressed in the just noted second contention. In other words, modern heterodoxy is, *qua* heterodoxy, first and foremost an orientation in ontology. It is to be distinguished from the mainstream by its willingness to approach theory and method in a manner informed by available insights into the nature of social reality.

The individual heterodox traditions are rendered distinct from each other by their particular substantive orientations, concerns and emphases, not by theoretical claims or results, empirical findings, methodological principles or policy stances.

The perspective sustained in this essay will surely be contested, not least by those economists who prefer to view themselves as heterodox but who believe that mathematical–deductivist reasoning is desirable in itself. But in the absence of any more coherent or empirically adequate thesis on the nature of modern heterodoxy, the broad thesis advanced here does have something to commend it. In particular, the set of contentions defended allows, without any obvious tension, a way of distinguishing the various heterodox traditions, collectively from the mainstream and individually from each other, in a manner that does not compromise their coherence as fruitful traditions in economics.

Notes

1 First published in *Cambridge Journal of Economics*, 2006, Vol 30, No 6, 483–505.
2 For an account of how the Association for Heterodox Economics was formed, see Lee (2002).
3 Go to http://l.web.umkc.edu/leefs/htn.htm
4 See, for example, http://www.orgs.bucknell.edu/afee/hetecon.htm, which currently lists various heterodox economics associations, heterodox economics

journals, heterodox publications (news, commentary and analysis), and heterodox discussion groups.

5 Briefly consider, for example, the project of old institutionalism, or anyway the manner in which it is commonly perceived. To speed up matters, let me rely on the commentary of the institutionalist historian Malcolm Rutherford. In his view, '[a]ll attempts to define American institutionalism, whether in terms of a set of key methodological or theoretical principles or in terms of the contributions of [major contributors] … have run into problems with apparent disparities within the movement' (Rutherford, 2000, p. 277). Rutherford notes the 'dramatic differences' in the methodological principles, theoretical positions and definitions of major contributors, and recognises the impression this has given: '[i]nstitutionalism easily appears as incoherent, as little more than a set of individual research programs with nothing in common other than a questioning of orthodox theory and method' (Rutherford, 2000, pp. 277–8). Thus Mark Blaug has stated that institutionalism 'was never more than a tenuous inclination to dissent from orthodox economics' (Blaug, 1978, p. 712), and George Stigler has claimed that institutionalism had 'no positive agenda of research', 'no set of problems or new methods', nothing, but 'a stance of hostility to the standard theoretical tradition'. This view still finds wide currency – for example, Oliver Williamson has recently argued that [in the light of its failures elsewhere] 'the older institutional economics was given over to methodological objections of the orthodoxy' (Williamson, 1998, p. 24).

6 Even Kanth notes the emphasis on mathematics but without quite appreciating its essentiality:

> The apparent rigour of mathematics was recruited avidly by neoclassicism to justify and defend its truistic, axiomatic, and almost infantile, theorems that deeply investigated but the surface gloss of economic life. Indeed, for the longest time, Marxists (in the U.S.) had to live in the academic dog-house for not being familiar with matrix algebra, until keen (if not always scrupulous) Marxist minds, with academic tenures at stake, realised the enormous (and inexpensive) potential of this tool for restating Marxian ideas in formalised language and instantly acquiring the gloss of high science, the latter-day pundits of repute here being Roemer in the U.S. and Morishima in England, who were of course soon emulated by a host of lesser lights to whom this switch in language alone promised hours of (well funded) computerised fun and games.
>
> Of course, all the formalisms did not advance a critical understanding of the organon of Marxian system, and its many difficulties, one iota; but it did succeed in generating grudging respect for the Marxist by the even more facile and shallow savants of neo-classicism.

(Kanth, 1999, p. 189)

7 William Baumol focuses on hurdles facing students in particular:

> [t]hese days few specialised students are allowed to proceed without devoting a very considerable proportion of their time to the acquisition of mathematical tools, and they often come away feeling that any piece of writing they produce will automatically be rejected as unworthy if is not liberally sprinkled with an array of algebraic symbols.

(Baumol, 1992, p. 2)

Roger Guesnerie focuses on research:

> [m]athematics now plays a controversial but decisive role in economic research. This is demonstrated, for example, by the recourse to formalisation in the discussion of economic theory, and increasingly, regardless of the field. Anyone with doubts has only to skim the latest issues of the

journals that are considered, for better or worse, the most prestigious and are in any case the most influential in the academic world.

(Guesnerie, 1997, p. 88)

And Robert Solow admits that

Today if you ask a mainstream economist a question about almost any aspect of economic life, the response will be: suppose we model that situation and see what happens ... modern mainstream economics consists of little else but examples of this process.

(Solow, 1997, p. 39–58)

Of course, heterodox economists do often capture the situation best. Consider the very apt assessment of Diana Strassmann, the editor of *Feminist Economics*. Like other heterodox economists, Strassmann certainly does not reduce economics to mathematical formalism but notices that this is an essential feature of the mainstream:

To a mainstream economist, theory means model, and model means ideas expressed in mathematical form. In learning how to 'think like an economist', students learn certain critical concepts and models, ideas which typically are taught initially through simple mathematical analyses. These models, students learn, are theory. In more advanced courses, economic theories are presented in more mathematically elaborate models. Mainstream economists believe proper models – good models – take a recognizable form: presentation in equations, with mathematically expressed definitions, assumptions, and theoretical developments clearly laid out. Students also learn how economists argue. They learn that the legitimate way to argue is with models and econometrically constructed forms of evidence. While students are also presented with verbal and geometric masterpieces produced in bygone eras, they quickly learn that novices who want jobs should emulate their current teachers rather than deceased luminaries.

Because all models are incomplete, students also learn that no model is perfect. Indeed, students learn that it is bad manners to engage in excessive questioning of simplifying assumptions. Claiming that a model is deficient is a minor feat – presumably anyone can do that. What is really valued is coming up with a better model, a better theory. And so, goes the accumulated wisdom of properly taught economists, those who criticize without coming up with better models are only pedestrian snipers. Major scientific triumphs call for a better theory with a better model in recognizable form. In this way economists learn their trade; it is how I learned mine.

Therefore, imagine my reaction when I heard feminists from other disciplines apply the term theory to ideas presented in verbal form, ideas not containing even the remotest potential for mathematical expression. 'This is theory?' I asked. 'Where's the math?'.

(1994, p. 154)

8 Essentially, the principle in question is a concrete universal underpinning the plethora of individual and singular contributions that collectively make up the mainstream output.

9 For a sustained discussion of the different forms of closed systems, including closures of causal sequence, see Lawson (2003, esp. chs 1, 2 and 4).

10 Most typically, such deductivist modelling endeavour encourages a specific conception of atomistic human agents (social atomism) where these are the sole explanatory units of social analysis (methodological individualism).

11 Though there are exceptions, such as Paul Davidson's concern with (non) ergodic systems (see Davidson, 1991, 1994, 1996).

12 Of course, where critics of the mainstream see the latter as substantive ideology, the emphasis on ontology promoted here can be viewed as a distraction (see, for example, Guerrien, 2004).

13 I do not wish to imply that individuals working mostly within heterodox traditions in economics could not themselves make a contribution to philosophical ontology. On philosophical matters, the flow of insights can be both ways between projects in ontology and the heterodox traditions in economics. Indeed, currently, there is real blossoming of insightful output by heterodox economists and others critically interacting with and seeking to shape (at the least the application of) the sort of ontological perspective described above, a perspective often systematised as critical realism in economics. See, in particular, Arestis *et al.* (2003), Beaulier and Boettke (2004), Davis (2004), Dow (1999, 2003), Downward (2003), Downward and Mearman (2003A, 2003B), Dunn (2004), Finch and McMaster (2003), Fine (2004), Graça Moura (2004), Hands (2004), Hargreaves Heap (2004), Kuiper (2004), Lee (2003), Lewis (2004B, 2004C), McKenna and Zannoni (1999), Nell (2004), Olsen (2003), Pagano (2004), Pinkstone (2003), Rotheim (1999), Setterfield (2003) and Smithin (2004).

14 I might note at this stage that there is surprisingly little comparative work in the literature that focuses on connections and distinctions between the various heterodox traditions. Some recent exceptions do exist (e.g., Danby, 2004). But there is a need for far more. Some insights can be gained though by considering those who have compared and likened one heterodox tradition (e.g., Beaulier and Boettke, 2004; Dunn, 2004; Kuiper, 2004) or more (e.g., Austen and Jefferson, 2004) with the ontological conception described above.

15 More specifically, I suggest that economics is the identification and study of the factors, and in particular social relations, governing those aspects of human action most closely connected to the production, distribution and use of the material conditions of well-being, along with the assessment of alternative really possible scenarios.

16 Such suggestions seem broadly substantiated explicitly by certain recent reflections of some heterodox thinkers concerned with the nature of the particular project with which they are associated (see Lewis, 2004A).

17 Of course, the question 'what is feminist theory?' is highly discussed among feminist writers and generates various, often very different responses. For a critical survey of the question that reaches a not dissimilar assessment to the very general suggestion advanced here, see Beasley (1999).

18 I use the word loosely. If findings are inconsistent, forms of critical resolution are clearly required.

References

Allais, M. 1992. The economic science of today and global disequilibrium, in Baldassarri, M. *et al.* (eds), *Global Disequilibrium in the World Economy*, Basingstoke, Macmillan.

Arestis, P. 1990. Post-Keynesianism: a new approach to economics, *Review of Social Economy*, vol. 48, no. 3, 222–46.

Arestis, P., Brown, A. and Sawyer, M. 2003. Critical realism and the political economy of the euro, in Downward, P. (ed.), *Applied Economics and the Critical Realist Critique*, London and New York, Routledge.

Austen, S. and Jefferson, T. 2004. 'Comparing Responses to Critical Realism', mimeo, Curtin Business School, Perth, Western Australia.

Baumol, W. J. 1992. Towards a newer economics: the future lies ahead!, in Hey, J. D. (ed.) *The Future of Economics*, Oxford, Blackwell.

Beasley, C. 1999. *What is Feminism?*, London, Sage.

Beaulier, S. A. and Boettke, P. J. 2004. The really real in economics, in Lewis, P. (ed.), *Transforming Economics: Perspectives on the Critical Realist Project*, London and New York, Routledge.

Blaug, M. 1978. *Economic Theory in Retrospect*, 3rd edn, Cambridge, Cambridge University Press.

Coase, R. 1999. Interview with Ronald Coase, *Newsletter of the International Society for New Institutional Economics*, vol. 2, no. 1.

Colander, D., Holt, R. P. and Rosser, J. B. Jr 2004. The changing face of mainstream economics, *Review of Political Economy*, vol. 16, no. 4, 485–500.

Danby, C. 2004. Towards a gendered post Keynesianism: subjectivity and time in a nonmodernist framework, *Feminist Economics*, vol. 10, no. 3, 55–76.

Davidson, P. 1980. Post Keynesian economics, *The Public Interest*, Special Edition, 151–73, reprinted in Bell, D. and Kristol, I. (eds), *The Crisis in Economic Theory*, New York, Basic Books, 1981.

Davidson, P. 1991. Is probability theory relevant for uncertainty?, *Journal of Economic Perspectives*, vol. 5, no. 1, 129–43.

Davidson, P. 1994. *Post Keynesian Macroeconomic Theory*, Aldershot, UK, Edward Elgar.

Davidson, P. 1996. Reality and economic theory, *Journal of Post Keynesian Economics*, vol. 18, no. 4, 479–508.

Davis, J. B. 2004. The agency-structure model and the embedded individual in heterodox economics, in Lewis, P. (ed.), *Transforming Economics: Perspectives on the Critical Realist Project*, London and New York, Routledge.

Davis, J. B. 2005. Heterodox economics, the fragmentation of the mainstream and embedded individual analysis, in Garnett, R. and Harvey, J. (eds), *The Future of Heterodox Economics*, Ann Arbor, MI, University of Michigan Press.

Dow, S. C. 1992. Post Keynesian school, in Mair, D. and Miller, A. (eds), *Comparative Schools of Economic Thought*, Aldershot, Edward Elgar.

Dow, S. C. 1999. Post Keynesianism and critical realism: what is the connection?, *Journal of Post Keynesian Economics*, vol. 22, no. 1, 15–33.

Dow, S. C. 2003. Critical realism and economics, in Downward, P. (ed.), *Applied Economics and the Critical Realist Critique*, London and New York, Routledge.

Downward, P. (ed.) 2003. *Applied Economics and the Critical Realist Critique*, London and New York, Routledge.

Downward, P. and Mearman, A. 2003A. Critical realism and econometrics: interaction between philosophy and post Keynesian practice, in Downward, P. (ed.), *Applied Economics and the Critical Realist Critique*, London and New York, Routledge.

Downward, P. and Mearman, A. 2003B. Presenting demi-regularities: the case of post Keynesian pricing, in Downward, P. (ed.), *Applied Economics and the Critical Realist Critique*, London and New York, Routledge.

Dunn, S. P. 2004. Transforming post Keynesian economics: critical realism and the post Keynesian project, in Lewis, P. (ed.), *Transforming Economics: Perspectives on the Critical Realist Project*, London and New York, Routledge.

Eichner, A. S. 1985. *Towards a New Economics: Essays in Post-Keynesian and Institutionalist Theory*, London, Macmillan.

Finch J. H. and McMaster, R. 2003. A pragmatic alliance between critical realism and simple non-parametric statistical techniques, in Downward, P. (ed.), *Applied Economics and the Critical Realist Critique*, London and New York, Routledge.

Fine, B. 2004. Addressing the critical and the real in critical realism, in Lewis, P. (ed.), *Transforming Economics: Perspectives on the Critical Realist Project*, London and New York, Routledge.

Friedman, M. 1999. Conversation with Milton Friedman, in Snowdon, B. and Vane, H. (eds), *Conversations with Leading Economists: Interpreting Modern Macroeconomics*, Cheltenham, Edward Elgar.

Fullbrook, E. (ed.) 2003. *The Crisis in Economics: Teaching, Practice and Ethics*, London and New York, Routledge.

Fullbrook, E. (ed.) 2004. *A Guide to What's Wrong with Economics*, London, Anthem Press.

Graça Moura, M. da 2004. A note on critical realism, scientific exegesis and Schumpeter, in Lewis, P. (ed.), *Transforming Economics: Perspectives on the Critical Realist Project*, London and New York, Routledge.

Guerrien, B. 2004. Irrelevance and ideology, *Post-autistic Economics Review*, no. 29, 6 December 2004, article 3, www.btinternet.com/,pae_news/review/issue29. htm.

Guesnerie, R. 1997. Modelling and economic theory: evolution and problems, in D'Autume, A. and Cartelier, J. (eds), *Is Economics Becoming a Hard Science?*, Cheltenham, Edward Elgar.

Hahn, F. 1970. Some adjustment problems, *Econometrica*, vol. 38, January; reprinted in *Equilibrium and Macroeconomics*, Oxford, Basil Blackwell.

Hahn, F. 1984. *Equilibrium and Macroeconomics*, Oxford, Basil Blackwell.

Hahn, F. 1985. 'In Praise of Economic Theory', 1984 Jevons Memorial Fund Lecture, London, University College.

Hahn, F. H. 1992A. Reflections, *Royal Economics Society Newsletter*, vol. 77.

Hahn, F. H. 1992B. Answer to Backhouse: yes, *Royal Economic Society Newsletter*, vol. 78, no. 5.

Hamouda, O. F. and Harcourt, G. C. 1988. Post-Keynesianism: from criticism to coherence? *Bulletin of Economic Research*, vol. 40, January, 1–34; reprinted in Pheby, J. (ed.), *New Directions in Post-Keynesian Economics*, Aldershot, Edward Elgar, 1989.

Hands, D. W. 2004. Transforming methodology, critical realism and recent economic methodology, in Lewis, P. (ed.), *Transforming Economics: Perspectives on the Critical Realist Project*, London and New York, Routledge.

Hargreaves Heap, S. 2004. Critical realism and the heterodox tradition in economics, in Lewis, P. (ed.), *Transforming Economics: Perspectives on the Critical Realist Project*, London and New York, Routledge.

Hodgson, G. M. 1989. Post-Keynesianism and institutionalism: the missing link, in Pheby, J. (ed.), *New Directions in Post-Keynesian Economics*, Aldershot, Edward Elgar.

Howell, D. 2000. *The Edge of Now: New Questions for Democracy and the Network Age*, London, Macmillan.

Kanth, R. 1999. Against Eurocentred epistemologies: a critique of science, realism and economics, in Fleetwood, S. (ed.), *Critical Realism in Economics: Development and Debate*, London and New York, Routledge.

Keynes, J. M. 1973. *The Collected Writings of John Maynard Keynes*, Vol. XIV, The General Theory and After: Part II Defence and Development, London, Royal Economic Society.

Kirman, A. 1989. The intrinsic limits of modern economic theory: the emperor has no clothes, *Economic Journal*, vol. 99, no. 395, 126–39.

Kuiper, E. 2004. Critical realism and feminist economics: how well do they get along?, in Lewis, P. (ed.), *Transforming Economics: Perspectives on the Critical Realist Project*, London and New York, Routledge.

Lavoie, M. 1992. Towards a new research programme for post-Keynesianism and new-Ricardianism, *Review of Political Economy*, vol. 4, no. 1, 37, 78.

Lawson, T. 1997. *Economics and Reality*, London and New York, Routledge.

Lawson, T. 2003. *Reorienting Economics*, London and New York, Routledge.

Lawson, T. 2005. The nature of institutional economics, *The Evolutionary and Institutional Economic Review*, vol. 2, no. 1, 7–20.

Leamer, E. E. 1978. *Specification Searches: Ad Hoc Inferences with Non-experimental Data*, New York, John Wiley.

Leamer, E. E. 1983. Let's take the con out of econometrics, *American Economic Review*, 34–43.

Lee, F. S. 2002. The association for heterodox economics: past, present and future, *Journal of Australian Political Economy*, vol 50, 29–43.

Lee, F. S. 2003. Theory foundation and methodological foundations of post Keynesian economics, in Downward, P. (ed.), *Applied Economics and the Critical Realist Critique*, London and New York, Routledge.

Leontief, W. 1982. Letter, *Science*, vol. 217, 104–7.

Lewis, P. (ed.) 2004A. *Transforming Economics: Perspectives on the Critical Realist Project*, London and New York, Routledge.

Lewis, P. 2004B. Transforming economics? On heterodox economics and the ontological turn in economic methodology, in Lewis, P. (ed.), *Transforming Economics: Perspectives on the Critical Realist Project*, London and New York, Routledge.

Lewis, P. 2004C. Economics as social theory and the new economic sociology, in Lewis, P. (ed.), *Transforming Economics: Perspectives on the Critical Realist Project*, London and New York, Routledge.

Lipsey, R. G. 2001. Successes and failures in the transformation of economics, *Journal of Economic Methodology*, vol. 8, no. 2, 169–202.

McKenna, E. J. and Zannoni, D. 1999. Post Keynesian economics and critical realism: a reply to Parsons, *Journal of Post Keynesian Economics*, vol. 22, no. 1, 57–71.

Nell, E. J. 2004. Critical realism and transformational growth, in Lewis, P. (ed.), *Transforming Economics: Perspectives on the Critical Realist Project*, London and New York, Routledge.

Olsen, W. 2003. Triangulation, time and the social objects of econometrics, in Downward, P. (ed.), *Applied Economics and the Critical Realist Critique*, London and New York, Routledge.

Pagano, U. 2004. The economics of institutions and the institutions of economics, in Lewis, P. (ed.), *Transforming Economics: Perspectives on the Critical Realist Project*, London and New York, Routledge.

Peukert, H. 2001. On the origins of modern evolutionary economics: the Veblen legend after 100 years, *Journal of Economic Issues*, vol. 35, no. 3, 543–56.

Pinkstone, B. 2003. Critical realism and applied work in economic history: some methodological implications, in Downward, P. (ed.), *Applied Economics and the Critical Realist Critique*, London and New York, Routledge.

Rotheim, R. 1999. Post Keynesian economics and realist philosophy, *Journal of Post Keynesian Economics*, vol. 22, no. 1, 71–104.

Rubinstein, A. 1995. John Nash: the master of economic modelling, *Scandinavian Journal of Economics*, vol. 97, no. 1, 9–13.

Rutherford, M. 2000. Understanding institutional economics: 1918–1929, *Journal of the History of Economic Thought*, vol. 22, no. 3, 277–308.

Sawyer, M. 1988. *Post-Keynesian Economics*, Aldershot, Edward Elgar.

Setterfield, M. 2003. Critical realism and formal modelling: incompatible bedfellows?, in Downward, P. (ed.), *Applied Economics and the Critical Realist Critique*, London and New York, Routledge.

Smithin, J. 2004. Macroeconomic theory, critical realism and capitalism, in Lewis, P. (ed.), *Transforming Economics: Perspectives on the Critical Realist Project*, London and New York, Routledge.

Solow, R. 1997. How did economics get that way and what way did it get? *Daedalus*, Winter, vol. 26, no. 1, 39–58.

Strassmann, D. 1994. Feminist thought and economics; or, what do the Visigoths know?, *American Economic Review*, Papers and Proceedings, 153–8.

Thomson, W. L. 1999. The young person's guide to writing economic theory, *Journal of Economic Literature*, vol. 37, 157–83.

Williamson, O. E. 1998. Transaction cost economics: how it works: where it is headed, *De Economist*, vol. 146, April, 23–58.

5   Economics as progress: the LSE approach to econometric modelling and critical realism as programmes for research[1]

Stephen Pratten

1. Introduction

Modern economics is very largely driven by fashion, with topics, themes, questions and categories appearing and disappearing without any clear line of progression.[2] The natural sciences, by contrast, are recognised as supporting numerous sustained projects. Think in particular of medical research, and the attempts to identify and understand diseases. Moreover, in such disciplines it is not unusual to find long-term projects in competition with one another. That is, one can find programmes of research addressing the same problems or phenomena but coming from different angles or perspectives, perhaps drawing upon different basic convictions about the nature of the problem or its solution. When two sustained competing programmes are found, a comparison of their relative strengths and weaknesses often facilitates insights which would otherwise not be apparent. Such comparisons allow us to see more clearly what is essential to the respective projects by deepening our understanding of their methodological presuppositions. Contrastive analysis of this type may also suggest ways in which it is vital to go forward by indicating more precisely what it is that requires further investigation and clarification for a reasoned choice to be made between the alternatives on offer.

While the characterisation of economics as fashion driven is undoubtedly correct as a broad generalisation, economics too can boast some sustained and competing programmes. And a failure to appreciate this can mean that the potential insights that can be achieved from contrastive exercises remain unrealised. In order to illustrate, and indeed to draw insight for modern economics, a comparison of two very important, if nominally quite different, programmes, which have each been under way for more than 20 years, is undertaken. Both programmes are addressing the same problem. Each has attracted a significant group of contributors. Numerous, albeit very different, advances have been made in the two projects. And the common question they address remains as important as it did when the two projects were initiated. By comparing the two, the nature of each, and the relevance of their common concerns, can be more easily appreciated. The comparison also enables us to identify the sort of evidence which would be required to move things forward, in the sense of providing a basis for selecting one project over the other. In this particular case, such a comparative assessment has a further rationale in that it helps us clear up a confusion perpetrated by the two main proponents of the respective projects more than 20 years ago. A disagreement between the two who have done most to develop these projects raised in an initial exchange but left unresolved can be clarified with the hindsight of seeing how the projects have developed.

The first of the two sustained, developmentally progressive, projects to be considered is the econometrics project of David Hendry and his colleagues, sometimes referred to as the *British tradition* or *LSE approach*.[3] The second is the project of Tony Lawson and his colleagues, mostly emanating from Cambridge, and systematised as *critical realism in economics*.[4] Focusing on these two particular programmes is not intended to suggest that there are no other constructive programmes of research in economics. A number of projects, especially those within heterodox traditions, such as post-Keynesian economics and Old Institutional economics, can be seen in this light. However, it is important to demonstrate that progressive long-term projects do exist, for the contrary opinion is widely held. Here two examples are provided that are important in many ways: their focus is of interest to all economics and their differences sum up the essence of the choices facing modern economists concerned with illuminating the social world.

Each project is seen by its proponents as developmental and progressive. Hendry, for example, explicitly invokes the notion of a *progressive research strategy for empirical modelling* (see Hendry, 1993: 177 and 210) and stresses the developmental nature of the project (see Hendry, Leamer and Poirier, 1990: 257). Critical realism, meanwhile, differentiates itself from certain projects in economic methodology which are, more or less, exclusively methodologically focused by insisting that the objective is to move *economics* forward (see Lawson, 1999b). In what sense can these self-consciously progressive and developmental research programmes be seen as dealing with the same problem? Both projects are, in fact, responding to the observation that modern econometrics has traditionally failed to identify event regularities of any satisfactory degree of strictness or durability, certainly not of a sort to facilitate successful forecasts. Hendry, for example, emphasises that '[f]ew of the main macroeconomic forecasting systems can produce sensible forecasts without the tender loving care of their proprietors. Many econometric equations in common use show significant deterioration in the accuracy with which they characterize data as time passes. And many economists are sceptical about empirical evidence, feeling it lacks "credibility"' (1985: 272). He even argues that '[a]ll models are crude simplifications, but many are hopelessly crude because of the methods used in their formulation, which camouflaged their inherent flaws, i.e. they were very badly designed. *The first hot blast of post sample reality ensured the conflagration of these straw-houses'* (1985: 279; italics added).[5] In similar vein, Lawson notes: 'Although econometric failure is manifest at many levels an outwardly familiar sign is the poor forecasting record of "econometric models" designed to track developments in the economy' (1997a: 301). More generally he notes:

> The most telling point against this econometrics project is the ex posteriori result that significant invariant event regularities, whether of a probabilistic kind or otherwise, have yet to be uncovered in economics, despite the resources continually allocated to their pursuit. Fifty years ago Haavelmo (1944) justified his efforts in developing 'the probabilistic approach to econometrics' with the observation that 'economics, so far, has not led to very accurate and universal laws like those obtaining in the natural sciences' (1944: 15). With the passage of time this situation does not seem to have changed significantly. *Econometricians continually puzzle over why it is that 'estimated relationships' repeatedly 'break down', usually as soon as new observations become available.*
>
> (1997a: 70; italics added)

The aim of this paper is to provide a comparison of these two programmes to see what can be learnt. In particular, the objective is to understand better the separate contributions of the two projects and to discover on what basis a choice between them could rationally be made by highlighting their many similarities and crucial differences in philosophical orientation. By providing such a comparison it will be seen that it becomes possible to resolve the confusion which characterised an early brief exchange between the two most prominent contributors to these programmes of research. Central to the original debate is an approach to econometrics delineated by Lawson (1981a) and designated the 'standard approach'. Lawson wrote of '[o]ne approach – which for the purposes of this essay will be labelled the "standard" approach – accepts the existence of "correctly specified" equations and "true" models and assumes the role of the econometrician is to utilise existing data in order to identify such structures' (1981a: 317). These true models, argued Lawson, were usually assumed to have stable parameters and a white noise error process. Against this 'standard', Lawson delineated a second approach, identified then as Keynesian, but thereafter systematised first as realist and eventually as critical realism in economics,[6] which does not start out with the presumption that correct econometric equations or (stable parameter) models exist only to be empirically identified.

At one stage, Lawson referred to Hendry and his colleagues as working within this standard approach. Hendry replied explicitly rejecting the claim that he worked within the approach Lawson designated as standard, arguing that, in his framework, all models are 'false' by definition. Hendry also accepted the possibility of unstable parameters (that structural breaks occur). Indeed, Hendry seemed even to accept many of the criticisms that Lawson levelled at much work carried out under the rubric of econometrics. Despite these clarifications, Lawson replied insisting that he had not misrepresented Hendry and that contrasting stances on the issues on which he focused, specifically the role of presuppositions of true models with constant parameters, were what divided the two projects. *Prima facie* both could not be correct. With the passage of time, it is clear that both participants have stuck to the basics of their own assessments of their own projects. But with the greater clarification, elaboration and progress that both projects have achieved, we can see how early misunderstandings occurred. As it happens, it is not that one was right and the other wrong. Rather, both were mostly right on their own terms. By examining how this is so, we obtain a better insight into both projects and are able to determine more clearly than hitherto the issues on which the relative performances of the two projects turn. The issues so brought into relief are fundamental to modern questions concerning the practice of empirical economics.

2. A common perception of the problem

In considering the output from the two programmes over the last 20 years, it would seem that Lawson must have misunderstood Hendry quite significantly. To situate Hendry's project as part of a 'standard' approach to econometrics that needs to be countered seems, at one level, to be almost wilful misrepresentation and, what is more, it appears to ignore certain striking correspondences between the two programmes. Lawson and Hendry's approaches actually share a common understanding of the difficulties of doing empirical research and also make similar criticisms of key questionable practices carried out within conventional econometrics. The features that the two projects share have grown to be quite substantial. In particular, both delineate a real world independent of our analysis of it and view it as complicated and evolving, and subject to structural changes. Both highlight the invalidity of much econometric practice, pointing out its inconsistency with most econometric theory. Both projects reject the idea that econometrics is analogous to experimental control. And both allow that models with 'nice' properties may be unobtainable. Yet the two projects proceed very differently. In eventually seeing how they do, we shall not only gain further insight into these projects but also see that Lawson was not so misguided in his initial drawing of contrasts after all. First, though, let me briefly elaborate on these claimed commonalities.

Realist propositions

Both programmes can be seen as adopting a realist orientation. Within critical realism, the thesis of the existential intransitivity of objects or ontological realism (the claim that things in general exist and act independently of our knowledge of them) is tied to the thesis of the historical transitivity of knowledge or epistemological relativism (that there is no way to know what exists except under particular, historically transient, descriptions). To elaborate, there are two types of object of knowledge: the things which are being expressed or described, etc., and the prior theories, hunches, facts, hypotheses, guesses, intuitions, speculations, etc., that are being transformed and drawn upon in arriving at current formulations. To describe certain objects or features as intransitive is to indicate that they exist at least in part independently of any knowledge of which they are the referent. Intransitive objects of knowledge need be no more fixed or enduring than transitive ones. With regard to the social realm, at the moment a social investigation is initiated the putative objects of that enquiry either do, or do not, exist, and if the former, possess whatever properties that they do, quite independently of the process of investigation which eventually ensues. This remains the case even if that investigation in due course informs a transformation in the object concerned. At the same time, if knowledge is not merely given in experience neither can it be seen as being created out of nothing. Rather, it must come about through a transformation of pre-existing knowledge-like materials. The argument critical realism develops is that

> the pervasive phenomena of scientific continuity and change is intelligible only if we recognise this distinction between intransitive and transitive objects of knowledge. For only then can we make sense of scientific discovery and change in our knowledge of the world on the one hand, and changes in the world itself on the other. That is unless knowledge and its intransitive objects possess relatively distinct beings and histories, scientific change and changes in the nature of things could not be distinguished, with the consequence that the former would be unintelligible while the latter would never be noted … the intelligibility of the phenomena of scientific continuity and change entails not only that creative subjects do not constitute the world (as in idealism including its post-modernist or pragmatist variants) but also that thought could be regarded as a mechanical function of the world (as in empiricism). Rather, knowledge must be seen as consisting of stuff that is socially produced, typically symbolically mediated and formed, historically specific, and materially irreducible to its intransitive objects. Both inside and outside science, when we talk or write of things, structures, events and states of affairs, we can speak or write of, and know, them only under particular descriptions that are neither reducible to, nor isomorphic with, the objects which … they nevertheless express.
>
> (Lawson, 1997a: 239)

Hendry, at times, explicitly adopts a realist perspective in the sense that the ultimate objects of scientific investigation are taken to exist independently of, or at least prior to, their investigation. For Hendry, '[t]here is an economic mechanism which operates in reality: This comprises the transacting, producing, transporting (etc.) behaviour of economic agents at some time and place' (1995a: 55). In adopting a realist orientation, Hendry is also concerned to provide some explicit commentary upon the nature of the object of analysis. Specifically, he suggests that the economic realm is highly complex:

> I certainly think that the real world exists. There are agents behaving in that world, and their interactions generate outcomes. We have a measurement process and a good idea of what it measures. The observables are generated by that joint mechanism, which is more complex than any model we think of.
>
> (Hendry, Leamer and Poirier, 1990: 189)

Hendry's references to an economic mechanism and a data generation process appear at times to be pointing to the distinction between an intransitive and transitive realm.[7] He notes: 'I find it very useful to think of the data generating process (DGP), the actual economic mechanism, as something external, and my model as something I am using to understand the DGP' (Hendry, Leamer and Poirier, 1990: 197). Elsewhere he notes that: 'We need different terms for the mechanism and models thereof, and will use the term DGP only for the actual process which generated the data' (1995a: 55). It would seem from these kind of remarks that Hendry is suggesting that the economic mechanism and models exist in distinct realms, the actual economic mechanism and the DGP in the intransitive realm, and the model in the transitive realm.

Structural breaks and the intrinsically dynamic nature of social reality

In a series of recent papers, Hendry and his colleagues have considered the implications for econometric modelling and forecasting of the existence of *structural breaks.* Hendry recognises that economies constitute highly dynamic complex processes and emphasises that they 'are often subject to major institutional, political, financial, and technological changes which manifest themselves as structural breaks in econometric models relative to the underlying data generation process' (Clements and Hendry, 1998a: 1). Hendry (1996: 412) provides an illustrative list of the kind of legislative, social, institutional and financial regime shifts that can generate such structural breaks. The existence of regime shifts and associated structural breaks is seen to undermine traditional forecasting procedures severely:

Unfortunately, the historical track record [of economic forecasting] is littered with less than brilliant forecasts. There have been major episodes of predictive failure when the model forecasts have system-atically over – or under predicted for substantial periods, and realised outcomes have been well outside any reasonable *ex ante* confidence interval computed from the uncertainties due to parameter estimation and lack of fit. Examples include the forecasts made by the major UK model based forecasting teams over the 1974–5 and 1980–81 recessions … . This suggests that it is inappropriate to use a theory of forecast-ing based on assuming a stationary process with constant parameters which are accurately captured by the model. Nevertheless, the major-ity of analyses adopt just such a perspective, and concentrate on a world in which a constant-parameter, unchanging relation … holds.

(Clements and Hendry, 1996: 102)

Essentially, the criticism of traditional forecasting procedures would seem here to be that they fail to take assessments of the nature of the underlying object of analysis sufficiently into account. Thus Clements and Hendry observe that

periods of economic turbulence resulting from structural breaks or regime shifts historically go hand in hand with episodes of dramatic predictive failure … The correlation between turbulence and pre-dictive failure is to be expected, but what is surprising is that most analyses of economic forecasting are firmly rooted in the assumption of a constant data generation process. For an econometric theory of forecasting to deliver relevant conclusions about empirical forecast-ing, it must be based on assumptions that adequately capture the appropriate aspects of the real world to be forecast.

(1996: 104–105)

The task Hendry and his colleagues set themselves, then, is that of con-sidering how econometric modelling can contribute to forecasting whilst acknowledging this feature of social reality.

To the extent that Hendry and his co-workers emphasise and acknowl-edge the dynamic and evolutionary nature of social reality, there is considerable correspondence with critical realism. Critical realism in economics argues that individuals are internally complex and cannot be conceptualised as passive automata. It insists that the subject matter of social science, including economics, cannot be reduced to principles governing the behaviour of individuals and descriptions of their situa-tions. In particular, in addition to acknowledging the centrality of human beings, human practices and contexts of action to all social life, critical realists establish the irreducibility of social structures including rules, relationships and positions. The conception of the social world sustained is of a network of continually reproduced inter-dependencies. As Lawson notes: 'Social reality is conceived as intrinsically dynamic and complexly structured, consisting in human agency, structures and contexts of action, none of which are given or fixed, and where each presupposes each other without being reducible to, identifiable with, or explicable completely in terms of, any other' (1997a: 159). On this view 'social structures ... cannot be regarded as somehow fixed; they can never be reified. There is always fluidity and movement. Even when, over restricted regions of time and space, a structure might be held to have been reproduced "intact" as it were (and ... given the holistic nature of much social structure all reproduction doubtless entails some change, just as change will rarely be total) this is always on the basis of the intrinsically dynamic and always potentially transformative, human practice' (ibid.: 171).[8] Just as Hendry and Clements criticise the traditional theories of forecasting for retaining the assumption of a constant *data generation process,* similarly Lawson criticises the ontological neglect he sees as characterising much economic modelling: 'any willingness of economic modellers to keep on attempting to forecast sufficiently accurately cannot establish that achieving this goal is a real possibility – that its conditions are everywhere or anywhere satisfied' (Lawson, 1998a: 359).

Econometric theory and practice

Lawson and Hendry also both acknowledge that econometric theory and practice are mutually inconsistent and see the respective programmes they support as responding constructively to this feature of contemporary economics. Lawson explicitly motivates his book *Economics and Reality* by identifying a series of theory-practice inconsistencies which he associates with contemporary mainstream economics. One such inconsistency relates to the way 'economists frequently employ methods, practices and techniques of enquiry and modes of inference, that are inconsistent with the theoretical perspectives on method which they claim to draw upon' (1997a: 4). According to Lawson:

> Econometrics is the paradigm example here. It is widely observed, for example, that when econometricians formulate and (often simultaneously) estimate their 'models' they frequently 'run' hundreds if not thousands of regressions, and in doing so contradict the classical theory of inference they explicitly acknowledge. Moreover, when their models are used to forecast unobserved (typically future) states of the economy, econometricians repeatedly make *ad hoc* revisions to estimated parameter values, or introduce 'add on' factors in order to generate results that are 'sensible' or believable, thereby contravening what Lucas designates the 'theory of economic policy'.
>
> (Lawson, 1997a: 6)

Lawson then goes on to attempt to render such inconsistencies intelligible.

Hendry too emphasises the distance between econometric theory and practice:

> At present there are peculiar gaps between theory and what people actually do: I think the sinners and preachers analogy in Leamer (1978) is the correct one here. The theoretical econometrician says one thing but as a practitioner does something different. I am trying to understand why economists do that, given that they know the theory, and they are obviously trying to solve practical problems.
>
> (Hendry, Leamer and Poirier, 1990: 179)

In their recent book on forecasting, Clements and Hendry (1999: xxiii) situate their own contribution as one which attempts 'to reduce the present discrepancy between theory and practice'. In an earlier paper, Hendry points to just the same set of tensions to which Lawson later refers when motivating his book. Hendry suggests that within conventional modelling:

> any misfit should lead to rejection of the model. Instead, to rescue their pet hypotheses, investigators may run literally 'hundreds of regressions' (cf. Friedman and Schwartz, 1982, p. 266), hoping that one of these will 'corroborate' their ideas. Thus, difficulties are camouflaged or papered over, not revealed; the resulting models are not robust and it is little wonder they break down when confronted with new data and/or new economic policies ... they do not even adequately characterise existing data.
>
> (1985: 277)

For Hendry, such tensions can be overcome only once an alternative approach to applied economics is adopted.

Experimental control and the data of the social realm

An explicit recognition that the data of the social realm are not amenable to being treated as if they were generated in conditions of experimental control is a further common component which the two programmes share. For Hendry, '[e]xperimentation may be useful as part of scientific method, and is a powerful instrument for discovery and evaluation, but it is not essential to either science or progressivity' (1997a: 168). He robustly criticises the view that econometrics represents a counterpart to experimental control in economics. He argues:

> Econometrics is sometimes viewed as the economics equivalent of experimental control. In such a framework, it is argued that although economists primarily obtain non-experimental data, the impact of

uncontrolled variables can be removed after the event by partialling out their effects using techniques such as multiple regression and its many sophisticated derivatives … However, that 'model' of econometrics would require that all relevant uncontrolled effects were measured and were indeed removed as covariates: since a major objective of econometric analyses is to determine what factors are relevant, there seems little hope of attaining that requirement.

(1997a: 173)

According to Hendry (1995a: 28), within the experimental context the modeller controls the environment and some of the factors (i.e. the inputs), traces their effects on certain other factors (i.e. the outputs) and establishes a causal relationship between inputs and outputs. Hendry sees it as highly misleading to treat observational data of the type typically available to the econometrician as if they represent measurements obtained in the context of a controlled experiment:

To apply the logic used by physicists (say) to the empirical analysis of data in econometrics requires the ominiscent assumption that the model is the mechanism which generated the data. In economics, we do not know how the data were actually generated, and we do not control the economy in the way that a physical scientist can control an experiment.

(1995a: 28)

Hendry suggests that it is important to recognise that economics departs significantly from the physical sciences in so far as 'rather little is known about the relevance of the states considered to the actual data generation process' (1997a: 171). Conventional econometrics fails to appreciate this difference: 'conventional modelling assumes that the model and data process coincide at the outset; i.e. that the data were actually generated by the factors in the model plus a random innovation impinging from nature' (1985: 277). As a consequence, conventional econometrics proceeds by asserting the existence of correct models whose parameters have only to be estimated.[9]

Lawson is equally critical of 'the pretence that economic phenomena are … generated under conditions equivalent to those achieved through experimental control' (1997a: 235). As we have seen, Lawson suggests that social reality is open, dynamic and holistic; the implication drawn from this is that neither it, nor stable bits of it, are amenable to isolation in conditions analogous to those of experimental control facilitating the production of event regularities. Thus he notes: '[i]t is certainly reasonable to doubt that controlled experimentation will ever be particularly meaningful in economics due to the impracticality of manipulating social structures and mechanisms in order more clearly to identify them' (1997a: 203–204).

Specifically, he suggests that 'the environment in which any mechanism acts need not be sufficiently homogenous. In the social realm, indeed, there will usually be a potentially very large number of countervailing factors acting at any one time and sporadically over time, and possibly each with varying strength' (1997a: 218). Further, 'the mechanisms or processes which are being identified are themselves likely to be unstable to a degree over time and space' (1997a: 219).

Event regularities and constant parameters

Both programmes see the existence of event regularities, and so models that presuppose constant parameters, as a fundamental issue, and Lawson and Hendry each consider the possibility of the absence of such regularities. Here Lawson's reference to 'event regularities' and Hendry's 'constant parameters' are viewed as essentially relating to the same phenomena. Hendry acknowledges that the assumption of data generation processes characterised by constant parameters can be questioned:

> ... the relevance to data analysis of arbitrarily postulated DGPs with constant parameters is open to question, since it is not obvious that there need exist any parameters in the empirical representations which economists consider ... For example, there may not be a marginal propensity to consume for any agents, any society, or any entities, however many theories postulate its central role, or data analyses claim its determination. I believe such constructions do exist, because (e.g., the aggregate marginal propensity to consume) apparently can be altered by changing taxes. Moreover, a substantial number of econometric relationships seem to persist through time. Finally, human behaviour, at both the individual and the social level, evolves slowly relative to the time-span of most econometric studies. Just as there is no criterion of truth for empirical models, so we cannot verify that parameters of interest exist to be discovered. Nevertheless, parameters of interest motivate and structure a study to come to a better understanding of the world in which we live. Historically, the existence of the initially postulated parameters may not be essential to scientific progress since, in the process of analysis, a better framework may emerge. Conversely, faster progress is likely if the selected parameters do reflect salient and constant features of reality. Parameters which prove to be constant empirically seem naturally to be of interest.
>
> (1995a: 348–349)

Hendry suggests that the adequacy of any underlying assumption concerning the existence of constant parameters can only be assessed *ex post*:

... economies seem prone to regime shifts, structural breaks and technological and financial innovations which require adaptation and
learning by economic agents. All of these induce different forms of
non-stationarity, which require careful empirical modelling if invariant parameters are to be established but do not *per se* preclude doing
so ... However, it is unsurprising that evidence in economics is less
secure than in the natural sciences, a difficulty exacerbated by the tiny
allocation of resources to data collection in economics. *The only issue of*
principle involved is the existence of underlying invariances, and on that, the
proof of the pudding is in the eating.

(1997a: 178; italics added)

Just as Hendry is prepared to question the validity of assuming the
existence of constant parameters, so Lawson examines the assumption
of the existence, and doubts the prevalence of constant conjunctions
of events. In order to facilitate discussion, Lawson sets out a number
of definitions relating to event regularities, perhaps the most basic of
which concerns *regularity stochasticism*. Regularity stochasticism is for
Lawson the thesis that

for every (measurable) economic event or state of affairs y there exists
a set of conditions or events, etc., $x_1, x_2 \ldots x_n$ say, such that y and x_1,
$x_2 \ldots x_n$ are regularly conjoined under some (set of) 'well behaved'
probabilistic formulations. In other words ... for any (measurable)
economic event y a stable and recoverable relationship between a set
of conditions $x_1, x_2, \ldots x_n$ and the average or expected value of y (conditional upon $x_1, x_2, \ldots x_n$) or some such, is postulated.

(1997a: 76)

Lawson and others developing critical realism have been especially concerned to identify the set of conditions on a system which would ensure
that such event regularities hold. These have been found to be rather strict.
Systems in which constant event regularities do not feature are referred
to as open. Closed systems relate to those situations where constant event
regularities obtain.

If Hendry insists that the existence of constant parameters is something
that can only be assessed *ex post*, then for Lawson too the question of whether
or not event regularities occur in the social realm remains essentially an
empirical matter. Thus he notes:

In *Economics and Reality* I maintain, as an ex posteriori assessment,
that event regularities that are both of sufficient strictness to be of use
to economic modellers, and of scientific interest (i.e. containing some
revelatory insight; acting behind our backs, as it were), are found to be
rather rare. Amongst other things, if fifty years of econometric failure

(in the face of billions of 'regressions') is suggestive of anything it is surely that regularities of the sort being sought after may after all be thin on the ground. In consequence, it seems at least reasonable that the hypothesis of the non-occurrence of event regularities of the sort being pursued be taken seriously.

(Lawson, 1998a: 357)

There exist then numerous points of contact between the LSE approach to econometrics and critical realism in economics. Both programmes can be seen as explicitly realist and provide commentaries on the nature of the object of analysis in elaborating the approaches they respectively defend. Both remain critical of others who do not take assessments of the nature of the underlying object sufficiently into account. Both recognise that econometric theory and practice are mutually inconsistent. Both explicitly recognise that the track record of econometric forecasting is poor. Both elaborate important sets of categories. Both programmes emphasise that the data of the social realm are not amenable to being treated as if generated in conditions of experimental control. Both understand the social world as evolving complex processes subject to structural breaks. Both see the existence of event regularities (and so constant parameter models, etc) as a point of contention. And both acknowledge that the existence or otherwise of event regularities (and hence constant parameters etc) is ultimately an empirical issue. Given these similarities, Lawson's original interpretation of Hendry's approach as a standard approach within econometrics does seem *prima facie* extraordinary. In fact, with so much in common, the relevant issue would seem to be how to differentiate at all between the two projects.

3. Identifying and accounting for the differences

The difference between the two programmes, in fact, begins with a further commonality. Most conventional econometric projects start by asserting the existence of correct models whose parameters have only to be estimated. They assume that social outcomes can be treated like phenomena produced in well-controlled experiments. Lawson and Hendry both reject the parallels with controlled experiments, both think that models with constant parameters are a special occurrence, and both set out to interpret such occurrences should they obtain. That is, both set out to provide general frameworks, against which specific occurrences of models with relatively stable parameters are a special case, and in terms of which they can be given a particular interpretation. Thus in providing these general frameworks Lawson and Hendry are again following similar lines, lines which take them away from the standard approaches. We can see again, then, why Hendry felt aggrieved in being referred to by Lawson as adopting a 'standard approach'. It is at this point, though, that their ways do part company. And we shall see that they do so in a manner that renders Lawson's assessment intelligible and, on its own specific terms, actually correct. Let me consider the two general frameworks in turn, starting with Hendry's approach.

Hendry on the DGP and the method of reduction

A fundamental feature of Hendry's approach is that it starts from the idea of a complex (considered to be) unknowable data generation process or DGP. There are, in fact, (at least) two ideas in play here. The first is the one already referred to above of a complex real world (ontological) mechanism (including measurement system) that gave rise to the economic data of interest. The second is a joint probability distribution defined over the entire sample space for all the observed random variables. Following Haavelmo (1944) it is *as if* the observable variables are produced in accordance with this distribution. It is the second idea, of the joint distribution, that is essential to Hendry's method of reduction, i.e. his account of 'how to analyse data in a non-experimental world' (1995a: 29). There may be some slippage in Hendry's writings, though, in that sometimes it is the former mechanism with a measurement system superimposed on it that is regarded as the DGP while at other times the term is used to refer to this *and/or* a probability distribution.[10] However, for our purposes it is sufficient that the concept of a joint distribution is relied upon. Thus Cook and Hendry write:

> In theory, one starts with the DGP which gives rise to the data, defined by the economic mechanism and the measurement system. In a non-experimental discipline such as economics, the DGP is a complicated, unknown function which is unlikely to be discovered … In practice, however, analyses are conducted within a framework defined by the Haavelmo distribution rather than the DGP (after Haavelmo who drew the attention of economists to the need to model in terms of joint distributions …). This joint distribution of the observed random variables over the entire sample period, which provides the most general description of the probabilistic information in the data and links the DGP to probability theory.
>
> (Cook and Hendry, 1994: 75–76)

They suggest:

> The analysis begins with the complete set of random variables U_T^1 relevant to the economy under investigation where $U_T^1 = (u_1, \ldots\ldots, u_T)$ defined on a probability space (Ω, F, P) where Ω is the sample space, F the event space, and P an appropriate probability measure. The assumption that economic events are measurable does not seem unreasonable: indeed Schumpeter (1933) went so far as to argue that

economics was inherently the most quantitative of the sciences since its measures arose from the ordinary business of life! The $\{u_t\}$ are not just the data to be analysed in the investigation, but also comprise all the potential data from the economic mechanism under study, so the DGP operates at the level of U_T^1. Thus, the vector u comprises details of every transaction of every agent at time t in all the regions of the geographical space relevant to the analysis. Obviously, U_T^1 is unmanageably large, and many of its components are either unobserved or so badly measured as to be unusable. The assumption that the behaviour of $\{u_t\}$ can be characterised by a joint distribution function is much more tenuous, although Haavelmo (1944) presented a powerful case for its generality. We make that assumption here ...

(Cook and Hendry, 1994: 78)

Now given this idea of a complex joint probability distribution, it is possible to see all actual econometric models as reduced forms of it. Conceptually, any model posited can be seen as derived from the general model through a reduction process which involves marginalisation – conditioning on certain variables (Hendry currently lists twelve distinct steps for reducing a complex distribution to a simple model; see, Hendry, 2000a).

So if all models can be interpreted as reductions of the general probability model defined over all relevant observable outcomes, the significant question, for Hendry, is whether reductions are achieved in the most useful way in some sense. The status of all the empirical models is the same: they are reductions of the general model. The aim, then, is not so much truth-seeking as one of engineering. The goal is to design a model that is useful.[11] And, typically, being useful means being found, first of all, to have a residual term that is unsystematic (and has relatively constant variance). It also means having parameters which are as constant as possible on subsets of existing data. It includes being consistent with economic theory. And it is desirable that variables treated as given are ones which economic agents could act contingently upon. It is held, too, that an acceptable model will encompass previously estimated models. Other criteria are also sometimes given, but those mentioned here should indicate the nature of the exercise. The important point is that, for Hendry, getting a 'good model' according to the sorts of criteria just listed is a question essentially of engineering or design. Consider how Hendry contrasts his approach to that which treats economic phenomena as if generated in a well-controlled experiment:

there is a key difference between a fully-controlled experiment described by a linear model, say, and a linear econometric model. The former can be represented schematically as:

$$y_t = f(z_t) + v_t \qquad (13.1)$$
$$\text{(output)} \quad \text{(input)} \quad \text{(perturbation)}$$

where y_t is the observed outcome of the experiment when z_t is the experimental input, $f(\approx)$ is the mapping from input to output, and v_t is a (hopefully small) perturbation which varies between experiments conducted at the same values of z. This equation entails that, given the same inputs, repeating the experiment will generate essentially the same outputs. The point is that causation is going from the right-hand side to the left-hand side in equation (13.1). Alternatively expressed, equation (13.1) is the DGP for y_t. It is this feature which validates, for example, regression analysis of the relation between y and z.

For econometrics to mimic experimental control requires data in which the outputs are in fact generated by the inputs, so the model must coincide with the mechanism which generated the data. But the economic mechanism is too complicated to be precisely modelled, and all econometric models must be simplifications and hence false. Since we neither know how the data were generated, nor control the economy, even though econometric equations might look like equation (13.1), there is in fact a fundamental difference, shown in equation (13.2):

$$y_t \quad = \quad g(z_t) \quad + \quad \varepsilon_t \qquad (13.2)$$
$$\text{(observed)} \quad \text{(explanation)} \quad \text{(remainder)}$$

Now, the left-hand side determines the right, rather than the other way round as in equation (13.1), and equation (13.2) merely shows that y_t can be decomposed into two components, $g(z_t)$ (a part which can be explained by z) and ε_t (a part which is unexplained). Such a partition is possible even when y_t does not even depend on $g(z_t)$, but is determined by completely different factors $h(x_t)$ say. In econometrics:

$$\varepsilon_t = y_t - g(z_t) \qquad (13.3)$$

describes empirical models: changing the choice or specification of z_t on the right-hand side alters the left-hand side, so (ε_t) is a derived process. In contrast to the process (v_t) in equation (13.1), (ε_t) in equation (13.2) is not a random drawing from nature: it is defined by what is left over from y_t after extracting $g(z_t)$.

(1997a: 174–175).

Hendry insists that in such circumstances it is necessary to approach modelling in a more engineering spirit

that is, as a process of designing models to achieve certain (albeit limited) objectives. Thus, the model is viewed as an inherently simplified mimic of behaviour, not a facsimile of the data process, and its unexplained component (residual) is derived as 'everything not elsewhere specified'. Then one designs the model such that (i)(a) the residual is unsystematic (i.e. is an innovation or 'news' relative to the available data) and has a relatively constant variance; (i)(b) the variables treated as given are ones which economic agents could act contingently upon; (i)(c) the parameters are as constant as possible on subsets of the existing data; (ii) it is consistent with theory; (iii) it is admissible given the properties of the measurement system (e.g., predictions of prices are positive, or of unemployment are less than 100 per cent etc); and (iv) it encompasses previous models (either historically or that and their forecasts).

(1985: 277)[12]

In recent years this framework has been supplemented with the category of a local DGP or LDGP. This is a particular reduction of the general probability distribution underpinning the whole analysis. It is defined over that subset of economic variables being considered in any analysis, and is conceived of as possessing unsystematic residuals, allowing that, should the LDGP be known, outcomes could be predicted up until an innovation error. The modelling exercise is then, in effect, to identify (or mimic) the LDGP:

> From the theory of reduction, there always exists a unique 'local DGP' (denoted LDGP) of the variables being modelled, formally derived from the actual DGP by reduction ... Any economy under study may comprise billions of decisions and millions of recorded variables, generated by the DGP of agents' behaviour and the recording procedures. The LDGP is the corresponding representation for the subset of variables under analysis such that, were the LDGP known, the outcomes could be predicted up to an innovation error. Thus computer-generated data from the LDGP would differ only randomly from the actual values, and would do so in the same way as equivalent data generated from the DGP itself ... The implication is that selection must be judged against the LDGP.

(2000b: 471)

Notice that the analysis does not at any stage require that the parameters of the LDGP or local model must be constant. Hendry is consistent throughout on this. If they are, this is an a posteriori occurrence, in effect it means that the DGP over the relevant period has been of such a nature that a model representing a specific reduction is found to possess constant parameters. Even where a constant parameter model is found, these parameters may not be easily interpretable in terms of economic theory. They do, after all, result from the complex reduction of a complex distribution. And Hendry emphasises this. Even so, he hopes that constant parameter models will be found which can be interpreted. Otherwise, as he admits, the models achieved would hardly be useful, even interpreted according to his general framework: 'No assumptions about "constant parameters" or stationary data are needed in justifying this analysis, although highly non-constant coefficients in any resulting econometric model would render it useless' (2000b: 471).

When invariant features of reality exist, progressive research can discover them in part without prior knowledge of the whole ... Indeed, a sequence of mutually encompassing LDGPs can be visualised, each of which is a valid representation of the phenomena under analysis. Should no invariant features of reality exist, neither theories nor econometric models would be of much practical value

(2000b: 474).

To summarise, within the actively controlled environment of the experiment, Hendry argues that it is possible to identify the DGP. In experimental contexts it is feasible to specify a relationship between the data in which different observations (repetitions of the same experiment) are connected by a common description (the same equation). The significance of the experimental context is that it allows an equation to be formulated which captures what is constant in the data. In economics, where researchers are dealing with a complex mechanism and historical, non-experimental data reported using limited measurement techniques, the DGP remains unknown and inaccessible. But Hendry insists a coherent and useful theory of econometrics can still be constructed. Crucially, he accepts that the relevance of his preferred method of reduction depends upon one central, essentially metaphysical, belief:

The nature of observations in macroeconomics is very different from that in some of the other sciences and must pose problems for any methodology. First economic time series are contingent on the particular historical path followed by the economy under study. This does not pose insuperable difficulties for reduction theory provided there exists an ahistorical (for example, stationary ergodic) innovation impinging on the dynamic evolution. Belief in the latter lies at a metaphysical level, although aspects are testable (for example, by developing homogenous explanations which survive for prolonged time periods).

(1997a: 177)

Hendry remains confident that it is possible to promote a progressive research strategy within econometrics despite the limitations of conventional approaches. He expresses hope not only that invariant features of reality exist but also that such constancy or invariance is systematically expressed at the level of regularities amongst measurable events. He admits that were these latter to be absent then econometric models would be stripped of much of their relevance or usefulness. Once Hendry's bold metaphysical assumption is accepted and if a sympathetic attitude is adopted toward his expression of hope that constant parameters obtain, his recommendations for the re-orientation of econometrics appear coherent.

Lawson's depth realism

Lawson's approach actually takes off where Hendry's leaves off. Lawson would certainly agree with Hendry that 'should no invariant features of reality exist, neither theories nor econometric models would be of much practical value'. The difference between Lawson and Hendry is where they look for the invariant features of reality. Hendry's approach ultimately relies on reasonably invariant correlations holding between observable variables, as we have seen. Lawson does not rule out the possibility of these being uncovered. But he develops an alternative approach in which explanatory success does not depend on their being found. This is a long story and I must summarise.[13]

Like Hendry, Lawson starts by giving an interpretation to such event regularities as do occur. But Lawson does not invoke the framework of DGPs and methods of reduction. Like Hendry, Lawson indicates the essentials of his approach by comparing it with what goes on in the well-controlled experiment. But Lawson provides a different interpretation of experimental work. By asking why natural scientific event regularities are mostly restricted to conditions of well-controlled experimentation and how it is that experimental results can be successfully applied outside the experiment where event regularities do not occur, Lawson provides a particular take on what is going on. He argues that we can only make sense of all this if we see experiments as seeking to isolate the stable causal mechanisms in which we are interested from countervailing mechanisms, in order to identify them empirically. The event regularity achieved is a correlation between the events triggering the isolated mechanism and its (undisturbed) effects. The results achieved can be applied outside the experiment because they relate to the underlying causal mechanism, not to the event regularity corresponding to its empirical identification. Thus, as Lawson often reminds us, the gravitational mechanism which gives rise to an event regularity when objects are dropped in a vacuum equally affects the paths of leaves as they fly over roof tops and chimneys.

Now the significant point here is that Lawson interprets the primary goal of experimental and all scientific work to be not the production of an event-regularity *per se* but the identification of the mechanism responsible for it. In Lawson's terminology this is causal explanation. Correlation analysis can be an aid to this process but it is not essential. And, according to Lawson, it is a knowledge of causal mechanisms that scientists mainly seek, and which can be used to send rockets to the moon, or cure disease. Data patterns are viewed more as useful epistemological features, where they occur, or can be produced, that enable underlying causal mechanisms to be identified.

Of course, because experimental control is typically not possible in the social realm, specific procedures are required to identify social causes. For this Lawson advances his theory of contrast explanation.

It is not necessary to discuss this idea here other than to say that the aim is to explain a surprising outcome: to explain 'why this rather than that (as expected)'. Whereas experimental work seeks to isolate a single mechanism physically, Lawson seeks to isolate one (or aspect of one) conceptually. He does this by focusing on two outcomes that unexpectedly have turned out to be different, when our current understandings led us to expect that they would have an identical causal history. *Prima facie* there is a case, in such situations, for supposing a single causal mechanism to be responsible.[14]

Competing philosophical frameworks

Lawson generalises his framework in a different manner to Hendry. Hendry produces a framework in which a joint probability distribution is defined over all observables, and against which any particular model is perceived as a reduced form. The generality comes with the move from variables of interest to a framework in effect covering all observable variables. Lawson's generalising move is from events of interest to the structures or mechanisms behind them, and responsible for them. Lawson's is a vertical ontological extension; Hendry's is a horizontal one. Lawson goes deeper; Hendry goes wider. Lawson seeks to uncover the nature of social reality, and advances a social ontology against which event regularities are a special case. On this conception, the limited occurrence of event regularities does not matter, because the explanatory goal is to uncover the (relatively enduring) mechanisms responsible for the movements in events or observables.

Why does Hendry not adopt this move as well? After all, there is nothing in Lawson's approach that necessarily invalidates Hendry's approach and interpretation. It mostly provides a more general way of proceeding, one that can be fruitful whether or not event regularities occur. The answer seems to be Hendry's prior philosophical orientation. Hendry acknowledges:

> I think 'causality' is only definable within a theory. I am a Humean in that I believe we cannot perceive necessary connections in reality. All we can do is to set up a theoretical model in which we define the word 'causality' precisely, as economists do with $y=f(x)$. What they mean by that in their theory is that if we change x (and it is possible to change x), y will change. And the way y will change is mapped by f, so we have a causal theory. They could give a precise or formal definition of the mapping $f(.)$. Empirically, concepts such as causality are extraordinarily hard to pin down. In my methodology, at the empirical level, causality plays a small role. Nevertheless, one is looking for models which mimic causal properties so that we can implement in the empirical world what the theorist analyses; namely, if you change

the inputs, the outputs behave exactly as expected over a range of interesting interventions on the inputs.

(Hendry, Leamer and Poirier, 1990: 184)

Hume denied the possibility of establishing the independent existence of things or the operation of natural necessity. In Humean philosophy, the only properties of which we can have any knowledge are those which give rise to distinct impressions. These properties include the perceptible qualities of bodies, such as their shape, size, colour, etc. We can observe the speeds and directions of say two colliding billiard balls immediately before and after they collide and we may identify a regularity in the way these speeds and directions are connected. What we do not observe is something beyond this that constitutes the capacity of one billiard ball to move another. On Hume's account of perception and causality, as traditionally interpreted, it is experiences, constituting atomic events and their conjunctions, that are viewed as exhausting our knowledge of nature. On such a view, generalities of significance in science must take the form of event regularities, for these are the only sort of generalities that such an ontological position can sustain. Hendry is restricted by his Humeanism to searching out correlations at the level of events and to sophisticated forms of data analysis.

Lawson is not restricted in this manner. Critical realism adopts a thoroughly *a posteriori* position, more Aristotelian in orientation, which defends the reality and knowledge of not only surface phenomena but also underlying structures, mechanisms, powers, tendencies, etc. As Lawson notes for critical realists:

> it is real things and their powers or ways of acting that are considered to be knowable and are taken to endure. Specific kinds of things have powers to act in definite ways in appropriate circumstances by virtue of certain relatively constant intrinsic structures or constitutions, or more generally, natures – which are discerned a posteriori in the process of science and general experience. It is these essential natures that designate what things are. And once we know what a thing is then, if certain 'activating' or 'triggering' conditions hold, we know how it will behave.
>
> (Lawson, 1989: 239)[15]

Without a structured ontology, the absence of strict event regularities necessarily threatens the search for scientific generalities. With a structured ontology of the kind elaborated within critical realism, persistence and generality can obtain at a different level. Moreover, as we have seen above, the realist account of deeper structures and mechanisms can render significant aspects of scientific activity, i.e. experimental activity and the application of scientific knowledge outside the experimental set-up, intelligible. Lawson, in committing himself to knowable deeper levels of reality, sets about elaborating ways of identifying underlying causes.

We can now clearly see the differences in the two projects despite their numerous commonalities, including their criticisms of others. Ultimately, they differ because Hendry's philosophical orientation prevents him from following the sort of path taken by Lawson. Probably Lawson would endorse Hendry's approach to the extent that models are found a posteriori to be successful. But Lawson does not need them, and as he does not expect useful econometric models to arise often he has committed himself to the alternative, ontologically explicit approach often systematised as critical realism.

4. Making sense of the original debate

Despite numerous similarities between the two programmes concerning the problems associated with carrying out applied research, and similar criticisms of conventional econometrics and reservations as to whether it is coherently grounded, there are after all key differences. Hendry's responses to the identified failures of conventional econometrics are from within a framework which holds fast to the hope that there are nonetheless event regularities of significance and durability in the social realm to be uncovered. The task is then to look both for procedures which would facilitate the identification of stable event regularities despite previous failures, and for ways to model what is going on after 'structural breaks' have undermined what were previously treated as regularised event patterns. Lawson's response is to fashion an alternative approach, one that makes no a priori commitment concerning the existence of strict event regularities. Both projects set out to provide general frameworks, against which special occurrences of models with relatively stable parameters are a special case, but herein lies the differences: for whilst Hendry might be said to consider the wider domain of surface phenomena, Lawson focuses on the underlying causal mechanisms ultimately generating the events and states of affairs that econometricians wish to correlate. These differences arise as a result of competing basic philosophical orientations being adopted. Hendry admits to being a Humean. This leads him to focus more or less exclusively upon measurable data. Hendry in fact defines science as 'a public approach to the measurement and analysis of observable phenomena' (1997a: 167). Lawson adopts a thoroughly a posteriori, more Aristotelian, position which concerns itself not only with surface phenomena but also with underlying structures, mechanisms, powers, tendencies, etc. Having identified where precisely and why these programmes diverge, can this help to explain the confusions which characterised the original exchange between Hendry and Lawson? Given Lawson and Hendry's competing philosophical orientations to science, both more fully elaborated over time, it now comes as no surprise that they differed as much as they did in their earlier debate. It is even possible to identify why misunderstandings arose.

In what sense does Hendry's approach remain 'standard'?

Lawson in his original paper (1981a) distinguished *standard* and other approaches according to belief in the likelihood of social event regularities being uncovered. His language though was about the possibility of finding *true* models. Thus he notes: 'Two different approaches to econometric modelling have been identified. The first assumes that there exists a "true" or "correctly" specified set of equations which have only to be identified' (1981a: 322). Given this notion of a true model it can be seen that true models and event regularities amount to very much the same thing. Moreover, Lawson was adopting this language in order to connect up explicitly with the terminology of Lucas (1976). For Lawson was responding to the Lucas critique of Keynesian modelling. Lucas used the language of true models of structures. Specifically, Lucas pointed out that his critique did not turn on the difficulty of finding a true model, but on the problem for modelling caused by the fact that the true model after a government intervention was not the same as the true model before it. Lawson was arguing that this criticism did not affect Keynesians because there was no presupposition of a true stable parameter model anyway: '[t]he Keynesian approach to modelling does not accept that reality has a "correct" representation in equation form' (1981a: 322). At another point in the paper Lawson draws the contrast explicitly between 'The standard approach which accepts the existence of a "true" model – that reality has a correct representation in equation form – and the Keynesian approach which, essentially, does not' (Lawson 1981a: 319). In this context, Lawson argued that Lucas's criticism applied not to the Keynesian approach but only to those who adopted the 'standard econometric approach'. And as an illustrative example Lawson mentioned Hendry:

> On reading the various contributions by Hendry and others, it is difficult not to be aware of the heavy emphasis on tests of, or ways of increasing, parameter stability and predictive accuracy. *This emphasis reflects an underlying belief that there exists a correct equation which needs only to be identified and which apparently possesses constant and stable parameters and usually a white noise error process.*
>
> (1981a: 318; italics added)

When Lawson said Hendry's approach was 'standard', he meant one thing only and something very specific: that its usefulness required invariant regularities or constant parameter models (however we refer to them). In all other senses, Hendry's approach is clearly non-standard. In this particular sense it remains standard. And it is obvious why Lawson picked out this one feature. For it is on this one feature that Lawson parted company with all other approaches to econometrics, including Hendry's.

It is now possible to see how confusion arose. If Lawson had said he was not convinced that there exist social event regularities to be uncovered, Hendry could have expressed his optimistic view to the contrary, both could have agreed it was ultimately an empirical matter, and they could have left it like that. Instead, Lawson expressed it as an (a posteriori) scepticism in the possibility of true models, noting Hendry's optimism. When Hendry replied saying that he did not claim to have identified a true model, Hendry seems to have misinterpreted Lawson's talk about possibilities as a claim that he – Hendry – had found a true model. Hendry mistook an ontological claim for an epistemological one. In particular, Hendry was eager to correct what he saw as a misrepresentation of his work and this involved quoting exactly a particular passage from an earlier jointly authored paper. Specifically, Hendry reproduced the following passage: 'However we do not [sic] conclude that our model represents the "true" structural relationship ...' (Hendry *et al*, quoted in Hendry 1983a: 69). Lawson replied that he never claimed that Hendry had found a true model, only that Hendry accepted the possibility. He took the following longer version of the above statement by Hendry as evidence of this: 'However we do not conclude that our model represents the "true" structural relationship since there are several important issues yet to be considered' (Hendry *et al*, as quoted by Lawson, 1983:78). Lawson pointed to other examples where phrases like correct models were deployed. Clearly, by phrasing his remarks in terms of a '*"true" model assumption*', Lawson left himself open to misunderstanding. Nevertheless, it is clear that his main point was that within the standard approach a specific representation of economic reality was being relied upon: for the standard approach to be coherent and useful it needs to be assumed that event regularities which could be expressed in equation form exist. Significantly, Lawson notes that this assumption is typically made a priori or adopted as an act of faith: 'the notion of a "correct" model or equation (and the usual presumption that this will involve stable parameters and a white noise error process) is ... no more than an act of faith or an assumption' (1981a: 319). In his reply Lawson states that: 'I wished to distinguish those econometricians who appear not to doubt the existence of (but not that they necessarily claimed to have found) true or correct relationships – that reality has a correct formal (if probabilistic) representation in (simple) equation form – which can in principle be identified, from those who at the very least are not convinced of this' (1983: 78). While Hendry is prepared to accept that it is an empirical issue as to whether event regularities obtain, the hope that they do exist is what renders his project coherent. In confusing Lawson's claim about possibilities for a claim about actual models, Hendry misread the basis on which Lawson was interpreting the standard approach. Hence, Hendry thought it enough merely to point out that he never considered any particular model as the true one. Here we have an explanation of Lawson's reply noted above.

Conceptions of truth and the status of econometric models

So far I have suggested that in attempting to clear up the confusions that surrounded the initial exchange it is important to recognise that Lawson, in characterising the standard approach, was concerned with the possibility of uncovering significant event regularities and was not suggesting that Hendry was claiming to have himself found a true model. However, this only constitutes part of the explanation. It is also crucial to recognise that Lawson and Hendry define truth in different ways. Both define it in relation to their own frameworks, and this leads to further differing views about the status of models.

For Lawson, truth is a relation (an expressive referential one) between theory and reality. For Hendry, it is a relation between a model and a more complex probability distribution or DGP (or statistical representation of the DGP). On Hendry's account, for truth the model and DGP must coincide (essentially be the same thing). But the whole point of Hendry's approach is that this rarely happens in the economic sphere. Indeed, the question is what to do *because it does not happen*. Hence Hendry's starting point is that all econometric models are false (because partial). When Hendry suggested in his response to Lawson that he accepted, and never claimed, that a true model or correct equation existed, he merely meant that any model derived, whether or not the parameters are stable, will be derived from a DGP and so necessarily simpler than it and so in *this sense* false. He wrote:

> A model is a simplified representation of some set of phenomena; as Hayek (1967, p. 14) expressed the matter ' ... a model always represents only some but not all the features of the original'. All models are, therefore, 'incomplete' pictures of reality and in that sense are 'false' by definition. Consequently, I generally drop the redundant qualifier, retaining the description 'false model' for a model that is rejected against another model. A 'true' model is virtually a self-contradiction as it would have to be as complicated as whatever it is supposed to represent.
>
> (Hendry, 1983a: 70)

This view of truth is one which Hendry has repeated and elaborated upon in later papers. For Hendry, models are engineered (designed) reductions of the DGP and, while they can be viewed as good/legitimate or not, it is not helpful to regard them as true. Hendry argues 'in favour of replacing a search for truth, which cannot be ascertained in economics, by a search for congruent encompassing empirical models which have a consistent and comprehensive theoretical interpretation' (Cook and Hendry, 1994: 73).

Lawson's goal is actively to seek truth. For truth is achieved when a theory or model adequately expresses that part of reality it is about. Lawson does not claim that we must obtain true theories, or even that we would know if we did. But he does not deny the possibility of truth, and recognises its importance as a regulatory ideal. In elaborating upon his expressive theory of truth, Lawson tries to draw links with what he takes to be the intuitions of many econometricians:

> To accept the fallibility and transformability of knowledge, however, is not thereby to deny the possibility of objective truth. Rather propositions are true, or contain truth, by virtue of the way that the world is. There is no need or possibility here of rejecting that implicit premise of the correspondence theory that truth can, under at least some of its numerous aspects, figure as an objective property of propositions. Here, the intuitions of many econometricians can be accepted. For it seems clear that when they reject either the possibility, or the actuality, of truth in formulating their models, especially when they declare that these models are not yet true ones, truth is being interpreted as something objective. It is being acknowledged as something which holds or exists independently of any individual's beliefs, and presumably, given the often found emphasis upon truth being unobtainable because of the complexity of reality, which turns upon the way that the world is. The implicit recognition of an objective aspect to truth is something I clearly retain.
>
> But in place of the conception of correspondence (or mapping) in knowledge and truth, the notion of expression is preferable. This term, as much as any, has connotations which capture that characteristic of knowledge that it is indeed fallible, historically transient, and transformable. It reminds us that there is no necessary relation of identity or correspondence involving knowledge. It indicates that what is expressed, the referent of any expression, can never be reduced to, or mapped onto, that which is expressed. But this latter situation, if to repeat, does not undermine the possibility of propositional truth. Indeed, the statement that 'contemporary western society is relatively complex', which in effect appears to be a premise for the familiar (if erroneous) claim that economic modelling must be unrealistic or false, may even be absolutely true – by virtue of the way the world is. Clearly, though, whether or not this is so, there is no question of a mapping or correspondence involved.
>
> (Lawson, 1997a: 239–240)

Thus when Hendry says his models are partial (and so in his terminology false), Lawson (in his terminology) would be likely to describe Hendry as making a probably true statement about the social world. For Lawson, partial claims can be true, and he explicitly argues that partiality does not necessitate falsity:

to focus upon particular features of something, for example a social system or a human being, is not per se to treat those features as existing
in isolation or otherwise subject to necessary distortion. If I focus on a
person's eyes in an attempt to gauge his or her reaction to what I am
saying, or if I describe them in reporting my impression to others, I do
not suppose that they exist in isolation; nor do I otherwise necessarily
miss-represent the person's reaction in any way. (Of course ... there
may not even be any distortion involved in expressing something as an
idealisation. It depends on the referent of that expression. Idealisations
can be real). To take a partial approach is not per se to deform. It can
involve distortion; but the one is not equivalent to the other.

(Lawson, 1997a: 240)

Assessment and implications

With hindsight, the central issue of the debate, masked by the discussion
of true models, is whether there is any alternative for empirical economics other than persisting with the narrow search for event regularities.
Hendry's view, rooted in his Humeanism, is that essentially there is no
alternative; Lawson's view, albeit initially only partially expressed,[16] is
that there is. With the acknowledged a posteriori difficulty of uncovering event regularities, or uncovering those that predict successfully,
Hendry's Humean orientation has taken his project one way; Lawson's
Aristotelianism has taken the project of critical realism in economics
a different way. Within their own specific frameworks, each is understandable, and clearly progressive. Hendry's approach ultimately rests
(with the rest of econometrics) on the faith that there are relatively stable event regularities to uncover (as Lawson in fact originally claimed).
However, his approach is not standard in any other sense. For Hendry,
econometric models are never true (thus their ability to express truth is
not a helpful/meaningful criterion). Rather, they are reductions that are
(or are not) legitimate/valid and potentially useful. Hendry's approach
provides a framework of interpretation, of constructive comparison and
much more. But it does not provide a method for progressing in a world
without some reasonably stable correlations between events. Lawson's
approach does. Given the relative paucity of social event regularities so
far, the Aristotelian approach, at this point in time at least, appears the
more promising.

There is a fundamental choice here which carries significant implications for how best to do empirical economics and it is at root a choice
between the two philosophical frameworks. At this fundamental level it
would seem that Lawson comes off best, in the sense that whilst Hendry's
Humeanism is largely a priori (and in any case now discredited in modern philosophy[17]) Lawson's orientation is a posteriori, grounded and
indeed can sustain Hendry's as a special case. For success to be achieved

in identifying even limited event regularities, closures (albeit local ones) must obtain. Now as Lawson notes:

> ... closures themselves have been shown, within critical realism, to presuppose, and indeed be a special configuration of, an open structured system, that is, a special case of the sort of system that does obtain ... Critical realism thus cannot and does not rule out a priori their limited occurrence. Rather, critical realism adopts an essentially ex posteriori orientation. And if the primary aim of the project of critical realism in economics in particular is to bring ontological considerations (back) into the economics picture and to indicate real possibilities in the social realm, it cannot determine a priori which possibilities are to be actualised in any local context. It can explain why ex posteriori closures do not seem to occur very often in the social realm (given the latter's human agency dependent, intrinsically dynamic and highly internally related nature), and it can and does indicate ways of proceeding in their absence.
>
> (1999a: 7–8)

Thus critical realism can accommodate the possibility of event regularities obtaining in the social realm. Were strict event regularities to be identified in the social realm, this would represent an interesting phenomenon requiring explanation, especially in the light of critical realist arguments concerning the nature of social material. Significantly, though, critical realism can also accommodate, and adequately account for, the non-prevalence of event regularities in the social realm, as well as the record of failure on the part of those searching for event regularities. Moreover, critical realism further provides some guidance concerning how to proceed with the task of identifying causal mechanisms in an essentially open social world.

5. Concluding remarks

In the face of claims that economics is increasingly driven merely by fashion, this paper has set out to consider two self-consciously progressive and developmental programmes, that have been promoted within the discipline over the last 20 years. The objective has been to draw out certain similarities and identify contrasts between these programmes. There are clearly points of contact between the two projects. Both programmes are seen by their proponents as standing opposed to an entrenched conventional or orthodox position. Both involve engagement at a methodological level, both have undergone considerable and significant extension and both have undertaken reassessments at the level of the history of thought. The paper has shown that there are also more substantial commonalities linking the two programmes. Both projects can be seen as responding to the observation that traditional attempts to identify event regularities within economics have hit upon severe problems. Both projects are realist at least to a degree, both provide explicit commentaries on the nature of the object of analysis in elaborating the approach defended, and both are critical of others who do not take assessments of the nature of the underlying object into account. Both recognise that econometric theory and practice are inconsistent. Both emphasise that it is not useful to treat the data of the social realm as if they are generated in conditions of experimental control. Both understand the social world as an evolving complex process subject to structural breaks, and so on. Yet despite all this the responses advocated by the programmes are very distinct. The different strategies advocated reflect their respective philosophical orientations and associated ontological commitments. Hendry adopts essentially a Humean orientation; Lawson does not. Hendry looks for patterns in surface phenomena; Lawson looks behind these for their deeper or underlying causes.

The present comparison of the two developed programmes has allowed some of the confusion surrounding an earlier exchange between the two main proponents of the programmes to be resolved. The point at issue in this earlier debate ultimately comes down to whether there is any alternative approach to empirical economics other than looking for patterns in surface phenomena. Lawson and Hendry's competing positions on this issue reflect the adoption of differing ontological positions, just as the developed programmes diverge as a consequence of their adherence to competing philosophical frameworks. Hendry accepts that at root his programme rests on a metaphysical or ontological claim: this is something to be welcomed since it constitutes a recognition that ontology is inexorable. What remains perplexing is the lack of concern with the sustainability of his ontological position. It is as if, for Hendry, it is enough to state his metaphysical claims. The sorts of circumstances which might lead Hendry to abandon or modify his ontological commitments are never identified. In considering a way forward for empirical economics – in choosing between Hendry and Lawson's respective approaches – what is required is reflection on the presuppositions being made by the competing projects in the light of an analysis of the ontological conditions of social reality.

Notes

1 I should like to thank David Hendry and the participants in the *Cambridge Realist Workshop* for useful comments on an early version of this paper. I also gratefully acknowledge the helpful criticisms and suggestions of two anonymous referees on an earlier draft. The usual disclaimer applies. First published in *Cambridge Journal of Economics*, 2005, Vol 29, No 2, 179–205.

2 This is a frequently made observation; Turnovsky (1992: 143), for example, writes:
There are several aspects of economics as it is currently practised which I find to be troubling and which I hope will be reversed over the next several

years. First, economics, particularly in the United States, is very much subject to fads. Certain topics become hot for a period, consuming a lot of research effort, only to become obsolete in a relatively short period of time and to be superseded by something else.

As David Hamilton notes: 'Fashions in economics are almost as fickle as those in dress and automobiles' (1984: 143).

3 The persistence of the LSE perspective has been highlighted as an aspect of the approach which marks it out from the changing and transitory fashions of much applied economics (see Faust and Whiteman, 1995: 171).

4 No attempt is made here to provide a general assessment of, or introduction to, either of these programmes. Rather the emphasis is upon relevant points of contact which highlight the similarities and contrasts between them. For a more general discussion of Hendry's approach see Cook (1999), Gilbert (1986), Pagan (1987) and Keuzenkamp (1995). For one useful attempt to place critical realism in context see Fleetwood (1999); for a general introduction see Boylan and O'Gorman (1995).

5 Hendry, in fact, could not be more severe in his criticism of the conventional approach to econometric modelling. He suggests that the conventional approach 'is inherently non-scientific and it would be surprising if it threw light on anything more than the investigator's personal prejudices' (1985: 273).

6 The re-examination of this debate serves as a useful corrective to the view sometimes expressed that critical realism in economics represents simply the attempt to impose a philosophy of science literature from outside as it were (see Mäki, 1998: 408). It is clear that the development of critical realism in economics has emerged from the problems and characteristics of economics itself.

7 While highlighting the relevance of such a distinction seems to lie behind Hendry's emphasis on the DGP, there appears to remain some ambiguity concerning the way in which Hendry himself deploys the term; for discussion see note 10 below.

8 More concretely, Lawson writes:

We live in an open economy, subject to the influences of erratic movements in world trade, multiple regionalised wars, frequent institutional collapses, the regular re-arranging of trading policies, agricultural gluts and failures, novel political developments including arbitrary, unannounced foreign policy changes bearing on matters relevant to domestic consumers and traders etc.

(1997a: 83)

9 Hendry writes:

Somewhat as a caricature the conventional approach in empirical economics is as follows: (i) postulate an arbitrary theory (arbitrary in the literal sense of being at the free choice of the investigator); (ii) find a set of data with the same names as the theory variables (such as 'money', 'incomes', 'interest rates', 'inflation', etc.); (iii) make a range of auxiliary simplifying assumptions (e.g., choosing a linear model, assuming away measurement errors); (iv) fit the theory-model to the data to see the degree of match. Corroboration is sought, and accepted, with minimal testing to check whether rejection is possible against interesting alternative hypotheses (such as non-random errors, and changing parameters).

(1985: 273)

10 For example, Hendry writes:

More generally, it is postulated that there exists a stochastic process generating all the variables (denoted by w_t) which are, and/or are believed to be, relevant (allowing for whatever measurement methods are involved). This vast complex is called the data generation process (abbreviated to DGP). In practice, the DGP may well be unknowable to our limited intellect, important variables may be unobservable, and/or the stochastic mechanism need not be constant over time. Nevertheless, I assume that there does exist a 'meta-parameterization', denoted by θ, which characterises what is relatively constant in the process. Less restrictively, the mechanism is assumed to generate outcomes sequentially over time. Empirical models result from reparameterising the process, through eliminating (marginalising with respect to) all but a small subset of variables (those remaining being denoted by x_t) and conditioning one sub vector y_t (called endogenous) of that remaining subset on another z_t (called 'exogenous' because it is not determined within the model). Here the basic statistical operations of conditioning and marginalising are used in their conventional senses: given any two continuous random variables a and b then their joint probability distribution D (a, b) can be expressed as

$$D(a, b) = D(a \mid b)D(b) \qquad (\text{or } D(b \mid a)D(a)) \qquad (18.1)$$

Where $D(a \mid b)$ is the conditional distribution of a given b and $D(b)$ is the marginal distribution b ...

Thus, the conceptual framework is that there exists some joint distribution denoted $D(w_1 \ldots w_T/\theta)$ which by repeated application of (18.1) corresponding to the notion of sequentially generating data yields the DGP:

$$D(w_1 \ldots w_T \mid \theta) = \Pi D(w_t \mid w_{t-1} \ldots w_1; \theta) \qquad (18.2)$$

$$(1983b: 422)$$

Hendry appears at least at times then to use the term the DGP to refer both to the underlying mechanism (plus measurement system) *and* to a probability distribution. In more recent work the argument is that the Haavelmo distribution constitutes a convenient statistical representation of the DGP. The implication is that the DGP and the probability distribution are different kinds of entity. This interpretation of the DGP is also evident in earlier work (see Hendry and Richard, 1982 and 1983). This ambiguity has been commented upon by Keuzenkamp, who suggests that: 'The DGP is reality and a model of reality at the same time. Philosophers call this "reification". Once this position is taken, weird consequences follow' (1995: 236).

11 Thus Hendry writes:

> Without an assumption of omniscience, there is no escaping the implication that all empirical econometric models are designed according to criteria specified by their proprietors ... The interesting issue is not whether or not models should be designed, but how they should be designed, and thus how the gap between theory and empirical evidence should be bridged.

(1995a: 359)

12 Hendry repeatedly draws a connection between econometrics and engineering; see Hendry and Wallis (1984: 4).

13 See Lawson (1997a) for a detailed elaboration and defence.

14 For discussion of the contrast explanation see Bhaskar and Lawson (1998) and Lawson (1997a, chapter 15, and 2003, chapter 4).

15 On the contemporary relevance of Aristotelian essentialism and its connections with critical realism, see Fleetwood, (1997). For further historical background see Cartwright (1992).

16 Lawson clearly attempts to identify two approaches to economic modelling. The standard approach is seen as presupposing that social reality has a correct representation in equation form while within the Keynesian framework: 'The presumption is neither that the models are in some sense "true" *nor even that there is a possibility of a true model in equation form*' (Lawson, 1981a: 318). Despite this it is sometimes unclear what precisely Lawson is defending. In particular, at times, he appears to be defending one, more or less, formalistic approach to modelling, namely Keynesian macroeconomic modelling, against other formalistic

approaches which presuppose event regularities i.e. the standard approach. The obvious question which arises here is, if the objective of the Keynesian macro-economic modellers is not to identify underlying event regularities: What are the objectives they pursue? Occasionally, the task Lawson seems to have set himself is to provide some such rationale. In certain passages (Lawson, 1981a: 322) the emphasis appears to be on formal modelling being one useful heuristic device. Running alongside and intermingled with this attempt to provide a rationale for formal Keynesian modelling is a second line of argument questioning the relevance of formalistic modelling altogether and pointing tentatively to some possible alternatives. For example, Lawson throughout stresses the continuously evolving and context-specific nature of social reality and also the relevance of case study work (Lawson, 1981a: 319). Indeed, if one considers Lawson's own substantive contributions dating from roughly the same period (see, in particular, Lawson, 1981b, and Kilpatrick and Lawson, 1980) it is clear that the favoured approach to empirical work is one of detailed case study analysis with little or no reference to formal modelling exercises. Interestingly, Lawson has recently returned to these two studies (1998b and 1997a, chapter 18, respectively) demonstrating how they can both be seen as consistent with critical realism. Lawson has not returned to the task of defending formal modelling from a developed critical realist stance. Indeed, it would seem he has become rather pessimistic about the contribution that such formal modelling strategies can perform in systems which are characteristically open (see for example Lawson, 2001). He notes that:

> Fundamental to the mainstream position is an insistence on working with formalistic models. Indeed, the primary objective of this mainstream project is to produce theories that facilitate mathematical tractability. In contrast my goal (naïve though it may sound) is to pursue true theories, or at least to achieve those that are explanatory powerful. I have found that the two sets of objectives, explanatory powerful theories and tractable models, are usually incompatible, just because of the nature of the social world. For whereas the latter has been found to be quintessentially open and seemingly unsusceptible to scientifically interesting local closures, the generalised use of formalistic economic methods presuppose that the social world is everywhere closed.
>
> (1999b: 273)

In retrospect it is apparent that what Lawson was groping toward was not an alternative basis for formalistic modelling at all but a rigorous alternative to it. Lawson's focus has increasingly been upon elaborating explanatory strategies which may prove fruitful within the structured and open social realm where the experimental production of event regularities is not feasible, and where few strict event regularities of any interest seem to occur spontaneously. It is crucial here to note that there is no consensus among critical realists concerning the likely contribution of formal methods within economics or more generally social science. Many argue from a critical realist position i.e. accepting the structured and open ontology outlined within the project, that specific types of formal techniques can be of considerable value; see for discussion: Finch and McMaster (2002), Porpora (2001) and Downward and Mearman (2002).

17 See Bhaskar (1978), Chalmers (1992, 1999) and Humphreys (1988).

References

Bhaskar, R, 1978, *A Realist Theory of Science,* Harvester, Sussex.
Bhaskar, R and Lawson, T, 1998, 'Introduction: Basic Texts and Developments', in M. Archer *et al.*, *Critical Realism: Essential Readings*, Routledge, London.

Boylan, TA and O'Gorman, PF, 1995, *Beyond Rhetoric and Realism in Economics: Towards a Reformulation of Economic Methodology*, Routledge, London.

Cartwright, N, 1992, 'Aristotelian Natures and the Modern Experimental Method', in J. Earman, ed, *Inference, Explanation and Other Frustrations: Essays in the Philosophy of Science*, University of California Press, Berkeley.

Cartwright, N, 1995, 'Causal Structures in Econometrics', in D. Little, ed, *On the Reliability of Economic Models*, Kluwer, Boston.

Cartwright, N, 1999, *The Dappled World: A Study of the Boundaries of Science*, Cambridge University Press, Cambridge.

Chalmers, A, 1992, 'Is a Law Reasonable to a Hume?', *Cognito*, Winter, 125–129.

Chalmers, A, 1999, 'Making Sense of Laws of Physics', in H. Sankey, ed, *Causation and Laws of Nature*, Kluwer Academic Publishers, Dordrecht.

Clements, MP and Hendry, DF, 1995, 'Macro-economic Forecasting and Modelling', *Economic Journal*, Vol 105, 1001–1013.

Clements, MP and Hendry, DF, 1996, 'Forecasting in Macro-economics', in D.R. Cox, D.V. Hinckley and O.E. Barndorff-Nielsen (eds) *Time Series Models in Econometrics, Finance and Other Fields*, Chapman and Hall, London.

Clements, MP and Hendry, DF, 1998a, 'On Winning Forecasting Competitions in Economics', mimeo, Oxford and Warwick.

Clements, MP and Hendry, DF, 1998b, *Forecasting Economic Time Series*, Cambridge University Press, Cambridge.

Clements, MP and Hendry, DF, 1999, *Forecasting Non-stationary Economic Time Series*, MIT Press, Cambridge, MA.

Cook, S, 1999, 'Methodological Aspects of the Encompassing Principle', *Journal of Economic Methodology*, Vol 6, No 1, 61–78.

Cook, S and Hendry, D, 1994, 'The Theory of Reduction in Econometrics', *Poznan Studies in the Philosophy of the Sciences and the Humanities*, Vol 38, 71–100.

Downward, P and Mearman, A, 2002, 'Critical Realism and Econometrics: Constructive Dialogue with Post Keynesian Economics', *Metroeconomica*, Vol 53, No 4, 391–415.

Faust, J and Whiteman, CH, 1995, 'Commentary on Progressive Modelling of Macroeconomic Time Series: The LSE Methodology by Grayham E. Mizon', in K. Hoover, ed, *Macroeconomics: Development, Tensions and Prospects*, Kluwer, Dordrecht.

Finch, J and McMaster, R, 2002, 'On Categorical Variables and Non-parametric Statistical Inference in the Pursuit of Causal Explanations', *Cambridge Journal of Economics*, Vol 26, No 6, 753–772.

Fleetwood, S, 1997, 'Aristotle in the 21st Century', *Cambridge Journal of Economics*, Vol 21, 729–744.

Fleetwood, S, 1999, 'Situating Critical Realism in Economics', in S. Fleetwood, ed, *Critical Realism in Economics*, Routledge, London.

Gilbert, CL, 1986, 'Professor Hendry's Econometric Methodology', as reprinted in C.W.J. Granger, ed, *Modelling Economic Series: Readings in Econometric Methodology*, Oxford University Press, Oxford.

Haavelmo, T, 1944, 'The probabilistic approach to econometrics', *Econometrica*, Vol 12, Supplement, 1–117.

Hamilton, D, 1984, 'The Myth is not the Reality: Income Maintenance and Welfare', *Journal of Economic Issues*, Vol 18, No 1, 143–158.

Hendry, DF, 1983a, 'On Keynesian Model Building and the Rational Expectations Critique: A Question of Methodology', *Cambridge Journal of Economics*, Vol 7, 69–75.

Hendry, DF, 1983b, 'Econometric Modelling: The Consumption Function in Retrospect', *Scottish Journal of Political Economy*, as reprinted in Hendry, 1993.

Hendry, DF, 1985, 'Monetary Economic Myth and Econometric Reality', *Oxford Review of Economic Policy*, as reprinted in Hendry, 1993.

Hendry, DF, 1993, *Econometrics: Alchemy or Science? Essays in Econometric Methodology*, Blackwell, Oxford.

Hendry, DF, 1995a, *Dynamic Econometrics*, Oxford University Press, Oxford.

Hendry, DF, 1995b, 'Econometrics and Business Cycle Empirics', *Economic Journal*, Vol 105, 1622–1636.

Hendry, DF, 1996, 'On the Constancy of Time Series Econometric Equations', *The Economic and Social Review*, Vol 2, No 5, 401–422.

Hendry, DF, 1997a, 'The Role of Econometrics in Scientific Economics', in A. d'Autume and J. Cartelier, eds, *Is Economics Becoming a Hard Science?*, Edward Elgar, Cheltenham.

Hendry, DF, 1997b, 'The Econometrics of Macroeconomic Forecasting', *Economic Journal*, Vol 107, 1330–1357.

Hendry, DF, 1997c, 'On Congruent Econometric Relations: A Comment', *Carnegie-Rochester Conference Series on Public Policy*, Vol 47, 163–190.

Hendry, DF, 2000a, 'Econometric Modelling', lecture notes for 'Econometric Modelling and Economic Forecasting', Department of Economics, University of Oslo, 24–28 July 2000.

Hendry, DF, 2000b, *Econometrics: Alchemy or Science?*, new edition, Oxford University Press, Oxford.

Hendry, DF, Leamer, EE and Poirier, DJ, 1990, 'The ET Dialogue: A Conversation on Econometric Methodology', *Econometric Theory*, Vol 6, 171–261.

Hendry, DF and Richard, JF, 1982, 'On the Formulation of Empirical Models in Dynamic Econometrics', as reprinted in Hendry, 1993.

Hendry, DF and Richard, JF, 1983, 'The Econometric Analysis of Econometric Time Series', as reprinted in Hendry, 1993.

Hendry, DF and Wallis, KF, 1984, 'Editors' Introduction', in *Econometrics and Quantitative Economics*, Blackwell, Oxford.

Humphreys, P, 1988, 'Causal, Experimental and Structural Realisms', *Midwest Studies in Philosophy*, Vol 12, 241–252.

Keuzenkamp, HA, 1995, 'The Econometrics of the Holy Grail – A Review of Econometrics: Alchemy or Science? Essays in Econometric Methodology', *Journal of Economic Surveys*, Vol 9, 233–248.

Kilpatrick, A and Lawson, T, 1980, 'On the Nature of Industrial Decline in the UK', *Cambridge Journal of Economics*, Vol 4, March, 85–102.

Lawson, T, 1981a, 'Keynesian Model Building and the Rational Expectations Critique', *Cambridge Journal of Economics*, Vol 5, 311–326.

Lawson, T, 1981b, 'Paternalism and Labour Market Segmentation Theory', in F. Wilkinson, ed, *Dynamics of Labour Market Segmentation*, Academic Press, London.

Lawson, T, 1983, 'Different Approaches to Economic Modelling', *Cambridge Journal of Economics*, Vol 7, 77–84.

Lawson, T, 1985, 'Keynes, Prediction and Econometrics', in T. Lawson and H. Pesaran, *Keynes' Economics: Methodological Issues*, Croom Helm, Beckenham.

Lawson, T, 1989, 'Realism and Instrumentalism in the Development of Econometrics', *Oxford Economic Papers*, Vol 41, 236–258.

Lawson, T, 1996, 'Econometrics, Data and Reality', mimeo, Cambridge.

Lawson, T, 1997a, *Economics and Reality*, Routledge, London.

Lawson, T, 1997b, 'Economics as a Distinct Social Science? On the Nature, Scope and Method of Economics', *Economie Appliquee*, Vol 50, No 2, 5–35.

Lawson, T, 1998a, 'Clarifying and Developing the Economics and Reality Project: Closed and Open Systems, Deductivism, Prediction and Teaching', *Review of Social Economy*, Vol 56, No 3, 356–375.

Lawson, T, 1998b, 'Social Relations, Social Reproduction and Stylised Facts', in P. Arestis, ed, *Method, Theory and Policy in Keynes: Essays in Honour of Paul Davidson: Volume Three*, Edward Elgar, Cheltenham.

Lawson, T, 1999a, 'Connections and Distinctions: Post Keynesianism and Critical Realism', *Journal of Post Keynesian Economics*, Vol 22, No 1, 3–14.

Lawson, T, 1999b, 'What Has Realism Got to Do with It?', *Economics and Philosophy*, Vol 15, 269–282.

Lawson, T, 2001, 'Mathematical Formalism in Economics: What Really Is the Problem?', in P. Arestis, M. Desai and S. Dow, eds, *Methodology, Microeconomics and Keynes*, Routledge, London.

Lawson, T, 2003, *Reorienting Economics*, Routledge, London.

Lucas, RE, 1976, 'Econometric Policy Evaluation: A Critique', reprinted in Lucas, R. E, 1981, *Studies in Business Cycle Theory*, Basil Blackwell, Oxford.

Mäki, U, 1998, 'Realism', in J.B. Davis, D. Wade Hands and U. Mäki, eds, *The Handbook of Economic Methodology*, Edward Elgar, Cheltenham.

Pagan, AR, 1987, 'Three Econometric Methodologies: A Critical Appraisal', in C.W.J. Granger, ed, *Modelling Economic Series: Readings in Econometric Methodology*, Oxford University Press, Oxford.

Porpora, D, 2001, 'Do Realists Run Regressions?', in C. Porter and J. Lopez, eds, *After Post Modernism*, Athlone Press, London.

Turnovsky, S, 1992, 'The Next Hundred Years', in J. Hey, ed, *The Future of Economics*, Blackwell, London.

6 An evolutionary economics? On borrowing from evolutionary biology[1]

Tony Lawson

The allure of an evolutionary economics

The idea of an evolutionary economics based on insights from evolutionary biology is clearly enticing to many modern economists. In the last few years especially, the number of economists attracted to it appears to be significantly on the increase (see, for example, Dopfer, 2001; Dugger and Sherman, 2000; Hodgson, 1997, 1998, 1999; Laurent and Nightingale, 2001; Loasby, 1999; Louçã and Perlman, 2000; Magnusson and Ottosson, 1997; Nicita and Pagano, 2001; Potts, 2000; Reijnders, 1997; amongst numerous others; and see Witt, 2001, for an interpretive survey).

The idea is not a new one. Marshall once famously concluded that 'the Mecca of the economist lies in economic biology rather than economic dynamics' (Marshall, 1961, p. xii). And Veblen inspired many in asking 'Why is economics not an evolutionary science?' Furthermore the issue has been frequently examined throughout the last century, not least in Nelson and Winter's (1982) *An Evolutionary Theory of Economic Change*.

Even so, many contributors have continued to urge caution, whilst debating the merits of borrowing from biology. For example, Penrose concludes a piece on biological analogies by arguing:

> But in seeking the fundamental explanations of economic and social phenomena in human affairs the economist, and the social scientist in general, would be well advised to attack his problems directly and in their own terms rather than indirectly by imposing sweeping biological models upon them.
>
> (1952: 819)

And Schumpeter (in a passage that has been interpreted as supporting the view that economics should eschew *all* metaphors from physical and natural sciences)[2] writes:

> … it may be … that certain aspects of the individual-enterprise system are correctly described as a struggle for existence, and that a concept

of survival of the fittest in this struggle can be defined in a non-tau-
tological manner. But if this be so, then these aspects would have to
be analyzed with reference to economic facts alone and no appeal to
biology would be of slightest use.

(Schumpeter, 1954: 789)

Others have been more obviously positive, although even amongst protagonists there is often an explicit recognition that borrowing from others,
including biology, is not a panacea (e.g., Hodgson, 1993). All in all, I think,
the jury is still out as to whether a fruitful evolutionary economics based
on principles drawn from evolutionary biology is a viable proposition.

The problem with the literature as it stands, it seems to me, is that too little
progress has been made on the question of what would justify drawing on
evolutionary biology (or indeed on any models first formulated outside the
social domain). And the reason appears to be not so much a lack of attention
to the details of evolutionary models (though there *is* often room for improvement here) as an insufficient attention paid to questioning the *nature* of the
social realm to which it is intended that the evolutionary models be applied.
Determining the nature of social material does matter, however. The nature
of the object of study always bears implications for how it can be studied.

Though seemingly obvious, even trite, this latter insight flies in the face
of much, if not most, of modern economics with its continual neglect of
explicit ontological analysis. Indeed modern economics is marked by a
widespread committal of the epistemic fallacy. This consists in the view
that questions about being can always be reduced to questions about our
knowledge (of being), that matters of ontology can always be translated
into epistemological terms. This fallacy assumes the form of an expectation that methods can be adopted from any sphere, and/or be of any kind
– mathematical, evolutionary, or whatever – and successfully applied irrespective of the nature of the object of study (see Lawson, 1997).

Even in the more insightful discussions bearing upon the possibility of an
evolutionary economics, questions of ontology have tended to be obscured
by a concentration on other matters. The latter have included such issues
as whether Darwin consistently proposed one sort of evolutionary theory
or mechanism only, the proper interpretation and relevance of the contributions of Lamarck, the nature of frontier modelling in modern biology,
and so forth. Whilst these sorts of inquiries have their interest they easily
distract from those more relevant to the question of whether it is feasible in
any useful way at all to abduct from biology into social theory.

In any case, whatever the reason for it, questions of ontology have been
largely neglected in discussions of borrowing from others, and here my
purpose is to help rectify this situation. It is the case that ontological considerations of some sort do already creep in here and there. However, they
rarely do so in a sufficiently explicit and systematic fashion.[3] My limited
aim here, as I say, is to contribute to helping redress this situation.

Perhaps it is useful if I anticipate at this point the conclusion I reach below on the worth of borrowing from biology. First let me say that by the term evolutionary I mean *not* any type of change, *but* the genealogical connection of all organisms along with an account of life and society regulated by descent with modification (essentially cumulative causation). Thus on my understanding, natural selection is but one evolutionary mechanism. However, by the term evolutionary many economists do seem to mean processes of natural selection. With this in mind the specific thesis defended in this chapter, and developed on the basis of ontological reasoning, is that there is no legitimate basis for an *evolutionary economics* as such if:

1   the term evolutionary (in 'evolutionary economics') is interpreted (as economists interested in borrowing from evolutionary biology tend to interpret the term) as denoting a process that in some way conforms to the natural-selection model that derives from (Darwinian) evolutionary biology, *and* if
2   the phrase 'evolutionary economics' is intended to signal a universal approach to economic analysis (implying that all economic phenomena can be treated as resulting from evolutionary [natural selection] processes).

Rather my thesis is simply that the social world is such that certain social phenomena *can* result from evolutionary processes of this sort, specifically from processes that manifest evolutionary natural selection aspects. Where this is so, an evolutionary explanation of the type in question, in part at least, is clearly called for. But this particular socio-evolutionary model ought not to be universalised *a priori*. Even Darwin thought that natural selection was but one mechanism amongst many regulating life on earth, albeit, in his view, the most important one. Thus in the final edition of *The Origin of Species*, Darwin (1872) writes:

> But as my conclusions have lately been much misrepresented, and it has been stated that I attribute the modification of species exclusively to natural selection, I may be permitted to remark that in the first edition of this work and subsequently, I placed in a most conspicuous position – namely at the close of the Introduction – the following words: 'I am convinced that natural selection has been the main but not the exclusive means of modification'. This has been of no avail. Great is the power of steady misrepresentation.
>
> (Darwin, 1872: 421)

As we shall see, in the social realm there is even greater reason to adopt such an open or pluralistic orientation in explanatory endeavour.

In truth, to insist on an 'evolutionary economics' modelled on the natural selection paradigm prior even to identifying the phenomenon to be understood and/or explained is ultimately no better than the modern mainstream's *a priori* insistence upon a deductivist or formalistic economics, that all phenomena be addressed using closed-systems deductivist modelling. The scope of relevance of this particular evolutionary model, as with all other methods or epistemological principles, can be determined only from context *a posteriori*. And the evidence is that the domain of relevance of this evolutionary model within the social realm is certainly not ubiquitous. Let me now briefly run through the argument.

The biological and social connection

As I say, recent years have witnessed something of a surge of interest in (the possibility at least of) borrowing from biology. But what explains the phenomenon that some, especially (but not exclusively) heterodox, economists appear so optimistic about gaining insight from biological writing, and in particular from theories of biological evolution? Much of the appeal seems intuitive. Certainly, I do not find this optimism well articulated even amongst the best of economic commentators. Although the formulation I proposed above, turning on the matching of evolutionary model or method to social ontological insight, seems simple enough, even the better parts of the literature do not always recognise that the relevant matter to be determined is indeed whether biological achievements provide a useful model for the social realm, given the latter's nature.

Actually, a study of the relevant literature reveals that very frequently several different lines of reasoning are run together. There is, in reality, not one type of connection of the biological to the social but three:

1 the biological as an *existential basis* for social phenomena;
2 the biological in *causal interaction* with social phenomena; and
3 the biological as the source of a *model* for the understanding of social phenomena.

Our understanding of capable human behaviour at any level requires an understanding of biological/social connections along the lines of types 1 and 2. But our primary concern here is actually with connections of type 3. The problem with much of the existing literature, it seems to me, is that these different forms of connection are rarely distinguished, with the consequence that support for type 3 is sometimes thought to be achieved by emphasising connections along the lines of type 1 and/or type 2. This is invalid. After all, whilst social phenomena and processes are, or include, an emergent surplus from the interactions of human beings (as opposed to being reducible to human beings themselves), it is the case that the physical realm (just like the biological) also provides an existential basis for, and exists in causal interaction with, social phenomena. Certainly if it is thought that connections of types 1 and 2 justify those of type 3, some argumentation is required. This, so far, is noticeably missing.

Evolutionary theory and metaphor

In order to assess the relevance of biological models for understanding social phenomena it is necessary to examine the nature of both social and biological modes of determination explicitly and in some detail. Before doing so, however, it is useful to consider the nature and role of metaphor. Discussions of borrowing from evolutionary biology are, as I say, usually couched in terms of the natural-selection metaphor, and I think it is necessary, before going further, to unpack how such applications relate to the current discussion.

Economists' discussions of metaphors, as with the practice of borrowing from other domains more generally, often include a good deal of suspect, if not clearly fallacious, reasoning. I am aware of economists arguing that if we borrow from biology we must take the latest aspect of that theory just because it is the latest. The same is often said to be the case if we borrow from physics. In order for economics to thrive, the claim runs, it is essential to copy from the cutting-edge of the hard sciences.

This attitude reflects an error I shall term the *abductionist fallacy*. This is the notion that insights, methods or theories of one domain of science or human reasoning, let me call the latter the *source domain*, can be abducted into another, the *target domain*, without prior consideration of the nature of the latter. The basic fact of the matter is that a particular theory of physics or biology or whatever, even if cutting-edge stuff, has no clear relevance for the social domain if it presupposes a type of material or configuration that is entirely absent from the social realm. If, for example, certain regions of the social realm are not in any way atomistic then no matter how hard nosed may be recent developments in atomic physics, they have no obvious automatic bearing on the regions of the social domain in question.[4]

For a metaphor or other form of abduction to be recognised as appropriate, something must be known about the target domain. This much is clear. And if the use of a metaphor is to prove successful as a means of illuminating the target domain it must generate new lines of analogous, and other forms of, reasoning in this domain. It will be expected, then, that once the categories in question have been abducted, they will take on their own meanings in the new context, i.e. meanings that are not wholly the same as those they carried in the source domain.

How exactly does metaphor work? I think we now know enough about the primary workings of metaphor (see, e.g., Boyd, 1993; Lewis, 1996, 2000b; Soskice, 1985; Soskice and Harré, 1982) to appreciate how they facilitate understanding and knowledge development. They do so, in essence, by making connections between two domains which hitherto may not have been recognised as having parallels. And they do so, in effect, by way of revealing that an object or feature in the source domain (the vehicle of the metaphor) and an object or feature in the target domain (the tenor) are both tokens of the same type, or each a concretisation of the same more abstract object.[5]

If, for example, we say John is a pig, we are suggesting there is a more general or abstract class of objects of which John and a pig are both tokens or particular sub-types. In this example the class may be of all creatures disposed to eating in a particular fashion. If we say that Jane is a donkey, we may in fact be meaning to suggest that Jane, like the donkey, is a special case of objects that are slow moving.

In these brief illustrations I use the qualifier 'may' in giving the noted interpretations just because the exact meaning will depend on context. The person formulating the metaphor for Jane may be wishing to imply not that Jane is slow like a donkey but stubborn in the manner that donkeys very often are. When John is described as a pig it may be because he has been sun-bathing and is (like certain varieties of pig at least) pink all over (although for this, references to strawberries and lobsters seem more common). In this particular case the relevant type-class is all pink objects. Use of metaphor capturing one token of this type, i.e. a pink object, signals that the tenor or target object of this metaphor is also a token of this type, i.e. is something that is pink. The particular nature of intended abstract conception or type, though, is something which can be determined only from context.

Often, of course, the context will be a general one, so that a wide body of people can interpret the metaphor in the manner its formulator intended. If, for example, it is said that trading is stagnant the general class is presumably that of all things where movement of activity is feasible but hardly happening. If it is said that prices have reached their ceiling the general class is presumably anything that has an upper limit and has reached it.

Metaphor works, then, by connecting objects or aspects, etc., previously regarded as unconnected, by showing them both to be special cases of the same general thing, to be tokens of the same type.

In making this connection, metaphor can indicate a possible model for the target object based on the object in the source domain. It allows us to set up a generic system, using insights from the source domain, which possesses the potential to provide lines of development in the target domain.

If we turn to the category of evolution, specifically, the first thing we can note is that were we to understand evolution quite generally as a form of change or development (as some do seem to) it need not be a metaphor for social processes at all. On this conception social processes just are evolutionary.[6]

Rather, biology becomes a more interesting source of ideas or resources, including metaphors, once we contemplate the suggestion that some social processes are evolutionary in a more particular sense, and specifically in accord with the idea of *natural selection*. Here, as we will see in due course, the idea of natural selection *is* a metaphor. The implicit intuition or hypothesis is that certain 'natural selection' mechanisms in the source or biological domain, and aspects of processes in the target or social domain, are indeed both tokens of the same, more abstract type.

But here we are jumping ahead of ourselves. My purpose with this slight detour was merely to clarify the role played by metaphor (or what I take to be its primary role). Metaphor, as with any form of abduction from one realm to another, requires appropriate conditions. As indicated earlier, in order to borrow usefully from biology in social theory we need to ensure sufficient commonalities between biological and social material. Our discussion of metaphor enables us to reinterpret that need as one for a general model of which there are both social and biological sub-types or tokens.

Advantages of the evolutionary model for social understanding: a preliminary orientation

Now, in embarking on the task of identifying relevant commonalities between the nature of biological and social materials, if any, we do not start from a position of complete ignorance of course. One very obvious (if rarely explicitly elaborated) reason for the prevailing optimism that the study of the biological realm can provide insights of relevance for analysing the social is that both worlds comprise open (i.e. highly unpredictable) and dynamic systems. In other words, there is a very general class of systems, namely those that are open and dynamic, of which the social and the biological are both immediately recognised as tokens. Let me elaborate.

The nature of social material

Certainly the social world can be recognised as an open, dynamic process. Indeed, according to the *transformational model of social activity* which I have defended at length elsewhere (Lawson, 1997, especially chapters 12 and 13; and 2003, chapter 2), social reality is found to be not only open and dynamic or processual, but an emergent realm, dependent upon, but irreducible to, transformative human agency, and comprising material that is structured and highly internally related, amongst other things.

More specifically, according to the transformational model, human agency, practice and social structures (including social rules, relationships, positions, etc.) are inter-dependent, but ontologically distinct, types of things. The social world turns on practice. In acting we both draw upon structures given to us, and contribute to reproducing and/or transforming them. Just as we usually do not acknowledge the structures we draw upon, so their reproduction or transformation is often unintended. Thus, we usually speak with a purpose in mind, which is typically to convey a thought or message to someone. But the rules of grammar we draw upon are unacknowledged, and their reproduction, depending as it does upon our collective speech acts, is usually unintended.

How do social structure and agency interconnect in this transformative process? Key categories here are social positions and social relations, especially internal ones. Two objects are said to be internally related when they are what they are, and do what they do, in virtue of this relation in which they stand to one another. Examples include teacher and student, employer and employee, landlord and tenant, etc.

Now it is typically not individuals *per se* that are internally related but the positions in which they stand. The crew on a passenger airplane have a range of duties and perks, etc. But they are not attached to the crew members personally. If one resigned and a second person were to take her or his place the second person would acquire access to the same positioned obligations and so forth as the first possessed. The same is even more clearly true of the passengers. As passengers they have rights and obligations. But as soon as others take their place these rights and obligations, etc., transfer. They do so because they are attached to positions the passengers occupy. We, all of us, choose, or (perhaps more typically) are allocated to, a multitude of positions (teacher, student, employer, employee, parent, child, European, Asian, old, young, male, female, salesperson, customer), each associated with a range of rule-conditioned obligations, rights, duties and prerogatives, etc., and related to other positions to which our practices are oriented. It is in virtue of our being slotted into social positions that we access social structures, and through acting according to position-related rights, obligations and interests that the social world is continually reproduced and/or transformed.

On this conception, then, the social world emerges as an inter-related network of dynamic totalities, of internally related processes. Practice, as I say, is the key to social being. Social structure depends on human agency and it is through human practice that specific structures are continually reproduced and transformed. This inherently dynamic and totalising human agency-dependent process, wherein social structure is both condition and consequence of action, I repeat, is the 'transformational model of social activity'. The central point for the moment, though, is that the social system is found to be intrinsically dynamic and open.

The biological model and mainstream economics

The same, of course, can be said of the biological realm. Indeed, a factor that spurred the development of evolutionary biology was precisely an acknowledgement that the biological realm too comprises dynamic and open systems. Such an assessment did not always prevail.[7] But the view that life on earth is a continuous process of transformation is by now sufficiently widely accepted that I shall not defend it here. Rather, my point is simply that the recognised successes of biological evolutionary models in addressing open and dynamic systems gives some immediate credibility to the idea that biological models can prove of relevance in some way in facilitating the analysis of social phenomena.

Certainly biological models are seen to have an immediate *prima facie* advantage over the competing mechanistic models of modern mainstream economics. For the latter are concerned with basically static or stationary scenarios. At best, these mechanistic models conceptualise change as exogenous shocks to systems (albeit to systems which respond by tending to re-equilibrate), or some such. Mostly, modern mainstream economics concerns itself with identifying positions and set-ups in which agents lack any incentive to change what they do. In comparison, as I say, evolutionary theory was developed to explain an intrinsically dynamic order, to account for processes of relatively continuous change. It is an explanatory theory with a potential purchase on any system recognised as being fundamentally open to the future.

If I appear to be labouring the point here, it is because these parallels between the two spheres, the social and the biological, seem to be less than always fully recognised. Rosenberg, for example, concludes 'that Darwinian theory is a remarkably inappropriate model, metaphor, inspiration, or theoretical framework for economic theory' (1994: 384). And his reservations boil down basically to one: evolutionary models in biology do not predict well:

> My pessimistic conclusions reflect a concern shared with economists who have sought comfort or inspiration from biological theory. The concern is to vindicate received theory or to underwrite new theory against a reasonable standard of predictive success. Few of these economists have noticed what the opponents of such a standard for economic theory have seen, that evolutionary theory is itself bereft of strong predictive power.
>
> (Rosenberg, 1994: 384)

Once we take a serious look at the nature of social material, however, we can see that evolutionary theory's lack of predictive power is no objection at all. Successful prediction presupposes closure, whereas the social system is found to be, like the biological realm, open and seemingly insusceptible to many, if any, scientifically interesting local closures, at least of the causal sequence sort. If the nature of the social realm is such that the successful prediction of social outcomes is unlikely, then to adopt methods premised on the necessity of achieving predictive accuracy is to abandon or ignore insights from ontology, to commit the epistemic fallacy. *Prima facie* the biological model gives *a posteriori* grounds for hope just because the social system is an open, mostly non-teleological, system of the sort with which evolutionary methods can in principle cope. In fact, I suspect it is this particular feature of the biological model that, implicitly at least, accounts for its current attractiveness to heterodox economists.

Natural selection

But this shared concern of the two sciences with open dynamic systems cannot be all of the story if the biological evolutionary model is to prove useful to social science. After all, we already have the transformational model of social activity in modern economics and social theory more widely. Biological evolutionary theory must provide something more if it is to enable social theorising to go further in some context.

As already signalled, that 'something more' in which we are interested appears to be bound up with the metaphor of natural selection. In economics there are already plenty of contributions claiming to show how order of sorts in society could come about (solely) by way of conscious (human) intervention or design. Biology deals with situations that equally are ordered in some sense, but where the form of order in question has not been brought about intentionally, i.e. by conscious design. This is a radical achievement undermining the idea of a benevolent prior design in history. And it is this insight, I suspect, that provides the relevant motivation for, and context of, seeking to apply the biological evolutionary metaphor in modern economics.

Actually this is not quite correct. I detect two motivations (at least) to the quest for borrowing from others. The first, the one I am myself interested in here, is a desire to understand and explain social reality, to be realistic, to seek for truth. But I cannot deny (and indeed have already acknowledged) that some contributors give a higher priority to drawing on the theories and practices of cutting-edge naturalistic sciences just because they are revered for being more naturalistic and/or 'cutting edge'. I return to this motivation towards the end of the chapter. For the time being I concentrate on the issues before us, accepting that the primary goal is social understanding including explanation. This, of course, is something I take largely for granted in arguing for an ontological turn in economics.

To return to the central argument I am concerned here specifically with the relevance to the social realm of the Darwinian model of 'natural selection'. Although the task of demonstrating that the characteristics of openness and dynamics are common to biological and social domains is fairly straightforward, that of determining whether insights systematised as the natural selection mechanism in evolutionary biology have parallels in the social realm requires a good deal more work.

A clear route to addressing such matters is to retroduce an appropriate (see below) general model of which the biological natural selection conception can be seen as a token, a general model which can in due course be examined for its applicability to social phenomena. In truth, there is no need to defer to a general model at all (even if this *is* the way metaphor works). All that is necessary is that the essential components are distilled from any biological natural selection example. The question I need to pose is merely whether these essential elements carry over to the socio-economic realm. However, by viewing them as features of a general model of which any biological example is viewed as a token, there is, I believe, less scope for confusion as to what is going on. In any case this will be my strategy here. I will consider a biological example, distil out the components essential to a natural selection mechanism and interpret these as features of a general model of which the specific (biological) example considered is a token. I will examine whether economic tokens of it are also feasible.

As a first step on this path, then, let me very briefly now consider a particular example of the biological model. I know that such examples are familiar enough to many modern economists, especially those working in the (old) institutionalist tradition. But I go through one here anyway partly for completeness, partly to convey my understanding of a natural selection process (there are of course competing understandings and emphases) and partly to keep the discussion focused not only on abstract models but also real-world processes.[8]

A biological example: the beaks of Darwin's finches

A well documented example that will serve my purposes concerns 'Darwin's finches' (so called because they were originally studied by Darwin), a group of finches inhabiting the relatively isolated Galápagos islands (visited by Darwin for five weeks during his voyage on the HMS Beagle). I focus, in particular, on a relatively recent episode in the process of evolution in sizes of their beaks.

The evolutionary episode in question took place on the specific island of Daphne Major between 1973 and 1978. It is an episode that has been documented by various scientific observers living on the island at the time (see, e.g., Weiner, 1994). Conditions were such that just about all the finches on the island were individually 'known' to these observers.

In the first four years of this period, fairly lush environmental conditions prevailed on Daphne Major. In particular, the rains fell in the early part of each year allowing seed-bearing plants to grow and attendant insects to flourish. There was thus a plentiful supply of food for birds produced in the early part of each year, and most of the finches were observed to survive the remainder of the year, whatever the conditions.[9] However, after the first week of January 1977 little rain fell for the whole of the rest of that year. Throughout this period the total mass of seeds on the island declined, and the average size and hardness of the seeds that remained uneaten increased steadily.[10] Hundreds of finches died.[11] Notably, those finches which survived were the bigger-beaked birds capable of cracking open the larger harder seeds that remained.[12] Mostly these were males, the average female beak (and body) having been smaller. In any case, following the drought the birds which survived and were able to mate were those birds which were distinguished within the original population by having larger beaks. And subsequently the offspring of the survivors were found also to possess big or deep beaks, typically about 4 or 5 per cent larger than those of their ancestors in the population of a few years earlier.[13]

In short, the result was evolution by way of a process of natural selection. The period saw a shift in the environment that 'favoured' (in a relative sense) those finches with larger beaks. Larger-beaked finches survived the environmental shift, and because their offspring inherited their parents' (larger) beak size, an evolutionary change was observed in the space of just a few years.[14]

Towards a general evolutionary model

So what are the essential features of the natural selection story here? What components are essential to this biological explanation of the mechanism of change or evolution via natural selection? Alternatively put, which abstract model(s) lies behind and systematises this specific illustration and others like it? What is essential to any (class of) model(s) for which the natural selection process whereby the beaks of finches evolved is a token example? Clearly there are several essential components to include.

A first feature of the explanation to retain is that it deals, at some level, with a *population* of individuals of a particular type (finches) and an aspect of the finch's environment or situation (food). Notice that the latter is indeed only an aspect. Finches need water, air, warmth and a host of other factors to survive. The environmental factor of selective causal influence here is food in the form of seeds in a context where substitutes are hard to come by.

The existence of *variety* of some sort within the relevant population is a second essential feature of this form of explanation. In the case of Darwin's finches the variety included the sizes of beaks. For, trivially, in order that finches with larger-than-average beaks were able to perform in a relatively successful manner, there clearly had to be finches with larger-than-average beaks present in the original population. Notice, then, that for a natural selection evolution story, the individuals of the population possess both traits that are essential to their qualifying as members of the relevant populations, and traits which differentiate them within that population.

A third essential feature of the explanation is that a mechanism of *reproduction* (or replication or inheritance) is included as part of the explanation. The story told could not count as an evolutionary one, as an explanation of the rise to prominence of the bigger-beaked finch in successive generations, if size of beak was something that the finches did not reproduce through their offspring. Relatedly, we have a conception of lineage here, a spatio-temporal sequence of entities in which later ones are in some sense descended from, and causally produced by, earlier ones.[15] Although over the period in question earlier generations of finches on the island had smaller beaks on average than later, ones they were still finches. There is a sense in which the bigger-beaked finches evolved out of, and constituted an evolution of, finches.

The specification of a mechanism whereby there is interaction between individual and environment is a fourth essential feature of the explanation. This is a mechanism whereby certain members of the population (with specific features) are *selected*. Following Hull (1981), I shall use the term *interactors* to refer to the entities in which interaction between the environment and the individual occurs. This will typically be a different entity to that which passes on its structure in replication. The latter, following Dawkins (1976, 1978), I refer to as a *replicator*. If a mechanism of gene replication is responsible for the reproduction or replication of finches with certain features, this is insufficient to explain the rise to prominence of birds with that gene. The interaction of the whole organism with its environment is an essential feature of the causal evolutionary process. In particular, the need for the finch to eat (in an environment of seeds as food) is an essential aspect of the story. (In biology the genetic constitution of the replicating individual is referred to as the genotype, the nature of the individual or organism the phenotype.)

A fifth relevant feature of the explanatory sketch is the fact of a degree of independence between the process whereby the variety of traits is produced and the manner in which the environmental mechanism doing the selecting has come about. Such independence is essential if the model is to explain the appearance of order or 'fit' (of beak size and seed size) in the absence of design. Otherwise there is nothing that necessarily distinguishes the explanatory schema from any other as found for example in modern economics. Specifically, without independence it can be argued that either trait or environment is produced in order to match the other, so that the puzzle of order in the absence of design is not, after all, addressed.

Notice further that evolutionary change in line with natural selection can come about over a period of time because either (i) a new trait emerges within a relevant population, one that is found to be favoured by the existing environment, or (ii) the environment shifts in a way such as to favour a trait that has long been in existence (or through a combination of these two types of development). In each such scenario, however, the *possibilities* turn on the processes generating the traits or variety, and the contribution of the environment lies in its 'selecting' amongst the particular set of features in evidence.

The PVRS model

Given that these identified elements are each essential to a natural selection story (such as illustrated by the evolving size of the beaks of Darwin's finches), all will be part of *any* abstract model of which the biological natural selection model can, *qua* a natural selection model, be viewed as a manifestation or token.

Let me refer to any model that contains these components as a Population–Variety–Reproduction–Selection, or the PVRS, model or system. We must keep in mind that for a process captured by a PVRS model to be one of natural selection, V (variety generation) and S (selection) conditions must be to a significant extent independent. The question is, how independent? In particular, should these conditions be strictly independent of each other, or is something weaker sufficient?

To clarify matters let me briefly consider three versions of the PVRS model distinguished according to the manner of the relation, if any, between the conditions of variety generation and those of environmental selection.

A PVRS model with variety and selection conditions strictly independent

Consider first a PVRS model in which the mechanisms influencing the variety of traits (V) and selection conditions or mechanisms (S) are *strictly independent*. This can be termed the polar, or neo- or strict, Darwinian version of the model.[16] This is the form of PVRS model usually thought to have most relevance in modern biology.

In the case of Darwin's finches, the presumption is that the conditions which select out the bigger-beaked finches (the availability of food only in the form of difficult-to-open seeds) are strictly independent of the (genetic mutation) mechanisms bearing on the process whereby a finch with a larger beak first emerged.

The advantage of distinguishing this version of the PVRS model is that it illustrates rather clearly that, and how, a mechanism, the natural selection mechanism, can bring about the appearance of order even in the complete absence of conscious design.

A feed-backward PVRS model

Second we can distinguish a PVRS model that allows S to feed back to, or causally influence, V. Let me refer to this version of the PVRS model as a feed-backward or S-to-V model. A biological token of this feed-backward version is the Lamarckian model,[17] a conception which (according to the manner in which it is most commonly interpreted) allows the inheritance of acquired characteristics. It proposes that acquisitions or losses, wrought through the influence of the environment, can feed back into the evolutionary process, being capable, in certain circumstances, of being preserved in the 'species' (or whatever) through reproduction.

To claim Lamarckian features for the evolutionary development of Darwin's finches would be to suppose the finches somehow acquired the advantageous feature of a larger beak directly in the process of interacting with their environment, and also somehow passed this characteristic on to its off-spring.[18]

A feed-forward PVRS model

Finally we can distinguish a PVRS model which allows V to feed forward and causally affect S. Let me refer to this as a feed-forward or V-to-S version of the PVRS model.

To suppose such a model has relevance to the example of Darwin's finches would be to maintain the mutation conditions giving rise to the longer beaks somehow affected the environment of selection, i.e. the nature, or causes, of the finches' food.

As the example of the beaks of Darwin's finches perhaps illustrates, the feed-backward and feed-forward forms of the PVRS model may have comparatively little application relative to the neo-Darwinian version in the biological realm. Or at least this was conceivably so prior to human intervention. With human manipulation via genetic modification we certainly find scope for the feed-backward model. And with the intervention of humans to ensure an environment prevails in which a particular desired variety of some species thrives, the feed-forward model also has some force.

But in other realms of the biological world, the polar or neo- Darwinian model is often thought to have most relevance. Variety and selection conditions, as in the case of Darwin's finches, are frequently found to be more or less strictly independent.

The natural selection mechanism

So with which version of the PVRS model are we concerned here? Notice that although in the case of Darwin's finches V and S conditions appear strictly independent, the degree or extent to which the strict or polar Darwinian model holds in biology is actually contested. More to the point, all we need here are the insights that relate to the natural selection mechanism. Clearly the strict Darwinian version best illustrates the workings of the natural selection mechanism. However, the openness of the social system means that even where a Darwinian mechanism is operative it is likely to be but one mechanism amongst many affecting the outcome. Remember we are motivated here by the recognition that, in an open changing world, mechanisms can exist (and in the biological realm clearly do exist) that ensure the appearance of order, the matching of part and whole, of individual and environment, even when this outcome is not the product of conscious design. All we need consider here is whether there are 'natural selection' tendencies of this sort at play in the social realm. No more need natural selection tendencies be the whole story on any occasion of change or persistence in the social realm than in the biological realm. The question is whether such an evolutionary mechanism is ever in play, whether there exists a tendency for certain selection conditions which are broadly independent of variety producing mechanisms to bear in any significant way upon the (sorts of) individuals of the population which come (via replication or reproduction) to dominate. The most relevant, or potentially useful, version of the PVRS model to investigate further, then, just is any version in which the V and S conditions are at least relatively independent. So the strict or polar or neo-Darwinian version of the PVRS model qualifies as a special case.

Back to social processes

The task awaiting us at this point is precisely to determine whether the biological evolutionary model as conceived here does, or could, have relevance to social analysis. If we accept that the PVRS model with S and V largely independent expresses a process which generalises the biological evolutionary model of natural selection in a manner that captures its essential features, we need now to assess whether there is any way in which it is able to be concretised usefully, i.e. be given a meaningful specific interpretation, in the social domain.

In fact, we can again be more definite here. Having accepted the (already elaborated) transformational model of social activity as capturing essential features of social reality, the specific questions we need to address are:

1   how, if at all, this version of the PVRS model ties in with the transformational model; and (assuming that it does tie in)
2   what might this PVRS model achieve that the transformational model does not already?

The PVRS evolutionary model as a transformational model of social activity

Although the relevance of the latter question presupposes a positive answer to the former, it is nevertheless possible here to address it first. For it is already clear that *if* a PVRS model can add anything to social analysis whilst remaining consistent with the transformational model, this is because the latter, more or less by 'design', is sufficiently abstract as to encompass all (so far) observed aspects of social reproduction/transformation. The latter was determined in the course of developing a general social ontology. But if this transformational model allows that both transformation and reproduction occur, it says little about either the conditions wherein one or the other is likely to dominate, or the *specifics* of any processes of social reproduction/transformation. The evolutionary model then, *if appropriate at all*, will presumably indicate one specification of the transformational model. It will provide a more concrete account of how reproduction and/or transformation of specific aspects of social structure can happen.

The more fundamental question here, though, is the former one. Given what we already know about social reality, as expressed in particular by the transformational conception elaborated above, does the PVRS model, constrained to conform to the transformational model, carry the potential to illuminate the social realm at all?

As an initial orienting strategy let me briefly recall the sort of model we are seeking. For a social-evolutionary story we require, at a minimum, some conception of a population of social individuals each with traits rendering them members of that population; a variety generation process giving rise to additional traits which differentiate members within the population; a notion of a relevant environment; a mechanism whereby individuals with various differentiated aspects are, or can be, reproduced or replicated; a mechanism whereby individuals of the population interact with their environment with different degrees of success; and an account of the process as a whole that conforms to the transformational model of social activity.

Consider, first, some likely candidates for social interactors (the social entities that interact with their environments). What sorts of individuals, if any, are various in their aspects, compete with others in social life, and ultimately are selected by the environment in which they occur? In particular, what answer to this question can be formulated that is in keeping with the transformational model of social activity? Of course, there may be many social scientific tokens. Any evolutionary framework developed here is very unlikely to be unique. Even so, it seems to me that a certain category of social phenomena does stand out more than others as a promising candidate for the set of social interactors we are looking for here. I refer to *social practices*.

Consider, for example, language use, including speech acts. Think of an international conference of academics. Although numerous languages will be spoken by the participants, especially in local restaurants and other off-conference meeting places, in the conference lecture by room the practice of speaking English invariably comes to dominate (at least currently). Some participants from countries where English is not the first language often try valiantly to get the discussion going in their own language, or in a different one to English, in some of the attendant seminars or even any main forum. But for various reasons, including, usually, the sheer number of native English speakers, and because non-native English speakers tend to speak English well, and native English speakers tend to speak other languages very poorly, the practice of speaking in English usually comes to dominate.

Notice that it is specific practices (in this case speaking in various languages), that are the individuals in competition here, not the human individuals *per se*. In my experience, the participants whose first language is *not* English are often in the majority at both international conferences as well as in the power echelons of the economics profession, including in the

UK and North America. It is not individuals *per se* whose first language is other than English that are squeezed out but the practice of speaking a language other than English in the public forum.

Of course, many young scholars going to an international conference for the first time will recognise this situation, and may, if their first language is not English or if their English is poor, perhaps take actions to acquire competency in speaking it. As such there is likely to be a feed-backward aspect to the process. But in the main, language speaking competencies are acquired independently of the constraining influences of international academic conference practices. Or at least, to the extent that this is so, the development of language practices of these conferences might be interpreted as conforming to the evolutionary 'natural selection' model.[19]

I think this example also indicates a further likely aspect of the most promising social-evolutionary framework of the relevant sort: that the environment of social selection will usually include, and often perhaps consist mainly in, the sum total of other related, including competing, social practices.

In keeping with the transformational model, then, I would suggest that the most promising, or anyway one conceivable, candidate for the social interactor is social practice, and the environment of selection includes all other social practices that are in some way related or connected. Interaction with the environment just is human interaction.

What sort of thing or aspect might be interpreted as a social replicator, the entity that passes on its structure in replication? The answer that fits most easily with the transformational conception of social activity, I suggest, is social structure and especially social rules including norms and conventions.

Think again of the practice of language use, say of French. This is governed by the structure of rules, etc., that make up the French langauge. These govern (though do not determine) speech acts. They are also reproduced just through people speaking French. In a manner characteristic of many social practices this drawing on rules of language in speech acts is sooner or later performed habitually.

Consider as a further example the (methodological) practices which dominate the modern economics discipline. Elsewhere (2003, chapter 10) I argue that the twentieth-century rise to prominence of the practices of formalistic deductivist economics warrants a social-evolutionary explanation along the lines of the PVRS model. Attempts to mathematise the discipline had been in place long before mathematical economics rose to dominance. The interactor here is the practice of attempting to render the study of social phenomena mathematical. The replicator just is the belief or (as some view it) 'convention' or 'cultural norm' (see Lawson, 2003, chapter 10) that mathematics is a fundamental component of all science and serious study. The rise to prominence of mathematical economics did not reflect any obvious breakthrough in terms of its relative explanatory performance (compared to that of other approaches). Rather it reflected a shift in the environment of academic practices more widely. Prior to the period in question, realisticness was a goal of all mathematical enquiry. With the turn of the twentieth century, mathematics became disconnected from models of sciences like physics (the mechanics model). Indeed, the need for any kind of interpretative orientation to mathematics became much reduced as the idea of 'mathematics for its own sake' became widely accepted. This removed the constraint (earlier strongly felt by Walras and others) that mathematical models in economics needed to be realistic, and allowed the mathematisation tendency in economics fuller sway. This change in the academic environment removed factors that previously were selecting against scientific research practices underpinned by the belief or convention that mathematics is an essential component. The shift in question thus allowed the latter mathematical practices more scope to become pervasive and even (as it eventually turned out) dominant. Of course, this evolutionary mechanism was never the whole story (and others are discussed in Lawson, 2003, chapter 10), but it appears to have been an important element of the relevant historical process nonetheless.

The above example (explored in some depth in Lawson, 2003, chapter 10) focuses on the mathematising tendency in economics as one set of practices within the population of all research practices. Because the explanatory puzzle is the varying fortunes and indeed survival of the mathematising tendency (whatever its form), the emphasis there is on environmental selection.

I might note, however, that if we narrow our perspective, the wide-ranging set of mathematising practices within economics can be construed as a population within its own right. And if we were to focus on this population as a candidate example of a natural selection process in the social realm, I believe the interest would likely fall more on processes of incremental adaption, i.e. on how this project has evolved over time. The likely or candidate replicators now appear to be (or to include) the enduring or core concepts, theories or methods (e.g., supply and demand analysis, general equilibrium, econometric method) underpinning the array of competing substantive contributions that are manifest. Such a hypothesis though is not something I shall explore further here.[20]

Disanalogies between evolutionary biology and evolutionary social science

If the above considerations are suggestive of the possibility that, and perhaps indicative as to how, the natural selection PVRS model may be concretised in the social domain, the transformational model is also especially useful as an aid to identifying some significant disanalogies between the biological and social realms.

Most obviously, it is only through the medium of human agency that variation is produced in the social realm, and that reproduction/replication and selection occur. Aspects of social structure may be reproduced by (collections of) individuals both over time, through these individuals repeatedly drawing on them (and adopting practices which presuppose and indeed manifest them), and also across people at a point of time, through (possibly sub-conscious) imitation, and so forth. Social systems are neither naturally reproduced nor self-reproducing. Rather such reproduction or transformation as occurs are the result of capable human beings purposefully going about their daily lives and tasks, interpreting themselves, their purposes and the social order in very definite ways, and continually interacting with (including copying) others. Although much of what occurs is unintended and perhaps misunderstood, intentionality is far more significant in the social than the natural domains. Human intentional activity is always the medium of both social reproduction and transformation.

The distinctiveness of the natural selection or biological evolutionary model

A further obvious difference between the social and the biological is that, whatever may be the precise relation between variety generation (V) and selection conditions (S) in the biological realm, these sets of conditions are likely more often to be inter-dependent or connected in the social (if and where they occur in the social realm at all). We need only think of the impact of market research, or indeed of almost any form of forward thinking or planning, to recognise that feed-backward linkages will have some force in the social domain, that selection conditions affect the variety produced. And we need only think of advertising, and then any form of persuasion, including use of power relations, to recognise the relevance of the feed-forward model in the social domain, to see how variety generation conditions can come to affect the environment of selection.

Indeed, and as I have already emphasised, it is precisely because of this contrast between conditions in the biological and those in social domains that reflection on the biological realm, and specifically the natural selection model, proves so useful to social explanation. For such reflection helps clarify the nature of a mechanism whereby order can be produced, whereby a matching of individual and environment (or part and whole) can emerge, that is not at all the result of conscious design.

Of course, just as social processes will rarely conform to the strict or neo-Darwinian model (which would mean that human practices were entirely autonomous of human intentionality – though see the discussion on 'memes' below) so they will not be purely or strictly Lamarckian or backwards determining (the functionalist–deterministic mistake of modern mainstream economics) nor conforming to a polar feed-forward or forwards determining model (the voluntarist or perhaps environment-as-putty model).

Nor should we expect that, if and where evolutionary features of a social process are identified, they are bound, or necessarily likely, to persist. Even where V and S conditions exist in a social process and are found at some point to be to a degree independent, it cannot be presumed that one and the same relation between V and S must hold throughout. That is, although environmental selection may have made a difference to the structure of the population over a period of space-time, this in itself is no guarantee that such a selection process will continue. Indeed, the past effects of any such mechanism in the social realm will likely provide a spur to power struggles, or to developments in technology, etc., designed purely to bring such a process under increased conscious control. It all depends on the situation.

Such considerations, then, lead us to anticipate that the natural selection biological model may well prove useful to social analysis. But if so, we can also anticipate that anything which can reasonably count as social-evolutionary explanation of the relevant (natural selection) sort will typically identify modes of interaction or influence between conditions of variety generation and of selection that are only relatively independent. In order to understand a social process adequately or fully it will likely also be necessary to identify patterns of accommodation and rejection, harmonious reinforcement and tension, between 'individuals' and the environment. The strict separation of both modes of replication and inter-action, and modes of mutation and selection, often thought to characterise the biological realm, give way, in the social realm, to processes of greater or more obvious causal interdependency and interpenetration. Indeed, in the end the contrast between the evolutionary and many other social explanatory scenarios may be one largely of degree rather than kind.

Evolutionary explanation as a limited epistemological case

Having, I think, found qualified support for the thesis that borrowing from evolutionary biology carries the potential to be of some use in the social realm, depending on context, I want (like many before me, if not necessarily for the same reasons) to conclude here by emphasising caution. For if there is reason for supposing the social-evolutionary explanation remains always a possibility, depending on context, the transformational model which helps us properly to see this also indicates that the evolutionary model is unlikely ever to be the whole story. It may even be a rather small aspect of the total picture.

The fuller story is provided precisely by the realist transformational model of social activity. Its scope of coverage includes merely develop-mental (including wholly planned) forms of change, forms of emergence, acts of whim, and so on. Indeed it includes forms of change where, amongst other things, there is either no variety in a population, or no meaningful concept of an identifiable environment playing a selecting role.

One difference between the transformational model and specific ver-sions of the PVRS model is of vital significance here. This is a contrast not between their particular specifications but the ways in which, in the social domain, the two explanatory models are derived or supported. The transformational model (unlike the PVRS model) has been derived in an *a posteriori* manner to explain highly generalised features of social experience (e.g., the prevalence of routinised forms of behaviour, segmentation of practices followed by different types of individuals – see Lawson, 2003, chapter 2). It has been derived by inferring (by way of transcendental argument) what the world must be like for generalised social phenomena to be in evidence. In other words it has been derived by considering the social realm directly. This contrasts with the manner in which the PVRS model has been derived, which is by way of abstracting from the natural selection model found to achieve explanatory successes in biological science. The relevance of the PVRS model to social analysis is thus always open to question, a matter to be assessed in context. In other words, the sustainable reason for focusing on the natural-selection model in the social domain is the possession of some *a posteriori* ground (turning, I have argued, on our understanding of the nature of social reality and seeing parallels between it and the material of the biological realm) for suspecting there *may* be some scope for its successful application to social phenomena.

The danger for 'natural selection' thinking which draws on insights from biology, then, is of universalising *a priori* what is but a particular insight, a set of principles, whose relevance in the social realm is found *a posteriori* to be highly dependent on context. I am not suggesting the PVRS model cannot have relevance in the social domain; indeed I have suggested some likely applications above. Obvious further cases to study for purposes of uncovering an evolutionary story are social processes where structures and practices are found *a posteriori* to be relatively enduring but wherein the outcome is not obviously a success story by any absolute, or even necessarily very wide, set of criteria. Possible candidates for social-evolutionary explanations of this sort are institutions (i.e. structured processes of interaction that reveal a degree of space-time durability and are recognised as doing so – see Lawson, 1997: 165, 317–18; 2003, chapter 8), as well as, or including, certain routines, habits, as well as some seemingly locked-in (additional, including technological) structures that will likely be bound up with the development of institutions and/or habits.

However, here I want to emphasise that, promising though such candidates may seem, we have not uncovered grounds for any insistence on, or universalisation of, the 'natural selection' evolutionary model. I repeat that to insist without investigation or argumentation that such an approach is everywhere relevant is to promulgate a reductionist *a priori* methodological injunction, on a par with methodological individualism, or deductivism.

My concern here, of course, is to urge the abandoning of all *a priori* injunctions where this is feasible, and to turn, instead, to trial-and-error experimentation as seems reasonable, but also to any approach which includes, as an essential element, the endeavour to fashion methodological principles in the light of social ontological insights obtained *a posteriori*.

Economics and metaphor

Why are reductionist tendencies of the sort I have just noted as prominent as they are in economics? One possible reason for it is the earlier noted belief, seemingly growing in popularity in some quarters, that economics, or the study of social phenomena in general, must borrow wholeheartedly from some other discipline, and, in particular, that it must draw wholesale on metaphors which connect it to other more naturalistic (and especially 'cutting-edge' or anyway currently fashionable) developments. This belief is apparently supported by a perception that economics has historically been driven by an attraction for the mechanistic metaphor. The coupling of this latter perception with an assessment that the discipline needs to be brought up-to-date, in consequence encourages the idea that the accepted task is to replace the mechanics metaphor with another drawn perhaps from biological, cyborg or some other science.

Actually, I believe the historical conception of economics as having been driven by mechanistic ideals or the metaphor of mechanics (an orientation often disparagingly attributed in turn to 'physics envy') is largely misleading. The drive to mathematise has always been the more dominant concern (see Lawson, 2003, chapter 10). It just so happens that the sorts of mathematical methods economists have pursued rest on an implicit mechanistic (essentially atomistic) ontology, thus encouraging mechanistic substantive conceptions.

Further, I think it is important to recognise that when the likes of Marshall, Penrose and Schumpeter make reference to biological models they are concerned not with any *necessity* to adopt metaphors *per se*, but with the possibility of achieving the goal of a more realistic account of social reality thereby.

Of course, if I am suggesting that it is inaccurate to portray the competition over metaphors as essential to the history or the scientificity of economics, I do not deny that the employment of metaphor has often been, and will continue to be, useful. Rather I maintain only that the usefulness of any particular metaphor to any science is something to be determined empirically, and relates to its appropriateness to the nature of the material under analysis.

Memes and memetics

Still there is undeniably, at present, a wish on the part of some economists to be seen to be abreast of state-of-the art science, or of branches of it most recently in fashion. Now as it happens there appears to be a somewhat imperialistic tendency emanating from elsewhere, and specifically evolutionary psychology, ready to embrace this particular disposition. I refer to the project of *memetics*. Indeed some readers may wonder why the discussion so far has made (almost) no reference to it. One reason is just that it is not clear from the literature that very many economists are aware of memetics anyway. So if achieving a short cut in my argument were the goal it is not obvious that reference to memetics would help.

But there are other reasons why I have not connected with the relevant literature before this point. Whilst I believe there may be value in the category at the centre of this project, namely the *meme*, memetics is seemingly most ardently promoted by those who give the appearance (whatever qualifying asides are also tagged on) of seeking to achieve two questionable forms of reduction. The first is a reduction of the natural selection mechanism to the achievements of the 'selfish replicator'. The second is a reduction of the study of society and culture to (aspects of) evolutionary biology or psychology. If this assessment is at all accurate I do indeed wish to maintain a critical distance. For these tendencies, and particularly the latter, are of just the sort that I have been cautioning against throughout. Let me quickly elaborate.

The term *meme* derives from the writings of the evolutionary biologist Richard Dawkins, in particular *The Selfish Gene* (Dawkins, 1976) and *The Blind Watchmaker* (Dawkins, 1986). Having introduced the idea of a *replicator* as anything of which copies are made, i.e. a feature which passes on its structure in replication, and accepting that genes are the replicators of biology, Dawkins asks if there are replicators in other domains. He suggests there are. These are units of cultural transmission or imitation:

> We need a name for the new replicator, a noun that conveys the idea of a unit of cultural transmission, or a unit of imitation. 'Mimeme' comes from a suitable Greek root, but I want a monosyllable that sounds a bit like 'gene'. I hope my classicist friends will forgive me if I abbreviate mimene to *meme*.
>
> (Dawkins, 1976: 192)

Memes then are social replicators. In fact they are bits of information which replicate between minds as individuals communicate. Dawkins writes of 'tunes, ideas, catch-phases, clothes-fashions, ways of making pots or of building arches' (1976: 192).

One specific item that may appear to qualify as a meme, so understood, is the already discussed cultural wisdom or belief that for research work to count as scientific (or substantial or serious) it must take a mathematical form. 'Mathematics is essential to science'. This idea, though false as a claim about reality (see Lawson, 2003, chapter 1), is one that is nevertheless easy to grasp and to believe (especially given the remarkable and continuing achievements of mathematics more widely). Many people (especially those who labour under the two-part impression that mathematics is merely a language, and any language is somehow neutral in scientific work) view the idea (that mathematical methods be always used in science) simply as a (scientific) convention. And as discussed in Lawson

(2003, chapter 10) this apprehension of the role of mathematics has long been an element of western culture.[21]

Of course the idea (or convention) that science requires mathematics is sufficiently abstract to have high fidelity, where accepted. And it is replicated as the practices, methods and theories it conditions are reproduced and transformed over time (and is implicit in, and grounding, the content of text books, research papers, lectures and the like). The basic belief or convention involved does not literally copy itself. Certainly it is not copied unaided by human beings. But then nor do genes replicate themselves unaided, certainly not outside the laboratory.[22] Moreover, if replication does depend on human agency, continuity of the kind achieved is not a matter of simple individual volition. The options available to economists are both informed and constrained by the current practices of the academy, as well as accepted canons of knowledge, and curricula. And for mathematical economists the goal is not to reproduce the basic convention as such; the latter is mostly an implicitly accepted belief serving as a means to an end. The perceived goal is a new theorem, or a stable econometric relationship, or some such. But in doing such work and displaying it, the relevant 'copy me' message is communicated to all would-be academic economists nevertheless.

As I say, it is conceivable, then, that we have here an example of a meme. But I am not sure, and I leave it for memeticists to decide. My hesitation in embracing memetics stems, first of all, from a perception that its proponents mostly employ a rhetoric which implies acceptance of the view that the replicator is the prime mover in all that happens. Environmental selection (if it is to happen) 'requires' some reproduced entities to work on. In the case of the finches, for example, reproduction and selection are clearly influenced in an essential way by the nature of the birds themselves (the phenotypes). It is not just down to their genes *per se* (the genotypes or replicators). Dawkins, however, appears often to suggest that, because there is always a genetic contribution to the form, behaviour and reproduction of any phenotype and because the contribution is inherited, the gene is therefore the unit on which selection must act. Dawkins includes numerous qualifications to such an interpretation in his writings. But the thrust of the argument is clearly that everything of functional importance and complexity is an adaptation fashioned by natural selection working only for the benefit of selfish replicators, that is, in the biological realm, for the 'selfish gene'.

Transposed to the social realm the selfish replicator becomes the selfish meme. To quote Dawkins again:

> When we look to the evolution of cultural traits, and at their survival value, we must be clear whose survival we are talking about ... A cultural trait may have evolved in the way it has, *simply because it is advantageous to itself* ... Once the genes have provided their survival machines with brains that are capable of rapid imitation, the memes

will automatically take over. We do not even have to posit a genetic advantage in imitation.

(Dawkins, 1976: 214–15, emphasis added)

Contributors to memetics appear mostly to accept this perspective, and write of people being victimised by 'viruses of the mind' (Dawkins, 1993; Brodie, 1996). Thoughts think themselves.[23] Just as, for Dawkins, our bodies are lumbering robots for our genes, so our brains become lumbering robots for our memes, the latter being an evolutionary agent that evolves in accordance solely with its own interests.

Now on the account defended throughout this book human beings are, amongst other things, intentional subjects. But further, the social realm is not just the result of mental processing by humans. Society is not even made up of people. Rather it is a realm of emergent phenomena comprising social relations of powers, institutions, positions, rules, processes and much more. Culture does not exist only in human minds. What many memeticists appear to lack is serious insight into real social processes, and of how human (intentional) agency and structure interact.

Above (and in Lawson, 2003, chapter 10) I suggest that the enduring dominance of formalistic deductive economics may involve natural selection tendencies. Here, then, I am acknowledging the possibility that this process (specifically the selection of practices which presuppose the replicator belief or convention 'mathematics is essential to science') constitutes an example of memetics. But if this is indeed thought to be the case, I must emphasise that in attempting to explain how the convention in question is reproduced I do not enquire (or write of) what this convention does for itself, or even what we do for it (which is seemingly the set of questions posed, or stance taken, by most memeticists). Rather I take for granted that, amongst those individuals who seek to mathematise the study of social phenomena, a quest for understanding or scientific advance, or at least for gratification in the form of scientific status, is involved. In other words, my argument is that the pursuance of mathematical economics is caused *not* by a self-interested, or selfish, parasite in our minds, but by (understandably) mistaken assessments of the nature and goals of science on the part of its human protagonists. It is because the proponents of mathematical economics are often mistaken in their views concerning the necessity of mathematics, and can be shown to be so, that it is worth engaging with them in order to effect a change (or at least to influence those thinking of joining in with the mainstream project).

Herein, then, lies one reason why I have not linked into the literature on memes from the outset (and am still cautious about doing so). If I have misinterpreted the intentions of memeticists here (and I do acknowledge the numerous tagged-on qualifications that are to be found in the relevant literature, here and there), I suspect the problem lies as much in the way the project is mostly presented as in this reading.[24]

But actually, there is a yet more compelling reason for my hesitancy here. This is the universalising and reductionist orientation taken (and even trumpeted) by many of those who contribute to the memetics program. Whatever insight there is in the literature on *memes*, and I believe there is a good deal[25] (and I do not accept all the criticisms made of it[26]) major problem is the propensity of many of its proponents to treat the approach from the outset as one that has universal bearing (even prior to any agreement amongst those working in the area over whether memes have been shown to exist; see for example the competing views of Robert Aunger and Susan Blackmore, both found in Aunger, 2000 [chapters 11 and 2 respectively]).

Darwin coped with abstract units of inheritance because he had a phenomenon to explain. But modern memeticists are not in the same situation. They lack not only a clear account of details of any proposed memetic explanation, but seemingly also a developed sustainable understanding of the nature of society and culture which they wish to account for. Certainly, nowhere do I find anything closely resembling the transformational model discussed above. Nor are social-ontological elaborations much in evidence at all. The driving force of the project, rather, is an apparent desire to reduce the whole of the social sciences and cultural studies (whatever the nature of the 'objects' the latter do study) to a form of evolutionary thinking.

Perhaps it is not surprising, then, to find that, of the contributors to a much-heralded edited volume on memes (Aunger, 2000), those most committed to the memetics project turn out to be biological in inclination, whilst those most opposed to it have a background of working more in psychology and/or social theory. It is certainly noteworthy that the quest for evolutionary understanding of the social world through using the category of memes has been systematised (by Dawkins) as *Universal Darwinism*, a heading that readily conveys the impression (whatever the strict definition)[27] that the endeavour is not modal, i.e. concerned with seeking *a posteriori* successes, but categorical, signalling an *a priori* thesis about the scope of relevance of the model. It is in this fashion, too, that we can appreciate Dennett's idea of 'universal acid'. It is formulated in his *Darwin's Dangerous Idea* (Dennett, 1995), a book which has contributed significantly to a diffusion of the memetics idea. The 'dangerous idea' in question is an abstract algorithm, sometimes called a replicator dynamic. It consists in repeated iterations of selection from among randomly mutating replicators. Couched in such terms a specific Darwinian evolutionary process, that of natural selection, is interpreted as an entirely general phenomenon characterising not just biological material (such as DNA) but any other kind as well, allowing application of Dennett's algorithm to anything:

> Darwin's dangerous idea is reductionism incarnate, promising to unite and explain just about everything in one magnificent vision. Its

being the idea of an algorithmic process makes it all the more power-ful, since the substrate neutrality it thereby possesses permits us to consider its application to just about anything.

(Dennett, 1995: 82)

If memetics, at least as perceived by these contributors and others, evades the charge of genetic determinism it does so only by embracing a univer-salist stance on socio-cultural evolution. That is, in (correctly) rejecting the idea that evolutionary biology or genetics can explain everything, memet-icists encourage the view that biology can explain the natural world and memetics can explain the rest.

As Susan Blackmore, who has perhaps contributed more than anyone to popularising the memetics project (see for example Blackmore, 1999a, 1999b, 1999c, 2000a, 2000b), observes: 'The new vision is stunning ... because now one simple theory encompasses all of human culture and creativity as well as biological evolution' (Blackmore, 2000b: 54).

In the end, it is difficult to avoid gaining the impression that, so far at least, this 'stunning' feature, this potential to facilitate a theory of every-thing, is actually the central drive of, and dominant explanation of much of the growing support for, the current memetics project.

My own position, defended throughout this book, is that a surer path to understanding turns on an avoidance of *a priori* universalising, where feasible, and the determining of relevance *a posteriori*. Certainly I welcome cooperative interdisciplinary endeavour concerned to explore the *scope* of evolutionary, including natural selection, mechanisms. But this is quite different from agreeing in advance that socio-cultural study, including eco-nomics, should be reduced to evolutionary psychology and/or biology.[28]

Tailoring to context

To draw the chapter to a conclusion, and to return to its central argument, the basic thesis I defend is that the borrowing by economists from others can benefit from a turn to ontology. Once ontology is brought into the pic-ture it is conceivable that little disagreement of substance will be found to remain amongst many of the imputed protagonists to the debate over the legitimacy of borrowing from evolutionary biology.

When Schumpeter argues that social phenomena 'would have to be analyzed with reference to economic facts alone and no appeal to biol-ogy would be of slightest use' (1954: 789), we can interpret him as saying that the relevance to the social realm of the (abstract PVRS model which generalises the) biological-evolutionary model can be determined only by examining directly the nature of (the relevant aspects of) the social phe-nomena in which we are interested. If so, Schumpeter's remark need not after all involve him in the view that economics should eschew *all* meta-phors from physical and natural sciences.

And when Penrose writes that

> in seeking the fundamental explanations of economic and social phe-
> nomena in human affairs the economist, and the social scientist in
> general, would be well advised to attack his problems directly and in
> their own terms rather than indirectly by imposing sweeping biologi-
> cal models upon them

(1952: 819)

this again need not be at odds with borrowing from biology. For the point
being made here is merely that the external imposition of models and metaphors, without any consideration of their potential relevance to the social
domain, is likely to be unhelpful.

The evolutionary natural selection model is merely a construct that
carries (now *a posteriori* grounded) potential for insightful social analysis. The call to look to such evolutionary processes, where appropriate,
has modal status only. The reasoned stance is to determine the relevance
of any specific evolutionary claim by examining it in context. Where the
interest is with natural selection mechanisms specifically, it is important
to recognise that the PVRS model (i.e. the PVRS model with S and V conditions significantly independent) is not the biological natural selection
model *per se*, but an abstract conception of which the biological model is
a token. However, the manner of its *a posteriori* usefulness in the biological realm (i.e. the fashion of its success as a biological token) can, given
what we know of the model and of the nature of the social domain, be
suggestive of leads to be followed and investigated, but never imposed,
in the social realm.

Two contentions are central to my argument. The more specific one
is that borrowing from evolutionary biology, or indeed from anywhere,
needs to be carried through informed by the perspective on the transformational model of social activity. The more general contention (of which
the former is a special case) is that, in borrowing from other disciplines,
economists can benefit from a commitment continually to shaping and
reshaping theories or models in the light of insights obtained (and continually updated) concerning the *nature* of social reality. Indeed, I conjecture
that problems of the sort that sometimes plague the discussion in question
will mostly be seen quickly to dissolve once an ontological turn is effected
in economics, with a greater take-up of the realist social theorising.

Notes

1 This chapter first appeared as chapter 5 in Lawson, T, 2003, *Reorienting
  Economics*, Routledge.
2 See Hodgson (1995: xv).
3 One recent exception is Vromen (2001). However, Vromen's emphasis is less
  with the ontological conditions of an evolutionary economics than with the

ontological presuppositions of the contributions of Nelson and Winters (1982) and of 'evolutionary game theory'. A further contribution I came across just as this was going to press is that by Carsten Herrmann-Pillath (2001). This is closer in orientation to the position defended here and in many ways complements it. Clearly there is a shared recognition of the need to bring ontology more explicitly into evolutionary thinking, a recognition of the openness of the world and its structured nature. Our emphases are different, however, and we do not cover the same ground. Herrmann-Pillath focuses very little on social process, being more concerned to stress that the mind has emerged from biological evolution and must be included in the acknowledged subject-matter of economics (and to demonstrate the superiority of realism over instrumentalism). Our approaches are different, too, in that Herrmann-Pillath writes as if the possibility of economics as an evolutionary economics is a foregone conclusion. And we differ most, perhaps, when Herrmann-Pillath interprets the philosophical discipline of ontology as a dogmatic one, with acceptance of one ontological 'dogma' over another being little more than a matter of taste.

4 Actually we can identify a string of related errors here. The *abductionist fallacy* is similar to the *epistemic fallacy* already mentioned, the belief that matters of ontology can be reduced to matters of epistemology, that questions about being can be rephrased as questions about knowledge (of being). The *linguistic fallacy*, denoting the error of supposing that questions of being can be reduced to questions of discourse (about being), is a further related category. We might also identify as the *moralistic fallacy* the error of reducing questions about human nature and well-being to questions of best policy and practical action (affecting well-being). This is a fallacy I intend to explore on a future occasion. All are species of the general case which might be termed the *conflationist fallacy*, the error of reducing (or misinterpreting) questions about one type of thing to (or as) questions about something quite different in nature or character.

5 Of course, metaphor like most other categories is a contested concept. Those who reject a realist orientation will no doubt disagree with the interpretation accepted here. But then they will probably take issue with the whole discussion.

6 As is well known evolutionary ideas have moved from economics to biology as much as vice-versa.

7 For early Christians it was a matter of faith that the living world was a replica of one which God originally created; neither extinction nor transformation of species was admitted. This led early investigators to interpret fossils as patterns which coincidentally resembled shellfish and other life forms. Eventually, the organic character of fossils was recognised, however, and by the end of the eighteenth century it was acknowledged that rocks provided a compendious record of previously existing life-forms. However, and much in the way that modern-day economists use their conceptions of 'exogenous shocks to the system' to explain what does not easily fit with their models, scientists of this time, wishing to avoid the blasphemous conclusion of continuous change, fell back on theories of their own exogenous shocks; in particular they invoked theories of periodic floods and other catastrophes. After each one God saw fit to replenish the world with a novel stock of living things. A difficulty for this type of explanation came with the eventual realisation that fossil levels revealed not only differences but advances in life-forms. The lowest (and oldest) strata of rocks recorded invertebrates, fish appeared on later ones, then reptiles and birds, later mammals including, finally, humans. Progressionists and other creationists argued that this merely meant that God had staggered the manner in which God's creations were introduced; there was no question

of transformation or descent involved in these changes. But in so doing the various contributors were by now acknowledging that the phenomena to be explained had changed.

A variety of positions designed to preserve the traditional view were developed. But by the end of the eighteenth century, science at large was taking paths which would foster a more transformative perspective in biology. Most significantly, the earth lost its place at the centre of the universe; the closed world opened to an infinite universe as the cosmos came to be regarded as a developing, if law governed, process. At the same time biologists recognised that many life-forms contained remnants of once, but no longer, functional organs (e.g., wings that no longer facilitated flight), undermining directly the arguments from design.

In due course, as further insights into the nature of life on earth were achieved, the notion of it as essentially unchanging became replaced by the recognition that it, like everything else, is in a state of relatively continuous transformation. It was in order to account for the mechanisms of transformation that theories of evolution were formulated.

8 It is my impression that economists and others concerned with drawing on biology give far too little to the nature of the biological processes themselves (as well as to social ones). Rather, arguments over models are reported as if debates can be resolved at this level independently of considering the nature of real world processes. In other words, it is frequently the case in the philosophy of biology (and, or including, psychology) that the epistemic fallacy is evident: questions of being are here, as elsewhere, too often treated as though reducible to questions about the knowledge or modelling of being.

9 The finches on Daphne Major were studied by Peter Boag and Peter and Rosemary Grant (see, e.g., Boag and Grant, 1981) and their findings are well summarised in Weiner (1994):

> In the Grants' first four years on this island, they never saw the struggle for existence get ... [very] intense. Those were the good years for Darwin's finches. By the end of the Grants' first season, for instance, there were about fifteen hundred *fortis* on Daphne Major. Nine out of ten of those *fortis* were still alive in December, just before the next rains came. There were also about three hundred cactus finches on the island that first April, and nineteen out of twenty of them survived the dry season and made it through to December.
>
> Their fourth year, in 1976, was especially wet and green. There were great bouts of rain in January and February, and light showers in April and May, a total of 137 millimetres of rain, which is a good year for Darwin's finches.
>
> (Weiner, 1994: 71)

10 The biologists involved in the study graded the seeds on the island according to the ease with which they could be opened. This resulted in a 'struggle index' with lowest numbers denoting the seeds that are easiest to eat. In June of 1976 there had been more than 10 grams of seeds in an average square metre of lava (the islands being volcanic). By June of 1977

> there were only 6 grams of seeds per square meter ... By December there would be only 3 grams.
>
> As they always do in dry times, the birds went on looking for the easiest seeds. But now they were sharing the last of the last of the pistachio nuts. They were down to the bottom of the bowl. In June of the previous year, four out of five seeds that a finch picked up were easy, scoring less than 1 on the Struggle Index. But as the small, soft, easy seeds of *Heliotropium* and other plants disappeared, the rating climbed and climbed, peaking above 6.

The birds were forced to struggle with the big tough seeds of the *Palo Santo*, and the cactus, and *Tribulus*, symbol of the struggle for existence, a seed sheathed in swords.

(Weiner, 1994: 74)

11 All through the drought the total mass of seeds on the island went down, down, down. The average size and hardness of the remaining seeds went up, up. The total number of finches on the island fell with the food supply: 1,400 in March 1976, 1,300 in January 1977, fewer than 300 in December.

Next they take the finches species by species. At the start of 1977 there were about 1,200 *Fortis* on Daphne. By the end of the year there were 180, a loss of 85 per cent.

At the start of the year there were exactly 280 cactus finches on the island. By the end of it there were 110, a loss of 60 per cent.

Of the smallest ground finches, *fuliginosa*, there were a dozen on the island at the start of 1977, and only one of them survived the year.

(Weiner, 1994: 77)

12 Weiner (1994) describes, almost with excited impatience, the process the scientists Peter Grant and Peter Boag go through in studying the data of the event of 1997. First these scientists discuss the deaths of many finches and other details.

At last … they look at the beaks of the survivors … Among *fortis*, they already knew that the biggest birds with the deepest beaks had the best equipment for big tough seeds like *Tribulus*; and when they totted up the statistics, they saw that during the draught, when big tough seeds were all a bird could find, these big-bodied, big-beaked birds had come through the best. The surviving *fortis* were an average 5 to 6 per cent larger than the dead. The average *fortis* beak before the draught was 10.68 millimetres long and 9.42 deep. The average beak of the *fortis* that survived the drought was 11.07 millimetres long and 9.96 deep. Variations too small to see with the naked eye had helped make the difference between life and death. The mills of God grind exceedingly small.

Not only had they seen natural selection in action. It was the most intense episode of natural selection ever documented in nature.

(Weiner, 1994: 78)

13 Now it became of great significance that variations of body and beak are passed on from one generation to the next with fidelity. As a result, the males' unequal luck in love helped perpetuate the effects of the drought. The male and female *fortis* that survived in 1978 were already significantly bigger birds than the average *fortis* had been before the drought. Of this group the males that became fathers were bigger than the rest. And the young birds that hatched and grew up that year turned out to be big too, and their beaks were deep. The average *fortis* beak of the new generation was 4 or 5 per cent deeper than the beak of their ancestors before the drought.

In the drought of 1977 the Finch Unit had seen natural selection in action. Now in its aftermath they saw evolution in action, in the dimensions of the birds beak's and in other dimensions too.

After that, the watchers on Daphne Major had to keep watching. They had to keep coming back. Not only is Darwin's process in action among Darwin's finches, not only can natural selection lead to evolution among their flocks, but it leads there much more swiftly than Darwin supposed possible.

(Weiner, 1994: 81)

14 This difference in beak sizes may not seem especially significant. And one can easily imagine how different unusual spells of climatic conditions can so

change the environment as to (re)select in favour of smaller-beaked finches. Indeed, such occurrences are also documented amongst those who have studied Darwin's Finches. Other evolutionary changes are certainly more enduring. No doubt many of us were brought up hearing natural selection explanations of the giraffe's seemingly enduring long neck. According to the standard account, there was once a time when giraffes had necks far shorter than those observed on giraffes today. Let us suppose so. The hypothesis, often recounted, is that something eventually happened whereby a long-necked giraffe appeared. That something, by most accounts (so let's accept this account here), consisted in a mutation at the level of the individual's genes. Such a long-necked giraffe was able to eat from the higher branches of trees out of reach to others and so thrived. So did the offspring who also had longer necks, in virtue of gene reproduction. Indeed, long-necked giraffes not only were able to cope better than others in general, they were able to survive in conditions that others could not: when available food was concentrated on the higher branches of trees. Gradually the advantage bestowed on long-necked giraffes led to their being the dominant group in the population of giraffes, and eventually indeed being the only group.

I do not know if there is evidence to support such an explanation. But whether or not there is, the *nature* of the process producing an evolution in the beak of the finch is much the same, if on a smaller scale, albeit with a seemingly less stable result. Indeed, it is surely a fundamental insight, one stressed by Darwin himself, that variations do not need to be large to make a difference. Small variations in some aspect of an organism can mean the difference between life and death.

15 Of course, because in biology all organisms have evolved, they contain features of their evolutionary, and typically highly path-dependent, past. In biology, as in all else, for an understanding, history matters.

16 I am not wishing to suggest that Darwin himself accepted this strict case.

17 The Lamarckian model is named after Jean Bapiste de Monet, the Chevalier de Lamarck (1744–1829). However, 'Lamarck' was far from unique in holding to the doctrine (admitting the possibility of the inheritance of acquired characteristics); nor was he its original formulator. Lamarck's acceptance of the doctrine is though clear when he writes:

> All the acquisitions or losses wrought by nature on individuals, through the influence of the environment in which their race has been placed, and hence through the influence of the predominant use or permanent disuse of any organ; all these are preserved by reproduction to the new individuals which arise, provided that the acquired modifications are common to both sexes, or at least to the individuals which produce the young.
>
> (Lamarck, 1984 [1809]: 113)

For further discussions see for example Burkhardt (1977, 1984) or Hodgson (1993, 2001).

18 Of course, it is possible that where traits *can* be developed as a response to environmental conditions, and these can be acquired only by some subset that has the capacity to develop them, and these traits are helpful to 'survival', it will appear as though we have a feed backwards mechanism when really we do not. That is, it will seem that the environment is determining genetic variation. For example, suppose a subset of finches developed a flying manoeuvre that is very helpful in avoiding predators or obtaining a type of food, or whatever. If only a subset of finches has the capacity to develop this technique (a result of genetic mutation), the environment will favour those that have this capacity *and* come to develop it. Thus it will seem that some finches are developing a

trait in the environment (which they are) and passing it on through inheritance (which they are not). Rather it is the capacity to develop the trait which is passed on through inheritance, and this capacity was (by my construction) first generated via genetic mutation, not environmental selection. The point is that such examples can give the appearance of not invoking a natural selection mechanism when ultimately they may do.

19 Of course, this example merely illustrates a selective tendency in play in many aspects of perhaps most societies (even in those, like France, where linguistic imperialism is fiercely resisted).

20 Let me, however, briefly elaborate a little further. Several characteristics of the mathematising project are evident. Its development is cumulative. Incremental changes in mathematical forms, when coupled with the selective effects of environmental pressures, have given rise to complex, multi-functional, economic theories, practices, projects and institutions. Further mathematical forms have been adaptive without being in any obvious way optimal. They reflect an internal dynamic of change which is shaped by historical conditions rather than predestined convergence on a single, uniquely efficient form of evolutionary optimum. One needs only think of how early empirical-statistical work evolved into the 'probability approach' or econometrics, which in turn adapted in form with the widespread introduction of computers to academic institutions; and later how, with availability of cheap high-powered computers available to all, computer simulation methodology rose to dominance. Further, evolution of basic mathematical concepts and techniques has operated, and continues to do so, through a process somewhat analogous to inheritance in the biological sphere, which involves vertical transmission (i.e. replication over time) of stored information. More specifically, mathematical concepts and techniques store coded information about theoretical adaptations in a way which parallels the form and function of the genetic code. Replication or inheritance occurs through the replication of basic methods and concepts over time. As a study of the history of mathematical economics reveals, although the content of substantive theorising often shifts considerably from one period to another, underpinning the more substantive contributions there is a significant degree of conceptual continuity. These replicated methods and concepts are put to use by econometricians and theorists when new ideas emerge.

In short, mathematical economics might be thought of as a particular mechanism of cultural transmission which works by coding information into conceptual form, often reproduced in text books, research papers and lectures, etc., thereby assisting its inter-temporal dissemination. Mathematical economics discourse currently appears to possess the degree of autonomy and self-reference sufficient to provide it with the capacity for self-replication, while at the same time it is linked to wider academic and other processes through co-evolution.

21 I note that according to the *Oxford English Dictionary* a meme just is 'An element of culture that may be considered passed on by non-genetic means, esp. imitation'.

22 It is sometimes said that, if memes do exist, they cannot be true replicators because, unlike genes, they replicate only as a consequence of some other agent's activity. Now first I do not think that if such differences do exist they matter. Rather the claim seems to reveal a misunderstanding of the nature of metaphor and analogy. The relevant issue is to identify a process whereby order can come about in the absence of design. But I think it is in any case incorrect to view genes as somehow self-sufficient in replication. There is no self-replicating molecule in biology. For its replication DNA relies on dozens of protein enzymes, which in their turn require (for their correct synthesis) many other factors (such as coded information embedded in the combinatorial

permutations of the four nucleotide bases of DNA – see, e.g., Stephen Rose, 2001; Dover, 2001).

23 For some memeticists, at least, the meme is to be found only in the brain, though they are (mostly) not generated from within the brain but acquired from others. On this view units of culture or some such replicator mutate inside human minds.

24 I do not refer here to all contributions to memetics. But my reading of many resonates with the basics of the following assessment, by Dover (2001), of the writings of Dawkins in particular:

> Dawkins can often be seen to face both ways (the selfish gene: now we see it, now we don't). Dawkins' hard line is that he has opened our eyes to a dramatic new way of thinking (what he terms a 'transfiguration') about the genetic motor of natural selection; his soft line is that he is saying nothing new of major importance, for, yes, deep down, he recognises that it is the phenotype which is the prime mover, as Darwin rightly conceived. This ability to look both ways at once was likened by Dawkins himself to the visual illustration of the Necker Cube presenting two simultaneous orienta-tions of a 3-D cube from a 2-D paper image. We should not be taken in by this edgy ambivalence; the perceived thrust of Dawkins's writing is about only one thing: everything of functional importance and complexity is an adaptation fashioned by natural selection working for the good of selfish replicators. The caveats, the qualifications, the 'ifs' and 'buts', are not part of the grand illusion.
>
> (Dover, 2001: 55–6)

25 Its truth is presumably that being social creatures we often assimilate the views and values of those around us. But this does not necessitate cultural determinism.

26 For example there is a demand that because the category of meme is created to sound like gene that the two are more closely related than they are, that a meme is a gene in more than a metaphorical way. Susan Blackmore is keen to avoid this:

> Gould seems to think that because memes and genes are related by analogy or metaphor we would somehow be doing a disservice to biological evolu-tion by making the comparison. Again he has missed the point that both are replicators but they need not work in the same way.
>
> (Blackmore, 1999a: 18)

Whether or not Gould is correctly portrayed here, I think the worry which Blackmore raises is more a reason for avoiding the term meme altogether. For it immediately invites greater comparison of the meme with the gene that rela-tions of analogy or metaphor warrant. If the term social replicator is instead used, it is then an open question whether the latter share with genes com-monalities over and above those that constitute them as replicators. Relatedly, it seems to me that other commentators too (especially those sympathetic to memetics but not [yet] prepared to acknowledge that memes exist) want to tie the meme and gene too closely and (without reflecting on the nature of metaphorical relations) set seemingly arbitrary requirements on memes to qualify as appropriate gene analogues (see, e.g., Sperber, 2000; Aunger, 2000). Further, Hull's (2000) observation that Blackmore's conception of a meme (her restriction of the subject-matter of memetics to 'information learned through imitation') serves to restrict this evolutionary theory to a single species, namely humans, is not a criticism at all.

27 I am aware that Universal Darwinism is defined as a project concerned with the possibility that Darwinian principles have wide application (with auxiliary

considerations specific to each domain). But if this is the stance, what a misleading label for it.

28 Worries about memetics which are in some ways similar to those discussed here are also expressed by Mary Midgley (2001).

References

Aunger, Robert (ed.) (2000) *Darwinizing Culture: The Status of Memetics as a Science*, Oxford: Oxford University Press.

Blackmore, Susan (1999a) *The Meme Machine*, Oxford: Oxford University Press.

Blackmore, Susan (1999b) 'Meme, Myself and I', *New Scientist*, March, 40–4.

Blackmore, Susan (1999c) 'The Forget-Meme-Not Theory', *Times Higher Educational Supplement*, February.

Blackmore, Susan (2000a) 'Can Memes Get off the Leash?', in Robert Aunger (ed.) (2000).

Blackmore, Susan (2000b) 'The Power of Memes', in *Scientific American*, Vol 283, No 4, 52–61.

Boag, Peter T. and Peter R. Grant (1981) 'Intense Natural Selection in a Population of Darwin's Finches (*Geospizinae*) in the Galápagos', *Science*, Vol 214, 82–5.

Boyd, Richard (1993) 'Metaphor and Theory Change: What is "Metaphor" a Metaphor For?', in A. Ortony (ed.) *Metaphor and Thought*, 2nd edition (1st edition, 1979), Cambridge: Cambridge University Press.

Brodie, Richard (1996) *Virus of the Mind: The New Science of the Meme*, Seattle: Integral Press.

Burkhardt, Richard W. Jr (1977) *The Spirit of the System: Lamarck and Evolutionary Biology*, Cambridge, MA: Harvard University Press.

Burkhardt, Richard W. Jr (1984) 'The Zoological Philosophy of J. B. Lamarck', in J. B. de Lamarck (1984 [1809]) *Zoological Philosophy: An Exposition with Regard to the Natural History of Animals*, translated by Elliot from the first (French) edition of 1809, Chicago: Chicago University Press.

Darwin, Charles (1872) *On the Origin of Species by Means of Natural Selection, or Preservation of Favoured Races in the Struggle for Life*, 6th edn. with additions and corrections, London: John Murray.

Dawkins, Richard (1976) *The Selfish Gene*, Oxford: Oxford University Press.

Dawkins, Richard (1978) 'Replicator Selection and the Extended Phenotype', *Zeitschrift für Tierpsychologie*, Vol 47, 61–76.

Dawkins, Richard (1986) *The Blind Watchmaker*, New York: W.W. Norton.

Dawkins, Richard (1993) 'Viruses of the Mind', in B. Dahbohm (ed.) *Dennett and his Critics: Demystifying Mind*, Oxford: Blackwell.

Dennett, Daniel (1995) *Darwin's Dangerous Idea*, London: Penguin.

Dopfer, Kurt (ed.) (2001) *Evolutionary Economics: Programme and Scope*, Boston, Dordrecht and London: Kluwer Academic Publishers.

Dover, Gabriel (2001) 'Anti-Dawkins', in Hilary Rose and Stephen Rose (eds) *Alas Poor Darwin: Arguments against Evolutionary Psychology*, London: Vintage.

Dugger, William M. and Howard J. Sherman (2000) *Reclaiming Evolution: A Dialogue between Marxism and Institutionalism on Social Change*, London and New York: Routledge.

Herrmann-Pillath, Carsten (2001) 'On the Ontological Foundations of Evolutionary Economics', in Kurt Dopfer (ed.) (2001).

Hodgson, Geoffrey M. (1993) *Economics and Evolution: Bringing Life Back into Economics*, Cambridge, UK, and Ann Arbor, MI: Polity Press and University of Michigan Press.

Hodgson, Geoffrey M. (ed.) (1995) *Economics and Biology*, The International Library of Critical Writings in Economics 50, Cheltenham: Edward Elgar.

Hodgson, Geoffrey M. (1997) 'Economics and Evolution and the Evolution of Economics', in J. Reijnders (ed.) *Economics and Evolution*, Cheltenham: Edward Elgar.

Hodgson, Geoffrey M. (1998) 'The Foundations of Evolutionary Economics: 1890–1973', in *International Library of Critical Writings in Economics*, Cheltenham: Edward Elgar.

Hodgson, Geoffrey M. (1999) *Evolution and Institutions: On Evolutionary Economics and the Evolution of Economics*, Cheltenham: Edward Elgar.

Hodgson, Geoffrey M. (2001) 'Is Social Evolution Lamarckian or Darwinian?', in John Laurent and John Nightingale (eds) *Darwinism and Evolutionary Economics*, Cheltenham: Edward Elgar.

Hull, David (1981) 'Units of Evolution: A Metaphysical Essay', in U. J. Jensen and Rom Harré (eds) *The Philosophy of Evolution*, Brighton: Harvester Press.

Hull, David (2000) 'Taking Memetics Seriously: Memetics Will Be What We Make It', in Robert Aunger (ed.) (2000).

Lamarck, John Baptiste de (1984 [1809]) *Zoological Philosophy: An Exposition with Regard to the Natural History of Animals*, translated by Elliot from the first (French) edition of 1809, Chicago: Chicago University Press.

Laurent, John and John Nightingale (eds) (2001) *Darwinism and Evolutionary Economics*, Cheltenham: Edward Elgar.

Lawson, Tony (1997) *Economics and Reality*, London: Routledge.

Lawson, Tony (2003) *Reorienting Economics,* London: Routledge.

Lewis, Paul (1996) 'Metaphor and Critical Realism', *Review of Social Economy*, Vol 54, No 4, 487–506. Reprinted in Stephen Fleetwood (ed.) (1999) *Critical Realism in Economics: Development and Debate*, London: Routledge.

Lewis, Paul (2000) 'Does Metaphor Have a Place in a Realist Methodology of Economics?', mimeo, Cambridge.

Loasby, Brian J. (1999) *Knowledge, Institutions and Evolution in Economics*, London: Routledge.

Louçã, Francisco and Mark Perlman (eds) (2000) *Is Economics an Evolutionary Science? The Legacy of Thorstein Veblen*, Cheltenham: Edward Elgar.

Magnusson, Lars and Jan Ottosson (eds) (1997) *Evolutionary Economics and Path Dependence*, Cheltenham: Edward Elgar.

Marshall, Alfred (1961) *The Principles of Economics*, 9th (variorum) edition, London: Macmillan.

Midgley, Mary (2001) 'Why Memes?', in Hilary Rose and Steven Rose (eds) (2001).

Nelson, Richard and Sidney Winter (1982) *An Evolutionary Theory of Economic Change*, Cambridge, MA: Harvard University Press.

Nicita, Antonio and Ugo Pagano (eds) (2001) *The Evolution of Economic Diversity*, London and New York: Routledge.

Penrose, Edith (1952) 'Biological Analogies in the Theory of the Firm', *American Economic Review*, Vol 42, No 5, December, 804–19.

Potts, Jason (2000) *The New Evolutionary Microeconomics: Complexity, Competence and Adaptive Behaviour*, Cheltenham: Edward Elgar.

Reijnders, Jan (ed.) (1997) *Economics and Evolution*, Cheltenham: Edward Elgar.

Rose, Stephen (2001) 'Escaping Evolutionary Psychology', in Hilary Rose and Stephen Rose (eds) *Alas Poor Darwin: Arguments against Evolutionary Psychology*, London: Vintage.

Rosenberg, Alexander (1994) 'Does Evolutionary Theory Give Comfort or Inspiration to Economics?', in P. Mirowski (ed.) *Natural Images in Economic Thought: Markets Read in Tooth and Claw*, Cambridge: Cambridge University Press.

Schumpeter, Joseph A. (1954) *History of Economic Analysis*, New York: Oxford University Press.

Soskice, Janet (1985) *Metaphor and Religious Language*, Oxford: Clarendon Press.

Soskice, Janet and Rom Harré (1982) 'Metaphor in Science', in D. S. Miall (ed.) *Metaphor: Problems and Perspectives*, Brighton: Harvester.

Sperber, Dan (2000) 'Why Memes Won't Do', in Robert Aunger (ed.) (2000).

Vromen, Jack (2001) 'Ontological Commitments of Evolutionary Economics', in Uskali Mäki (ed.) (2001).

Weiner, Jonathan (1994) *The Beak of the Finch: A Story of Evolution in Our Time*, London: Jonathan Cape.

Witt, Ulrich (2001) 'Evolutionary Economics', in Kurt Dopfer (ed.) (2001).

7 Structure, agency and causality in post-revival Austrian economics: tensions and resolutions[1]

Paul Lewis

1. Introduction

One of the most significant recent developments in the methodology of economics has been the increasing attention devoted to the ontological commitments of economic theories, that is, to what those theories presuppose about the nature of socio-economic reality. Whereas methodological debate in economics in the 1970s and 1980s focused on the epistemological issues associated with the construction and evaluation of theoretical claims, the 1990s witnessed an upsurge in interest in examining the assumptions that economists make about the constituents of the socio-economic world. Advocates of this 'ontological turn' in economic methodology argue that it is impossible to engage in any sort of ordered thinking about the socio-economic world without making a commitment (if only implicitly) to some social ontology, because any attempt to conceptualise socio-economic phenomena of interest inevitably involves the adoption (if only implicitly) of some picture of the nature of social being.[2]

In the vanguard of this 'ontological turn' is an approach known as critical realism. This approach, whose most prominent exponent in economics is Tony Lawson (1997, 2003), is prescriptive in orientation, being predicated on the claim that research into socio-economic life is most likely to bear fruit if it uses tools which are tailored to suit the nature of the socio-economic material under investigation. To this end, critical realists deploy philosophical arguments in order to develop an abstract account of the nature of the socio-economic world, which is subsequently used to characterise the methods appropriate for studying socio-economic life.

Supporters of critical realism maintain that they share a good deal in common with various heterodox schools of thought, stemming from the fact that heterodox economists have frequently invoked ontological arguments in a way that seems quite compatible with critical realism. A critical realist reading of heterodox economics suggests that many Austrian, Evolutionary, Feminist, Old Institutionalist, Intersubjectivist, Marxist, Post-Keynesian and Social economists have emphasised the importance of adopting a methodology that is tailored to suit the nature of the socio-economic material under investigation, pitching their criticisms of orthodox economics and the case for their own preferred methods of economic analysis on ontological grounds (Lawson, 1997, pp. xiii–xiv, xvii; Fleetwood, 1999a).

Proponents of critical realism argue that it provides philosophical resources that can help heterodox economists to make explicit, clarify and systematise their insights into the nature of socio-economic being and its implications for appropriate methodology for economics. The sustained, explicit reflection about ontological issues facilitated by critical realism, its advocates contend, is useful in a number of ways: it allows intuitions to be more fully articulated and developed; it helps to reveal and resolve internal inconsistencies in theoretical positions and arguments; it facilitates a greater sensitivity to the trade-offs involved in adopting one analytical framework in preference to another; and it enables researchers to identify more accurately the differences between competing approaches, thereby promoting a more informed, and therefore hopefully respectful and productive, dialogue between their proponents.

The current paper aims to illustrate the benefits that accrue from the sort of sustained, explicit reflection about ontological issues facilitated by critical realism. It does so by examining the work of radical subjectivist Austrian economists as it has developed since the post-1974 revival in the fortunes of the Austrian school, focusing in particular on their account of the generation of socio-economic order in decentralised market economies (Section 2).[3] Section 3 argues that ambiguities and tensions can be discerned in the radical subjectivist account, centring in particular upon the latter's account of the causal forces at work in the market process. The conceptual resources required to resolve those tensions and ambiguities, it is argued, are to be found in critical realism (Section 4). The final section of the paper draws out some of the broader implications of the suggested resolution for radical subjectivist Austrian economics (Section V).

2. Radical subjectivism and the role of tradition in the generation of socio-economic order

The defining characteristic of the Austrian school of economics is its commitment to the principle of subjectivism, that is, the idea that the driving force of socio-economic life lies not in objective states of affairs *per se* but in what they mean to people. 'Economics is not about things and tangible material objects,' Mises (1949, p. 92) writes. '[I]t is about men, their meanings and actions.'

However, the Austrian school's understanding of subjectivism has been far from static (Lachmann, 1990b, pp. 243–246). The principle of subjectivism has its origins in the marginal revolution in the 1870s as a 'subjectivism of wants', the idea behind which is that different people have different tastes and so attribute different values to the same object. The second stage of subjectivism, which has its origins in the work of Ludwig Mises, extends the principle of subjectivism to encompass the fact that people's actions are driven by their subjective interpretations of their circumstances and so are not rigidly determined by the latter (O'Driscoll and Rizzo, 1996, pp. 1–2). This second stage of subjectivism suggests that because the external circumstances which influence the outcome of any one individual's conduct include the creative and so often unpredictable behaviour of their fellow men, people must act in the face of (radical) uncertainty in the sense that they do not have even a probabilistic knowledge of the best means of achieving their desired ends (Mises, 1949, pp. 105–118). This 'subjectivism of means and ends', as Ludwig Lachmann (1990b, p. 246) has christened it, suggests that faced with such uncertainty people may pursue similar ends in dissimilar ways, acting on the basis of different subjective ideas about the best way to further a particular goal.

More recently, however, Ludwig Lachmann has extended the principle of subjectivism still further by arguing that uncertainty renders problematical not just people's choice of means but also the ends towards which their activity is directed. To see why, note that if uncertainty renders people unaware even of the existence (let alone the likely magnitude) of some of the factors that influence the consequences of their actions, then the question arises of how purposive conduct is possible at all. Lachmann, following Shackle, answers by arguing that people deal with their ignorance of the future, and so manage to act in a purposeful, goal-driven fashion, by using their imagination to envisage desirable future scenarios and then deciding which actions might bring them about:

> Economic choice does not consist in comparing the items in a list, known to be complete, of given fully specified rival and certainly attainable results. It consists in first creating, by conjecture and reasoned imagination on the basis of mere suggestion offered by visible or recorded circumstance, the things on which hope can be fixed. These things, at the time when they are available for choice, are thoughts and even figments.
> (Shackle, 1972, p. 96, quoted in Lachmann, 1990b, p. 246)

As Lachmann (1976) famously put it, '[T]he future is to all of us unknowable, though not unimaginable' (p.230). In other words, for Lachmann (as for Shackle), far from being 'given' unproblematically, the ends which people seek are actually a creative product of their imaginations, implying that subjectivism embraces not just people's choice of means but also the ends they strive to achieve. In a world of radical uncertainty, people must continuously reflect upon their goals, assessing whether in the light of the unforeseen changes in circumstances that accompany the passing of time the ends initially selected are still worth pursuing or whether other objectives (perhaps not formerly envisaged) have now become worthy of attention. In this way, Lachmann advocates the extension of the principle of subjectivism to encompass people's goals and the expectations of the future which inform them, a third, radical stage for which Lachmann coins the phrase 'the subjectivism of active minds' (Lachmann, 1982, pp. 36–39, 45–48; 1990b, p. 246).

While Lachmann regards the extension of the principle of subjectivism to people's goals and expectations as a natural development of the central theme of Austrian economics, many Austrians have argued that Lachmann's radical subjectivism, as it is also known, nihilistically undermines the scope for economic theory to explain how decentralised market economies are able to generate an orderly allocation of resources. To see why, note that economic activity will be coordinated successfully only if people's plans are mutually compatible, which in turn requires they hold similar expectations. The problem with Lachmann's radical subjectivist account of expectations-formation, its critics argue, is that it makes the requisite convergence of expectations look highly improbable, leaving economic theory incapable of explaining how it is possible for decentralised market economies to generate an orderly allocation of resources.

Recent contributors to the Austrian tradition have argued that the key to explaining how the socio-economic order is generated lies in a reappraisal of the account of the relationship between human agency and social structure which informs Austrian economic theory. More specifically, they contend that a satisfactory account of how market economies generate an orderly allocation of resources requires Austrians to eschew the atomistic or under-socialised model of man with which their approach has sometimes been associated in favour of an account which portrays people not as isolated Robinson Crusoes but rather as social beings who are embedded in networks of shared meanings and traditions of interpretation.[4]

To see why this is thought to be the case, observe first of all that contemporary radical subjectivists view the under-socialised model of man as an isolated, atomistic Robinson Crusoe as a legacy of the Cartesian and Enlightenment ideal of the detached observer who can free herself from the biases, prejudices and preconceptions of traditional modes of thought in order to gain a pure, unadulterated understanding of the world (Lavoie, 1991a, p. 482, 1991b, p. 48, 1994a, pp. 57–58; Prychitko, 1994b, pp. 264–271; Horwitz 1995, pp. 261–265; Lavoie and Chamlee-Wright, 2000, pp. 40–45). This Cartesian perspective implies that people attempt to solve the epistemological problem of acquiring knowledge of one another's future conduct (Mises, 1957, p. 311) by interpreting events and forming expectations in ways that are unprejudiced by the social, cultural and historical context in which they are situated. However, as soon as it is acknowledged that every effort to understand the world relies on some theoretical scheme or other (Lavoie, 1990c, pp. 2, 6; Chamlee-Wright, 1997, p. 24; Boettke *et al.*, 2004), then it becomes apparent that the atomistic approach risks descending into a form of solipsism. For by locating the origin of meaning in the unfettered imagination of the sovereign ego, acting in complete isolation from shared interpretive frameworks, the Cartesian approach implies each person's interpretations and expectations are purely private and subjective, and therefore potentially idiosyncratic and arbitrary. And in that case, it is indeed extremely difficult to see how people's expectations can cohere well enough to facilitate a significant degree of coordination of economic activity (Addleson, 1995, pp. 73–74, 88; Boettke *et al.*, 2004).

This line of reasoning suggests that the key to rebutting the charge of nihilism that dogs the subjectivism of active minds lies in recognising that the minds in question, far from being isolated Cartesian egos, are in fact thoroughly social in nature (Lavoie, 1991b, p. 48). Building on the work of Lachmann (1971, 1990a),[5] and drawing also on the philosophical hermeneutics of Paul Ricoeur (1971, 1981) and (in particular) Hans-Georg Gadamer ([1975] 1993), the post-revival radical subjectivists have argued that the key to overturning the charge of nihilism lies in replacing the under-socialised model of man as an isolated Robinson Crusoe with an account which portrays people as social beings whose values, beliefs and conduct are profoundly shaped by the social, cultural and historical context in which they are embedded (Granovetter, 1985). As we shall see below, contemporary radical subjectivists attempt to sustain a 'sophisticated' version of individualism that threads its way between the under-socialised, Cartesian conception of human nature and the opposite, over-socialised extreme according to which people are so completely socialised that their attributes and behaviour are completely determined by their social environment (Boettke, 1989a, pp. 76–77, 1990b, pp. 15–22, 1998a, pp. 58–65; Boettke and Storr, 2002, pp. 162–176; Prychitko, 1989–90, 1994b, p. 268; Vaughn, 1994, pp. 130, 132–133).

We can elaborate on the above by observing that the current generation of radical subjectivists follow Gadamer (1975, pp. 262, 265–277, 304) in conceptualising people as finite or historically situated beings who, in virtue of being born and raised in a culture that pre-exists them, are 'thrown' into a socio-economic world that is not of their own making and which as a result has already been interpreted according to the 'prejudices' – the traditional, historically given shared interpretive frameworks and conceptual schemes – of their predecessors (Boettke, 1989b, p. 195 n. 7; Kibbe, 1994, p. 104; Addleson, 1995, p. 83). It follows that at any given moment in time people face social structures (shared interpretive schemes and meanings) that are 'relics of the … efforts of former generations' (Lachmann, 1971, p. 68) in the sense that they are the product of actions undertaken, not in the present, but in the past. The fact that these social structures pre-exist current agency implies that they are not simply created *ex nihilo* by the latter: 'We constantly operate in a world that, in some fundamental sense, we have not created. We are born into a world of pre-existing social structures and meanings' (Horwitz, 2004, p. 3). The upshot of this, as Shackle ([1972] 1992, p. 122) has observed, is that the structures in question are inherited *involuntaristically* by the current generation: 'We cannot *choose* the present:

it is too late. The present is unique ... and [already] determined', whereas 'choice requires rival possibilities'. And this leads post-revival radical subjectivists to reject 'the ontological prejudice ... that the "parts" [people] are more real than the "whole" [society]' and to conclude as a result that it is desirable to 'reinstate the intersubjective as an irreducible realm' in social and economic theory (Madison, 1990b, pp. 41, 42). For contemporary radical subjectivists, then, pre-existing social structures, inherited ready made from the past, are 'entities with their own identities, not just collections of individuals', and should therefore be understood as constituting an ontologically irreducible realm with 'an existence and a role separate from the people ... who are associated with them' (Addleson, 1995, p. 126).

The fact that people are situated within such a pre-interpreted world has the important consequence that their beliefs and actions are profoundly shaped by the 'horizon of established meanings' (Lachmann, 1990a, p. 139) they inherit from the past. 'As a thinking and acting being', Mises (1949, p. 43) writes, 'man emerges from his pre-human existence already as a social being':

> Inheritance and environment direct a man's actions. They suggest to him both the ends and the means. He lives not simply as man *in abstracto*; he lives as a son of his family, his people, and his age; as a member of a definite social group; as a practitioner of a certain vocation; as a follower of definite religious, metaphysical, philosophical ideas; as a partisan in many feuds and controversies. He does not himself create his ideas and standards of value; he borrows them from other people. His ideology is what his environment enjoins upon him.
> (Mises 1949 p. 46; quoted by Boettke and Storr, 2002, pp. 174–175)

On this view, people's beliefs and actions are thoroughly conditioned by the legacy of the past or, as Gadamer (1975, pp. 276, 300–302) terms it, 'effective history'. Quite contrary to the contention, spawned by Cartesian and Enlightenment thought, that inherited schemes of thought are simply impediments to understanding, post-revival radical subjectivists follow Gadamer (1975, pp. 270–283 and 360–361) in maintaining that the intellectual traditions bequeathed by past generations are indispensable to current thought, for it is only by drawing on the prejudices and preconceptions embedded in tradition that people are able to conceptualise both themselves and the world in general (Lavoie and Chamlee-Wright, 2000, pp. 39–45, 104–127; Horwitz, 2004). Tradition, far from being inimical to reason and purposeful conduct, is on this account a condition of their very possibility. As Madison (1994, p. 46) puts it, '[I]ndividuals are truly empowered to do things – and indeed, can be "individuals" in, as Hayek would say, the "true" sense of the term – only within the context of appropriate *institutional* ("societal") frameworks.'[6]

For post-revival radical subjectivists, it is the fact that people are situated within a common tradition of thought that enables them to understand and successfully to negotiate their world, and thereby to generate an orderly allocation of resources (Bernstein, 1983, pp. 128–130; Ebeling, 1986, p. 47; Lavoie, 1987, pp. 581–582, 585–588, 1990c, pp. 2, 6; Boettke, 1989b, p. 185; Chamlee-Wright, 1997, pp. 24–26). The existence of shared interpretive traditions is of paramount importance because in attempting to divine the significance of price signals, say, people are able to transcend a purely subjective (and therefore potentially arbitrary and idiosyncratic) viewpoint, and so avoid lapsing into solipsism, only by drawing on the traditional conceptual schemes they share with other members of their society. These widely accepted interpretive schemes act as 'points of orientation' (Lachmann, 1971, p. 38) which enable people to reach common or intersubjectively agreed interpretations of the meaning and significance of prices and other relevant phenomena, and thereby to form expectations which are consistent enough to facilitate mutually compatible plans (Ebeling, 1986, pp. 47–52, 1990, pp. 186–190; Boettke, 1990b, pp. 20–21; Kibbe, 1994, p. 104; Boettke *et al.*, 2004).

What this line of reasoning reveals, radical subjectivists argue, is that the charge of nihilism so often levelled against the work of Lachmann and his followers is unwarranted (Lavoie, 1991b, p. 48; Boettke *et al.*, 2004). The apparent inability to explain how decentralised economies generate an orderly disposition of resources, far from being an inevitable consequence of subjectivism of active minds, is in actual fact no more than an artefact of the Cartesian model of man, a 'pseudo-problem' created by a failure to appreciate the true significance of the fact that people are social beings. For as soon as it is admitted that the basis of all knowledge lies not in the pure reason of the isolated (subjective) mind but rather in shared interpretive traditions, then the solipsistic isolation of Robinson Crusoe can be avoided and the convergence of expectations that underpins the successful coordination of people's plans explained (Lavoie, 1994a, p. 57).

While, as we have seen, those post-revival radical subjectivists who draw on Gadamer's writings argue that social structures (understood as sheared meanings and traditions of interpretation) are ontologically irreducible to current human agency, and indeed profoundly shape the latter, they are (as we shall see, acutely) conscious of the need to avoid two dangers: the first is that of reifying social structure by treating it as something which exists completely independently of human agency; the second is that of over-stating the impact of social structure to such an degree that it is thought to determine people's actions, reducing them to the status of mere cultural dupes who lack the capacity creatively to (re)shape their social environment (Boettke, 1998a, pp. 58–61; Boettke and Storr, 2002, pp. 170–175). Gadamer and radical subjectivists avoid the danger of reification by acknowledging that while people are born and raised in a world of *pre-existing* traditions, the latter's *continued* existence depends upon the activities of the *current* generation of people:

Even the most genuine and solid tradition does not persist by nature because of the inertia of what once existed. It needs to be affirmed, embraced, cultivated. It is, essentially, preservation, and it is active in all historical change.

(Gadamer, 1975, p. 281)

On this view, tradition not only informs and shapes people's actions but is itself continuously being remade (reproduced or transformed) by them (Gadamer, 1983, p. 130; Ebeling, 1987, p. 56; Addleson, 1995, p. 94; Boettke, 1998a, p. 59). In addition to acknowledging the importance of human action for the continued existence of social structure, both Gadamer and the radical subjectivists contend that their emphasis on the importance of tradition does not exclude the scope for creative human agency. For while shared conceptual schemes impose limits on people's interpretive activities, they do not circumscribe the latter so severely that people are reduced to the status of puppets whose beliefs and expectations are completely determined by the traditions in which they stand. On the contrary, inherited interpretive frameworks cannot be used just as they stand but must always be modified to fit the concrete circumstances of the current generation. Gadamer (1975, pp. 324–330) argues, is exemplified by the legal process. The law is not an algorithm that can simply be mechanically applied to determine the outcome of a particular case. On the contrary, judges must exercise their discretion in assessing precisely how the law bears upon the peculiarities of each particular case, a process that may on occasions involve them re-interpreting (and thus transforming) established legal precedents. For Gadamer, then, people do not slavishly adhere to tradition, allowing it to dictate their interpretations of events. On the contrary, people actively (and sometimes creatively) appropriate tradition in order to establish its precise relevance for their own particular circumstances. Consequently, the meanings which emerge from this process, far from being dictated either by the interpreter's subjective imagination or by tradition alone, are the joint product of the interplay – the 'fusion of horizons', the 'conversation' or the 'dialogue', to use Gadamer's (1975, pp. 306–307, 362–389) metaphors – between the two. Understanding, Gadamer (1975, p. 293) argues, 'is neither subjective nor objective' but rather involves 'the interplay of the movement of tradition and the movement of the interpreter.' And in a similar vein, modern radical subjectivists maintain that while people's attempts to divine the meaning of prices are informed by traditional interpretive frameworks, the latter do not uniquely determine people's interpretations and expectations. For, like Gadamer, the radical subjectivists acknowledge that people actively appropriate interpretive frameworks, applying them in the light of what Hayek (1945, p. 80) termed their 'knowledge of the particular circumstances of time and place' in order to reach a reasoned assessment of the course of future events (Ebeling, 1986, pp. 50–52, 1990, pp. 188–189; Boettke, 1989b, p. 84 n. 1, 1990b, p. 21).

What this suggests is that radical subjectivists seek a middle way between determinism and voluntarism, according to which historically given traditions channel people's interpretations and therefore their actions narrowly enough to enable them to form reliable expectations of each other's behaviour but so not so rigidly as to exclude the possibility of entrepreneurial creativity: 'Human action is not determinate, but neither is it arbitrary ... In other words, human action is free within an area bounded by constraints' (Lachmann, 1971, p. 37).

Pre-existing traditions both facilitate and constrain current human understanding and socio-economic activity – they are, as Lachmann (1971, p. 141) puts it, both 'instruments of, *and* constraints upon, human action' – while current agency leads in turn either to the reproduction or transformation of those inherited traditions. On this view, social science deals with a pre-interpreted world where shared interpretive traditions and meanings are both an (ontological) condition of the possibility of human action and also a continually reproduced outcome of the latter (Lavoie, 1987, p. 588, 1991b, pp. 48–49, 1994a, p. 58; Boettke, 1998a, pp. 59, 62; Boettke and Storr, 2002, p. 171).[7]

The vantage point provided by post-revival radical subjectivism suggests, then, that socio-economic life is the result of a 'mutually dependent process in which both the individual and his social context are informing and informed by each other' (Kibbe, 1994, p. 104):

> To ask: 'Which is prior, the individual or society?' may be to ask a misleading question ... A properly dialectical approach might be fruitful ... The question, 'Which is prior and which is to be explained in terms of the other, the individual or society?' is an epistemological-foundationalist question which we, in a post-modernist age, would perhaps be best not to raise in the first place.
> (Madison, 1990b, pp. 42–43; also see Lavoie, 1987, p. 585)

The picture of the market sponsored by this approach is one of a process of continuous change, situated within a nexus of economic and non-economic institutions and driven by people's purposive activities. And the aim of the discipline of economics, on this view, is to construct an 'economics of meaning' (Lavoie, 1994b, p. 9, 1997, p. 223; Boettke *et al.*, 2004) which provides causal explanations of how the dialectical interplay or 'tacking back and forth' (Boettke, 1989a, pp. 77–78, 1989b, p. 185, 1998a, p. 62; Horwitz, 2004, pp. 1–5) between people's purposive activities and inherited traditions and institutions causes changes in prices, outputs, methods of production and so forth, and thereby generates an orderly allocation of resources (Lavoie, 1994a, p. 56; Boettke and Prychitko, 1998; Boettke *et al.*, 2004).[8]

3. Radical subjectivism and the causal efficacy of social structure: tensions and ambiguities

The following section examines in detail the ontological commitments of the 'sophisticated' version of individualism advocated by radical subjectivists, that is to say what it presupposes about the nature of socio-economic reality. A number of ambiguities in the positions taken by radical subjectivists on these issues will be identified. These interpretive puzzles, it will be argued, reflect underlying tensions in post-revival radical subjectivism. A subsequent section of the paper will suggest how these tensions might be resolved.[9]

Consider first the ontological issue of (the nature of) the relationship between social structure and human agency that underpins the radical subjectivist account of the market process. As we have seen, the 'sophisticated' version of methodological individualism to which post-revival radical subjectivists subscribe is designed to thread its way between two extreme analyses of the structure–agency relationship. The first is the under-socialised approach, according to which social structure is ontologically reducible to human agency. On this view, social structure is simply the voluntaristic creation of human agency and exerts no causal influence on people's attributes or behaviour. The second, diametrically opposed extreme – the over-socialised approach – suggests that human agency is ontologically reducible to social structure, portraying people as so thoroughly socialised that their characteristics and actions are completely determined by the nexus of social structures in which they are situated. According to such over-socialised accounts, people are so slavishly obedient to the dictates of social norms and customs that their conduct is causally determined by social structure. The middle way between these two reductionist approaches advocated by radical subjectivists conceptualises social structure and human agency as ontologically distinct but mutually dependent features of the socio-economic world.

In the light of the above, one might quite reasonably pose the (ontological) question, is the interplay between social structure and human agency *causal* in nature? That people's actions exert a causal influence on socio-economic events seems clear enough; Austrians of all hues regard the actions of entrepreneurs as the 'driving force' (Kirzner, 2000) – or, to use an Aristotelian term on which we shall elaborate below, the efficient cause (Mäki, 1990a, pp. 158–161, 1992, pp. 41–44) – of the market process. This leaves the question of whether social structures also exert their own, *sui generis* causal influence on socio-economic events. As we shall see, it is not immediately obvious where radical subjectivist Austrians stand on this issue.

Consider first the following passage, where radical subjectivists Peter Boettke and Virgil Storr elaborate on their preferred account of the structure–agency relationship by observing that radical subjectivism 'overcomes the pitfalls of positing either an *over-* or *undersocialised* view of the individual by maintaining that his or her behaviour is *affected* by, *influenced* by, even *directed* by social structures and relations but not *determined* by them' (Boettke and Storr, 2002, p. 166).

David Prychitko comments in a similar vein that:

> [C]ontrary to a general misunderstanding (in part caused by some of the more polemic-like overtones of some Austrian writings), collective, social institutions are not *mere* mental constructs ... Collectives do have real influences; they are not only hypothetical tools. And any Austrian worth his salt would agree with this.
>
> (Prychitko, 1989–90, p. 13)[10]

How should these passages be interpreted? In particular, is the influence that social structures are said to exert on people's actions *causal* in nature?[11]

Evidence in favour of an interpretation which suggests that this question should be answered in the affirmative can be found if we examine in greater detail the radical subjectivist account of how shared interpretive schemes facilitate an orderly allocation of resources. As we have seen, radical subjectivists argue that social structures (understood as traditional interpretive schemes and commonly held meanings) help people to reach similar interpretations both of their circumstances and also of the type of action that counts as an appropriate and/or morally acceptable response to those circumstances. Such structures 'prescribe certain forms of conduct and discourage others' and so 'reduce uncertainty by circumscribing the range of action of different groups of actors', thereby enabling people to anticipate one another's actions successfully enough to act in concert and so achieve an orderly allocation of resources (Lachmann, 1990a, pp. 139, 141; also see Lachmann, 1971, pp. 12–13, 37, 49–50, 60). In this way, social structures play a 'vital role in affecting the expectations, beliefs and behaviour of the various economic actors and in promoting ... social coordination' (Boettke, 1990b, p. 17; see also Boettke *et al.*, 2004; Horwitz, 2004). What this reveals is that radical subjectivists acknowledge that social structures make a difference to people's behaviour. And given that it is just such a capacity to help bring about changes in observable events and states of affairs (such as people's actions) that is the hallmark of causal efficacy (Miller, 1987, p. 61),[12] then the radical subjectivist account appears to acknowledge (if only implicitly) that social structures are causally efficacious. As Birner (1995, p. 305) observes apropos Lachmann's claim that institutions enable socio-economic actors to cope with their ignorance of the future by moulding and channelling people's actions, 'This is the same as saying that the institutions causally influence the behaviour of individuals.'[13]

However, while the interpretation advanced above suggests that the 'sophisticated' version of methodological individualism sponsored by post-revival radical subjectivism implicitly acknowledges the causal efficacy of social structure, other comments made by contemporary radical subjectivists appear to cast doubt on this conclusion. A notable example of the type of statement in question is to be found in Gary Madison's paper, 'How Individualistic is Methodological Individualism?' where he claims that although social structures are more than merely collections of individual people, 'these irreducible "wholes" are nevertheless not things – ontological entities (such as a group mind) capable of exerting efficient causality on individuals' (Madison, 1990a, pp. 49–50). But if social structures are not efficient causes, then what (if any) causal powers do they possess?

The remarks concerning causation and social structure scattered about the radical subjectivist literature do not provide a definitive answer to this question. For example, Lavoie and Chamlee-Wright (2000, p. 14) argue that social structure is 'an *aspect* of virtually any causal factor one might identify, not a separate causal factor of its own', a comment that might reasonably be taken to indicate that they deny that social structures possess their own, *sui generis* causal powers. Yet Lavoie and Chamlee-Wright go on to write that social structure 'make[s] other "causal factors" what they are. It does not stand as a separate cause of changes; it constitutes the meaning of the factors which do cause the changes' (Lavoie and Chamlee-Wright, 2000, p. 23).

This sits a little uncomfortably with Lavoie and Chamlee-Wright's earlier comments, for one might think that something which determines what the other causal factors are would itself count as a 'cause' of socio-economic events. While Lavoie and Chamlee-Wright's remarks are (as we shall see) suggestive, then, their precise significance is far from clear.

Nor does contemporary radical subjectivists' use of quotations from the work of Ludwig Mises to illustrate their arguments help us to find a compelling answer to these interpretive questions. Both Addleson and Boettke illustrate their accounts of the 'sophisticated' version of methodological individualism sponsored by radical subjectivism by quoting Mises's claims that 'social entities have real existence' and that they are 'real factors determining the course of human events' (Mises, 1949, p. 42; quoted by Addleson, 1995, p. 126, and Boettke, 1990b, p. 19, respectively). Yet the support that the citation of these excerpts seems to provide for the claim that radical subjectivists regard social structure as causally efficacious is undermined almost immediately by Boettke's approving citation of Mises's reductionist assertion that 'definite actions of individuals constitute the collective' (Mises, 1949, p. 43; quoted in Boettke, 1990b, p. 20). For if Mises is correct in maintaining that social wholes are constituted by the actions of individuals – if 'a social collective has no existence and no reality outside of the individual members' actions' (Mises, 1949, p. 42) – then little (conceptual) room is left for them to be real, ontologically irreducible entities which can influence the course of socio-economic life.

If one turns to the entry on 'Causation and Genetic Causation in Economic Theory' in the *Elgar Companion to Austrian Economics* in order to clarify the radical subjectivist position, one might be led to conclude that radical subjectivists do indeed deny that social structures exert any causal influence whatsoever on human agency. For the entry states that according to the genetic-causal approach to economic theory (to which, as we have already noted, radical subjectivists claim are committed): 'Market outcomes are causally related to individual actions. Market outcomes are thus causally reducible to the desires and beliefs of agents' (Cowan, 1994, p. 63).

If it is really the case that radical subjectivists regard market outcomes as causally reducible to people's beliefs and desires, then once again there appears to be little conceptual room left for the possibility that social structures are causally potent entities that influence people's actions. Yet one might hesitate before drawing this conclusion, for two main reasons. First, while the author of the entry, Robin Cowan, is an Austrian economist, he is not a fully paid-up member of the radical subjectivist wing of the Austrian school. His views may, therefore, be more representative of other factions within Austrian economics which adopt a more atomistic view of human nature and who therefore are less inclined to acknowledge the causal efficacy of social structure than radical subjectivists. Second, the conclusion that social structures do not possess irreducible causal powers threatens to undermine the radical subjectivist account of the role of institutions in the generation of socio-economic order because, as we have seen, the latter presupposes that social structures are causally efficacious *vis-à-vis* human agency.

Students of radical subjectivist Austrian economics appear, then, to be faced with something of an interpretive puzzle. On the one hand, the radical subjectivist account of socio-economic order seems implicitly to invoke and to rely on the causal efficacy of social structure. On the other hand, however, radical subjectivists at times appear to deny that social structure possess the very causal powers upon which their capacity to coordinate socio-economic activity depends.[14] In fact, as I shall argue below, the radical subjectivist position *can* be interpreted in a way that resolves the aforementioned puzzle, but this is possible only if conceptual repertoire of radical subjectivism is expanded to allow for a more elaborate understanding of (the varieties of) causality in operation in the socio-economic world. And the requisite concepts are to be found, it will be argued below, in recent developments in social theory systematised under the heading of critical realism.

4. Radical subjectivism and the causal efficacy of social structure: resolution

Like radical subjectivists, critical realists argue that the socio-economic world can be divided into the ontologically distinct but interdependent realms of social structure and human agency.[15] According to critical realists, social structure and human agency are recursively related; each is both a necessary condition for, and also a consequence of, the other. Critical realists reject the reductionist extremes of voluntarism and determinism in favour of the view that socio-economic life issues from the interplay of social structure and human agency over historical time. Critical realists agree with Gadamer and the radical subjectivists that people are 'thrown' into a socio-economic world which is populated by pre-existing social structures. They argue that this implies that human agency must be understood as reproducing or transforming those structures rather than (voluntaristically) creating them out of nothing (Archer, 1995, pp. 71–72, 137–141; Lawson, 1997, pp. 168–171). According to this *transformational model of social activity*, as it has been christened, social structure and human agency are mutually dependent; pre-existing social structures both facilitate and constrain human agency, while the continued existence of social structures hinges on people's actions.

Critical realists concur with radical subjectivists that historically given social structures are a prerequisite for intentional human agency because they are the repository of much of the (often tacit) knowledge which informs (albeit imperfectly) people's actions (Fleetwood, 1995, pp. 77–105, 125–134; Lawson, 1997, pp. 30–31, 1998, pp. 357–362).[16] However, and also like radical subjectivists, critical realists recognise that social structures do not just facilitate people's actions; they also constrain them. According to critical realists, the fact that social structures pre-date and therefore are ontologically irreducible to current human agency implies that they enjoy a measure of autonomy from and influence over the latter (Archer, 1995, pp. 137–139). It is possible to see why this is so by means of an example. Consider the predicament of foreign visitors to Great Britain who wish to understand the conversations of British people. The visitors *must* use the English language to do so; anyone who insists on attempting to interpret the speech acts of British people using a different language is highly unlikely to be able to render them intelligible. Merely wishing that things were different, or acting as if they were, will not suffice. This does not necessarily reflect sheer awkwardness on the part of the person's British interlocutors but rather the fact that while the rules of English grammar facilitate successful communication in Great Britain, their (pre-)existence also implies that one must have a command of the English language if one does indeed wish to understand what British people are saying. However sincerely British people wish to make themselves intelligible to a visitor by speaking in that person's native tongue, they are unlikely to be able to do so because, thanks to the activities of the parents and teachers who educated them in the past, they were brought up to speak English rather than the visitor's native language.

What this suggests more generally is that people will be able to interpret, and so understand and anticipate, the behaviour of their fellow men only by drawing on the relevant, pre-existing social rules and interpretive schemes. Moreover, they are likely to have a reasonable chance of successfully implementing their own plans only if their conduct is guided by those same interpretive traditions. Lachmann (1966) captured the element of compulsion which the existence of historically given social structures introduces into socio-economic life, writing in words that critical realists would wholeheartedly endorse, that 'There are certain super-individual schemes of thought, namely institutions, to which ... [people's] plans *must* be oriented. They constitute, we may say, "interpersonal orientation tables"' (p. 62; emphasis added). Social structures – the 'norms [and] institutions ... to which all individual action *has* to be oriented' (Lachmann, 1971, p. 21; emphasis added) – can thus be seen to exercise a degree of coercive power over people's behaviour, in the sense that they militate in favour of particular sorts of action being undertaken and thereby make a difference to people's behaviour. Unlike radical subjectivists, however, critical realists *do* explicitly acknowledge that this capacity to make a difference to people's actions is the hallmark of causal efficacy and as such implies that social structures are causally efficacious (Archer, 1995, pp. 139, 147–148, 176; Lawson, 1997, pp. 31–32, 57–58; Lewis, 2000, pp. 251–252). And critical realists are able to do so, I shall argue, because they possess a more sophisticated portfolio of concepts for articulating their understanding of causality than do radical subjectivists.

Critical realists conceptualise the causal efficacy of social structure in terms of an Aristotelian framework (Bhaskar, 1989, p. 34). The paradigm of the Aristotelian approach is a sculptor. A sculptor produces works of art using the raw materials and tools available to him. The sculptor is the *efficient* cause – the prime mover or driving force – of this artistic activity. Nonetheless, while the material upon which the sculptor works clearly does not initiate activity (it does not sculpt itself of its own accord) and hence does not qualify as an efficient cause, it does affect the final outcome by influencing the sculptor's actions (cf. Koppl, 2002, p. 35). Different types of material lend themselves to different types of sculpture and may as a result induce the sculptor to employ different tools and techniques and also to pursue different goals. Thus, the material makes a difference to the sculptor's actions, thereby exerting a causal influence over the ensuing outcome. And it is in recognition of this that the medium in which the sculptor works is described as a *material* cause of that outcome.

Critical realists regard the behaviour of the sculptor as the exemplar of social action in general. Just as a sculptor fashions a product out of the raw materials and tools available to him, so social actors produce their actions out of pre-existing social structure. Like the medium in which the sculptor works, pre-existing social structure lacks the capacity to initiate activity and to make things happen of its own volition. It is indeed the case that people are the only efficient causes or prime movers in society. Nevertheless, as we have seen, social structures constitute indispensable prerequisites for human agency and *do* affect the course of events in the social world by influencing the course of action that people choose to pursue (Archer, 1995, pp. 195–201, 2000, p. 465; Lawson, 1997, pp. 187–188). And by influencing people's actions, pre-existing social structure makes a difference to and hence exerts a (material) causal influence over social life (Lewis, 2000, pp. 263–265).[17]

Critical realism suggests that one way of explaining and resolving the tensions in the work of post-revival radical subjectivists identified above is to argue that they rely on two notions of causality, only one of which is made explicit. In their explicit discussion of causality, such as those found in Madison (1990a, pp. 49–50) and Cowan (1994), Austrians reduce causal efficacy to the capacity to initiate trains of events, that is to efficient causality. However, the transformational model of social activity makes clear that if 'causality' is understood as the ability to make a difference to the course of social events, then efficient causation does not exhaust all the varieties of causality in the social world.[18] For although people are the only efficient causes in the social world, there are also material causes such as social structure. And it is on something like the notion of material causation that radical subjectivists seem implicitly to be relying in their accounts of how traditional interpretive schemes and shared meanings orient people's actions and thereby facilitate socio-economic order. For example, the claim that social structures are material causes enables us to make sense of Lavoie and Chamlee-Wright's remarks – reported above – concerning the causal efficacy of social structure. The vantage point provided by critical realism suggests that Lavoie and Chamlee-Wright (2000) are correct to state that social structure 'does not stand as a separate cause of changes' (p. 23) if their claim is understood to mean that social structure is not an efficient cause of socio-economic events. But it is nevertheless an 'aspect of' (p. 14) the efficient causes in the sense that social structure is material cause of people's actions, helping to 'make [them] what they are' (p. 23) by conditioning which actions people choose to pursue.

Significantly, the addition of 'material causality' to radical subjectivists' conceptual portfolio would enable them to acknowledge explicitly the causal efficacy of social structure without lapsing into a form of naïve holism that anthropocentrically and erroneously attributes human properties such as intentionality, motivation and efficient causality to social structures and reduces people to the passive slaves of some over-arching structural imperative. This is important because the fear that ascribing causal efficacy to social structure inevitably leads to such untenable forms of naïve holism accounts for much of the reluctance of radical subjectivists to admit that social structures are causally efficacious. For example, Madison's (1990a) denial of the causal efficacy of social structure, reported above, centres on his belief that acknowledging that social wholes are causally efficacious entails postulating 'a group mind' (p. 49) which enjoys 'greater reality' than individual people and which has the (efficient) causal power to engage in purposeful action (pp. 51, 50). Such an approach, Madison (1990a, p. 51) contends, amounts to a form of 'methodological reification' that reduces people to the mere bearers of social forces that are beyond their control (p. 50). Other radical subjectivists display a similar concern to avoid those varieties of structuralism and structural-functionalism which attribute an over-arching purpose or some other human property to social wholes and which reify social structure by failing to relate it back to the actions of individuals.[19]

Critical realism shows how it is possible to ascribe causal efficacy to social structure whilst avoiding the aforementioned errors of naïve holism. The ontological distinction between actors and social structure enables critical realists to argue that the two may possess very different properties (Bhaskar, 1989, p. 35; Fleetwood, 1995, p. 88). Thus, critical realists can without tension or contradiction claim that purposefulness, the ability to interpret and ascribe meaning to events and the capacity to initiate activity characterise people without anthropomorphically attributing such properties to social structure. The theoretical framework provided by critical realism suggests that while social structure possesses its own distinctive property of material causality, it is neither a conscious decision-making entity – a 'supermind in the image of the individual mind', as Hayek (1952, p. 101) put it – nor an efficient cause that subordinates people to the dictates of a (reified) group mind. Moreover, critical realists do not reify social structures by denying their ultimate dependence on human agency. Indeed, far from denying the significance of human action for the continued existence of social structures, critical realists take care to specify precisely whose actions are responsible for the existence of the social structures that are in place at any particular moment in time (Archer, 1995, pp. 66, 72, 141–154). There are two aspects to this. First, critical realists readily acknowledge that *historically given* social structures are the product of human action. However, as we have seen, critical realists wish to emphasize that their activity-dependence is *past tense*; the structures in question are the product of actions undertaken *in the past*, possibly by actors long since dead, not in the present, and as a result are ontologically irreducible to *current* agency (in the *present* tense, so to speak). Second, critical realists also accept that while the historically given social structures extant at a particular moment in time are the result of actions undertaken in the past, their *continued* existence depends upon *current* human agency. Critical realists would endorse Menger's (1883) claim that 'Each generation in every society has as its calling the evaluation and revision of received institutions' (pp. 223–224; quoted in Beaulier and Boettke, 2000, p. 550; also see Mises, 1949, pp. 46–47, quoted in Boettke and Storr, 2002, p. 175). However, while critical realists readily acknowledge the ultimate activity-dependence of social structure, and the potential for structural and institutional transformation it brings, they also eschew voluntaristic accounts which ignore the fact that extant structures condition people's actions and so help to decide whether the inherent potential for change is realised. For, as has been touched upon above, and as I have elaborated at length elsewhere (Lewis, 2000, pp. 258–262, 2004), the human agency on which the reproduction or transformation of existing social structures hinges is itself conditioned in a variety of ways by those selfsame structures: the pattern of incentives which motivate people to seek either to preserve or to transform extant structures, the distribution of the resources required successfully to act on those incentives and the interpretive frameworks in terms of which people conceptualise their circumstances and aspirations, are all embodied in existing social structures, which as a result constitute an ontologically irreducible influence on current behaviour. It is in recognition of the fact that the activity on which the continued existence of social structures hinges is itself dependent upon those structures that critical realists describe structure and agency as being recursively related. And it is to conceptualise the impact of social structure in this regard that critical realists employ the notion of material causality.

5. Conclusion

It has been argued above that the addition of the concept of material causation to radical subjectivists' conceptual portfolio will enable them to do (explicit) justice to their (hitherto implicit) reliance on the notion of the causal efficacy of social structure, and thereby to resolve various tensions and ambiguities in radical subjectivist Austrian economics, whilst avoiding the limitations of naïve holism. This final section of the paper will examine some of the broader implications of the suggested, critical realist resolution of the noted tensions and ambiguities in radical subjectivism. The discussion will centre on the model of explanation to which the suggested resolution gives rise, and more specifically its implications for radical subjectivists' commitment to an explanatory approach that can reasonably be described as methodological individualism.

We have seen that, according to critical realism, people make their own history but not in circumstances of their own choosing. Pre-existing social structures, bequeathed to the current generation of actors by actions undertaken in the past, constitute the setting in which current action takes place and influences (without determining) the latter. And the structures which are the product of current behaviour form the context for the next round of action. On this view, socio-economic events are generated by a complex causal nexus that involves both the efficient causation of actors and the material causation of social structure. Consistent with this, the model of explanation sponsored by critical realism suggests that explaining some socio-economic phenomenon of interest consists in giving an abstract, usually discursive and always fallible account of its causes: socio-economic phenomena of interest are to be explained not monocausally but rather as the result of the causal interplay over (historical) time between (antecedent) social structure and (subsequent) human agency.

More specifically, according to critical realists, the initial stage of an explanation involves the identification of the practices responsible for the phenomenon under investigation, after which it is necessary to uncover the social structures which make those practices possible, along with any unconscious psychological factors which motivate them (Archer, 1995, pp. 15, 71, 165–344; Lawson, 1997, pp. 56–58, 191–271).

Now while the model of explanation sponsored by critical realism shares much common ground with the genetic-causal approach preferred by radical subjectivists – both approaches suggest that explaining some socio-economic phenomena of interest involves giving discursive, fallible accounts of its causes – there is at least one important difference between the two that has potentially significant implications for radical subjectivists. For an approach such as critical realism, which suggests that socio-economic events of interest are best explained in terms of the causal interplay between social structure and human agency, sits very uneasily under the heading of methodological *individualism* and might be more accurately described as methodological *interactionism* (C. Lawson *et al.*, 1996, pp. 144–148; C. Lawson, 1999, p. 56). Hence, if radical subjectivists do indeed accept the critical realist resolution of the tensions and ambiguities noted above, then they would be committing themselves to an approach which, by suggesting that social and institutional factors can quite legitimately be invoked as elements within causal explanations, effectively calls into question their long-standing commitment to methodological individualism (Vaughn, 1997, p. 1258). In this way, the suggested resolution of the tensions in radical subjectivism noted above thus exemplifies Boettke's (1996, p. 33) claim that the incorporation into Austrian economics of recent developments in the philosophy and methodology of the social sciences (such as critical realism) 'will not be benign in terms of the self-understanding of the Austrian social-scientific project'.[20]

In truth, as Samuels (1989, pp. 57, 66) has observed, the commitment to (even a sophisticated form of) methodological individualism found in the explicit methodological pronouncements of radical subjectivists is not always mirrored in their actual research, where radical subjectivists on occasions invoke social and institutional factors as part of their causal explanations. The way in which radical subjectivists implicitly rely on the causal efficacy of social structure in their explanations of how socio-economic order is possible in decentralised market economies is a specific example of this. Similar examples are to be found in the radical subjectivist literature on comparative economic systems and economic development, a recurrent theme in which is that 'institutions matter' (Boettke, 2001, p. 4) and that the comparative performance of different economies is best explained in terms of the relative capacity of the institutions of capitalism to disseminate the information and provide the incentives required for the successful coordination of people's plans and wealth creation. As Boettke and Prychitko (1998, pp. xiii, xix, xxi–xxii) have put it:

Market process theories (of all varieties) ... strive to explore how the institutional environment affects the behaviour of individuals and thus the manner in which they interact with others within the market economy. The focus of a modern ... political economy asks how the institutional environment impacts on individuals by structuring the incentives they face and the flow of information they must process ... [Austrians argue that] the institutional configuration of the private property competitive economy provided both the incentives and the information for individuals to coordinate their plans, whereas socialism – an institutional configuration of collective property and comprehensive planning – would provide neither the incentive nor information required for participants to *learn* how to coordinate their activities ... [What this suggests is that] [w]e cannot just presuppose and thus leave unexamined the institutional environment – it must become a main topic of investigation ... if we want to advance our understanding of how alternative institutional configurations affect the learning of economic participants.[21]

However, if it is indeed true that in their substantive research radical subjectivists rely on social and institutional factors to explain variations in the performance of different economies, say, then they would appear in practice to be deviating so far from what is commonly understood as 'methodological individualism' that, as was noted above, the latter is rendered misleading as a description of their methodological commitments, which once again seem to be more accurately described as a form of methodological *interactionism*. And if it is the case that radical subjectivists in practice adopt a methodology that seems to be rather different from what most people understand by the term 'methodological individualism', then perhaps they might not be too unwilling to ascent to a new description of their approach as methodological interactionism.

Justification for the idea that radical subjectivists should make an explicit commitment to a methodological interactionism, and thereby openly legitimise the presence of social and institutional factors in causal explanations, rests not just on the desirability of ensuring (internal) consistency between their explicit methodological pronouncements and their actual practice, important though that is, but also because doing so bears upon their external relations with other, heterodox schools of thought. Perhaps most notably, radical subjectivists' official commitment to methodological individualism is a major impediment to closer relations with (old) institutionalists (Hodgson, 1986; Clark, 1993; Gloria-Palermo, 1999, pp. 116–160).[22] The reformulation of radical subjectivism proposed in this paper, whereby radical subjectivists explicitly acknowledge the causal efficacy of social structure and adopt an interactionist approach to causal explanation, will remove this stumbling block and thereby promises not only to improve the internal coherence of radical subjectivism but also to facilitate improved relations to other heterodox schools of thought (Lewis, 2002). Given that, as radical subjectivists themselves have noted (Boettke, 1994, pp. 610–611; Boehm *et al.*, 2000, p. 403), the capacity to form strategic alliances with other heterodox schools is likely to prove an important determinant of the future health of Austrian economics, this is potentially an important, beneficial consequence of the incorporation of critical realist insights into radical subjectivism advocated in this paper.

Notes

1 I am grateful to Bruce Caldwell and to participants in seminars at Cambridge University and at the 2002 meeting of the Southern Economic Association for comments on an earlier draft of this paper. I would also like to thank the members of the Austrian Economics Colloquium at New York University, especially Roger Koppl, for helpful conversations about some of the arguments advanced below. Any remaining deficiencies are of course solely my responsibility. First published in *Review of Political Economy*, 2005, Vol 17, No 2, 291–316.

2 The term 'ontology' is used here to refer to the nature of (what exists in) the world, that is, the nature of being (Harré, 1988, p. 100; Butchvarov, 1995, p. 489).

3 For a valuable account of the post-1974 revival of the Austrian school, see Vaughn (1994, pp. 92–111).

4 Prominent contributions to this line of thinking, many of whose authors either are or have been associated with George Mason University, include Addleson (1995), Boettke (1989a, 1989b, 1990b, 1990c, 1998a), Boettke *et al.* (2004), Chamlee-Wright (1997), Ebeling (1986, 1987, 1990), Horwitz (1992, 1994, 1995, 1998, 2002, 2004), Lavoie (1986, 1987, 1990a, 1990b, 1990c, 1991a, 1991b, 1994a, 1994b), Lavoie and Chamlee-Wright (2000), Madison (1989, 1990a, 1990b, 1994, 1998), Prychitko ([1989–90], 1995, 1994a, 1994b) and the essays collected in Lavoie (ed., 1990d) and Prychitko (ed., 1995).

5 The extent to which Lachmann himself succeeded in devising an analysis of socio-economic order that eschews the use of the equilibrium concept whilst simultaneously avoiding nihilism is a contentious issue in contemporary, radical subjectivist Austrian circles. See, for instance, Vaughn (1994, pp. 155–161, 171), Lavoie (1994b, 1997) and Prychitko (1994a, 1997a, 1997b).

6 'The first thing that should be said,' Hayek (1945, p. 6) writes apropos the 'true', sophisticated version of individualism to which contemporary radical subjectivists subscribe, 'is that it is primarily a *theory* of society, an attempt to understand the forces which determine the social life of man … This fact should by itself be sufficient to refute the silliest of the common misunderstandings: the belief that individualism postulates (or bases its arguments on the assumption of) the existence of isolated or self-contained individuals, instead of starting from men whose whole nature and character is determined by their existence in society.' For more on this point, see Boettke (1989a, 1990b), Prychitko (1989–90, 1995), Madison (1990a, 1994), Lavoie (1994a), Fleetwood (1996, p. 743) and Caldwell (2001, pp. 548–551).

7 As Gadamer (1975, p. 293) puts it:

> Tradition is not simply a precondition; rather, we produce it ourselves inasmuch as we understand, participate in the evolution of the tradition and hence determine it ourselves. Thus the circle of understanding … describes an ontological structural element in understanding.

8 This is the so-called genetic-causal approach to economic methodology (Mayer, 1932; Cowan, 1994; Cowan and Rizzo, 1996).

9 The account that follows is intended to adhere to the 'principle of charity in interpretation' advocated by scholars such as Deirdre McCloskey and Ludwig Lachmann, according to whom one should attempt wherever possible to read a text or body of work in a way that imputes coherence to it wherever possible and which yields interpretations that the author(s) would be willing to acknowledge as their own (Lavoie, 1994b, p. 16; Boettke and Sullivan, 1998, p. 163).

10 Similar comments about social structure 'influencing', 'affecting' or exerting 'feedback' effects on people are to be found in Boettke (1990b, pp. 16, 19, 1998a, p. 73), Boettke and Prychitko (1998, pp. xiii, xxii), Boettke and Storr (2002, pp. 175, 181, 187–188 n. 29), Chamlee-Wright (1997, p. 39) and Horwitz (2004, pp. 3, 10).

11 While Boettke (1990b, p. 24) describes modern radical subjectivists as *institutional individualists* in the sense of Agassi (1975), recourse to Agassi's paper sheds little light on the question under investigation here. For while Agassi (1975, p. 154) notes that 'individuals are affected by social conditions, and in turn affect them', he does not address the issue of whether this influence is causal in nature.

12 As Cowan and Rizzo (1996, p. 286) comment, 'If there is no change in a system, then *ipso facto* there can be no causation.' Also see Cowan (1994, pp. 63–64) and O'Driscoll and Rizzo (1996, p. 62). However, and significantly for the argument developed below, the approach to causation adopted here suggests *pace* Cowan (1994, p. 67) that it is not only the episode which triggers an event (for example, the spark which leads to a fire) but also the conditions necessary for the triggering (such as the presence of oxygen) which count as causes (in a sense to be made more precise below) of that event (Miller, 1987, pp. 60–61).

13 Additional support for this line of interpretation is provided by the fact that commentators on Gadamer's writings (upon which, as we have seen, post-revival radical subjectivists rely heavily) have understood his notion of 'effective history' to mean that interpretive traditions exert a (non-deterministic) causal influence over current activity (Wachterhauser, 2002, p. 61).

14 This tension has also been alluded to in passing by Mäki (1990b, p. 302) and Addleson (1995, pp. 126–127).

15 Considerations of space preclude a detailed statement of the reasoning by which critical realists justify their preferred socio-economic ontology. Consequently, the following section will tend simply to state the conclusions reached by critical realists, elaborating only on those aspects of the underlying argument that are particularly important for resolving the tensions in radical subjectivism, and leaving the interested reader to find elsewhere a detailed explanation and justification of the critical realist position. The socio-economic ontology sponsored by critical realism is discussed at length by Archer (1995). Book-length treatments of the project of critical-realism-in-economics can be found in Lawson (1997, 2003). Fleetwood (1995) uses the vantage point provided by critical realism to analyse the evolution of Hayek's work. Shorter accounts that compare and contrast critical realism with Austrian economics include Runde (1993, 2001), Lawson (1994), Fleetwood (1996), C. Lawson (1999) and Lewis (2005).

16 Critical realists would also argue that in addition to serving as points of orientation for people's plans, social structures are repositories of power and other resources, and are also sites of vested interests (Lewis, 2005).

17 Of course, none of this should be taken to imply that social structures act behind people's backs or that people's actions are completely determined by social structures. While the transformational model of social activity suggests

that social structure is causally efficacious, it does not reduce people to the status of mere puppets whose actions are causally determined by social structures. For, as we have seen, critical realists argue that social structures influence the course of socio-economic affairs only by the way they condition people's choice of action, not by acting autonomously (behind people's backs, as it were). Consequently, critical realists can speak of the causal influence that social structures exert on socio-economic events without denying either the mediating role of people's interpretations (and hence the necessity of a hermeneutic moment in social science) or the possibility that people may act in a creative fashion, and therefore without making any deterministic claims about the connection between people's socio-economic circumstances and their conduct. For example, while a foreigner who is in Britain and who wishes to understand and to communicate with other people will have to use the pre-existing rules of English grammar in order to produce intelligible speech acts, those rules do not determine what (s)he says or writes. The possibility also remains open that the person in question may be a taciturn character who chooses not to communicate at all. Likewise, an entrepreneur can ignore traditional interpretive schemes in formulating his or her plans, so long as (s)he is prepared to accept the consequence that those plans are unlikely to reach fruition. But if people wish to communicate, or to have a realistic chance of carrying out their plans, then they do indeed need either to adapt their actions so that they acknowledge the importance of inherited social structures. For more on these issues, see Archer (1995, pp. 195–196), Lawson, (1997, pp. 34–35, 200–201), Layder (1997, pp. 201–202), Porpora (1998, pp. 346–347) and Sayer (2000, pp. 17–18).

18 Cowan and Rizzo's (1996, p. 274 n. 1) comment that '[W]e do not claim that there is only one concept that has legitimate claim to being called "causation"' perhaps indicates that the claim that efficient or genetic causation does not exhaust all the varieties of causation in socio-economic life will not prove to be too uncongenial for Austrians. For more common ground on this issue, compare Cowan and Rizzo (1996, pp. 291–292 n. 31) with Lewis (2000, pp. 263–265).

19 See, for example, Hayek ([1952] 1979, pp. 100–101), Lachmann (1971, pp. 7, 73–74), Prychitko ([1989–90], 1995, p. 10, 1994b, p. 268), Boettke (1989a, p. 76, 1996, p. 35, 1998a, pp. 54–55), Lavoie (1994a, p. 56) and Boettke and Storr (2002, p. 170).

20 Significantly, there is a considerable volume of literature suggesting that Hayek ultimately abandoned methodological individualism and acknowledged the causal-explanatory importance of social structures (Fleetwood, 1995, 1996; Sciabarra, 1995; Caldwell, 2000, 2001).

21 Also see Boettke (1989a, p. 78, 1990b, pp. 15–16, 1998a, pp. 69–74, 2001, pp. 240–241, 253–254), Lavoie and Chamlee-Wright (2000, pp. 53–80), Boettke and Storr (2002, pp. 179, 181) and Boettke and Subrick (2002).

22 This has not gone wholly unnoticed by Austrians. For example, Roger Koppl writes in a recent book that 'I use the term "methodological individualism" with some misgivings. It has come to hurt, not help, communication' (Koppl, 2002, p. 35).

References

Addleson, M. (1995). *Equilibrium Versus Understanding: Towards the Restoration of Economics as Social Theory*. London and New York: Routledge.

Agassi, J. (1975). 'Institutional Individualism.' *British Journal of Sociology*, 26, 144–155.

Archer, M.S. (1995). *Realist Social Theory: The Morphogenetic Approach*. Cambridge: Cambridge University Press.

Archer, M.S. (2000). 'For Structure: Its Reality, Properties and Powers. A Reply to Anthony King.' *The Sociological Review*, 48, 464–472.

Beaulier, S. and P.J. Boettke (2000). 'Of Norms, Rules and Markets: A Comment on Samuels.' *Journal des Economistes et des Etudes Huamaines*, 10, 547–552.

Bernstein, R.J. (1983). *Beyond Objectivism and Relativism*. Oxford: Basil Blackwell.

Bhaskar, R. (1989). *The Possibility of Naturalism: A Philosophical Critique of the Contemporary Human Sciences*. 2nd edition. Hemel Hempstead: Harvester Wheatsheaf.

Birner, J. (1995). 'Interpretation and its Consequences.' *Journal of Economic Methodology*, 2, 304–311.

Boehm, S., I.M. Kirzner, R. Koppl, D. Lavoie, P. Lewin, C. Torr and L. Moss (2000). 'Remembrance and Appreciation Roundtable: Professor Ludwig M. Lachmann (1906–1990).' *American Journal of Economics and Sociology*, 59, 367–417.

Boettke, P.J. (1989a). 'Evolution and Economics: Austrians as Institutionalists.' *Research in the History of Economic Thought and Methodology*, 6, 73–89.

Boettke, P.J. (1989b). 'Austrian Institutionalism: A Reply.' *Research in the History of Economic Thought and Methodology*, 6, 181–202.

Boettke, P.J. (1990a). *The Political Economy of Soviet Socialism: The Formative Years, 1918–1928*. Boston: Kluwer Academic Press.

Boettke, P.J. (1990b). 'Individuals and Institutions.' *Critical Review*, 4, 10–26.

Boettke, P.J. (1990c). 'Interpretative Reasoning and the Study of Social Life.' In D. Prychitko (ed.), *Individuals, Institutions, Interpretations: Hermeneutics Applied to Economics*. Aldershot: Avebury, 1995.

Boettke, P.J. (1994). 'Alternative Paths Forward for Austrian Economics.' In P. Boettke (ed.), *The Elgar Companion to Austrian Economics*. Aldershot: Edward Elgar.

Boettke, P.J. (1996). 'What is Wrong with Neoclassical Economics (and What is Still Wrong with Austrian Economics)?' In F.E. Foldvary (ed.), *Beyond Neoclassical Economics: Heterodox Approaches to Economic Theory*. Cheltenham: Edward Elgar.

Boettke, P.J. (1998a). 'Rational Choice and Human Agency in Economics and Sociology: Exploring the Weber–Austrian Connection.' In H. Giersch (ed.), *Merits and Limits of Markets*. Berlin: Springer-Verlag.

Boettke, P.J. (1998b). 'Formalism and Contemporary Economics: A Reply to Hausman, Heilbroner and Mayer.' *Critical Review*, 12, 173–186.

Boettke, P.J. (2001). *Calculation and Coordination: Essays on Socialism and Transitional Political Economy*. London and New York: Routledge.

Boettke, P.J. and D.L. Prychitko (1998). 'Introduction: Varieties of Market Process Theory.' In P.J. Boettke and D.L. Prychitko (eds), *Market Process Theories, Volume I: Classical and Neoclassical*. Cheltenham: Edward Elgar.

Boettke, P.J. and V.H. Storr (2002). 'Post-Classical Political Economy: Polity, Society and Economy in Weber, Mises and Hayek.' *American Journal of Economics and Sociology*, 61, 161–191.

Boettke, P.J. and J.R. Subrick (2002). 'From the Philosophy of the Mind to the Philosophy of the Market.' *Journal of Economic Methodology*, 9, 53–64.

Boettke, P.J. and S.T. Sullivan (1998). 'Lachmann's Policy Activism: An Austrian Critique of Keynesian Proclivities.' In R. Koppl and G. Mongiovi (eds), *Subjectivism and Economic Analysis: Essays in Memory of Ludwig Lachmann*. London and New York: Routledge.

224   *Paul Lewis*

Boettke, P.J., D. Lavoie and V.H. Storr (2004). 'The Subjectivist Methodology of Austrian Economics and Dewey's Theory of Inquiry.' In E. Kahlil (ed.), *Dewey, Pragmatism and Economic Methodology*. London: Routledge.

Butchvarov, P. (1995). 'Metaphysics.' In R. Audi (ed.), *The Cambridge Dictionary of Philosophy*. Cambridge: Cambridge University Press.

Caldwell, B. (2000). 'The Emergence of Hayek's Ideas on Cultural Evolution.' *Review of Austrian Economics, 13*, 5–22.

Caldwell, B. (2001). 'Hodgson on Hayek: A Critique.' *Cambridge Journal of Economics, 25*, 539–553.

Chamlee-Wright, E. (1997). *The Cultural Foundations of Economic Development: Urban Female Entrepreneurship in Ghana*. London and New York: Routledge.

Clark, C.M.A. (1993). 'Spontaneous Order Versus Instituted Process: The Market as Cause and Effect.' *Journal of Economic Issues, 27*, 373–385.

Cowan, R. (1994). 'Causation and Genetic Causation in Economic Theory.' In P. Boettke (ed.), *The Elgar Companion to Austrian Economics*. Aldershot: Edward Elgar.

Cowan, R. and M.J. Rizzo (1996). 'The Genetic–Causal Tradition and Modern Economic Theory.' *Kyklos, 49*, 273–317.

Ebeling, R.M. (1986). 'Towards a Hermeneutical Economics: Expectations, Prices, and the Role of Interpretation in a Theory of the Market Process.' In I.M. Kirzner (ed.), *Subjectivism, Intelligibility and Economic Understanding: Essays in Honour of Ludwig M. Lachmann on his Eightieth Birthday*. New York: New York University Press.

Ebeling, R.M. (1987). 'Cooperation in Anonymity.' *Critical Review, 1*, 50–61.

Ebeling, R.M. (1990). 'What is a Price? Explanation and Understanding.' In D. Lavoie (ed.), *Economics and Hermeneutics*. London: Routledge.

Fleetwood, S. (1995). *Hayek's Political Economy: The Socio-Economics of Order*. London and New York: Routledge.

Fleetwood, S. (1996). 'Order Without Equilibrium: A Critical Realist Interpretation of Hayek's Notion of Spontaneous Order.' *Cambridge Journal of Economics, 20*, 729–747.

Fleetwood, S. (1999a). 'Situating Critical Realism in Economics.' In S. Fleetwood (ed.), *Critical Realism in Economics: Development and Debate*. London and New York: Routledge.

Fleetwood, S. (ed.) (1999b). *Critical Realism in Economics: Development and Debate*. London and New York: Routledge.

Gadamer, H-G. (1975). *Truth and Method*. Second, revised edition. Translated by J. Weinsheimer and D.G. Marshall. London: Sheed and Ward, 1993.

Gadamer, H-G. (1983). *Reason in the Age of Science*. Translated by F.G. Lawrence. Cambridge, Mass: MIT Press.

Gloria-Palermo, S. (1999). *The Evolution of Austrian Economics: From Menger to Lachmann*. London and New York: Routledge.

Granovetter, M. (1985). 'Economic Action and Social Structure: The Problem of Embeddedness.' *American Journal of Economics and Sociology, 91*, 481–510.

Harré, H.R. (1988). *The Philosophies of Science*. Oxford: Oxford University Press.

Hayek, F.A. (1945). 'Individualism: True and False.' In F.A. Hayek, *Individualism and Economic Order*. Chicago: University of Chicago Press, 1948.

Hayek, F.A. (1952). *The Counter-Revolution of Science Studies on the Abuse of Reason*. Second edition. Indianapolis: Liberty Fund, 1979.

Hodgson, G.M. (1986). 'Behind Methodological Individualism.' *Cambridge Journal of Economics, 10*, 211–224.

Horwitz, S. (1992). 'Monetary Exchange as an Extra-Linguistic Social Communication Process.' *Review of Social Economy*, 50, 193–214.

Horwitz, S. (1994). 'Subjectivism, Institutions and Capital: Comment on Mongiovi and Lewin.' *Advances in Austrian Economics*, 1, 279–288.

Horwitz, S. (1995). 'Feminist Economics: An Austrian Perspective.' *Journal of Economic Methodology*, 2, 259–279.

Horwitz, S. (1998). 'Hierarchical Metaphors in Austrian Institutionalism: A Friendly Subjectivist Caveat.' In R. Koppl and G. Mongiovi (eds), *Subjectivism and Economic Analysis: Essays in Memory of Ludwig M. Lachmann*. London and New York: Routledge.

Horwitz, S. (2002). 'The Functions of the Family in the Great Society.' Mimeo, St. Lawrence University.

Horwitz, S. (2004). 'Money and the Interpretive Turn: Some Considerations.' *Symposium*, 8, 249–266.

Kibbe, M.B. (1994). 'Mind, Historical Time and the Value of Money: A Tale of Two Methods.' In P.J Boettke and D.L. Prychitko (eds), *The Market Process: Essays in Austrian Economics*. Aldershot: Edward Elgar.

Kirzner, I.M. (2000). *The Driving Force of the Market: Essays in Austrian Economics*. London and New York: Routledge.

Koppl, R. (2002). *Big Players and the Economic Theory of Expectations*. Basingstoke: Palgrave.

Lachmann, L.M. (1966). 'The Significance of the Austrian School of Economics in the History of Ideas.' In W.E. Grinder (ed.), *Capital, Expectations and the Market Process: Essays on the Theory of the Market Economy*. Kansas City: Sheed, Andrews and McMeel, 1977.

Lachmann, L.M. (1971). *The Legacy of Max Weber*. London: Heinemann.

Lachmann, L.M. (1976). 'From Mises to Shackle: An Essay on Austrian Economics and the Kaleidic Society.' In D. Lavoie (ed.), *Expectations and the Meaning of Institutions: Essays in Economics by Ludwig Lachmann*. London and New York: Routledge, 1994.

Lachmann, L.M. (1982). 'Ludwig von Mises and the Extension of Subjectivism.' In I. Kirzner (ed.), *Method, Process and Austrian Economics: Essays in Honour of Ludwig von Mises*. Lexington, MA: D.C. Heath and Company.

Lachmann, L.M. (1990a). 'Austrian Economics: A Hermeneutic Approach.' In D. Lavoie (ed.), *Economics and Hermeneutics*. London: Routledge.

Lachmann, L.M. (1990b). 'G.L.S. Shackle's Place in the History of Subjectivist Thought.' In D. Lavoie (ed.), *Expectations and the Meaning of Institutions: Essays in Economics by Ludwig Lachmann*. London and New York: Routledge, 1994.

Lavoie, D. (1986). 'Euclideanism Versus Hermeneutics: A Reinterpretation of Misesian Apriorism.' In I.M. Kirzner (ed.), *Subjectivism, Intelligibility and Economic Understanding: Essays in Honour of Ludwig M. Lachmann on his Eightieth Birthday*. New York: New York University Press.

Lavoie, D. (1987). 'The Accounting of Interpretations and the Interpretation of Accounts: The Communicative Function of "The Language of Business".' *Accounting, Organizations and Society*, 12, 579–604.

Lavoie, D. (1990a). 'Understanding Differently: Hermeneutics and the Spontaneous Order of Communicative Processes.' Annual Supplement to *History of Political Economy*, 22, 359–377.

Lavoie, D. (1990b). 'Computation, Incentives, and Discovery: The Cognitive Function of Markets in Market Socialism.' *Annals of the American Academy of Political and Social Science, 507,* 72–79.

Lavoie, D. (1990c). 'Introduction.' In D. Lavoie (ed.), *Economics and Hermeneutics.* London: Routledge.

Lavoie, D. (ed.) (1990d). *Economics and Hermeneutics.* London: Routledge.

Lavoie, D. (1991a). 'The Progress of Subjectivism.' In M. Blaug and N. de Marchi (eds), *Appraising Economic Theories: Studies in the Methodology of Research Programmes.* Aldershot: Edward Elgar.

Lavoie, D. (1991b). 'The Discovery and Interpretation of Profit Opportunities: Culture and the Kirznerian Entrepreneur.' In B. Berger (ed.), *The Culture of Entrepreneurship.* San Francisco: Institute for Contemporary Studies Press.

Lavoie, D. (1994a). 'The Interpretive Turn.' In P.J. Boettke (ed.), *The Elgar Companion to Austrian Economics.* Aldershot: Edward Elgar.

Lavoie, D. (1994b). 'Introduction: Expectations and the Meaning of Institutions.' In D. Lavoie (ed.), *Expectations and the Meaning of Institutions: Essays in Economics by Ludwig Lachmann.* London and New York: Routledge.

Lavoie, D. (1997). 'On Regrouping the Intellectual Capital Structure of Lachmann's Economics.' *Advances in Austrian Economics, 4,* 219–226.

Lavoie, D. and E. Chamlee-Wright (2000). *Culture and Enterprise: The Development, Representation and Morality of Business.* London and New York: Routledge.

Lawson, C. (1999). 'Realism, Theory and Individualism in the Work of Carl Menger.' In S. Fleetwood (ed.), *Critical Realism in Economics: Development and Debate.* London and New York: Routledge.

Lawson, C., M. Peacock and S. Pratten (1996). 'Realism, Underlabouring and Institutions.' *Cambridge Journal of Economics, 20,* 137–151.

Lawson, T. (1994). 'Critical Realism and the Analysis of Choice, Explanation and Change.' *Advances in Austrian Economics, 1,* 3–30.

Lawson, T. (1997). *Economics and Reality.* London and New York: Routledge.

Lawson, T. (1998). 'Clarifying and Developing the *Economics and Reality* Project: Closed and Open Systems, Deductivism, Prediction, and Teaching.' *Review of Social Economy, 56,* 356–375.

Lawson, T. (2003). *Reorienting Economics.* London and New York: Routledge.

Layder, D. (1997). *Modern Social Theory: Key Debates and New Directions.* London: UCL Press.

Lewis, P.A. (2000). 'Realism, Causality and the Problem of Social Structure.' *Journal for the Theory of Social Behaviour, 30,* 249–268.

Lewis, P.A. (2002). 'Austrians and (Old) Institutionalists on the Possibility of Socio-Economic Order: Towards a Rapprochement.' Mimeo, Cambridge University.

Lewis, P.A. (2004). 'Structure and Agency in Economic Analysis: The Case of Austrian Economics and the Material Embeddedness of Socio-Economic Life.' In J.B. Davis, A. Marciano and J.H. Runde (eds), *The Elgar Companion to Economics and Philosophy.* Cheltenham: Edward Elgar.

Lewis, P.A. (2005). 'Boettke, the Austrian School, and the Reclamation of Reality in Modern Economics.' *The Review of Austrian Economics, 18,* 83–108.

Madison, G.B. (1989). 'Hayek and the Interpretive Turn.' *Critical Review, 3,* 169–185.

Madison, G.B. (1990a). 'How Individualistic is Methodological Individualism?' *Critical Review, 4,* 41–60.

Madison, G.B. (1990b). 'Getting Beyond Objectivism: The Philosophical Hermeneutics of Gadamer and Ricoeur.' In D. Lavoie (ed.), *Economics and Hermeneutics*. London: Routledge.

Madison, G.B. (1994). 'Phenomenology and Economics.' In P.J. Boettke (ed.), *The Elgar Companion to Austrian Economics*. Aldershot: Edward Elgar.

Madison, G.B. (1998). *The Political Economy of Civil Society and Human Rights.* London and New York: Routledge.

Mäki, U. (1990a). 'Practical Syllogism, Entrepreneurship and the Invisible Hand: A Critique of the Analytic Hermeneutics of G.H. von Wright.' In D. Lavoie (ed.), *Economics and Hermeneutics*. London: Routledge.

Mäki, U. (1990b). 'Mengerian Economics in Realist Perspective.' Annual Supplement to *History of Political Economy*, 22, 289–310.

Mäki, U. (1992). 'The Market as an Isolated Causal Process: A Metaphysical Ground for Realism.' In B.J. Caldwell and S. Boehm (eds), *Austrian Economics: Tensions and New Directions*. Boston: Kluwer Academic Publishers.

Mayer, H. (1932). 'The Cognitive Value of Functional Theories of Price.' In I.M. Kirzner (ed.), *Classics in Austrian Economics: A Sampling in the History of a Tradition. Volume II: The Interwar Period.* London: William Pickering, 1994.

Menger, C. (1883). *Investigations into the Method of the Social Sciences with Special Reference to Economics.* New York: New York University Press, 1985.

Miller, R.W. (1987). *Fact and Method: Explanation, Confirmation and Reality in the Natural and the Social Sciences.* Princeton, NJ: Princeton University Press.

O'Driscoll, G. and Rizzo, M. (1996). *The Economics of Time and Ignorance.* Second edition. London and New York: Routledge.

Porpora, D.V. (1998). 'Four Concepts of Social Structure.' In M.S. Archer, R. Bhaskar, A. Collier, T. Lawson and A. Norrie (eds), *Critical Realism: Essential Readings*. London and New York: Routledge.

Prychitko, D.L. (1989–90). 'Methodological Individualism and the Austrian School.' In D. Prychitko (ed.), *Individuals, Institutions, Interpretations: Hermeneutics Applied to Economics*. Aldershot: Avebury, 1995.

Prychitko, D.L. (1994a). 'Ludwig Lachmann and the Interpretive Turn in Economics: A Critical Inquiry into the Hermeneutics of the Plan.' *Advances in Austrian Economics*, 1, 303–319.

Prychitko, D.L. (1994b). 'Socialism as Cartesian Legacy: The Radical Element within F.A. Hayek's *The Fatal Conceit*.' In P.J. Boettke and D.L. Prychitko (eds), *The Market Process: Essays in Austrian Economics*. Aldershot: Edward Elgar.

Prychitko, D.L. (ed.) (1995). *Individuals, Institutions, Interpretations: Hermeneutics Applied to Economics*. Aldershot: Avebury.

Prychitko, D.L. (1997a). 'Lachmann's Plan, and its Lesson: Comment on Lavoie.' *Advances in Austrian Economics*, 4, 209–217.

Prychitko, D.L. (1997b). 'The Dangers that Court Hermeneutics: Rejoinder to Lavoie.' *Advances in Austrian Economics*, 4, 227–229.

Ricoeur, P. (1971). 'The Model of the Text: Meaningful Action Considered as a Text.' *Social Research*, 38, 529–562.

Ricoeur, P. (1981). 'What is a Text? Explanation and Understanding.' In P. Ricoeur, *Hermeneutics and the Human Sciences*. Translated by J.B. Thompson. Cambridge: Cambridge University Press.

Runde, J.H. (1993). 'Paul Davidson and the Austrians: Reply to Davidson.' *Critical Review*, 7, 381–397.

Runde, J.H. (2001). 'Bringing Social Structure Back into Economics: On Critical Realism and Hayek's Scientism Essay.' *Review of Austrian Economics*, *14*, 5–24.

Samuels, W.J. (1989). 'Austrian and Institutional Economics: Some Common Elements.' *Research in the History of Economic Thought and Methodology*, *6*, 53–71.

Sayer, A. (2000). *Realism and Social Science*. London: Sage.

Sciabarra, C.M. (1995). *Marx, Hayek and Utopia*. Albany: State University of New York Press.

Shackle, G.L.S. (1972). *Epistemics and Economics: A Critique of Economic Doctrines*. New Brunswick and London: Transaction Publishers, 1992.

Vaughn, K.I. (1994). *Austrian Economics in America: The Migration of a Tradition*. Cambridge: Cambridge University Press.

Vaughn, K.I. (1997). '*Hayek's Political Economy: The Socio-Economics of Order*. By Fleetwood (Steve).' *Economic Journal*, *107*, 1257–1258.

Mises, L. (1949). *Human Action: A Treatise on Economics*. Third, revised edition. Chicago: Contemporary Books Inc., 1966.

Mises, L. (1957). *Theory and History: An Interpretation of Social and Economic Evolution*. Auburn, AL: Ludwig von Mises Institute, 1985.

Wachterhauser, B. (2002). 'Getting it Right: Relativism, Realism, and Truth.' In R.J. Dostal (ed.), *The Cambridge Companion to Gadamer*. Cambridge: Cambridge University Press.

Part III

Interventions in the history of economic thought

8 Smith and Newton: some methodological issues concerning general economic equilibrium theory[1]

Leonidas Montes

1. Introduction

There is general consensus that in economics Adam Smith is, in the words of Jevons, the 'father of the science'. In this setting it has regularly been argued that neoclassical and modern mainstream economics carry through the methodological impetus brought into the discipline by Smith. Moreover, economists conventionally take it for granted that Smith applied Newton's method to political economy. Because Newton's method is thought to be similar to that of modern mainstream economics, the association of Smith with Newton is taken to further bolster the claim that modern mainstream economics continues the Smithian tradition. Support for this commonly accepted view is gathered from Smith's panegyric attitude to Newton's conception of philosophy. This shared conviction among economists underpins some interpretations of the 'invisible hand' and of the intention behind the controversial chapter 7 of Book I of the WN,[2] baptising Smith as a forerunner, if not the founder, of theories of general economic equilibrium (e.g., Robbins, 1962 [1932]; Schumpeter, 1994 [1954]; Arrow and Hahn, 1971; Jaffé, 1977; Hollander, 1973, 1987; Samuelson, 1977, 1992). As an offspring of the same tradition Walras, the architect of the 'equilibrium system', has been set alongside Newton, the discoverer of the 'world system' (Samuelson, 1952, p. 61). In this framework, Newton's atomistic/mechanistic description of the celestial order provides evidence that Smith initiated the tradition of neoclassical and modern mainstream economics, having the same underlying ontological preconceptions that are pervasive and fundamental in the development of general economic equilibrium theory since Walras, whose achievement represents 'the peak of neoclassical economics' (ibid.).

This paper will argue that this is wrong. In the second half of the eighteenth century, Newton was the intellectual hero, venerated by all the *philosophes*, and Smith was certainly no exception. However, while shared admiration does not necessarily imply a common methodology, I suggest not only that Smith was not a Newtonian in the commonly received sense, but also that Newton was not either. Specifically, I shall argue that Smith did not have an atomistic–mechanistic view of the world in the tradition of neoclassical and later modern mainstream economics, and that Newton did not simply conform to the axiomatic–deductive methodology fostered and adopted by 'mechanical philosophy'. Mainstream economists have ignored this situation, relying on too narrow a reading of Newton. As a consequence, Adam Smith's rich, complex and broadly philosophical approach has been overshadowed by a biased and obsolete positivistic interpretation of the Newtonian method.

It will be helpful to my argument if I start, in section 2 below, by considering Newton's method and its impact. The image of Newton as the father of the 'Age of Reason' will be questioned. More emphatically, it will be argued that this inherited association of Newton with the axiomatic–deductive tradition is misleading. Newton's analytic–synthetic method is broader, and his all-encompassing philosophical project, including theology and alchemy, reveals that their influence and his intentions were much more complex. I suggest that the positivistic interpretation of Newton's method is a product of the French Enlightenment that paradoxically adopted a mechanical philosophy founded on the success of his *Principia*.

In section 3, I examine the nature and viability of the widely held view of 'Smithian Newtonianism', i.e. the idea that Adam Smith simply applied a particular mechanistic version of society that presupposed an atomistic view of human beings. This interpretation will be jettisoned; I show that Smith's methodological position is radically different from this narrow neoclassical and mainstream misunderstanding of Newton's methodology. In arguing my case I shall focus, in particular, on the popular version of Smith as a precursor of general economic equilibrium theory. Section 4 will contrast Walras's idealistic position concerning pure economics with what I consider to be the realist Smithian view. Also, the controversial chapter 7 of Book I of the WN is reassessed in order to bring to an end the flawed but relatively common view of Smith as the founder or forebear of general equilibrium theory.

In section 5, I suggest some similarities between Smith's broad and interdisciplinary project and some recent developments in methodology and economics represented by critical realism (see, in particular, Lawson, 1997). Finally, in section 6, I present a brief conclusion underlining the main issues at stake and their relevance for modern economics.

2. Was Newton a Newtonian?

Before questioning whether, or in what sense, Smith is a Newtonian, let me ask the same question of Newton himself. The argument, in brief, is that Newton's contribution can be viewed under two aspects: his method and his results. These have been confused by neoclassical and mainstream economists. The former is a combination of analysis and synthesis, terms I shall expand upon below. His discovery was a system of mechanics, which under certain conditions – but certain conditions only, namely those of a closed system – gives rise to event regularities facilitating the use of mathematics. Neoclassical and modern mainstream economists, following the tradition of the French Enlightenment thinkers, have mistakenly interpreted as Newton's general method one particular case of his results. They have focused on Newton's results as they pertain to a closed system with a production of event regularities, relying upon a narrow axiomatic–deductive methodology. Noticing the latter's conduciveness to methods of mathematical modelling, they have supposed that reliance upon mathematics represents Newton's a priori methodological orientation. This, though, is not correct. His method was that of analysis and synthesis, and primarily analysis in search of underlying causes. This is the true method of Newton, and it is the philosophical conception adopted by Smith. Thus the method of the modern mainstream is neither Smith's nor Newton's, but simply a procedure used in a particular case of Newton's highly specific results that has been erroneously universalised. Let me first elaborate on Newton's methodology and its setting.

A characteristic feature of the Enlightenment in general was a confidence in the power of human reason, in which Newton epitomised the triumph of human intellectual capacity over nature. Alexander Pope's (1730) intended epitaph for Newton is a clear reflection of this belief: 'Nature and nature's laws lay hid in night: God said, Let Newton be! And all was light.'

However, during the last few decades, the image perpetuated by the Victorians of Newton as the father of the 'Age of Reason', and our understanding of the nature of Newtonianism, have radically changed. John Maynard Keynes was quite original in challenging the received apotheosised image of Newton with his biography 'Newton, the Man' (Keynes, 1972). This essay was path breaking in anticipating a renewed interest in the life and character of Newton, and much speculation regarding certain previously omitted aspects of these.[3] Today, Stukeley's devotional account of his hero and friend (*Memoirs of Sir Isaac Newton's Life*, 1752), and Brewster's classical biography (*Memoirs of the Life, Writings, and Discoveries of Sir Isaac Newton*, 1831), are to be taken *cum grano salis*. But regarding the nature of Newtonianism, Keynes, who in 1936 bought at Sotheby's 120 lots of Newton's papers and studied them, failed to realise the importance of Newton's manuscripts when he declared that his 'secret heresies and scholastic superstitions' were 'wholly devoid of scientific value' (1972, p. 370).[4] Although this view was widely accepted until recently, today the image of Newton as the father of modern science, thinking 'on the lines of cold and untinctured reason' (ibid., p. 363), is open to question, especially as more research is carried out on his writings about theology and alchemy. The last decades have witnessed a rapid growth in the 'Newtonian industry'.[5] It is clear that Newton not only pursued alchemical studies with great vigour, but also that his theological quest occupied a great part of his intellectual energies. If the public Newton was the Cambridge Lucasian Professor, the Master of the Mint and the President of the Royal Society, privately he was an Arian, a doctrine unacceptable to orthodox Anglicans,[6] and a devout alchemist.

The reception of Newton's legacy during the eighteenth century was multifaceted, especially when we discuss what has commonly been labelled 'Newtonianism'. It is widely believed that Newton synthesised, but also transformed, the mathematical rationalism developed by Descartes with the experimental emphasis in vogue in Great Britain after Francis Bacon. Although from a general perspective this is accurate, nevertheless 'Newtonianism' has many meanings depending on the setting.[7] Nowadays, when we refer to Newton's system, we commonly mean his *Principia* (*Philosophiae naturalis principia mathematica*, 1687), and the *Opticks* (1704) essentially represents for the layman a piece of interest only to the historian of science. The former, written in 'the mathematical way', was extremely difficult to understand even for the educated. In fact, Newton made his *Principia* strenuous to read expressly to avoid 'being baited by Smatterers in Mathematicks' (quoted in Westfall, 1980, p. 459).[8] But the *Opticks*, written in English by Newton rather than Latin,[9] was then much more accessible to the general public. The impact of the *Opticks*, reaching a wider audience during the eighteenth century, perhaps exceeded that of his *magnum opus*. If celestial mechanics was the grand science, the subject of the *Opticks* was not only more spectacular, but also inherently speculative.

Although the *Opticks* presents some important discoveries, it deals with experiments and hypotheses, not concluding with irrefutable propositions, like his *Principia*, but simply stating at the end 31 'queries'.[10] But Newton's *Principia*, founded on the three laws of motion, establishes the law of universal gravity. Implications for the motion of many different kinds of observed phenomena are then drawn from it.[11] This is the great achievement of Newton's 'experimental philosophy', which consists in the method of analysis (method of resolution) and synthesis (method of composition), and is defended not only in the *Principia*, but even more vehemently in his *Opticks*.

In his famous *General Scholium*, appended to the end of the second edition of the *Principia*,[12] Newton adds that '[i]n this experimental philosophy, propositions are deduced from the phenomena and are made general by induction' (Newton, 1999 [1687], p. 943). But probably the best expression of his analytic–synthetic method is given in the last query of his *Opticks*. There Newton clearly states that:

> Analysis consists in making Experiments and Observations, and in drawing general Conclusions from them by Induction ... Synthesis consists in assuming the Causes discover'd, and establish'd as Principles, and by them explaining the Phaenomena proceeding from them.
>
> (Newton, 1931 [1704], pp. 404–5)

Then, analysis allows the philosopher to infer causes from phenomena, and synthesis to establish a (or some) principle(s) from which we can explain other phenomena.

It is worth noting that Newton's method was understood by the *philosophes* of the Scottish Enlightenment.[13] For example, according to Maclaurin, a famous Scottish mathematician supported by Newton[14] and author of the popular *An Account of Sir Isaac Newton's Philosophical Discoveries* (1748):[15]

> [Sir Isaac Newton] proposed that, in our enquiries into nature, the methods of *analysis* and *synthesis* should be both employed in a proper order; that we should begin with phenomena, or effects, and from them investigate the powers or causes that operate in nature; that, from particular causes, we should proceed to the more general ones, till the argument end in the most general: this is the method of *analysis*. Being once possest of these causes, we should then descend in a contrary order; and from them, as established principles, explain all the phenomena that are their consequences, and prove our explications: and this is the *synthesis* ... the method of *analysis* ought ever to precede the method of composition, or the *synthesis*.
>
> (Maclaurin, 1750 [1748], p. 9, original emphasis)

This is a lucid expression of Newton's analytic–synthetic method. Indeed, the law of universal gravitation, as a 'power' or 'cause' that operates in nature, is the cornerstone of Newton's 'system of the world', from which all other natural phenomena are derived. The philosophers of the Scottish Enlightenment assimilated this method as one of dissecting nature into its constituent parts, establishing a (or some) principle(s) from which phenomena could be explained. The fundamental role of the method of resolution or analysis was given its priority and precedence.[16] Maclaurin is also clearly aware that whereas the *Principia*

> describes the system of the world ... [*Opticks*] enquires into the more hidden parts of nature ... the subject is more nice and difficult ... Hence it is what he has delivered in the first (though full capable of improvement) is more complete and finished in several respects; while his discoveries of the second sort are more astonishing.
>
> (Ibid., pp. 20–2)

Certainly the curious nature of the *Opticks* fascinated the eighteenth century, but people were also well aware of the *Principia*'s irrefutable scientific success.

But regarding the nature of Newton's methodology, more recently Kuhn has observed that, although Newton

> has seemed to support the further assertion that scientific research can and should be confined to the experimental pursuit of mathematical

regularity ... Careful examination of Newton's less systematic published writings provides no evidence that Newton imposed upon
himself so drastic a restriction upon scientific imagination.

(1958, p. 45)[17]

Achieving 'mathematical regularity' was not Newton's goal *per se*, nor a
precondition of his method. It is worth emphasising that at the beginning
of Book III of the *Principia*, 'The System of the World', Newton develops his *Regulae Philosophandi* (Newton, 1999 [1687], pp. 794–6), putting
forward four rules for the study of natural philosophy. None of them
mentions mathematics at all, and the fourth strongly stresses the role of
induction.[18] The emphasis on mathematical regularity was a consequence
of his spectacular results that fostered synthesis, rather than of his actual
methodology. The former has overshadowed the latter. The *Principia*'s
success in creating a mathematical system of nature has determined a
particular interpretation of Newton's method, in which the results of his
mathematical natural philosophy encouraged the method of synthesis,
universalising this procedure as the scientific method par excellence.

In a fragment on method that was most likely intended for the *Opticks*,[19]
Newton referred to the method of resolution and composition, adding
that: 'he that expects success must resolve before he compounds. For
the explication of Phaenomena are Problems much harder than those in
Mathematicks' (McGuire, 1970, p. 185).

This passage is extremely important for my argument. Newton is not
only responding to the dominant 'mechanical philosophy', a point that I
elaborate below, but again reveals the fundamental aspect that has been
ignored in the axiomatic–deductive interpretations of Newtonianism, i.e.
the priority of analysis or resolution. Furthermore, it carries a lesson. For
one of the greatest mathematicians of all time considered the task of uncovering natural phenomena more difficult than the synthesis or composition
that necessarily follows.[20] Traditionally, the method of composition has prevailed over the method of resolution in modern interpretations of Newton,
leading to a biased axiomatic–deductive interpretation of his methodology
based on the *Principia*'s success. In my view, this phenomenon most probably started during the French Enlightenment. The 'Age of Reason', relying
on Newton's achievement, privileged composition, instigating a historical
process that increasingly ignored the central role that resolution played
in Newton's great discoveries. The attention given to the role of reason,
on deducing from already given principles, in explaining other phenomena, was detrimental to a rounded understanding of Newton's actual
methodology, ignoring the importance of creative thought. Undoubtedly
imagination and creative power played a fundamental role in identifying celestial gravity with simple attraction, and in introducing dynamics
into cosmology. But neither can Newton's method of analysis simply be
reduced to the famous legend of the fall of an apple on Newton's head.

From an ontological perspective, the *Opticks* presents a dialectical movement between the experimental–mathematical description of rays and colours, and the uncertain philosophical nature of light, and the *Principia* between the mathematico–deductive description of natural phenomena, and the uncertain philosophical nature of gravity. Indeed, universal attraction, although observable in nature, remained a mystery and a source of controversy for many philosophers. On the Continent it was objected that Newton's concept of gravity was a mere 'hypothesis' analogous to the invisible causes that fascinated the Schoolmen.[21] This allegation, mainly fostered by Leibniz, infuriated Newton, who, loyal to his Christian but rather unorthodox beliefs, added to the second edition of the *Principia* (1713) the famous *General Scholium*. This begins by insisting that Descartes's theory of vortices ought to be eliminated. Then Newton explains that:

> This most elegant system of the sun, planets, and comets could not have arisen without the design and dominion of an intelligent and powerful being ...
> He rules all things, not as the world soul, but as the lord of all.
>
> (Newton, 1999 [1687], p. 940)

Finally, Newton acknowledges that he has 'not yet assigned a cause to gravity' (ibid., p. 943). If the father of modern physics wanted 'to treat of God from phenomena' (ibid.) as part of natural philosophy, he also needed Him in his rebuttal of Leibniz's attempt to reduce universal attraction to a mechanical cause. Newton repeatedly criticised 'mechanical philosophy', as he considered that mechanical principles were inadequate to explain all phenomena. His intellectual foes, Huygens, Hooke and Leibniz, followed the mechanical philosophy tradition that had been fostered by Descartes. For Descartes, as for Galileo, a force should be caused by a mechanism. Newton's philosophy could not agree with the imposition of mechanical necessity, as a cause of force. Gravity, which is observable but without a known cause, is the paradigmatic example. In addition aware of the limits of a purely mechanical interpretation of nature, Newton denied that, ontologically, reality could be treated as a simple machine, complete and self-sufficient in itself.[22] Mechanical laws do not explain all phenomena of reality. As Drennon put it, for Newton ultimately: 'the universe, in its true essence, is not a mechanism, for mechanical laws cannot account for its origin and sustained existence' (1933–4, p. 405).

Newton was a realist in his search for explanatory phenomena. Although he might appear to be suggesting a theological explanation for the cause of gravity, he clearly asserts that in explaining the motions of the heavenly bodies 'it is enough that gravity really exists' (Newton, 1999 [1687], p. 943). In fact, Koyré brilliantly argued that Newton found a new metaphysical approach to nature in which the classic cosmos disappears, giving birth to 'an open, indefinite, and even infinite universe' (1965, p. 7). Indeed, Newton, the father of the universal law of gravitation, was even open to the possibility 'that there may be more attractive Powers' (Newton, 1931 [1704], p. 376). Before his death he is reported to have said:

> I don't know what I may seem to the world, but, as to myself, I seem to have been only like a boy playing on the sea shore, and diverting myself in now and then finding a smoother pebble or a prettier shell than ordinary, whilst the great ocean of truth lay all undiscovered before me.
>
> (Quoted in Westfall, 1980, p. 863)

Newton believed in truth; he very successfully uncovered part of it, but he was aware that much more underlay the realm of actuality.[23] He believed in an all-encompassing natural philosophy; his theological and alchemical interests were not simple leisure pursuits, but part of his scheme of thought.[24] His project even suggests a general micro–macro move between his *Opticks* and the *Principia*, founded on the intuition that 'if Nature be most simple & fully consonant to herself she observes the same method in regulating the motions of smaller bodies which she doth in regulating those of the greater' (quoted in Westfall, 1980, p. 521). In fact, modern interpretations of Newtonianism mostly rely upon the *Principia*'s stunning results, confining the complexity of his methodological orientation to mathematical modelling, ignoring the importance of analysis in seeking for underlying causes. A purely materialistic or mechanistic natural philosophy was utterly impossible for Newton. In particular, the Cartesio–Leibnizian reduction of natural phenomena to a pure, self-sustaining and self-perpetuating mechanism was against Newton's philosophy, but ironically became the landmark of 'Newtonianism'. As Koyré pointed out, one consequence of the Newton–Leibniz debate (especially through Clarke's famous polemic with Leibniz between 1715 and 1716)[25] was that:

> The force of attraction which, for Newton, was a proof of the insufficiency of pure mechanism, a demonstration of the existence of higher, non-mechanical powers, the manifestation of God's presence and action in the world, ceased to play this role, and became a purely natural force, a property of matter, that enriched mechanism instead of supplanting it.
>
> (Koyré, 1957, p. 274)

When we turn to the study of social phenomena, there is one passage of Newton's *Opticks* that perhaps adumbrated an ambitious Enlightenment undertaking. In query 31, the final paragraph of the *Opticks*, Newton remarked: 'And if natural Philosophy in all its Parts, by pursuing this Method, shall at length be perfected, the Bounds of Moral Philosophy will be also enlarged' (Newton, 1931 [1704], p. 405).

This suggestion was taken seriously at the time. The belief that Newton's 'experimental philosophy' could be applied to social phenomena was commonplace amongst the eighteenth-century *intelligentsia*, initiating a longstanding intellectual tradition (see Myers, 1983). The idea of a universal order that could be explained from the simple principle of gravitation was a discovery that fascinated the minds of the period. As Newton had discovered the laws governing natural phenomena, it was the task of moral philosophers to unveil the social realm. Therefore the methodological move from the celestial bodies to human society, based on what has been labelled the 'principle of design', could not wait any longer. Hume's project to develop a 'science of human nature', or the 'science of man', was a clear example of this pursuit.[26] With no barriers between the different branches of knowledge, the problem was not whether the Newtonian method could be transferred to the social realm, but *how* this new generation of 'social scientists' would attain this goal.

The overwhelming success of Newtonian natural philosophy made it practically inevitable that the social sciences would try to conform to an empirico–deductive pseudo-Newtonian pattern. But it was the spectacular nature of Newton's results that dominated this process, not the method used in achieving those results. This focus on results rather than on method is mainly a consequence of the paradoxical fact that the intellectuals of the French Enlightenment retained the Cartesio–Leibnizian precepts of 'mechanical philosophy', but underpinned by Newton's successful discoveries. It was Condorcet, a friend and close collaborator of the Physiocrat Turgot, who later formulated his project of *mathématique sociale*. It was Laplace who answered, when asked by Napoleon about the place of God in his cosmological system, 'I do not need that hypothesis'. In political economy, the Physiocrats followed this pseudo-Newtonian tradition, which was later adopted and adapted by Walras and played an important part in the subsequent development of general economic equilibrium theory.

The thinkers of the Scottish Enlightenment, and Smith in particular, are different in the respect that their project was supported by an unmistakably distinctive philosophical approach (see Dow, 1987).[27] Certainly, the views shared by Montesquieu, Diderot, d'Alembert, Helvétius, Condorcet and d'Holbach were different from those shared by their Scottish counterparts such as Smith, Hume and Ferguson, although there are clear mutual influences. The role of 'natural history' as an account of progress from the 'early and rude state' to 'polished society' is fundamental for the Scottish philosophers. Smith's four stages theory is a way to understand the successive steps from the hunting stage, pastoral life and agriculture towards commercial society. This was the objective of natural history, and no wonder why the Scots were fascinated with the American natives. Yet the general search for first principles was encompassed within a larger project: the spring of social science.

I have already questioned the widely accepted positivistic version of Newton that has been taken for granted by the main proponents of the marginal revolution and by mainstream economists alike.[28] To put it mildly, Newton was neither sympathetic to the mechanistic view of the world, nor did he unconditionally endorse an axiomatic–deductive approach to reality. Rather, his central method was primarily oriented to uncovering causes, not to tracing the consequences of event regularities given initial conditions. Now it is time to turn our attention to Adam Smith, the 'father of our science'.

3. Smithian Newtonianism

3.1 Some common views of Newton's influence

Between 1752 and the beginning of 1764 Adam Smith was Professor of moral philosophy at Glasgow University. His lectures on this subject, as reported by his student and friend John Millar, basically comprised theology, ethics, jurisprudence and political economy or 'expediency' (EPS, pp. 274–5). This classification reveals the humanistic character of his project and reminds us of the noble origins of the discipline of economics.[29] Indeed, an important feature of the Scottish Enlightenment in particular, and of the Enlightenment in general, was that the intellectual atmosphere was intensely multidisciplinary.[30] The classical breakdown of philosophy into logic, moral philosophy and natural philosophy was still applied, but only meant that Scottish men of letters were simply *philosophes* in its wide etymological sense. Certainly '[t]he highest compliment a Scottish scholar could receive was that he commanded a knowledge of wide-ranging subjects' (Redman, 1993, p. 221; 1997, p. 110). Knowledge, without bounds, was part of a systematic inquiry to discover some simple philosophical principles governing all kinds of phenomena. It is therefore not surprising that Smith wrote about metaphysics, natural history, ethics, political economy, astronomy, rhetoric and jurisprudence,[31] had a perfect command of Greek and Latin, and was also interested in mathematics and physics.

It has become almost commonplace to label Smith as Newtonian, a 'system-builder' (Skinner, 1976) who not only found inspiration in the father of modern physics, but also relied heavily on his method. In the General Introduction to the WN's Glasgow Edition, the editors consider that 'Smith sought to explain complex problems in terms of a small number of basic principles, and each conforms to the requirements of the Newtonian method in the broad sense of the term' (WN, intr., p. 4). Skinner also believes that Smith's economics 'was originally conceived in the image of Newtonian physics' (1979, p. 110). For Blaug, the pivotal role of sympathy in TMS and that of self-interest in the WN 'must be regarded as deliberate attempts by Smith to apply this Newtonian method first to ethics and then to economics' (1992 [1980], p. 52).[32] Few scholars, to my knowledge, have assumed a different position.[33] But the problem is not whether Smith was or not a Newtonian, but what the actual nature of 'Smithian Newtonianism' is. We have already seen that the epithet 'Newtonian' raises complex issues, and I have demonstrated that the positivistic interpretation of Newtonianism is not only biased, but also flawed. In this section we shall see that the answer to the question 'How did Newton actually influence Smith?' is also not straightforward.

In particular, there is a widespread view that:

> Adam Smith took Newton's conception of nature as a law-bound system of matter in motion as his model when he represented society as a collection of individuals pursuing their self-interest in an economic order governed by the laws of supply and demand.
>
> (Hetherington, 1983, p. 498)

And also that Smith's methodology 'presupposed the view that society is a compound of independent individuals, i.e. an aggregate of Robinson Crusoes' (Freudenthal, 1981, p. 135). Moreover, Smith has come to be known as a precursor of Walrasian general equilibrium theory, because 'both authors [Smith and Walras] looked to Newtonian celestial mechanics as a model for their vision of social science' (Jaffé, 1977, p. 19).

I shall refute this mechanistic and atomistic view that, for Smith, individuals are no more than self-interested atoms that interact in society.[34] And I shall question the interpretation of Smith as a forerunner of general equilibrium theory.[35] But before I do so, it is useful to analyse some clues Smith gives about his methodological position.

3.2 Smith's methodological stance and some misinterpretations

Smith not only refers to 'the great work of Sir Isaac Newton' (TMS, III.2.2, p. 124), but also acknowledges numerous times his admiration for Newton's philosophy.[36] He is reported to have lectured that 'the Newtonian method is undoubtedly the most Philosophical, and in every science whether of Moralls or Naturall philosophy' (LRBL, p. 146), restating Newton's suggestion of his method of natural philosophy as being adequate to moral philosophy.

Although the view that natural philosophy constituted a model for the development of moral philosophy was widely accepted, in my opinion Adam Smith did not unconditionally support it. In fact, he was aware that the complexity of human phenomena, of which political economy was a part, could not be simply reduced to a mechanistic analogue of the natural realm. For Smith, human affairs cannot be reduced to a mathematical–deductive method in order to emulate Newton's success in his *Principia*. Smith did not view man as an isolated atom but, following the 'civic humanistic tradition' (Pocock, 1975, 1983, 1985), as a *zôon politikón*. In my view, he has too readily been assimilated to the natural jurisprudential tradition, neglecting the evidence that he is thinking within a more 'humanist' tradition. The latter implies a broader view of human beings as members of society, as human beings situated in an economic/societal position.[37] For example, his reaction against the 'man of system' constitutes clear evidence of his view of human beings as members of society, and not as isolated atoms. Using the metaphor of individuals as pieces upon a chess-board, the 'man of system' who intends to control individuals as mere pieces forgets that 'in the great chessboard of human society, every single piece has a principle of motion of its own' (TMS, VI.ii.2.17, p. 234). But this movement is not uniform; neither is it the result of homogeneous human natures. It is the member of society moving autonomously, as an internally structured and complex human being who lives in an open and changing society. That is why no one can control human affairs. In corroboration of this point, Smith is continuously aware of the ineluctable 'unintended consequences' that are pervasive in reality. Therefore, to restrict Adam Smith to a mechanistic–empiricist–positivist view of human beings is to ignore his humanistic legacy.

In his early essay 'The Principles Which Lead and Direct Philosophical Enquiries; Illustrated by the History of Astronomy' – 'the pearl of the collection', according to Schumpeter (1994 [1954], p. 182) – Smith hints at his methodological position.[38] Before investigating the different stages of astronomical discoveries, he explains how psychological principles direct scientific endeavour. Surprise ('what is unexpected'), wonder ('what is new and singular') and admiration ('what is great and beautiful') correspond to the different and successive mental stages of our 'philosophical enquiries'. Surprise is '[t]he violent and sudden change produced upon the mind, when an emotion of any kind is brought suddenly upon it' (EPS, p. 35). Wonder is 'that uncertainty and anxious curiosity excited by its singular appearance, and by its dissimilitude with all the objects he had hitherto observed' (EPS, p. 40). The sentiment of surprise exalts the novelty of wonder, 'the first principle which prompts mankind to the study of Philosophy' (EPS, p. 51). Finally, admiration is attained with the discovery of 'the real chains which Nature makes use of to bind together her several operations' (EPS, p. 105). Curiosity, intellectual dissatisfaction and scientific success that will soothe the mind represent these three states of the mind.

The philosophical move underlying Smith's methodology is that these 'sentiments' (surprise, wonder and admiration) must lead to uncovering the 'nature and causes' of natural and social phenomena. Therefore this particular psychological development of science entails not only an aesthetic view, but also a methodological position that must not be exclusively constructed by looking to reason (Descartes), and certainly not to hidden causes (Scholastics), but by surveying reality in its broad realm. Experience, induction and also introspection play a relevant role in this process. Smith defines recurrently philosophy 'as the science of the *connecting principles* of nature' that 'endeavours to introduce order into the chaos of jarring and discordant appearances' (EPS, pp. 45–6, emphasis added). Moreover, its aim is to 'lay open the *concealed connections* that unite the various appearances of nature' (EPS, p. 51, emphasis added).

Smith's philosophy, following Newton, gives priority to the method of resolution, i.e. to uncovering the real structures underlying phenomena, as the task of the philosopher is finally to reveal these 'concealed connections'.

One particular feature of Newton's natural philosophy, completely different from Smith's moral philosophy, is that the *Principia*, and to a lesser extent the *Opticks*, is highly mathematical. In the Preface to the *Principia*'s first edition, Newton declared 'it has seemed best in this treatise to concentrate on *mathematics* as it relates to natural philosophy' (Newton, 1999 [1687], p. 381), and certainly he went very far in this relation.[39] However, Smith is very cautious, and rather sceptical about the use of mathematics in moral philosophy. He explicitly declares, 'the utility of those sciences [the higher parts of mathematics], either to the individual or the public, is not very obvious' (TMS, IV.2.7, p. 189). In a letter regarding Webster's compilation of Scottish population figures for a pension scheme, Smith declares: 'You know that I have little faith in Political Arithmetic and this story does not contribute to mend my opinion of it' (Corr., p. 288). Again, Smith declares in his WN: 'I have no great faith in political arithmetic' (WN, IV.v.b.30, p. 534). His method in economics (and *a fortiori* in ethics),[40] with the exception of some simple arithmetical operations such as averages, is not mathematical at all.

Jevons's attempt to treat economics as a 'Calculus of Pleasure and Pain' that 'must be mathematical science in matter if not in language' (Jevons, 1965 [1871], p. vii) is an important feature of the so-called marginal revolution that has been exceedingly influential in modern mainstream economics. Smith, in contrast to the general emphasis on mathematics that characterises neoclassical economics, which has been taken even further by modern mainstream economics, was sceptical about the use of mathematics in the social sciences.[41] But for Jevons, even Adam Smith, 'the father of the science, as he is often considered … is thoroughly mathematical' (ibid., p. xxii). Indeed, celebrating the centennial of the publication of the WN, Jevons emphasised that

> a hundred years ago it was very wise of Adam Smith to attempt no subdivision, but to expound his mathematical theory (for I hold that his reasoning was really mathematical in nature) in conjunction with concrete applications and historical illustrations.
>
> (Jevons, 1905, pp. 200–1)

It seems no mere coincidence that almost a century later, for the WN's bicentenary, Samuelson briefly endeavours a vindication of Smith, but this time 'to raise his stature as an economic theorist' (Samuelson, 1977,

p. 42). Apparently his well-known dictum, 'equations are sentences, pure and simple' (Samuelson, 1952, p. 59), not only establishes a necessary relation between mathematics and language, but also a sufficient one, as Samuelson states that: 'Smithian functions, never before written down explicitly in quite this way, are concave and first-degree-homogeneous' (ibid., p. 48). Adam Smith must be looking forward to the year 2076!

These misinterpretations have fostered the generally accepted view of a peculiar 'Smithian Newtonianism', not only restricting Newton's method to just its mathematical and deductivist parts, but also confining Smith's broad philosophical project to the narrowness of mainstream econom-ics' emphasis on axiomatic–deductive models. Indeed, one consequence of this 'Smithian Newtonianism' is to make Adam Smith a forerunner of general equilibrium theory. Chapter 7 'Of the natural and market Price of Commodities' of Book I of the WN has been routinely considered as the foundation of general equilibrium, and the 'invisible hand' is the popular metaphor used to explain this idealised order. For example, Schumpeter, not an admirer of Smith, considers Walras's general equilibrium as the 'Magna Charta of economic theory' (Schumpeter, 1994 [1954], p. 968), and repeatedly complains about Smith's lack of originality. But Schumpeter praises the 'rudimentary equilibrium theory of Chapter 7, by far the best piece of economic theory turned out by A. Smith' (ibid., p. 189).

Similarly, Robbins eulogises the achievement of the WN, which is 'in harmony with the most refined apparatus of the modern School of Lausanne' (1962 [1932], p. 69). Hollander, applying our modern knowledge of general equilibrium to an understanding of Smith's price mechanism, refers to 'the remarkable chapter' (1973, p. 117). Later he argues that 'still a price–theoretic orientation to the *Wealth of Nations*' has not been con-tradicted (Hollander, 1987, p. 61), concluding that chapter 7 'contains an embryonic account of general equilibrium theory' (ibid., p. 65). And Arrow and Hahn, in their first chapter, written by Arrow, consider the invisible hand as 'a poetic expression' and ascribe Smith as 'a creator of general equilibrium theory' (1971, p. 2).[42]

The expression 'invisible hand' occurs three times in Smith's writings, in his essay in EPS, 'The History of Astronomy', in the TMS and also the best-known version in the WN. Its first appearance is definitely ironic, reacting, as usual, against 'the poison of enthusiasm and superstition'. Smith refers to the origin of polytheism: 'fire burns, and water refreshes; heavy bodies descend, and lighter substances fly upwards, by the necessity of their own nature; nor was the *invisible hand* of Jupiter ever apprehended to be employed in those matters' (EPS, p. 49, emphasis added). In the TMS he mentions the 'natural selfishness and rapacity' of rich people who 'are led by an invisible hand to make nearly the same distribution of the nec-essaries of life' (TMS, IV.i.10, pp. 184–5). Not in terms of distribution, but when analysing the restraints upon importation, does Smith in the WN refer explicitly to the beneficial consequences of promoting self-interest, as people are 'led by an invisible hand to promote an end which was no part of his intention' (WN, IV.ii.9, p. 456). There has been a vast industry interpreting the invisible hand. Recently Grampp (2000) has detected ten possible interpretations for Smith's metaphor (including his own),[43] but the version that relates it to general equilibrium is probably, as we have already suggested, the most popular and widely accepted among mainstream economists.

Samuelson, embodying the view of economic theorists, follows Schumpeter's insight, claiming that 'these partial equilibrium relations are well-determined by Smith's relations of general equilibrium', as with 'the INVISIBLE HAND doctrine, self-interest, under perfect competition, can organize a society's production efficiently' (Samuelson, 1977, p. 47, original emphasis). Elsewhere, he praises openly 'the genius of Smith's formulation of a general equilibrium model' (Samuelson, 1992, p. 5). Before analysing the famous chapter 7 to see whether it is somehow a precursor of Walrasian general equilibrium, and thus confirming this generally accepted interpretation, I shall comment briefly on Walras's methodological position.[44] This is necessary to reveal a fundamental and curiously neglected methodological difference between the architect of general equilibrium and its foremost forerunner. In addition, this contrast will shed light upon Smith's methodology, showing that the view of Smith as a precursor of general equilibrium theory is simply instrumental to the neoclassical economics project.

4. Walras versus Smith

4.1 The Walrasian methodology of economics

In his *Elements of Pure Economics or The Theory of Social Wealth*, Walras states in the Preface to the fourth edition (1900) that '[i]t is already perfectly clear that economics, like astronomy and mechanics, is both an empirical and a rational science' (Walras, 1954 [1900], p. 47), foreshadowing his concluding remark that in '[t]he twentieth century … mathematical economics will rank with the mathematical sciences of astronomy and mechanics; and on that day justice will be done to our work' (ibid., p. 48). It appears that even as we enter the twenty-first century, Walras's aspiration still dominates our discipline.

Walras complains that Smith's definition of political economy is inadequate,[45] arguing that '[t]he primary concern of the economist is not to provide a plentiful revenue for the people or to supply the State with an adequate income, *but to pursue and master purely scientific truths*' (ibid., p. 52, emphasis added). Emphasising the *is* and *ought* distinction, Walras states that pure economics is as scientific as natural science, a clear expression of the character of the Newtonian revolution applied to the social realm. What happens in reality or what is normative is a different issue:

What ought to be from the point of view of material well-being is the concern of applied science or art; while what ought to be from the point of view of justice is the concern of moral science or ethics.

(Ibid., p. 60)

Therefore, in the *ought to* realm, we have applied economics (category of relations between persons and things: industry) and ethics (category of relations between persons and persons: institutions).[46]

In conclusion, Walras posits a three-fold classification of political economy as a social science into pure, applied and social economics (ibid., pp. 60–4). Science, or pure economics, differs from art and ethics in that it deals with natural phenomena, not with human phenomena. Regarding human phenomena, Walras distinguishes between art (applied economics) and ethics (social economics). They differ, since the former category comprises the relations between persons and things, and the latter category comprises the relations between persons. Walras's classification may be dissected as follows:

	Domain	*Criteria*	*Object*	*Generic phenomena*
Pure economics	Science	Truth	Universals	Value in exchange
Applied economics	Art	Useful	Material well-being	Industry or production of wealth
Social economics	Ethics	Good	Justice	Property or distribution of wealth

I refer deliberately to Walras's object of pure economics as 'universals' in order to underline his explicit, but neglected, Platonic view of science: 'A truth long ago demonstrated by the Platonic philosophy is that science does not study corporeal entities but universals of which these entities are manifestations' (Walras, 1954 [1900], p. 61). Also, in a letter he declares: 'I am an idealist. I believe ideas reshape the world after their own image … I am swimming against the current of my century. Facts are now the fashion' (quoted in Jaffé, 1980, pp. 532–3, note 14).

Walras not only has a Platonic view of science in itself, but the leap from pure economics to applied economics is done in a Platonic way.[47] As economists we should proceed by reaching the world of ideas, and then, like the philosopher–king, we should descend to our worldly reality. In his own words:

the pure science of economics should then abstract and define ideal-type concepts in terms of which it carries on its reasoning. The return to reality should not take place until the science is completed and then only with a view to practical applications.

(Walras, 1954 [1900], p. 71)

Moreover, pure economics represented by 'the theory of value in exchange is really a branch of mathematics' (ibid., p. 70), and it 'must precede *applied economics*; and this pure theory of economics is a science which resembles the physico-mathematical sciences in every respect' (ibid., p. 71). If Newton, observing the attraction between bodies, could infer the law of gravity, Walras's intention, after contemplating the phenomenon of exchange, was to derive an analogous general equilibrium theory.[48] This conflation of pure economics with mechanics was a natural consequence of the 'mechanical philosophy' tradition, which, since the French Enlightenment, and especially among the *Economistes*, adopted Newton's success as its scientific archetype. The application of mathematics to social phenomena, as one fundamental characteristic of the so-called marginal revolution, is an offspring of this tradition.[49] Not surprisingly, Walras wrote that 'the natural economic mechanism is, within certain limits, a self-moving and self-regulating mechanism' (quoted in Ingrao and Israel, 1990, p. 386). This reduction of social phenomena to mathematics evolved with Pareto until Debreu finally made the crucial step: the theory's axiomatisation, the culmination of Walras's Platonic ideal.

For Walras, ideas not only precede but also surpass reality,[50] or, in other words, pure economics has a ubiquitous priority over practical and ethical issues. Jaffé (1980) summed up this argument: 'It is clear that Walras had no liking for realism as such. In fact, he vehemently denounced it in all its manifestations: in art and in literature as well as in philosophy, science and economics' (ibid., p. 532).

4.2 Smith's controversial Chapter 7 of Book I

In Chapter 7, 'Of the natural and market Price of Commodities', of Book I of the WN, Adam Smith succinctly develops what has been commonly considered as the foundations of general equilibrium theory. He refers to the natural (ordinary or average) rates of wages, profit and rent, which define the natural price of commodities. This natural price differs from the market (or actual) price that is determined by effective demand. Smith explains how a decrease in the quantity supplied triggers competition among consumers, thereby increasing prices, and how an increase in the 'quantity brought to the market' forces suppliers to lower prices. And, as a conclusion, we have the following influential passage:

> The natural price, therefore, is, as it were, the central price, to which the prices of all commodities are continually *gravitating*. Different accidents may sometimes keep them suspended a good deal above it, and sometimes force them down even somewhat below. But whatever may be the obstacles which hinder them from settling in this *center of repose and continuance*, they are constantly tending towards it.
>
> (WN, I.vii.15, p. 75, emphasis added)

The use of the word *gravitating* and the idea of a *center of repose* have been commonly accepted as additional evidence of Newton's influence.[51] Furthermore, Smith twice in this chapter refers to his system of 'perfect liberty', suggesting a perfectly competitive market, a harmonious order constituted by crypto-atomistic consumers and producers. This has been fundamental to interpreting Smith as a precursor of general equilibrium theory, and of the theorems of welfare economics. But after a couple of pages discussing some facts about price volatility and how fluctuations affect rent, wages and profits, Smith continues:

> But although the market price of every particular commodity is in this manner continually *gravitating*, if one may say so, towards the natural price, yet sometimes particular accidents, sometimes natural causes, and sometimes particular regulations of police, may, in many commodities, keep up the market price, for a long time together, a good deal above natural price.
>
> (WN, I.vii.20, p. 77, emphasis added)

It is noteworthy that, in this passage, Smith carefully adds after *gravitating* 'if one may say so', underlining its metaphorical character. Certainly, the tone of this second passage is different, but the basic economic idea of a tendency, in its vernacular sense, remains. But Smith then immediately explores the three reasons why market prices can exceed natural prices. Thus his attempt is to explain the *causes* of deviations in natural price, to discover the nature of these 'different' and 'particular' accidents, not to reduce these phenomena to a final state.

To conclude that Smith had a view of prices as teleologically 'gravitating' towards an equilibrium in which individuals behave as isolated atoms motivated simply by self-interest – and thus a clear indication of 'Smithian Newtonianism' – is a conclusion that has to be laid to rest. The universal law of gravitation, as I have already stressed, was fundamental during the Enlightenment. It was the cornerstone of scientific success, and its terminology was widely used. Smith was no exception,[52] as most intellectuals not only relied on Newton's success, but also borrowed directly from his rhetoric. But is Smith's realistic account of economic phenomena paving the way for an ontologically atomistic–mechanistic general equilibrium theory? My answer is emphatically negative.

First of all, we know that general equilibrium theory, since Walras's early contributions, has become increasingly mathematical, basically emulating the results of what Cohen (1980) terms the *Principia*'s 'Newtonian style'. But we have already argued that Smith opposed the use of sophisticated mathematics in political economy.

Second, unconditional faith in a rational order, characterised by harmony, stability, balance or equilibrium, was a particularly French phenomenon, pervasive in Lavoisier, Laplace, Condillac, Lagrange,

Condorcet and particularly in the Physiocrats. The thinkers of the Scottish Enlightenment, and Smith in particular, did not consider that social phenomena could be reduced simply to such an assumption. Indeed, Smith used the word equilibrium only once in the WN, when criticising the doctrine of the balance of trade (WN, IV.iii.c.2, p. 489). The word equilibrium, that had been previously been introduced into the language of political economy by the Physiocrats,[53] the real forebears of general economic equilibrium theory, does not appear in other relevant passages that might suggest a relationship with general equilibrium theory. Moreover, regarding Smith's teleological view of the market, he is considering a process, not a final state. Blaug has expressed this view bluntly:

> The effort in modern textbooks to enlist Adam Smith in support of what is now known as the 'fundamental theorems of welfare economics' is a historical travesty of major proportions. For one thing, Smith's conception of competition was … a process conception, not an end-state conception.
>
> (Blaug, 1997 [1962], p. 60)[54]

And third, the development of general economic equilibrium theory has produced progressively more idealised models, inspired by the Walrasian Platonistic picture of pure economics,[55] and increasingly removed from reality. If the Walrasian tradition of pure economics, and especially its contemporary mainstream inheritors, are highly idealist, Smith's political economy is definitely realist.

These three points are intertwined. Smith not only belonged to a tradition that reacted against the metaphysics of Plato (third point), but also against the Cartesian rationalism that influenced mechanical philosophy (first and second points). He evidently shared Newton's apprehension about reducing all phenomena to mechanical causes. This is ontologically fundamental. Mechanical reductionism applied to economics demands the use of sophisticated mathematics to explain the harmony of market forces within an idealised general equilibrium model. In conclusion, this reductionism presupposes a closed system, an assumption that is at the core of mechanical philosophy and at the heart of mainstream economics, especially in relation to general equilibrium theory.

The conviction, held by mainstream economists, that social phenomena can be treated mechanically, and individuals atomistically, has been wrongly ascribed to something that might be called 'Smithian Newtonianism'. The latter is a doubly spurious interpretation of Newton and Smith that has pervaded neoclassical and mainstream economics and underlies the development of modern economic general equilibrium theories. If mainstream economists have simply relegated Newtonianism to forces in equilibrium, neglecting Newton's method of resolution, this mechanical order, in their view, influenced Smith's conception of the market mechanism. Moreover, economic theorists share the widespread interpretation that Smith's conception of market forces has been enhanced by an atomistic conception of human beings. This mechanistic–atomistic reading of Smith has been used to make him the 'father of the science', but only of the science of neoclassical and mainstream economics.

5. Some possible methodological connections with critical realism

Smith's general attempt to uncover the nature of political economy, and in particular to illuminate the 'different accidents' (WN, I.vii.15, p. 75) of the market mechanism, cannot be considered either a philosophical or a theoretical predecessor of general equilibrium theory. If the theories of general economic equilibrium presuppose a closed system, Smith's realism in political economy cannot be confined to the narrowness of this project. Indeed, 'Adam Smith's portrayal of the economy is hardly reducible simply and unambiguously to a system of spontaneous harmonious order' (Lawson, 1994, p. 531).

I shall now briefly emphasise some similarities between Smith's philosophical position and the project recently systematised as critical realism. I argue that a proper interpretation of 'Smithian Newtonianism', a serious assessment of what Smith does share with Newton, reveals his project to be closer to that of critical realism than to the axiomatic–deductive programme embraced by modern mainstream economists. The intuition that we live in an open system in which tendencies are 'transfactual', i.e. they *are* (or are in play) irrespective of what *happens* (the actual outcome that emerges), is implicit in Smith's general attempt to uncover the 'nature and causes' of the market mechanism. I maintain not only that critical realism sheds further light on our understanding of Smith, but also that critical realism can find in the 'father of the science' an eminent ally for arguing against the mainstream insistence on axiomatic–deductive models.

The idea of celestial order, strengthened by the ontology of mechanical philosophy, proved to be extremely influential for the development of economics. Lawson has argued of the celestial closure associated with Newtonian mechanics that

> it is precisely its spectacular nature that accounts for some part of the general failure from Laplace onwards to realize that the situation is relatively uncommon, to appreciate that the celestial closure is far from being indicative of the phenomenal situation that can be expected to prevail more or less everywhere.
>
> (1997, pp. 29–30)

Smith's aim was not the realisation of a theoretical model of the market mechanism from which a conjunction of events can be deduced. Neither was he the traditional empiricist confining his philosophical mind exclusively to the empirical and actual domains of reality. His ambitious intellectual pursuit was to uncover the real structures underlying social and moral phenomena, and the aim of Chapter 7 of the WN is to unpack the 'nature and the causes' of the market. The mainstream project of general economic equilibrium, in particular, deviates substantially from Smith's intention. If prices potentially tend to a natural price, Smith never reduces the potentiality of the price mechanism as exercised to an actuality defined in a closed system. In general, Smith's political economy does not presuppose a deductivist view of the world as a set of theories erected upon the event regularity conception of laws.

Critical realism poses the concept of tendency as fundamental to its scientific project. In its broader sense, tendencies are potentialities that may not be actualised because we live in an open system (ibid., pp. 22–3, and *passim*). They belong to the real or 'deep' domain of underlying structures, powers and mechanisms that do or may 'exist', regardless of being identified. Tendencies are non-empirical; they are rather 'transfactual'. They can either be manifest, as in Newton's explanation of the movement of planets, or underlying observable phenomena, like gravity. It is the latter that reveals the real stability. Even planetary motion may be disrupted, say by an undetected massive meteoroid (ibid., pp. 29–30). This is a common and important feature of tendencies that has been routinely ignored within modern mainstream economics. Although Smith is using 'tending towards' in a vernacular sense, his elucidation of the price mechanism, encompassed within his methodological position, is an attempt to reveal the 'real' causes underlying the phenomena, which is the primary object of social science. Therefore his emphasis on uncovering 'the particular accidents ... natural causes, and ... particular regulations of police' (WN, I.vii.20, p. 77) does not necessarily imply a ubiquitous and all-encompassing closed system.

Tendencies, simply viewed as manifest strict event regularities, miss the 'real' but not necessarily actualised nature of most social phenomena. This failure is represented by an unreal 'decentralized economy motivated by self-interest and guided by price signals' (Arrow and Hahn, 1971, pp. vi–vii), disguised as a clear, simple and abstract, but closed mathematical model. Uncovering the nature of the market mechanism phenomenon was part of Smith's intention. Looking for the causes was his scientific motto. In this sense his aim was to reveal the 'nature and causes' underlying social phenomena. Furthermore, Smith's project, as an interdisciplinary endeavour seeking to uncover the real causes behind social phenomena, is not compatible with the currently dominant idealised neoclassical and mainstream economics. It forms part of an open system, not only in terms of its evident but neglected multidisciplinary aim, but also in its methodological stance.

Newton's analytic–synthetic method emphasises the precedence of the method of resolution over the method of composition, underlining his assessment that the major difficulties are in the former, and not in the synthetic and mathematical deductions that necessarily follow. Smith adopted the spirit of Newton's method, but he does not favour induction, and neither does he favour deduction. Both Newton and Smith react against reducing phenomena to mechanical causes, sharing in common a philosophical project, in Smith's words, to 'lay open the concealed connections that unite the various appearances of nature' (EPS, p. 51). Critical realism has defended a retroductive mode of inference, which is neither deduction, nor induction. Its aim is also to reveal the 'concealed connections', i.e. to uncover the mechanisms that exist at a deeper level. Retroduction, as a mode of inference, involves a dialectical movement that attempts to identify the factors responsible for phenomena, and not simply to generalise them. It appears to me clear that critical realism as a philosophical position, and retroduction, as a primary method of uncovering the causes of phenomena, is closer to Smith, and also to Newton, than is the restrictive mainstream economists' emphasis on axiomatic–deductive models.

Smith's methodological stance regarding 'surprise, wonder and admiration' (see *supra* section 5.3.2), which has a longstanding philosophical pedigree, is also similar to that of modern-day critical realism:

> theoretical explanatory enquiry is likely to be initiated or further stimulated where contrastive demi-regs occasion a sense of surprise, doubt or inconsistency, either between the observed phenomenon and a set of prior beliefs, or between competing explanations of it, and so forth.
>
> (Lawson, 1997, p. 211)

It is certainly 'surprise' and the sense of doubt occasioned by 'wonder' that play a central role for philosophy, triggering a process of uncertainty that finally transforms our understanding into the illumination of reality. Also, Smith's definition of philosophy as aiming to 'lay open the concealed connections' clearly reflects his conception of the nature of reality as not always actualised. Therefore we can infer that Smith's philosophical position presupposes existence, while acknowledging that it is usually concealed.

In addition, the idea of change, as inherently embedded in social life, and the evidence of 'unintended consequences' are fundamental to Adam Smith and fully shared by the project of critical realism, with its criticism of mainstream models that attempt to control reality as if human beings were uniform molecules in a laboratory.

6. Conclusions

The popular and biased version of 'Smithian Newtonianism' that I have attempted to expose has fostered a mechanistic reduction of social phenomena, and an atomistic view of human beings. Indeed, Newton's

Principia inspired a succession of *Principles* (Bentham, Ricardo, Malthus, Mill, Jevons and Marshall, to name the most influential), but Smith's *Inquiry into the Nature and Causes of the Wealth of Nations*, with its suggestive and original title, definitely inspired but did not necessarily lead to the neoclassical project. The question that must be asked is: What happened to the real 'Smithian Newtonianism'? Regarding its neglect, I believe there is a shared responsibility between what might be called an enlightened mechanical reductionism of social phenomena and an atomistic philosophical utilitarianism.[56] In this context, the emphasis on measuring, presupposing atomistic behaviour in a closed system, represents the twilight of the Scottish political economy tradition.

In particular, as I have argued above, Walras's methodological approach in pure economics, as the foundation of general economic equilibrium theory, is the historical predecessor par excellence of what Lawson (1997) has defined as the ubiquity of spontaneous closed systems that characterise deductivism in modern economics. Walras's explicit reliance upon Plato's ideals clearly contrasts with the realist view of phenomena, which prevailed during the Scottish Enlightenment, and was fully endorsed by Smith. The Walrasian legacy of pure economics, as a particular version of Newtonianism applied to economics, ignores the fundamental feature that individuals are internally structured and inherently complex, and that we act in an open and changing world. Faith in reducing the complexities of economic behavior to a mathematical model, inspired by mechanical philosophy, is simply inconsistent with Smith's broader project.

The Scottish political economy tradition, represented by Adam Smith, has been increasingly marginalised in contemporary economics (Dow, 1987). Even worse, Smith has been unjustly confined to the tight quarters of mainstream economics. He became the father of a highly deductivist science: pure economic theorising. He has been praised as the founder of general equilibrium theory, a Walrasian offspring whose spirit could hardly be more contrary to Smith's philosophical position. Were he alive today, Smith would certainly lament the divorce of economics and ethics, epitomised by the hackneyed fact/value distinction. He would regret that currently mathematical axioms or assumptions not evident in themselves have replaced familiar principles. He would also complain that mathematics has become the method of economics. It is not without relevance that the often quoted but rarely read WN was written for the general public, not for the expert mathematician.

Political economy was a broad and interdisciplinary subject within moral philosophy. Its realism and practical insight in tackling policy matters are lacking in today's mainstream economics. Such straightforward characteristics are not only shared by critical realists and the majority of historians of economic thought, but are at the core of their project. Unfortunately, the original aim of Smith's broad philosophical inquiry has been ignored, leading to diverse, and usually opposing, versions of the legacy of 'the father of the science'. The voice of critical realism is a healthy call for a more 'realistic' approach to our discipline, and Adam Smith's enduring whisper embodies a vigorous tradition of political economy that has been overshadowed by somewhat naïve if influential interpretations.

Notes

1 Earlier versions of this paper were presented at the Workshop on 'Realism and Economics', at King's College, University of Cambridge, 26 February 2001, and at the 28th Annual Meeting of the 'History of Economics Society', held at Wake Forest University, North Carolina, 2 July 2001. This paper has greatly benefited from these discussions. In particular, I am indebted to Phil Faulkner, Clive Lawson, Adil Mouhammed and Warren Samuels for helpful comments on earlier drafts, and also to Avi Cohen for his suggestions. I am also grateful to Sir Martin Rees, and especially to Peter Lipton for helpful and acute comments on section 2 of this paper. Eric Schliesser, who independently reached some similar conclusions, provided me with very useful comments. Finally, comments by two anonymous referees are gratefully acknowledged. The usual caveats apply. First published in *Cambridge Journal of Economics*, 2003, Vol 27, No 5, 723–747.

2 Herein I shall refer to five of the six standard books of *The Glasgow Edition of the Works and Correspondence of Adam Smith* by their abbreviation for references and quotations. These are, in addition to *An Inquiry into the Nature and Causes of the Wealth of Nations* (WN) and *The Theory of Moral Sentiments* (TMS): *Essays on Philosophical Subjects* (EPS), *Lectures on Rhetoric and Belles Lettres* (LRBL) and *The Correspondence of Adam Smith* (Corr.).

3 For example, Manuel's iconoclastic *Portrait of Sir Isaac Newton* (1968) offers a Freudian account of Newton's life, although sometimes it is overspeculative. In my view, Westfall's *Never at Rest: A Biography of Isaac Newton* (1980) is still the best and most objective biography of Newton. Andrade (1954), Hall (1992) and White (1998) are also worth reading.

4 Keynes even declared that Newton's manuscripts 'have, beyond doubt, no substantial *value*' (1972, p. 368, emphasis added). He was mistaken not only in academic, but also in economic, terms: recently Cambridge University Library has paid over £6 million for the Macclesfield Collection. However, ironically, in 1888 the University Library returned some of Newton's manuscripts because they lacked scientific value.

5 For a perceptive but perhaps outdated review of the 'Newtonian industry', see Westfall (1976). In his *Guide to Newton's Principia*, Cohen provides additional references (Newton, 1999 [1687], pp. 293–8). He also announces George Smith's forthcoming *Companion to Newton's 'Principia'*.

6 Arianism denied Trinitarianism, and it was specifically excluded from the Toleration Act of 1689, which offered religious freedom to all faiths, except Catholicism and any form of Unitarianism (which included Arianism).

7 Schofield distinguishes Baconian, Leibnizean, Cartesian and Newtonian 'Newtonianisms', and argues that during the eighteenth century 'it seems clear that Newton was not a Newtonian in any one of the many versions which can be identified' (1978, p. 177). For a challenging and insightful account of these issues, see Buickerood (1995) and also the essays in Jones (1989).

8 At the beginning of Book III 'The System of the World', Newton declares that he had 'composed an earlier version of book 3 in popular form, so that it might be more widely read' but that in order 'to avoid lengthy disputations,

I have translated the substance of the earlier version in a mathematical style, so that they may be read only by those who have first mastered the principles' (Newton, 1999 [1687], p. 793).

9 The *Opticks* was published in 1704 a year after the death of Newton's life-long rival Hooke (Newton had sworn not to publish it while Hooke was alive). A second edition in Latin was published in 1706, followed by a second English edition in 1717.

10 The first English edition contains, at the end, 16 queries; the Latin edition increases the number by seven new queries (numbered 25–31) and the second English edition adds eight more queries (numbered 17–24).

11 The laws of 1) inertia, 2) force and change in motion, and 3) action and reaction, are in Book I. Newton acknowledged his debt to Galileo for the first two laws, and to Wren, Wallis, Huygens and Mariotte for the third. In Book III he states the law of universal attraction, and then applies it to the 'system of the world'.

12 *Principia*'s first edition was published in 1687. The second, edited by Cotes, in 1713, and the third, edited by Pemberton, was published in 1726. The first complete English translation of Newton's *Principia* was made by Andrew Motte, and published posthumously in 1729. A revised version by Florian Cajori was published in 1934. Recently Whitman and Cohen's long-awaited complete translation of *Principia*, with Cohen's excellent *A Guide to Newton's Principia*, was published in 1999.

13 For the importance of Scottish Universities, see Cant (1982).

14 Redman calls Maclaurin an 'associate' (1997, p. 106) of Newton and Drennon 'a close friend of Newton' (1933–4, p. 407). However, Hall says categorically 'they never met' (1992, p. 367).

15 I choose Maclaurin's work not only because he was Scottish, and his book was probably read by Adam Smith, but also as I believe it is the best early explanation of Newton's method. Pemberton, the editor of the *Principia*'s third edition, wrote *A View of Sir Isaac Newton's Philosophy* (1728), but it lacks Maclaurin's clarity. Voltaire's *The Elements of Sir Isaac Newton's Philosophy* (1738) is also deficient, as he did not have the necessary mathematical knowledge.

16 As Wightman, the editor of EPS, acknowledges, in particular 'Smith's methodology would seem to conform to the requirements of the Newtonian method properly so called in that he used the techniques of analysis and synthesis in the appropriate order' (EPS, intr., p. 12).

17 Similarly Hall has recently argued that 'though Newton did not assert hypotheses as truths, he framed them throughout his life, and indeed made them known to the world' (1998, p. 58).

18 Rule IV states that inductions 'should be considered either exactly or very nearly true' until new phenomena may make them 'either more exact or *liable to exceptions*' (Newton, 1999 [1687], p. 796, emphasis added). I am indebted to Eric Schliesser for calling my attention to the significance of these last three words.

19 Unfortunately, Newton suppressed the fragment. According to McGuire, in this fragment 'Newton gives a more elaborate account of his methodology than is found in the later editions of the *Opticks*' (1970, p. 179).

20 Although Newton developed, independently of Leibniz, 'the calculus of fluxions' – differential calculus – and his 'method of flowing quantities, or fluents' – integral calculus – he would refer to his mathematical pursuits as 'divertissements'.

21 Hypothesis is the Greek word for supposition. According to Koyré, 'hypothesis' became for Newton 'toward the end of his life, one of those curious terms, such as "heresy", that we never apply to ourselves, but only to others' (1965,

p. 52). His aversion to the word 'hypothesis' definitely began in 1672, when he published *The New Theory of Light and Colours*. Hooke considered Newton's theory only a hypothesis and Huygens a 'probable' one. Newton's reaction against the insistence upon this accusation is the reason for his *General Scholium*'s famous dictum *hypothesis non fingo*, and not the erroneously popular belief that in general he dismissed hypothesis (a belief that would certainly contradict his *Opticks*). Recently Hall, who had earlier denied the importance of Alchemy for Newton, has argued for the importance of hypothesis for Newton (cf. *supra* note 17). Although the famous phrase has been usually given as 'I frame no hypothesis', following Motte's 1729 translation, it should be better translated as 'I feign no hypothesis' (Newton, 1999 [1687], p. 943), as has been convincingly argued by Koyré (1965, p. 35), because feign implies falsehood. On this, see also Cohen's *Guide to Newton's Principia* (Newton, 1999 [1687], pp. 275–6).

22 In a letter dated 1715, Leibniz complained that '[a]ccording to their [Newtonians'] Doctrine, God Almighty wants to *wind up* his Watch from Time to Time' (Clarke, 1717, p. 5), reflecting the idea of a complete and self-sufficient world. It is important to point out that when Newton argued that the cause of gravity could not be mechanical, he is implying that gravity cannot be simply attributable to or determined by mechanical cause, i.e. matter and motion, which is at the core of Descartes' theory of vortices. Koyré points out: 'As for the "mechanical" hypothesis, that is, *those of Descartes, Huygens and Leibniz*, they have no place in experimental philosophy [Newtonian method] simply because they attempt to do something that cannot be done' (1957, p. 230, original emphasis).

23 In the suppressed introduction to the *Opticks* Newton asserts that

> [t]o explain all nature is too difficult a task for any one man or any one age. Tis much better to do a little with certainty & to leave the rest for others that come after you than to explain all things without making sure of anything.
> (McGuire, 1970, p. 183)

24 On alchemy's importance to Newton's system, Dobbs left us her wonderful *Foundations of Newton's Alchemy* (1975) and then *Janus Faces of Genius: The Role of Alchemy in Newton's Thought* (1991); see also Figala (1977, 1992 [1984]). McGuire and Rattansi, based on the 'classical' Scholia, give a fascinating analysis of the influence of *prisca sapientia* in Newton (see also White, 1998), concluding that 'the heart of Newton's philosophy of nature, the world of forces and active principles, lay categorically beyond the systems of the *Opticks* and the *Principia*' (McGuire and Rattansi, 1995 [1966], p. 108). Nowadays there is no doubt that alchemy, theology (for references see Verlet (1996, p. 337, note 20)) and the traditions of ancient sages and philosophers played a role shaping Newton's conception of natural philosophy. However, the extent of its influence is still a matter of debate. In *A Guide to Newton's Principia*, Cohen provides an excellent account of this issue (Newton, 1999 [1687], pp. 56–64), arguing that certain concepts of Newton's natural philosophy are closely intertwined with his general concerns in alchemy, ancient wisdom and theology.

25 Samuel Clarke, an intimate friend of Newton, represented the philosophical views of his master replying to Leibniz's famous five letters in a polemic that finished with the latter's death, in 1716. Clarke published Leibniz's letters and his replies in 1717 as *A Collection of Papers which passed between the learned late Mr. Leibniz and Dr. Clarke, in the years 1715 and 1716. Relating to the Principles of Natural Philosophy and Religion*.

26 In the Introduction to his *Treatise on Human Nature*, Hume refers explicitly to the 'application of experimental philosophy to moral subjects' (Hume, 2000

[1739–40], p. 4), and in his *Enquiry Concerning the Principles of Morals*, Hume compares his attempt to 'Newton's chief rule of philosophizing' (Hume, 1998 [1751], p. 98), certainly referring to Newton's four rules, in the beginning of Book III of *Principia* (cf. Newton, 1999 [1687], pp. 794–6).

27 I believe that the character of the Scottish Enlightenment emerged from a unique and challenging atmosphere. After the parliaments of Scotland and England passed the Act of Union in 1707, for various reasons a provincial feeling among the Scottish intellectual community sprang up. A kind of 'keeping up with the English' feeling spread. This influenced the quality of their education. In addition, if the Scots would refer to the British after the Union, the English would still distinguish between them and the Scottish. Smith's protests that in Oxford 'the great part of the publick professors have, for these many years, given up altogether even the pretence of teaching' (WN, V.i.f.8, p. 761) is not only a consequence of personal bitterness, but also reflects a well-founded belief. Smith's point against Oxbridge was that '[t]he great fault which I find with Oxford and Cambridge, is that Boys sent tither instead of being Governed, become Governors of the Colleges, and that Birth and Fortune there are more respected than Literary Merit' (Corr., p. 37). Smith's opinion that the Scottish universities were 'the best seminaries of learning that are to be found anywhere in Europe' (Corr., p. 173) was generally accepted. They had an outstanding reputation in Europe.

28 Cohen states categorically that 'Newton was not a positivist' (Newton, 1999 [1687], p. 279), arguing that Ernst Mach's influential *Science of Mechanics: A Critical and Historical Account of Its Development* had set out a biased interpretation of Newton (cf. Newton, 1999 [1687], p. 277). Mach considered that '[a]ll that has been accomplished in mechanics ... has been a deductive, formal, and mathematical development on the basis of Newton's laws' (Mach, 1960 [1893], p. 226; note that, if we replace 'mechanics' by 'economics', this has a curious relationship to the current state of our discipline; see also his interesting section 'The economy of sciences', ibid., pp. 577–95). Incidentally, the mathematician Karl Menger, son of Carl Menger, wrote the introduction to the sixth American edition, and it was in his famous colloquium that Wald and von Neumann presented in 1934 and 1937, respectively, important papers for the development of general economic equilibrium theory (see Weintraub, 1983, pp. 5–15).

29 It was Marshall who, before retiring in 1908, finally won the battle to establish economics as an independent subject of study. But the 'moral philosophy tradition' of economics remained in Cambridge, with Keynes writing to Harrod in 1938, 'I want to emphasize strongly the point about economics being a moral science' (1973, p. 300).

30 This feature of the Enlightenment, and the role of reason, is evident when Kant, in his *Answer to the Question: What is the Enlightenment?*, replies with Horace's motto '*Sapere aude*! Have courage to make use of your *own* understanding! Is thus the motto of enlightenment' (Kant, 1996 [1784], p. 17, emphasis in the original). *Sapere aude* literally means 'dare to be wise' or 'dare to learn'.

31 Before his death, Smith ordered his executors to burn sixteen folios that presumably contained part of his ambitious project of a treatise on jurisprudence.

32 Soon after, Blaug adds that Smith 'had a naïve view of what constituted Newton's method' (1992 [1980], p. 53), which is very disputable. I would rather agree with Cohen, who thinks that 'Smith was well educated in Newtonian science' (1994, p. 66).

33 Deane cautiously declares that '[h]ow far Smith did apply a Newtonian scientific method to his inquiry into the nature and causes of the wealth of nations is debatable' (1989, p. 61), and Redman, whose work has been very influential for

this chapter, regardless of some points of disagreement, argues that 'persisting today in labeling Smith's method Newtonian would be deceptive' (1993, p. 225).

34 The literature on the generalised view that self-interest is the foundation of Smith's economics is enormous, but I think the quotation that best reflects my point here is Stigler's comment that the WN is 'a stupendous palace erected upon the granite of self-interest' (Stigler, 1982, p. 136). Also interesting is Stigler's claim, at the bicentenary conference of the publication of the WN, that 'Adam Smith is alive and well living in Chicago' (Skinner, 1988, p. 2), though it must be acknowledged that during 2001–2002 five PhD dissertations related to Smith were submitted at the University of Chicago.

35 Winch convincingly argues against those who still want to view Smith as a precursor of general equilibrium theory, but he believes that '[w]hat Smith praised as "Newtonian method" fits his own work as well as that of general equilibrium theorists' (1997, p. 399).

36 For example, '[t]he superior genius and sagacity of Sir Isaac Newton, therefore, made the most happy, and, we may now say, the greatest and most admirable improvement that was ever made in philosophy' (EPS, p. 98).

37 Lawson has underlined the nature of social conflict in Smith's WN as proof of his non-atomistic view of human beings (1994, pp. 528–33). On Smith and different aspects of civic humanism, as it is clear in chapter 3, I am indebted to some influential essays in Hont and Ignatieff (1983) and to Winch (1978, 1996, 2002) who, although cautious and even critical at times, is influenced by this historical approach.

38 I use 'hinting at' advisedly as this essay was written before 1758 (see EPS, p. 103), and perhaps much earlier, while Smith was studying in Oxford. However, this does not mean that the *History of Astronomy* represents simply a juvenile work. Its importance is evident, as Smith did not include it amongst those essays that were burned just before his death. Moreover, it seems that he cared about this piece, because in 1773, when Smith was ill, and Hume was his literary executor, Smith mentions this essay as publishable (cf. Corr., p. 168).

39 Cohen (1980) argues that the uniqueness of Newton's revolution was the creation of a 'mathematical' system of nature. He labels the 'Newtonian style' as an unmatched stage of scientific progress, as Newton applied geometry, algebra, fluxions, limit procedures and infinite series to natural phenomena. In his *Guide to Newton's Principia*, he summarises this position (Newton, 1999 [1687], pp. 148–55).

40 For example, 'the never to be forgotten Dr. Hutcheson' (Corr., p. 309) would occasionally resort to 'applying mathematical calculation to moral subjects' (Hutcheson, 1726 [1725], p. 194). See especially *An Inquiry into the Original of Our Ideas of Beauty and Virtue* (1726 [1725], pp. 182–90) and *An Essay on the Nature and Conduct of the Passions and Affections, with Illustrations on the Moral Sense* (1728, pp. 34–40).

41 Smith's position probably reflects the Scottish reaction against abstract mathematics and their preference for geometry (Olson, 1971), which, by the way, is very 'Newtonian'. Redman (1997, pp. 250–3) defends the thesis that Smith was not an opponent of statistics, but only that he was simply reacting against a lot of guessing. However, she endorses the view that Smith was against the use of mathematics in political economy.

42 Kerr (1993) rebuts this neoclassical interpretation of Smith simply in terms of the market mechanism, proposing a framework for understanding his theory as one of endogenous technical change and growth.

43 Warren Samuels is working on a project on the invisible hand, and he has already detected 48 different senses for Smith's metaphor. Regarding the invisible hand in general, I believe that its importance should not be overstated, and

I would agree with Galbraith for whom 'the invisible hand, the most famous metaphor in economics, was just that, a metaphor' (1987, p. 64).

44 I shall concentrate exclusively on Walras not only because he is the father of general equilibrium theory, but also because his methodological position permeates the modern development of general economic equilibrium theory, in which the latter's emphasis on existence surpasses even the former in terms of its detachment from reality. However, a caveat must apply: we must not 'confuse Walras with the present day Walrasians' (Morishima, 1977, p. 5).

45 Jaffé suggests that 'it is doubtful that Walras ever read the *Wealth of Nations* attentively' (ibid., p. 26), and attributes Walras's neglect of Smith as a predecessor of his theory of general equilibrium to his 'fanatical anglophobia' (1977, p. 31).

46 This distinction is part of the partially unfinished project of Walras's second book, *Elements of Applied Economics of the Theory of the Agricultural, Industrial, and Commercial Production of Wealth*, and his third book, *Elements of Social Economics or The Theory of Distribution of Wealth via Property and Taxation*. Two papers on these issues were published in 1898 and 1896 (*Études d'économie politique appliquée* and *Études d'économie sociale*, respectively).

47 Pokorny (1978) rightly underlines the Platonic nature of Walrasian economics, to which Smith was clearly opposed, as their main and insurmountable difference. Unfortunately this philosophical feature of Walras has been generally ignored.

48 It is well known that Walras developed his general equilibrium theory with the image of the equilibrium of mechanical forces in his mind, inspired by Poinsot's 1803 treatise *Eléments de statique*.

49 Cohen argues that the social sciences have failed in their attempt to emulate the Newtonian sciences. He even claims, against those who would like to see general equilibrium theory as Newtonian, that '[o]ne cannot even make a mechanical model of the Newtonian system. In the Newtonian system ... there is no equilibrium' (1994, p. 61).

50 I agree with Walker (1984) who challenges Jaffé's interpretation of Walrasian general equilibrium as normative. The view of Walras's methodology as 'realistic utopia' (Jaffé, 1980, p. 533) is disputable, at least in its modern versions. See Lawson (1989, p. 73, note 2) for a brief but insightful account of how contemporary general equilibrium theory has become more idealised. For a perceptive treatment of the intellectual development of general economic equilibrium theory Ingrao and Israel (1990) still provide, in my view, the best account. Weintraub (1983) presents an interesting account of the modern development of competitive equilibrium.

51 Redman's view that '[i]n Smith's day invoking Newton's name and borrowing his terminology was a commonly used rhetorical device' (Redman, 1993, p. 225) is quite relevant. For the intellectually widespread use of this rhetoric and its philosophical significance, see especially Myers (1983).

52 Cohen not only affirms that Smith understood Newton better than did Montesquieu and Carey, but also shows that Smith's notion of prices is closer to the real Newtonian system (1994, pp. 65–6).

53 Rothschild points out that 'Turgot and Condorcet use the word "équilibre" fairly frequently in their economic writings' (2001, p. 312, note 147). For example, Turgot wrote that

[t]he market value of commodities, the revenue, the prices, the salaries, the population, are things which are linked to one another by mutual dependence and which find themselves their *equilibrium* according to a natural proportion; and this proportion will always be maintained so long as commerce and competition are entirely free.

(Turgot, 1770, quoted in Fry, 1992, p. 170, emphasis added)

a closer forerunner of general economic equilibrium theory. I am indebted to Jochen Runde for pointing out that not mentioning equilibrium does not necessarily imply not believing in it. However, I still believe that the point, although far from conclusive, is important to my argument, and to me the possibility that Smith might have consciously avoided the use of the word 'equilibrium' seems perfectly plausible.

54 For example, Mas-Collel *et al.*'s popular *Microeconomic Theory* reads:

> The first fundamental theorem of welfare economies states conditions under which any price equilibrium with transfers, and in particular any Walrasian equilibrium, is a Pareto optimum. For competitive market economics, it provides a formal and very general confirmation of Adam Smith's asserted "invisible hand" property of the market.
>
> (Mas-Collel *et al.*, 1995, p. 549; see also pp. 327 and 524)

55 Walras's project is perhaps the most radical precursor of the conditions Lawson attributes to what today would be termed as 'economic theory' or 'pure theory' (Lawson, 1997, pp. 86–7). Certainly, this idealised mathematical pure economics project has become archetypal for mainstream economists with their emphasis on formalistic deductivist models.

56 'It was this view of individuals as members of society, rather than isolated atoms, which provided the basic principles underlying Scottish political economy, differentiating it from formal utilitarianism' (Dow, 1987, p. 341). Veblen defends the same thesis: 'After Adam Smith's day, economics fell into profane hands … it was the undevout utilitarians that became the spokesmen of the science' (Veblen, 1933 [1899–1900], p. 130).

References

Andrade, E. N. da C. 1954. *Sir Isaac Newton*, London, Collins, St James's Place.

Arrow, K. J. and Hahn, F. 1971. *General Competitive Analysis*, San Francisco, Holden-Day.

Blaug, M. 1992 [1980]. *The Methodology of Economics or How Economists Explain*, Cambridge, Cambridge University Press.

Blaug, M. 1997 [1962]. *Economic Theory in Retrospect*, Cambridge, Cambridge University Press.

Brewster, D. 1831. *Memoirs of the Life, Writings, and Discoveries of Sir Isaac Newton*, London, John Murray.

Buickerood, J. G. 1995. Pursuing the science of man: some difficulties in understanding eighteenth century maps of the mind, *Eighteenth Century Life*, vol. 12, no. 2.

Cant, R. G. 1982. Origins of the Enlightenment in Scotland: the Universities, in *The Origins and Nature of the Scottish Enlightenment*, edited by Campbell, R. H. and Skinner, A, Edinburgh, John Donald.

Clarke, S. 1717. *A Collection of Papers which Passed between the Learned Late Mr. Leibniz and Dr. Clarke, in the Years 1715 and 1716. Relating to the Principles of Natural Philosophy and Religion*, London, James Knapton.

Cohen, I. B. 1980. *The Newtonian Revolution: With Mustrations of the Transformation of Scientific Ideas*, Cambridge, Cambridge University Press.

Cohen, I. B. 1994. Newton and the social sciences, with special reference to economics, or, the case of the missing paradigm, in *Natural Images in Economic Thought: 'Markets Read in Tooth and Claw'*, edited by Mirowski, P., Cambridge, Cambridge University Press.

Deane, P. 1989. *The State and the Economic System: An Introduction to the History of Political Economy*, Oxford, Oxford University Press.

Dobbs, B. J. T. 1975. *The Foundations of Newton's Alchemy: The Hunting of the Greene Lyon*, Cambridge, Cambridge University Press.

Dobbs, B. J. T. 1991. *Janus Faces of Genius: The Role of Alchemy in Newton's Thought*, Cambridge, Cambridge University Press.

Dow, S. C. 1987. The Scottish political economy tradition, *Scottish Journal of Political Economy*, vol. 34, no. 4.

Drennon, H. 1933–4. Newtonianism: its method, theology, and metaphysics, *Englische Studien*, vol. 68, pp. 397–409.

Figala, K. 1977. Newton as alchemist, *History of Science*, vol. 15, no. 1.

Figala, K. 1992 [1984]. Newton's alchemical studies and his idea of the atomic structure of nature, appended to Hall, A. R. *Isaac Newton: Adventurer in Thought*, Cambridge, Cambridge University Press.

Freudenthal, G. 1981. Adam Smith's analytic–synthetic method and the 'system of natural liberty', *History of European Ideas*, vol. 2, no. 2.

Fry, M. 1992. *Adam Smith's Legacy: His Place in the Development of Modern Economics*, London, Routledge.

Galbraith, K. 1987. *A History of Economic Thought*, London, Penguin.

Grampp, W. D. 2000. What did Smith mean by the invisible hand?, *Journal of Political Economy*, vol. 108, no. 3.

Hall, A. R. 1992. *Isaac Newton: Adventurer in Thought*, Cambridge, Cambridge University Press.

Hall, A. R. 1998. Isaac Newton and the aerial nitre, *Notes and Records of the Royal Society of London*, vol. 52, no. 1.

Hetherington, N. S. 1983. Isaac Newton's influence of Adam Smith's natural laws in economics, *Journal of the History of Ideas*, vol. 44, no. 3.

Hollander, S. 1973. *The Anomalies of Adam Smith*, London, Heinemann Educational Books.

Hollander, S. 1987. *Classical Economics*, Oxford, Basil Blackwell.

Hont, I. and Ignatieff, M. 1983. *Wealth and Virtue: The Shaping of Political Economy in the Scottish Enlightenment*, Cambridge, Cambridge University Press.

Hume, D. 1998 [1751]. *An Enquiry concerning the Principles of Morals*, edited by Beauchamp, T. L., Oxford, Oxford University Press.

Hume, D. 2000 [1739–40]. *A Treatise on Human Nature*, edited by Nonon, D. F. and Nonon, M. J., Oxford, Oxford University Press.

Hutcheson, F. 1726 [1725]. *An Inquiry into the Original of Our Ideas of Beauty and Virtue*, London, J. Darby.

Hutcheson, F. 1728. *An Essay on the Nature and Conduct of the Passions and Affections, with Illustrations on the Moral Sense*, Glasgow, J. Darby and T. Brown.

Ingrao, B. and Israel, G. 1990. *The Invisible Hand: Economic Equilibrium in the History of Science*, Cambridge, MA, MIT Press.

Jaffé, W. 1977. A centenarian on a bicentenarian: Leon Walras' *Elements* on Adam Smith's *Wealth of Nations*, *Canadian Journal of Economics*, vol. 10, no. 1.

Jaffé, W. 1980. Walras' economics as others see it, *Journal of Economic Literature*, vol. 18, no. 2.

Jevons, W. S. 1905. Future of political economy, in *The Principles of Economies: A Fragment of a Treatise on the Industrial Mechanism of Society and Other Papers*, London, Macmillan.

Jevons, W. S. 1965 [1871]. *The Theory of Political Economy,* New York, Augustus M. Kelley.

Jones, P. 1989. *The 'Science of Man' in the Scottish Enlightenment: Hume, Reid and their Contemporaries,* Edinburgh, Edinburgh University Press.

Kant, I. 1996 [1784]. An answer to the question: What is the Enlightenment?, in *Practical Philosophy: The Cambridge Edition of the Work of Immanuel Kant,* edited by Gregor, M. J., Cambridge, Cambridge University Press.

Kerr, P. 1993. Adam Smith's theory of growth and technological change revisited, *Contributions to Political Economy,* vol. 12, pp. 1–27.

Keynes, J. M. 1972. 'Newton, the Man', in *Essays in Biography,* Vol. X in *The Collected Writings of John Maynard Keynes,* edited by Moggridge, D., pp. 363–81, London, Macmillan for the Royal Economic Society.

Keynes, J. M. 1973. *The General Theory and After: Defence and Development,* Vol. XIV in *The Collected Writings of John Maynard Keynes,* edited by Moggridge, D., London, Macmillan for the Royal Economic Society.

Koyré, A. 1957. *From the Closed World to the Infinite Universe,* Baltimore, Johns Hopkins University Press.

Koyré, A. 1965. *Newtonian Studies,* London, Chapman & Hall.

Kuhn, T. S. 1958. Newton's optical papers, in *Isaac Newton's Papers & Letters on Natural Philosophy,* edited by Cohen, I. B., Cambridge, Cambridge University Press.

Lawson, T. 1989. Abstraction, tendencies and stylised facts: a realist approach to economic analysis, *Cambridge Journal of Economics,* vol. 13, no. 1.

Lawson, T. 1994. The nature of Post Keynesianism and its links to other traditions, *Journal of Post Keynesian Economics,* vol. 16, no. 4.

Lawson, T. 1997. *Economics & Reality,* London, Routledge.

Mach, E. 1960 [1893]. *The Science of Mechanics: A Critical and Historical Account of Its Development,* Illinois, The Open Court Publishing Company.

Maclaurin, C. 1750 [1748]. *An Account of Sir Isaac Newton's Philosophical Discoveries,* London, Printed for A. Millar.

Manuel, F. E. 1968. *Portrait of Sir Isaac Newton,* Cambridge, MA, Belknap Press of Harvard University Press.

Mas-Collel, A., Whinston, M. D. and Gereen, J. R. 1995. *Microeconomic Theory,* Oxford, Oxford University Press.

McGuire, J. E. 1970. Newton's 'Principles of Philosophy': an intended preface for the 1704 *Opticks* and a related draft fragment, *British Journal for the History of Science,* vol. 5, pp. 178–86.

McGuire, J. E. and Rattansi, P. M. 1995 [1966]. Newton and the 'Pipes of Pan', in *Newton: A Norton Critical Edition,* edited by Cohen, I. B. and Westfall, R. S., New York, W. W. Norton.

Morishima, M. 1977. *Walras' Economics: A Pure Theory of Capital and Money,* Cambridge, Cambridge University Press.

Myers, M. L. 1983. *The Soul of Modern Economic Man,* Chicago, The University of Chicago Press.

Newton, I. 1931 [1704]. *Opticks: or, a Treatise of the Reflections, Refractions, Inflections and Colours of Light,* London, Printed for William Innys.

Newton, I. 1999 [1687]. *Mathematical Principles of Natural Philosophy,* edited by Cohen, I. B. and Whitman, A., Berkeley, University of California Press.

Olson, R. 1971. Scottish philosophy and mathematics 1750–1830, *Journal of the History of Ideas*, vol. 32, no. 1.

Pocock, J. G. A. 1975. *The Machiavellian Moment*, Princeton, NJ, Princeton University Press.

Pocock, J. G. A. 1983. Cambridge paradigms and Scotch philosophers: a study of the relations between the civic humanist and the civil jurisprudential interpretation of eighteenth-century social thought, in *Wealth & Virtues: The Shaping of Political Economy in the Scottish Enlightenment*, edited by Hont, I. and lgnatieff, M., Cambridge, Cambridge University Press.

Pocock, J. G. A. 1985. *Virtue, Commerce, and History: Essays on Political Thought and History, Chiefly in the Eighteenth Century*, Cambridge, Cambridge University Press.

Pokorny, D. 1978. Smith and Walras: two theories of science, *Canadian Journal of Economics*, vol. 11, no. 3.

Redman, D. A. 1993. Adam Smith and Isaac Newton, *Scottish Journal of Political Economy*, vol. 40, no. 2.

Redman, D. A. 1997. *The Rise of Political Economy as a Science: Methodology and the Classical Economists*, Cambridge, MA, The MIT Press.

Robbins, L. 1962 [1932]. *An Essay on the Nature and Significance of Economic Science*, New York, Macmillan.

Rothschild, E. 2001. *Economic Sentiments: Adam Smith, Condorcet, and the Enlightenment*, Cambridge, MA, Harvard University Press.

Samuelson, P. 1952. Economic theory and mathematics: an appraisal, *The American Economic Review*, vol. 33, no. 2.

Samuelson, P. 1977. A modem theorist's vindication of Adam Smith, *The American Economic Review*, vol. 67, pp. 42–9.

Samuelson, P. 1992. The overdue recovery of Adam Smith's reputation as an economic theorist, in *Adam Smith's Legacy: His Place in the Development of Modern Economics*, edited by Fry, M., London, Routledge.

Schofield, R. E. 1978. An evolutionary taxonomy of eighteenth-century Newtonianisms, *Studies in Eighteenth Century Culture*, vol. 7, pp. 175–92.

Schumpeter, J. A. 1994 [1954]. *History of Economic Analysis*, Oxford, Oxford University Press.

Skinner, A. 1976. Adam Smith: the development of a system, *Scottish Journal of Political Economy*, vol. 23, no. 2.

Skinner, A. 1979. Adam Smith: an aspect of modern economics?, *Scottish Journal of Political Economy*, vol. 26, no. 2.

Skinner, A. 1988. 'Adam Smith and Economic Liberalism', Hume Occasional Paper no. 9, Edinburgh, David Hume Institute.

Smith, A. 1981 [1776]. *An Inquiry into the Nature and Causes of the Wealth of Nations*, edited by Campbell, R. H. and Skinner, A. S., Indianapolis, Liberty Fund.

Smith, A. 1982. *Essays on Philosophical Subjects*, edited by Wightman, W. P. D., Indianapolis, Liberty Fund.

Smith, A. 1984 [1759]. *The Theory of Moral Sentiments*, edited by Macfie, A. L. and Raphael, D. D., Indianapolis, Liberty Fund.

Smith, A. 1985. *Lectures on Rhetoric and Belles Lettres*, edited by Bryce, J. C., Indianapolis, Liberty Fund.

Smith, A. 1987. *Correspondence of Adam Smith*, edited by Mossner, E. C. and Ross, I. S., Indianapolis, Liberty Fund.

Stigler, G. J. 1982. *The Economist as a Preacher,* Oxford, Basil Blackwell.

Stukeley, W. 1936 [1752]. *Memoirs of Sir Isaac Newton's Life,* London, Taylor & Francis.

Veblen, T. 1933 [1899–1900]. The preconceptions of economics, in *The Place of Science in Civilization and Other Essays,* New York, Viking Press.

Verlet, L. 1996. 'F=MA' and the Newtonian revolution: an exit from religion through religion, *History of Science,* vol. 34, no. 3.

Walker, D. A. 1984. Is Walras' theory of general equilibrium a normative scheme?, *History of Political Economy,* vol. 16, no. 3.

Walras, L. 1954 [1900]. *Elements of Pure Economics or The Theory of Social Wealth,* edited and translated by Jaffé, W., London, George Allen & Unwin.

Weintraub, E. R. 1983. On the existence of a competitive equilibrium: 1930–1954, *Journal of Economic Literature,* vol. 21, no. 1.

Westfall, R. S. 1976. The changing world of the Newtonian industry, *Journal of the History of Ideas,* vol. 36, no. 1.

Westfall, R. S. 1980. *Never at Rest: A Biography of Isaac Newton,* Cambridge, Cambridge University Press.

White, M. 1998. *Isaac Newton: The Last Sorcerer,* London, Fourth Estate.

Winch, D. 1978. *Adam Smith's Politics: An Essay in Historiographic Revision,* Cambridge, Cambridge University Press.

Winch, D. 1996. *Riches and Poverty: An Intellectual History of Political Economy,* Cambridge, Cambridge University Press.

Winch, D. 1997. Adam Smith's problems and ours, *Scottish Journal of Political Economy,* vol. 44, no. 4.

Winch, D. 2002. Commercial realities, republican principles, in *Republicanism and Commercial Society,* edited by Skinner, Q. and van Galderen, M., Cambridge, Cambridge University Press.

9 Metatheory as the key to understanding: Schumpeter after Shionoya[1]

Mário Graça Moura

1. Introduction

You are somewhat confused. Having consulted Schumpeter's major works and the literature devoted to his writings, you find (a) that it is often the case that interpreters present contrasting views on him and (b) that almost invariably there exists textual support for their contrasting theses. In fact, you are beginning to wonder whether you are ever going to be able to *understand* Schumpeter. This could demand that you study his entire work – a considerable enterprise, at the end of which it could be that you remain confused.

As it happens, this enterprise has meanwhile been undertaken by Yuichi Shionoya. In his *Schumpeter and the Idea of Social Science* (1997), which builds on several of his papers, he argues that attempting to interpret Schumpeter on the basis of fragments of his *oeuvre* involves the risk of a misunderstanding. '[R]ather than reading him in snatches', it is necessary to 'consider all of his work' (ibid., p. xi) – not least his metatheoretical writings. Shionoya's book is actually subtitled *A Metatheoretical Study*, for he endeavours to show that Schumpeter's metatheoretical framework provides the key to understanding the underlying unity and real significance of his scientific achievements.[2]

The centrepiece of this project is Shionoya's attempt to demonstrate Schumpeter's consistent adherence to a particular version of instrumentalism. In Section 2, I consider the scope and meaning of this thesis, decomposing it into a series of claims. I then proceed to examine these claims (Section 3). I conclude that Shionoya does not succeed in establishing what he aims to establish and, indeed, that he is sometimes simply wrong. This critique paves the way for an alternative route to understanding Schumpeter's discourse. A very different hypothesis on Schumpeter is put forward (Section 4), and its contribution to rendering his mercurial work intelligible is assessed, albeit incompletely (Section 5). This hypothesis, too, is of a metatheoretical nature. It is influenced by Tony Lawson's writings, which are at the centre of critical realism (see Lawson, 1997). Brief concluding comments follow in Section 6.

2. Shionoya's thesis: context and meaning

2.1 *Preliminaries*

Shionoya's book endeavours to reconstruct Schumpeter's metatheoretical framework with a view to clarifying the meaning of his substantive theories. This metatheoretical framework is presented as a system comprising the methodology of science, the sociology of science, and the history of science; whereas Schumpeter's substantive theory is argued to consist of three blocks – economic statics, which turns on general equilibrium theory; economic dynamics, which builds on statics and attempts to encompass innovation and its implications; and economic sociology, which focuses on institutions and their evolution, attempting to integrate theory and history.

These definitions cannot convey the complexity of Shionoya's plan. But they are indicative of its scope. In fact, Schumpeter connoisseurs will have no doubt that it is impossible to do justice to an argument of this breadth – *a fortiori* to any subtleties, of which there are many in Shionoya's book – within the space available. For my purposes, however, it suffices to concentrate on a single, original element of Shionoya's argument, which is ultimately decisive for the success of his book. I refer to the claim – for which I henceforth reserve the label 'Shionoya's thesis' – that Schumpeter is an instrumentalist.

The centrality of this thesis within Shionoya's book is apparent from the fact that it is repeatedly retrieved in order to illuminate Schumpeter's theories, to the effect that all of Schumpeter's substantive work is ultimately claimed to have an instrumentalist cast. In addition to this, Schumpeter is argued to defend instrumentalism in his metatheoretical writings.[3] Consider the following passages:

> Chapter 5 takes up [Schumpeter's] maiden work, *Das Wesen und der Hauptinhalt der theoretischen Nationalökonomie*, and interprets his methodology as instrumentalism, which was first developed to lay a foundation for neoclassical economics but later functioned as an anchor in his attempt to construct a universal social science designed for the integration of theory and history.
>
> (Shionoya, 1997, pp. 9–10)

> When we leave *Wesen* and come to dynamic theory and the analysis of historical development in Schumpeter's subsequent works, we find him dealing with facts explicitly in terms of statistical and historical concepts … But this neither meant, nor was there a reason, that he had to change his instrumentalist view.
>
> (Ibid., p. 121)

I shall show that Schumpeter applied his instrumentalist method-ology, as forged first for static economic theory, *mutatis mutandis* to economic sociology ...

(Ibid., p. 196)

The broad contours of Shionoya's thesis are apparent from these state-ments. An investigation of its merits requires, however, a more precise formulation. Let us attempt to specify what exactly Shionoya is claiming.

2.2 *Shionoya's claims about Schumpeter's instrumentalism*

Shionoya's thesis claims that Schumpeter is an instrumentalist in two senses. On the one hand, he is claimed to defend instrumentalism. On the other hand, his substantive work – all of his substantive work – is deemed to have an instrumentalist basis. In other words, Schumpeter is argued to practise consistently the methodology that he preaches – a feature that it would be unwise simply to take for granted.

Shionoya implies, moreover, that recognising Schumpeter's instru-mentalism is the key to solving interpretative controversies and avoiding interpretative mistakes. These mistakes, of which there seem to be quite a few (see, e.g., Shionoya, 1997, pp. 75–6, 82, 243–4), are apparently due to 'reading Schumpeter in snatches' and failing to take account of his metatheory. In Shionoya's words, 'locating [Schumpeter's substantive contributions] within our metatheoretical framework will clarify the logi-cal connection between them and dispel existing misinterpretations about them' (ibid., p. 10). Accordingly, it is incumbent upon Shionoya to demon-strate that, by interpreting Schumpeter as an instrumentalist, one exposes, and avoids, flaws that blemish Schumpeterian exegesis.

Finally, there is a third claim implicit in Shionoya's thesis. His aim is to unveil the underlying unity and consistency of Schumpeter's work. 'In Schumpeter's system', Shionoya (ibid., p. 310) writes, 'statics, dynamics, and economic sociology are coherent, though they are concerned with different problems and methods.' The key to grasping this coherence is Schumpeter's metatheory. It follows, then, that the latter must be coherent. This implies, in turn, that Shionoya regards instrumentalism as a coherent position. In fact, Shionoya himself seems to be committed to instrumen-talism. 'My interpretation', he writes (ibid., p. xii), 'might be criticized for being too well ordered and artificial. Yet in science theoretical models imposed on reality are always systematic and artificial creations of the human mind, and both the depiction and the reconstruction of theories and thought are in themselves theoretical activities.'

To sum up, Shionoya's thesis encompasses three claims, which can be summarised as follows:

Proposition 1:   Schumpeter is an instrumentalist, and consistently so.
Proposition 2:   Recognising Schumpeter's instrumentalism is the key to understanding his theories.
Proposition 3:   Schumpeter's instrumentalism is a coherent position.

We have already gone some way towards describing the content of these propositions. It remains to specify Shionoya's conception of Schumpeter's instrumentalism.

2.3 Shionoya's conception of Schumpeter's instrumentalism

In the minds of economists, instrumentalism probably recalls Milton Friedman's irrepressible 1953 essay; and instrumentalism is typically regarded as the conception that theories are neither true nor false but only convenient instruments for generating successful predictions logically. Shionoya dissents. To begin with, he argues that it is Schumpeter – not Friedman – who should be credited with methodologically defending instrumentalism. But he adds that it is inappropriate to restrict instrumentalism to its currently more usual meaning. Instrumentalism, Shionoya observes, entails that theories are nothing but tools, but not that they must be computational rules for prediction; and it is in this broader sense that Schumpeter is an instrumentalist:

> [I]t is more appropriate to interpret [Schumpeter's] point of view in light of the broad conception of instrumentalist philosophy that was held by his contemporaries and by which he was actually affected. Hence we should understand the *central* claims of instrumentalism as the belief that, first, with regard to the role of theories, they are merely tools, and second, with regard to the cognitive status of theories, they are neither true nor false.
>
> (Shionoya, 1997, p. 98)

> The instrumental roles of a theory ... include organization, classification, reconstruction, and – through all these efforts – the understanding of otherwise chaotic facts. For Schumpeter, the latter roles were much more important than prediction ... It was from this standpoint of moderate instrumentalism that Schumpeter opposed ... the conception of prediction as the ultimate test of a theory.
>
> (Ibid., p. 122)

As is apparent, the first passage above implies that there are some subsidiary claims of instrumentalism. And Shionoya goes on to argue that some, but not all, variants of instrumentalism are opposed to realism – a rather problematic point.[4] Schumpeter's position, however, is suggested to be anti-realist (see, e.g., Ibid., p. 110).

In short, Shionoya's definition of Schumpeter's alleged stance can be accepted in that it incorporates the constitutive traits of instrumentalism as traditionally understood in philosophy, i.e. the conception of theories as nothing more than tools, hence as neither true nor false. We can now proceed to examine his thesis.

3. Diagnosing Shionoya's thesis

3.1 On instrumentalism as the key to understanding Schumpeter[5]

As remarked, Shionoya sometimes points to errors and confusions in Schumpeterian exegesis, which the recognition of Schumpeter's metatheoretical position is supposed to dispel. One of these interpretative errors concerns Schumpeter's thesis that the capitalist process has a tendency to self-destruction. In Shionoya's opinion,

> [Schumpeter's] thesis that capitalism will decline because its economic success will lay the groundwork for social circumstances unfavorable to it should not be interpreted as historical determinism. It has nothing to do with a historical hypothesis or prediction; rather, it is a theoretical hypothesis derived from certain assumptions about the interaction between economic and social factors, and its validity rests on the instrumental roles [of theories] in understanding reality.
>
> (Shionoya, 1997, p. 220)

The claim that Schumpeter's thesis on the self-destruction of capitalism is not a deterministic prediction is actually true. Clearly, though, Schumpeter could be an instrumentalist if this claim were false. And the fact that it is true does not require that Schumpeter be committed to instrumentalism.[6] This case, then, provides no grounds to accept that the recognition of Schumpeter's (alleged) instrumentalist orientation is the key which dispels misinterpretations of his substantive theories.

Now, the most obvious difficulties in Schumpeterian exegesis ultimately turn on his repeated, and not merely rhetorical, invocation of both Walras and Marx. Schumpeter is committed to general equilibrium theory, and yet innovation, or creative destruction, and capitalism's structural transformation are his main topics. This has always puzzled Schumpeterians. If there is one issue that we would want Shionoya to explain, then it is certainly this one. He should convince us that Schumpeter's apparent dualism is intelligible – i.e. does not yield an inconsistency – once we recognise his adherence to instrumentalism. This is what Shionoya offers in his most elaborate comment on Schumpeter's commitment to Walras and Marx:

> More than a few authors writing about Schumpeter have criticized the paradox and inconsistency in his admiration for, and indebtedness

to, both Walras and Marx. This criticism is rooted in the popular mis-interpretation ... that fails to understand the coordination of statics and dynamics in Schumpeter's thought; it is no wonder that this mis-interpretation is now extended to relations between economic and noneconomic areas in a wider perspective ... Social events are related to each other, not only simultaneously but also intertemporarily. Simultaneous relationships are the subject of the Walrasian general equilibrium theory; intertemporal relationships are the theme of the Marxian theory of evolution. Both relationships are necessary ... to explain any event at any point in time ... The apparent contradiction [in Schumpeter] is refuted by the idea, based on historical experience, that the very success of the capitalist economy will produce noneco-nomic factors that are inconsistent with it ... Accounting for the fact that the changes in noneconomic factors are the result of economic development, we can assume a grand general equilibrium between the economic and noneconomic spheres and its evolution over time. This was Schumpeter's integrated vision ...

(Shionoya, 1997, p. 82)

But this, I think, is hardly what we are entitled to expect. Surely this 'grand general equilibrium' – or 'enlarged version of the general equi-librium analysis', as Shionoya (1986, p. 759) previously called it – has nothing to do, and is incompatible, with Walrasian general equilibrium? And, in any case, where is instrumentalism? Elsewhere in the book Shionoya gives a clue:

[T]here is the often repeated criticism that [Schumpeter's] simultane-ous acceptance of Walras's idea and Marx's idea is a contradiction. [But i]t is quite natural that a theoretical structure differs according to the objectives and problems of researchers. It is unnecessary from a meth-odological standpoint to demand that all theories be monolithic even if they are entertained by one person. To use Schumpeterian rhetoric, does it cause any inconvenience or contradiction that one has a key for a room and another key for a car? Because only the usefulness of instru-ments is important, no one thinks that one must have one master key.

(Shionoya, 1997, p. 310)

But this statement is somewhat at odds with the one quoted before. And if it is intended to suggest that theories are just tools – and there-fore it is legitimate to resort to Walras for some purposes, and to Marx for other purposes – then it misses the target. For, even if instrumental-ism allows for mutually inconsistent theories, it presumably requires that they be internally consistent; and it is emphatically not the case that some of Schumpeter's writings are consistently 'Walrasian' and others consistently 'Marxian'. What renders Schumpeterian exegesis most difficult is precisely his proclivity to be inconsistent within the same piece.

There are several instances of this but I shall select just one.[7] As is well known, Schumpeter's *Theory of Economic Development* (Schumpeter, 1934) provides an account of the emergence of innovators, or entrepreneurs, who disrupt the tradition-based 'circular flow of economic life'. Yet this circular flow is identified with a competitive equilibrium system (which, the absence of interest apart, is basically Walrasian); and this equilibrium system seems to rule out the possibility of real novelty, i.e. to emasculate Schumpeterian entrepreneurship. How a creative entrepreneur is to emerge in such a scenario as Schumpeter fashions is something of a mystery.

Now, can instrumentalism serve to demonstrate that this apparent inconsistency is actually an optical illusion? I am not convinced – particularly since Shionoya does not really discuss this issue. The verdict must be that Proposition 2 is unsubstantiated.

3.2 On Schumpeter as an instrumentalist

The fact that Proposition 2 is unsubstantiated makes it harder for Shionoya to defend Proposition 1. But he attempts to validate the latter following yet another route. He argues that Schumpeter advocates instrumentalism in his writings on the methodology of economics (first and foremost *Das Wesen und der Hauptinhalt der theoretischen Nationalökonomie* (Schumpeter, 1908)) and on the methodology of economic sociology (primarily *Gustav v. Schmoller und die Probleme von heute* (Schumpeter, 1926)). Since theorists do not necessarily follow their methodological prescriptions, these pronouncements are insufficient to establish that Schumpeter is – or is not – an instrumentalist. But they can be suggestive. Consider the economic methodology implied in the following passages:[8]

> If mechanics had wanted to satisfactorily answer what 'force', 'movement', 'mass', etc., actually 'are', then the proud edifice which we now admire could never have been erected.
>
> (Schumpeter, 1908, p. 24)

> One usually contrasts explanation and description, and demands that theory find the 'causes of facts', and the 'forces' and 'laws' that 'rule' them. But, on closer observation, it is easy to convince oneself that the core of any theory, *what it truly says*, is always and only a statement about functional relationships between some quantities; all the rest is ... unessential. This is most evident in those sciences that are farthest away from speculation, the exact natural sciences, and has found its clearest expression in Kirchhoff's famous definition of mechanics. To find ... causes is impossible for us, but we do not need them either in order to arrive at concrete results.
>
> (Ibid., pp. 37–8)

The conception of theory defended here does seem to point towards Shionoya's thesis.[9] There are, however, some complications. Compare the following excerpts:

> The explanation that our theory provides is a description of functional relations between the elements of our system by means of formulas as concise and general as possible. *These formulas we now call 'laws'.*
>
> (Schumpeter, 1908, p. 43)

> We do not philosophise about what must be because of some 'necessity' but instead describe what in many cases *is*. In so doing we expect that the same *be* in other cases which we have not observed ...
>
> (Ibid., p. 44)

> [T]here are no grounds to refer to our laws as 'statements of tendencies', as Marshall does. What this is intended to mean is simply that circumstances may intervene which lead to results different from those that our laws entitle us to expect. But this is evident ... Each law in natural science is also subject to this possibility. A stone on a table cannot fall to the ground. If, for this reason, one wants to classify the law of gravity as a 'description of tendencies', one may do so: in principle, there is nothing to object. But there is no characteristic in here that would be specific to *our* laws.
>
> (Ibid., p. 45)

> If what the theory predicts does not occur, then the 'practical person' simply dismisses the theory as false. This is unjustified. Our laws are at work even then, and the concrete result would be *different* if they were not.
>
> (Ibid., p. 466)

In short, whilst Schumpeter puts forward an instrumentalist conception, he also seems to be implying that theories (or 'laws'), rather than being mere creations of theorists, refer to (causal) mechanisms which *exist* and, even if they are not fully manifest, make a difference. This is a realist stance.

If we turn to the methodology of economic sociology, we find further difficulties. 'From Schumpeter's standpoint', Shionoya (1997, p. 195) writes, 'if economic sociology is a theory at all, then its epistemological status must be construed as an instrument'. And he adds: 'Schumpeter's view was that economic sociology is part of theory ..., although its subject matter is different from that of economic theory' (ibid., pp. 205–6). In short, because for Schumpeter economic sociology is a kind of theory, and he regards theories as (mere) instruments, his economic sociology is instrumentalist.

Yet it is not clear that economic sociology is a theory in the sense that Shionoya's inference demands. Thus, in his *History of Economic Analysis* Schumpeter refers to theory as a 'box of tools' (Schumpeter, 1954, p. 15); he argues that history is more important, to begin with, because 'the subject matter of economics is essentially a unique process in historic time' (ibid., p. 12); he submits that theory is nonetheless neither impossible nor useless, because 'economic history itself needs its help' (ibid., p. 13, fn. 3); and eventually he brings in economic sociology, on the grounds that history and theory, 'while essentially complementing each other, do not do so perfectly' (ibid., p. 20).[10]

However, he also distinguishes between historical and theoretical hypotheses (see ibid., pp. 14–15) – a distinction already present in *Wesen* (see Schumpeter, 1908, pp. 531–2; Shionoya, 1997, p. 112). The former are claimed to imply a cognition, whereas the latter are methodological tools only. Since there is no possibility of a compromise between realism and instrumentalism, it follows, then, that the epistemological status of economic sociology – which, somehow, is supposed to serve as a bridge between theory and history – becomes obscure.

Shionoya does attempt to strengthen his argument in other ways. In his discussion of *Gustav v. Schmoller* ... he argues that

> Schumpeter wanted to put a brake on what might have appeared to be an endless process of data collection in Schmoller's research program, a bottomless pit into which historical economists were liable to fall. To do so, he had to resort to a methodological perspective ... Instrumentalism facilitates deductive attempts even when empirical data are not sufficient according to the [realist] Schmollerian standard ... One need not engage in the never-ending process of fact-finding in order to finally develop realistic assumptions.
>
> (Shionoya, 1997, pp. 202, 206–7)

Yet this is, again, unacceptable. Shionoya is, amongst other things, confusing realism with realisticness (see Mäki, 1994). He is implying that realism entails the belief that assumptions can, and indeed must, be 'finally ... realistic'. And, to the extent that he lapses into this misrepresentation, he is ultimately implying that it is *impossible* not to be an 'instrumentalist' – and thus depriving his own thesis of meaning.

It is, I think, unnecessary to persevere. Shionoya does not succeed in showing that Schumpeter's pronouncements consistently yield a defence of instrumentalism, much less that he *is* an instrumentalist. This, of course, does not entail that he is not. Is it possible, then, to falsify Shionoya's claim?

As François Perroux (1965, pp. 45 ff.) observes in his critique of Schumpeter's *Theory of Economic Development*, if a theory is to have explanatory value, then, starting from the 'essential economy' proposed, however abstract, one should be able to reconstruct the 'concrete economy'. If, on the contrary, this reconstruction attempt leads to contradictions, then the theory is *une simple construction de l'esprit*. In the latter case, that is, a method or form of reasoning has been adopted independently of, or with insufficient attention to, insights into the nature of things.

Now, as Lawson (1997) explains, a method necessarily presupposes a theory of knowledge, which in turn presupposes a theory of what is – a theory to the effect that what *is* is knowable by resorting to that method. Ontology is a category that it is impossible to eliminate. Accordingly, an a priori commitment to any method (the logico-deductive method, for instance) may be conducive to a clash with a theorist's actual world view – and give rise to tensions and inconsistencies.

Tensions and inconsistencies, as remarked, are pervasive in Schumpeter's writings – which may suggest the existence of such an a priori commitment (we shall investigate this shortly). At any event, the existence of internal tensions and inconsistencies suffices to establish that Schumpeter cannot be consistently instrumentalist.

3.3 On Schumpeter's instrumentalism as a coherent position

The considerations presented so far suffice, I think, to undermine Shionoya's thesis. Before developing an alternative hypothesis along the lines just hinted at, however, it is worth establishing that Proposition 3 is also false. And to this end, it is convenient to introduce two contrasting conceptions of the nature of the social world – to distinguish between *closed systems* and *open systems* (see Lawson, 1997).

In a closed system, conditions of action are identified with, or taken to imply, results of action. Indeed, such a system is characterised by regularities of the form 'whenever conditions x then outcome y'.[11] In such a scenario, social order can only rest upon the global coherence of these regularities – whence the necessity of some orthodox notion of equilibrium. There is no room for choice in that, if it is to be real, choice cannot be confused with the conditions of its exercise. Real novelty is thus preempted; and, relatedly, knowledge is certain and its growth monistic.

In an open system, on the other hand, regularities of the form 'whenever conditions x then outcome y' do not typically obtain: the future is indeterminate, as it must be if choice is to exist. Since choice presupposes intentionality and knowledgeability, and knowledge requires some endurability in its object, there must exist (relatively enduring) structures that facilitate, and constrain, but are not reducible to, human action. Capacities, then, are not identified with actual outcomes, and real novelty is possible. Social order now rests upon the dynamic interdependence of action and structure and is therefore an order of a transformational, perhaps evolutionary, kind. And knowledge is necessarily precarious and open to revision: ignorance and surprise are pervasive.

In the light of these definitions, it is clear that Friedman's (1953) position rests on the implicit premise that the social world is a closed system (see Lawson, 1992). Accordingly, the possibility of prediction is taken for granted. And the truth of assumptions does not matter if they yield true predictions. In fact, explanation is not even an option in Friedman's conception. He assumes that a theory is a hypothetico-deductive system, and correctly implies that one cannot logically infer the truth of its assumptions from the truth of its conclusions (see Boland, 1979). Accepting its premises, then, Friedman's 'instrumentalism' cannot be criticised on the grounds of coherence.

Schumpeter's alleged instrumentalism, however, differs from Friedman's. Schumpeter is categorical that prediction of events is typically impossible (see, e.g., Schumpeter, 1939, p. 13). But why? What kind of social world is Schumpeter implicitly assuming to reach this conclusion? Given his insistence on novelty and entrepreneurship, it would seem likely that he conceives of the social world as an open system. He certainly does *not* regard it as a closed system in our sense.

Yet, if this is correct, it appears to be the case that his putative instrumentalist position involves an incoherence. On the one hand, prediction of events is deemed typically unfeasible; on the other hand, contrary to Shionoya, instrumentalism cannot legitimately claim an explanatory role for theories, in as much as explanations cannot usefully be based upon assumptions supposedly without truth status. Such 'explanations' cannot provide but the pretence of knowledge. But theories which can neither predict nor explain would seem to be *useless* for the purpose of illuminating the social world or, in Shionoya's (1997, p. 122) expression, for understanding facts.

4. An alternative hypothesis

The preceding critique points to an alternative (realist) hypothesis on Schumpeter. This hypothesis seeks to make sense of Schumpeter's writings on the basis of a metatheoretical *inconsistency*, which is supposed to be reproduced in his substantive work. Whilst Schumpeter conceives of the social world as an open system, he simultaneously accepts a conception of the structure, or form, of scientific theories which presupposes a closed world.

That he conceives of the social world as an open system seems to follow from his views on entrepreneurship and innovation. Entrepreneurship is argued to involve creative idiosyncrasy, and accordingly innovation 'cannot be predicted by applying the ordinary rules of inference from the pre-existing facts' (Schumpeter, 1947, p. 222). Rather, it is a 'creative response' – where 'response' means that entrepreneurship is not a 'Shacklean leap into the void' (Boehm, 1990, p. 226). As Schumpeter (1991, p. 409) notes, 'objective' conditioning factors 'have as much claim to being dubbed "causal" as has the action they condition'.[12]

That he accepts a conception of science which implicitly supposes a closed world – the conception that science requires the framing of regularities of the form 'whenever conditions x then outcome y' – is suggested by his enduring commitment to equilibrium and its ultimate justification:

> [O]ur objects of investigation are certain *relations of dependence* or *functional relations*. The fact that economic quantities stand in such relations to one another legitimises their separate treatment provided that they are uniquely determined. The unique determination of a system of quantities is a scientific fact of the utmost importance. It means that, when certain *data* are given, we have all the necessary elements to '*understand*' the magnitude of those quantities and their movement. In this case, a separate, independent discipline about such phenomena is possible, and this is therefore what must be established before anything else. If a system of equations yields absolutely nothing but the proof of a uniquely determined interdependence, this is already very much: it is the founding stone of a scientific structure.
>
> (Schumpeter, 1908, pp. 33–4)

> Whoever knows the origin and the workings of the exact natural sciences knows also that their great achievements are, in method and essence, of the same kind as Walras'. To find exact forms for the phenomena whose interdependence is given us by experience, to reduce these forms to, and derive them from, each other: this is what physicists do, and this is what Walras did.
>
> (Schumpeter, 1910, p. 79)

> Lest [the reader] should ... turn away from Walras' construction [*tâtonnement*] on the ground of its hopeless discrepancy from any process of real life, I wish to ask him whether he ever *saw* elastic strings that do not increase in length when pulled, or frictionless movements, or any other of the constructs commonly used in theoretical physics; and whether, on the strength of this, he believes theoretical physics to be useless.
>
> (Schumpeter, 1954, p. 1015)

Let us analyse this justification. This is quite important in that my hypothesis may *prima facie* appear eccentric. I am proposing, after all, that Schumpeter is committed to equilibrium not because of but despite his *Weltanschauung*. Yet it *is* quite comprehensible that Schumpeter accepts the conception that science rests on regularities of the form 'whenever conditions x then outcome y' – a conception in which equilibrium, or the global coherence of a set of functional relationships, is the only conceivable notion of order. For his acceptance of this conception does *not* result from sustained reflection on the nature of the social world. Rather, Schumpeter believes that this conception of the structure of science is the conception of the 'true' sciences.

In these sciences, exact regularities are non-empirical, and yet this has not precluded practical success. 'Many a historian ... who is so critical of [our] theory', Schumpeter (1908, p. 559) submits, 'would think just the same about exact mechanics, were it not for ... its connection with the achievements of modern technology.' Accordingly, the theorems of 'pure economics' should be regarded as 'interesting scientific results and very promising beginnings' (ibid., p. 579); but, as in physics, it is unwarranted to expect that they should yield immediate practical gains.

Yet is it true that 'pure economics' is on a par with the exact natural sciences? Is it correct to identify 'laws' with exact regularities or 'formulas'? An affirmative answer would entail that laws of nature are *mere constructs*; which makes it incomprehensible why they should have facilitated any achievements. Where, then, lies the confusion?

As Lawson (1997, pp. 29–30) explains, it *is* true that exact regularities in natural science are, typically, not a spontaneous occurrence but a result of human contrivance. As a rule, they obtain – approximately – under experimental conditions. However, scientific experiments do not *constitute* laws. Instead, they ought to be understood as attempts to isolate, and so facilitate the empirical identification of, mechanisms *which are at work independently of human intervention and act both inside and outside those engineered conditions.* Law-statements are statements that elucidate these mechanisms. For on this conception, but not on the one that Schumpeter is making his own, the usefulness of law-statements outside experimental situations *is* intelligible (see ibid., pp. 27 ff.).

Of course, the misunderstanding is not specifically Schumpeter's. It was propagated by the philosophy of his time. He can be charged only with rather uncritically (a priori) accepting the conception that science supposes the framing of regularities of the form 'whenever conditions x then outcome y' – as just about every economist did. In fact, tensions in the work of some of his contemporaries have been explained on the basis of a similar mismatch between their world view and the ontology implicit in their conception of science (see, e.g., Fleetwood, 1995; Pratten, 1994, ch. 2).

Let me emphasise, finally, that this mismatch has nothing to do with an acceptance or rejection of instrumentalism as a philosophy. What matters is that Schumpeter ends up defining economic theory in terms of a particular structure of explanation: 'whenever conditions x then outcome y'. In his words, a (theoretical) 'explanation' is 'nothing but the specification of a uniquely determined magnitude for our unknowns and of their laws of motion' (Schumpeter, 1908, pp. 340–1).[13] This structure of explanation is sometimes defended on instrumentalist grounds *and sometimes not*[14] – which in itself suggests that Schumpeter accepted it largely a priori, and strengthens the plausibility of my hypothesis.

5. An incomplete assessment

A proper assessment of my hypothesis cannot be offered here.[15] This would involve demonstrating that there is a *pattern* to Schumpeter's tensions and inconsistencies throughout his entire work, and that this pattern is explicable on the basis of his metatheoretical stance. A brief illustration will nevertheless be *sketched*, focusing on the opening stages of Schumpeter's *Theory of Economic Development* – a book marked by a 'constant tension' between an approach 'in which the observed nature of reality is kept to the fore' and 'the logico-deductive approach' (Oakley, 1990, p. 57).

I shall first provide some background notes on the *Theory*.[16] I then attempt to show that there are two mutually inconsistent models mixed up in Schumpeter's text. One of them refers to an open and structured system, the other appears to rest on an a priori commitment to an inadequate conception of science – a commitment that leads him to frame his conception of capitalism in terms of a closed system.

5.1 Some background notes on Schumpeter's 'Theory'

Schumpeter's *Theory* rests on the opposition of two categories: the 'circular flow' and 'development'. The circular flow represents adaptive behaviour. Development, in contrast, is 'spontaneous and discontinuous change in the channels of the flow' (Schumpeter, 1934, p. 64). It is the carrying out of innovations, by entrepreneurs, encompassing the introduction of new goods and production methods, the discovery of new markets and sources of materials, and the implementation of new forms of industrial organisation.

Second, the opposition of these two categories is suggested to encapsulate the difference between acting within a framework of customs and traditions, on the one hand; and deliberately changing that framework, on the other. The circular flow is founded upon custom and experience, whereas development 'consists precisely in breaking up old, and creating new, tradition' (ibid., p. 92).

Third, there is another dimension to the distinction between continuous adaptation and discontinuous innovation. According to Schumpeter, the circular flow 'describes economic life from the standpoint of the economic system's tendency towards an equilibrium position' (ibid., p. 62); whereas development is 'that kind of change arising from within the system *which so displaces its equilibrium point that the new one cannot be reached from the old one by infinitesimal steps*' (ibid., p. 64, fn. 1).

Fourth, Schumpeter's two basic categories, the circular flow and development, are not exclusive to capitalism. However, it is impossible to conceive of capitalism apart from development. This is because, for Schumpeter, the distinctive characteristics of capitalism are related to its *particular* method of generating development. In his *Theory*, Schumpeter focuses on this particular method.

In so doing, however, he does not want to address capitalist develop-ment as it is empirically manifest. He acknowledges that '[e]very process of development creates the prerequisites for the following', so that 'things will turn out differently from what they would have been if every con-crete phase of development had been compelled first to create its own conditions' (ibid., p. 64). But he insists that, 'if we wish to get at the root of the matter, we may not include in the data of our explanation elements of what is to be explained' (ibid.). He therefore starts his explanation of capitalist development from a circular flow that has not been affected by antecedent capitalist development. And this circular flow – which refers to a market economy rather than to Schumpeterian capitalism – carries no historical meaning (see, e.g., ibid., pp. 10, 245).

Finally, this circular flow is ultimately taken as a downright change-less system. Schumpeter submits that the assumption of stationarity 'recommend[s] itself' in that 'one can exhibit the fundamental form of the economic course of events with the maximum simplicity in an unchang-ing economy' (ibid., pp. 82–3, fn. 1).

5.2. Problems and tentative explanations: a sketch

For Schumpeter, in sum, entrepreneurship entails the ability to transcend and transform custom and tradition by exercising creative capacities. On the other hand, the immanent tendency of the circular flow is to reach a position of equilibrium. In order to highlight the 'essence' of development, Schumpeter actually assumes that the economy is in a full-employment equilibrium.

Under such conditions, innovation can consist only in 'the different employment of the economic system's existing supplies of productive means' (ibid., p. 68), and entrepreneurs must command the power to draw these means from their traditional uses. But there are no reser-voirs of purchasing power. Indeed, money 'adds nothing new' to the circular flow, and 'nothing essential is overlooked in abstracting from it' (ibid., p. 51). Innovation requires, then, the creation of purchas-ing power *ex novo*; which entails that money becomes essential (see, e.g., ibid., p. 71). And this method of financing innovation, by credit creation – 'the only one … available in strict logic' in the absence of previous development (ibid., p. 72) – is capitalism's *differentia specifica*. Significantly, 'capital' is the purchasing power with which the entre-preneur pays for productive means.

Yet Schumpeter's notion of equilibrium, whatever its peculiarities, is orthodox: it yields closure. As such, it rules out choice, creativity and entrepreneurship. How, then, is the entrepreneur to emerge in the first place? How is development conceivable? In order to understand this, let us simply *assume away* Schumpeter's conspicuous invocation of equilib-rium mechanisms. As will be apparent, there are fragments left which enable us to reconstruct a conception of development.

According to this conception, individuals typically act on the basis of certain signals, the interpretation of which is facilitated by tacitly known rules and traditions. Long experience, in part inherited, is argued to have taught the individual (see ibid., pp. 5–6), who acts 'according to certain symptoms of which he has learned to take heed' (ibid., p. 21). 'He acts in the ordinary daily round according to general custom and experience' (ibid., p. 39). Still, there is always a degree of deliberation in tradition-based, everyday behaviour:

> [T]he necessity of making decisions occurs in any work. No cobbler's apprentice can repair a shoe without making some resolutions and without deciding independently some questions, however small. The 'what' and the 'how' are taught him; but this does not relieve him of the necessity of a certain independence. When a worker from an electrical firm goes into a house to repair the lighting system, even he must decide something of the what and the how ... Now the director or independent owner of a business has certainly most to decide and most resolutions to make. But the what and the why are also taught him.
>
> (Ibid., pp. 20–1)

Individuals, however, are capable of breaking up old, and creating new, traditions. They can act as entrepreneurs. Yet this kind of action necessitates a higher level of reflection than everyday behaviour. It implies transcending, hence becoming consciously aware of, rules which, ordinarily, are not reflected upon:

> [O]utside these accustomed channels the individual is without those data for his decisions and those rules of conduct which are usually very accurately known to him within them. Of course he must still foresee and estimate on the basis of his experience. But many things must remain uncertain, still others are only ascertainable within wide limits, some can perhaps only be 'guessed' ... There will be much more conscious rationality in this than in customary action, which as such does not need to be reflected upon at all; but this plan must necessarily be open not only to errors greater in degree, but also to other kinds of errors than those occurring in customary action ... Carrying out a new plan and acting according to a customary one are things as different as making a road and walking along it.
>
> (Ibid., pp. 84–5)

And the human mind is not powerful enough constantly to work at the level of awareness which entrepreneurship requires. '[E]very man would have to be a giant of wisdom and will, if he had in every case to create anew all the rules by which he guides his everyday conduct' (ibid., p. 83). Thus these rules will be relatively enduring; and this stability is a condition of entrepreneurship.

How entrepreneurs operate depends, naturally, on the institutional setting which in turn they contribute to transforming. In any case, however,

entrepreneurial action, and hence development, are not exclusive to capitalism. They can occur independently of *ad hoc* credit creation. For there
always exist innovative opportunities, which can be carried out depending on the availability of savings, etc.[17] As a market economy must be a
money economy (see, e.g., Schumpeter, 1917), the emergence of capitalism
in the Schumpeterian sense involves no analytical break.

Of course, the capacity of private banks to produce purchasing power
is hardly a detail. This institutional innovation has a profound impact on
the morphology of development. But we need not discuss this here. The
above considerations suffice to suggest that Schumpeter has a model in
mind, which rests on a conception of the social world as open and structured and is coherent.

The problem is that he superimposes upon this conception a framework
presupposing closure. There is a very different, more explicit model in
the opening stages of Schumpeter's *Theory*. In this model adaptive action
founded upon custom and experience is made equivalent to a particular
kind of rational conduct: 'In so far … as it is a question of adapting himself
to the conditions and of simply complying with the objective necessities
of the economic system without wishing to change them, one and only
one particular way of acting commends itself to the individual, and the
results of this action will remain the same as long as the given conditions
remain the same' (Schumpeter, 1934, p. 40). Indeed, 'in practice people
act in accordance with well-tried experience, and … in theory we regard
them as acting in accordance with a knowledge of the best combination of
present means under the given conditions' (ibid., p. 42).

The wages and rents of these people are determined by the marginal
productivities of labour and land, whereas the prices of products are
equal to the prices of the services of labour and land embodied in them.
Production flows profitlessly because, if a surplus over the value of the
services of labour and land accrues to employers, employees switch to
the task of combining productive resources in accordance with the prevalent techniques. Since produced means of production are regarded as
'transitory items' and as 'accumulated productive forces which can at
any moment and without loss or friction be turned into any specific commodities wanted' (ibid., pp. 44, 10, fn. 2), innovation is reduced to new
combinations of (perfectly adaptable) labour and land.

In short, it is possible to detect, albeit in fragmentary form, two irreconcilable models that appear mixed up in Schumpeter's *Theory*. What can
explain this? In particular, what is the motivation for his closed system
framework? Clearly, Schumpeter's crucial insights – on variable levels
of consciousness in human action, on the interdependence of individual creativity and institutional arrangements, on the essential nature of
money and the specifically capitalist role of the banking system – cannot
have their source in this equilibrium framework. This suggests that this
framework is not so much a product of ontological reflection as of a priori

methodological preferences: that it is the product of a preconception of how what is must be fashioned so as to qualify as science.

Schumpeter's rationalisations of his own style of theorising certainly point in that direction. As remarked, he argues that, 'if we wish to get at the root of the matter, we may not include in the data of our explanation elements of what is to be explained' (ibid., p. 64), and proposes to offer an account of development as it would arise out of a position without development. He wants to describe capitalist development starting from the *logical*, rather than historical, absence of the distinctive characteristics of capitalism. And this is surely not an ontologically grounded move. In fact, it cannot result but of a preconception of how to frame scientific results – a preconception causing unnecessary, but in Schumpeter's case hardly avoidable, tensions. For, in as much as a phenomenon is truly new, its emergence cannot possibly be accounted for on a purely logical basis. This is why Schumpeter cannot explain how entrepreneurs, or capitalism, are to arise out of equilibrium.

6. Concluding comments

I have argued that Shionoya's thesis is unsuccessful. The alternative hypothesis put forward is, like Shionoya's, of a metatheoretical nature. But, as I now want to emphasise, it rests on an interpretative strategy distinct from Shionoya's – and from the strategy underlying most Schumpeterian interpretations.

As observed earlier, it is easy to find irreconcilable exegeses of Schumpeter. Clearly, then, his work must exhibit tensions and inconsistencies; otherwise it is difficult to see how interpretative controversies could be so conspicuous. Yet the existence of tensions and inconsistencies does not necessarily mean that Schumpeter's writings license a plethora of contrasting exegeses. It is at least conceivable that these interpretative contrasts be due to methods of exegesis that cannot adequately address the kaleidoscopic character of Schumpeter's text.

And, as I see it, this is indeed the case. Many interpretations of Schumpeter rest upon the implicit assumption that there exists a Schumpeterian essence, which can be disentangled from random 'noise' – even though the persistence of disagreement suggests that this assumption is not well founded. Facing Schumpeter's mercurial text, interpreters have little difficulty in finding support for a variety of putative Schumpeterian 'essences'.

In contrast, I reject the implicit postulate that tensions and inconsistencies must be of peripheral importance, and attempt to make sense of Schumpeter's discourse *by explaining why these tensions and inconsistencies obtain*. This project rests upon the conception that inconsistencies, to the extent that they are interesting, are due to the resilience of discourses which imply different ontologies; and upon the theory that this enduring coexistence of contrasting ontologies can originate not so much in the fact that science is an ongoing, fallible project to understand the world as in a *pre*conception of the structure, or form, of scientific theories. In accordance with this theory, I have proposed that the tensions and inconsistencies in Schumpeter's writings reflect his inability to discard a conception of science the ontological presuppositions of which are not congenial to his *Weltanschauung*.[18]

As for Shionoya's argument, it represents a third strand in Schumpeterian interpretation. He argues that Schumpeter's metatheory provides the key to solving the confusions that *his interpreters* have propagated, and *denies* that Schumpeter is inconsistent. Thus, to repeat, Shionoya (1997, p. 10) promises that locating Schumpeter's substantive theories within his metatheoretical framework 'will clarify the logical connection between them and dispel existing misinterpretations about them'; and he insists that '[i]n Schumpeter's system, statics, dynamics, and economic sociology are coherent, though they are concerned with different problems and methods' (ibid., p. 310).

In order to avoid misunderstandings, finally, it is perhaps not superfluous to contrast my hypothesis with Shionoya's with regard to the importance of Schumpeter's work. *Prima facie*, my hypothesis may appear to be more critical of Schumpeter than Shionoya's. Yet does this impression stand up to scrutiny? Shionoya attributes to Schumpeter an instrumentalist position that has been severely criticised – even in its strongest, 'predictivist' version – though Shionoya is sympathetic to that position. My argument, on the other hand, emphasises Schumpeter's enduring and a priori commitment to an inadequate conception of science. But is it really surprising that Schumpeter should have rather uncritically imported the conception of science of *his* time? More importantly still – and in contrast with Shionoya – I contend that much of what Schumpeter writes does not really depend upon that (now philosophically discredited, but still widely held) conception. Though this conception constrained the expression of his insights, he could not avoid transcending its limitations and producing a body of work as remarkable as that of any great economist. And *that* ought to be regarded as much more important than mere coherence.

Notes

1 Previous versions of this paper were presented at the *Cambridge Realist Workshop Conference*, University of Cambridge, May 2000, and at the 27th Annual Meeting of the History of Economics Society, University of British Columbia, Vancouver, June/July 2000. I am grateful to António Almodovar, Maria de Fátima Brandão, Tony Lawson and two anonymous referees for their comments and suggestions. Part of the present argument builds on my PhD thesis, for which I gratefully acknowledge financial support from FEP-UP and INVOTAN. First published in *Cambridge Journal of Economics*, 2002, Vol 26, No 6, 805–821.

2 Shionoya has meanwhile returned to Schumpeter, along the same lines. See his papers in Shionoya (2001).

3 Schumpeter's main work on statics is actually a metatheoretical treatise: *Das Wesen und der Hauptinhalt der theoretischen Nationalökonomie* (Schumpeter, 1908).

4 Shionoya (1997, p. 99) writes that some instrumentalists 'admit that some theoretical entities are real. This is the reason why the difference between instrumentalism and realism is sometimes viewed as blurred.' Yet this difference is hardly blurred (see Lawson, 2000). The acceptance that theoretical entities are real or that theories can be considered true or false does not in itself imply a (realist) commitment to

truth. Indeed, it may even be possible to define instrumentalism as the thesis that falsity is irrelevant to the theoretical enterprise.

5 My examination of Shionoya's thesis begins with Proposition 2 because this proposition is relevant to assessing the truth of Proposition 1.

6 Consider the following passage, which Shionoya quotes:

> Analysis ... never yields more than a statement about the tendencies present in an observable pattern. And these never tell us what *will* happen to the pattern but only what *would* happen if they continued to act as they have been acting in the time interval covered by our observation and if no other factors intruded. 'Inevitability' or 'necessity' can never mean more than this.
>
> (Schumpeter, 1942, p. 61)

It is at least conceivable that this statement means (a) that capitalism is subject to various tendencies – which, if they persist and fully work themselves out, would bring about a particular observable pattern; (b) that these tendencies need not persist nor work themselves out, in that they may be counteracted by other tendencies; and (c) that, whatever observable outcome ensues, these tendencies are *real* because they impact upon empirical reality and are not invented by Schumpeter.

7 I return to this inconsistency below. But, as I say, there are other examples of 'internal inconsistencies'. Thus, Schumpeter's quite Austrian argument on competition as a process in *Capitalism, Socialism and Democracy* (Schumpeter, 1942) is irreconcilable with his positivist analysis of the economics of socialism in the same book. In addition to this, Schumpeter is inconsistent in yet another way. His comments on the ontological status of equilibrium (see below) – or on perfect competition – vary in the course of his work. Yet it is not the case that he revises his stance for good at some point; rather, he oscillates between irreconcilable positions. Naturally, inconsistencies such as these entail that contrasting claims about Schumpeter can be easily documented on the basis of quotes. 'With Schumpeter', as Stephan Boehm (1990, p. 233, n. 19) puts it, '*that* is hardly ever a problem'.

8 Translations from *Wesen* are my own.

9 Schumpeter (1908, p. 32) actually distinguishes between 'pure theory' (or *theoretische Ökonomie*) and 'economic theory'. 'Pure theory' is static equilibrium theory, whereas 'economic theory' is a broader category. However, Schumpeter's 'dynamic' theory is insisted to rest upon static 'pure theory' (see, e.g., Schumpeter, 1912, pp. 511 ff.). Statements coherent with those quoted above can be found throughout Schumpeter's work, up to his *History of Economic Analysis*. See, e.g., Schumpeter (1954, pp. 15, 824, fn. 25), where the purely instrumental nature of theory is emphasised.

10 Schumpeter also brings in statistics as a technique of economic analysis. But that is irrelevant to the present argument.

11 Lawson (1997) uses the expression 'whenever event x then event y'.

12 Or, from a different angle:

> Manifestly, the captured surplus value *does not invest itself* but must *be invested*. This means on the one hand that it must not be consumed by the capitalist, and on the other hand that the important point is *how* it is invested. Both factors lead ... from the *objective* to the *subjective* ... [T]he crucial factor is that the social logic or objective situation does not unequivocally determine *how much* profit shall be invested, and *how* it shall be invested, *unless individual disposition is taken into account.*
>
> (Schumpeter, 1927, p. 242)

Interestingly, Schumpeter writes (in a comment on Marschak, published in Stolper, 1994, p. 375) that his system is 'ex ante indeterminate and in this sense "open" ... [T]here is something of évolution créatrice about it (as there is ... about every true evolution, a biological "sport" for instance or de Vries' "mutation").'

13 Incidentally, this is why the differences between Schumpeter and Menger are ultimately less significant than Shionoya (1997, pp. 115 ff.) believes. Schumpeter, unlike Menger, cautions against dabbling in 'metaphysical' issues. Yet he accepts the same structure of science as Menger, and his arguments on why an 'exact orientation' should be favoured likewise reduce to the assertion that it has proved successful in natural science.

14 Schumpeter recognises the fictitious, instrumental nature of equilibrium, but he also writes that 'this mechanism for establishing or reestablishing equilibrium is not a figment devised as an exercise in the pure logic of economics but actually operative in the reality around us' (Schumpeter, 1939, p. 47).

15 A very preliminary attempt at such an assessment has been made in Graça Moura (1997).

16 I quote from the English translation of the second edition (Schumpeter, 1934). The original (1912) edition is different in some respects. For the limited present purposes, however, there seems to be no clear advantage in using the original German text.

17 The circular flow admits of improvements which may, eventually, 'make a great department store out of a small retail business' (Schumpeter, 1934, p. 62), and there is no reason why the implementation of such changes should not be considered an entrepreneurial act.

18 Whilst I think that there is a tendency to turn a blind eye to, rather than make sense of, Schumpeter's protean inclinations, I am not suggesting that my interpretative strategy is somehow unique within Schumpeterian studies. Oakley (1990), for instance, follows similar lines. Others point to a mismatch between Schumpeter's 'vision' and his 'technique' (see Minsky's (1992) comment on a Shionoya paper). Indeed, all the studies that attempt to understand why Schumpeter is inconsistent, rather than merely registering or even ignoring that fact, ultimately point in the same direction. Still, critical realism could be the key for a thorough rationalisation of Schumpeter's tensions and inconsistencies.

References

Boehm, S. 1990. The Austrian Tradition: Schumpeter and Mises, pp. 201–41 in Hennings, K. and Samuels, W. J. (eds), *Neoclassical Economic Theory, 1870 to 1930*, Boston, Kluwer

Boland, L. A. 1979. A Critique of Friedman's Critics, *Journal of Economic Literature*, vol. 17, 503–22

Fleetwood, S. 1995. *Hayek's Political Economy: The Socio-Economics of Order*, London and New York, Routledge

Friedman, M. 1953. The Methodology of Positive Economics, pp. 3–43 in Friedman, M., *Essays in Positive Economics*, Chicago, University of Chicago Press

Graça Moura, M. da 1997. 'Schumpeter's Inconsistencies and Schumpeterian Exegesis: Diagnosing the Theory of Creative Destruction', PhD thesis, University of Cambridge

Lawson, T. 1992. Realism, Closed Systems and Friedman, *Research in the History of Economic Thought and Methodology*, vol. 10, 149–69

Lawson, T. 1997. *Economics and Reality*, London and New York, Routledge

Lawson, T. 2000. 'Two Responses to the Failings of Modern Economics: The Instrumentalist and the Realist', paper presented in Tokyo, National Institute of Population and Social Security Research, March 2000

Mäki, U. 1994. Reorienting the Assumptions Issue, pp. 236–56 in Backhouse, R. E. (ed.), *New Directions in Economic Methodology*, London and New York, Routledge

Minsky, H. P. 1992. Commentary, pp. 363–70 in Scherer, F. M. and Perlman, M. (eds), *Entrepreneurship, Technological Innovation, and Economic Growth: Studies in the Schumpeterian Tradition*, Ann Arbor, University of Michigan Press

Oakley, A. 1990. *Schumpeter's Theory of Capitalist Motion: A Critical Exposition and Reassessment*, Aldershot, Edward Elgar

Perroux, F. 1965. *La Pensée Economique de Joseph Schumpeter: Les Dynamiques du Capitalisme*, Genève, Librairie Droz

Pratten, S. 1994. 'Forms of Realism, Conceptions of Science and Approaches to Industrial Organisation', PhD thesis, University of Cambridge

Schumpeter, J. A. 1908. *Das Wesen und der Hauptinhalt der theoretischen Nationalökonomie*, Leipzig, Duncker & Humblot

Schumpeter, J. A. 1910. Marie Esprit Léon Walras, *Zeitschrift für Volkswirtschaft, Sozialpolitik und Verwaltung*, vol. 19. English translation in Schumpeter, E. B. (ed.) 1952. *Ten Great Economists: From Marx to Keynes*, London, Allen & Unwin, pp. 74–9

Schumpeter, J. A. 1912. *Theorie der wirtschaftlichen Entwicklung*, Leipzig, Duncker & Humblot

Schumpeter, J. A. 1917. Das Sozialprodukt und die Rechenpfennige: Glossen und Beiträge zur Geldtheorie von heute, *Archiv für Sozialwissenschaft und Sozialpolitik*, vol. 44, 627–715

Schumpeter, J. A. 1926. Gustav v. Schmoller und die Probleme von heute, *Schmollers Jahrbuch für Gesetzgebung, Verwaltung und Volkswirtschaft im Deutschen Reiche*, vol. 50, 337–88

Schumpeter, J. A. 1927. Die sozialen Klassen im ethnisch homogenen Milieu, *Archiv für Sozialwissenschaft und Sozialpolitik*, vol. 57. English translation in Sweezy, P. M. (ed.) 1951. *Imperialism and Social Classes*, Oxford, Blackwell. Reprinted in Swedberg, R. (ed.) 1991. *The Economics and Sociology of Capitalism*, Princeton, Princeton University Press, pp. 230–83

Schumpeter, J. A. 1934. *The Theory of Economic Development: An Inquiry into Profits, Capital, Credit, Interest, and the Business Cycle*, Cambridge, Mass, Harvard University Press

Schumpeter, J. A. 1939. *Business Cycles: A Theoretical, Historical and Statistical Analysis of the Capitalist Process*, 2 volumes, New York and London, McGraw-Hill

Schumpeter, J. A. 1942. *Capitalism, Socialism and Democracy*, 5th edition (1976), London, Allen & Unwin

Schumpeter, J. A. 1947. The Creative Response in Economic History, *Journal of Economic History*, vol. 7. Reprinted in Clemence, R. V. (ed.) 1989. *Essays on Entrepreneurs, Innovations, Business Cycles, and the Evolution of Capitalism*, New Brunswick and London, Transaction Publishers, pp. 221–31

Schumpeter, J. A. 1954. *History of Economic Analysis*, London, Allen & Unwin

Schumpeter, J. A. 1991. Comments on a Plan for the Study of Entrepreneurship, pp. 406–28 in Swedberg, R. (ed.), *The Economics and Sociology of Capitalism*, Princeton, Princeton University Press

Shionoya, Y. 1986. The Science and Ideology of Schumpeter, *Rivista Internazionale di Scienze Economiche e Commerciali*, vol. 33, 729–62

Shionoya, Y. 1997. *Schumpeter and the Idea of Social Science: A Metatheoretical Study*, Cambridge, Cambridge University Press

Shionoya, Y. (ed.) 2001. *The German Historical School: The Historical and Ethical Approach to Economics*, London and New York, Routledge

Stolper, W. F. 1994. *Joseph Alois Schumpeter: The Public Life of a Private Man*, Princeton, Princeton University Press

10 Order without equilibrium: a critical realist interpretation of Hayek's notion of spontaneous order[1]

Steve Fleetwood

Introduction

If the various entities that comprise a system fit together so that the system displays order as opposed to mere chaos, some *principle of organisation* must then be in operation. When the system under investigation is the socioeconomic system, the following question is warranted: what is the principle of organisation in operation ensuring that socioeconomic order as opposed to chaos occurs? There appear to be two generic principles on offer each one rooted in a philosophical and methodological position. The first principle of organisation, and the one typically adopted by most economists, is *equilibrium*. Hahn treats equilibrium as the 'central organising idea' of neoclassical theory (1973, p. 1). Since there are far too many notions of equilibrium to deal with individually,[2] I shall make use of the following generic, working definition given by Dow:

> The equilibrium concept is pervasive in economics because it imposes order on complex relationships: it provides a natural point at which to look at the *outcome* of particular forces. Even if it is the process itself by which the forces are exerted which is the primary interest, the end point provides a useful benchmark for analysis.
>
> (1985, p. 112, emphasis added)

Equilibrium, by this working definition, might for example occur when, via market exchange, a particular set of prices is so established that the actions of all agents have resulted in a situation that could not be improved upon or perhaps when the economy generates signals that do not cause agents to change their expectations and therefore their actions. What differentiates the various notions of equilibrium is, for our purposes, irrelevant; what unites them, however, is not. I shall demonstrate below that all these notions (a) presuppose an empirical realist ontology, (b) presuppose a mode of theorising encouraged by this ontology, and (c) display a preoccupation with defining an end state.

The second principle of organisation, and the one adopted by the mature Hayek (i.e. after circa 1960), is *radically different* from any mainstream notion of equilibrium. Hayek adopts what I refer to as a *transformational principle of spontaneous socioeconomic order.*[3] I shall demonstrate below that this alternative principle (a) presupposes a quasi-critical realist ontology, (b) presupposes a mode of theorising encouraged by this ontology, and (c) displays a focus upon processes as opposed to end states.

This paper aims to show that the mature Hayek (a) abandons empirical realism and adopts something approaching critical realism, and (b) abandons equilibrium and adopts the alternative transformational principle of order. The ultimate aim of this paper, however, is merely to use Hayek's work to demonstrate the possibility of something that is, typically, denied by most contemporary economists – namely, that *one can abandon equilibrium without having to fall into analytical anarchy.*

In order to achieve these aims, I rely on the transcendental method. This method is similar to that employed by a detective faced with a dead body. He or she must work backwards from the available evidence to find who *must* have committed the murder, faced with the problems that the murderer will not own up to the crime and that the body cannot offer any verbal assistance. In effect, I ask the following transcendental question: what *must* Hayek be presupposing about ontology, given that he utilises a particular mode of theorising to generate a particular explanation about how the market process results in socioeconomic order?[4] Answering the question necessitates two steps. First, I set up the hypothesis that Hayek *must* be presupposing something approaching a critical realist ontology and a mode of theorising engendered by it, if the observations that he does not use the principle of equilibrium, focuses upon transformational processes and does not use the axiomatic–deductive method are all to be consistent with his ontology. Second, I then go on to explore his work on social rules, the telecom system and their articulation in the market process to demonstrate that the hypothesis can be sustained in the case of the mature Hayek.

These two steps are carried out in five sections. Section 1 outlines the two key philosophical positions of empirical realism and critical realism – including the transformational model of social action (TMSA), which will form the basis for the alternative, transformational principle. Section 2 demonstrates how the ontology of empirical realism encourages the use of equilibrium, whilst Section 3 notes Hayek's complete break with equilibrium. Section 4 demonstrates how the ontology of critical realism encourages the adoption of a transformational principle, paving the way for the introduction of an (abstract) Hayekian version of the TMSA. The final part demonstrates that Hayek's work on the market process, involving as it does the articulation between social rules of conduct and the telecommunication system (i.e. the structures and mechanisms that facilitate the discovery, communication and storage of knowledge), can usefully be interpreted as a concrete illustration of the abstract quasi-TMSA depicted in Section 4.

1. Two philosophical and methodological positions

This section identifies the two main strands of philosophical thought underlying (virtually all) economic theory. Empirical realism (ER) underlies mainstream economics, whilst critical realism (CR) underlies Hayek's socioeconomics. The reason for elaborating these philosophical positions is that every scientific statement presupposes an ontology of some kind – whether or not the scientist recognises it. And if it is the case that the presupposed ontology encourages the use of a particular organising principle, an elaboration of the presupposed ontology, and the relationship between it and the organising principle, will assist in evaluating the latter. Moreover, if one is troubled by the use of a particular principle (as Hayek clearly is *vis-à-vis* equilibrium), locating the source of the trouble at the ontological level will assist in formulating a satisfactory alternative.

Empirical realism

Drawing upon the work of Bhaskar (1978, pp. 40–41), one can summarise ER by the following three points:

1   ER prioritises epistemology. The empiricist presupposes an ontology grounded in sense experience. Knowledge about the external world is reduced to knowledge about what can be perceived, so that to exist is to be perceived. What cannot be perceived cannot be known about and is therefore inadmissible to science.
2   What can be perceived are unique, unconnected, fragmented, punctiform, atomistic episodes or events. Events given in sense experience cannot be other than atomistic, since any connection or relation between them is impervious to sense observation.
3   Knowledge of reality given as events in sense experience is taken to be isomorphic with, or fused with, the reality known to science. This epistemology has implications for ontology. If sense experience delivers atomistic events, and these events are presumed fused with reality, that reality must be atomistically constituted. This epistemology, then, conceals an atomistic ontology.

One more point, the most important one for this paper, follows from the previous three:

4   If knowledge of reality is given as events in sense experience, these events form the basis for scientific knowledge.

Lawson explains this succinctly:

> [I]f particular knowledge is of events sensed in experience, then any possibility of general, including scientific knowledge must be of the constant patterns, if any, that such events reveal. On this Humean view, clearly, these are the only forms of generalisations conceivable. Such constant patterns, i.e. regularities of the form 'whenever event x then event y', of course constitute the Humean or positivist account of causal laws.

> (1995)

From the ER perspective, general knowledge is available only on the possibility of discovering regular patterns in the flux of events given in sense experience of the form 'whenever event x then event y' referred to here as Humean laws. Science proceeds by using Humean law(s) to deduce consequences from initial axioms buttressed by assumptions. I shall refer to this henceforth as the axiomatic deductive method.[5]

Critical realism

CR prioritises ontology. The nature of the world is thought to determine the way in which one can actually go about obtaining knowledge of it. So what, according to CR, is the nature of the world? The next two sections illustrate that, from the CR perspective, the world is *layered* and *transformational*. The final section highlights the switch in the mode of theorising encouraged by this layered and transformational ontology.[6]

Layered ontology

Bhaskar[7] establishes the possibility of a layered ontology via an inquiry into the practice of science, with particular emphasis upon the notion of Humean law. He makes two key observations from this understanding of law, identifies two key problems and then draws implications for ontology. First, virtually all of the constant conjunctions of events that are of interest to science occur not spontaneously but only in experimental situations.[8] The point of experiment is to *'close the system'* by creating a particular set of conditions that will isolate the interesting causal mechanism from all those that are not of interest. The interesting causal mechanism is then allowed to operate unimpeded, and the results, the constant conjunctions, are recorded. Hence, the Humean law is more accurately styled as 'whenever event x, then event y, *under conditions z'. Second, the results obtained from experimental situations where conditions z exist (i.e. in closed systems) are often successfully applied outside experimental situations (i.e. in open systems).

Two problems follow. First, if Humean law is based upon a constant conjunction of events, and such constant conjunctions are, typically, not found outside closed systems, one must conclude that, outside closed systems, there are no laws.[9] Second, if Humean law is based upon a constant conjunction of events, and such constant conjunctions are, typically, not found in open systems, then the question of what governs events in open systems is left unaddressed. Moreover, it leaves the observation that the results obtained from closed systems are often successfully applied in open systems without any valid explanation.

If events manifesting themselves as constant conjunctions are, typically, not found in open systems, so that Humean law cannot govern and explain them, something else must govern and explain them. The governing mechanism cannot be predicated upon a constant conjunction of events, because whatever does govern events does so even when the events do not manifest themselves in constant conjunctions. The mechanism (gravity) that governs the fall of the autumn leaf does not cease to govern when the leaf fails to conform to any empirical regularity, i.e. when the leaf is acted upon by a series of other (possibly counteracting) mechanisms such as aerodynamic and thermodynamic mechanisms. This has implications for ontology.

Domain	*Entity*	
Empirical	Experience	
	Impression	
	Perception	These 3 domains are, typically,
Actual	Events and actions	'out of phase' with one another
'Deep'	Structures	
	Mechanisms	
	Rules	
	Powers	
	Relations	

The best way of understanding what this layered ontology entails is via an example:

Domain of the empirical
One might perceive agents engaging in satisfactory transactions, i.e. exchanging goods or services without resort to swindling or theft.

Domain of the actual
Most agents actually do engage in satisfactory transactions.

Domain of the deep
There are 'deep structures' such as the rules of private property that causally govern this actuality.

These domains are, typically, *unsynchronised* or *out of phase with one another*. For example, although for most of the time most agents participate in satisfactory transactions, on occasion some do not. This deviant action occurs irrespective of whether or not it is perceived and despite the fact that the rules of private property persist throughout. Being out of phase means that structures existing at the level of the deep, for example rules of private property, might (a) be only indirectly observable, and (b) act *transfactually*. The indirectly observable nature of deep structures implies that science has to take the domain beyond the actual and empirical seriously. The transfactual nature of deep structures carries two implications – both of which assist in the explanation of the non-existence of constant conjunctions of events. Transfactuality implies that deep structures such as the rules of private property continue to govern the flux of events even when the events (a) are not manifest *at all* at the level of the actual or empirical, or (b) are not manifest as constant conjunctions. This is because other, countervailing, structures (e.g., high rates of poverty) might also be governing the behaviour of the agents engaged in the transaction. Typically, then, one will not be able to make the empirical observation that all transactors, at all times, engage in satisfactory transactions. The actual resultant events depend upon the interplay of a range of causally governing structures.

Although this section opened with a discussion of the practice of natural science, it is evident that it can readily be extended into social science. This extension is strengthened by making the following claims about human agency. If human agency is real, (a) human agents could always have acted otherwise, and (b) human action must make a difference to the social world.[10] The implication arising from (a) and (b) is that the social world is open. The conclusions derived from an investigation of the practice of natural science, therefore, hold for social science. The social world constitutes an open system, and the social ontology is layered.

Transformational ontology

The ontology adopted by CR is not only layered but also transformational. Bhaskar establishes the possibility of a transformational ontology from an investigation into the nature of society.[11] Whilst, traditionally, most commentators recognise that society consists of agents and (in some sense) structures, the debate centres upon the way in which they interact. With the TMSA, Bhaskar enjoins this debate. He proceeds to identify, and retain, the correct parts of the three traditional social ontologies, synthesising them to form a new position.

From the reificationist position,[12] represented by Durkheim, Bhaskar retains the notion that structural elements exert constraint upon agents. From the voluntarist position represented by Weber,[13] he retains the notion that social material is concept-dependent, i.e. depends upon the intentional and meaningful behaviour of individuals. From the 'dialectical' position represented by Berger,[14] he retains the notion that the other two positions are reductionist, and the task of social theorists is to find a way of avoiding the Scylla and Charybdis of reification and voluntarism, whilst elaborating a *meaningful* interaction or relation between agents and structures.

Nothing happens out of nothing. Agents do not create or produce structures *ab initio*; rather they recreate, reproduce and/or *transform* a set of pre-existing structures. Society continues to exist only because agents reproduce and/or transform those structures that they encounter in their social actions. Every action performed requires the pre-existence of some social structures upon which agents draw in order to initiate that action, and in doing so reproduce and/or transform them. For example, communicating requires a medium (e.g.) language, and the operation of the market requires the rules of private property. This ensemble of social structures, according to Bhaskar, simply *is* society. As Bhaskar observes:

> [P]eople do not create society. For it always pre-exists them and is a necessary condition for their activity. Rather society must be regarded as an ensemble of structures, practices and conventions which individuals reproduce and transform, but which would not exist unless they did so. Society does not exist independently of human activity (the error of reification). But it is not the product of it (the error of voluntarism).
>
> (1989, p. 36; see also 1987, p. 129)

The transformational principle, then, centres on the mechanisms and structures that are the *ever-present condition, and the continually reproduced and/or transformed outcome, of* human agency. Agents, acting purposefully or consciously, unconsciously draw upon, and thereby reproduce, the structures that govern their actions in daily life. People do not marry with the conscious aim of reproducing the nuclear family, yet this is nevertheless an unintended consequence of, as well as a necessary condition for, their activity.[15]

Switch in the mode of theorising

Operating with a layered and transformational ontology, the emphasis of investigation necessarily switches (ontologically speaking) from the domains of the empirical and actual to the domain of the deep and the deep structures that govern these events/actions. With the recognition that the events/actions of experience are not manifest in the form of constant conjunctions, the notion of Humean law becomes untenable. As a consequence, the axiomatic deductive mode of theorising is also rendered untenable. When this is combined with the further recognition that something must govern the events/actions of experience, the mode of theorising, if it is to bear fruit, must switch.

Although the consequences of particular events/actions *cannot* be deduced, one does not have to give up on 'scientific' or systematic investigation: the conditions for the possibility of these events/actions *can* be excavated. The deep structures that act with transfactual necessity to govern the events/actions given in sense experience can be uncovered and their operation illuminated and explained. Hence the domain of the deep is where investigation must focus. As Bhaskar puts matters:

> Looked at in this way [TMSA] ... the task of the various social sciences [is] to lay out the structural conditions for various conscious human actions – for example, what economic processes must take place for Christmas shopping to be possible – but they do not describe the latter.

> (1989, p. 36)

Metaphorically speaking, the *modus operandi* of economics is *not* to move (horizontally) between actions/events, trying to ascertain or generate constant conjunctions, but to move (vertically) from events/actions to the deep structures that govern them. Economics, from the CR perspective, proceeds by inquiring into, illuminating and explaining the conditions (i.e. the reproduction and/or transformation of deep structures) necessary for the existence of some observed socioeconomic activity. Illumination and explanation supplant deduction and prediction.[16]

What has just been adumbrated is extremely important if one is to understand that Hayek's explanation of the market process is an example of a transformational principle, so let us pause to take stock. Once a layered and transformational ontology is (explicitly or implicitly) recognised, and the alternative mode of theorising that is engendered by it is adopted, the possibility is open to conceive of a radical alternative to the principle of equilibrium. As will become clear in Section 3, an equilibrium is an end state: a state where all that is going to happen has happened.[17] A theory of equilibrium focuses upon and defines the spatiotemporal co-ordination of some events/actions; its ontological orientation is upon the domains of the actual and empirical.

A transformational order, by contrast, is a process: a process involving the mechanisms and structures that are the ever-present condition, and the continually reproduced and/or transformed outcome, of human agency. A theory of transformational order focuses not upon the outcome of events/actions but upon the conditions that make these events/actions possible; its ontological orientation is upon the domain of the deep. The source of the 'order' in the transformational principle of order, therefore, lies with the mechanisms and structures. The task of socioeconomics is to illuminate and explain what these mechanisms and structures are, and how they are reproduced and/or transformed.

2. From ER ontology to the organising principle of equilibrium

The ER ontology presupposed by mainstream economists, contrary to that postulated by CR's, is not layered, but (metaphorically) flat. Since the domain of the deep is not recognised, investigation *cannot* focus upon this domain and must necessarily remain within the fused domains of the empirical and actual.[18] The events/actions given in sense experience are taken as the particulars of the world, and attempts are made to establish general scientific knowledge by discovering regular patterns in, or constant conjunctions of, these events/actions, i.e. Humean laws.

Since all economic theory purports to make some valid claim about the way the world really is (even if this often requires a tortuous explanation of the correspondence between theory and reality), statements and laws derived in theory must (be thought to) have some resonance with the real world. Now most economists recognise, of course, that the events/actions occurring in the real world are not perfectly constant. Laws do not hold with perfect regularity. No mainstream economist using (e.g.) the Law of Factor Substitution would claim that whenever the price of factor l rose, it would be substituted for, *in each and every case*, by factor k. In more general terms, no mainstream economist would actually expect (Humean) laws to hold perfectly in reality. What is necessary for theory construction, i.e. constant conjunctions of events/actions, appears not to exist in the real world.

What, then, is the mainstream economist to do? The fact that reality is not perfectly regular makes it impossible to find any constancy in the flux of events/actions and therefore no laws. There are two possible ways out of this dilemma. The first requires the switch in mode of theorising noted above, from the fused domains of the empirical and actual to the domain of the deep. Adhering to a flat ontology, however, the mainstream economist simply *cannot* take this route, and must opt, therefore, for the second possibility, namely the resort to (typically violent and therefore illegitimate) analytical abstraction.[19] The really existing complicating factors that cause the irregularities in events/actions are, typically, spirited away via the use of (often completely fictitious) axioms and assumptions in the modelling exercise. A closed system is engineered whereby the complicating factors have been removed, regular patterns in the flux of events/actions created and Humean law resurrected. Economics can then proceed by using the axiomatic–deductive method.

The mainstream economist attempting to deal with the generalised co-ordination of economic activity must combine a law(s) with axioms of behaviour buttressed by assumptions such that it is possible to predict *ex ante* that if agent A initiates event/action x, event/action y follows under conditions z. This, typically, involves describing and predicting the movement between the two states: from one state of rest (no matter how temporary) to another such state.[20]

It appears, then, that commitment (implicit or explicit) to an ER ontology encourages a particular mode of theorising. This is not simply a matter of subjective preference or whim, for the major alternative mode of theorising, that which focuses upon the domain of the deep, is quite simply ruled out. One is, therefore, committed to theorising solely in terms of the fused domains of the empirical and actual, i.e. in terms of events/actions given in sense experience. Any co-ordination must be based upon regular patterns in the flux of events/actions. This is, however, precisely the domain in which regularity does not exist. Also, since it is impossible to find any pattern in the flux of events/actions, it is impossible to use, or discover, Humean laws. In order to cope with this lack of regularity, the system is closed via the construction of a model wherein all complicating factors that might lead to irregularity have been exorcised. The economist is, thereby, enabled (or more accurately perhaps, enfeebled) to do no more than describe the conditions under which the consequences of agents' action co-ordinate with one another, at which point socioeconomic order in the guise of equilibrium is said to exist. Equilibrium carries two negative implications: (a) the emphasis is upon end states and not upon the processes by which these end states allegedly come about or tend to come about,[21] and (b) the emphasis is necessarily upon a closed model rather than reality.[22] These negative implications have been known to Hayek from the mid-1930s. As will become clear below, when he abandons ER and adopts a quasi-CR ontology, his understanding of socio-economic order simply has no need for equilibrium and the negative implications it carries.

3. Order versus equilibrium

In 1968 Hayek explicitly abandons the notion of equilibrium for the alternative notion of order, writing:

> Economists usually ascribe the order which competition produces as an equilibrium – a somewhat unfortunate term, because such an equilibrium presupposes that the factors have already been discovered and competition therefore has ceased. The concept of an 'order' which … I prefer to that of equilibrium, has the advantage that we can speak about an order being approached to varying degrees, and that order can be preserved throughout a process of change.
>
> (1968, p. 184)

He defines order as

> a state of affairs in which a multiplicity of elements of various kinds are so related to each other that we may learn from the acquaintance with some spatial or temporal part of the whole to form correct expectations concerning the rest.
>
> (1973, p. 36)

The progressive nature of the shift lies in understanding that *order is not an alternative (to equilibrium) as a description of an end state but rather a process.* A system that displays order is one in which a process of reproduction and/or transformation is occurring. A theory of order is a theory that explains this process. Moreover, the process implies no (temporary or permanent) termination point. Boettke *et al.* argue that the nature of the ordering process is an alternative conception that works without reference to any equilibrium construct. They add: 'An evolutionary process is open-ended, in that the process does not tend towards any state. Consider what it would mean for human evolution to tend towards a final state. No biologist would ever say that we need to have a fully evolved human to understand the process of evolution' (1986, p. 8). It cannot go unremarked, however, that in places Hayek gives the impression that, owing to the discovery or learning possibilities involved in the market processes, there is a tendency for expectations to converge gradually over time.

> The correspondence of expectations ... is brought about by a process of trial and error which must involve constant disappointment. The process of adaptation operates, as do the adjustments of any self organising system, by what cybernetics has taught us to call negative feedback: *responses to the differences between the expected and the actual results of actions so that these differences will be reduced. This will produce an increased correspondence of expectations ...*
>
> (1976, pp. 124–125, emphasis added)

This could be interpreted to mean that negative feedback will generate a learning process and thereby an 'increased correspondence of expectations'. It is hard to ignore the possibility that, given enough time and effort, expectations will become so co-ordinated that they terminate in some end state. In other words, if expectations become gradually more co-ordinated, what is to prevent their perfect co-ordination terminating in some end state, some form of equilibrium? Once, however, one breaks with thinking in terms of end states, another possibility opens up. What Hayek has in mind is most definitely not a correspondence or tendency towards an end state on any description. 'Increased correspondence' for Hayek, and this is the important claim, is *relative to the level of correspondence that any other system of socioeconomic organisation could achieve.*

I agree therefore with Rizzo's (1990) observation that Hayek's 1968 paper marks the site of Hayek's complete break with the notion of equilibrium as a never-attained 'benchmark' and his acceptance of a 'more radically relativistic' conception of order as a more co-ordinated state relative to that attainable in any other social system. One suspects that Hayek would agree with O'Driscoll and Rizzo's observation that '[a] theory of evolved orders is not a theory of optimality or efficiency, precisely because it is a process not an end state theory ... It is not what competition does to fulfil our expectations that commends it; it is what we would not have expected it to do that commends it' (1985, pp. 109–111).

The notion, then, of order and a tendency towards order is fundamentally different from the notion of equilibrium and a tendency towards equilibrium. Hayek long ago abandoned any such notion, and to look for an alternative, a 'looser concept of equilibrium' (Rizzo, 1990, p. 30), is to miss the point – no such alternative exists. The tendency is not towards any end state but is a tendency to co-ordinate expectations better than any alternative socioeconomic system. Hayek's claim to the superiority of the market-based socioeconomy over any alternative form does not turn on the ability to construct a theoretical model and 'prove' or describe a unique or stable equilibrium that is Pareto optimal or some such. Rather, it turns on the power of the explanation of how and why a market-based socio-economy (allegedly) makes use of the totality of dispersed knowledge to co-ordinate actions and consequences, and thereby brings about socioeconomic order, better than any alternative. As Hayek himself puts it:

> The discovery procedure which we call competition aims at the closest approach we can achieve by any means known to us to a somewhat more modest aim which is nevertheless highly important: namely a state of affairs in which all that is in fact produced is produced at the lowest possible costs.
> ... Only because the market induces every individual to use his unique knowledge of particular opportunities and possibilities ... can an overall order be achieved that uses in its totality the dispersed knowledge which is not accessible as a whole to anyone.
>
> (1967C, p. 91)

4. Hayek's quasi-critical realist ontology, method and the organising principle of transformation

Whilst it is quite clear that Hayek rejected equilibrium for a principle of order, it is also clear that he never presented his alternative in any systematic fashion. The aim of this penultimate part of the paper is to introduce the possibility that, by using a CR (i.e. layered and transformational) ontology and a mode of theorising appropriate to it, one can provide the meta-theoretical system that Hayek lacks and augment his principle of order without doing violence to it.

Hayek's quasi-TMSA[23]

According to the Hayekian quasi-TMSA presented here, the socioeconomy is the ensemble of resources (knowledge), mechanisms (telecommunications system) and structure (rules). These elements are, however, not merely thrown together in a heap; there is a principle of organisation in operation, and that principle is transformation. These elements are the ever-present condition, and the continually reproduced outcome, of human agency.

Agents, being equipped with the cognitive apparatus that facilitates rule-following action, in possession of resources in the form of localised 'knowledge of time and place' (Hayek, 1945, p. 527), and motivated by the desire to increase their own welfare, initiate courses of action and attempt to bring about certain desired consequences. This action necessitates the drawing upon, and thereby reproduction and/or transformation of, social rules of conduct. In the absence of formal mechanisms that facilitate the communication and storage of knowledge (e.g., the trade press), access to a sufficient quantity of knowledge would be severely limited. In the absence of informal mechanisms, the telecom system being central, communication would (allegedly) be so cumbersome that no-one would know enough about relatively distant economic activity even to begin to co-ordinate their plans and actions with others. In the absence of social rules of conduct, however, no social action at all would be possible, since agents can only act at all by following rules. Agents cannot initiate action that might bring about a desired goal without working with resources, mechanisms and structures and, in working with them, they are reproduced and/or transformed.

Switch in the mode of theorising

Note that it is in virtue of the transformational nature of social being that no termination point in the market process is ever reached. Whilst what exists is continually reproduced, it is also, typically, transformed in the process so that it is not reproduced exactly.[24]

With the adoption of something approaching a CR ontology, an extremely important development in Hayek's method appears to occur. His mode of theorising switches from what he himself refers to as 'narrow technical economics' (1964A, p. 91),[25] i.e. from what might be described as a focus upon the domains of the actual and empirical to the domain of the deep. It switches from a preoccupation with events/actions given in sense experience, to a preoccupation with the deep structures that govern them. Economics, for Hayek, becomes an inquiry into, and explanation of, the various resources, mechanisms and structures that are drawn upon, reproduced and/or transformed in establishing socioeconomic order. Although Hayek does not, of course, explain his *modus operandi* with this terminology, it appears to be a perfectly acceptable interpretation. It fits with his rejection of the notions of equilibrium and (Humean) law, and explains why, as an economist, he needs to focus upon social rules of conduct.

5. The market process or catallaxy: the articulation of social rules and the telecommunications system

This final part begins by exploring the nature and historical evaluation of Hayek's problematic, before going on to show that his work on the market process or catallaxy is a concrete illustration of the rather abstract quasi-TMSA depicted in Sections 1 and 4. Hayek's understanding of the market process focuses upon the structures and mechanisms (i.e. social rules of conduct and the telecom system) that are the ever-present condition, and the continually reproduced and/or transformed outcome, of human agency.

The evolution of Hayek's 'problematic'

Although 'Hayek's work' undergoes what Lawson refers to as a 'continual transformation' (1994B), two significant sea changes can be detected. Whilst the change, dated from the publication of 'Economics and Knowledge' (1936), is now well established,[26] the second, dated from the publication of *The Constitution of Liberty* (1960), is not. It appears that Hayek sets out *the* crucial question for economics in 1936 but cannot answer it satisfactorily until 1960. The question is this: how can the socioeconomic activity of millions of unconnected individuals be co-ordinated when this requires the prior co-ordination of their plans, which in turn requires the discovery, communication and storage of an enormous amount of knowledge that exists only as a decentralised and fragmented totality?[27]

The answer comes in two temporally divided parts. In a 1945 paper, Hayek argues that co-ordination occurs owing to the discovery, communication and storage of knowledge being facilitated by the telecommunications system – Hayek's term for the price mechanism. By itself, however, the telecom system cannot perform this facility since, as Hayek is aware, there is a range of knowledge that is discovered, communicated and stored by mechanisms other than the telecom system.[28] In his work after 1960, Hayek argues that the discovery, communication and storage of knowledge is facilitated not by the telecom system *alone* but by the telecom system articulating with, and embedded within, a dense web of social rules of conduct.[29] As Hayek puts it: 'Although the price mechanism is an imperfect guide ... it is still an indispensable guide ... if all knowledge and foresight dispersed among many men is to be used' (1960, p. 350).

> [I]t is mainly changes in price that bring about the necessary adjustments. This means that, for it [price system] to function properly, it is not sufficient that the rules of law under which it operates be general rules, but that their content must be such that the market will work tolerably well. The case for a free system is not that any system will work satisfactorily where coercion is confined by general rules, but

that under it such rules can be given a form that will enable it to work ... [The] efficiency of the system will depend on the particular content of the rules.

(Ibid., p. 229)

Hayek, it appears, comes to recognise that the telecom system alone cannot facilitate the discovery, communication and storage of the knowledge necessary for socioeconomic order to occur, yet occur it does. Some other knowledge-facilitating device must, therefore, be in operation, and this something else turns out to be social rules. This, however, raises the following question: what properties do rules possess that enable them to articulate with the telecom system to facilitate the discovery, communication and storage of knowledge? The short answer is: because social rules are the embodiment of social knowledge.[30] In one place Hayek writes that:

In such spontaneous formations [as a market society] is embodied a perception of the general laws that govern nature. With this cumulative embodiment of experience in tools and forms of action will emerge a growth of explicit knowledge, of formulated generic rules that can be communicated by language from person to person.

(1960, p. 33)

Whilst Hayek only uses the term 'embodied' very occasionally (e.g., 1973, p. 119; 1960, p. 157), the sentiment is echoed in numerous passages, especially in 1960, chs. 2 and 3, 1973, ch. 1 and 1988, pp. 19–20. Hayek describes an historical, evolutionary process of trial and error whereby agents discover new rules or modify existing ones, using them as a basis for action. The reason rules can serve as a basis for action is because they embody the collected wisdom of the society. As Hayek puts it:

Like all general purpose tools, rules serve because they ... help to make the members of the society ... more effective in pursuit of their aims ... The knowledge that has given them [rules] their shape ... is knowledge of the occurrence of certain problem situations.

(1973, p. 21)

[By] guiding the actions of individuals by rules ... it is possible to make use of knowledge which nobody possesses as a whole.

(Ibid., p. 49)

Most knowledge ... is obtained ... in the continuous process of sifting learnt tradition ... The tradition is the product of a process of selection ... which without anyone knowing or intending it, assisted in the proliferation of those who followed them ... The process of selection that shaped custom and morality could take account of more factual circumstances than individuals could perceive, and in consequence tradition is in some respects superior to, or 'wiser' than, human reason.

(1988, p. 75)

By embodying the collected wisdom of society, this knowledge becomes available to all individuals, giving what Butler refers to as an 'instant and unconscious summary of how to act' (1983, p. 23).[31]

With the nature of Hayek's 'problematic' now firmly understood, all the parts of this paper can be brought together. It is now possible to demonstrate that the market process *just is* the process of reproduction and/or transformation of the deep structures and mechanisms (i.e. the social rules and the telecom system) that facilitate the discovery, communication and storage of knowledge, so as to make co-ordinated socioeconomic activity a possibility. When Hayek elaborates upon the market process or catallaxy, he is, I suggest, drawing upon the transformational principle. If so, it appears that he must be presupposing something approaching the (CR) ontology necessary to sustain this principle. This final section, then, considers Hayek's work on the market process to see whether this interpretation is defensible.

The market process or catallaxy

Whereas the term 'economy' might refer to a planned system (which could be an individual agent), the term 'catallaxy' contains no such constructivist connotations. A catallaxy is the order spontaneously 'brought about by the mutual adjustment of many individual economies in the market' (1976, pp. 108–109), and has four key characteristics.

First, whilst the individuals that populate the catallaxy are isolated, they are not *asocial* but *social* individuals. They are situated within, and depend for their ability to act upon, a web of social rules of conduct. Hayek offers a social theory rather than a set of claims about the behaviour of (fictitious) atomised individuals.

Second, each agent possesses differing fragments of knowledge. The precise extent of their knowledge is dependent upon the type of knowledge they have, lack or seek. For example, an agent may have fairly extensive knowledge of the immediate environment, but be virtually ignorant of the remote environment and radically ignorant of the future.

Third, agents have expectations, formulate plans and subsequently initiate courses of action to pursue their own goals, possibly selfishly, possibly with great altruism; the motive makes no difference. The point is that there is no one mind in control directing agents to initiate certain actions, to pursue certain goals and thereby attempting to make their actions and goals compatible with one another.

At first glance this looks like a recipe for chaos: isolated individuals with small parcels of localised, fragmented and partial knowledge and on occasion being ignorant, pursuing their own (possibly) self-serving goals, with no

conscious co-ordinating agency in control. It is, however, the fourth important characteristic which, according to Hayek, prevents this slide into chaos
and holds the key to establishing socioeconomic order, namely social rules of
conduct. Since agents are only able to initiate social action (including reacting
to price signals) by drawing upon social rules, their actions are simultaneously individually motivated and socially sanctioned. According to Hayek:

> What reconciles the individuals and knits them into a common and
> enduring pattern of a society is that ... they respond in accordance
> with the same abstract rules ... What ... enables ... men to live and
> work together in peace is that in the pursuit of their individual
> ends the particular monetary impulses which impel their efforts ...
> are guided and restrained by the same abstract rules. If emotion or
> impulse tells them what they want, the conventional rules tell them
> how they will be able and be allowed to achieve it.

(1976, p. 12)

'A catallaxy is thus the special kind of spontaneous order produced by the
market through people acting within the rules of the law of property, tort
and contract' (ibid., p. 109).

*Owing to the existence of a set of deep structures in the form of social rules
of conduct,* a high degree of compatibility of actions and consequences is
ensured, where incompatibility appears to be the more likely outcome.[32]

Social rules have two important characteristics: they relate not to specific but to general action, and they are, more often than not, limiting in
the sense that they forbid certain classes of action. The kind of rules Hayek
has in mind are not of a kind that specify that a particular commodity must
sell at a particular price, or that a certain distribution of income must be
maintained, or that a particular bankruptcy must be avoided, etc.[33] These
are examples of constructivist, i.e. consciously designed and implemented,
rules. The rules he does have in mind appear as a complex web of rules
of the laws of property, tort and contract, although equally important for
Hayek are a series of tacit rules such as integrity, honesty, keeping promises, etc. Whilst these rules are perhaps better known as a 'code of ethics'
or 'norms', the term 'rule' is better suited to Hayek's needs. Not only is this
term Hayek's choice, but, unlike 'norms' or 'ethics', it can also be extended
to cover phenomena like social action such as speaking a language, physiological action such as riding a bicycle, or cognitive activity such as learning.

Whilst the complex web of rules acts to decrease uncertainty in general,
it will almost inevitably increase uncertainty in particular instances. Rules
can only ensure that agents have the potential to interact in a potentially
fruitful manner; they cannot guarantee that they will do so. 'But all that
rules can achieve in this respect is to make it easier for people to come
together and to form [a] match: abstract rules cannot actually secure that

this will always happen' (1973, p. 99). This increase in local uncertainty is germane, although it at first appears paradoxical, with respect to price. By following rules, agents are able to utilise the knowledge content of prices and thereby decide upon a course of action. However, the rules do not extend as far as stating what the price should be:

> The abstract rule of conduct can (and, in order to secure the formation of a spontaneous order, should) thus protect only the expectations of command over particular physical things and services, and not the expectations concerning their market value.
>
> (1976, p. 124)

> It may at first appear paradoxical that in order to achieve the greatest attainable certainty it should be necessary to leave uncertain so important an object of expectations as the terms at which things can be bought and sold.
>
> (Ibid., p. 125)

Prices have a very important temporal aspect to them, captured in Jevons's phrase 'bygones are forever bygones' (Hayek, 1976, p. 121). Only current prices are important, since they inform on what action ought to be taken in the present, i.e. they suggest how much time, effort, resources, etc., it is currently worth putting into a product. Resources already expended cannot be recovered if, over the passage of time, conditions that were thought stable actually change. In this case, there is a likelihood that the action will lead to disappointed expectations. Prices, then, will typically be the 'wrong' ones; they will contain the 'wrong' information.

Considering prices, along with social rules of conduct, there appears to be a complex interaction between the social structures of rules, and the mechanisms of the telecom system. According to Ioannides:

> The price mechanism is not however the only knowledge-dispersion system in a market society ... the *rules of conduct and the social institutions which have evolved through centuries ... themselves constitute a knowledge disseminating system.* Through them, the knowledge of the legal, political and moral framework of any social activity is conveyed to all market participants.
>
> There is thus a major difference between the information disseminating functions of the price system and those rules and institutions. The knowledge dispersed by the former is of a dynamic nature, in the sense that it leads individuals to a constant revision of their plans. The knowledge dispersed by the latter is stabilising, in the sense that it constantly affirms the stability of the social framework in which individuals act.
>
> (1992, p. 38, emphasis added)

Ioannides recognises not only that social rules are structures that facilitate the discovery, communication and storage of knowledge in their own right, but also that there is a concatenation or articulation between them and prices. This places social rules on an equal footing with the telecom system *vis-à-vis* discovery and communication of knowledge, and makes it necessary for *economists* interested in the operation of the market to understand social structures.

Hayek appears to be arguing that, whilst following abstract, general rules and monitoring price signals, agents proceed by trial and error, which must inevitably involve a constant stream of disappointed expectations for a number of them. The continual process of trial and error, disappointed expectations and the communication of failure to others triggers a process of adaptation as agents strive to correct them. Once certain plans or expectations are shown to be false, the consequences are then perceived by other agents who might attempt to avoid acting on the same false expectations. As Lachmann puts it: 'Nobody can profitably [or, one might add, unprofitably] exploit his knowledge without conveying hints to others' (1976, p. 59).

However, since the ability of the mechanisms and structures that facilitate the discovery, communication and storage of knowledge are far from perfect, socioeconomic co-ordination must also be far from perfect, efficient, optimal, etc. Activity in the market place, proceeding by trial and error and therefore via the never-ending necessity of continual successes and disappointment, generates a socioeconomic order that, whilst impossible to describe as an equilibrium or perfect co-ordination of actions, is far from mere chaos. If the socioeconomy is neither perfectly co-ordinated nor chaotic, some alternative principle of organisation must be in operation. The most likely candidate is some form of transformational principle along the lines described here.

The mature Hayek appears to adopt a *transformational principle of spontaneous socioeconomic order*. The conditions for socioeconomic order in a market economy, namely resources in the form of knowledge, mechanisms such as the telecom system that facilitate the discovery, communication and storage of this knowledge, and structures in the form of social rules of conduct, are the ever-present condition, and continually produced outcome, of market-based action. Hayek's elaboration of the market processor catallaxy is the substantive manifestation of this transformational social ontology. The market process *just is* this transformational process, and the aim of Hayek's socioeconomic theory of order is to explain this process.

Conclusions

The presupposition of an ER ontology encourages a mode of theorising focusing upon the domains of the empirical and actual, which encourages, in turn, a preoccupation with the definition of end states or equilibria. The presupposition of a CR ontology, by contrast, encourages a mode of theorising focusing upon the domain of the deep, which encourages, in turn, a preoccupation with processes, more specifically with the reproduction and/or transformation of the structures and mechanisms that make socioeconomic activity possible. In the specific case of Hayek, the adoption of something approaching a CR ontology encourages his adoption of the transformational principle. Hayek's transformational principle of spontaneous socioeconomic order, offering, as it does, one of the best explanations of the market process, is a clear illustration of how one can abandon the principle of equilibrium without having to fall into analytical anarchy.

Notes

1 I wish to thank Steve Pratten and the two anonymous referees for their thoughtful comments on earlier drafts. First published in *Cambridge Journal of Economics*, 1996, Vol 20, No 6, 729–747.
2 Weintraub (1986) gives a useful summary of some notions of equilibrium and its close relative, disequilibrium. Note also that some form of the equilibrium concept is used by Sraffian and Sraffian-inspired Marxists and some Austrians.
3 I shall not elaborate upon the *spontaneous* nature of order partly because the point Hayek makes is moot. The argument that the Great Society is the result of human design (at least in terms of nineteenth and twentieth century thought) is an argument without an opponent. Kukathas was forced to remind Hayek that 'there can be no doubt that Hegel and Marx did not think of society as the product of conscious design' (1989, p. 208; see also ch. 6.2).
4 In general, transcendental inquiry is an inquiry into the conditions of the possibility of an entity. In effect, one asks: what *must* be the case for X to be possible? The 'must' here requires some clarification; Lawson (1996) offer a most succinct one:

> [Must] does not signify some ahistoric, infallible conception of the acquisition of knowledge … A theory which results from transcendental analysis is, at best, the only known theory at the time to be consistent with the acceptable premises. Instead the *must* relates to a two-stage structure of the transcendental argument: the first, positive stage is to show that the existence of some Y makes X intelligible; the second, negative part is that in which it is shown, how counter intuitive, contradictory, or incoherent results follow from the failure to sustain Y.

What Hayek *must* be presupposing, then, does not signify an infallible claim on my part; it has to be reasoned for and reasoned against by those who oppose my hypothesis or interpretation.
5 The axiomatic deductive method, as used here, is grounded in empirical realism and is an extension of the more general philosophy of empiricism. Missing this subtle point leads to difficulty in recognition that (pure) economic theorists who never attempt to confront their models with data can still be characterised as empirical realists (see Bhaskar, 1978, pp. 12–30, especially pp. 15 and 24–25). The critical realist critique of mainstream economics, therefore, applies to both the explicitly empirical and the explicitly formal branches of the subject. Closed systems and Humean laws are used irrespective of whether the laws are (a) obtained by recording the events of experience; (b) via some alleged axiom of human behaviour; (c) adhered to following empirical testing; or (d) adhered to on other criteria – for example, logical consistency. They are also used irrespective of whether the point is to make a prediction in historical time

(forecast) or logical time. See Lawson (1994C, pp. 259–261, especially fn 1) and Lawson (1995, pp. 1–11).

6 A CR ontology, or something approaching it, is implicitly presupposed in certain aspects of N. Kaldor (Lawson, 1989); Marx (Pratten, 1994); Post Keynesians (Lawson, 1994A); and J. Commons (Lawson, 1994). Lawson (1994B) and Peacock (1993) also noted Hayek's possible CR credentials. I have also made the case for Hayek approaching a CR position in Fleetwood (1995).

7 Bhaskar (1978, chs. 1 and 2 and postscript); Collier (1994, ch. 2).

8 Hayek's discussion of 'complex phenomena' (by which he means primarily social phenomena) indicates his recognition that there are no constant conjunctions of events to be found in the social world and hence no Humean laws – although he does not, of course, put matters this way (1955, p. 8; see also pp. 3–4, 9).

9 Note that the move into statistical theory does not overcome the problem that event regularities cannot be discovered. The 'whenever x then y' format is essentially the same as the 'whenever x then y on average' or some such. Stochastic closure is still closure. On closure see Lawson (1989).

10 Henceforth, and in recognition that the social scientific analogue of the natural scientific term 'event' is 'action', I shall refer to 'events/actions'.

11 Bhaskar (1987, pp. 104–136; 1989, ch. 2).

12 'Reification' refers to the notion that society exists independently of human action. Put bluntly, agents' actions are merely the result of their being buffeted by social structures. Schematically: structures→(create)→agents' actions.

13 'Voluntarist' refers to the notion that agents merely produce society in their actions. Not only are constraints on action not taken seriously, but structures that *enable* action are also ignored. Schematically: agents' actions→(create)→structures.

14 'Dialectical' refers to the notion of reciprocal causality where agents' action causes structure which then causes agents' action and so on. Schematically: agents' actions→(create)→structures→(create)→agents' actions→, etc., etc. On all this, see Bhaskar (1989, pp. 27–44).

15 It is important to note that, while social structures are necessary for action, i.e. they facilitate or causally govern action, they do not determine it. Social conventions may put pressure on people to marry but they do not determine whom they should marry. By using *this* conception, CR *is* able to maintain an active role for human agency whilst at the same time avoiding the error of voluntarism and retaining constraining (and enabling) structures.

16 This is merely to claim that the mode of inference switches from deduction to retroduction. For a comparison of deduction and retroduction, see Lawson (1994A), and for an elaboration of retroduction, see Collier (1994, pp. 160–167).

17 See Hayek (1936, especially sections IV to V, and 1946, pp. 92–94).

18 Note that an ER does not qualify as a CR simply by positing the existence of some entity that he or she chooses to call a 'deep structure'. There is a world of difference between an abstract theoretical entity that is used because it is thought to exist and have real causal power, and a theoretical entity that is used not because it is thought to exist, or have causal power, but because it is a convenient fiction – typically, its use is to close the system, i.e. to ensure 'whenever event x occurs, event y follows'. A CR might (e.g.) make use of a deep structure like a social rule of conduct. An ER might (e.g.) make use of a 'deep structure' such as the psychology of rational behaviour, recognising fully that such behaviour is entirely fictional. A defence of the use of fictional entities would follow if challenged, possibly by invoking Friedman's famous (1953) essay. Note, however, that since rationality is not (with certain exception) defended on the basis of it being realistic, it cannot be posited as a really

existing deep structure. Whilst one is, of course, quite entitled to call a fictitious entity a deep structure, one must recognise that this might constitute
misuse of a term that has a very specific meaning (see Bhaskar, 1978, p. 15).

19 Whilst abstraction is necessary for all theoretical endeavours, this necessity
has been (mis)used by mainstream economists as a smokescreen for using
mathematically tractable, but completely fictitious, concepts – with disastrous
results. Apart from a few Marxist economists (A. Sayer, 1981; D. Sayer, 1983),
this crucial issue has been virtually ignored.

20 See Machlup (1978, pp. 77–78) for a neat summary of the use made by mainstream economists of (static) equilibrium.

21 Whilst it is true that notions of *process* can be used without adopting CR, many
such uses are, upon closer scrutiny, quite vacuous. Fisher, for example, claims
that the following equation 'characterises' the *process* known as 'tatonnement'
(1989, pp. 20–23):

$$Pi=Fi[Zi(P)]$$

Pi is the price of the ith commodity, *Zi* is the total excess demand, and *Fi(.)* is
a continuous sign preserving function *(sic)*. He explains this as follows: '[T]he
price of the ith commodity adjusts in the same direction as the excess demand for
that commodity, the exact adjustment being a continuous function of the excess
demand (and therefore price).' Whilst the notion (or metaphor) of tatonnement
is no doubt intended to refer to the market process involved in the formation of
socioeconomic order, the reduction of these multidimensional processes to (a) a
relation between price and quantity, and (b) the one dimension of an equation
is banal – although absolutely necessary if the *system is to be closed*. One only has
to compare this notion of process against the quasi-CR notion of market process
elaborated by Hayek (Section 5 below) to understand that describing the former
as a process is misleading and vacuous. See also note 19 above.

22 According to Dow, GE theory

> abstracts from intractable aspects of reality to provide a watertight rigorous
> framework for analysis of those aspects which are tractable … [I]t is not clear
> how one translates a statement expressed in terms of a GE model into a state-
> ment about a world which it does not describe. The precision refers to the
> model, not the economic events which reflect theoretically intractable elements.
>
> (1985, p. 123)

23 The term 'quasi' in this sense means 'something approaching', and implies that
Hayek does not actually adopt the entire corpus of CR, nor TMSA, although I
cannot elaborate here upon this point.

24 This is sufficient to violate a key requirement of mathematics, namely that the
variable under consideration does not change in the act of computation – algebraic or empirical. In CR language, one might say that the variable is intrinsically
closed, i.e. its internal state is completely defined and unchanging in the course
of computation. As Sayer, drawing upon Georgescu-Roegen, observes:

> Only if the objects are qualitatively invariant is the order in which we meas-
> ure or change them irrelevant. The transformation of the objects refereed to
> by the variables of an equation interact in a way which produces qualitative
> change (e.g., through a learning process), the variables will not be able to
> make stable reference.
>
> (Sayer, 1992, p. 177)

The transformational nature of social being, of course, means a mathematical treatment of Hayek's notion of spontaneous socioeconomic order is quite impossible.

25 Hayek appears to consider that he himself was, prior to the late 1930s, a positivist – and therefore an ER by my definition. In 1942 he writes:

I myself originally approached my subject thoroughly imbued with the belief in the universal validity of the method of the natural sciences. Not only was my first technical training largely scientific in the narrow sense of the word but also what little training I had in philosophy or method was entirely in the school of Ernst Mach and later of the logical positivists.

(Hayek, 1942, pp. 57–58)

26 See Caldwell (1988, p. 515).

27 'Clearly there is here a problem of the Division of Knowledge which is quite analogous to, and at least as important as, the problem of the division of labour' (Hayek, 1936, p. 49).

28 I shall cite just one example:

Their knowledge of the alternatives before them is the result of what happens on the market, of such activities as advertising, etc., and the *whole organisation of the market* serves mainly the need of spreading the information on which the buyer is to act

(Hayek, 1946, p. 96, emphasis added)

Hayek's reference to the 'whole organisation of the market' indicates his awareness that there are institutions other than the telecom system that facilitate the discovery, communication and storage of knowledge.

29 This periodisation is often missed by commentators who look for both the question *and* the answer in Hayek's early work. They fail, therefore, to see the relevance of his more sophisticated (yet still economic) mature work on rules (cf. Desai, 1994).

30 The idea that rules embody knowledge is not unique to Hayek: institutionalist economists have long known of what one thinker calls the 'informational function of institutions' (Hodgson, 1993, pp. 7, 10; see also 1988, ch. 6).

31 For further elaboration of his work on rules, see Hayek (1962, 1964A.B, 1967B, 1970 and 1979 epilogue).

32 Hayek's use of the term 'catallaxy' is extremely illuminating here. The word derives from ancient Greek, and means not only to exchange, but more importantly, 'to change from an enemy into a friend' (1976, p. 108). The harnessing of a potentially destructive force lies at the heart of Hayek's spontaneous socio-economic order.

33 Hayek (1976, p. 4; ibid., chs. 7 and 10; 1960, ch. 4; 1962, p. 57; 1988, p. 12).

34 To allow the historical progression of Hayek's thoughts to be seen clearly, the dates of his work appearing in the text and the bibliography refer to the date of presentation or publication, whichever is earlier.

Bibliography[34]

Bhaskar, R. 1978. *A Realist Theory of Science,* Hemel Hempstead, Harvester Wheatsheaf

Bhaskar, R. 1987. *Scientific Realism and Human Emancipation,* London, Verso

Bhaskar, R. 1989. *The Possibility of Naturalism,* Hemel Hempstead, Harvester Wheatsheaf

Boettke, P., Horwitz, S. and Prychitko, D. 1986. Beyond equilibrium analysis: reflections on the uniqueness of the Austrian tradition, *Market Process,* vol. 4, no. 4

Butler, E. 1983. *Hayek: His Contribution to the Political and Economic Thought of Our Time,* London, Temple Smith

Caldwell, B. 1988. Hayek's transformation, *History of Political Economy,* vol. 20, no. 4

310   *Steve Fleetwood*

Collier, A. 1994. *Critical Realism: An Introduction to Roy Bhaskar's Philosophy*, London, Verso

Desai, M. 1994. Equilibrium, expectations and knowledge, in Birner, J. and Van Zijp, R. (eds), *Hayek, Co-ordination and Evolution*, London, Routledge

Dow, S. 1985. *The Methodology of Macroeconomics*, Oxford, Basil Blackwell

Fisher, F. 1989. *Disequilibrium Foundations of Equilibrium Economics*, Cambridge, Cambridge University Press

Fleetwood, S. 1995. *Hayek's Political Economy: The Socio-economics of Order*, London, Routledge

Friedman, M. 1953. *Essays in Positivist Economics*, Chicago, Chicago University Press

Hahn, F. 1973. *On the Notion of Equilibrium in Economics*, Cambridge, Cambridge University Press

Hayek, F. 1936. Economics and knowledge, *Economica*, 1937, no. 4

Hayek, F. 1942. The facts of the social sciences, in Hayek, F. (1949)

Hayek, F. 1945. The use of knowledge in society, *American Economic Review*, vol. 35, no. 4

Hayek, F. 1946. The meaning of competition, in Hayek, F. (1949)

Hayek, F. 1949. *Individualism and Economic Order*, London, Routledge & Kegan Paul

Hayek, F. 1955. Degrees of explanation, in Hayek, F. (1967A)

Hayek, F. 1960. *The Constitution of Liberty*, London, Routledge

Hayek, F. 1962. Rules, perception and intelligibility, in Hayek, F. (1967A)

Hayek, F. 1964A. Kinds of rationalism, in Hayek, F. (1967A)

Hayek, F. 1964B. Kinds of order in society, *New Individualist Review*, vol. 1, no. 3

Hayek, F. 1967A. *Studies in Philosophy, Politics and Economics*, London, Routledge & Kegan Paul

Hayek, F. 1967B. Notes on the evolution of systems of rules of conduct, in Hayek, F. (1967A)

Hayek, F. 1967C. The confusion of language in political thought, in Hayek, F. (1967A)

Hayek, F. 1968. Competition as a discovery process, in Hayek, F. (1978)

Hayek, F. 1970. The errors of constructivism, in Hayek, F. (1978)

Hayek, F. 1973. Rules and order, in Hayek, F. (1982)

Hayek, F. 1976. The mirage of social justice, in Hayek, F. (1982)

Hayek, F. 1978. *New Studies in Philosophy, Politics and Economics*, London, Routledge & Kegan Paul

Hayek, F. 1979. The political order of free people, in Hayek, F. (1982)

Hayek, F. 1982. *Law, Legislation and Liberty*, London, Routledge & Kegan Paul

Hayek, F. 1988. *The Fatal Conceit: The Errors of Socialism*, London, Routledge

Hodgson, G. 1988. *Economics and Institutions*, Cambridge, Polity Press

Hodgson, G. 1993. The economics of institutions, *European Association for Evolutionary Political Economy Newsletter*, no. 15, July

Ioannides, S. 1992. *The Market, Competition and Democracy*, Aldershot, Edward Elgar

Kukathas, C. 1989. *Hayek and Modern Liberalism*, Oxford, Clarendon Press

Lachmann, L. 1976. From Mises to Shackle: an essay on Austrian economics, *Journal of Economic Literature*, vol. 54, no. 14

Lawson, C. 1994. The transformational model social activity and economic analysis: a reinterpretation of the work of J.R. Commons, *Review of Political Economy,* vol. 6, no. 2

Lawson, C., Peacock, M. and Pratten, S. 1996. Realism, underlabouring and institutions, *Cambridge Journal of Economics,* vol. 20, no. 1

Lawson, T. 1989. Abstraction, tendencies and stylised facts: a realist approach to economic analysis, *Cambridge Journal of Economics,* vol. 13, no. 1

Lawson, T. 1994A. The nature of post Keynesianism and its links to other traditions, a realist perspective, *Journal of Post Keynesian Economics,* vol. 16, no. 4

Lawson, T. 1994B. Realism and Hayek: a case of continuous transformation, in Colona, M. and Hageman, H. (eds), *Capitalism, Socialism and Information: The Economics of F.A. Hayek,* Aldershot, Edward Elgar

Lawson, T. 1994C. A realist theory for economics, in Backhouse, R. (ed.), *New Directions in Economic Methodology,* London, Routledge

Lawson, T. 1995. A realist perspective on contemporary economic theory, *Journal of Economic Issues,* vol. 29, no. 1

Lawson, T. 1996. Developments in Hayek's social theorising, in Frowen, S. (ed.), *Hayek the Economist and Social Philosopher: A Critical Retrospect,* London, Macmillan

Machlup, F. 1978. *Methodology of Economics and Other Social Sciences,* New York, Academic Press

O'Driscoll, G. and Rizzo, M. 1985. *The Economics of Time and Ignorance,* Oxford, Basil Blackwell

Peacock, M. 1993. Hayek, realism and spontaneous order, *Journal for the Theory of Social Behaviour,* vol. 23

Pratten, S. 1994. Structure, agency and Marx's analysis of the labour process, *Review of Political Economy,* vol. 5, no. 4

Rizzo, M. 1990. Hayek's four tendencies towards equilibrium, *Cultural Dynamics,* vol. 3, no. 1

Sayer, A. 1981. Abstraction: a realist interpretation, *Radical Philosophy,* no. 28

Sayer, A. 1992. *The Method of Social Science: Realist Perspective,* London, Routledge

Sayer, D. 1983. *Marx's Method: Ideology, Science and Critique in 'Capital',* Brighton, Harvester

Weintraub, E. 1986. *Microfoundations: The Compatibility of Microeconomics and Macroeconomics,* Cambridge, Cambridge University Press

PART IV

Methods

11 Methods of abstraction and isolation in modern economics[1]

Tony Lawson

[...]

A central plank of Hodgson's critique is the charge that the distinction I draw between methods of abstraction and theoretical isolation does not hold. Or rather Hodgson claims, 'the distinction is, at least in prominent practical instances, difficult to sustain'. I believe, to the contrary, that the distinction (elaborated below) is very easy to sustain, and that it is vital to social analysis that we do sustain it.

Why does Hodgson single out this particular issue? The answer is not totally clear to me. Hodgson notes that I regard abstraction as both unavoidable and useful but that I am rather wary of the method of theoretical isolation, associating it implicitly with the mainstream. I think Hodgson's goal is to persuade that the sorts of methods that I advocate (and more especially abstraction) face essentially the same problems as those confronting the mainstream. In other words, Hodgson seems to be working on two fronts. On the one hand he wishes to suggest that formalistic methods can be more useful than I allow. On the other hand he wishes to convey the impression that any alternative methods that I have advocated share any difficulties that can be associated with formalism.

[...]

Abstraction and theoretical isolation

How first does Hodgson argue that abstraction presupposes closure? In truth, he does not; that is, he does not provide an argument. Rather he asks the question: 'If abstraction is necessary, and it involves the limitation of the sphere of consideration and the exclusion of additional relations or disturbing forces, then doesn't this too imply the assumption of a closed system?' And he gets Stephen Nash to answer it for him: 'Stephen Nash (2004) has recently argued in the affirmative, suggesting that Lawson too must assume conditions or forms of closure.'

Hodgson adds nothing to this, though he perhaps believes that his case is bolstered through his suggesting that I use the distinction (between abstraction and theoretical isolation) as a form of protection: '[Lawson] uses this distinction to protect his argument against the objection that his method of abstraction also implies the assumption of closure; he argues that abstraction does not imply closure but isolation does.'

Hodgson notes that in referring to the method of theoretical isolation I draw on the work of Uskali Mäki. This is correct; the method is not one I myself defend or have sought to develop. Let me then restate the conception of it I set out in *Economics and Reality*, which makes reference to Mäki's (1992) conception, and seems to be Hodgson's notion. There I write of it:

> According to Mäki, [the method of theoretical isolation] is a method 'whereby a set of elements is theoretically removed from the influence of other elements in a given situation' (1992: 318). Mäki adds that 'In an *isolation*, something, a set X of entities, is "sealed off" from the involvement or influence of everything else, a set of Y entities; together X and Y comprise the universe' (ibid.: 321). Of course, even in experimentation no such isolation occurs literally, only physical rearrangement. But the aspect of all this that I find most problematic is Mäki's notion of *theoretical* or *ideal isolation*, an apparently 'traditional forceful procedure ... in economics' wherein no material re-arrangement is involved at all. Rather 'a system, relation, process, or feature ... is closed from the involvement or impact of some other features of the situation' by way of 'an intellectual operation in constructing a concept, model or theory' (ibid.: 325). In fact, Mäki goes further and distinguishes 'internal' and 'external isolation': 'In an *internal isolation*, one isolates a system from influences coming from within the system, while *external isolation* closes a system from influences that have sources which are external to the system.' Mäki adds that both 'internal and external isolation are relevant in economics' (ibid.: 326).
> (Lawson, 1997, pp. 131–2)

The distinction before us is easy enough to grasp. To abstract is to focus on aspects of something whilst *not* assuming the non-existence, or non-impact, of features not focused explicitly upon (that are abstracted from). To theoretically isolate is precisely to treat those aspects not focussed upon as non-existent, or at least as sealed off, as having no systematic influence.

The difference between the two is easily demonstrated if we consider an aspect of some team game, say football or hockey, on television. Suppose we see on the television screen a player, say a footballer, running with the ball down the side of the pitch, towards the end at which the opponent's goal is situated. If we are abstracting we will be interpreting this footballer's actions in a manner that takes into account the fact that supporting players on the same side will be moving in the same direction, and defenders of the opponent's team will be facing up to make a challenge. If instead we treat these other players as somehow sealed off from the action, as momentarily non-existent, then we are using the method of theoretical isolation. Clearly this creates a different world to the actual one addressed via abstraction. In the isolationist's world as described, if scoring is the player's objective all he or she has to do is take the ball to the goal and kick it between the two posts. There will be no opposition, because all other players not focused upon are assumed to have no impact.

A sports example such as this is useful because the game is clearly an internally related whole. The parts, the various movements of individual players, only get their meaning from the whole, so that any attempt to interpret one bit whilst ignoring the rest must fail if it is meaningful at all. I throw in the TV screen just to get the abstractionist and the isolationist to focus on the same part.

Clearly abstraction, but not theoretical isolation, will be relevant wherever the whole is not just the mechanical sum of parts. Composers, surgeons, artists as well as social theorists deal with internally related wholes. As such, abstraction, not theoretical isolation, will be the appropriate method of analysis.

Now it should be clear, although it is worth emphasising it anyway (not least because this may be a source of the confusion), that these two methods, *though distinct*, are not strict alternatives. Because the world in which we live is so complex, abstraction is always involved. It will be so even where an isolationist approach is adopted (indicating that the presumption of 'isolation', or being sealed off, can only ever be a relative one). For example, in considering the sports game above, in the scenarios of *both* the abstractionist and the theoretical isolationist, the causal force of gravity is presupposed, but abstracted from. That is, in each case gravity is not mentioned or analysed but accepted as acting; it is not assumed to be sealed off or inoperative; in neither case are the players treated as being propelled into outer space[2].

In contrast the method of isolation has very restricted conditions under which it is relevant or anyway useful. The paradigm case is provided by a situation of controlled laboratory experiment. Here a mechanism is physically insulated from countervailing features in order to be empirically identified: an event regularity is generated correlating the triggering of the mechanism and its unimpeded effects. Once more abstraction will be involved. We may momentarily concentrate on the 'isolating' of the mechanism, then on the triggering of it, then on some of its effects. We may at all times abstract from colour, smell, sound, cost of apparatus, and so forth; but then again we may not: it all depends on the context.

Of course, the controlled experiment represents a physical, not a theoretical, isolation. But a theoretical isolation is a process of imagining what would occur if a physical isolation could be achieved. A theoretical isolation is indeed a thought experiment. And where physical conditions are such as to inhibit in principle (as opposed to providing practical difficulties for) the physical isolation of certain features, then it seems that the method of theoretical isolation is without utility.

For example the interconnectedness and mutual constitution of the numerous different features of social reality are such that it is impossible to experimentally isolate individual components, such as money, firms or markets, and examine how they so operate when isolated from each other and from everything else. Equally, it is meaningless to *theorise* these features as if sealed off from the influence of each other and everything else. Of course, stated explicitly, this all seems obvious. Nevertheless such isolationist procedure dominates the specific methodological practices of modern economics.

If it seems clear enough that abstraction and theoretical isolation are indeed rather distinct (albeit not strict alternatives), I must now turn and examine how Hodgson argues to the contrary. There are essentially three strands to Hodgson's endeavour. First, seemingly accepting that closure is presupposed by the employment of methods of theoretical isolation, Hodgson seeks to associate closure with abstraction too. Second, drawing on Schelling's (1969) analysis of 'racial' segregation, Hodgson seeks to show that the use of heuristics, clearly presupposing the method of isolation, is equivalent to the process I describe under the heading of abstraction. Third, Hodgson claims that the distinction I draw between the methods of abstraction and isolation is too vague to be of practical import. Let me run through each of these charges in turn indicating why I believe each to be unsustainable.

1) Abstraction and closure

How first does Hodgson argue that abstraction presupposes closure? In truth, he does not; that is, he does not provide an argument. Rather he asks the question: 'If abstraction is necessary, and it involves the limitation of the sphere of consideration and the exclusion of additional relations or disturbing forces, then doesn't this too imply the assumption of a closed system?' And he gets Stephen Nash to answer it for him: 'Stephen Nash (2004) has recently argued in the affirmative, suggesting that Lawson too must assume conditions or forms of closure.' Hodgson adds nothing to this, though he perhaps believes that his case is bolstered through his suggesting that I use the distinction (between abstraction and theoretical isolation) as a form of protection: '[Lawson] uses this distinction to protect his argument against the objection that his method of abstraction also implies the assumption of closure; he argues that abstraction does not imply closure but isolation does.'

Now whatever else Stephen Nash (2004) does or does not do, as far as I can see he nowhere mentions abstraction, let alone argues that it presupposes a closure. Nash does suggest that the explanatory method I advance presupposes closures but fails to draw a distinction between closures of concomitance and closures of causal connection, and so to appreciate that it is the former variety that are significant for the explanatory approach I defend. He further fails to note that (perceived) closures are significant precisely when they break down. But this is all beside the point. The topic of abstraction is not addressed.

If there is no argument advanced either by Hodgson or by Nash, there is seemingly none (here) to which I must determine a response. And to the point it should be very clear from all that has gone before that of course abstraction does not imply closure. At least it does not if by abstraction we mean focusing on a part of a whole whilst leaving the rest of the whole momentarily out of focus, and if by closure we mean, as I do throughout, a system supporting an event regularity. Clearly, abstraction can be applied to all types of systems, to those that support strict event regularities, to those that support partial ones and equally to those seemingly not supporting any. It can be applied to matters that are real or fictitious. If I talk only about the horn (or white colour, or billy-goat beard, or lion's tail, or cloven hoofs) of a unicorn, I am abstracting in the context of discussing a fiction. To say of the social system, or of any specific part of it, that it is fundamentally open is to abstract. To suggest that abstraction presupposes closure is simply to misunderstand one or other or both of the two terms.

2) *The use of heuristics is equivalent to the method of abstraction*

A second point of difference between us concerns the way in which Hodgson believes that formalistic models might serve as heuristic devices. Once more Hodgson is concerned to connect abstraction to theoretical isolation. The latter method is closely connected to the notion of heuristics as used in economics, and this seems to account for Hodgson's concern to relate the latter in turn to abstraction. Here the analysis gets more interesting. Hodgson writes:

> The purpose of a heuristic is to identify possible causal mechanisms that form part of a more complex and inevitably open system. Heuristics can be useful without necessarily making adequate predictions or closely matching existing data. Their purpose is to establish a plausible segment of a causal story, without necessarily giving an adequate or complete explanation of the phenomena to which they relate.

It is this belief that appears to ground Hodgson's suggestion, which I am disputing, that the use of heuristics and abstraction are closely related if not equivalent, that 'heuristics relate to the very process of abstraction that Lawson himself highlights'.

Hodgson's contention that the 'purpose of a heuristic is to identify possible causal mechanisms' is, I believe, simply wrong (at least if I am interpreting him correctly, a matter to which I return in due course). It may well be the case that heuristics can be useful for some yet-to-be-explicated purposes 'without necessarily making adequate predictions or closely matching existing data'. But their contribution is not 'to establish a plausible segment of a causal story'. Rather any usefulness they possess, or so I shall argue, can stem only from the fact that a plausible segment of a causal story has already been established[3].

However, I realise that this last claim is likely to be contentious; that others too will likely be uncomfortable with it. So let me defend it at length. It is in the context of suggesting that heuristics achieve the same outcome as abstraction that Hodgson refers to Schelling's (1969) model of 'racial' segregation (to illustrate his argument). This latter focus is useful in that, unlike many economic contributions, Schelling's analysis does indeed seem to carry insight and be somewhat persuasive. This, no doubt, is why Hodgson draws upon it. So eventually below I run through my argument referencing Hodgson's example of Schelling as is relevant.

Heuristic and the method of successive approximation

First, though, I should establish the meaning of the term heuristic. Of course, specific categories can be made to mean anything we want them to. But all have a context, and most have a history. The term heuristic originally meant something like 'serving to find out'. How the latter is interpreted does vary according to context. In education it usually relates to a system in which pupils are trained to find out things for themselves. In philosophy and science it most commonly means a rule of thumb that has been found to be useful in making progress towards solving a problem. A heuristic computer program is one that begins with only an approximate method of solving a problem within the context of some goal, and then uses feedback from the effects of the solution to improve its own performance.

It is worth emphasising that in all such cases, the heuristic (the method, system or whatever) is observed to work; it is found successfully to serve some process of finding out. If something new is proposed as a heuristic device there is presumably an expectation at least that it will serve its intended purpose.

The way the term heuristic is usually employed in economic methodology is bound up with developing theories by way of relying on assumptions or conceptions believed to be false[4]. Heuristic assumptions are often said to be those that are used to simplify the analysis as a first step with the expectation (or perhaps, with hindsight, with a knowledge) that the picture is to be (or has been) rendered more realistic through complicating it at a later stage.

Such a process of gradually complicating the picture with the aim of making it more realistic is presumably what Hodgson has in mind when he notes that 'heuristic models [...] are literally unrealistic' and he writes that Schelling's 'model is simply a heuristic step along the road towards that more complete end'. In a later version of his paper (presented at the Cambridge Realist Workshop in November 2005) Hodgson also refers approvingly to Musgrave (1981), who in fact provides the classic statement of the step-wise procedure in terms of heuristic devices or assumptions:

> [A scientist] may wish to *develop* ... a theory in two stages: in the first stage he takes no account of factor F, or 'assumes' that it is negligible; in the second stage he takes account of it and says what difference it makes to his results. Here the 'assumption' that factor F is negligible is merely a heuristic device, a way of simplifying the logical develop-ment of the theory. Let us call such assumptions *heuristic assumptions*.
>
> (1981, p. 383)

It is thus easy to see how the method of theoretical isolation 'whereby a set of elements is theoretically removed from the influence of other elements in a given situation' (Mäki, 1992, p. 318) relates to the making of heuristic assumptions in economics. For both advanced knowing that significant causal influences (and perhaps other significant features) are omitted.

The step-wise approach of moving from initial conceptions of iso-lated features to a more realistic or complete theory is often referred to as the method of successive approximation, particularly when there are (possibly many) more than two steps involved. It is something I discuss explicitly in *Economics and Reality*, where I look at the practice of accept-ing certain sorts of believed-to-be-false assumptions as a 'heuristic device in a step-wise process of moving from simplified or ideal conceptions to others of greater complexity and so, it is supposed, realisticness' (Lawson, 1997, p. 127). What is required here is some analysis of heuristic assump-tions interpreted as unrealistic claims, and how they serve to facilitate theory development.

Hodgson himself does not give any analysis of why, or when, a con-ception regarded as unrealistic might be illuminating. He does, though, appear to suggest that it might be provided by Robert Sugden's (2000) account of 'credible worlds', which also makes reference to Schelling's (1969) contribution. Sugden's idea is that if a model captures a 'credible counterfactual world' we apparently have some inductive warrant for its relevance to our world. Hodgson writes:

> Robert Sugden (2000) asks probing questions concerning the role and 'realisticness' of this and other heuristic models in economics. These heuristic models have the paradoxical claim that they are literally unrealistic yet they seem to illuminate important aspects of reality. Using the Schelling model alongside George Akerlof's (1970) famous article on the 'market for lemons', which again claims to establish

meaningful propositions about the world on the basis of an admittedly unrealistic model, Sugden (p. 28) describes these models as 'credible counterfactual worlds' that give 'some warrant for making inductive inferences from model to the real world'.

Now inductive inferences concerning states of affairs are problematic at the best of times. But even overlooking this, we are entitled to ask: what does it mean to talk of 'credible counterfactual worlds'? It appears to be accepted that worlds such as those described by Schelling could not come about. So in what sense are they credible? We surely need to know this if Hodgson's reference to Sugden is to help us understand when or why some conceptions that are acknowledged as unrealistic remain useful.

It so happens, as I say, that in *Economics and Reality* I set out an analysis of possible heuristics and related issues that can make sense of all this. This is something to which I now need to return. Let me give a brief summary.

The method of successive approximation and heuristic assumptions

In *Economics and Reality*, in fact, I argue that two conditions are essential (though by no means sufficient) to the success of this method of successive approximation (relying on heuristic assumptions as interpreted by Musgrave and others). These are:

1   that the factors considered in 'isolation' be real causal factors, structures and/or transfactually acting mechanisms or tendencies; and
2   that the effects of the factors so considered in 'isolation' combine or interact mechanically.

(Lawson, 1997, p. 129)

These conditions, and the need to satisfy them, are easily grasped. Basically the idea is to move from an understanding of a part of a causal story to an understanding of more, or of all, of it.

This requires, first, that the features (treated as) isolated in thought be causal mechanisms and that the nature of the causal parts, or individuals, viewed in isolation as a first step, are not knowingly portrayed incorrectly. In other words, it is essential that the intentional fictionalising concerns *not* the manner of acting of the parts considered separately (in isolation) but only the (heuristic) assumption of their acting in isolation from (some) other factors affecting the total outcome.

Of course, this requirement, in its turn, presupposes that the way a causal mechanism operates as it is found in reality is the same as it would operate in 'isolation from (some) other factors affecting the total outcome' (or under the conditions assumed in the heuristic exercise).

Notice, too, that this requirement rules out the vast majority of theoretical conceptions that are bound up with modern mainstream formalistic modelling.

A second condition that must typically be satisfied if we are successfully to utilise the method of successive approximation (or heuristics), that is if we are to achieve an understanding of the whole by way of considering the workings of parts considered in isolation, is that the effects of the different parts or causal elements can be aggregated, that is combined additively or mechanistically. In contrast, if there are, say, emergent powers of the more complex entity or whole irreducible to those of its parts considered separately, then it is not clear that it is especially useful to proceed by seeking to understand (or speculating about) how each part might act in isolation.

Notice, too, that to make sense of the first condition (that the way a causal mechanism operates as it is found in reality is the same as it would operate in isolation from [some] other factors affecting the total outcome) we need the notion of transfactuality. Something is said to be acting transfactually when it is having its effect *whatever the actual outcome*. Gravity is pulling my computer keyboard to the floor even as my desk acts to counteract this force and leave the keyboard at rest (relative to myself) in front of me. In other words, the keyboard does not need to be dropped in an experimental vacuum for gravity to have its effect. Similarly, the aspirin acts to offset my headache even if my noisy environment and heavy drinking countervail its effects and leave my head in a worse state. Such factors as gravity and the aspirin, when triggered, act not counterfactually but transfactually. We can talk not just of how they would (counterfactually) act in different non-actual but ideal circumstances, but also of how, when triggered, they are continually transfactually acting, whatever other forces are in play. The category of a tendency is reserved for the effects of forces that are acting transfactually, i.e. whatever the actual outcome.[5] It is when a mechanism is insulated from countervailing factors that (as in a well-controlled experiment) its tendencies and the outcome produced coincide.

Although advocates of the method of successive approximation, or the making of heuristic assumptions, typically do not identify the two noted conditions for the method of successive approximation to be successful, they can be seen to be built into their illustrations. Consider the classic exposition of Alan Musgrave, concerning Newton's analysis of inter-planetary motion:

> When Newton sought to discover what his theory predicted about the solar system, he first neglected inter-planetary gravitational forces by 'assuming' that there was only one planet orbiting the sun. He proved that, if his theory was correct, the planet would move in an ellipse with the sun at one of its foci. This assumption was not a negligibility assumption: Newton knew that planets would sometimes have detectable

gravitational effects on one another. Nor was it a domain assumption: Newton was not saying that his theory only applied to one-planet solar systems. You miss the point if you object that Newton's assumption is false, because our system has more than one planet. You also miss the point, though less obviously, if you object that the *consequence* of Newton's assumption was false, because planets do not move exactly in ellipses. The consequences drawn from heuristic assumptions do not represent the precise predictions of the theory in question; rather, they are steps towards such precise predictions.

(Musgrave, 1981, p. 383)

Clearly, the method of successive approximation is found to be successful in the case of Newton's analysis of inter-planetary motion, both because it is real (gravitational) tendencies that are so considered (in isolation), tendencies that seemingly operate transfactually whatever else is going on, and also because gravitational tendencies do appear to combine mechanically.

Equally clearly, however, the conditions in question, and in particular the requirement that causes combine mechanically, do not hold in general. Perhaps their lack of universality is most readily apparent if we think of chemical reactions and combinations. But mechanistic combining is hardly typical of social phenomena either. For example, the network of social relations so central to social life cannot meaningfully be broken down into parts with some bits treated as though existing in isolation before others are eventually added back in. It makes no sense at all to treat any feature in isolation from another to which it is essentially related. In studying family behaviour, say, it is clearly quite irrelevant to study conceptions of parental mechanisms apart from conceptions of the nature, including needs, of children or the mutual relationship in which parents and children stand. Equally, it is incoherent to consider the situation of landlords/ladies in isolation from (conceptions of) tenants, or conceptions of employers in isolation from those of employees, and nor does it make sense to consider capitalist firms, markets and money in isolation from each other, and so on.

Pure and applied explanation

There is a further point I want to pull out from all this, one that can perhaps be made in the clearest way if I first distinguish *pure* from *applied* modes of explanation. Briefly put, pure explanation is concerned with identifying and understanding causal mechanisms; applied explanation is concerned with working out how already-known mechanisms conspired to bring about some concrete real world event or state of affairs (see e.g., Lawson, 1997, chapter 15). For example, meteorologists pretty much know the separate causal mechanisms that govern weather patterns; much of the pure explanatory component has been done. Each day, though, at least in the UK (and probably everywhere else after some novel weather pattern has been experienced), an applied explanatory endeavour is initiated: the object becomes to explain the pattern of behaviour just experienced utilising an understanding of causal mechanisms already available (and drawn upon in explaining every other day's weather patterns).

Now the point of drawing attention to this latter distinction here is to emphasise that, to the extent that the method of successive approximation, or the making of heuristic assumptions as understood here, have relevance at all in scientific methodology, it is as a component of applied, not pure, explanation. The method in question can be put to work only after the pure-explanatory work has been done. For example, the heuristic assumption that only causal mechanism X is in play (or need be considered), albeit as a first step, presupposes that causal mechanism X has already been uncovered.

Thus in Musgrave's analysis, Newton's goal is not to construct a theory of gravitational forces. This he already possessed. Rather the purpose (we are informed[6]) was to show in a step-wise manner how his theory could ultimately correctly predict inter-planetary movement.

Grounding counterfactuals

The reason I draw attention to this distinction is to indicate that it is only *after* a causal hypothesis of interest is obtained, that is after the pure-explanatory stage, that it may be legitimate for counterfactual insights concerning it to be generated. In other words, a statement about a tendency that is transfactually in play will often license a subjunctive conditional about what would have happened at the level of the course of events if the system had been insulated from the activities of (some) other actually operative mechanisms, or indeed if it had been in any other state.

How we obtain our understanding (or hypotheses) of causal mechanisms of interest is itself a complex process that I discuss at length elsewhere (see especially Lawson, 2003, chapter 4; but also see my responses to Caldwell and Ruccio in Fullbrook, 2009). Contrast explanation will often be important (operating under a logic of analogy and metaphor amongst other things). But it may be merely that we abduct insights obtained in other spheres (as I think may be the case of Schelling's analysis; see below).

Now I think it is this overall framework or understanding that Sugden is edging towards with his notion of 'credible counterfactual worlds'. If a mechanism does act transfactually it licenses a hypothetical statement about how things might be in a different world. Descriptions of the different worlds to our own may be more or less realistic. There is a sense in which alternative worlds seem more credible if the only unrealistic aspect is the absence of actual mechanisms, as opposed to claims about how identified mechanisms do, or could, actually work. This, I suspect, is the basis for Sugden regarding such a counterfactual world as in some sense credible, despite never being expected to occur.

But if it is, notice that it is not the fact of 'credible counterfactual worlds' that give 'some warrant for making inductive inferences from model to the real world', as Hodgson, following Sugden, puts it. Rather, it is a prior understanding of the real world that licenses subsequent claims about certain counterfactual 'worlds' appearing credible.

Notice, too, that no matter how insightful a counterfactual analysis of this sort might be, a comprehensive understanding of the causal process under study cannot typically be captured or conveyed in this manner. Rather, to obtain a full (and indeed ultimately practically useful) understanding of the situation, tendency statements must be interpreted as categorical and indicative, to the effect that, if triggered, a mechanism is really in play whether or not its effects are fully manifest.

In other words, to focus only on actual outcomes in counterfactual scenarios (real or impossible) is typically to miss the main insights available. For if a mechanism licensing a focus on 'credible counterfactual worlds' is indeed operative, then it is having its effects anyway (transfactually); there is a tendency continuously in play in our actual world, whatever the outcome. And this can be acted on. For example, policy can consequently be devised to reinforce or countervail such a tendency as required.

The dominant-mechanism special case

Of course, if a domain of reality is such that a causal mechanism focused upon (and treated as acting in isolation as a first theoretical step) is not only stable but dominating of other causal factors (and especially if all mechanisms in play do combine mechanistically), it is likely that event patterns that the theory predicts are recognisable in the outcomes actually achieved. But where this is so, the method fares well not because false claims are providing insight in some mystical fashion, but because the conceptions of mechanisms acting in relative insulation from counteracting others are not that unrealistic after all (and so barely qualifying as heuristics). Of course, it was in part to deal with such scenarios that I introduced the notion of demi-regularities or demi-regs[7]

In other words, isolationist methods appear most legitimate and insightful (though their ability to actually add much is questionable) precisely in situations where a causal mechanism is so dominant it is (momentarily) effectively insulated from the countervailing effects of other factors. That is, methods of theoretical isolation are legitimised and express reality in a recognisable fashion precisely on occasions where the isolation is not merely 'theoretical' but effectively actual. Needless to say, to suppose that such occasions license the ubiquitous reliance on such methods is to overlook the rarity of the former.

An example of such a special case is the celestial patterning addressed by Newton and referred to by Musgrave. Indeed, I suspect that Newton was as much concerned to explain a demi-reg (the approximate ellipse traced out by the paths of many planets) as to launch a project of successive approximation (in conditions where the mathematics of dealing with the movements of more than two planets had yet to be developed, and indeed was achieved only after Newton's death). The celestial pattern arises because of rather *peculiar* conditions that hold in the case of the planets, in that both their intrinsic states as well as the extrinsic forces acting upon them are, in relevant respects, sufficiently stable, at least over the time period with which most people are usually concerned, i.e. over human life-spans. Properly interpreted, Newtonian mechanics posits theories of how bodies (tend to) act; celestial phenomena function merely as evidence of the postulated tendencies. Thus, if the intrinsic or extrinsic states of the planets in our solar system were not so stable but were to change in some way, perhaps a massive meteor were to pass through the solar system, then such a mechanics would entail a consequent disruption of the familiar celestial phenomenal patterns.

The point is that although the celestial example is spectacular in nature, it represents a relative rarity in constituting a spontaneous demi-reg of its sort. No doubt it is precisely its spectacular nature that accounts in some part for the general failure from Laplace onwards to realise that the situation *is* relatively uncommon, to appreciate that the celestial demi-reg, or near closure supporting it, is far from being indicative of the phenomenal situation that can be expected to prevail more or less everywhere. This failure, in turn, appears to be largely responsible for the widespread, if tacit, acceptance, formerly in philosophy, and currently in the social sciences in particular, of a ubiquity of constant conjunctions of events in nature, and thus of the doctrine of the actuality of 'causal' laws. It no doubt also encourages the idea that methods of theoretical isolation, or of successive approximation, or of heuristics and such like, have ubiquitous relevance, when in fact conditions under which they are relevant, certainly as they are formulated in modern mathematical–deductivist economics, appear to be circumscribed indeed.[8]

Schelling

We are finally in a position to interpret the contribution of Schelling. And we can now appreciate that Schelling's analysis can be expected to be insightful if it captures a real mechanism that operates transfactually, that is, that produces tendencies towards 'racial' segregation, whatever else is going on.

As I understand Schelling's (1969) analysis, the basic idea is as follows. In a context in which

1   individuals perceive themselves as belonging to one or other of two mutually exclusive and exhaustive groups and

2   (at least a significant number of) individuals prefer not to be located in a situation where they are dominated or overwhelmed by members of the 'other' group, and

3   space that can be occupied is confined or restricted, or where grouping of some kind must (for whatever reason) occur, there will be a tendency towards (some) segregation.

I doubt this was ever news. Indeed, do we not all experience situations in which a tendency of this sort is so dominant that it is even actualised? I certainly have, and regularly. My earliest memories include glimpses of physical education lessons in primary school where the teacher regularly asked the class of about 30 children to form four or so groups. Invariably, as I recall, the groups were wholly male or wholly female but not mixed. Today, I cannot but notice that in my workplace (Cambridge) coffee room, the 'support staff' invariably avoid sitting next to 'academic staff' except on occasions (such as outside of lecture term) when the number of academics present is much reduced (and indeed no greater than the number of support staff).

Schelling's contribution, I think, is to suggest that the mechanism in question – basically a preference not to be dominated by perceived 'others' in a confined space – is relevant to understanding racial segregation in the US, at least at a certain moment and place in history. He points out that for purposes of the US census individuals are (or were) classified as white or as black, and that many at least view themselves in this fashion. Now to the extent that a majority of (and perhaps almost all) individuals prefer not to be overwhelmed by others of a different 'colour', and there is a restricted area in which some population is located, we have reason to expect a tendency to racial segregation.

Schelling suggests several more concrete claims that seem likely realistic and consistent with his basic, more abstract conception. Thus he mentions mechanisms whereby '[w]hites may prefer to be among whites and blacks among blacks' (p. 489); or 'whites may prefer the company of whites, while blacks don't care' (p. 489); or whereby '[w]hites and blacks may not mind each other's presence, even prefer some integration, but [where there is] […] a limit to how small a minority either colour is willing to be' (p. 489).

Schelling, though, does not develop an ontology of transfactual tendencies as set out above. Instead, he writes as though countervailing factors are absent and tendencies in play will all be realised (as outcomes or movements). For example:

Whites and blacks may not mind each other's presence, even prefer some integration, but, if there is a limit to how small a minority either colour is willing to be, initial mixtures more extreme than that will lose their minority members and become one colour; those who leave may move to where they constitute a majority, increasing the majority there and causing the other colour to evacuate.

(p. 489)

Clearly, this passage is easily rewritten in terms of tendencies and greater contingency ('tend to lose' in place of 'lose', etc.). When it is, it is this revised formulation in terms of tendencies that licenses the passage as written (not the other way round).

Of course it may be that Schelling believes that 'colour preferences' dominate all countervailing factors. If so then his formulation might be accepted as it is, as a claim intended to be realistic with respect to the real world.

Schelling and counterfactuals

Alternatively, the implicit claim that *only* 'colour preferences' are effective (or that they dominate) can be interpreted as a heuristic assumption. Proceeding on this interpretation seems legitimate, although the point of it is not clear. The language of tendencies conveys all the insights that could be so expressed (and indeed more). The aim could be to do as Musgrave suggests and add in complicating factors bit by bit. But then we would need to know that the effects of Schelling's mechanism, and of those yet to be identified, aggregate in a mechanical fashion. I see no reason to expect this, and Schelling reveals no inclination to proceed in this fashion.

Instead, Schelling continues by imagining yet more concrete or detailed scenarios that conform *not at all* to the world in which we live or to one we could reasonably expect to occur. He constructs fictitious set-ups (e.g., 'a line along which blacks and whites [...] have been distributed in equal numbers and random order' [p. 489]), and assumes that individuals can move freely (and repeatedly move) according to fixed rules, identical for everyone, without costs or countervailing forces of any kind, and so forth.

I am not at all sure that this additional analysis provides any insight other than to the very specific properties of the very particular set-ups or 'models' considered. Any understanding concerning the real world is already contained in the analysis of tendencies. What is going on is that the concern with modelling for its own sake at this point takes over.

Interestingly enough Schelling (1969) does not actually construct any *mathematical* model as such. As a result, Hodgson's claim that Schelling's contribution is a demonstration of the benefits of 'a formal heuristic' is erroneous from the outset. Still there is little doubt that the just-discussed assumptions introduced by Schelling facilitate or encourage a mathematical modelling approach. And it is also clear that whatever the precise nature of Schelling's own early piece it eventually stimulated many papers of a more formalistic kind.

The point to emphasise, though, is that these later papers, or modellers, did not generate the insights we associate with Schelling, but rather they drew upon them in an attempt to legitimise their modelling endeavour. Any new insights obtained concerned merely the properties of the (increasingly complex and unrealistic) formalistic models. Assumptions are made just to get certain desired patterns or results (elegantly) to emerge.[9]

If I am correct in my analysis of all this the question that clearly arises is 'why bother?' Why the interest in models for their own sake? The answer, of course, is the situation I have been actively attempting to counteract throughout much of my writing: the widespread idea that mathematical modelling is in itself a necessary feature of any respectable economic theorising.

Heuristics and causal mechanisms

Let me at this stage return to Hodgson's particular critique. It will be remembered that according to Hodgson: 'The purpose of a heuristic is to identify possible causal mechanisms that form part of a more complex and inevitably open system.' I have shown that, to the contrary, the heuristic assumptions can go to work in economic methodology only after causal mechanisms of interest have already been identified or at least hypothesised. Schelling (1969), I have suggested, illustrates just this.

After setting out his own outline of Schelling (1969) Hodgson adds:

> I have suggested above that heuristics are appropriate if they successfully abstract an important causal mechanism in reality. Accordingly, heuristics relate to the very process of abstraction that Lawson himself highlights. But Lawson suggests that heuristics are isolations rather than abstractions. So here I must return to Lawson's (1997, p. 236) attempted distinction between isolation and abstraction, as quoted above. According to him, the key difference is 'between leaving something (temporarily) out of focus and treating it as though it does not exist'. Again take the Schelling model as an example. Schelling himself accepts that bigoted racists exist, yet he leaves them out of his model. The purpose of the model is not to excuse or deny racism, but the more severe forms of racism are deliberately removed. Nevertheless, the model is extremely and worryingly persuasive.

Here Hodgson seems to make the same mistake as before. Let us be clear. Where a causal mechanism is in play we can focus momentarily upon it, and leave countervailing factors and so forth aside. If the causal mechanism is of a sort that it will have these effects whatever the context, i.e. whatever the relations in which it stands to other causal structures, then clearly it follows that the way it would operate in isolation is equivalent to the way it will operate as we find it in the real world. In such a scenario, it is not illegitimate, and there may be some utility, if, as a first step to an analysis, we adopt the heuristic assumption that the causal factors left out of focus do not exist, or are sealed off. This will clearly be especially the case if the omitted factors appear insignificant compared to the factor on which we focus.

But to describe this situation with the words 'heuristics are appropriate if they successfully abstract an important causal mechanism in reality' is to get things the wrong way round. A correct statement is rather of the sort that 'heuristics are appropriate (if at all) where an isolatable causal mechanism has already been abstracted'. And from this it does not quite follow, as Hodgson would have it, that: 'Accordingly, heuristics relate to the very process of abstraction that Lawson himself highlights.' Rather it follows only that the appropriate use of heuristics *depends* (like everything else) on the very process of abstraction that I highlight.

The heuristic, in the given context, is the assumption that factors out of focus have no effects, that they can be treated as sealed off or non-existent, that the mechanism in focus is acting in (relative) isolation. It is thus indeed the case that 'heuristics are isolations rather than abstractions'.

In the second part of the passage Hodgson writes that although Schelling ignores factors such as 'bigoted racists', Schelling's 'model is extremely and worryingly persuasive'.

I myself am not sure how useful it is to treat Schelling's mechanism as a heuristic first step, as I have already indicated. But whether or not it is useful to do so, any insight to Schelling's analysis arises only because it first captures a case (albeit a special one) of a mechanism that can be regarded as realistic. Why any persuasiveness thereby imparted should be worrying I do not know. Moreover, the consequences of some individuals holding racist views are likely incorporated anyway; certainly Schelling does not examine or distinguish the various grounds for preferences regarding racial segregation, so there is no reason to suppose that bigotry is excluded.

Now I am well aware that I have only provided an interpretation of what is going on and that it is open to contestation. But I do believe I have set out a defence of a framework that can render coherent the various issues before us. Certainly, I do not find much that is coherent in Hodgson's few criticisms; and nor actually am I aware of an equally coherent alternative framework provided elsewhere. Hodgson is very wide of the mark indeed when he suggests that I do not consider the possible heuristic value of formal models, and that I ignore the role of context. At the very least, I think we must accept that if there is insight to be gained from treating formal models as heuristic devices the case for this has yet to be made. If Hodgson feels compelled to establish this point I think he must first do a bit more work. In any case there is nothing here to encourage the view that abstraction is the same as theoretical isolation.

An alternative interpretation

Let me, though, add a qualification to all this. For many reasons it is vital to be charitable in debate, and perhaps there is a more charitable reading of what Hodgson is saying. The preceding discussion does seem to me to be the most accurate reading of Hodgson, in that he writes that the *'purpose* of a heuristic is to *identify* possible causal mechanisms', and that the *'purpose* [of heuristics] is to *establish* a plausible segment of a causal story, without necessarily giving an adequate or complete explanation of the phenomena to which they relate', and so forth. And I did want to respond to what seems to be the most comprehensive as well as accurate interpretation of Hodgson's position. But it is possible that Hodgson is simply suggesting that when we make heuristic assumptions and consider features as if in isolation it is important that those features treated as isolated be real causal mechanisms. That is, it is feasible that Hodgson is *not* at all suggesting that heuristic is somehow bound up with the process of *identifying* a causal mechanism but rather that heuristic (to be successful) needs to be employed in an analysis in which a mechanism has *already been identified*.

If this is the correct interpretation of his position, Hodgson has seemingly expressed himself rather misleadingly, but at least this would be a claim on Hodgson's part that seems sustainable.

However, the nature of my response is still much the same (albeit I could perhaps have made it significantly shorter). Specifically, it remains the case that it is an achieved understanding of the actions of a transfactually active causal mechanism that licenses the subjunctive conditional or counterfactual, that sets the boundaries of, and illuminates, 'credible counterfactual worlds'; it is not the other way round. And fundamentally, it still does not follow that theoretical isolation or 'heuristics relate to the very process of abstraction' in the sense of being much the same thing.

For sure, to consider a transfactually active mechanism as if it were isolated from countervailing factors involves abstraction. But to assume thereby that this method of isolation, or the use of heuristics involved, is the same as abstraction (even if the focus is a scenario of a single dominant mechanism in operation) is simply a mistake. Abstraction, as earlier noted, is involved in theorising both the real and the fictional, the open and the closed and equally both the isolated and non-isolated; indeed it is a part of all forms of conceptualisation or theorising. To conclude that because abstraction is involved in some special case it thereby reduces to, or is somehow intrinsically bound up with, that special case is a conflation that simply does not bear considering further.

So, in short, we can see that, whichever way Hodgson is arguing it, the distinction between abstraction and theoretical isolation cannot be dissolved and in fact (especially given the apparent rarity of the conditions in which the latter is likely useful) remains vital to successful explanatory endeavour.

3) The distinction drawn between abstraction and theoretical isolation is insufficiently precise

Hodgson's third charge is that the distinction I draw between abstraction and theoretical isolation is insufficiently precise. I hope, though, that it is by now clear that this is not so, and that I have said enough to demonstrate that the two methods are indeed irreducible one to the other. Still let me go through Hodgson's last strand of argument to illustrate this one more time.

Hodgson considers a case in which some factor X (trade with other nations) is ignored (in an analysis of the workings of a national economy), and questions whether ignored meaning being-not-mentioned (abstraction) is not the same as ignored meaning treated-as-having-no-influence or not-existing (theoretical isolation).

He writes of the former (abstractionist) scenario:

> Surely, some verbal statement would be required, acknowledging the existence of international trade, explaining its omission from the current discussion, and suggesting that further work must be done to incorporate it into the analysis. But this is also the kind of necessary qualification that we should expect from the best presentations of heuristic models.

Actually, I think it is typically only in the case of theoretical isolation that mention of specific omissions is warranted. Analysis never starts from complete ignorance; much is always taken for granted but remains unstated. As I noted earlier, most social theorists take gravity as given (they abstract from it) in social analysis, but rarely acknowledge or explain that omission. If in contrast they wanted to assume its effects were absent or sealed off, this would most certainly warrant a mention, and an explanation. For under such a heuristic assumption our planet (if indeed there was one at all) would be very different indeed.

In similar fashion, when an economist discusses aspects of an economy such as the UK, its trade with other nations might not get a mention (be abstracted from); but it would nevertheless be presupposed. The focus may be on the workplace, say on improving work security, or on gender mainstreaming in employment strategy. In each such case trade may not be mentioned (it may be abstracted from), because most social theorists take for granted the fact that the UK is a trading nation. But if trade were assumed away, rather than treated as a background causal factor, this once more would certainly warrant a mention and an explanation. For life in the UK, under such an assumption, would be very different indeed to life in the UK as we currently know it[10]. There is no support here for the thesis that abstraction and theoretical isolation cannot be distinguished.

Hodgson continues:

> On the other hand, it would be impossible to mention all the things that we have left out of the account. In this sense all theory is 'temporary'. But do such unmentioned omissions amount to treating some causal linkages as though they do not exist? If this were the case, then every theory, including non-formal, discursive theory, by Lawson's criteria is a failure. Once we try to apply Lawson's criteria, then their insufficiency and vagueness become apparent, and his attempted distinction between abstraction and isolation is revealed as highly problematic.

The first two sentences here are surely correct. But it does not at all follow that to not mention a causal linkage is thereby, of necessity, to treat it as not existing, or as being sealed off. As I say, it is not at all the case that a social analysis that neglects to mention the gravitation is necessarily operating thereby under the assumption that gravity does not exist. That is one reason abstraction is so useful.

In short, it is clear that there is nothing in all this that in any way threatens the distinction between abstraction and theoretical isolation or renders it 'highly problematic'. It may well be that the method of isolation is found to have little utility. But the distinction in question, between the practice of not focusing on something and assuming its effects are somehow absent or sealed off, remains as clear and vital to social theorising as ever.

Concluding comments

Despite the emphasis that mainstream economists place on methods of formalistic modelling (or perhaps because of it), they make relatively few attempts to justify their orientation. This is surely a significant absence leading in and of itself to an impoverishment of the discipline, whatever else might be going on. Hodgson's spirited intervention to make a substantial defence of forms of formalistic modelling, and/or the manner in which mathematical–economic models might fruitfully be interpreted or utilised, is thus to be welcomed. He performs an important service. For reasons given, however, I am not convinced by Hodgson's efforts so far. But knowing Hodgson, I suspect he will persevere further in this, and I am confident we will all be the better for it, whatever may be the conclusions that are reached along the way.

Notes

1 This is an abridged excerpt from chapter 12 of *Ontology and Economics* (Fullbrook, 2009), in which Tony Lawson is responding to some criticisms formulated by Geoffrey Hodgson. The excerpt is included because it contains a relatively recent statement on (an ontologically grounded) assessment of the use of mathematical methods in economics. The original chapter is entitled 'On the Nature and Roles of Formalism in Economics'. In the excerpt the focus is

on abstraction as a method compared to various methods of theoretical isolation advocated by defenders of modelling in economics, and I have substituted a new title accordingly (SP).

2 In other words, in cases where isolationist methods are adopted, and it is assumed that some factor X operates in isolation, it will be clear from the context of analysis that some (and which) factors are being treated as operative but unmentioned as opposed to being sealed off.

3 In other words, I am suggesting that any insight attached to a formal model is typically not the result of the modelling or heuristic exercise itself but derived first in a different context. For a mainstream economist, the overriding objective is to produce a mathematical model. Obviously, modellers are uncomfortable with the charge of irrelevance, so attempts will be made to render models as realistic as possible; real insights will be tagged on wherever feasible. But as I say, I believe the real insights are typically independent of, and indeed achieved prior to, the construction of the mathematical model.

4 This is the conception shared by others who work in this field. For example, Steve Keen recently considers heuristics, emphasising clearly that 'a heuristic assumption is one which is known to be false, but which is made as a first step towards a more general theory'.

5 Notice that the point of a controlled experiment is to insulate some real causal factor (in order to better empirically identify, or, just as commonly, to empirically verify [or not], the manner in which a mechanism works). Significantly, however well the mechanism is insulated (and insulation will rarely, if ever, be perfect), knowledge of the mechanism's workings will often allow us to say that, and how, it will operate outside the experiment, in the open system of complex interacting reinforcing and countervailing forces. Clearly it is because many mechanisms act transfactually that we can successfully apply knowledge achieved in the (controlled) experiments, where event regularities are produced, to conditions where event regularities are absent; for the results achieved apply first and foremost to transfactual tendencies, not to highly restricted and rare event regularities.

6 Actually, I am not so sure of Musgrave's explanation of Newton's intentions (see below), even if, as in this case, the conditions for the method of successive approximation to be successful appear to be satisfied.

7 Which in *Economics and Reality* I characterised as 'a partial event regularity which *prima facie* indicates the occasional, but less than universal, actualization of a mechanism or tendency, over a definite region of time–space' (see also *Reorienting Economics*, chapter 4). In Lawson (1997) I suggested that a demi-reg:

> indicates the likely effects of a causal mechanism that frequently but not uniformly are actualised over a particular region of time–space. The patterning observed will not be strict if countervailing factors sometimes dominate or frequently co-determine the outcomes in a variable manner. But where demi-regs are observed there is evidence of relatively enduring and identifiable tendencies in play.

8 Perhaps too it is a focus upon the rare (if sometimes rendered prominent) scenario, wherein some mechanism dominates others (so that treating it as if acting in isolation is not so different from treating it realistically), that most encourages Hodgson in his view that 'the distinction (between theoretical isolation and abstraction) is, at least in prominent practical instances, difficult to sustain'.

9 At this point I am reminded once again of Frank Hahn's awakening to the nature of this sort of state of affairs (even if Hahn mistakenly supposes that those who recognise it more immediately are disposed to being anti-mathematics [as opposed to being anti the abuse of mathematics]):

[...] there is [...] a lesson which has only gradually been borne in on me which perhaps inclines me a little more favourably to the 'anti-mathematics' group. The great virtue of mathematical reasoning in economics is that by its precise account of assumptions it becomes crystal clear that applications to the 'real' world could at best be provisional. When a mathematical economist assumes that there is a three good economy lasting two periods, or that agents are infinitely lived [...] everyone can see that we are not dealing with any actual economy. The assumptions are there to enable certain results to emerge and not because they are to be taken descriptively.

(Hahn, 1994, p. 246)

10 Any resulting analysis would be extremely different. This absence would mark most of the UK's internal economic institutions, as well as the sorts of political activities undertaken. All goods, including technology, would be home produced. Competition would presumably be internally generated. International pressures affecting security-at-work policies would be absent. The economy would not (need to) be part of trading blocs. Presumably factors like the European Employment Strategy would have no impact. There would be no scope for policies like export-led growth or import quotas. There is no obvious reason why movements in world commodity prices would have any impact, etc.

References

Akerlof, George A. (1970) 'The Market for "Lemons": Quality Uncertainty and the Market Mechanism', *Quarterly Journal of Economics, 84*(3), August, pp. 488–500.

Blaug, Mark (1997) 'Ugly Currents in Modern Economics', *Options Politiques, 18*(17), September, pp. 3–8.

Fullbrook, Edward (ed.) (2009) *Ontology and Economics: Tony Lawson and his Critics,* London and New York: Routledge.

Hahn, Frank H. (1985) 'In Praise of Economic Theory', the *1984 Jevons Memorial Fund Lecture,* London: University College.

Hahn, Frank H. (1992a) 'Reflections', *Royal Economic Society Newsletter, 77*.

Hahn, Frank H. (1992b) 'Answer to Backhouse: Yes', *Royal Economic Society Newsletter, 78.*

Hahn, Frank H. (1994) 'An Intellectual Retrospect', *Banca Nazionale del Lavoro Quarterly Review, XLVIII*(190), pp. 245–258.

Hodgson, Geoffrey M. (2006) *Economics in the Shadows of Darwin and Marx: Essays on Institutional and Evolutionary Themes,* Cheltenham: Edward Elgar.

Lawson, Tony (1981) 'Keynesian Model Building and the Rational Expectations Critique', *Cambridge Journal of Economics, 5,* pp. 311–326.

Lawson, Tony (1997) *Economics and Reality,* London and New York: Routledge.

Lawson, Tony (2002) 'Mathematical Formalism in Economics: What Really is the Problem?', in Philip Arestis and Sheila Dow (eds), *Methodology, Microeconomics and Keynes: Festschrift for Victoria Chick,* London: Taylor and Francis.

Lawson, Tony (2003) *Reorienting Economics,* London and New York: Routledge.

Lawson, Tony (2004) 'On Heterodox Economics, Themata and the Use of Mathematics in Economics', *Journal of Economic Methodology, 11*(3), September, pp. 329–340.

Leamer, Edward E. (1978) *Specification Searches: Ad Hoc Inferences with Non-Experimental Data,* New York: John Wiley and Sons.

Leamer, Edward E. (1983) 'Let's Take the Con out of Econometrics', *American Economic Review*, 73(3), pp. 34–43.

Lipsey, Richard G. (2001) 'Successes and Failures in the Transformation of Economics', *Journal of Economic Methodology*, 8(2) June, pp. 169–202.

Mäki, Uskali (1992) 'On the Method of Isolation in Economics', in C. Dilworth (ed.), *Intelligibility in Science*, Poznan Studies in the Philosophy of the Sciences and the Humanities, 26, pp. 317–351.

Musgrave, A. (1981) 'Unreal Assumptions in Economic Theory: The F-Twist Untwisted', *Kyklos*, 34, pp. 377–387.

Nash, Stephen J. (2004) 'On Closure in Economics', *Journal of Economic Methodology*, 11(1), March, pp. 75–89.

Schelling, Thomas C. (1969) 'Models of Segregation', *American Economic Review*, 59(2), pp. 488–493.

Sugden, Robert (2000) 'Credible Worlds: The Status of Theoretical Models in Economics', *Journal of Economic Methodology*, 7(1), March, pp. 1–31.

12 Applied economics, contrast explanation and asymmetric information[1]

Tony Lawson

1. Introduction

The modern discipline of economics, or at least its dominant mainstream branch, has, to a fairly significant extent, lost touch with the real world. This is a view that Brian Reddaway repeatedly expressed to me as we jointly lectured a Cambridge undergraduate paper in applied economics in the 1980s. It is a view that I also had come to accept. A further belief we both held was that the reason for this unfortunate state of affairs is the more or less compulsory focus on formalistic models: we shared the assessment that, *by their nature*, the sorts of models that economists use preclude the uncovering of very much real insight into social reality, *given its nature*. Furthermore, we were both convinced that realistic assessments of economic developments remained entirely feasible.

Thereafter, though, Reddaway and I parted company; our research strategies diverged somewhat. We did not actually disagree significantly on anything. But we did do things rather differently.

Reddaway, as is well known, maintained an overtly practical orientation throughout, and focused very much on seeking 'rough and ready' patterns in data, and using them in such a manner as the prevailing context seemed to warrant. Although he did not coin it, Reddaway very much liked repeating the *aphorism*: 'It is better to be roughly right than precisely wrong.' In his view, if the complexity of social reality is such that formal models would always get things wrong, the use of these models leads us to results that are spuriously 'precise'. He regarded this presentational precision as overly pretentious. In place of using the latest formalistic techniques Reddaway encouraged his students to make 'back of envelope calculations', to follow 'simple rules of the thumb', and such like. Reddaway mostly concerned himself with data as published in official sources. And the nature of this data, he believed, was such that only rough and ready methods of analysis could provide insight.

As I say, my path was a different one. Like Reddaway I was of the view that the nature of social reality is such that formalistic methods are unlikely very often to be appropriate to its analysis. But my concern has been to elaborate this nature, and to investigate whether any insights obtained by so doing can provide some kind of aid to socio-explanatory enquiry. In short, my preferred path has been to turn to the philosophy of social science, and in particular to social ontology (the study of the nature of social reality).

Reddaway was supportive of this project, such as it was explicitly formulated in those days. However, he did often impress upon me the following point. If one of my goals was to seek out and emphasise approaches to social explanation that went largely unrecognised in the discipline, it would always be helpful to provide illustrations of how they work.

Looking back on my output of recent years I suspect I have failed in this. Certainly, I have given support to certain explanatory approaches, most especially to dialectical explanatory approaches (I indicate what I mean by this below), and in particular to a specific form of dialectical reasoning that I refer to as *contrast explanation*. But the illustrations I have provided have perhaps been too brief. Moreover, where I have given more detailed illustrations I have mostly used my own empirical-explanatory studies (see, e.g., Lawson, 1997, ch. 18, 1998). A possible drawback of this is that it may encourage a suspicion that I am trying to give support to my own preferred substantive conclusions as much as illustrate an explanatory approach.

With this in mind, I use the opportunity of this occasion to illustrate an explanatory approach I believe to be potentially fruitful for social analysis, focusing upon a contribution that is already widely regarded as persuasive, but whose explanatory underpinnings have not been elaborated as explicitly as I think is warranted, and which do indeed conform to the explanatory moves I regard as significant.

Mindful that, from 1955 to 1970, Reddaway was Director of the Cambridge Department of Applied Economics, I here focus on explanation of a mostly applied kind. This also helps remedy a further area of neglect; for previously I have concentrated on explanation of a pure kind. Before I can turn to an illustrative example of applied economic explanation as I conceive it, however, I must indicate how I interpret the difference between pure and applied explanation in the context of the explanatory approach I often advocate.

2. Causal explanation

The conception of explanation I have come to defend as potentially fruitful for economics is a causalist one (see, e.g., Lawson, 1997, 2003). On this view the primary goal of science, whether natural or social, is to seek out and identify the causes of phenomena of interest. Typically the causes identified will not be (just) events, but underlying mechanisms, powers, structures, processes, totalities or whatever, which produced, or at least facilitated, the phenomenon of interest.

Thus, when cows in the UK in the 1980s started wobbling their heads and falling over, the goal of researchers was to identify the causes of the symptoms of this apparent illness ('mad cow disease' or Bovine Spongiform Encephalopathy) in order, in due course, to find a solution and/or prevent its reoccurrence.

As I say, I think this same causalist orientation is the appropriate one for economics. On this conception, when, or if, social theorists are engaged in identifying the causes of phenomena that lie within the social domain, I am suggesting they are practising science in precisely the sense of natural science. Parenthetically, then, I am suggesting that economists can be scientific in the sense of natural science irrespective of whether or not they choose to apply formalistic techniques.

How are pure and applied explanation to be distinguished? *Pure explanation*, I have argued elsewhere (Lawson, 1997, ch. 15), is the identification of previously unknown or ill-understood causal mechanisms. *Applied explanation* is the employment of knowledge of already identified and understood mechanisms to understand how some outcome of interest has come about. Typically, the latter involves applying knowledge achieved at the stage of pure explanation, along with an assessment of prevailing conditions, to determine how all (or many of) the relevant causal factors combined to produce some (aspect of some) outcome of interest.

If the identification of the prion as causing mad cow disease is an example of pure explanation, an example of applied explanation is provided by 'everyday' meteorology. The principles or causal mechanisms underpinning the various weather patterns are by now well known. But it is not always possible to see in advance how the various mechanisms will interact to produce weather patterns yet to occur. Thus, after the event, an applied explanatory process is undertaken to identify the particular conditions and combinations that must have prevailed for the patterns observed to have occurred.

How are we to reveal or identify relevant social causes? In certain advantaged natural–scientific explanatory contexts, it is possible to experimentally insulate causal mechanisms of interest, and thereby to empirically identify them. The challenge is to achieve causal explanation in the absence of experimental control.

The problem in non-experimental scenarios is that any phenomenon – the behaviour of cows, the yields of crops in a field, the pattern of measured unemployment – will likely be governed by a multiplicity of non-physically isolatable factors, many unobservable and/or transient and/or unstable, with each in turn being the result of, or depending on, its own causal conditions. How, then, do we go about identifying the different causal factors bearing on a phenomenon? How, furthermore, might we successfully discriminate amongst competing causal hypotheses?

3. Contrast explanation

The method to which I have previously given most emphasis is a dialectical procedure that can be systematised as *contrast explanation*. Before describing it, let me emphasise that I do not seek to suggest that it is the only approach that is useful to social science, though as it happens I have found it to be as useful an approach as any, not least because it seems to encompass many other approaches as special cases (see Lawson, 2003, ch. 4). Rather, the reason I have chosen to emphasise and defend any particular approach to explanation at all is to combat the claim often made that, if social reality is complex, it is necessary to simplify and fictionalise in order to proceed. From accepting the latter claim, it is but a simple step to suggesting that the formalistic methods of modern economics, with their admitted fictions, are as justified as any other approach. In my writing I have shown, over and again, that not only is it not necessary to simplify and thereby fictionalise, but doing so can lead us astray. My emphasis on contrast explanation is thus part of an endeavour to demonstrate that the complexity of social reality does not justify the modern reliance on practices that have proven to be so inadequate to the achievement of explanatory insight.

So what is contrast explanation (or the method of explaining critical contrasts)? The gist of it is as follows. Rather than to seek to explain some outcome x, the goal is to explain some contrast 'x rather than y' and to do so in conditions where we might have expected the contrasted outcomes to be the same, because, as far as we could discern, they shared the same causal history. The approach thus turns on explaining *differences* in outcomes, but differences that, from the point of view of existing understandings, are considered to be surprising, noteworthy, inconsistent, disturbing, doubt-inducing or otherwise interesting.[2]

Thus, for example, the goal is to explain *not* the yield of crops in the field but why the crop yield is, say, twice as high as the average down one side of the field; to explain not movements in unemployment in total in a given area, but why unemployment in this area, in a particular time interval, grew far more rapidly in, say, the north than everywhere else.

Let me refer to any region (of time, or space or culture, etc.) in which we expect outcomes to be roughly the same (because we believe them to share the same or a similar causal history) as a *contrast space*. The point of applying the approach I am describing is that if outcomes in such a contrast space are expected to be the same, but one (or a small subset) is found, in fact, to diverge from the others, there is a *prima facie* case for supposing that a single (set of) factor(s) is responsible. In this scenario we are effectively standardising for all the factors in operation throughout the contrast space except the one that makes the difference.

Thus, a complex array of factors may be bearing on crop yield. But we expect them to be roughly the same throughout the field. To the extent that the yield is significantly and systematically higher at one end, there is at least some reason to suppose that a single factor is responsible – perhaps a passing river. If cows in the UK in the 1980s started wobbling their heads and falling over when previously they did not or others do not, we can hope to identify a single factor making the difference – as it turns out, the prion. If unemployment is falling throughout a region except in one part we can hope to explain the difference – perhaps the concentration, in the affected area, of a previously major industry now in decline.

Notice that not just any old contrast will do here. It does have to be surprising, or doubt inducing, or otherwise of interest, from the point of view of current understandings. If I notice that the colour of the walls in my house is different from that of the walls of my neighbour down the street, this, *per se*, is unlikely to spark an explanatory endeavour. If, however, I happen to own both properties and have paid someone to decorate them in identical fashion then my discovery that they are actually different may well initiate the search for an explanation.

This is not an insignificant point. I fear that a lot of contrastive or 'comparative' social research is undertaken where the researchers have no prior reason to expect similar causal histories in play, say in firms or labour markets in different continents. Rather the institutions or locations selected are chosen for some other convenient reason, such as ease of access, attractiveness of location, etc.

4. Experiments

The described manner of standardising for all causal factors except one over a particular space is a feature of experimental situations too. Thus, the latter can be seen as special cases of contrast explanation.

Some experiments occur outside the laboratory. Consider experiments in plant breeding. One question often addressed is whether a particular chemical compound acts as a fertiliser for a given crop. A field is divided into numerous plots and the compound is added to some plots but not others. If it is found that the eventual crop yield is systematically and significantly higher than average where the compound has been added it is reasonable to conclude that the compound indeed acts as fertiliser. Here the contrast to be explained is between the yields of crops on the plots receiving the compound and yields on the remaining plots; because except for the addition of the compound to some plots the causal history throughout the field seems to be the same.

In the successful controlled indoor laboratory experiment, a causal mechanism is effectively insulated from the effects of countervailing forces and triggered. Its own unimpeded effects are thereby observed and recorded. Here there is a contrast between what happens after the mechanism is triggered and what happened before it was triggered. The two situations are the same except for the triggering of the mechanism.

In the latter example, the background factors not under consideration are held constant or held off (or rendered orthogonal) where possible. Out in the open field this is no longer the case. However, if the experiment is well conceived there will be reason to expect background factors, though varying, to be the same throughout the contrast space (the field). Thus, although the weather is constantly changing throughout the period of a plant-breeding experiment, at any point in time each part of the field is experiencing the same amount of sunlight, rainfall, etc., as any other part.

In the successful experiment (whether indoor or outdoor) a contrast is deliberately stimulated. In the more typical non-experimental scenario the aim is to seek out surprising contrasts ex posteriori; that is, to seek out contrasts in conditions where outcomes were expected to be the same because they are believed to have shared similar causal histories.

So the approach to contrast explanation I describe in effect generalises the types of explanatory endeavour that surround situations of experimental control. And if the latter are special cases of the approach I am defending, then to universalise methods that presuppose outcomes are of the sort that are produced in well-controlled experiments, as economists often do, can now be seen to be as unnecessary as it is illegitimate.

Of course, even when faced with a surprising or otherwise interesting contrast to explain, there remains the task of identifying the causal mechanisms responsible for this difference. But here the problems are no different from those facing many experimental natural sciences. There can be no formulaic way of moving from phenomena at one level to their underlying causes. But let me run through what I believe can be said.

5. Retroduction and retrodiction

Let me briefly contrast the modes of reasoning employed in getting at causal processes as appropriate to theoretical and applied explanation, respectively. In each case the aim is to redescribe some phenomenon under a new scheme of concepts designating the structures, mechanisms or agents that are, to some degree, responsible for it.

Pure or theoretical explanations are characteristically *analogical* (scientists first searched, albeit unsuccessfully, for a virus responsible for 'mad cow disease' because viruses have so frequently been found to be responsible for disorders in animals previously) and *retroductive* (positing novel mechanisms that, if they were to exist and act in the postulated manner, would account for phenomena singled out for explanation). In short, theoretical explanations entail transforming existing cognitive resources into plausible theories of novel mechanisms responsible for identified patterns of phenomena. These theories are then empirically assessed and, when found to be empirically adequate, themselves explained in turn, in the continuous unfolding of explanatory knowledge.

Applied explanations, in contrast, are characteristically *resolutive* and *retrodictive*. They entail, first of all, the resolution of conjunctions or complexes, and the redescription of their components. This is followed by the determination (retrodiction) of possible antecedents of these components, and the empirical elimination of possible causes. For example, if we attribute weather pattern x to a particular combination of (already understood) causal mechanisms y, it is necessary to determine (retrodict) the conditions for y and then to check empirically whether these conditions are actually obtained.

Where the causes bearing on some phenomenon are many, it may well be that any applied explanatory endeavour can, at best, achieve only a highly partial explanation of some concrete phenomenon. That is, it may be possible to explain some phenomenon of interest only under one or a few of its aspects.

Where the causes in question are already known to operate, but have not previously been connected with the phenomenon in question, the distinction between applied explanation and the discovery of hitherto unknown mechanisms, or pure explanation, may not be especially sharp; indeed the two may run into each other.

In any case, in the social domain, which appears quintessentially open in the sense that a large number of factors are likely to bear on any phenomenon, a somewhat partial approach to applied explanation is likely to be typical. And to the point, to account for any resolved component of some phenomenon, in applied, as in pure, explanation it may well prove useful to adopt a contrastive explanatory approach.

How might we discriminate between competing causal hypotheses? One obvious way is to check their relative explanatory powers with respect to contrasts on which they both bear. How this will work out will vary from situation to situation. Consider the case where crop yield down one side of the field is significantly and systematically greater than the average yield of the field. One explanation could be a passing stream. But a competing explanation may be the shade provided by trees aligning the side of the field. If so, one obvious resort is to see if there is a point where the stream and trees part company. Perhaps the same crop has been planted in an adjoining field that is similar to the first one in all obvious respects except that the river veers across the middle of the field. If, say, the crop yield remains higher only along the edge of the field we might reasonably conclude that it is the shade and not the stream that is making the difference. At this stage, of course, someone may object that it is bird droppings from roosting birds rather than shade that makes the difference. If so, we need to think of an additional way of discriminating between shade and bird droppings. For this we might look to where birds also roost on field-crossing telegraph wires that provide little shade, and so forth. As I say, how we (are able to) proceed is always a matter of context.

Notice that the more contrasts of relevance that can be explained according to a causal hypothesis being defended, the more confidence we are entitled to hold in that hypothesis.

6. Dialectics

Why do I suggest that contrast explanation is dialectical? I do so because I understand dialectical learning as repeatedly involving three basic components (or steps or moments or stages) where these form the basic structure of contrast explanation. These three components can be summarised as follows:[3]

1   An achieved level of understanding or knowledge of the relevant domain, giving rise to expectations and grounds for action
2   Reason(s) to challenge the achieved level of understanding involving:
   i   Psychological factor(s), such as surprise, doubt, concern, interest, curiosity, dissatisfaction in some situation and incomprehension
   ii   Epistemological factor(s), such as error, contradiction, inconsistency, constraint, ignorance and over-partiality
3   A process of revising the original understanding to meet the challenge posed at stage 2.

The primary dialectical moment is at stage 2, of course, where previous understanding is 'negated', or found to be 'contradicted', or anyway inadequate. Contrast explanation starts at this stage with observations that are contrary to expectations and so are surprising. They are surprising because they do not conform to the understanding achieved at step 1, regarding the causal history of a particular contrast space. Resolving the problem, that is, providing an explanation of the surprising contrast, moves us on to the revised understanding at step 3 where, in principle, the process can start over again. Thus, like all dialectical processes of explanation, contrast explanation is an error theory of learning. Unlike with modern economics, outliers, errors, noise, 'structural breaks', anomalies, etc., are not problems to be put aside but opportunities for explanatory advance.

Having briefly described the explanatory framework I have advocated elsewhere (e.g., Lawson, 1997, 2003), let me now illustrate the process of applied explanation it encompasses through drawing on an influential example from economics. The pressing question of course is: which example to use? Economics is not exactly awash with explanatory contributions widely held to have provided insight. In fact, if I am to start from an economic study widely believed to have provided insight, it is clear that I am going to have to find something acceptable to, and indeed accepted by, the mainstream. Thus, I already seem to be faced with an almost impossible task. For if the nature of social reality is such that mainstream economics, through its reliance upon mathematical deductivist methods, is unable usually to provide much insight, it is seemingly going to be difficult to locate a study well known to, and appreciated by, the mainstream that appears to be explanatorily successful.

Paradoxically, or not, there do seem to be one or two studies that fall into this category of being both appreciated by the mainstream and widely regarded as explanatorily successful. One such is George Akerlof's (1970) highly successful study of the market for 'lemons'. Why this has been accepted by the mainstream is less important for my immediate needs than the fact that it has been.[4] More fundamentally, it does not take much to see that, with a bit of reconstructing, Akerlof's well-known study is indeed an example of contrast explanation of an applied sort (even though it is usually classified as pure theory). I thus turn to it below as a means of illustrating the explanatory approach I am defending. However, the puzzle that this paper is widely known to, and in a sense is accepted by, the mathematical mainstream of modern economics does bear on the broader picture I am presenting. In consequence, this puzzle is itself something I shall eventually address below.

7. Contrast explanation in practice

In his paper 'The Market for "Lemons": Quality Uncertainty and the Market Mechanism', Akerlof (1970) focuses on the market for used cars. If this study is to be interpreted as an example of contrast explanation there must be a surprising or puzzling phenomenon to explain, one that is at least suggestive that an explanatory enquiry is called for. Akerlof puts the phenomenon he intends to address as follows: 'From time to time one hears either mention of or surprise at the large price difference between new cars and those which have just left the showroom. The usual lunch table justification for this phenomenon is the pure joy of owning a "new" car. We offer a different explanation' (p. 489).

Here, then, to reconstruct Akerlof's analysis in our own terms, we have a surprising or interesting contrast. The subject matter is the selling prices of cars recently out of the showroom and the contrast addressed is that these prices are significantly below those of new cars rather than close to or equal to these prices. The contrast space is modern US markets for used cars.

Notice that the objective is not to explain a set of prices. This would require a knowledge of too many factors, a significant proportion of which are likely to be highly contingent and transient as well as unobservable. The contrast is regarded as interesting because the quality of new cars and of those that have recently left the showroom appear, on the face of it, to be reasonably similar, leading to the expectation that their prices would not be especially far apart. Yet this proves not to be the case.

In seeking to explain the contrast in question, namely the large and surprising discrepancy between the prices of new and almost new cars, Akerlof, in effect, seeks to identify a causal mechanism adversely affecting the price of used cars that does not affect the price of new ones.

The term 'lemon' that appears in the title of Akerlof's paper is US slang for a commodity that is regarded as substandard or inferior compared to the average of those available at the going price. In many markets the products sold are found to be of variable quality; and this is likely to be as true of the car market as of any other.

Akerlof's proposed explanation of the contrast here in question is, in the first instance, a mechanism resulting in a tendency for the proportion of lemons amongst cars being re-traded to be significantly higher than amongst those yet to be sold.

Simply put, Akerlof reasons that if, or where, the price of used cars stays at, or close to, the price of new ones, there will be a tendency for the worse-than-average cars, or 'lemons', to be re-traded; it is dissatisfied customers who are most likely to off-load their cars in order to acquire (in the hope of and some reasonable grounds for expecting) better ones. Thus, there will a tendency for those relatively new cars that reappear in the used market to be sub-standard. But, realising this, would-be buyers are unlikely to be prepared to pay anything like the full cost for a used car. In consequence, the prices of used cars will tend to be lower.

So the basic mechanism is one that is hardly a novel discovery. It is the interaction of different groups of individuals, and specifically those with a clear interest in off-loading/trading known-to-be-substandard goods if they can get their money back, and those with an equally clear interest in avoiding purchasing likely-to-be-substandard goods at a price for which they can buy the same item from a retailer, where the proportion of 'lemons' is expected to be significantly lower (than amongst second-hand sellers).

This retrodicted mechanism can be considered to be operating in the car market to reduce the resale price of newly purchased cars only under certain conditions of course. These are the following:

- cars, including new ones, are known to be of variable quality
- the relative quality of cars cannot be determined from their appearance
- through purchasing a new car the owner acquires a knowledge of the quality of that car not available to others (and in particular a knowledge of whether the quality is above or below the [assumed to be roughly known] average quality of a car of a given make and model)
- a basic lack of trust between traders.

Having identified (retrodicted) the relevant mechanism responsible, along with the relevant conditions in the car market, Akerlof draws out further implications of his theory. One such is that the mechanism identified will be, in effect, self-reinforcing. In the circumstances described, anyone with a good car will find that they cannot sell it at a price that reflects its (high) relative value, just because no one will trust her or him that the car is indeed as good as a new one is expected to be. In consequence, owners of 'better' cars are unlikely to trade them.

Further, whatever the level to which the price of a particular model may fall, there will be a tendency for owners with cars regarded as sub-standard-at-that-price to want to trade. To the extent that potential buyers realise this, the market for used cars will tend to diminish everywhere, as, in effect, bad cars push out the good ones and nobody wants to buy.

Although starting from a contrast concerning the prices of new and slightly used cars, Akerlof focuses on an explanatory mechanism, which reasonably can be expected to impact more widely. Abstracted from the example of used cars, the implicit, but essential, conditions for the hypothesised mechanism to operate more widely are:

- a scenario in which items that are being traded vary in quality;
- a scenario in which the appearances of these items do not straightforwardly signal relative quality;
- an asymmetry in information between potential parties to a negotiation;
- a basic lack of trust between potential negotiators.

In such conditions there will be tendencies for a reduction in either/both the average quality of items traded or acted upon and/or in the size of the market.

Notice that although Akerlof does not use the language of tendencies, this is indeed what he, in effect, identifies; a tendency – let me refer to it as the *lemon tendency* – that may on occasion be offset to some extent by countervailing tendencies. Akerlof identifies a tendency that, if in play, could explain the contrast noted. And it is a hypothetical tendency whose reality can be further assessed by considering its explanatory power with respect to empirical contrasts it bears upon more widely.

What other scenarios or set-ups satisfy the conditions of the tendency? According to Akerlof, certain insurance markets do. Specifically, older people in particular are systematically better informed than insurance companies of their likely need for insurance, 'for error in medical check-ups, doctors' sympathy with older patients, and so on make it much easier for the applicant to assess the risks involved than the insurance company' (p. 492). As prices rise, if the lemon tendency is in play, the people who insure themselves will be those with most grounds for believing that they will need insurance. And with the tendency for the average medical condition of insurance applicants to deteriorate as the price level rises, a point may well come where no insurance sales takes place at any price.

An implication of the analysis is the contrast between insurance opportunities between older and younger people. And this is seen to be borne out. Akerlof starts from the empirical claim that '[i]t is a well-known fact that people over 65 have great difficulty in buying medical insurance' (p. 241). He also reproduces findings that support this contention,[5] backing these up with a range of supportive statistics.[6]

A basic condition for the working of the mechanism to which Akerlof draws our attention is the lack of a relationship of trust between buyer and seller. Thus, an implication of the theory of the lemon tendency is that the latter tendency will operate in an unimpeded fashion only where relations of trust, or mechanisms guaranteeing quality, cannot be, or anyway are not, established. It is perhaps an implication of the hypothesis that used cars will trade at a price closer to worth if the traders are friends or at least acquaintances. But the general point is that where quality variation is large (this is also a condition of the lemons mechanism) trade will occur only where some kind of quality control (friendship or close relationship, membership of some small community or some other basis for relationship of trust; existence of some agency checking for and/or guaranteeing quality control, etc.) is in place.

I emphasised earlier that we are entitled to have greater confidence in a causal hypothesis the more explanatory powerful it is found to be in relation to significant contrasts of which we are aware. It is thus of interest that Akerlof seeks to impress that his hypothesis can render intelligible a range of (surprisingly) contrasting phenomena.

In this light we can observe that, according to Akerlof, there 'is considerable evidence that quality variation is greater in underdeveloped than developed areas' (p. 496). It follows that trade between developed and less developed countries will tend to be small unless the less developed countries find a way of checking/guaranteeing quality. In support of this Akerlof seeks to demonstrate that where trade takes place various sorts of controls are in place (in contrast to the situation in developed countries). For example, he notes that in India, under the Export Quality Control and Inspection Act of 1963, about 85 per cent of Indian exports are covered under one or another type of quality control (p. 496).

Akerlof also indicates how, in less developed countries, markets in credit depend, for their existence, upon institutions that are reputable or which, in being limited to local groups, can use communal ties to encourage honest dealings. For example, he notes that a majority of industrial enterprises are controlled by 'managing agencies', which have generated a reputation. In turn, these managing agencies are dominated by caste or communal groups. He finds that:

> In this environment, in which outside investors are likely to be bilked of their holdings, either (1) firms establish a reputation for honest dealing, which confers upon them a monopoly rent insofar as their services are limited in supply, or (2) the sources of finance are limited to local communal groups which can use communal – and possibly familial – ties to encourage honest dealing *within* the community.
>
> (p. 498)

A further seemingly supportive example of the lemons mechanism is the 'extortionate rates' that the local money lenders in India have been able to charge clients. Akerlof notes that high interest rates have been a leading factor in landlessness. This was a problem that the 'Cooperative Movement' was intended to counteract by setting up banks to compete with the local money lenders. This, however, merely led to another 'interesting' contrast warranting an explanation: that the interest differential between banks in the city and those of the local moneylenders remained large rather than disappearing (as might be expected with opportunities for intermediaries to gain from any lasting difference). But, again, the lemons mechanism can account for this, adding to the explanatory power of the hypothesis. Akerlof addresses the issue as follows:

> While the large banks in the central cities have prime interest rates of 6, 8, and 10 per cent the local moneylender charges 15, 25, and even 50 per cent. The answer to this seeming paradox is that credit is only where the granter has (1) easy means of enforcing his contract or (2) personal knowledge of the character of the borrower. The middle man who tries to arbitrage between the rates of the money lender and the central bank is apt to attract all the 'lemons' and thereby make a loss.
> (pp. 498, 499)

In sum, then, Akerlof produces a hypothesis of a mechanism capable of explaining his original contrast of interest, and demonstrates the explanatory power of this hypothesis with respect to further empirical (contrastive) phenomena that the hypothesis is considered to bear upon. Akerlof's study thus provides a good illustration of the applied explanatory approach earlier elaborated.

8. Reception by the mainstream

It will be apparent that the discussion set out has not made any reference to any form of mathematical deductivist modelling. Clearly such modelling is unnecessary, and on the face of things, given that it typically introduces fictions, would only clutter the analysis. Why then was Akerlof's analysis accepted by the mainstream at all given the latter's prioritisation of formalistic modelling procedures?

Before continuing let me stress that I am not suggesting (and have never suggested) that mathematical modelling cannot provide insight in the social realm. Certainly, if certain closure conditions hold – essentially if spheres of social reality approximate to closed isolated systems of atomistic agents – then the models can be expected to have relevance. However, I have argued that social reality in general is open and structured, constituted by phenomena with emergent powers that are processual in nature, constituted in relation to other phenomena and so forth. Only rarely are real world social conditions likely to approximate those (closed and atomistic) scenarios that would guarantee that formalistic models can provide insight. Having said that, have I not also suggested that it is plausible that Akerlof's 'lemons mechanism' operates in a number of scenarios? How then do I explain its acceptance by the mainstream?

Part of the answer, no doubt, is that Akerlof does provide the compulsory mathematical model. This was likely a necessary condition for the paper's acceptance. But it is not clear that this is sufficient to explain it, even less does it explain the degree of attention the paper has since received, especially in recent years. For in truth Akerlof's paper is hardly mathematical at all, and what little maths there is gives the appearance of being tagged on (in just over two pages) to provide a suggested and clearly unrealistic numerical example of the mechanism after the latter has already been elaborated. In addition, the example provided is clearly unrealistic, portraying a closed world significantly different to our own. If this section were dropped, the paper would certainly be none the worse, and, I believe, much the better. Presumably it is included merely as a sop to the mathematical mainstream.

As the modelling part of the paper is so clearly marginal to the analysis, giving the appearance, in fact, of being a rather unhelpful add-on, it still seems to be a bit of a puzzle that the paper was acceptable to the mainstream. One would have expected the mainstream journals to dismiss this paper as 'trivial' or 'not economics', just as they do most heterodox non-formalistic contributions. Here then we still seem to have a further surprising contrast to explain: why the paper was accepted by the mainstream where non-formalistic contributions mostly are not.

Perhaps it is tempting to suppose that in the late 1960s the emphasis on formalism was not as rigid and dogmatic as it currently appears. It can be argued that the wave of compulsory formalism was only just beginning to roll in. Prominent journals did make some exceptions.

In any case we should remember that many mainstream journals did in fact reject the paper, and seemingly precisely because of its non-formalistic nature. For, in line with the treatment of other papers where formalism is equally minimal or non-existent, the paper was considered too simplistic to publish. The paper was eventually accepted by the *Quarterly Journal of Economics* (*QJE*) and published in 1970. Before that it was sent to the *American Economic Review* in 1967 but was rejected, without even a referee's report, because, as Akerlof himself recounts, the *Review* 'did not publish such trivial stuff' (Akerlof, 1995, p. 52). Next it went to the *Journal of Political Economy*, which at least sent a report. Finally, before the *QJE*, it went to the *Review of Economic Studies* (on the urging of one of the editors) but 'was rejected on the grounds again that it was "trivial"' (Akerlof, 1995, p. 53).

Examining this particular episode and others like it, George Shepherd (1995) concludes that, in the period in question

> [t]he technical tide rolled in. Leading journals filled with theorems and equations. The same wave that pushed in the math dragged away the words: articles that contained only clear ideas in clear prose began to be rejected because they contained insufficient markets. For example, journals rejected important articles by George Akerlof and

> [others] because they were 'trivial', 'chatty' or 'lacked a formal model'
> – editor code for too many words and too few symbols and numbers.
>
> (Shepherd, 1995, p. 11)

Maybe, then, the timing is the explanation that the limited amount of formal modelling was just enough to scrape home in at least one mainstream journal at that time. However, there is a related puzzle that is not so easily resolved. For not only did one journal eventually accept the paper, but, with time, the paper became widely acknowledged by mainstream economists and even won Akerlof the Nobel Memorial Prize in Economics.

What then is the explanation of this phenomenon? I believe that the paper became widely accepted for a reason bearing mostly on aspects of it that I have so far emphasised little, and which I think are actually limitations.

In addition to the contrastive explanatory analysis set out above (and his largely meaningless formalistic, supposedly illustrative, model) Akerlof suggests many counter-tendencies to the lemons mechanism, but does so in an overly functionalist way. That is, he at times implies that institutions, etc., which end up guaranteeing quality/honesty in some way, were explicitly designed to offset the quality uncertainty that is a basic condition for the lemons mechanism to be in play.

This is true of the examples discussed above, and to some extent I have re-jigged the presentation. Towards the end of the paper Akerlof also adds the following:

> Numerous institutions arise to counteract the effects of quality uncertainty. One obvious institution is guarantees. Most consumer durables carry guarantees to ensure the buyer of some normal expected quality. One natural result of our model is that the risk is borne by the seller rather than the buyer.
>
> A second example of an institution which counteracts the effects of quality uncertainty is the brand name.
>
> (p. 499)

Akerlof goes on to claim that the advantage of brand naming is not only that it indicates quality, but gives the purchaser a 'means of retaliation' – curtailing future purchases – if the quality does not meet expectations. Under the head of brand naming, Akerlof discusses the practices of hotel and restaurant chains. And he further considers the role of licensing practices – of doctors, lawyers and barbers – as also working to reduce quality uncertainty.

The reason I question the presentation of some of this is that Akerlof seems to use expressions like 'institutions arise to counteract' to mean 'in order to counteract'. This may or may not be so, and in any case is not necessary to his argument. Horses' tails are functional in swishing away flies but it is not clear that horses grew them in order to do this. Certain institutional/community relations may be functionally appropriate to counteracting the 'lemons mechanism' but it does not mean that they were designed for this effect. They (or aspects of them) sometimes may have been. But to suppose that they always were without empirical examination is merely to give an unnecessary sop to the rationalistic tendencies of mainstream economics.

And this is the point. Enamoured by their mathematical–deductivist modelling activities, economists need to construct worlds that conform to the systems of isolated atoms these models presuppose (see Lawson, 1997, 2003). The main (though not the only conceivable – see Lawson, 1997, ch. 8) atomistic assumption so employed is that everyone is rational in the sense of acting as an isolated selfish calculator. Akerlof's contribution can be, and indeed has been, read as suggesting that all institutions and other social structures (previously regarded as impediments to the optimising process) are now to be interpreted as the results of optimising decisions of rational agents acting in the context of asymmetric information.

Furthermore, armed with this theory, mainstream economists have sought to extend the 'explanatory' scope of their project not only to institutions as such, but also to culture, customs, norms, habits, trust and such like. Thereby, with the latter treated no longer as exogenous or irrational, but rather as rational or optimising responses to market imperfections, the mainstream has been able to extend into, or inaugurate, new sub-fields such as new economic sociology or new economic geography.

In other words, this aspect of Akerlof's contribution can fairly be interpreted as initiating a novel imperialistic tendency on the part of mainstream economists. For those social structures that economists previously disregarded as the preserve of other social sciences are now to be explained as the efficient outcomes of the optimising economic agents that populate mainstream economic theorising. Ben Fine (2003) makes the same point:

> [I]n the presence of market imperfections, it becomes rational for individuals to establish, or at least to conform with once established, the non-market mechanisms for addressing these imperfections. In case of the market for lemons, for example, traders might decide to run a warranty scheme. This would be an elementary form of institution for handling the informational imperfections that accompany transactions. Consequently, institutions in general can be understood as the non-market response to market imperfections [...]
>
> At this stage, it is possible to make explicit what has so far been implicit as far as the current phase of economics imperialism is concerned. With the incorporation of institutions, customs culture, norms, trust and so on into economics, so are addressed the traditional concerns of the other social sciences from the perspective of market and informational imperfections. The result has been the creation or renewal of a range of 'new' fields within and around economics, with a corresponding extension of economics to previously neglected

topics – the new institutional economics, the new economic sociology, the new political economy, the new growth theory, the new labour economics, the new economic geography, the new financial economics, the new development economics, and so on.

(Fine, 2003, p. 7)

None of this is essential to Akerlof's central explanatory argument. However, it does likely explain its eventual widespread adoption by the mainstream. In an evolutionary world, nature will give the appearance of design if it gives the appearance of anything. And in an evolutionary social world, if the conditions of the 'lemons tendency' hold, then institutions that facilitate markets will give the appearance of being designed to do so, if the markets are in evidence at all.

To defend (what I am interpreting as) Akerlof's basic hypothesis as explanatory powerful, Akerlof needs only to demonstrate that where markets exist under the conditions of his hypothesis, there must be some countervailing factor serving (whether by design or otherwise) to facilitate at least limited exchange (there is no need at all to suppose that the latter are always the intentional design of optimising agents concerned with the problem of asymmetric information). And by exploring situations where markets do and do not exist, and their nature, Akerlof does indeed demonstrate empirical support for his hypothesis. Appropriately conceived it is an example of contrast explanation of an applied sort in practice.

9. Conclusion

In previous writing I have argued that even if, as seems to be the case, social reality is not everywhere a closed system, then successful social analysis remains possible. However, the latter is likely to require the application of not merely analytical methods but also, and perhaps especially, those, like contrast explanation, that are primarily, or more overtly, dialectical in nature.

My limited objective with the current paper is to illustrate the dialectical explanatory approach in question, drawing upon an example of a successful and widely accepted piece of applied economics that it effectively underpins. The example utilised to this effect is George Akerlof's 'The Market for "Lemons": Quality Uncertainty and the Market Mechanism'. Hitherto the reasons for the success of Akerlof's analysis have remained largely unpacked. Here, in part, I have endeavoured to repair that omission.

Notes

1   First published in *Cambridge Journal of Economics*, 2009, Vol 33, No 3, 405–419.
2   Various aspects of the account here defended are paralleled in writings elsewhere, especially in the philosophy of science literature. See, for example, van Frassen (1980), Garfinkel (1981) and Lipton (2004).

3 I think Hegel's approach can indeed be systematised as a special case of this schema. But then so, I believe, can the approach of numerous others, even including those of Mill and Popper, though this is not the occasion to elaborate.

4 An alternative possible example suggested by a referee of this article is Ronald Coase's (1937) paper on 'The Nature of the Firm', which poses the contrastive question of why there is internal organisation in a situation in which production coordination seems best achieved by the price mechanism. A reconstruction of this paper likely would provide more insight into the relevance for contrast explanation. For the time being though, Akerlof's study gives me more than enough to work with.

5 For example, he reports the findings of Dickerson (1959) in *Health Insurance*:

> Generally speaking policies are not available at ages materially greater than sixty-five ... The term premiums are too high for any but the most pessimistic (which is to say the least healthy) insureds to find attractive. Thus there is a severe problem of adverse selection at these age.
>
> (p. 493)

6 Akerlof records:

> While demands for health insurance rise with age, a 1956 national sample survey of 2,809 families with 8,898 persons shows that hospital insurance coverage drops from 63% of those aged 45 to 54, to 31% of those over 65. And surprisingly, this survey also finds average medical expenses for males aged 55–64 of US$88, whereas males over 65 pay an average of US$77. While noninsured expenditure rises from US$66 to US$80 in these age groups, insured expenditure declines from US$105 to US$70. The conclusion is tempting that insurance companies are particularly wary of giving medical insurance to older people.
>
> (Akerlof, 1970, p. 493)

References

Akerlof GA 1970. The Market for 'Lemons': Quality Uncertainty and the Market Mechanism. *Quarterly Journal of Economics*; 84(3): 488–500.

Akerlof GA 1995. In: Shepherd G, editor. *Rejected: Leading Economists Ponder the Publication Process*. Sun Lakes, Arizona: Thomas Horton and Daughters, pp. 52–53.

Coase R 1937. The Nature of the Firm. *Economica*; 4: 386–405.

Dickerson OD 1959. *Health Insurance*. Homewood, IL: Irwin.

Fine B 2003. 'A Brief History of Economic Imperialism', mimeo, London School for Oriental and African Studies; paper presented at the Cambridge Realist Workshop. 3 November 2003.

Garfinkel A 1981. *Forms of Explanation*. New Haven, CT: Yale University Press.

Lawson T 1997. *Economics and Reality*. London and New York: Routledge.

Lawson T 1998. Social Relations, Social Reproduction and Stylized Facts. In: Arestis P, editor. *Essays in Honour of Paul Davidson, Vol. 3*. Cheltenham: Edward Elgar.

Lawson T 2003. *Reorienting Economics*. London and New York: Routledge.

Lipton P 2004. *Inference to the Best Explanation*. London and New York: Routledge.

Shepherd G 1995. *Rejected: Leading Economists Ponder the Publication Process*. Sun Lakes, Arizona: Thomas Horton and Daughters.

van Frassen BC 1980. *The Scientific Image*. Oxford: Clarendon Press.

PART V
Ethics

13 Critical ethical naturalism: an orientation to ethics[1]

Tony Lawson

The social realm consists of emergent phenomena with their own irreducible causal powers, phenomena whose novelty and irreducibility facilitate, and indeed warrant, a relatively autonomous science of society. This, in brief, is a thesis I have long defended (e.g., Lawson, 1997, though most recently in Lawson, 2012, 2013a, 2013b). The conception thereby sustained remains, however, thoroughly naturalistic in the sense that social phenomena are demonstrated to be diachronically coherent with phenomena posited in our best theories of the natural domain, and in particular with those of quantum mechanics and evolutionary biology. Alternatively put, it can be shown how social phenomena emerge from, whilst remaining consistent with, and indeed dependent upon, phenomena studied within the non-social natural sciences. The account of social reality defended thus (or in this sense) constitutes a *socio-ontological naturalism*.

My concern here is to determine the most sustainable ethical orientation that remains consistent with this specific naturalist orientation. That is, my concern here is with elaborating and defending a version of *ethical–ontological naturalism*, or, as more conventionally stated, an *ethical naturalism*.

The account developed, it will be seen, is sufficiently challenging of many systematised alternative ethical positions, as well as of popular conceptions of the nature of moral theorising, as to warrant the label of *critical ethical naturalism*.

I Ethical naturalism

The term emergent in the opening sentence expresses the idea of novelty, of something unprecedented or previously absent, that somehow arises out of phenomena already in existence. Previously I have argued that emergent phenomena arise as, or as properties of, novel totalities, coming about through a recombination (perhaps involving a modification) of pre-existing elements. In this, the relational organisation of any emergent totality constitutes an essential (emergent) feature of the totality, rendering the causal properties of the latter irreducible to those of the elements that come to be incorporated as components.

In particular I have argued that social phenomena specifically, i.e. those whose existence and/or reproduction depend necessarily on human inter-action, are, or are bound up with, totalities or systems that emerge from, and can causally act back upon, whilst yet remaining dependent upon, though causally and ontologically irreducible to, a pre-existing non-social reality. That is, I have argued that there exists a relatively autonomous or separate realm of ontologically and causally irreducible social phe-nomena; marking the site for a relatively autonomous social science (see especially Lawson, 1997, 2003a).

In pursuing the possibility of a sustainable ethical naturalism, a first question to pose is whether there similarly exists a relatively autonomous or separate realm of emergent moral phenomena. In other words, are there moral phenomena that are both emergent and ontologically and causally irreducible in the just-noted sense of social phenomena, and to which our moral terms (like good and bad, etc.) uniquely apply?

I believe the answer is clearly no. Unlike the case of social reality *per se*, the naturalistic orientation I find most sustainable in regards to ethical concerns is somewhat reductionist. Although moral discourse indeed has its own categories, such as good, bad, right, wrong and so forth, it is not clear that these terms refer to irreducible phenomena of some emergent moral realm. Rather they are seemingly always used to pick out phenom-ena that can equally be referred to using other forms of social, biological, psychological, physical, etc., descriptions (such as human well-being, interest, action facilitative of human well-being, and so forth).

So the kind of ethical naturalism that I find compelling and seek to defend is, as I say, a somewhat reductionist stance in that it holds that there are no separate emergent moral properties that are irreducible to the (rest of the) real/natural world including social reality. Rather, ethical or moral terms pick out features of the world that can be, and typically are, simultaneously referred to in more clearly naturalistic terms; moral terms share the same referents as non-moral terms.

Taking a stand

An argument sometimes thought to undermine such ethical positions such as I am seeking to develop turns on the assessment, usually associated with David Hume, that an 'ought' cannot be derived from an 'is', that, at the meta-ethical level of analysis pursued in the paper so far, a prescrip-tive claim cannot be derived from merely factual or descriptive claims. Although I believe such an argument to be erroneous (we can for example reason that: person X needs to live, the house that X is in [alone] is on fire and the only way for X to survive is to leave the house, so X *ought* to leave; see Lawson, 2013c), the insight it contains is that we can draw specific conclusions about conduct only through also making assessments of what is in the interests of a relevant subject or group of subjects, their needs and desires or whatever. The point, then, is that although a naturalistic theory is not undermined by considerations of how prescriptive assessments are formed, it is recognised that factual assessments must include judgements of interests (for example, that it is not in one's interest to be burnt), which in turn explain why other factual judgements (the house is on fire) constitute reasons for action (leaving the house).

This, however, is precisely what ethical naturalist positions do; they advance substantive theories about human interests. Of course, up until this point I have been writing only *about* the position of ethical naturalism; I have adopted an outsider or *meta*-perspective. But to say more, and indeed to hold (as opposed to talk about) an ethical naturalist stance, it is necessary to take a stand. Given the sort of reductionist ethical naturalist account I am proposing, this requires committing oneself to a specific social theory, and specifically to a definite account of that which has so far been described as the human interest. Once this is taken, ought-statements can be inferred directly, though of course conditioned ultimately by a conception of human interest that is thereby (provisionally) taken for granted. It is this latter insight that human interests are always at some level taken for granted that I assume Hume was really observing.[2]

Here I draw on my own research reported elsewhere (see, for example, Lawson, 2003a, 2003b), and mostly I do little more than summarise (fallible) results that bear clear relevance for the current topic of discussion. I will though elaborate some of the more contentious claims. According to the conception defended:

1 Human beings have natures such that each does indeed have 'interests'; more usefully human beings are the sorts of beings that can flourish. Generalised flourishing is thus the basis of ethical thinking, the referent of the ethically good.

2 Morality exists throughout the human world. It concerns actions and objectives and the like. People everywhere act in accordance with actions and/or objectives assessed as being right or wrong or good and bad, etc.

3 Human interests, the bases of our conditions for flourishing, that allow each to flourish, do not reduce to our preferences. Rather, each human being is a bundle of needs including those of realising various capacities, capabilities and so forth, where flourishing depends on the fulfilment of these needs. A subset of human needs including capacities and/or capabilities are seemingly shared/universal (e.g., needs and/or powers to develop capacities/capabilities of language use, or generally to partake in forms of social interaction); and others are not. All are developed in specific historical and socio-cultural contexts. And all are in some ways subject to continuous transformation.

4 Human beings are inherently relational. By this I do not mean merely that we are embedded in society. Rather we are social–relationally

constituted. From the moment we are conceived we are being socially formed. Certainly, from birth onwards, it is very apparent that we are positioned according to gender, class, nation, culture and so on; and according to our positions we have rights and (eventually) obligations, that relate us to others, whether similarly positioned or positioned contrastively (with our rights matched by the [internally related] obligations of others, and so on). We are thus necessarily socio-relational beings.

5   Human beings have evolved in communities where the survival and flourishing of each depends on the survival and flourishing of the community, and so ultimately of all others. Thus we are essentially, as a result of evolutionary development, beings whose ability to flourish is bound up with the ability of all others to do so. It is in the interests of each of us that others around us, and ultimately everyone, flourishes; this is so regardless of similarities and differences, so long as the necessary conditions of flourishing of any one is not necessarily undermining of the flourishing of others.

6   By similar reasoning to 5) we are born into non-human nature too, and constituted through our relations to it. Thus it is in our interests that all of nature flourishes, at least in so far as it is not (intrinsically) harmful to us.

Propositions 5 and 6, especially the former, are fundamental here. Far too much time and effort of modern social theory, not least economics, is spent, often under the head of rational choice theory, or social choice theory, 'modelling' human beings as though the interests of any one can be determined in isolation of any consideration of the interests of all others.

Only a slight advance in insight is made by those who argue that this is a little extreme and we must recognise that it is not irrational for each person to be concerned for others too. I am suggesting both positions share a false premise: that the real interests of any individual can even be conceived apart from the interests of all others. We have evolved in communities and we have community-oriented natures. We are not merely embedded in society, as some commentators wary of too much individualism are apt to put it; we are societal creatures. Our flourishing will be flourishing in society.

I am not suggesting that we value others just to the extent that their well-being pleases us as self-contained individuals, as if their well-being is something like an argument in a utility function.[3] Rather, others are a part of what we are, or at least their flourishing is a part of our own, and in this we recognise intrinsic worth in others as we do in ourselves; we are all part of the same valued human project going forward; the flourishing of each of us is bound up with that of everyone else.

In fact, just as parents have a responsibility (to the community) for their young children, as do babysitters, say, and just as doctors have responsibilities for patients, etc., so each of us have responsibilities *to the community* for looking after ourselves. After all, we are often best placed to know our own specific needs, and be aware of physical pain, etc. Thus, in caring for ourselves we are caring simultaneously for everyone else, for the wider community of which we are part, and we can do so only in ways that are consistent (or not notably inconsistent) with the flourishing of the members of the wider community. Again, we do not care for ourselves just for the benefits of others; we do it for ourselves too. The ethical project is a shared one.

This then is the basis of the position I am systematising as *critical ethical naturalism*. If terms like good or goodness have the same referent as human interests as construed here, we can say that the ultimate ethical good is generalised human flourishing. This is what we all ultimately value. Given our social natures this will entail a form of society or community in which we are situated. Of course, as well as having certain commonalities with *all* others (e.g., capacity for language) and other commonalities with *but some* others (e.g., age or specific languages or culture), we each are unique in a multitude of ways. So the *ethical goal* of generalised flourishing will be of a form in which we flourish in our own very *different* ways; a situation in which the flourishing of each and any of us is a condition of the flourishing of all others.

So the ethical goal that informs moral activity is a form of society that provides such conditions. This, following Aristotle, can be called the good society or *eudemonia*.[4] It seems to be the sort of formulation that Marx and Engels have in mind when, in the communist manifesto, they contemplate an 'association, in which the free development of each is the condition for the free development of all'.

Given that there are obstacles blocking the achievement of any such good society, including those social mechanisms that frequently prevent each of us from fully recognising the nature of our own real interests (for example, that they include the flourishing of all others), then action that can be considered derivatively as *morally good or right* is action oriented to removing such obstacles.

Of course, of the imaginable forms of action that could be utilised to remove such obstacles, only those that are consistent in themselves with the goals of human flourishing qualify as morally good (the good society cannot be brought about by harming or eliminating those that are slow to recognise its value).

As I say, because dominant accounts of ethics and morality are often (formally at least, albeit typically less so in their unexplored presuppositions; see below) amongst the obstacles to such a society, as are prevalent layperson accounts which treat an individual's concerns as somehow isolatable from those of most others, the position being defended is, I think, appropriately distinguished as a critical version of ethical naturalism.

II Moral realism

It follows, too, that such an ethical naturalism is equally a form of moral realism. Why so? Any realism has it that there is a world that exists at least in part independently of, and certainly prior to, any knowledge claims that are formed about it. Accordingly, all claims or beliefs about this reality are fallible, and the truth status of any such claims and beliefs depends not on us but on the way the world is.

I have suggested that (axiological) goodness relates to human flourishing, and that this requires conditions in which we can all flourish in our differences. Hence a goal or action is derivatively morally good if our adopting it contributes (or would contribute) to fulfilling this end, to enabling us to move towards eudemonia, including, especially, via the removal of existing obstacles.

Clearly whether or not an action or objective does fulfil this criterion is something about which we, in forming a judgement, may be mistaken. Morally good objectives and actions thus exist independently of our knowledge of them. There is thus a truth of the matter as to whether certain objectives or actions are (morally) good in the relevant sense that it holds independently of what we judge, always fallibly, to be the case. So the position I am elaborating is a moral realist one in a fairly strong sense.

Moreover, to the extent that all actions and objectives are affecting of others, all are moral. The social and the moral domain essentially have the same referent.

How do we seek to identify morally good objectives and actions? We do so through empirically informed processes of reasoning, oriented to identifying structures and practices that obstruct (the path towards achieving) generalised human flourishing, and thereafter forming strategies for transforming them.[5] Such processes are obviously fallible. But then so are the reasoning processes followed in any other form of science.[6]

From the perspective of the conception I am defending, of course, the plurality of actually existing moralities can be (fallibly) explained, evaluated and criticised, and transformative programmes formulated (at best in democratic forums).

Because social reality is open, as indeed are all future forms of social determination, it will be evident that, unlike in the favourite hypothetical setups of professional philosophers, there will rarely be a single objective or course of action to uncover, or form of action of consideration to be brought to bear in decision taking. Openness underpins plurality in ethics just as it does in social science.

It follows, then, that *transfactuality* is as relevant a category in moral science as in the other sciences. This term can be contrasted with that of counter-factuality, i.e. something that would happen if certain conditions were different than they are. Rather, transfactuality refers to something that, if triggered, is in play whatever is happening at the level of *actual* events. For example, gravity as a force does not just operate when isolated in an experimental vacuum. That is, it is not something that would merely operate counterfactually if an experimental vacuum were produced; it is something that operates transfactually all the time whatever the outcome. It affects the autumn leaf even as it flies over roof tops and chimneys.

The same, I am suggesting, is the case of the moral standing of various objectives and actions in any given context. If it is morally bad to kill others, then this remains true transfactually even if conditions arise whereby other moral considerations dominate in determining a correct *actual* course of action. Thus the dichotomies of deontology versus consequentialism are seen to be false. Both presuppose closed systems where few exist in the social realm; and obligatory and consequential (deontological and consequentialist) considerations both play a transfactual role in the open system that is the real world.

The difference between moral considerations and the forces of nature, clearly, is that whereas in the latter case what actually ensues when various forces act in countervailing ways (say the action on the autumn leaf of gravitational, thermodynamic and aerodynamic tendencies) is independent of our deliberations, this is not so in the moral case. The correct (set of) resolution(s) of conflicting moral considerations may be objective, even if consisting in a range of possibilities, but our reasoning processes are always fallible; we have to seek our best assessments of the right or correct resolutions, where the most useful forum is presumably a democratic, inclusive one facilitative of critical, respectful engagement with others. Certainly any such forum has to be consistent with our understandings of the possibilities for eudemonia.

Decision-making

Any decision-making processes involved in considering how to remove obstacles seemingly lying on the path to moving towards the good society will no doubt often be complex. They may involve exercises in formulating, and thinking in terms of, possible scenarios that appear desirable and consistent with our understanding of (developing) human nature, potentials for technology and for society, as well as ideas about means of transition to a better world. But however complex they may be, any such decision-making process could never seek to produce a blueprint. The good society can only be an open one in which it is up to the totality of concretely singularised individuals together to determine what is to be done as they go along. There is obviously some difference between emancipatory and emancipated action, even if it is desirable that the values underpinning the former are informed by considerations of the latter.

Parenthetically, there is little in common between the process envisioned here and the use of forecasting models in modern mainstream economics. The latter models are constructed in the hope of predicting and so controlling the economic states of affairs that would result from specific changes to certain variables designated 'exogenous'. But future outcomes at the level of events are always open.

From the perspective I am defending, practical judgement can focus instead on formulating actions for absenting constraints on human flourishing (say, removing gender hierarchies in society), identifying the supportive conditions of unwanted constraints, and discussing different strategies, if such exist, for transforming the structures concerned in the desired direction (a procedure elaborated somewhat in Lawson, 1997, chapter 19).

But little can be determined in advance of the events that would thereby occur of the choices that people emancipated from existing forms of structural constraints or oppression would make.

The concrete judgemental exercise necessarily entails a conception of human nature that is revisable. And, of course, the evolutionary openness of human nature itself entails that any objective morality too is open. Obviously the human capacity for wisdom will greatly benefit the process. But in this exercise much speculation is inevitable.[7]

Virtue

If the moral goodness or otherwise of actions and objectives is derivative of how they relate to the flourishing of beings (in these examples of human beings), the same is presumably true of other moral features or orientations besides actions. In particular, this seems to be the nature of many, although probably not all, virtues. It is easy to see that dispositions to be firm, stubborn, unyielding and so forth might be morally good or virtuous in some situations (when undergoing torture in prison with the fate of many others depending on one's silence) but not others (when, perhaps, taking decisions with a partner who has ideas different to one's own about, say, which holiday destination would be most conducive to everyone's flourishing). Determining whether or not a disposition can count as virtuous or morally good also mostly entails reference to the nature and well-being of others, in context.

Other virtues, like honesty, sensitivity and intelligence, dispositions that appear virtuous largely independent of context, may well qualify as virtues because of their ontological status as fundamental aspects of human beings. The same sort of argument might be made of some (virtuous) actions which may thereby be considered to possess intrinsic value. Even if this is so, however, such actions remain bound up with recognition of goodness in forms of being.[8]

III Ethical naturalism and moral realism as generalised presuppositions

I now want to suggest that the ethical naturalism and moral realist positions briefly sketched are not only coherent but also are (or positions very similar to them are) actually presupposed by the doings of us all. If this is so, the conception I am developing lays claim to be as much descriptive as prescriptive in character; with elaborating in effect both a need and a tendency for us all to be authentic, to become as coherent as possible with who we already really are. I start with the doctrine of ethical naturalism.

Ethical naturalism as a general presupposition

For most people, life throws up numerous difficulties, and many of us, at least for lengthy periods, can become preoccupied with problems and difficulties relating to the survival and/or the well-being of those very close, more or less continuously. In this it is easy to be attracted to seemingly simple solutions or explanations that pit us against specific others. But that recognised, I actually think it takes very little reflection to see that when we are not so distracted by matters that obstruct clear thought, we are all continuously oriented to the flourishing of us all.

We can see this in making sense of the importance we attach in such moments to a widespread set of recurrent observations. Throughout human culture and history there are repeated instances of people rushing, spontaneously, to the aid of others, including strangers, perceived to be in distress. This is a generalised feature of human experience; we regularly hear or read of individuals passing by some situation that is perceived as harmful to various unknown individuals, and rushing to help; they unthinkingly rescue others from burning houses, rivers into which they have fallen, the fallout of car or train accidents, and so forth. Moreover, if such acts are everywhere observed, just as relevantly they are everywhere highly regarded; all communities are seen to give praise or make awards to those who have rushed spontaneously to the aid of others.

As an illustrative indicator I might note that many cultures and religions have their own version of the parable of the good Samaritan (Luke 10:25–37). This is an account of a wounded person lying in the road, bypassed by an overly distracted/worried priest too focused on his own apparent concerns and by others who might also have been expected to offer help, and eventually aided, in a generous fashion, by someone who might have been thought to be almost an enemy. The wounded man, we can infer, was Jewish, and the helper was a Samaritan. Samaritans at the time were not well liked by the Jews. The products of intermarriages between Israelites and pagans, the Samaritans, who had built a rival temple on Mount Gerizim, were essentially viewed by the Jews as heretics, and publicly cursed in the synagogues.

The point I make here is how such an account of other-helping action resonates seemingly with all of us (when in the late 1990s I first drafted these lines, an internet search for the 'good Samaritan' revealed over 120,000 sites of hospitals, centres for the homeless, help centres, clinics and so forth wishing to be associated with the other-person-in-distress-serving image that the 'good Samaritan' expression has come to denote; by June 2013, when I reread the original version of this paper, the number had risen to 28.4 million). We all recognise that it is good to help the other, and *prima facie* not so good just to pass on by.

It seems to me that we can (best) make sense of these sorts of general-ised observations (and resonances), and others like them (which, as I say, in some form appear to apply to all cultures – albeit subject to culture-specific countervailing tendencies), by understanding all of us as finding value in others. It is because we do so that we will their survival and flourishing and (derivatively and critically) evaluate actions concerned with facilitating that end (actions which we endeavour to undertake) as morally good.

A significant part of this explanatory claim is just that we do recognise (or invest) intrinsic value in others. This is quite different from supposing that someone or something has, or is of, value only to the extent it is con-ducive to our own welfare and so of value only (or at most) for us. Have we not all accepted opportunities to help strangers in this *sort* of fashion? Perhaps a person has fallen off a bike in front of us, or just fallen over. When we, and others around us, rush to help, we do not do so (merely) for our own satisfaction or welfare; we do not do it merely to attend to feel-ings about ourselves; we do it spontaneously for the sake of the hurt and perhaps endangered individual. The quality of having-to-be-helped lies in the individual who has fallen over, off a bike, into a river, or whatever. Helping is not done for the helper or rescuer but for the helped or rescued. The latter could have been anyone, even perhaps a perceived enemy or possibly an animal.

Mostly, we help in this way anonymously, not looking to be rewarded in any way other than believing we have helped. This is perhaps most evidently the case when monetary or other forms of support is sent, often by way of contributing via charities or other international organisations, to people we will almost surely never meet in parts of the world that have experienced tsunamis, earthquakes, destructive typhoons and other disasters.

A central point of the parable of the good Samaritan is that the latter had nothing to gain by his (we are told it was a man) action other than seeing a fellow human being restored to health. This indeed was in the Samaritan's real interest. Certainly there was a cost involved. The Samaritan attended to, and wrapped, the injured man's wounds, set the injured man on his own donkey (leaving the Samaritan with no option but to walk), delivered the wounded man to an inn and took personal care of him. On departing on his way the Samaritan paid the inn keeper 'two silver pieces' to look after the wounded stranger, and promised to pay any extra costs incurred on his return journey. Indeed, it is not uncommon for those who 'go to the rescue' of others to suffer serious injuries or even the loss of their own life at the hands of those who see less clearly where their real interests lie (which is presumably why, in the parable, the priest and others hurried on their way).

The relevant matter here, of course, is not that the parable relates a true account (whether or not it is true is not the issue), but that we all appear to recognise the moral worth of the Samaritan's actions as related, or more generally of the moral goodness of helping other beings in need, in particular human beings. In other words, we often, and spontaneously, go to the help of others because we recognise, and act upon, what is good for them; we recognise or perceive value existing independently of us (or at least independently of our own willing) and we can and do act on it. And if we are ourselves somehow in fear of helping the other-in-need, we judge as morally good the actions of those others who do so go to help.

Human rights

Additional support for the claim that we are all critical ethical naturalists is revealed I believe by the very existence of a widely supported human rights movement. Taken at face value, of course, the contemporary assertion of human rights is in numerous instances untenable, if not quite the 'nonsense upon stilts' that Jeremy Bentham supposed (or considered of its predecessor in the form of natural rights). In human societies, all rights are tied to social positions, and are constituted in (internal) relation to obligations attached to other positions, obligations which must be met if rights are to be exercised. A university lecturer in, say, the modern UK cannot exercise the right to give lectures, if students do not turn up, or where no one meets the obligations of maintaining lecture halls, admitting students to the university, etc.

By and large, however, being human, and so claims of human rights *per se*, are not (in most parts of most modern-day societies at least) positionally constituted, certainly not so in relation to obligations that are assigned to, and are fulfilled by, others. Yet the rhetoric of human rights talk remains clearly attractive to very many. Even those (typically philosophers and legal theorists) who reject the rhetoric of human rights as overly loose tend to acknowledge that there is something very appealing about the idea that everyone on the planet, irrespective of country, class, gender or any other status, has basic rights to conditions in which they can flourish.

Most observers acknowledge, too, that the rhetoric can be, and has been, politically strategically effective in improving some conditions here and there. In addition, it is clear that those propounding rights talk are confident that the assertions made will withstand public scrutiny.

Few, though, stop to question the basis of this appeal and rhetorical success, or the confidence of the proponents. The explanation of it, I suggest, just is that it is a manifestation of a universal (if often implicit) dedication to a world of generalised human flourishing; in effect a manifestation of an implicit commitment to what I am calling critical ethical naturalism.

Although the current manner of organisation of human society, i.e. capitalism, does not permit generalised human flourishing, the expression of generalised human rights reveals a devotion to the goal in practice. When declarations of human rights are made it is clear that no individual or body is (yet) offering systematically to meet them; rather they consist of conditions of human survival, dignity and flourishing that seemingly most of us agree should everywhere prevail. The popularity of human rights talk, movements, declarations and projects, as I say, is revealing of the widespread implicit attachment to something like an ethical stance such that I am systematising as critical ethical naturalism. Declarations of human rights in particular signal the widespread support for the conditions of freedom and flourishing incorporated within the various formulations.

Of course, and as I have indicated in passing, if the above set of numerous observations and interpretations are broadly correct, so that we can accept that we are not egoists, i.e. we acknowledge and can act upon the worth of others, there is no clear reason to suppose that the only intrinsic worth we recognise or act to facilitate is the flourishing of members of our own species. All beings are of intrinsic worth, and their flourishing is ultimately bound up with our own, even if we perceive the worth of human beings as ranking highest (on the latter assessment, see e.g. St Augustine and Andrew Collier, 1999). But all organisms have needs and reveal active tendencies to their fulfilment, with some non-human forms seemingly conscious and experiencing pleasure and pain. Thus, for all such beings there are conditions and developments which are for their good,[9] and in all cases we flourish on this planet as one.

Moral realism as a general presupposition

Observations on how we act when not overly distracted and misled by immediate practical concerns do, I believe, reveal us all to be not merely (critical) ethical naturalists but also moral realists. That is, when we weigh up how to act, we assess moral activities as right or wrong according to their contribution to the removal of obstacles on human flourishing; we understand that our assessments of the moral worth of actions are derivative and fallible.

Consider a situation where someone is spotted apparently floundering in the river. A passing stranger, who happens to be a strong swimmer, jumps into the river and pulls the first person out. If this is all we know of the situation, we may well judge the action to be morally good. I suspect we all tend to do this. Suppose, though, that the 'rescued' person informs us that he or she did not fall into it, but jumped in to save a pet dog or small child, say, that had fallen in, and in fact the action of the passer-by has resulted in the dog or child drowning.

The basic activity of pulling someone from the river no longer appears as morally good (even if in the former case the intention was well meaning). We may even criticise the 'rescuer' for being overly hasty and ignoring the apparent pleas of the rescued person to stop interfering. In other words, the moral value of even a (well-meaning) action like jumping into a river with the intention of rescuing someone is something we can wrongly evaluate, and later recognise as wrongly evaluated; certainly an action is never good (or bad) just because we assess it as so.

A significant number of those people who in 2003 supported the invasion of Iraq now view it as having been morally wrong.[10] Clearly, if criticism can be made of an action, there must be a position from (or standard by) which it is done. In the example of the rescued swimmer the action of the passer-by can be criticised from the standpoint of our increased understanding of the nature and needs of the first person whose good included the worth of the dog or child.[11] In the case of the Iraq War those involved presumably revised their whole understanding of the actions taken in terms of the actual, and threats to the, well-being of the very many people involved and especially those that have suffered directly or indirectly as a result of the invasion. It is the survival and flourishing of some relevant party that allows us to determine whether (or which) actions in a given context qualify as morally good. The moral worth of an action is derivative of the good or flourishing of some being(s).

I am suggesting, then, that the widespread experience of certain (other-helping) actions which many individuals in appropriate contexts undertake presuppose (as a condition of their intelligibility) a generalised regarding of others as worthy, of value, involving a willing of their generalised flourishing, and that such actions are assessed to be morally good just because of this. In other words, the moral worth of actions is derivative of how they relate to the survival and flourishing of forms of, and typically of human, being. It is being as being that is of (or is invested with) intrinsic worth,[12] and the sought-after flourishing of which grounds our moral deliberations.

IV The possibility of eudemonia

Clearly, any case for critical ethical naturalism being a coherent orientation rests on a presupposition that a society of generalised human flourishing remains feasible. Is there any reason to suppose it might not be? This is a significant consideration; for if the sort of society conceived were known to be out of the question then to condition practical judgement on such a conception could even do unnecessary harm.

Imagine a scenario in which, say, there is a seriously injured person who is in the process of dying unless adequate hospital care is provided. We have transport of sorts and are faced with choosing between two hospitals lying in opposite directions to where we are situated, with one known to be far more reliable/successful in its provision of medical aid than the other, but, unlike the second-best hospital, is located at such a distance away that it would be impossible to reach before the injured person dies. In such a situation it would surely not be morally good to embark on a journey towards this more reliable, but unreachable, hospital.

If the good society were shown to be a practical impossibility, it *might* similarly be the case that we are better off seeking to achieve some alternative form of society that has numerous benefits for fairly generalised flourishing, but is actually obtainable. I am not at all suggesting that the good society is beyond our reach. But if the good society were shown to be not achievable, such considerations would likely come into play. Moreover, I suspect it is often the case that many commentators give verbal support to the current social order just because they doubt the possibility of reaching anything better (and perhaps fear the possibility of making things worse).

But what could render such a conception of eudemonia as formulated above an *all time* impossibility? Such a result requires that, in any and all *achievable* forms of society, there will always be some individuals whose conditions of flourishing necessarily entail aspects which undermine the possibilities for the flourishing of others. Such an enduring scenario can be posited, it seems to me, only by way of either maintaining an extreme form of essentialism which fixes the (physiological, psychological, social or cultural) natures of some as necessarily antagonistic to those of others, or arguing that all societal structures are necessarily contradictory and oppressive as totalities.

Such universal constraints, as far as I know, have yet to be demonstrated. Paedophilia might be suggested. But I doubt it is other than socially determined. If not, then the aimed-for society would have to deal with the tension that arises. But I can think of very few other examples that even suggest themselves as significant potential challenges to the sort to society under consideration here, i.e. to a society that is organised to facilitate generalised flourishing in our differences.

Of course many take a somewhat pessimistic view of human nature in general. It is conceivable, though, that most of the ills of human life are rather manifestations of human weakness in the face of a system that is just not organised to facilitate human flourishing. To the contrary, society currently is structured in a manner that encourages atomistic behaviour and incentivises the domination of one over the other. But there is nothing especially natural about the manner in which affairs are currently organised, and every reason to think that all structures that so encourage such ultimately irrational behaviour can be transformed. Certainly, I see no compelling reason to suppose that the perspective defended here, of developing human personhood and identities, through individual and social transformation, is infeasible in principle. So I persist in the view that eudemonistic society or something very close to it remains a real possibility.

A *prima facie* complication, of course, is that in any decision context there will be some forms of action possibilities which in appearing to remove immediate obstacles to the flourishing of some will equally appear to work simultaneously to the detriment of others.

But, this need not be true of all feasible remedial responses. There are various grounds for optimism here. One is recognition that human beings seemingly all share certain species-level features (such as the already-noted capacities to enter natural and social being, including to acquire language). Another is the fact that our species being appears to be evolving relatively slowly (compared to social structures and technology).

A further ground for being positive is that there exists gaps between our (of course, always to some extent historically specific and evolving) real needs, our wants, and the various ways of meeting or satisfying our needs. It is the gaps between needs (e.g., of respect) and far more transient wants (e.g., under current Western conditions to own various status-symbolising commodities) and satisfiers (large houses, expensive cars) which lay the basis for the happy fact that there will often be very many ways of meeting current individual needs, through transforming wants and so allowing different items to serve as satisfiers, with at least the possibility of doing so in ways that do not harm others, especially through dynamic adjustment, or co-determination of persons, practices and structure over time.

Indeed, this malleability or under-determination in respect to meeting the conditions of human flourishing or fulfilment is a major cause for optimism on matters of ethics. It means we can continually rethink the conditions of human flourishing and ways of transcending constraints, to uncover ways to human flourishing in a multitude of forms, which nevertheless do not turn on abusing others, the environment or whatever. The challenge, indeed, is very much to find ways in which we *all* in our own ways can live fulfilling, meaningful lives without social ills and without too much damage to nature. As I say, the under-determination of the means of our fulfilment, the gap between satisfiers and needs, even noting that the latter are neither fixed nor homogeneous, allows the possibility that the challenge can be met.[13]

As a result, I think we can embrace the goal of working to bring about the good society as conceptualised here, and so interpret objectives oriented to absenting constraints on its emergence as morally good. It perhaps bears repeating once more that because we start from here, and the here and now counts as well, we can accept as morally good only those actions and/or objectives which both work to remove impediments to the good society that are themselves, *as far as possible*, developmentally consistent with it. That is, if we are to be true to ourselves including our goals, we ought to endeavour to ensure that, as far as possible, the actions and goals adopted in seeking to bring about the good society are consistent with the values of the sort of society we wish to usher in. This, of course, will likely mean that we work at least as much on transforming our structurally conditioned selves as the structures of society.

Needless to say, it remains always the case that all social aspects of the future, including forms of human being, our conceptions of the latter and our technological and other possibilities, are open. It is for this reason that we can aim only at being developmentally consistent; we can only do our best to move in the direction that seems the most sustainable starting from here.

As time passes, certain once-realisable possibilities for the good society are likely to be realisable no longer. But short of destroying ourselves as a species, or somehow losing our (of course, always societally realised) capacities for reason, for capable social interaction and concern for all others that seem so essential to our species being, I see no grounds to suppose that the eudemonistic society need not remain a real possibility for some set of concrete manifestations.

In summary, I suggest there are indeed numerous reasons for supposing that the good society is feasible so that it is right and good that conceptions of it inform our understandings of morally good actions, i.e. those that are to be pursued where feasible. Given our (fallible but hopefully developmentally progressive) understanding of (developmentally open) human nature, of the relation of human beings to social structure and (the rest of) nature, and of the developmental possibilities in all aspects of society and non-social nature including their inter-relations, we can with reason continue to seek to identify constraints upon human flourishing, and work to discover ways of absenting them consistent with our conception of the good society (itself an open process).

V Tending to eudemonia?

One clearly interesting question that can be raised at this point is whether, rather than our being inhibited in principle from reaching the eudemonistic society or process, there is actually a mechanism of sorts at work in the social world tending to bring us towards it. Without some such ethical mechanism, moral deliberations may yet be largely pointless, if meaningful.

By posing this question I do not of course ask, 'Must the good society come about?' The answer to this would have to be no.[14] The future, clearly, is open, and we are quite capable even of destroying ourselves as a species. What I mean is: is there a mechanism, a tendency at work, giving us a perpetual prodding, an impulse, towards the good society?

I believe there is. Moreover, it is implicit in the account already elaborated, in the thesis that we are all in effect critical ethical naturalists, including moral realists. In other words, the mechanism lies just in the drive basic to all of us to work, *ceteris paribus*, to remove obstacles on the flourishing of all others, as well as ourselves.

This is a feature of our basic human nature and being, even if our specific positioning in society leads us to be frequently mistaken and/or weak and so to act also in ways that are inconsistent with ourselves. The main obstacle that prevents us helping others to flourish, I suspect, is fear, and in particular fear of the unknown. The obvious remedy for this fear is to interact with others and see that the basis for fear is misplaced. Thus, a methodology for bringing about eudemonia is *travel*, both in a literal and metaphorical sense.

The assessment that we are all critical ethical naturalists, put differently, is that we are disposed as a species to care for others. This entails that when we recognise constraints on the flourishing of others, we feel compelled to support action designed to remove them *ceteris paribus*. However, it is through interacting with others that this abstract tendency to care becomes concretised. In a sense we learn how to act in a manner that is beneficial to others, that is consistent with their needs. As we do so, we learn how to act in ways that are consistent with the flourishing of those we encounter as well as ourselves.

As I write, it appears that our interactions with others are increasing in scope, a process that is revealing to all, and far more clearly than hitherto, both the nature and ways of others as well as the inescapable interconnectedness of us all. Thus the process of wider-spread interaction informs our dispositions to care in a manner that builds the good society into all our actions. Let me elaborate these comments a little.[15]

Knowing the other and learning how to care

If it is part of our condition to be disposed to care for others, then to realise that disposition it is essential that we are sufficiently knowledgeable of others, of their natures, needs and conditions, in order to be able to act in an appropriate fashion. It is indeed likely that the major obstacle to our caring more widely, indeed to the good society, is ignorance of others *per se*,[16] perhaps bound up, as I say, with a common place and comprehensible fear of the unknown.

It is the case that ignorance and/or fear of 'others' can be overcome in many ways. But the seemingly most generalised and systematic manner of doing so is simply via increased human interaction. Individuals often note how they have started out with negative feelings towards someone (or something) acquired indirectly, only to revise these feelings through direct interaction. I believe that in similar fashion interaction enables us to understand, and thereby lose any ungrounded fear of, others in general.

The fact that we are able to learn the needs of others through interacting with them is everywhere apparent. We can see that even young children, taking pleasure in feeding wild (or not so wild) animals and birds, quickly learn, through attempting to attract them, to be patient, to stand (or sit) still and quiet, consistent with an assessment of the nervous disposition of these creatures. Individuals mostly act in a quiet and respectful fashion, even as tourists, when entering places of worship, in keeping with the nature of the forum. And so I believe we all learn through interacting with other people the appropriate way to do so. In interacting successfully with others we assess something of their natures, whether of children, older people, potential partners, mere strangers, people of different cultures, police people, opponents in games or debates, members of one's own teams, those threatening us and/or seemingly losing their self-control, and so on. Similarly, in many daily affairs we need to know the natures of various institutions, social processes or whatever.

It is certainly true, as I have already acknowledged, that when acting in a moral way we *feel* for those we help; we are influenced by emotions. But, it would be wrong to suppose that emotion is divorced from reason; in a certain sense feelings are as cognitive as our thoughts, and can be equally right or wrong.

If feelings include a cognitive element, it follows that, even if feelings are a central component of moral (and other) actions, our potential to act rationally in morality, as in other forms of action, increases with knowledge of the nature of the world around us, indeed of the whole universe, but especially of those aspects with which we interact.

Personal identities

In fact, it is apparent that through interaction with others we can come not only to care for them but even to identify with them. Certainly we must recognise the usual fixed and context-independent conception of selves and identities not as a legitimate abstraction, but merely an illicit theoretical idealisation. We are always in a process of change or becoming particularly in our relations to others.

Think of football supporters, certainly as found in the UK. Very often they seem not merely to support a football club; they identify with it. They internalise the club as part of themselves, as part of their own identity. They reach a point at which they do not choose to care; they care because the club has become an extension of themselves. When a team is doing badly, supporters frequently grumble that they cannot avoid caring about what is happening to the team.

It appears to me that this extending of our essential selves to incorporate those with whom (or with which) we interact is rather general. People come to identify with musical (and other) artists, religious or political groups, places of work, their gardens, (features of) the local countryside or places frequently visited, whole regions, and even nations. In each such case, people do not just choose to care; the other becomes part of them, so that caring for oneself and the other coincide.

Think of the care shown by most pet owners to their pets. Think too of occupations and the way many people identify with their places of work, especially where the work is a form of craft (some even say of institutions for which they work, or of the work itself, that 'it is in my blood'). People equally seem to identify with material objects like musical instruments, cars, bicycles or computers. And is it not also significant how far some people go to protect (aspects of) the world's ecological environment?

In many ways we are who we are because of what we (come to) care about; in identifying and extending our ultimate concerns and commitments we define and extend ourselves. I do not suggest that in extending ourselves to incorporate others the latter lose their own identities. I do, though, think that we all become transformed in the process, and in ways that connect all of us all the more.[17] In truth the ontology I defend reveals the social world to be a dynamic interconnected whole. The goal really is to recognise our interconnectedness and transform the connecting relations in ways that allow us all to flourish.[18]

My claim, then, is that we care more just because, and as, we interact with others, where interacting with others is part of our (always relationally dependent and developing) rational being. Indeed, caring becomes triggered by a disposition to care itself being the result of caring through interacting. Through interacting with more others, we understand more, and in doing so we come to extend ourselves further, incorporating the others to a greater or lesser degree into ourselves. And to the extent that we all have a tendency to act rationally, this becomes the tendency of our extended self; it becomes a drive to preserve and flourish in terms of all our self, including any newly acquired parts.[19] Thus as we, each of us, become more interactive, as is part of our rational nature (-in-society), so we come to care for more of those around us, first for our immediate, and then for our not-so-immediate, environment, as those with which or whom we interact become more integral to our own selves or being.

Or to put things slightly differently, because the self is to a significant extent relationally constituted, there cannot be a self-interest that exists independently of the interests of others; the interests of the self and others both are mutually constitutive and interlay and overlap. The fundamental connectedness at the heart of human reality, and the implicit grasping of this brought about by human interaction, and the continuous reconstitution of the self, ensures, I believe, that a tendency is in play to care (habitually) for the other as oneself.

Globalisation

The reason I suggest that all this may represent a tendency to eudemonia, rather than, say, to a state of caring for, and acting on behalf of, others restricted to our local community, lies in the way in which the contexts of, and possibilities for, social interaction are changing.

I have in mind here the globalising tendencies of wider economic and social forces. Globalisation is the ever larger, faster and deeper impact of regional flows and patterns of social interaction. Currently, the industrial world is experiencing sets of processes embodying the transformation of spatially organised social relations and transactions, in a way that vastly extends the possibility (and actuality) of transcontinental or interregional flows of human interaction.

We can all now (say, through air-travel or use of the internet) inter-act more quickly and easily with others far afield. And more significantly the institutions (including systems of law) and general social structures in which we act and are shaped are increasingly internally related to (constituting of, and constituted by) those to be found elsewhere (and increasingly everywhere else). As a result, our horizons of interaction are advancing continually, just as the spatial conditions of our interaction are becoming ever more internally related. Socialism always was impossible in one country or region, and so is eudemonia. The tendency for greater integration and mutual constitution or co-development that comes with globalisation (partly manifested in the widespread public demonstra-tions of resistance to the worst aspects of these developments, including a resistance oriented to safeguarding threatened [often highly localised] cultures, social systems, environments and species), though fraught with tension and dialectical inconsistencies (in need of sublation), nevertheless serves to absent previous constraints on tendencies to care-within-the-community fully expressing themselves as tendencies to eudemonia. In other words, as we learn and understand more about others, and recog-nise the nature of our inescapable interconnectedness, the more it seems that the activation of our tendencies to care will mean acting consistently with the noted formulation of the good society.

My contention, then, is that we have a disposition to care with the result that an impulse to freedom or emancipation, to human fulfilment or flour-ishing, is present in all our actions. However, we learn how better to care in concrete circumstances through human interaction. Further, to a signif-icant extent we are who we are because of what we (come to) care about. In identifying and extending our ultimate concerns and commitments we define and extend ourselves simultaneously. However, we do this in con-ditions not of our own choosing. Our situations in society condition the sorts of persons we become and influence the personal and social iden-tities we achieve. With the possibilities for interaction stretching across space and shrinking the time it takes, and given our (presumably con-tinuing) rational inclination ever to interact more, along with an increased recognition of the connectedness of us all to others, eudemonia is indeed a real and ever-closer tendential possibility.

I do, of course, recognise that we typically act in contexts where the possibility of a clear recognition that the goal is the pursuit of human flour-ishing is frequently undermined by countervailing masking mechanisms, leading us (also) to act against ourselves. As I write, in fact, there are many world-wide developments suggesting these are, momentarily at least, espe-cially powerful. But actually, I believe these countervailing tendencies are ultimately the weaker ones just because they are usually parasitic upon the more positive ones. Dishonesty and deception, etc., arise only because of capacities for honesty, truth and knowledge, and so forth. Being untrustworthy only impacts where people trust. Selfishness achieves benefits only through the unselfishness of others. And even irrealism makes any points it can by presupposing realism. All such countervailing ideas or factors appear to depend on others which are more consistent with the developing of our true natures. And all countervailing factors can be undermined, I believe, by way of increased interaction and understanding.

Even so, whether or not this is the case, my aim here is merely to argue the possibility that there is an identifiable tendency to the good society in play. In every interaction there necessarily is a commitment to understanding others, to solidarity, trust, honesty and other conditions of human fulfilment of some sort. As long as, and because, this is so, the attaining of the good society eventually remains, in the context of an ever more internally related global system, an always real (and ever-present) tendential possibility.

That is not to say that discoveries made in projects systematised explicitly as ethical ones cannot help the process along. But the impulse or tendency to the good society, I believe, is there already, and lies at the level of everyday practice. Of course, if this is indeed the case, it cannot be forgotten that this tendency exists alongside numerous countervailing drives and commitments, processes and interpretations, which serve to mask the real nature of human being, the conditions of human flourishing, including the value of everyone flourishing. But it can be argued that the tendency to the good society is there. And because it is there (and because countervailing tendencies seem to be largely parasitic upon it) projects that explicitly embrace a critical ethical naturalism as well as science can, because they are concerned with illumination and understanding, be harnessed to help it along.

Final comments

Although I have defended an account of ethics that could be described as somewhat objectivist, this has not involved my positing ethical objects of any kind.[20] Rather the ethical naturalism I have advanced is reductionist in that the terms of its discourse make reference to features that are known by other names. I have suggested that the ethical goal is generalised human flourishing in our differences, and so a society that renders this feasible. Actions and objectives that are morally good or right are those that take us coherently in this direction. That we care enough to move in this direction, though, is not so much a prescription as a description of an operative tendency. But in this we can and do clearly and repeatedly make mistakes and show weakness, as we all are also continuously directed, and very often misdirected, by countervailing concerns. If there are implications of a practical sort it is for a need to seek to identify, understand and transform or remove all obstacles that lie in the path to eudemonia, and perhaps most especially those that prevent us recognising who we really are. In the context of modern economics specifically, it seems especially urgent that we more clearly recognise and embrace the insight that rationality itself is not about adopting a narrow self-oriented individualism of the sort that populates modern texts but about acting as far as possible in ways that facilitate the flourishing of us all.

Notes

1 This is a significantly abridged (and very slightly updated) version of a paper originally intended as a chapter of *Reorienting Economics* (Lawson, 2003a). The original paper (some of the ideas of which were trialled in Lawson, 2000) was eventually omitted from the latter book because in its unabridged form it became very long, too long for a single chapter (several times longer than this abridged version); and at that time I was less confident than I wished (and am currently) in the sustainability of some of the central ideas being advanced (and preserved in this current version). I am very grateful to Stephen Pratten for requesting (and repeatedly prodding me to retrieve and shorten) the paper for this publication. For generous financial support that facilitated the final revisions I am grateful to the *Independent Social Research Foundation*.

2 Of course, even to make a factual statement to another is already ultimately to presuppose that their well-being is bound up with truth, communicative interaction, learning and so forth.

3 I use this formulation to convey an assessment to those familiar with modern economics. In truth I do not believe that utility functions exist, or that the phenomena they are supposed to express conform in a manner that allows them to be so represented. Rather the utility function is no more than a fictitious device contrived merely in order to extend the domain of mathematical modelling; its postulation has nothing to do with being realistic, explanatory or otherwise insightful.

4 In the *Nichomachean Ethics* Aristotle argues that there must be an ultimate good, one which is pursued for its own sake. This is eudaemonia, or eudemonia (the spelling I employ here), often translated as happiness. It has long been debated whether happiness is the best (or proper) translation, but there is widespread agreement that, if it is, our modern notion of happiness does not accord with that of Aristotle and the early Greeks. Rather, eudaemonia or eudemonia is taken as indicating a life of a human being fulfilled, a life of flourishing. Hence, use of the term eudaemonistic or eudemonistic for designating a society in which all human beings flourish is not obviously inappropriate.

5 Of course, this will typically be difficult and requires more than insight. Even if, as many now conclude, resources allocated to mathematical modelling in economics are largely wasted and so thereby an obstacle on the path to generalised flourishing, and even if the attachment to modelling stems from a misconception of science, as I believe it does, and even if it is easy to demonstrate and explain the misunderstandings involved, as I believe it is, any such demonstration does not guarantee an impact if, as is the case, the modellers themselves manifest no readiness to listen or otherwise seriously engage, and this refusal meaningfully to engage has no bearing on their ability to control all the resources.

6 So such a position is quite consistent with an epistemological relativism, i.e. with the recognition that all knowledge claims are partial, fallible, situated

and likely transient (as I have argued at length elsewhere [Lawson, 1997]). I emphasise this explicitly here just because many commentators interested in developing an ethical stance similar to that pursued here appear to suppose otherwise. An example is provided by Martha Nussbaum, who cautions:

> ... the attack on realism has been sufficiently deep and sufficiently sustained that it would appear strategically wise for an ethical and political view that seeks broad support not to rely on the truth of metaphysical realism, if it can defend itself in any other way.

> (1995, p. 69)

Nussbaum is clear that she means '[b]y metaphysical realism [...] the view [...] that there is some determinate way the world is, apart from the interpretive workings of the cognitive faculties of living beings' (p. 68). But if (in this otherwise excellent contribution) Nussbaum is accepting that realists necessarily suppose either/both that all reality is independent of us and our practices, or/and that somehow we grasp it in a manner unmediated by our human capacities and limitations, culturally and socially and physically situated perspectives, current understandings and so forth, she is quite wrong; she is reducing realism to a naive absolutist version indeed. In truth, Nussbaum is ceding too much ground to her postmodernist or 'relativist' opponents. It seems, then, important that I emphasise at the outset that realists are no more committed to absolutism than relativists are to irrealism. Rather the relevant matter is to determine the forms of realist and relativist perspectives which are most appropriately to be combined in specific contexts. By combining ontological (scientific) realism and epistemological relativism we obtain not judgemental relativism but judgemental rationality of just the sort that Nussbaum wishes to sustain.

7 I should also note, however, that even the forming of a concrete practical judgement does not by any means guarantee its realisation. Of course any agent is always acting in some fashion. Thus normative reasoning of the sort in question, if carried through, will condition action in some way. But if, and presumably only if, conditions allow that the concrete practical judgement *can* be realised, that the agent is able to exercise the necessary powers for it, and does not suffer from a lack of will power, the action prescribed, assuming it is also sincerely wanted, will materialise as part of the course of events.

8 The conception of human being defended above does carry further implications bearing on moral value. To this point, I have examined certain consequences for practical action stemming from the fact that we are concerned with a society of people comprising very different and perpetually developing concrete identities. A further, if related, consideration, and a possible constraint on the realisation of morally good actions, is the seeming impossibility of continuous moral reflection in the face of the continuity of moral action. For it follows from the social ontology defended earlier that all our actions presuppose, and causally affect, our relations with other people and things and so have a moral aspect. But because moral behaviour appears, therefore, to be unavoidably continuous – all action has a moral aspect – it seems to follow that not all (indeed only a small proportion of) moral doings can be prosecuted on the basis of conscious deliberation and reflection.

However, the difficulty raised here affects action under all of its aspects, whether moral or otherwise. As I have elsewhere argued (especially Lawson, 1997, chapter 13), because action (i.e. intentional human behaviour) is a continuous flow, most of it, especially action chronically concerned with going on in life, must be carried out at the level of sub- or practical consciousness; a continuous commentary or reflection on our doings seems infeasible. Much of our action is tacitly or subconsciously performed. And its possibility appears to presuppose dispositions (constrained or weighted capacities or competencies) that we have already developed. Specifically, by acting in similar ways in given conditions over and again we build up dispositions so to behave in this fashion, with the result that the actions called into play in the relevant conditions eventually become habitual.

And this reasoning is relevant for our moral behaviour equally. Specifically, it suggests that the possibility of undertaking morally good actions more frequently, indeed habitually, requires a building up of dispositions so to do, the latter themselves resulting from repeated efforts at acting in morally good ways. This leads to the conclusion, prominent in Eastern philosophy and religion especially, that it is good precisely to develop 'wholesome' dispositions or orientations to action (or *kun long* as they call it in Tibetan; see, e.g., Gyatso, 2001). This recognition must caution against any complete separation of questions of morally good actions and virtue. The point here, though, is that despite the fact that all behaviour has a moral aspect this in itself need not prove a barrier to the possibility of good actions being regularly undertaken.

Parenthetically, I might also observe that these sorts of considerations do not undermine the somewhat cognitivist emphasis already defended. Although I may, say, drive from Cambridge to London, 'lost' in thought or conversation, and so guided by practical consciousness, the latter still enables me skilfully and successfully to negotiate the numerous obstacles that confront me on my journey. Practical or subconscious action, if largely habitual, need be no less appropriate to its object than that which is fully reflective. There are differences, but the quality of aboutness, i.e. of being about something, is not one of them. Practical consciousness, like conscious reflection, can be more or less adequate to its object, and open to assessment and criticism by others; it too is partial and fallible. And so it can be in morality.

9 In fact, or for some at least, there is no obvious reason even to draw the line with organic being; there is a sense in which mountains and lakes have a tendency to persist in their being. This is a position recently developed in an interesting way by Andrew Collier (1999) who, building on the writings of St Augustine and Spinoza in particular, argues that all being thereby has worth in some measure. Actually, drawing on Augustine, Collier argues for a ranking of being according to their intrinsic worth, with human beings ranked highest, and the least sentient beings lowest. Collier does not really justify this ordering. It may be that justifications can be connected to discussions of emergence. Elsewhere (most recently in Lawson, 2013b) I have examined how it is that, despite the second law of thermodynamics, according to which there is a tendency for entropy to increase, or for everything to break down into messiness, order, whether simple or complex, emerges at all. From this perspective, any form of emergent order seems absolutely remarkable, and the more complex the form, the more it is dependent on more basic forms of emergent order, the more remarkable still. Perhaps it is reasonable to suggest that the claim that all being has value is related to the fact that all emergent forms and their continuity are something remarkable and indeed incredible in the circumstances. Perhaps, too, it is reasonable to suggest the more complex the form, incorporating as it does less complex forms as components, the greater thereby its value.

10 As I write this particular passage (June 2013), a Google of the passage 'the Iraq war, I was wrong' throws up 141 million entries.

11 Indeed we may go on our way thinking this was a bad action never knowing that the 'rescued' person was none-too-well and actually fabricating the claim about there being a dog or child.

12 The more common criticisms of, or challenges to, moral realism pick up on the cognitivist aspirations of the latter. Specifically they focus on moral realism's claim that moral reasoning proceeds in broadly the manner of (our best conception of) science. The goal in this is to highlight differences between the conditions of science and ethics which would seem to render moral realism untenable.

More often than not, however, the claimed contrasts turn on a misconception of science, one I have often criticised elsewhere (e.g., Lawson, 1997, 2003a). For example, it is not infrequently suggested that ethics must be unlike science in that it can make no claims to certainty, its objects are necessarily constructs of human beings, it lacks value neutrality and opportunities for experimental testing, and so forth. I have argued often enough by now, however, that science too is a fallible social process lacking in certainty, that society is dependent on human agency without this compromising the possibility of social science, that all science is value-dependent, and that its explanatory work can proceed without (and certainly does not reduce to) possibilities of experimental testing (on all of this see Lawson, 1997, 2003a).

Other challenges are based more on a questionable assessment of the possibilities for moral realism itself. These include the suggestion that ethics cannot be like science because there is nothing which plays the role of empirical observation, and there is no objective order to be uncovered in ethics. From the (reductionist) version of (critical) ethical naturalism set out, however, we can see that observation plays precisely the same role in ethics as in science and both science and ethics have a domain of objects to be discovered (as well as a realm of human assessments of these objects).

A related challenge (Rawls, 1971) focuses on the weighing of possibilities that occur in moral deliberation; it is observed that typically a coherent moral position can be achieved only by trading off moral beliefs to obtain a harmonious equilibrium assessment. It is thereby concluded that the moral realm is necessarily a social construction of the practitioners in that field, whereas science is a process of discovery of an objective order.

But even *pure* explanatory science, the identification of causal mechanisms, is itself a process of negotiation between a range of different (often contradictory) observations and a set of competing theories. In any case, the substantive moral theory here is that ethics is concerned with identifying the conditions of, and means to, human flourishing. And *applied* explanatory science faces a situation very much as found in ethics concerning the forming of practical judgements. For in an open system that which happens at the level of actual phenomena is usually determined by a multiplicity of causal factors just as, in ethics, at least according to the conception outlined above, that which is to be done depends on a multiplicity of moral factors. Once the transfactual force of both causal factors and moral objectives is recognised it can be seen that ethics is like science on these considerations as well. The difference, as already noted, is that decision makers must decide how to resolve the competing claims whilst the applied scientist (or the applied scientist unconcerned with prediction) can wait and see what emerges. This is a difference of practicality, not in objectivity.

A further challenge to moral realism highlights the cultural variability in moral beliefs. It first observes that scientists throughout the world, and with different cultural backgrounds, can usually agree in their assessments of scientific evidence, with the result that science progresses. It then argues that the fact of culturally variable moral beliefs is evidence that ethics is not open to justificatory procedure and does not progress in the manner of science.

Clearly, this objection takes a stereotypical image of conditions surrounding some natural sciences as a model of all science. How easily and often do social scientists agree? But more to the point, the evidence does not damage the position defended here. My claim is that the moral worth of any actions or orientations is derivative of the way they facilitate human flourishing or well-being. There is nothing in my assessment that requires either that human development and so conditions of flourishing are everywhere the same, or that the contexts in which the conditions of flourishing can be met are other than highly varied. Indeed, they clearly are so varied. Thus the fact of cultural variability in human moralities in and of itself undermines neither the moral realist assessment that ethics can, in relevant respects, proceed in the manner of science nor the possibility that ethics can make, and has made, progress.

Indeed it is clear that the question of progress boils down to whether over time we have improved our understanding both of the human condition in all its developed variety and also of the conditions of, and for ways of satisfying, its well-being. And the answer, it seems fairly clear, is that (if only slowly and with difficulty) we have.

Incidentally the moral realist need not deny that many assessments of what is morally good contain falsehood. Indeed, it is precisely a presupposition of the position defended here that moral claims can be true or false. There is no need for the moral realist to defend all aspects of moralities in all cultures any more than the scientist must stick with all (aspects of all) scientific theories. Both types of knowledge claim are varied, fallible, contested and open to critical development. It is a fair challenge for the moral realist to explain the content of the various folk and other moralities that abound. This, though, can be undertaken only on a case-by-case basis.

13 I make no claim to the effect that we can (or cannot) avoid being members of restricted communities within the larger society. If, however, it turns out that we can only function in a manner beneficial to ourselves and others through being members of 'local' communities, with community-conditioned needs, interests and so forth, it follows that, for our actions to be morally good, we must respect, and help facilitate, the meeting of any contrasting needs of members of other communities (as well as of our own).

14 At least regarding human life on planet earth over the imaginable future.

15 This is a topic that requires a book in itself. Here I must be brief, so my argument, at best, will be but suggestive.

16 Of course, this position is hardly novel (if almost entirely absent from modern economic discussion). The best recent argument for it of which I am aware, and to which I am indebted, is provided by Collier (1999), who traces the argument back to Macmurray (1932, 1933, 1935). In particular Collier observes:

> Of course, all human action is in terms of how some other people or other beings are, in that it involves some beliefs about them, and, in the case of any action within the bounds of sanity, some true beliefs about them. But immoral action involves inadequate ideas about others. Action is moral insofar as it relates to others as they are in themselves, rather than as they are for us. But of course this is not any Kantian distinction between an unknowable 'thing in itself' and its appearances. The point is rather that what someone or something is 'for us' is a shot at an account of them as they are in themselves, and the shot may be nearer to or further from its mark.
>
> (p. 26)

In making his points Collier draws on the following earlier assessments of Macmurray – 'reason is the capacity to behave in terms of the nature of the object, that is to say, to behave objectively' (Macmurray, 1935, p. 19); and:

> We are in the habit of saying our feelings are just felt. They can't be true or false. About that we have no difficulty. Yet, if we think carefully, we shall realise that there is no special difference between feelings and thoughts in this respect ... True thoughts are thoughts which refer properly to reality,

and which are thought in terms of the nature of the object to which they refer. Why should our feelings be in any different case? It is true that they are felt and that they are what they are felt to be, just like our thoughts. But they also refer to things outside us. If I am angry I am angry at something or somebody, though I may not be able to say precisely what it is.

(Macmurray, 1935, pp. 24–5)

From this perspective, we might now say that morality is a demand to act rationally in our regard for others, both in helping others and also in recognising, or seeking an understanding of, their real natures, in order that we may act according to their own needs and not our personal sympathies.

17 I am here talking of tendencies in play. In no way am I arguing that others – whether humans, animals or the environment – should be valued just because and to the extent that they become part of our extended selves. To the contrary, I am arguing that they have separate identities and are always more than extensions of ourselves, and this affects the nature of our moral obligations towards them. Here I am concerned with the ways in which, in our daily lives, we do come to care.

18 Interestingly, when I have proposed to others (including philosophical opponents) the formulation of the good society accepted here – i.e. a society in which the free flourishing of each is a condition of the free flourishing of all – one very common initial response has been something like: 'the problem with that formulation is that it is so abstract or formal as to be acceptable to almost everyone'. I agree with this latter assessment. And it is essential to my position that this assessment is correct. The point at which participants in normative discourse mainly disagree, I believe, is in putting substance to this formulation: deciding the degree to which there are indeed commonalities in human nature; how the fulfilment of human needs are best facilitated; and so forth. In other words, our disagreements concern matters that science in particular can help us to sort out. As long as the formal criterion is acceptable to, and accepted by, us all (albeit in implicit and vague ways), it follows that at least an impulse to the good society is continually in play. It also follows that social theory, including economics, can play a role in facilitating and strengthening this impulse, that economics properly executed, indeed, just is moral philosophy *albeit itself necessarily conceived as science*.

19 Again I find this insight in Collier (1999), who in turn locates the basic argument in Spinoza. Whilst I personally prefer to talk in terms of our extending ourselves or our identities, Collier writes instead of our extending our bodies. But the position defended is much the same:

> First … a human conatus must itself be conceived (under the attribute of extension) as a drive for greater interaction, that is, both greater interaction with more things and hence greater extension of the part of the world that counts as part of the extended body; in short, greater extent and integratedness of the (extended) body. Under the attribute of thought of course, the conatus is a clear drive for understanding, for rationality.
>
> But insofar as the conatus realises its tendency, it becomes the conatus of an extended entity. It comes to include the drive to preserve the being of its new parts also. It becomes care for one's environment – care of the same sort (though not necessarily of the same degree) as our care for our own bodies in the narrow sense. And this is plausible enough in many homely instances. The more one is involved with something (say, one's garden) through sensitivity of perception and active work, the more will one care about the fate of its contents.

(Collier, 1999, p. 41)

20 Since this paper was originally written (the first version emerged some time in the late 1990s), Amartya Sen's capability approach to ethics has been developed

and become fairly well known at least to some heterodox economists. This is not the place to start a comparison, though it would be easy enough to show that Sen's reasoning presupposes an ethical naturalism and a moral realism. What I do want to comment upon is Sen's reluctance to embrace explicit systematic ontological thinking (in practice he cannot avoid it of course) due seemingly to an (erroneous) belief that this requires a commitment to a realm of emergent ethical objects.

From the ontological perspective I am defending, human flourishing is bound up with the opportunities we all have to satisfy our needs, including developing and utilising various (combinations of) capacities, not least those to act knowledgably and capably in society, to make informed choices, and live in peace, good health and harmony with others. As far as I can tell, actualised outcomes, such as acting knowledgably and capably in society, making informed choices, and living in peace, good health and harmony with others, are what Sen calls 'functionings'; the capacities (including the opportunities, freedom of deliberation, etc.) to actualise or achieve such outcomes are what Sen terms capabilities.

It is inevitably the case that such features frequently come to prominence in any form of ontological reasoning about the nature of human beings in society; this has seemingly always been the case. What is surprising is that, despite his clearly travelling this same ground, Sen seems to want to avoid any suggestion that ontological systematisation might be involved. Rather, he mentions the term ontology only rarely and then usually just in order to signal a distancing orientation from a very specific (and implausible) ontological conception. Thus, in his relatively recent comprehensive book *The Idea of Justice*, Sen (2009) mentions ontology in the text only once. He does so only after first asserting that 'objectivity is itself a rather difficult issue in moral and political philosophy' and in response to a question of his own worrying about the place of 'ethical objects':

> Does the pursuit of ethical objectivity take the form of the search for some ethical *objects*? While a good deal of complex discussion on the objectivity of ethics has tended to proceed in terms of ontology (in particular, the metaphysics of 'what ethical objects exist'), it is difficult to understand what these ethical objects might be like. Instead, I would go along with Hilary Putnam's argument that this line of investigation is largely unhelpful and misguided. When we debate the demands of ethical objectivity, we are not crossing swords on the nature and content of some alleged ethical 'objects'.
>
> (Sen, 2009, p. 41)

This passage suggests that underpinning Sen's desire to take a distance from explicit ontological elaboration may be a belief that the latter will necessarily involve making a commitment to the reality of some such 'ethical objects'. If this is so, it is hopefully clear from the current paper that no such commitment is necessary. Of course, I go further and argue that the avoidance of explicit ontological reasoning is itself actually debilitating of ethical analysis, not least (though of course not only) in regard to resolving difficulties in addressing issues like objectivity in moral and political philosophy. For an excellent very recent contribution to political economy and its history that fully covers Sen's contribution to ethics, explicitly taking in the sorts of issues raised here including Sen's reluctance to acknowledge fully the objectivism of his own account, see Nuno Martins (2013).

References

Aristotle (1881) *Nicomachean Ethics*, translated by F.H. Peters, London: Kegan and Paul.

Collier, Andrew (1999) *Being and Worth*, London: Routledge.

Gyatso, Tenzin (2001) *Ancient Wisdom, Modern World: Ethics for the New Millennium*, London: Abacus.

Lawson, Tony (1997) *Economics and Reality*, London and New York: Routledge.

Lawson, Tony (2000) 'Evaluating Trust, Competition and Co-operation', in Yuichi Shionoya and Kiichiro Yagi (eds), *Competition, Trust and Co-operation: A Comparative Study*, New York, Berlin and Tokyo: Springer Verlag.

Lawson, Tony (2003a) *Reorienting Economics*, London and New York: Routledge.

Lawson, Tony (2003b) 'Ontology and Feminist Theorising', *Feminist Economics*, 9:1, March, 119–50. Reprinted in John B. Davis (ed.), *Recent Developments in Economic Methodology*, 2006, Cheltenham: Edward Elgar.

Lawson, Tony (2012) 'Ontology and the Study of Social Reality: Emergence, Organisation, Community, Power, Social Relations, Corporations, Artefacts and Money', *Cambridge Journal of Economics*, 36(2):345–85.

Lawson, Tony (2013a) 'Emergence and Social Causation', in John Greco and Ruth Groff (eds), *Powers and Capacities in Philosophy*, London and New York: Routledge.

Lawson, Tony (2013b) 'Emergence, Morphogenesis, Causal Reduction and Downward Causation', in Margaret Archer (ed.), *Social Morphogenesis*, New York: Springer.

Lawson, Tony (2013c) 'Ethical Naturalism and Forms of Relativism', *Society*, 50:570–5.

Macmurray, John (1932) *Freedom in the Modern World*, London: Faber and Faber.

Macmurray, John (1933) *Interpreting the Universe*, London: Faber and Faber.

Macmurray, John (1935) *Reason and Emotion*, London: Faber and Faber.

Martins, Nuno (2013) *The Cambridge Revival of Political Economy*, London and New York: Routledge.

Nussbaum, Martha C. (1995) 'Human Capabilities, Female Human Beings', in Martha C. Nussbaum and Jonathan Glover (eds), *Women, Culture, and Development: A Study of Human Capabilities*, Oxford: Clarendon Press.

Rawls, John (1971) *A Theory of Justice*, Cambridge, Massachusetts: Harvard University Press.

Sen, Amartya (2009) *The Idea of Justice*, London: Penguin Books.

14 Realism, universalism and capabilities[1]

Nuno Martins

1. Introduction

Amartya Sen criticises ethical theories that use resources, commodities, goods, income, wealth or other material conditions as the only bases of well-being and advantage. One reason for this is the existence of diversity between human beings. Different human beings will attain different levels of well-being when given the same resources, commodities, goods, income, wealth or other material conditions. Sen suggests his 'capability approach' as an alternative that takes into account human diversity. Nevertheless, diversity also poses difficulties for the capability approach itself: the existence of empirical diversity renders generalisations less obvious, but the selection of capabilities implies making generalisations and comparisons.

I will argue that the key to this imbroglio consists in recognising an ontological distinction between an empirical level, where diversity between individuals exists, and an ontologically distinct level of structures and causal powers, about which more general, and at times even universal, statements can be made. The main argument will be that human subjectivities, human experiences and underlying structures are ontologically distinct (albeit highly interdependent) modes of being. If human subjectivities (and/or human experiences) and underlying structures cannot be reduced to one another, there is no contradiction in recognising diversity at one level while making general, and at times even universal, claims about structures and causal powers at another level, in a context where individuals are free to act based on the structures that condition (by enabling and constraining) their activity.

This is an alternative to attempts of generalising and universalising which proceed by providing a universal list of capabilities (e.g., Nussbaum 1992, 2000, 2003). The present argument maintains Nussbaum's emphasis on (Aristotelian) realism and universalism, but addresses these questions from a social ontology perspective, and not by providing a list of universal capabilities (the differences between the conception of capabilities suggested here and Nussbaum's own account of the latter will become clearer in section 4).

I will start by describing the capability approach (and its concern with finding an informational space for assessing equality that takes into account both human diversity and human needs) in section 2. In section 3 I will address the problems involved in using the capability approach in order to evaluate advantage and to make universal welfare judgements. In section 4 I will describe Tony Lawson's structured ontology, and argue that Lawson's framework helps us to reconcile the existence of human diversity with the possibility of making universal welfare judgements. In section 5 I shall give some illustrations of how a structured ontology can provide guidance to the selection of relevant capabilities. In section 6 I will argue that Lawson's framework is consistent with the non-deterministic conception of human agency that underpins the capability approach. In section 7 I will argue that a realist view of underlying structures and human needs was already implicit in Sen's original formulation of the capability approach, while in section 8 the main argument will be that epistemological relativism and a realist view of capabilities are compatible. Some concluding remarks will follow.

2. Informational bases of welfare analysis

In the context of the assessment and examination of inequality, Amartya Sen criticises perspectives that only take into account *achieved* welfare. Sen argues that human advantage and equality should rather be assessed in terms of the *freedom* to achieve. In fact, a central concept (perhaps the central concept) in Sen's contributions is that of freedom, which is specified as an account of positive freedom (that is, freedom as a real power *to* achieve, and not just freedom *from* constraints). This concern with going beyond 'achieved welfare' towards 'freedom to achieve' has been a characteristic not only of Sen's conception of freedom, but also of John Rawls' (1971) theory of justice: both conceptions take note of the range of opportunities and potentialities each individual has at her or his disposal.

Nevertheless, Sen has argued against a particular feature of Rawls' theory of justice, namely the use of *primary goods* (which include wealth, income, rights, liberties, opportunities and the social bases of self-respect) as the space for assessing human advantage and well-being. One must recognise that: (i) primary goods are only a means to well-being and advantage (not the end we aim for); and (ii) that diverse human beings need different endowments of primary goods. In fact, diversity is, in addition to freedom, another central concept in Sen's analysis. Sen argues that diversity is an essential feature of reality, not an additional complication to be added on later – and this view of diversity as a fundamental aspect of reality is essential to Sen's argument against Rawls' conception of equality. Sen argues:

[...] the importance of the distinction between seeking equality in different *spaces* relates ultimately to the nature of human diversity.

It is because we are so deeply diverse, that equality in one space frequently leads to inequality in other spaces. The force of the question 'equality of *what*?', thus, rests to a great extent on the empirical fact of our dissimilarity – in physical and mental abilities and disabilities, in epidemiological vulnerability, in age, in gender, and of course, in the social and economic bases of our well-being and freedom.

(Sen 1992:117)

Sen's critique of Rawlsian equality can be extended to perspectives that demand equality in the space of commodities, goods, resources, incomes, wealth, entitlements or the material conditions each person possesses. The diversity between human beings leads to a shift from a space of goods to a space defined in terms of the person–goods relationship: it is in the latter space, not in the former, that inequality can be assessed in a more appropriate way. These two central categories of Sen's analysis – viz., freedom and diversity – are also related: the fact that diverse individuals are free to act in different ways further enhances the existent diversity.

One example of an approach that, unlike Rawls', takes into account the person–goods relationship, is the utilitarian approach. Sen argues that '[u]tility has a "personal" dimension that indices of primary goods do not; the latter have to be "impersonal" in this sense' (Sen 2002:342). And he continues:

[...] the real contrast to draw [...] is not so much between primary goods and *specifically* utilities, but between primary goods and other indices that can accommodate personal variability in the conversion of goods into personal achievements. Utility is, arguably, one such index (under each of its respective interpretations as happiness, choice, fulfilment of desire, etc.).

(Sen 2002:343)

In this passage, Sen argues that his major concern is to find a space that can encompass personal differences 'in the conversion of goods into personal achievements'. Even though Sen claims that 'utility is, arguably, one such index', he rejects utility theory as an account of human advantage and equality. One reason for this rejection is that utilities reflect achievements, and Sen argues that the appropriate space to assess human advantage and equality is that of freedom to achieve, not the space of actual achievements – as we saw previously. Furthermore, Sen criticises utility theory on the grounds that it uses a metric that focuses on the person's 'mental reaction'. As an example of this latter point, Sen (1982) notes that if someone is 'hard to please', utility theory would recommend giving this person a higher level of goods (if the aim was to bring her or him to a level of utility equal to that of an 'average' person). But Sen argues that such a psychological feature should not entitle that person to extra goods. Furthermore, Sen argues that some desires a person may have, such as the desire of a disabled person to have the same opportunities as people who are not disabled, seem more legitimate than the desire of someone to be 'deluged in champagne and buried in caviar', even if the disabled person already feels a higher degree of utility or happiness (without even having the same opportunities) than the other person would feel after being 'deluged in champagne and buried in caviar'.

In addition, Sen notes how a person in a situation of deprivation might adapt her or his preferences to such a situation, and end up feeling a level of utility similar to that of someone who is not similarly deprived. Hence, the notion of utility will not capture the full extent of this deprivation. If someone adapts her or his preferences to a situation of deprivation, there is still a real loss in well-being, and hence advantage should be assessed in terms of these real losses, not in terms of the utility level that those losses generate.

In this context, Sen proposes his *capability approach*, which is a perspective that accounts for how goods and resources affect different human beings by focusing on the 'functionings' and 'capabilities' each different person can achieve using these goods and resources – and not on the person's 'mental reaction' or degree of happiness (often identified with 'utility'). Functionings are the actual achievements of the person, that is, what the person is or does. Capabilities are the set of potential functionings that a person can achieve. In Sen's analysis, the appropriate space to assess human advantage and equality consists in the capabilities that people have reason to value.

3. Applying the capability approach

Sen's distinction between relevant capabilities and wants (or desires) is essential to his argument against utilitarianism. But Sen does not specify how such a distinction (between relevant capabilities and other wants) can be established and used for practical purposes. Effectively, Sen's original formulation of the capability approach was mainly concerned with providing the philosophical underpinnings for a different perspective, not with the practical application of the approach. Sen's notion of a capability that one has reason to value is a somewhat abstract concept, which surely needs further specification.

One example of work done in the pursuit of further specification can be found in the writings of Martha Nussbaum. Nussbaum argues for: (i) the importance of universal values (see Nussbaum 2000); (ii) an Aristotelian account of human functioning (see Nussbaum 1992); and (iii) further specifying the capability approach in order to apply it in practice (see Nussbaum 1992, 2000, 2003), for 'Sen's "perspective of freedom" is too vague', and 'we must make commitments about substance' (Nussbaum 2003:33). Within this background, Nussbaum suggests a list of capabilities considered to be universal, central and non-negotiable, which, she argues, should be provided to every individual.

There is much merit in Nussbaum's defence of universal values, and in her grounding of the capability approach (or at least of its notion of human functioning) in Aristotelian thinking (on which see, for example, Nussbaum 1992, or Sen 1999b:289, who also recognises an Aristotelian vein in his approach). Like Sen, Nussbaum points towards a realist account of human functioning that moves beyond the emphasis on subjective welfarism or utilities on the one hand, and resources or incomes on the other hand, that dominates contemporary welfare analysis. Besides, Nussbaum is right in noting that commitments of substance are needed in order to render the capability approach applicable.

Nevertheless, to provide a universal list of capabilities is not an easy task, to say the least. As Sen recognises: 'There are, of course, many difficulties with the notion of "basic capability equality". In particular, the problem of indexing the basic capability bundles is a serious one' (Sen 1982:368). Sen continues:

> [...] whatever partial ordering can be done on the basis of broad uniformity of personal preferences must be supplemented by certain established conventions of relative importance. The ideas of relative importance are, of course, conditional on the nature of the society.
>
> (Sen 1982:368)

Developments of the capability approach have placed greater emphasis on going straight from Sen's original formulation of the approach towards empirical analysis. Here I argue instead that such applications should be mediated by a detailed *ontological* analysis of biological, social and economic structures, which shape our capability space by facilitating or constraining human agency.

The aim here is not to provide a universal list of capabilities, but rather to clarify the structural causes that must be taken into account in the process of broadening the capability space. If the capability space arises from underlying structures, possessing the (emergent) causal power to shape people's capacities and actions, a careful scrutiny of the latter is essential to the project of human emancipation. Welfare analysis and socio-economic policy should then be addressed by investigating the extent to which underlying structures promote (or not) capability enlargement and human emancipation.

Now, there are three fundamental questions that must be distinguished at this stage. The first question is whether there can be any general (or possibly universal) statements about human capabilities and well-being. This central question depends on a second question, and a third question. The second question concerns which structures and corresponding capabilities are fundamental to our well-being. The third question is whether we share any common (or even universal) structures and capabilities. Both these two last questions must be answered before the first can even be addressed. Here, I will argue that an analysis of underlying biological, social and economic structures is fundamental to address all these three questions. The study of ontologically distinct structures can help us to understand which structures and corresponding capabilities are *important* to our well-being and advantage, which structures and capabilities are *general* or common (and possibly universal), and hence which general (or even universal) statements can be made about human well-being (and the structures that contribute to well-being).

However, remember that any attempt to answer these questions must take into account the fact that diversity is, as Sen has pointed out, an essential and irreducible feature of reality. In the next section I will argue for the use of a structured ontology in order to reconcile the existence of diversity with the possibility of general (possibly universal) ethical evaluations.

4. Diversity, universalising and Lawson's structured ontology

The aim of the capability approach is to find a space for assessing human advantage and inequality. In order to do so, there must be some generalisation if not universalising, a necessity that has also been recognised by Martha Nussbaum (2000). Effectively, there must be some commonality of capabilities, otherwise there would be no criteria to move from a world of differences towards social policy making. As Tony Lawson argues:

> The possibility of human freedom presupposes the existence of shared human objectives, i.e. real interests and motives, ultimately rooted in common needs and capabilities. If everyone's needs are purely subjective, with the possibility of being irreconcilably opposed, then projecting the goal of social emancipation is indeed likely to be question-begging from the outset.
>
> (Lawson 2003:240)

Lawson continues:

> [...] the possibility of moral theorising can, at least in part, be based on a recognised common human nature, a recognition grounded on our biological unity as a species. However, because this common nature is always historically and socially mediated, human needs will be manifest in potentially many ways. It follows [...] that the pursuit of social goals always takes place in a context of conflicting position-related interests. [...] Certainly, conflicts centring on the interests of class positions, age, gender, nation, states, regions, culture, and so forth, are as real and determining as anything else. Even so, different groups may cooperate allowing different, and even opposed, interests sometimes to be met. The point remains, though, that opposed, position-related

interests or developed needs exist. And it may be upon our unity as a species and the more generalised features of our social and historical experience and make-up, that the greater possibility of unambiguous and more enduring progress rests.

(Lawson 2003:240, 241)

In this passage, Lawson argues how some commonality of needs can be found at least in 'our biological unity as a species'. This seems a suitable starting point, since this commonality appears to be an unquestionable one, and Sen himself resorts to examples related to this aspect, noting how physical and biological disabilities are cases of capability deprivation. Furthermore, Sen also emphasises the importance of the concept of needs that Lawson refers to here, arguing that: 'My contention is that *even* the concept of *needs* does not get adequate coverage through the information on primary goods and utility' (Sen 1982:367, emphasis in original).

Lawson explains that 'because this common nature is always historically and socially mediated, human needs will be manifest in potentially many ways' (2003:240). Hence, one must also take note of economic, social and cultural factors. For example, people without physical disabilities might find their capability space reduced due to the social position they occupy in a given social structure. Sen (1999b) also provides some examples of this, such as cases of gender inequality, or of impossibility of political participation, and notes the need of analysing 'the social and economic bases of our well-being and freedom' (Sen 1992:117). So the application of the capability approach cannot be confined to identifying physical or biological disabilities, for socio-economic structures and social (and historical) processes may also lead to inequality in the capability space.

Now, how is it possible to move from empirical differences (which can exist at a physical, biological, psychological or socio-economic level) towards generalisations and universalising (while taking into account contextual elements like 'culture', 'established conventions of relative importance' and the 'nature of society', as Sen puts it)? Doing so is essential in order to go from empirical diversity towards some systematised understanding of inequality and disadvantage. But if, as Sen argues, diversity is an essential feature of reality (not an additional complication to be added later), how can generalisations be made? Lawson (2003) suggests a solution for this problem: he argues that empirical diversity and structures exist at *different ontological levels*:

[...] an individual's manifest nature and experiences may be unique. But this is quite consistent with commonality or generality lying at a different level, an insight we can recognise only when we pass beyond an ontology of the actual and specifically of experience.

(Lawson 2003:240)

As the term 'ontology' will likely be unclear to those unfamiliar with philosophy of science, metaphysics or economic methodology, I shall clarify what I mean by it as well as by such expression as 'different ontological levels'. By 'ontology' I mean an enquiry into the nature of 'being', as 'being qua being'. It is an analysis of the underlying categories of reality. It is important to understand that ontological commitments are always present in any theory, for any theory refers (if only implicitly) to some reality, which is described through our categories and conceptions. Hence, ontology is something that is done by *any* theorist, either explicitly or implicitly.

If ontology refers to the nature of being, then the expression 'different ontological levels' implies some heterogeneity in this ultimate nature of reality, otherwise there would be no ontological differences, i.e. differences and diversity in the 'stuff' that constitutes the fundamental nature of being.

According to Lawson's structured ontology, reality is constituted not only by events, but also by the underlying structures, including physical, biological, psychological and social structures. The social realm (and psychological structures) can be seen as emergent from the biological realm, which in turn is emergent from the physical realm. Lawson (1997:63) writes:

> Emergence may be defined as a relationship between two features or aspects such that one arises out of the other and yet, while perhaps being capable of reacting back to it, remains causally and taxonomically irreducible to it.

This means, for example, that although the biological realm constitutes the basis for the social realm, the latter is not reducible to the former.

Ontology can be global, when analysing all aspects of reality, or local, when it is concerned with a given part of reality (for example, the biological realm, or the social realm). Lawson's analysis is concerned with the social realm, and hence with elaborating social categories in the context of a structured *social* ontology, according to which social reality is constituted not only by specific individuals, but also by the underlying social structures.

These social structures comprise social rules that are attached to each social position. Social positions are *internally related*. Aspects of reality are said to be internally related when they are what they are because of the relations in which they stand to one another. Accordingly, when parts of a given phenomena are internally related, these parts in isolation will not possess essential properties of the 'whole'. Social structures are reproduced and/ or transformed through time, as specific individuals slot into each social position and follow (or change) social rules through their social practices. Socio-economic structures arise in the context of human interaction, but are not reducible to the latter. The joint activity of structures and human agents co-produces empirical phenomena, and hence structures are the underlying (material) *causes*, in conjunction with (the efficient causation of) human agency, of observed events – and also the causes of the broadening or reduction of the human agent's capability space (the distinction between material and efficient causation will be clarified in section 6; I discuss in more detail the impact of underlying structures in the capability space in Martins 2006).

For Lawson, the reality of an entity can be inferred not only from our perception of it, but also from its causal effects. So even though we do not observe structures, the existence of the latter can be inferred from the observance of their effects. Structures are ontologically real, just like their effects in observable events, and cannot be reduced to the latter.

Now, events and states of affairs are diverse because of the different ways in which they are intrinsically structured. But the underlying causal structures are ontologically distinct from the events and states of affairs they govern. In the biological realm, this means that there is an ontological distinction between biological structures and specific organisms. In the psychological realm, this signifies that there is an ontological distinction between the (neuro)psychological structures behind our needs, and our concrete subjectivity that is shaped not only by (neuro)psychological structures, but also by our individual experiences and context. In the social realm, this entails that since social structures and human individuals are ontologically distinct, not only social structures are irreducible to specific individuals, but human agency is also irreducible to the social structures by which it is (to a greater or lesser extent) constrained or enabled.

Hence, one can make general statements about the underlying causes behind a particular capability space while maintaining Sen's view that human diversity is an irreducible feature of social reality, because diversity refers to empirical phenomena, whilst universal claims are made about ontologically distinct (biological, psychological or social) causal structures. Of course, the level of generality will vary depending on how many individuals share the relevant structures. For example, biological structures will be shared by all human individuals (exceptions are, for example, cases of physical disability). Social structures will be shared by particular groups and, while being a source of commonality within that group, will often be a source of diversity between groups.

5. Some illustrations of how the analysis of structural causes may help

Nussbaum (2003) addresses the issue of the selection of relevant capabilities by providing a universal list of central human capabilities. It must be noted that Nussbaum's list already implies the recognition of underlying biological and social structures that foster human functioning. Capabilities such as '[b]eing able to live to the end of a human life of normal length' (Nussbaum 2000:78), 'Bodily Health' and 'Bodily Integrity' depend on the underlying biological structures of a human being.

Yet, these three capabilities that Nussbaum points out are manifestations of how underlying biological structures and powers of the human being enable human functioning. Of course, since human beings share a similar biological structure (with very similar biological needs), Nussbaum's reference to those three manifestations of underlying biological structures is fairly uncontroversial, for similar biological structures and powers will bring about similar manifestations of the latter.

But biological structures are not the only structures shaping human capabilities. Social structures, for example, are also essential to the broadening of human capabilities, as Nussbaum (2000:79, 80) notes when referring to 'Emotions', 'Practical Reason', 'Affiliation' and 'Play' as central capabilities. The role of socio-economic structures is also important, as Nussbaum (2000:80) notes when pointing out the capability of 'Control over One's Environment'.

Nussbaum's endorsement of a list of specific capabilities is unproblematic when addressing functionings which depend mostly on biological structures, for the latter are identical between human individuals (hence are general), and are recognised as important for our well-being. The problem comes when addressing specific functionings which depend on social (and also economic) structures. The latter are not identical across different cultures and regions, and in many cases it is not clear which social structure better promotes our well-being. So the endorsement of a definite list of capabilities becomes problematic, at least without a careful scrutiny of how underlying structures contribute to our well-being. The question one may now ask is: but what are the biological and social structures behind any of the capabilities in Nussbaum's list? How can we move beyond Nussbaum's list towards the analysis of underlying structures?

The study of the underlying structures at play in a particular spatio-temporal setting cannot start at an ontological level, for it first requires empirical analysis of such a concrete situation. Ontology can play a very important role in providing general categories and in the scrutiny of competing methodologies. But assessing which underlying structures are important for our well-being, and whether there are common or general structures (the two issues on which the question of universalism in ethics depends), in a given concrete situation, requires more than ontological analysis – it requires empirical evidence as well. The recognition of the irreducibility of empirical diversity means that the analysis of concrete situations must begin with empirical analysis, and only afterwards move towards the ontologically distinct underlying structures, about which general (and possibly universal) statements can be made.

Therefore, clarifications of how a structured ontology may help in the analysis of concrete situations can only be illustrations, conditional on the empirical claims used in each particular illustration. In order to illustrate how the analysis of ontologically distinct biological and social structures can provide a better basis for more general (possibly universal) claims concerning well-being, I will provide two examples in which the conception of a structured ontology outlined above is combined with further empirical claims about biological, social and economic structures. This will be done in order to elucidate how a structured ontology can be applied in practice.

The first illustration will address the underlying structures behind emotions (a central capability in Nussbaum's list), and in the second illustration I shall discuss the 'control over one's environment' (another central capability in Nussbaum's list). The two illustrations cover different types of structures: the first illustration is mainly concerned with biological and social structures, and the interaction between both; while the second illustration is primarily concerned with socio-economic structures.

Illustration 1: Emotions

Before going into detail about how a structured ontology can help address the role of emotions in human well-being, let us first briefly discuss Nussbaum's perspective on emotions and well-being. Nussbaum (2000:79) argues that the capability 'to love, to grieve and to experience longing, gratitude and justified anger' are central (emotional) capabilities. She adds that emotional development must not be blighted by 'overwhelming fear and anxiety, or by traumatic events of abuse or neglect'. But what is Nussbaum's basis to choose which of those emotions, if any, constitute central human capabilities?

For example, why do we need emotions like 'justified anger'? Is not anger a negative emotion? Now, some emotions could be seen as constitutive of well-being (in the sense that they directly generate well-being) or instrumental to well-being, when they help us to act in a way that will increase our well-being in the long run (even though they do not directly generate well-being). Maybe Nussbaum wants to note that 'justified anger' strengthens our capability to respond to threatening or oppressive situations, and thus it is instrumental to (albeit not constitutive of) our well-being.

However, whether 'justified anger' will help us to increase our well-being still depends on the particular context we face. In some situations 'justified anger' will be a useful instrument to achieve well-being, but in many other social situations it will not. So whether 'justified anger' is a central capability depends on context, including the underlying social structures that facilitate or constrain the emergence of concrete social situations.

Furthermore, other emotions that Nussbaum classifies as obstacles to our emotional development (at least when we are 'overwhelmed' by them), such as fear and anxiety, also have instrumental value. Like (justified) anger, fear and anxiety have proved to be evolutionarily useful for our survival. So if instrumental value is accepted as a criterion for selecting relevant capabilities (as Nussbaum seems to do when defending the capability for 'justified anger'), why exclude fear and anxiety from the list of central capabilities?

Maybe Nussbaum wants to suggest that fear and anxiety are negative emotions only when we experience them beyond a certain degree, for she uses a qualifier: '*overwhelming* fear and anxiety' (Nussbaum 2000:79, my emphasis). But still, the criteria used in the selection of capabilities, concerning for example the instrumental value of emotions, remain far from clear, for it is still conditional on underlying (biological and social) structures, which, although implicit in Nussbaum's analysis, are not explicitly discussed. In fact, the question of whether any emotion has instrumental value for our well-being depends on the particular social contexts we face (the same emotion can have a positive instrumental value in a particular situation, and a negative instrumental value in other situations), hence the need to study the underlying social structures that shape different situations.

Thus, Nussbaum's list would be universal only if, by chance, the structures she implicitly assumes as being the triggering causes of emotions like 'justified anger', 'fear' and 'anxiety', are common to all human beings (a premise that could be accepted in what biological structures are concerned, but not in what social structures are concerned).

Now, in order to provide a more complete illustration of how the study of biological and social structures helps in more general (possibly universal) welfare analysis, I shall have to provide a more detailed explanation of some empirical facts concerning biological structures at this stage – for, remember, ontological analysis must be combined with empirical evidence before it can provide guidance to the selection of relevant capabilities.

Recent advances in the neurosciences have provided a better understanding of the neurobiological basis of emotions (see, for example, Damásio 1994 or LeDoux 1996), and shed some light on the issue of which emotions can be said to be universal. Damásio (1994) distinguishes between primary emotions and secondary (or social) emotions. Primary emotions include emotions like fear, anger, happiness, sadness, surprise and disgust. Primary emotions occur when, after a stimulus, a given brain area (like the amygdala, or the cingulated cortex) is directly triggered, and executes the appropriate bodily responses through brain circuits and regions that include the hypothalamus, the basal forebrain and the brain stem as key agents. In a primary emotion like fear, for example, a stimulus will directly trigger the amygdala, and afterwards be executed by regions like the hypothalamus, the basal forebrain and the brain stem.

Secondary emotions include emotions like sympathy, compassion, embarrassment, shame, guilt, pride, jealousy, envy and gratitude. Secondary emotions are derived from primary emotions, for they combine the brain machinery involved in primary emotions with other brain areas that categorise objects and situations, including social situations.

In secondary emotions, the stimulus is firstly processed in regions like the ventromedial prefrontal cortex, which is sensitive to contextual and social categorisation of external objects and situations. It is through the ventromedial prefrontal cortex that brain regions like the amygdala or the cingulated cortex are afterwards (and hence indirectly) activated, and the bodily responses are then executed through the hypothalamus, the basal forebrain and the brain stem.

While the brain areas involved in primary emotions contain innate dispositions that cause similar reactions to similar stimuli by different human agents, at least one of the brain areas involved in secondary emotions (the ventromedial prefrontal cortex) can change its neurobiological dispositions, and acquire new dispositions, at any stage of our life. Since the ventromedial prefrontal cortex categorises external objects and situations (including social contexts), our reaction towards social situations can change through our lifetime.

Hence, primary emotions are universal to all human beings (provided no damage occurs in their neurobiological structures), for primary emotions depend on neurobiological dispositions and responses that are essentially innate, while secondary emotions will be much more dependent on the external environment, including our particular experiences, social context and underlying social structures, since secondary emotions rely not only on innate dispositions, but also on acquired dispositions (see Damásio 1994).

As a first point, note that on the basis of this understanding we can, as Lawson argues, recognise the possibility of universalising at the level of our biological unity as a species (in this case, through an analysis of our neurobiological structures and innate dispositions), while also recognising the ontological distinctiveness of human experiences and social structures, which have a causal impact on our acquired dispositions. The analysis of underlying neurobiological structures can provide a basis for the recognition of universal primary emotions, while general statements about secondary emotions require the analysis of both neurobiological and social structures (in what secondary emotions are concerned, our knowledge of common (neuro)biological structures can provide guidance to the formulation of general claims about how social structures affect well-being in virtue of the way in which social situations trigger and shape acquired dispositions).

For example, let us now examine how the previous analysis can help us to study the causal impact of these structures on well-being. The examination of underlying structures shows us that the neurobiological structures that trigger fear, for example, are biologically innate and universal, so unless we want to violate our biological integrity (for example, damaging our amygdala in order to avoid the triggering of the emotion of fear in our brain) our focus should be on the situations that trigger this emotion. This then directs us towards the need for transforming the social structures that may facilitate or constrain situations of overwhelming fear or anxiety.

The way in which social structures can help balance emotions is, of course, a complex mechanism which again requires the study of the social and psychological structures involved. Anthony Giddens (1984), for example, notes how the repetition of daily and familiar routines works as an anxiety-controlling mechanism (and aids the control of the emotions of fear and anxiety), by providing a feeling of sameness and continuity in our everyday life. The existence of a stable social structure is often crucial to enable these familiar routines to take place, providing the agent with what Giddens calls, following Laing (1965), 'ontological security'. A stable social structure that provides a stable environment can then be identified as an essential component of the capability space of a person.

But even though these routines can be seen as a response to a basic anxiety-regulating mechanism we all possess (for it depends on neuropsychological structures that can be said to be similar in every human being), we can only observe the latter's manifestations in the particular wants and desires that human beings may have, which will be shaped by social context as well. Such wants may vary across regions, time and cultures, and the endorsement of a list of functionings which promote social capabilities will depend on context (the concrete routines and experiences observed across regions, time and different cultures can be immensely diverse). In such cases, universal claims can only be made at the ontologically distinct level of the neuropsychological structures that influence ontological security, and the more general features of the underlying social structures, not at the level of the social functionings which will be different across regions, time and cultures.

To repeat, the point to note is that the question of whether any emotion, routine or practice is a central human capability depends on underlying biological and social structures, and any list of valuable emotions will be conditional on the latter. To bypass the study of these structures undermines the grounds for generalising and universalising, for it is the underlying structures, and not their empirical manifestations, that can be said to be general or possibly universal.

Illustration 2: Control over one's environment

In the previous illustration the emphasis was on the interaction between neurobiological and social structures. In this second illustration I will focus on the role of socio-economic structures. To do so, I will discuss another item of Nussbaum's list, namely the 'control over one's environment'. Here, Nussbaum (2000:80) refers to the ability of 'being able to hold property (both land and movable goods) not just formally but in terms of real opportunity; and having property rights on an equal basis with others'.

Now, to hold property may be an important capability within a given socio-economic structure, but it can only be justified within the context of such particular structure, and may not be an important capability in other possible socio-economic structures. Karl Polanyi (1944) famously distinguished between different modes of distribution of goods, like reciprocity (the mutual exchange of goods as part of a long-term relationship), redistribution (which requires the existence of a central entity or figure, to which all goods are directed, and who then distributes them through the community) and (market) exchange (the exchange of goods through a market mechanism, i.e. according to a price system).

Under socio-economic structures other than that a market economy, the social position of an individual in a network of social relations governed through reciprocity or redistribution is far more important for her or his well-being than the possession of property. So the possession of property cannot be said to be a universal capability regardless of the underlying socio-economic structure. Nussbaum's claim that all individuals should hold property seems to presuppose the socio-economic structure of a market economy, for only in such a case is the existence of property rights (distributed through the members of the community) essential to the equality of central capabilities.

But a market economy cannot be assumed to be a universal socio-economic structure. In our economic history, for the most part market exchange played a minor role in the distribution of material resources and goods, and the guiding principles of distribution were reciprocity or redistribution. Even today, principles like reciprocity are still fundamental in many family economies, and play a major role in numerous developing regions.

Furthermore, the material means (including property) to achieve valuable capabilities may vary across regions, time and cultures, even under similar modes of distribution. For example, the level of income and wealth of an individual that enables one to achieve certain social capabilities (such as 'appearing in public without shame') may vary depending on the culture and the values of the society (s)he lives in, as Sen (1999b) notes. The point, again, is that it is not possible to universalise the possession of property as a fundamental capability without an analysis of the underlying socio-economic structures. In fact, to provide a list of capabilities as specific as Nussbaum's list, without a scrutiny of underlying structures, ultimately leads to the rejection of the irreducibility of empirical diversity, because no distinction is made between empirical diversity and ontologically distinct structures, and a particular structure is implicitly assumed as being common to all cultures and individuals.

6. Freedom and structural causation

The illustrations presented in the last section were concerned with specific capabilities in Nussbaum's list. However, there is a more general problem concerning structural causation and human agency that must be addressed at this stage. Having argued that biological and social structures are the ultimate basis for general (possibly universal) statements, an important question remains to be addressed: whether these structures preclude the freedom of human action or not.

The recognition that the social realm is emergent from, and irreducible to, the biological realm enables Lawson's ontology to support the hypothesis that biological structures do not completely determine human action. Biological structures are recognised as a condition of possibility for social activity, but the latter is not totally determined by the former.

What about the causal efficacy of social structures? Do social structures, as the underlying causes of events, totally determine human actions in Lawson's conception? If this were the case, then the causal efficacy of social structures would be inconsistent with the freedom of the human agent, which is essential to Sen's (and Nussbaum's) perspective. Diversity, freedom and choice are central concepts for the capability approach, and for Sen's understanding of human action. Hence, any social theory that is to be made compatible with the capability approach (and with Sen's conception of social reality) must place these as real constituents of reality.

The recognition of freedom as an ontological constituent of reality means one needs a social theory where there is both: (a) the possibility of free choice, where such freedom is also a source of diversity in behaviour; and (b) some generalisation and classification, in order to understand 'culture' and 'established conventions of relative importance' which, Sen argues, depend on the 'nature of society'.

To satisfy condition (a), it would be enough to argue that the world is constituted by diverse human beings endowed with freedom of choice, but without any further ontological level there would be no criteria for classifying and generalising – condition (b) would not be verified. To satisfy condition (b), one could endorse a social theory where social structures are reified and cause individual actions according to a fixed pattern, but then there would be no freedom of action for diverse human beings – condition (a) would not be verified.

The solution to this problem consists in noting the previously mentioned fact that social structures, on the one hand, and empirical phenomena and human subjectivity, on the other hand, are at ontologically distinct levels. Lawson explains

> [...] it is now clear that there is no contradiction in recognising each of us as a unique identity or individuality, resulting (in part) from our own unique paths through life, and *also* accepting that we can nevertheless possess similar needs or interests as well as stand in the same or similar positions and relations of domination to those of others around us, including gender relations. From this perspective there is no contradiction in recognising both our different individualities and experiences as well as the possibility of common interests in transforming certain forms of social relationships. Fundamental here

> is the fact that human subjectivities, human experiences and social structures cannot be reduced to one another; they are each ontologically distinct, albeit highly interdependent, modes of being.
>
> (Lawson 2003:241, emphasis in original)

Thus, general judgements on how socio-economic structures promote or constrain human capabilities are consistent with the postulate that human agents are not totally determined by socio-economic structures. Social structures are related to human agency because social structures are reproduced and transformed by human agency (hence structures depend on agency), and also because the social structures so reproduced and transformed will in turn promote or constrain human capabilities (and hence human agency and capabilities also depend on structures). But both structure and agency interact as ontologically distinct realities. This is not a deterministic model where one part of reality (social structures or human agency) determines the other. It is still left to the human agent to choose from the capability space that is shaped by social structures (hence human agency is not reducible to social structures).

Social structures are the material causes of action in the sense that they provide a set of social rules that may be used or not by the human agent when formulating an action. In this sense, social structures are a material available for the human agent to use if she or he wishes to do so, but its use is still conditional on the choice of the agent, which constitutes the efficient causation of human action (on the distinction between social structures as a material cause of events, and human agents as the efficient cause of events, see Paul Lewis 2000). Hence, one can reconcile: (i) empirical diversity with universalising (as argued previously), and (ii) human freedom with the causal efficacy of socio-economic structures (as argued in the present section).

Without taking note of the ontological distinction between social structures and human agency, one would be led to adopt a solution similar to Nussbaum's. Remember that if we do not recognise the ontological irreducibility of social structures and human agency to each other, we are led to either assume that social structures are reducible to (or can be explained only in terms of) human agency, or assume that human agency is reducible to (or can be explained only in terms of) social structures.

In the latter case, we would have a deterministic model of structural causation where agents do not have the freedom to act in a different way than the one determined by social structures. As we saw before, such a deterministic model of structural causation would be inconsistent with the freedom of human agency, which is central to Sen's and Nussbaum's writings.

Hence, without recognising the ontological distinction between social structures and human agency, the only way to safeguard freedom of agency is to focus only on human agency, thus ignoring the social structures that may enlarge or constrain the capability space – thus, Nussbaum suggests a universal list of capabilities without analysing the structural causes behind a given capability space.

But the absence of a careful investigation of structural causes behind events and experiences implies that there can be no criteria for generalisations and universalising from events and experiences, if the latter are recognised as irreducibly diverse. This is why it becomes important to recognise the above-mentioned ontological distinction between underlying (biological, psychological, economic or social) structures and the particular way in which they become manifest in human experiences, human subjectivity and human wants and desires, a distinction which can provide guidance to the process of selecting relevant capabilities.

7. The implicit ontological commitments of Sen's capability approach

Notice that the notion of structural causation has not been absent from Sen's own writings. Sen's (1981) study of poverty and famines, for example, has been especially concerned with the structures and causal factors behind real variations of well-being. Besides, Sen's (1999a) own argument for rejecting utility theory already points in this direction. Sen argues that physical or biological disabilities are a real cause of capability deprivation that cannot be assessed in terms of utility. Remember that Sen explains how people might end up adapting their preferences to a worse situation, and hence utility will not capture the real loss in advantage and well-being that occurs in virtue of this physical or biological disability. Sen's argument implies a distinction between the sorts of desires that people have. The desire of a disabled person, to have the same range of opportunities as anyone else, corresponds to a basic *need*, which is a consequence of an unfortunate physical condition. A disabled person is constrained with relation to something that is essential to human functioning, given the nature of human beings.

The desire to be 'buried in caviar', on the other hand, seems to be a particular *want* of a person with a highly exigent personal taste, which may be a result of several factors, but does not seem to be caused by a basic need (it is not essential to human functioning). Therefore, it seems to be the case that Sen's argument already points (at least implicitly) to an ontological analysis of the real physical and biological causes of deprivation (I provide a more complete assessment of the ontological commitments of Sen's capability approach in Martins 2006, 2007).

In addition to physical and biological causes of deprivation, Sen suggests some other causes, such as economic, social or cultural factors which are, Sen argues, 'conditional on the nature of the society' (Sen 1982:368). Sen (1999b) notes how many people see their capability space reduced in virtue of the social position they occupy in a society (e.g., cases of gender inequality). The physical, biological, psychological, social and cultural factors add to economic factors accounting for deprivation, such as entitlement of goods or means to purchase and exchange goods, these latter identified by Sen in his book *Poverty and Famines* (Sen 1981). So one can find some analysis of physical, biological, psychological and socio-economic structures already present in Sen's writings, albeit in a somewhat implicit way.

This analysis of physical, biological, psychological and socio-economic structures can provide us with some criteria for knowing which structures endow a person with a capability space that permits responding to more pressing needs. Sen argues:

> The existence of social variation does not, of course, rule out various agreements on what is to count as serious deprivation. Indeed, it can be argued that if we concentrate on certain basic functionings and the corresponding capabilities, there may be much more agreement on their importance, than there would be if we concentrated on particular commodity bundles and particular ways of achieving those functionings.
>
> (Sen 1992:108)

So even though Sen argues that diversity is an essential feature of reality (not an additional complication to be added later), he also seems to be optimistic about the possibility of generalising.

8. Ontology, realism and epistemological relativism

A note on ontology and epistemology is required at this stage. The suggested realist ontological analysis shares much with an Aristotelian account of human functioning that underpins the capability approach, which both Nussbaum (1992, 2000) and Sen (1999b:289) recognise. But it must be emphasised that engaging with the suggested (realist) ontological analysis does not mean adopting the view that objects of knowledge are other than transient. Effectively, knowledge of any socio-economic reality proceeds by means of previous knowledge, within human experience and human preconceptions. The present argument is much in line with what Nussbaum calls an 'internalist essentialism' (Nussbaum 1992:207), and also an 'historically grounded empirical essentialism', that 'takes its stand within human experience' (Nussbaum 1992:208), not with some sort of externally imposed realism that does not take into account the fact that knowledge and conceptions depend on past knowledge and past conceptions (for another perspective on this distinction, see also Hilary Putnam 2002).

Having a realist approach simply means that *knowledge is not totally produced by context*; rather, knowledge must be about ontologically real objects, even though our conceptions of these real objects are partially (but not totally) influenced by past knowledge, conceptions and context. As Lawson notes

> [...] there is nothing essential to scientific or ontological realism that supposes or requires that objects of knowledge be naturalistic or other than transient, that knowledge obtained is other than fallible, partial and itself transient, or that scientists or researchers are other than positioned, biased, interested, and practically, culturally and socially conditioned.
>
> (Lawson 2003:220, emphasis in original)

Nussbaum's (1992) attack on 'externalist metaphysical-realist essentialism' may generate some confusion because it mixes two different concerns: an ontological concern with the nature of things; and an epistemological concern with the knowledge we can obtain of those things. Ontological realism (or scientific realism) is a claim about things, not about knowledge of things, and the two domains (the ontological and the epistemological) should not be conflated (see Lawson 1997, 2003). This fallacy, of reducing the ontological domain to the epistemological domain (that is, of taking *being* to be exhausted by our *knowledge* of being), is frequent in much philosophical analysis (on this, see Lawson 1997).

So having a realist position about the ontological properties of objects does not convey anything about whether knowledge of objects is 'internal' or 'external' to human experience. The prefixes 'externalist' and 'internalist' refer to an epistemological issue, while 'realism' (or 'essentialism') refers to an ontological issue, even though this distinction is not explicitly acknowledged by Nussbaum, who seems to conflate these different concerns in the idea of 'internalist essentialism'.

In fact, as it seems obvious that all our knowledge must be obtained from 'within human experience', the terms 'externalist (metaphysical-realist) essentialism' and 'internalist essentialism' seem misplaced. For if the internalist/externalist distinction refers to whether knowledge is historically mediated (and relative) or not, it seems obvious that 'externalist essentialism' is an impossible stance, and there cannot be any sort of 'essentialism' other than 'internalist essentialism'.

The existence of some features of human nature and society that are in some sense absolute and essential, and ground the possibility of universalising, is also suggested by Sen: '[P]overty is an absolute notion in the space of capabilities, but very often it will take a relative form in the space of commodities or characteristics' (Sen 1984:335). David Crocker also notes how

> [t]he important point is that the capabilities approach can retain the notion of a culturally invariant (absolute) core to both well-being and

deprivation while at the same time construing any *specific* means of provisioning as relative to historical and cultural contexts.

(Crocker 1992:592, emphasis in original)

Furthermore, a realist view of universalising, in the context of a structured ontology, also helps address many critiques that are made to the capability approach. Crocker, for example, argues:

> Sen impales the BNA [Basic Needs Approach] on the horns of a dilemma. Either the BNA collapses into a commodity approach (with respect to certain capabilities) or it does not. If it does, then it will not be able to specify the commodities in a culturally invariant way. [...] If the BNA takes the other horn, however, then the 'needs of commodities may not be absolutely specifiable at all' [Sen, Resources Values and Development (1984:514)]. In contrast, Sen claims, we can specify absolute or culturally invariant deprivation and achievement in terms of capabilities. Unfortunately, Sen provides no argument for this contention, and it may be that needs and capabilities would be on the same boat.

(Crocker 1992:605)

Realist social theorising and social ontology can bring useful clarifications to this distinction, so that one can 'specify absolute or culturally invariant [or at least to some extent invariant] deprivation and achievement in terms of capabilities'. Furthermore, without a structured ontology, Sen's emphasis on the freedom of diverse individuals could easily take us back to a subjective welfarist (individualistic) approach to ethics, where the 'reason to value' a functioning would depend on a subjectivist assessment that could be at odds with a realist Aristotelian account of human functioning. Whilst it is true that subjective valuation will be undertaken by free, diverse and historically situated individuals (hence the existence of *epistemological relativism*), this valuation exercise refers to real capabilities and functionings, within an Aristotelian view of human functioning (hence the need of *ontological realism*).

9. Concluding remarks

Lawson's structured ontology helps us to reconcile (a) empirical diversity and (b) the existence of real and general structures: general structures and causal powers exist as intrinsic and essential to social entities, but these latter are empirically diverse because of the different ways they are intrinsically constituted or structured.

Because of this ontological distinction, general statements can be made about causal factors (such as underlying structures) while recognising the irreducibility of empirical diversity. This distinction can help us to evaluate the person–goods relationship in terms of the capabilities one has reason to value. Welfare analysis and social policy can then contain general (and possibly universal) prescriptions while recognising the uniqueness of human experiences and empirical diversity: for causal analysis of underlying structures, and structural transformation aimed at broadening the capability space, are issues to be addressed at an ontological level that is distinct from that of actualities and empirical phenomena.

Besides, this ontological distinction enables both freedom of human agents and the causal efficacy of structures to coexist, for now one can recognise the existence of both: (1) real (biological and social) structures that constrain or facilitate human agency; and (2) free and diverse individuals who continuously reproduce and/or transform these structures they draw upon. This realism about (biological and social) structures avoids falling back into subjective welfarist (and voluntaristic) perspectives, while the emphasis on freedom prevents us from supposing the reification of social structures.

The selection of a list of capabilities also becomes less ambiguous once these ontological underpinnings are clarified. The suggested perspective maintains Nussbaum's emphasis on (i) pursuing universal values, and (ii) an Aristotelian view of human functioning, potentials and capabilities (a view that Sen also recognises in his approach). However, to these important contributions of Nussbaum, I would add a conception of a structured ontology, which enables us to reconcile empirical diversity and individual freedom on the one hand, with the possibility of universalism and ontological realism on the other hand. One cannot proceed directly to substantive analysis without further scrutiny of the social processes that generate each concrete state of affairs.

Sen emphasises the need for public scrutiny and democratic discussion before the selection of concrete capabilities. Such public scrutiny can be fruitfully informed by the ontological analysis previously described. Nussbaum argues that 'Sen's "perspective of freedom" is too vague' (Nussbaum 2003:33), but it might be that such 'vagueness' implies not the absence of a practical goal, but rather the necessity of analysing each particular social context before identifying real needs and selecting relevant capabilities. The ontological distinction mentioned above shifts our attention to the general structures that cause capability reduction or enlargement, without neglecting Sen's view that diversity and freedom are irreducible constituents of social reality.

Note

1 For extremely valuable comments I am most grateful to Tony Lawson, Jochen Runde, Stephen Pratten and three anonymous referees. I gratefully acknowledge financial support from the Portuguese Foundation for Science and Technology (Fundação para a Ciência e a Tecnologia), given through the POCI (Programa Operacional Ciência e Inovação) 2010. First published in *Review of Social Economy*, 2007, Vol 65, No 3, 253–278.

Bibliography

Crocker, D. A. (1992), Functioning and Capability: The Foundations of Sen's and Nussbaum's Development Ethic, *Political Theory*, 20(4):584–612.

Damásio, A. (1994), *Descartes' Error: Emotion, Reason, and the Human Brain*, New York: G. P. Putnam's Sons.

Giddens, A. (1984), *The Constitution of Society*, Cambridge: Polity Press.

Laing, R. D. (1965), *The Divided Self*, Harmondsworth: Penguin.

Lawson, T. (1997), *Economics and Reality*, London: Routledge.

Lawson, T. (2003), *Reorienting Economics*, London: Routledge.

LeDoux, J. (1996), *The Emotional Brain: The Mysterious Underpinnings of Emotional Life*, New York: Simon & Schuster.

Lewis, P. A. (2000), Realism, Causation and the Problem of Social Structure, *Journal for the Theory of Social Behaviour*, 30(3):249–268.

Martins, N. (2006), Capabilities as Causal Powers, *Cambridge Journal of Economics*, 30(5):671–685.

Martins, N. (2007), Ethics, Ontology and Capabilities, *Review of Political Economy*, 19(1):37–53.

Nussbaum, M. C. (1992), Human Functioning and Social Justice: In Defense of Aristotelian Essentialism, *Political Theory*, 20(2):202–246.

Nussbaum, M. C. (2000), *Women and Human Development: The Capabilities Approach*, Cambridge: Cambridge University Press.

Nussbaum, M. C. (2003), Capabilities as Fundamental Entitlements: Sen and Social Justice, *Feminist Economics*, 9(2&3):33–60.

Polanyi, K. (1944), *The Great Transformation: The Political and Economic Origins of Our Time*, Boston: Beacon Press.

Putnam, H. (2002), *The Collapse of the Fact/Value Dichotomy and Other Essays*, Cambridge, MA, and London: Harvard University Press.

Rawls, J. (1971), *A Theory of Justice*, Cambridge, MA: The Belknap Press of Harvard University Press.

Sen, A. (1981), *Poverty and Famines: An Essay on Entitlement and Deprivation*, Oxford: Oxford University Press.

Sen, A. (1982), *Choice, Welfare and Measurement*, Oxford: Blackwell; Cambridge, MA: MIT Press.

Sen, A. (1984), *Resources, Values and Development*, Cambridge, MA, and London: Harvard University Press.

Sen, A. (1992), *Inequality Reexamined*, Oxford and New York: Oxford University Press.

Sen, A. (1999a [1985]), *Commodities and Capabilities*, Oxford and New York: Oxford University Press.

Sen, A. (1999b), *Development as Freedom*, Oxford: Oxford University Press.

Sen, A. (2002), *Rationality and Freedom*, Cambridge, MA: The Belknap Press of Harvard University Press.

PART VI

Elaborating conceptions of social reality

15 Ontology and the study of social reality: emergence, organisation, community, power, social relations, corporations, artefacts and money[1]

Tony Lawson

1. Introduction

Research activity or reports presented as contributions to social science are often met with suspicion if not outright derision as inevitably not contributing to, or constituting, real or proper science.[2] Underpinning this reception is a widespread apprehension that, unlike the sciences of 'nature', such a would-be or proclaimed (social) science does not have a proper 'object' of study, one with its own properties, its own dynamic, its own mode of being, requiring (and permitting) specialist study. If political commentators are sometimes interpreted as announcing that there is no such thing as society,[3] others, and not least philosophers of science, frequently charge, and not always without reason, that social theorists mostly invent their subject matter, creating theoretical entities that are not to be treated as realistic in any way, being without referents in the real world.[4]

What would it take to demonstrate that such negative receptions are unwarranted, that a meaningful social science is after all entirely feasible? A sufficient response, I take it, would be to identify causal factors, properties and/or entities that can reasonably be categorised as *social*, which possess their own distinct mode of being, yet are as real or objective[5] as the objects studied within the traditional 'natural' sciences, and in a relevant sense irreducible to the latter.

Primary candidates for features to be classified as social so conceived, I suggest, are those (if there are any) that arise out of, and depend necessarily upon, human interactions (clearly constituting a unique mode of being); those, if any, that *could not* exist in the absence of human beings and their doings.

My contention is not only that there are indeed such features reasonably so identified as social – and collectively constituting the social domain or social reality – but also that such features are just as real or objective as those of any other domain, bearing their own irreducible causal powers, justifying and indeed warranting their separate, specialised and relatively autonomous form of scientific study.[6] In other words, I contend that, whatever the achievements of 'social science' to date, the material conditions for a social science that is scientific in the sense of existing natural science are entirely present.

An apparent obstacle to my grounding this contention is the widely accepted doctrine of ontological naturalism, the thesis that everything can be explained in terms of natural causes. This is a non-dualist orientation that entails that even features such as life, choice and intentionality are integrated with the (rest of the) natural world and not composed of some separate (non-naturalistic) stuff. From the perspective of this doctrine it may seem unlikely that many of the usual categories of social theory can be accommodated, not least those such as social position, social power and social relation that figure centrally in my own conception of social reality. Instead, from the perspective of ontological naturalism, it may well be held that such categories at best serve as placeholders for features that can be more properly described in terms of the traditional objects of some (non-social) natural science.

I too accept the doctrine of ontological naturalism. My objective here is not to resist it, but to suggest that this doctrine is not after all contravened by the conception of social reality I have previously defended, despite the latter including the noted causal features, features that are held both to have a distinct mode of being and also to be (in relevant senses to be defined below) *ir*reducible to phenomena studied in the traditional 'natural' sciences. Thus I shall be defending an account whereby social reality is seen to be distinct from, and yet dependent upon, non-social material.

1.1 A philosophical contrast

The systematic consideration of issues such as these falls under the head of social ontology, the study of the nature of social being. This is a branch of philosophy that I believe to be overly neglected in both philosophy and science (see, e.g., Tony Lawson, 1994, 1997, 2003; Edward Fullbrook, 2009).

This neglect is not total, however. One contributor who in recent times has written explicitly on social ontology and in a sustained and systematic way is the philosopher John Searle (e.g., 1995, 1999, 2010), and here I advance my arguments by way of initially making some comparisons between Searle's position and my own. For although in our respective contributions we focus largely on the same set of issues and generate results and frameworks that, in very many ways, are extremely similar, in certain fundamental respects relevant to my concerns here our positions also appear very different, at least at first sight.

An immediate relevant difference concerns the manner in which Searle and I have gone about our theorising, and in particular our contrasting starting points. The latter especially reflect the different priorities given to the constraint of ontological naturalism.

My own approach is multifaceted, but a central component has been to proceed by first identifying generalised features of experience concerning (aspects of) human interactions and then to question whether any of their preconditions (i.e. the conditions that must be in place for these experienced interactions and aspects to be possible) include those that are additionally irreducible *outcomes* of human interactions (and if so to explore their natures, etc.). If such human-interaction-dependent features are so identified, then, being causally efficacious conditions of (further) human interaction, they can be accepted as real, and being products of human interaction they are seen additionally to be social. The conception of social ontology I defend (and elaborate upon in due course below) is to a significant extent a result of such endeavour (see, e.g., Lawson, 2003, especially ch. 2).

If my approach might be appropriately described as *working backwards* (from actual social interactions to their conditions of possibility), Searle's alternative is perhaps best described as *working forwards* – by way of building on the results of natural sciences regarded as the most sound. Specifically, according to Searle, there are 'two features of our conception of reality that are not up for grabs' and within which any theory of society must fit: 'the atomic theory of matter and the evolutionary theory of biology' (Searle, 1995, p. 6).[7]

Searle's mode of theorising, then, is not only consistent with, but also guided by, the constraint of *ontological naturalism*. By explicit intent Searle is concerned to understand how anything that might be termed 'human society' has arisen out of material that is traditionally studied by the natural sciences. Whether or not Searle holds to there being something distinct about social reality, it is clear that dependence and continuity are stressed throughout.

If it is the case that by starting from human interactions and working backwards in the manner briefly sketched I have given insufficient explicit attention to ontological naturalism in previous contributions, the latter, as I say, is nevertheless a thesis I broadly accept. My previous neglect of a naturalistic assessment of my position is, thus, to repeat, something I seek explicitly to rectify here.

1.2 Emergence

In naturalistic discussions of how novel elements or properties come about in any domain of reality, a critical analytical category is that of *emergence*. It is a term used to express the appearance of novelty, or something previously absent or unprecedented. It figures in Searle's writings as well as in my own. And whilst there are numerous competing accounts of emergence to be found in the literature, it is clear that both Searle and I seek non-dualist conceptions (i.e. that do not portray social or any emergent reality as consisting in non-naturalistic material, totally separated from other material). Even so, it is precisely over issues covered by the category emergence that, *prima facie* at least, Searle and I seemingly part company the most in elaborating our basic frameworks. Let me briefly indicate how.

Typically, emergence is conceived in terms of entities and their properties found at a particular level of reality, but composed out of entities (components) existing at a lower level of reality. Specifically, an entity and its properties are said to be *emergent* from some lower (or different) level where they arise through the relational organising of lower-level elements and the emergent properties in question are not possessed by any of the lower-level elements that get to be organised.

The foregoing is sufficient to give a general (non-dualist) conception of emergence. Searle and I and seemingly most others who advance emergentist positions accept this conception as far as it goes, with Searle referring to it as 'emergence1' (Searle, 1992, p. 111).

Emergence so understood however is not an explanatory term but rather one that marks the spots where (diachronic) explanatory work remains to be undertaken to reveal how the higher-level entities do (or have) emerge(d).[8] In particular the above conception of emergence leaves open the precise nature of the relationship between higher-level emergent causal powers and the powers of the lower-level components.

Whether or not it is built into the idea of emergence *per se*, I additionally hold to the notion that although any higher-level emergent entity and its properties are conditioned by and dependent upon lower-level elements or components, they are nevertheless synchronically both causally and ontologically (and not merely taxonomically and epistemologically) irreducible to them.

At first sight at least, Searle, as we will see, appears to reject this latter thesis of (synchronic) causal and ontological irreducibility. If this is indeed a difference between us, then it is a significant one. For it is the composite or stronger view additionally positing (synchronic) causal and ontological irreducibility (a conception which Searle terms 'emergence2') that, when applied to social phenomena specifically, grounds most securely my assessment that a relatively autonomous social science is entirely feasible.

In fact, as far as I can discern, most philosophers prepared at all to defend non-dualist accounts of emergence appear to disallow causal and ontological irreducibility. Such stances are understandable. For, as already noted, any notion that starting from the atomic theory of matter we are somehow able to end up with irreducible items such as social relations, with their own equally irreducible causal powers, can easily seem altogether far too mysterious. It is thus easy to suppose that any claim that I have found space for such supposedly irreducible social causes in my own framework means that I have, after all, exempted myself from the constraint of producing an account that is coherent with ontological naturalism.

As I say, I do propose to provide an explicitly naturalistic account of my position here. But in so doing I shall maintain the stronger view of emergence that posits causal and ontological *ir*reducibility, nevertheless, and take the opportunity to indicate that there is nothing especially mysterious involved in accepting it. I shall argue indeed that it is quite consistent with our best accounts of the physical sciences, at least as I understand them.[9]

To achieve these ends, however, does require my running through aspects of my analysis of emergence in greater detail than I have hitherto. This, and specifically a defence of causal and ontological irreducibility in the context of emergence, is the focus of the following section. Whether Searle and I really do disagree on the relevant issues here (a matter that I shall explore), it is certainly the case that Searle's seemingly opposed formulations provide a useful foil or contrast at this point, enabling me more easily to draw out and explore the issues I regard as most significant for the questions being addressed. In Section 2 the discussion will focus on emergent reality in general, without specific reference to any putative social domain.

In Section 3 I turn to argue that the version of emergence that I am defending equally underpins the development of phenomena that can reasonably be defended as social. In this part of the discussion the challenge I take up is to run through my previously presented account of specific social emergents (see, e.g., Lawson, 1997, 2003), not least my account of social relations, powers and positions, to demonstrate their coherence with the doctrine of ontological naturalism.

In Section 4 I briefly indicate that the conception to that point set forth, which focuses mainly on human beings in social relations, also extends, in important respects, to the analysis of inanimate social objects, including artefacts and (aspects at least of) money.

2. Emergence, reduction and organisation

At the heart of the competing conceptions of emergence under consideration here, then, are apparent differences regarding possibilities of certain forms of reduction, namely causal and ontological. Actually, in wider discussions regarding the nature of emergence, the focus is often on causal reduction alone. Nevertheless, both forms are pertinent here and clearly the meanings of both warrant elaboration.

Searle (1992) himself provides explicit formulations of each. Of *causal reduction* Searle writes:

> This is a relation between any two types of things that can have causal powers, where the existence and a fortiori the causal powers of the reduced entity are shown to be entirely explainable in terms of the causal powers of the reducing phenomena.
>
> (Searle, 1992, p. 114)

And Searle's conception of *ontological reduction* is a situation in which 'objects of certain types can be shown to consist in nothing other than objects of different types' (Searle, 1992, p. 112).

If the account of emergence that I am defending is such that the possibilities both of causal and of ontological reduction are, in the senses just noted, foreclosed, for Searle not only is this seemingly not the case but causal reduction follows automatically from emergence1 and such a reduction usually leads itself to an ontological reduction. Thus after reviewing numerous examples, Searle summarises his findings as follows:

> The general principle in such cases appears to be this: Once a property is seen to be *emergent1*, we automatically get a causal reduction, and that leads to an ontological reduction, by redefinition if necessary. The general trend in ontological reductions that have a scientific basis is toward greater generality, objectivity, and redefinition in terms of underlying causation.
> So far so good.
>
> (Ibid., p. 116)

Searle goes on to argue, however, that although consciousness is emergent1 and so, by his reasoning, causally reducible, it is also somewhat exceptional in being at the same time ontologically *irreducible*.

My seemingly somewhat more radical contention is that whilst consciousness is indeed ontologically irreducible, it is, like everything else regarded by Searle as emergent1, actually also causally irreducible. But then my assessment is that every emergent phenomenon is both ontologically and causally irreducible. Moreover, if *prima facie* paradoxically, I do also want to suggest that in maintaining this contention my position is ultimately not so different from that of Searle. That is, despite explicit statements such as those noted above, I am not convinced that Searle is ultimately appropriately represented as supporting causal and ontological reductionism at all.

2.1 Emergence and causal and ontological irreducibility

So how do I propose to defend a version of emergence that resists the theses of causal and ontological reductions in particular? Furthermore, how do I propose to do so in a manner in which the resulting conception remains consistent with (ontological) naturalism and thereby (or otherwise) avoids the charge of mysteriousness that tends to accompany claims of strong emergence? Further still, how do I propose to sustain a non-causally and non-ontologically reductionist account of emergence in a manner that implicates Searle as holding to a similar thesis?

Before setting out the argument it may be useful to emphasise the distinction between *synchronic* (at a point in time) and *diachronic* (over time) forms of reduction and explanation. I doubt that many commentators who accept ontological naturalism deny that where higher-level features have arisen, there will have been a historical process whereby these features came about. That is, there is always a historical explanation of higher-level phenomena to be uncovered and so *in that sense* there is a possibility of a historical or diachronic reduction.

This anyway is not in contention here. Rather, the debates over stronger versus weaker forms of emergence are concerned with the possibility of synchronic (not diachronic) reducibility, with whether higher-level elements or features or powers can be reduced to lower-level ones *alone and at a given point in time*. This is the way the issue is framed by Searle above, for example when he speaks of causal reducibility in terms in which 'the existence and a fortiori the causal powers of the reduced entity are shown to be *entirely explainable* in terms of the causal powers of the reducing phenomena' (emphasis added) and of ontological reducibility in terms whereby 'objects of certain types can be shown to consist in *nothing other than* objects of different types' (emphasis added). It is the possibility of such *synchronic* causal and ontological reductions that I am disputing and indeed rejecting.

On what basis do I do so? In quoting Searle in the last paragraph I use italics to emphasise the expressions 'entirely explainable' and 'nothing other than' just because it is these over which, at first sight at least, we seemingly disagree and which are essential to a position that qualifies as reductionist here. I do not deny that the causal powers of lower-level phenomena are contributory to higher-level ones or that these lower-level elements are components of higher-level entities (albeit perhaps after modification, as, say, when the electrons of atoms are rearranged if two combine to form a molecule). But there is always more going on.

An emergent property or power is the property or power of something (that possesses it), i.e. it is a property of an object, entity or element, where the latter is usually formed by way of a combination of pre-existing (lower-level) elements or entities. On this there is seemingly widespread agreement. However, the components of emergent entities (unlike members of aggregate collections) do what they do *qua* components only because of the manner in which they are organised (arranged, structured or related) as parts of the whole. Quick examples are the properties of liquidity of any material, the affordances of a home, the movement of the car, the validity or conclusion of a deductive argument. It is precisely when, and due to the manner in which, the lower-level elements are (perhaps with or through modification) so organised that emergent entities with emergent powers are feasible, and component parts make the contribution they do to the emergent result.

I do not think this is especially denied in the philosophical literature. However, in discussions of emergence, two sets of phenomena tend, between them, to receive the dominant if not the sole emphasis. The first set consists of (emergent) entities or 'elements' with powers of efficient causality conventionally described as lying at the higher level. The second consists of entities or 'elements' with powers of efficient causality conventionally located at the lower level, and which (perhaps through modification) come to comprise components of emergent higher-level entities.

I have already noted that missing from the analysis is any account of the manner in which the lower-level phenomena become *organised* (*arranged, related or structured*) in the process through which the higher-order entities emerge. This is an absence that is significantly masked by the repeated use of the noted categories. A result is that this relational organisation, which entails an arrangement of lower-level elements, is very often left largely under-elaborated or little discussed, and treated implicitly as part of the lower level and mostly as a given.

My contention is simply that the organisation of the lower-level phenomena is itself always a novel phenomenon, emerging *along with* any higher-level totality. In other words, the relational-organisation itself must be regarded as a higher- (not lower-) level feature, and indeed a causal property of the emergent totality or entity. Typically it is a form of formal causation. Think of the components of a building, comprising, say, bricks, mortar, blocks of wood, panes of glass and so forth. Imagine a particular building dismantled and its bricks and other components then rearranged differently, and perhaps randomly or blindly. It is easy to imagine configurations whereby the house, along with house properties of affording shelter, etc., would no longer emerge. The arrangement, the configuration or organising relations of the components, makes a difference. It is a form of causation; it is formal causation. It emerges along with any emergent totality and indeed is a property of the latter. And it is easy to see that the arrangement of lower-level components is a causal feature of higher-level entities generally (for an elaboration of this latter assessment see Lawson, 2012).

It is a recognition that organising structure is an emergent higher-level phenomenon, as we will see, that grounds my claim that emergent phenomena are in the relevant sense ontologically and causally irreducible.

I should perhaps quickly note here that the term organisation has two inflections. In processes of emergence the lower-level elements become organised as components of the emergent entity or whole, and so we can refer to the organisation *of* the components. But the category organisation is also regularly employed to refer to the totality including the lower-level elements that have become (re)organised.[10] Hopefully it will be clear from context which meaning is intended here. When the term refers to the emergent entity or totality, i.e. when organisation is a whole or a *system*, then it includes not just the lower-level elements that (perhaps with or through modification) have become components, along with their context, but also an organising structure comprising emergent relations between components (as well as, of course, others that bind these components to features in their environment).

2.2 The impossibility of synchronic reducibility

Once (or where) it is recognised that the emergent phenomenon is a system in which components are constrained to act within organising structures, the argument against ontological reducibility is straightforward. For if, as I am suggesting, the emergent entity or system includes organising relations that are external to the lower-level elements, then the totality is necessarily ontologically irreducible to the lower-level components alone, components which in fact become organised (and, to repeat, thereby very often indeed being significantly modified[11]) in the process of emergence.

The argument against causal reducibility is no less straightforward. For it is clear enough that any emergent higher-order forms of efficient causation are precisely powers of the emergent system, whole or organisation, and depend as much on the organising structures and relations as on the lower-level components that the latter organise.

I am not sure that put like this my claim is especially contentious. Far too often, though, the organising structure, despite involving relations that are externally related to lower-level components, is left implicit and taken for granted in the relevant discussions.[12] I am suggesting that this neglect of attention to organising structure is unhelpful at best, and serves almost unwittingly to deflect challenges to the dominant presumption that the causal powers of emergent phenomena are somehow always reducible to the causal powers of lower-level phenomena alone.

Once recognition of organising structure as a higher-level phenomenon is made fully explicit, I think it follows straightforwardly that synchronic reductions are not feasible.

2.3 Searle

Is this really a very different position from that of Searle? I am not so sure. Certainly there do at first sight appear to be very clear differences. For as we have seen, Searle explicitly embraces the doctrine of causal reducibility according to which causal powers of any higher-level phenomenon are said to be 'entirely explainable' in terms of the causal powers of lower-level components, as well as the doctrine of ontological reducibility, according to which 'objects of certain types can be shown to consist in nothing other than objects of different types'.

We also find, however, that a notion of organisation or system does usually figure as a presupposition in Searle's more detailed formulations, albeit as one that is usually left largely unexamined.

Thus when in his 1992 book (that most discusses these issues) Searle introduces the notion of 'emergence', he writes explicitly in terms of 'causally emergent system features':

But some other system features cannot be figured out just from the composition of the elements and environmental relations; they have to be explained in terms of the causal interactions amongst the elements. Let's call these 'causally emergent system features'. Solidity, liquidity, and transparency are examples of causally emergent system features.

(Searle, 1992, p. 111)

Although in using the category system here Searle does not write explicitly in terms of the relational structuring of components, when elaborating a little on the example of solidity he adds:

Thus, for example, some objects are solid and this has causal consequences: solid objects are impenetrable by other objects, they are resistant to pressure, etc. But these causal powers can be causally explained by the causal powers of vibratory movements of molecules in lattice structures.

(Ibid., p. 114)

We can see then that this statement does not amount to reducing solidity to the causal powers of molecules alone, for emergent organisation in the form of lattice structures is clearly essential. Whatever Searle's formal claims about causal reductions, it seems clear enough that any emergent causality also depends upon the organisation of lower-level phenomena, where the former is irreducible to the latter.

I am suggesting, then, that when Searle, on accepting causal reduction, insists that any higher-level causal powers are 'entirely explainable in terms of the causal powers of the reducing phenomena' this may yet be correct, *but only to the extent that we add the qualification*: 'when these latter phenomena, perhaps through a process of modification, are organised via structures or relations that are themselves an emergent part of the higher-level emergent entity'.

I am suggesting, too, that Searle appears to be accepting the latter qualification at least up until (though perhaps without also accepting) the point that the organising structures are interpreted as an emergent part of the higher-level emergent entity.

In other words, the real difference between us, if there is one, is seemingly not over the question of whether organisation plays an explanatory role (in addition to the explanatory contribution of the components) but over what sort of recognition or emphasis or status is to be given to the category of organisation. I believe organisation has to be seen as itself an emergent phenomenon (requiring diachronic explanation), and one that significantly forecloses the possibility of (synchronic) causal and ontological reduction. Searle, at times at least, seems to take relational-organisation as something like an implicit lower-level background factor, one that is explicitly acknowledged when writing abstractly of causally emergent ('system') features, but neglected when defending causal reductions.

In short, I am suggesting that in Searle's conception of emergence there is a mostly present but underplayed referencing of a relational structure (organising the lower-level components) in his accounting for higher-level powers that interest him, and that it is this underplaying of organisational relations that allows or leads him to sanction the idea that causal and ontological reductions are (almost) everywhere feasible. In contrast (and whatever may be Searle's position), I am suggesting that the organising structure of an emergent entity is itself an ever-present emergent feature. And because any emergent powers of efficient causation possessed by the emergent whole are dependent upon the organising structure, synchronic causal and ontological reduction as understood throughout are proscribed.

2.4 Historical emergence

Let me elaborate my argument a little further. I have acknowledged that there is always a historical explanation to any object or property that emerges. Reality is seen to be processual in the sense (or to the extent) that novel entities continually arise out of, and through (re)organisations of, what was there before (albeit with the latter possibly transformed in the process). So, to repeat, a full understanding of any emergent form of reality requires concrete (diachronic) causal accounts of emergent organisational order. In other words, a significant task facing any science is to provide detailed empirically informed accounts of how, in different domains, relatively stable organisations of lower-level phenomena do arise (or have arisen).

Very often this will be no easy task. All such emergent order somehow results in the face of, and despite, the second law of thermal dynamics, according to which everything tends to entropy or basically messiness. It thus seems clear enough that emergent order must arise and act *via the workings of* this law, rather than somehow negating or acting against it. In fact, it appears to be the case in many situations and levels of complexity that emergent organisation is essentially a contingent configuration that is left over after thermodynamic and numerous other processes have worked to eliminate the vast majority of a priori potential configurations of lower-level properties. These are issues I explore more systematically elsewhere.[13] For now I merely report that in all cases examined the emergence of the totality and of the organising structure are simultaneous and linked developments. Because of this, higher-order properties are not synchronically reducible to lower-level components *alone*. And this is the form of reducibility in which the relevant debates (over the nature of emergent properties) have occurred and which ultimately matters most if we are interested in questions of academic disciplinary autonomy.

2.5 Modern physics

Though I cannot elaborate further here on substantive processes of emergence, my concern not only to adhere to the doctrine of naturalism but also to be seen to be doing so, does perhaps mean that I need to indicate how I suppose the anti-(synchronic) reduction thesis I am defending coheres with (or anyway is not obviously inconsistent with) those results of modern natural science (particularly of physics) that appear most to challenge the conception I am defending.

Obviously this is a huge topic and, since the development of quantum theory especially, physics itself, as well as its philosophy, are areas of high contestation. So it is impossible to be comprehensive or inclusive here, or indeed be more than indicative. Even so there is an onus on me, I suspect, to at least touch on the manner in which I believe coherence can be sustained, at least against the seemingly strongest challenge from reductionism; and I do believe the antireductionist thesis is no less coherent with the results or findings of modern physics than is the doctrine of synchronic reductionism. So in support of this latter contention, and with the foregoing qualifications in mind, let me very briefly focus on particle physics specifically, which may seem to provide the biggest challenge to the position here defended.

Proponents of the thesis that emergent phenomena are synchronically reducible have understandably been especially interested in seeking out any fundamental elements from which *all* others ultimately have emerged, and to which *all* are ultimately reducible. Particles have traditionally been regarded as the primary candidates for any such fundamental elements. And in particle physics, specifically, the categories of *elementary particle* or *fundamental particle* have been fashioned to express just such elements. These categories are applied to phenomena interpreted as particles but not known to have any substructure, i.e. they are believed *not* to be made up of smaller particles. With elementary particles believed not to have structure – and in the *standard model*, quarks, leptons and gauge bosons are currently regarded as elementary particles[14] – they tend to be interpreted as amongst the basic building blocks of the universe from which everything else is ultimately formed. From such a standpoint it is easy to suppose that only causation at the level of elementary particles is real or of proper scientific interest.

Clearly, from the alternative perspective I am defending, the latter set of inferences, if attractive to many, is not sustainable simply because, even in such a scenario, the emergence of any higher-level causal properties would still depend upon the organisation of lower-level elements, even supposedly fundamental ones. Thus even here any higher-level causation, being a real property of emergent forms of organisation, would, like the emergent organisation from which it derives, be synchronically irreducible and so warranting of scientific investigation at its own level, no matter how fundamental the elements so organised.

But as much or more to the point, any supposition that it is causation only at the level of elementary particles that is real or of proper scientific interest is no longer supported even within leading branches of modern physics, just because, strictly speaking, there are no particles, at least not as conventionally understood. Specifically, according to quantum field theory, or at least its seemingly more explanatorily powerful interpretations,[15] if there is anything that underpins everything else it is quantum field processes,[16] and the phenomena that appear to be particles are the resulting effects of the quantisation of field excitatory activity. The particle-like elements are in fact said to be 'quanta of excitation' or 'field quanta'. As such they are effectively emergent forms of organisation displaying particle-like behaviour.

Organisation, in other words, is found to be a fundamental category and a feature of emergent phenomena even in modern physics concerned with 'particles'; particle-like phenomena are but emergent features, i.e. essentially organisations, of quantum field processes (although they are not so much like little balls as organised ripples in a field).

Moreover, according to quantum field theory, at least as I interpret it, there is also little reason to concentrate on searching out fundamental forms of organisation (to ground a reductionist programme). For, quantum field processes seemingly occur at many different and perhaps all levels, at many different scales and degrees of complexity. It follows that although there are, or can be, relations of dependency between organisations at different levels, there need be no ultimate or base level in quantum field theory, and so no reason for asserting that any one pattern or organisation of process is more fundamental, elementary, genuine, real or basic than any other; all remain of potential interest to science.

So, even from the perspective of modern quantum theory, the basic reductionist thesis can be challenged, and a stronger version of emergence of the sort I am defending appears grounded.

2.6 Searle again

Interestingly, I find resonances of all this once more in the contributions of Searle. Specifically, in a chapter preceding the one in which he indicates his preferred notion of emergence, Searle (1992) discusses the nature of the physical phenomena of the atomic theory of matter. He acknowledges of these phenomena that it is 'convenient, though not entirely accurate, to call [them] "particles"' (1992, p. 86). He notes, too, that when these are not interfered with they in fact behave more like waves. And he suggests that such 'particles' in all the examples considered 'are organized into larger systems' (p. 86), adding:

> Essential to the explanatory apparatus of atomic theory is not only the idea that big systems are made up of little systems, but that many

features of the big ones can be causally explained by the behaviour of the little ones.

(Searle, 1992, p. 87)

Here I primarily want to emphasise Searle's apparatus of systems or organisations consisting of (organised) subsystems. Of course Searle is also supposing of organisations or systems that 'many features of the big ones can be causally explained by the behaviour of the little ones'. As noted above, I hold that this is correct *only* if we add the qualification: when these latter 'little ones', perhaps through a process of modification, are organised via structures and relations that are themselves an emergent part of the higher-level emergent system or organisation. But putting that qualification aside, it seems that Searle too is of the view that everything is emergent organisation.

2.7 Entities

If emergent organisation is seemingly characteristic of all reality, and if features of reality are continually being reorganised (as well as de- or dis-organised), it appears that everything is effectively in process. From this perspective it is perhaps opportune to clarify what, if anything, taken-for-granted categories such as *things* or *entities* might mean. At this point, in other words, I should probably state explicitly what I have in effect been supposing these categories to mean throughout the discussion of emergence. I suggest that a category such as *entity* is appropriately used just to express (or can be thought of as expressing) a *relatively stable* actualisation of a feasible emergent organisation or system of underlying processes.

The latter clearly do abound. Field quanta can be relatively stable, and physicists do reasonably continue to use the term 'particle' to refer to such stable organisations that reveal 'particle-like' behaviour. But examples more immediately relevant to social analyses include human beings, artefacts and, I will argue below, human society or anyway social communities and the like, which are simply relatively stable social organisations.

Such a response does prompt the further question of what might be meant here by the notion of organisational *stability*. Abstractly speaking, stable organisation comes in at least two forms or 'systems', the first of which we might refer to as an environmentally closed, or equilibrium, system, and the second of which we can label an environmentally open, or far-from-equilibrium, system. Briefly put, equilibrium systems are stable if there are no disturbances from the outside environment; far-from-equilibrium systems require perpetual inputs from the environment to endure and be stable. A naturalistic example of the former is perhaps an atom and of the latter a home fire (or a garden bonfire) that needs constant inputs of oxygen and (possibly varying forms of) fuel.

Notice that there is no reason in principle why a far-from-equilibrium system cannot evolve in a relatively stable fashion over time, due to a (possibly gradual) transformation in its manner of organisation and/or to variation (possibly systematic) in the nature of the stability-facilitating external inputs. I think it is evident that such is the case with both living beings and human societies. I come to discuss the social realm explicitly below. For now it can be noted that widespread organisational stability is evident but, wherever it is found, is always warranting of explanation.

2.8 Naturalism

That the account defended, at least in terms of the aspects so far touched upon, coheres with naturalism should by now be clear. But let me address the issue explicitly. As far as I can discern, dismissals of 'stronger' accounts of (synchronic) emergence as being somewhat mysterious and inevitably non-naturalistic turn on two central presuppositions. The first is just that the organisation of lower-level phenomena is itself (implicitly) part of the lower level or otherwise something not warranting explicit attention. The second is the assumed completeness of contemporary accounts, or the asserted causal closure, of the physical world at lower levels, a position seemingly accepted by Searle, as well as others (e.g., Jaegwon Kim, 1993A, 1993B).

It follows from the latter presupposition alone, if true, that the stronger version of emergence positing irreducible novel causal powers must be untenable. But it is the former presupposition that prevents the second presumption from encountering any effective challenge.

I am suggesting, however, that there is a sense in which the lower-level *components* indeed do *not* contain all that is causally relevant; and this is precisely because higher-level properties depend in part on how the lower-level components come to be organised involving relations external to the components organised, where this organisation is itself part of the higher level. On this conception, although nothing can emerge or happen that was not in some sense already possible, the future is entirely open and possibilities of emergence that are realised are so contingently.

To so argue, however, is not to adopt some inescapably anti-naturalistic stance; I am suggesting nothing here that violates the thesis that all explanations are in terms of natural causes. Nor is there anything particularly mysterious about the picture conveyed. Moreover, I am not even proposing that there is anything to be added to the picture that is not already presupposed by opponents of the view of strong emergence. For it is clear that even if the organisation of the lower-level elements be recognised as a higher-level emergent phenomenon, *it remains something that is already included as part of the standard naturalistic picture*, albeit something that is typically left implicit and treated as a lower-level feature. If the organisation (of lower-level elements) is not viewed as a challenge to naturalism when regarded as a lower-level feature or anyway left implicit and undiscussed, this must presumably remain the case if instead it is interpreted itself as a higher-level emergent phenomenon.

It remains the case, then, that the account of strong emergence I am defending, both in principle and at least on the issues covered so far (I turn to the specifics of social emergence below), is quite consistent with ontological naturalism.

I have argued throughout that emergent phenomena are neither causally nor ontologically reducible. I have acknowledged, however, that the differences between the position taken here and those of contributors accepting the feasibility of such reductions may not be as large as they first appear. Perhaps in some cases the differences on the matters discussed are even mostly presentational. I suspect not, but even presentational differences matter. For the form of presentation can have practical consequences, not least to those interested in examining the possibility of, and doing, social science. For if my own account is correct then it follows that all forms of established science have objects of study that are synchronically irreducible emergent forms of organisations-in-process. And a putative social science is likely to be no different. Indeed, I will argue below that this is so. But it is important to recognise first that this is indeed the appropriate formulation if the possibility of a social science is a motivating question and issue. And this is something easily masked where relational-organisation is treated as a lower-level given.

I fear, too, that accounts of emergent causal powers that treat the relational-organisation as a background given will tend to result in a failure to examine how this organisation, itself an emergent phenomenon, not only comes into being (morphogenesis) but, of especial significance to understanding, how it persists when in fact it does (morphostasis). An account of the mode of reproduction of social organisational structure, indeed, is a feature I believe to be vital to any sustainable account of social ontology, a matter to which I turn shortly below.

To sum up the argument so far, I have suggested that philosophical rejections of stronger conceptions of emergence are due in part to an inadequately elaborated ontology, to a failure to incorporate or emphasise process organisation or organisation-in-process sufficiently, and specifically as a central form of emergent. However, once it is recognised that in standard accounts of emergence the actual relational-organisation of 'lower-level' elements is usually everywhere presupposed, the move I have made here is I believe almost unavoidable and perhaps even trivial, albeit one that is nevertheless consequential. The more challenging task, as I see it, is to give explanatorily powerful accounts of actual emergents.

It is with this latter undertaking in mind that I turn now to focus on the social realm specifically, to analyse the nature of society or social reality. In particular my aim is to demonstrate that the emergentist conception I have elaborated in earlier contributions (Lawson, 1997, 2003; Fullbrook, 2009) is not only sustainable but consistent with naturalism, and indeed consistent with the specific (naturalistic) account of emergence elaborated above.

3. Social systems

I turn, then, to the study of social reality and examine whether a would-be social science has a legitimate claim to be dealing with an emergent (irreducible) object or field of study.

Basic to everyday and indeed all human life is human interaction. I take it that this is not contentious. Here I want to elaborate aspects of its nature. A first property to note is that modern interaction takes place mostly within communities. I will (further) elaborate the notion of *community* in due course (once relevant additional categories of what is found to be a highly interdependent social reality are developed), but for now it will suffice to conceive it as an identifiable, restricted, relatively enduring (if typically evolving) coherent grouping of people who share some set of (usually equally evolving) concerns.

So conceived a specific community may or may not be regional, and where it is regional it can be pan-national or very highly localised or situated anywhere on a spectrum spanned by such cases. Different communities may, and clearly do, overlap, intersect and/or nest. We, each of us, interact with others within many different communities simultaneously. I take it that, pitched, as it is, at this relatively high level of abstraction, the observation that interaction occurs in communities so conceived is not especially contentious.

A second feature of human interaction to emphasise is that it is structured by the prevalence of what can be termed collective practices. By a *collective practice* I mean a specific way of going on that:

1   is recognised, over an interval in time and within some specific community, as the *accepted* way of proceeding with regard to achieving a particular outcome;
2   involves the *participation* of all members of the community, either through their direct adherence to the given accepted way of proceeding, or through their acting in other ways that facilitate, presuppose or otherwise maintain the latter, including avoiding intentionally impeding the actions of those more directly participating.

Let me immediately stress that by describing a collective practice as an *accepted* way of proceeding or going on, the manner in which I am interpreting the category of *acceptance* here has nothing to do with preference, agreement, support or approval, etc. Indeed, many individual participants in a collective practice may be particularly dissatisfied. Rather, the term indicates a way of proceeding that is in fact widely adhered to or observed or recognised by members of a specific community, whatever its intrinsic appeal. As such the term acceptance here, a form of collective or community acceptance (in contrast to the more evaluative notion of *individual acceptance* that I consider in due course), is effectively a status. It carries, and rests upon, community-wide recognition and serves to constitute a way of proceeding as the done way.

So a collective practice, put differently, is precisely a way of proceeding that (implicitly) has attached to it the status of being a (collectively) accepted way of proceeding within a community. It indicates something that is the case. Various ways of proceeding might be imagined that could serve any outcome that (whether or not by design) happens to be facilitated through generalised conformity with the accepted way, i.e. with the specific collective practice; but for whatever reason, one way has turned out to be the way that is generally observed.

Driving on the left side of the road in the contemporary UK might be a simple example of a way of proceeding that is recognised within a community. Using specific words or sentences to convey particular intended meanings is another. So, too, is queuing in a specific aisle to pay for goods at a local store.

Notice that there is always a range of behaviours consistent with any given collective practice. Typically, moreover, a collective practice will encompass several components or subpractices. Thus the accepted way of shopping at a local store may involve using a metal basket or trolley (provided by the store) as a means for carrying selected goods before purchase; queuing in a specific aisle; paying in one of several accepted ways to a person sitting behind a counter; and so on. But all are part of the collective practice of shopping at the store.

Notice, too, that as a precondition both for a collective practice to be recognised as such, i.e. as a way of proceeding that is accepted within a community, and so of successful participation, individuals within the community must have a sense of the scope or boundaries of the relevant community and recognise any such practice as in effect the property of that community.

Very often practices such as those I am discussing are referred to as social conventions. But given the many very different and often contested (and frequently inconsistent) interpretations of the category 'convention' that are to be found in the social theory literature, and a desire not to be side-tracked by debates over how this particular category is best employed, I shall stick with the notion of collective practice.[17]

A feature of social interaction, then, is the widespread conformity to collective practices, where the latter are everywhere to be found in human societies. I take this assessment also to be reasonably non-contentious; the ubiquity of collective practices, along with widespread conformity to the range of behaviours consistent with each, is seemingly a generalised feature of experience.

3.1 Coordination

It is clear that these accepted ways of going on, however they originally came into being, can be, and very often are (in being so 'accepted'), functional in the sense of facilitating what is, in effect, a form of social life. In particular they can and do serve to coordinate social interaction, by indicating to all would-be (and permitted-to-be) participants within a specific community how, amongst various conceivable ways of proceeding to a certain end, things are in fact done by other members of a community, so facilitating relative stability and thereby a degree of predictability.

In making these latter observations I do not wish to imply a functionalist *explanatory* orientation. The fact that a specific set of collective processes may be functional to a particular outcome or form of life, in particular through facilitating coordination and predictability, does not necessitate that this is their explanation, the reason they came into being. It can be, but this is not an essential feature of collective practices; a chance meeting, say, repeated and then further repeated, and so on, can result in a regularised set of originally unforeseen and unintended collective practices.[18]

The point I do want to focus on, however, is that whatever may be the manner in which specific collective practices come into being, and whatever their *formal* status, they are widely to be found; individuals everywhere (whether consciously or otherwise) regularly use the a posteriori (relative) stability and widespread acceptance of such practices as a basis on which to get by, to form expectations and to decide appropriate action in order to coordinate with the actions of others.

3.2 Normativity

It is no doubt in large part because collective practices, where they are successfully produced and reproduced, are functional in various ways, not least in contributing to social co-ordination, stability and predictability, that the idea of acceptance not only expresses the done thing (or things) but usually also carries connotations of normativity. Indeed, collective practices are often referred to just as norms.

Normativity arises because, or when, the noted indicative aspect of any collective practice is also interpreted as stipulative, as indicating how an individual *ought* to proceed. Collective practices, in order to facilitate coordination, etc., need to persist and this usually *requires* that relevant individuals conform to (various interacting sets of) them.

It seems clear that through an upbringing in modern communities we all learn not merely to recognise the widespread prevalence of collective practices (even, or perhaps especially, as infants we do so in learning accepted ways to eat, drink, speak and even sleep, etc.), but also to respect them *qua* collective practices, to conform to, and so help to preserve, those of the communities we 'inhabit' (irrespective of any support or opposition to content); and to seek out knowledge of collective practices of other communities we may have the occasion to 'visit' – in order to conform.

The normative aspect of collective practices thus gives rise to the notion of *obligations*, a category that, along with the associated category of *rights*, will be seen in due course to be central to the conception of reality being developed. Obligations refer to accepted ways in which relevant community members are expected to proceed; rights express accepted ways of going on in which relevant individuals may proceed. If we are a part of, or wish to 'enter' or 'join', a community then, when appropriate, we are under the obligation to adhere to its norms or collective practices. At the same time, when we are part of a community we are permitted to enter into at least some of the community's collective practices, and where this is so these must be seen as rights (I will come to the issue of the segmentation of, and differentiated access to, certain practices below).

It may seem strange to interpret participation in the collective practices of, say, speaking English or shopping in a local store as rights. Yet even these practices exist only as community properties; they allow various individual activities just because the collective practices in question are accepted in the wider community. In other examples the rights' aspects of collective practices are clearer. In the UK not everyone has the right to drive on a motorway; a licence is required. Also in the UK, individuals under a certain age are not allowed to vote; and not so long ago neither were women of any age. Rights of individual property ownership have not always been the norm, etc. And of course even speaking English may not be a right in some courts, say, of the non-Anglophone world.

Notice that the role of rights and obligations in structuring social life presupposes the human capacities of being trustworthy and trusting others, of being willing and able to make and keep to promises and other commitments and to believe that others can and will also do so. As is clear in activities like driving on motorways, any co-operative interaction and ultimately any form of collective action, these human capacities are necessary conditions for the interactions involved to occur, for obligations in particular to be efficacious. As such these capacities of trusting and being trustworthy, etc., qualify as much as anything for being categorised as the glue of social reality, as the adhesive that enables the organisational structure to achieve a degree of binding.

I elaborate upon many of these issues below. But for now I am primarily emphasising that we all find ourselves under the obligation of respecting the collective practices or norms of the communities of which we are a part, or in which we wish to participate, and fulfilling this obligation is a condition of enjoying the rights of participating directly in, and so benefiting from, at least some of the practices of those communities. I might add that a widely interpreted additional right, if not quite an obligation, in many contexts, is that of criticising in various ways individuals who, though situated within a community, show signs of deviating from, or of acting in ways that serve to undermine, community collective practices or norms.

3.3 Organisation-in-process

So community life is relationally organised. Amongst other things it is organised by way of the collective practices and their inherent rights and obligations that structure human interaction. Taken together, human beings, their trusting capacities and their interactions, along with the structural features of collective practices that organise the interactions, amount to a social totality or set of totalities.

It is important to avoid reification, however. Notice that collective practices are inescapably processual in nature. The network of existing collective practices is a condition of individual practices, and the sum total of individual practices, each a token of a collective practice, serves to reproduce and/or transform the total network of collective practices. Collective practices are both condition and consequence of the individual practices they facilitate. Their mode of being is precisely that of being reproduced and/or transformed through the individual practices or activities they facilitate; they are inherently processual. The overall conception then is one of organisation-in-process.

We can thus appreciate that any stability provided by a given collective practice is always *relative* and *contingent*. Collective practices are indicative of how it is possible to go on in ways that are currently accepted within a community, but it is only through individuals participating in available collective practices that the latter are reproduced (when they are). Equally, through such participation, whether by design or by accident, practices or aspects of them are frequently (and sometimes continuously) transformed. Technological developments or physical transformations often make a difference. Language styles and vocabulary are transformed to meet the needs and restrictions of mobile phone communication; a structural alteration to a grocer's shop may affect the positioning of queues; developments in computer technology impact practices involved with buying and selling, banking, and so much else.

Of course, even when certain practices are collectively accepted within a community, the evaluative orientations of the individuals involved are not irrelevant to their stability. Collective acceptance, though by no means the same thing, cannot stably exist without at least some form and degree of generalised *individual acceptance*, unless of course there is physical coercion or huge personal or community 'costs' to desired changes.

Here it is useful to distinguish *individual acceptance to participate* in a collective practice and *individual acceptance of the merit or legitimacy* of the practice. Sufficient conditions for individual acceptance to *participate* in a collective practice are seemingly that the individual (i) understands the practice; (ii) recognises that it is regarded as 'accepted' within the community and so is operative, i.e. that it is a collective practice; and (iii) is willing (for whatever reason, including purely instrumental ones) to go along with the (range of behaviours consistent with the) collective practice.

In contrast, individual acceptance of the *legitimacy* of a collective practice additionally turns on evaluations made of the practice's intrinsic merit, how it was instigated (fairly, openly or otherwise), the nature of its consequences (e.g., whether it involves a community subgroup being oppressed as a result), etc. Of course, the fact of a given practice being accepted within a community is typically in itself some ground for it being regarded as legitimate. In many cases, however, this may not be sufficient, at least for specific individuals.

Clearly, then, it is interesting to consider how (if at all) the *stability* of collective practices varies according to the degree of individual acceptance of their legitimacy; and perhaps, in particular, how negative individual evaluations of the legitimacy of a given collective practice can and often do emerge and/or gain a voice and/or give rise to forms of action that lead to the collective practice in question being transformed or replaced.

Of course everything moves forward from 'here', i.e. is path dependent, so that there is always continuity in change, just as there is usually change in continuity. The point, though, is that with collective practices being given to individual actions, and being reproduced and/or transformed only through the sum total of those actions, everything is in process, so that such stability as is found, though often relatively enduring a posteriori is always contingent and never fixed.

3.4 Social emergence

The picture so far laid out is only a very partial version of the conception of social reality that I have defended previously and I will extend it significantly below. But even this brief sketch, which I am hoping is relatively non-contentious, is indicative of how social reality fits with the general account of (synchronically irreducible) emergent organisation-in-process elaborated above.

Certainly the conception of social reality so far elaborated (though highly partial), turning on the category of collective practice, is of an emergent form of organisation; it is a (normative) mode of organisation of individuals that facilitates forms of coordinated interaction, (relative) stability and predictability that would be unavailable to each individual in the absence of any such organisation.

In other words, certain powers of coordinated interactions are available to individuals *qua* community members, constituting affordances, involving rights and obligations that would not have emerged if human individuals were instead mere biological beings that just happened to be situated in close time–space proximity of others but without much, if any, sense of group collective practices. So we already can recognise a form of organisation (of human interactions) that is ontologically irreducible, involving powers or affordances that are thereby causally irreducible.

Notice that it is because such collective practices, as emergent forms of organising structure, are efficacious in facilitating coordinated interaction that their reality is established. And it is because they are irreducible to the individuals and individual practices that they organise that their relative autonomy is equally grounded, as is that of an appropriately oriented social science.

When and how human collective practices first appeared on the scene is a question for historical investigation. It is feasible that amongst early groupings of our ancestors, found-to-be-useful patterns of behaviour gave rise to physical dispositions or inclinations to act in certain ways, which eventually morphed into collective practices with associated rights and obligations.

The existence of the rights and obligations seems to presuppose the ability to *represent* obligations and rights in some at least rudimentary manner. This is an ability, parenthetically, that Searle believes only appeared with the emergence of language (see especially Searle, 2010).[19] I am not so sure; language, it seems to me, especially a language capable of representing rights and obligations, is in part built on, and presupposes, the (prior) existence of normative collective practices (concerning how words and sentences or at least basic sounds and signs are to be interpreted, etc.). But however that may be, we certainly live now in a linguistically infused universe, and community-relative collective practices carrying rights and obligations that serve to organise social life are seemingly ubiquitous.

3.5 Social rules

I turn now to develop or extend the conception of social reality so far given. In so doing let me first observe that it is with respect to the normative aspects of collective practices that *social rules* come into play. These, as I interpret them, are basically expressions of the content of acceptances under their purely indicative aspect, *interpreted as stipulations*. They are representations of norms, interpreted as *generalised procedures for action* (see Lawson, 1997, ch. 12; 2003, ch. 2). As such they can always be (though they need not be and are not always) expressed in a codified form along the lines of:

In C, if X then Y

Here C is the relevant community or context, X is type of activity and Y is the content of a collective practice. For example, if in the relevant community C an individual wishes to drive on public roads, to wear appropriate dress for a particular event such as a wedding or a funeral, or communicate a certain idea to others, all being instances of X, then the content of some Y, such as drive on the left, etc., indicates the accepted way of doing it.[20]

I am not wishing to suggest that rules are always a posteriori features of spontaneously evolving collective practices. Clearly rules may equally be introduced in an a priori fashion via a decision or declaration by a relevant body or subgrouping of the community and designed to facilitate new forms of collective practice or coordination, or to transform the manner in which forms of coordination have previously been achieved, etc.

But either way a rule is an expression or formulation of a normative aspect of a collective practice, whether as emergent representation or by design. Thus, on this understanding, a rule is something that may be broken, or never codified, or conformed to without acknowledgement, misinterpreted, etc., and so is clearly ontologically distinct from the practices with which it is associated.[21]

3.6 Division of practice, process and events

A further elaboration of the picture so far set out (slightly touched upon above in noting that community-wide collective practices are effectively rights) is that, whether the concern is with the declared rules or with more spontaneously emergent rules, not only are specific collective practices limited by the stretch or jurisdiction of the community of which they are the properties but, within any community, specific practices are typically limited further and differentially allocated. In short, *there is a division of collective practice.* It is accepted that certain practices can be followed by some but not by others. To follow particular practices it is necessary to belong to specific subgroups within a community.

Further still, particular practices accessible to some community members are always oriented to and indeed are constituted in relation to (i.e. are *internally related* to) different practices accessible to others. Thus accepted (highly restricted) practices associated with teachers and students are not just oriented to, but presuppose, each other; as is the case of the (equally restricted) practices associated with employers and employees, landlords/ladies and tenants, parents and children, leaders and followers (e.g., in partner dances such as jive or tango), buyers and sellers, etc. Similarly, even those practices of shopping in the local corner shop are not merely different from, but presuppose, those entered into by the owner, the cashier, the supplier of goods to the store, the store cleaner, etc. Collective practices, then, cohere and interrelate with others, and indeed are constitutively interdependent.

Parenthetically, a question that might reasonably be put at this point is whether all internally related interactions are best considered as part of the same collective practice. Are the accepted ways of going on for the cashier part of the same collective practice as shopping in the store? If university lecturing presupposes (and is a presupposition of) the activities of others participating as members of a student audience, are all implicated activities part of the same collective practice? Is goalkeeping in a football game part of the same collective practice as being an outfield player?

In part this is a matter of choice of use of categories. But I think things are clearest and simplest if we interpret lecturing as a separate (multi-component) collective practice to that of being a student, shopping as a separate practice to cashiering, goalkeeping as a separate practice within a football game, etc., though always recognising that all distinguishable collective practices are oriented to and mostly, indeed, constituted in relation to those of others.

Any internally related combinations of practices we might term a *collective process*. Examples are the continuous interactions on a university campus or in a market place, or the incessant traffic on a motorway.[22]

And a collective process often supports distinguishable episodes or sub-processes that we might identify as *collective events*, such as a particular lecture, or concert, or wedding, or game of football, or perhaps a specific purchase.

In all this, once more, the framework of acceptances is fundamental. Within any community it is accepted that one set of practices constitutes an accepted way of proceeding for group X and a second set, perhaps constituted in relation/orientation to the first, is an accepted way of going on for group Y. Similarly there are usually accepted ways of allocating some individuals to group X and others to group Y; processes of allocation that are themselves clearly each a form of collective practice. Thus the appointment/allocation of certain individuals to the category 'university lecturer' in the UK will proceed according to university and nationally accepted ways of making such appointments, etc.

3.7 Positions

It is these different groupings, each with its own associated accepted sets of ways of proceeding, that I have previously identified (and continue to identify) through use of the category *position*. This is a central and significant category in the conception I defend. A position or rather 'position occupancy' is an accepted status that confers a social identity; to be allocated to a specific position is to acquire the social identity of being so positioned. For example, an individual allocated to the position university lecturer acquires the social/positional identity of (is accepted within the community as possessing the status of) university lecturer.

Notions of rights and obligations are now clearly seen to be associated with positions and thereby group membership. If some positional practices *may* be participated in by a specific set of appropriately positioned individuals, it is typically only a subset of those same practices that *should* be undertaken by these positioned individuals.

To continue with the example of a university lecturer, an individual so positioned in the modern-day UK is typically allowed to use a faculty library or work in her/his faculty office at any time of the day; these are included amongst the employment *rights* that go with the post and are not available to all members of the wider UK community. But the individual is typically not only allowed but additionally required to give lectures, and set and mark examinations, etc.; these are included amongst the employment *obligations* of the position.

Positional rights and obligations, so conceived, always go together; certainly the former presuppose the latter. So a position is essentially a locus of a set of specific rights and obligations, where the accepted position occupants are the agents or bearers of these rights and obligations and typically acquire a status or identity associated with them.

Notice, however, that it is not just the incumbents of specific positions that incur obligations associated with them. Some others or some agency somewhere must ensure that rights such as those mentioned above can be met. Some positioned individuals or groups have the obligation to ensure there are processes in place serving to fund and facilitate universities, schools and libraries, to maintain lecture halls, etc.

3.8 Power

Notice yet further that positional rights and obligations ultimately relate to ways of influencing the behaviours of others, whether directly (as in teachers' powers to instruct students) or indirectly, through having influence over restricted community resources (such as academics' [right of] access to libraries and other publically funded research facilities that constitute resources that are not available to all). Even obligations involved in serving time in prison or acting as servants possess this characteristic. It thus seems reasonable to refer *both* to rights and to obligations as (positional) *powers*. Indeed they are constitutive of what might reasonably be termed social, collective or positional power. Such power, in other words, expresses positioned rights and obligations to participate in specific others-affecting collective practices that are granted to accepted occupants of relevant positions.[23]

A fundamental feature of modern social reality, then, is a multitude of interrelating multicomponent collective practices, processes and events constituting or grounding a complex (clearly equally emergent) structure of positional powers, comprising rights and obligations, in process.

Incidentally, it is not just human beings that acquire social identities through being socially positioned; inanimate objects do too. Obvious examples are those that when suitably positioned take on the identity of cash, passports, other identity cards, deeds of ownership, wedding rings, etc. But this process applies to all objects that (or when they) are brought into social being; all acquire social identities through being positioned in various ways and their being so always depends on community acceptance. Of course, when inanimate objects are so socially positioned, the capacities or powers most closely associated with their (system) positioning take the form *not* of rights and obligations but of (system) functions. I return to this topic in Section 4 below; for the remainder of this section I focus on positions occupied by human individuals.

3.9 Social relations

All forms of social being, then, depend upon positions and are associated with some form of positioned powers. The most fundamental are those immediately occupied by human beings. It is reasonable therefore that the category *social relation* be used to express the manner of connection of social positions, or at least those occupied by human individuals. But such social positions are connected precisely through the accepted rights and obligations associated with them. Thus, on the conception I am elaborating, a *social relation* is just (or is first and foremost) an accepted set of rights and obligations holding between, and connecting, two or more positions or occupants of positions. Social interaction can be understood as the contingent actualisations of such social relations.

It follows that because rights and obligations are forms of power, there is a sense in which all social relations are power relations.

Social relations, so understood, are not restricted to connecting those positions we tend *explicitly* to acknowledge as social identity constituting, such as those of teacher and student, employer and employee, landlady/lord and tenant, parent and child, etc. Others are to be found to hold so widely in a community that we may overlook the positionality involved. These include relations of creditor and debtor, or of gendered man and woman, or even citizen and non-citizen.

In some cases the positionality may (erroneously) seem to be (merely) one-sided just because the relation is between one explicitly positioned (or small group of) individual(s) and *all* others. A property relation is of this latter sort, at least within much of the modern world. If someone in a specific community, e.g., the contemporary UK, owns, say, a house or a lake, then everyone else in that community is *in the position* of not owning this house or lake. The owner has rights of access, use and disposal of it; the rest of us have the obligations involved in respecting and facilitating the owner's rights.

Of course, at an appropriate level of abstraction an identical set of rights and obligations is available to all current UK domestic property owners. But such considerations usefully serve to remind us that there is nothing preordained about ownership *per se*; rather the latter is seen to be a human community construct, a merely conventional, if at this time a highly customary, feature of certain specific geo-historical and cultural forms of human organisation. When members of a community accept or observe a situation of property ownership, even if there is only a single person in the community for whom property rights are to hold (say a tribal chief in regard to her or his dwelling), the members are accepting or observing consequences for everyone.

This recognition reinforces the idea, implicit if not explicit throughout, that *all* collective practices are positioned and other-oriented. As such it is evident that human beings *qua* social beings are always beings in social relations.

3.10 Power and its pursuit

I might briefly note how the conception laid out bears on how we understand activities concerned with the *pursuit* of power, a fundamental activity of modern societies. Clearly if, as I argue, community-sanctioned power (over others) mostly takes the form of positional rights (and obligations), it follows that much of the intentional *pursuit* of power in modern societies takes the form of human activities whereby those involved seek either (i) to acquire occupancy of existing relatively powerful positions; (ii) to transform (or defend) the rights and obligations associated with existing positions already occupied; or (iii) to create, and thereupon occupy, novel positions with emergent associated rights.

The practices both of individuals seeking to gain entry to established powerful positions, and also of positioned individuals and groups concerned to improve/defend/undermine existing positional rights and obligations, are familiar enough topics of social theory, especially within industrial relations, human resource management and labour market studies. But the manner in which particular individuals and groups are able, often with relative ease, to increase their power over others just through creating *novel* positions that they then frequently themselves occupy perhaps deserves more attention.

This is usually achieved via the device of declaring novel 'legal entities' or some such, which are effectively statuses or placeholders allowed by, and within, a wider community (and established by way of following procedures and/or collective practices of the relevant community). The establishment of these formal entities tends to disguise the fact that basically what is pursued and created is a new structure of power relations.

This is a topic that I can do little more than mention here, though I can perhaps note that an obvious way in which an individual or group can create novel forms of power over others in contemporary Western society is by establishing/registering a novel company (UK) or corporation (USA) that serves the goals of its establishers. Very little need be involved in creating the relevant powers; typically not even buildings are necessary. Indeed, in order to register or be incorporated (in the UK or the USA), little more is required than for the individuals concerned to supply a company name and address (the latter can even be that of a third party such as an accountant), officer details (a director can be sufficient, though a secretary is also typical), details of any share capital and shareholders, and a payment; and to file a memorandum and articles of association. But the process is straightforward and incorporation can even be completed online/electronically.

Following a successful application, the resulting company or corporation is thereby 'granted' many of the same legal rights as an actual person, but usually with limited liabilities. Companies or corporations, which may be made up of a single person or a group of people, thus effectively exist as virtual or fictitious persons, providing or constituting in effect legal devices that provide (typically) limited protection to the actual people involved in the activities of the company or corporation. And power for those involved is thereby achieved over numerous others and, not least, where profit seeking is involved, over those that are unable to raise capital themselves and so must serve (somewhere) as company employees.[24]

These are not matters I can elaborate upon here. I merely emphasise that significant if perhaps undertheorised features of social reality are the various endeavours to set up legal entities and other formal organisations or formal titles, motivated by the goal of establishing, and thereafter exercising, novel forms of power (always over others). If the conventional route of those involved is to present the situation as one in which the positioning of individuals, and the subsequent activities of positioned individuals, are derivative of, and subservient to, the goals of some seemingly neutral, or perhaps laudable, legal entity, associated organisation or some such, the fact is that the creation of the latter entity is often, and perhaps usually, derivative of, and subservient to (and tends to work either to legitimise or mask), the power aspirations of the individuals involved. The point of establishing and maintaining devices like companies and other formal bodies is to establish a novel structure of power relations between people.[25]

To return, however, to the more general point, modern societies are characterised by social relations that are constituted in terms of positional rights and obligations, representing forms of positional powers (always over others). The community-based opportunities available to us all depend upon the positional powers we can access. So not surprisingly, a significant feature of social life in modern communities is the prevalence of activities oriented to getting access to, transforming (or just maintaining/defending) and/or creating novel forms of positional powers (over others).

3.11 Community

At the start of the discussion of the nature of social reality the community was conceptualised as an identifiable, restricted, relatively enduring (if typically evolving) coherent grouping of people who share some set of (usually equally evolving) concerns. I need now to elaborate this conception so that the community, too, is seen *not* as a foundational category (there clearly are no social foundations) but as an emergent and also contingent component of a human-practice-dependent social reality in process.

Some way into the discussion I argued both that collective practices are effectively properties of communities and also that even the most general or open of a community's collective practices carry rights and obligations. I have since argued that rights and obligations are actually always associated with social positions. It follows, then, that each community is precisely a totality comprising the set of occupants of a certain specific social position along with (and organised through) all the structures

bearing upon those positions, including, not least, the rights and obligations associated with the relevant position.

As such the concerns that community members share may or may not
be reducible to the powers and interests that derive from position membership, but the latter will be a major part of the members' concerns. And
significantly, with every community (even very short-lived ones) being
associated with certain (positioned) rights and obligations, there is a clear
sense in which each community must be seen to be a *moral community*.

Notice, incidentally, that from the start I used the category 'collective
practice' or 'norm' to express what is essentially a community status con-
ferred on a way of proceeding by way of its being (collectively) accepted. I
am now suggesting that community membership or participant (i.e. position occupant) is, in the same way, itself a status, so that any associated
collective practices can indeed be viewed as status practices, where participation in such collective practices is amongst the rights and obligations
of community membership.

If every community corresponds to or is underpinned by a social position, a reasonable question to pursue is whether it is equally the case that
every social position supports a community.

Notice that on the conception I am defending any given community
may (i) contain subdivisions or subgroupings, each with its own differentiating and internally related positional powers; and/or (ii) be itself a
subgrouping of a broader group so that its members have access to the
positioned powers of the broader grouping, though also possessing some
of their own, defined relationally to other such subgroupings. So the question before us includes enquiring whether all such sub- or meta-groupings
of a given community are equally communities.

I suggest that any position *can* be said to support a community. An
intuitive difficulty with so responding in the affirmative, perhaps (at least
for those social positions that are occupied by more than one individual,
which is typically the case), is that everyday notions of community often
carry a sense of a *coming together* over some concerns, whereas it is always
possible that there are positions where occupants do no such thing, or at
least do not do so regularly or universally.[26]

However, this difficulty, if such it is, can be circumvented by distinguishing between a community *in itself* and a community *for itself*, with
positional identity associated with the former. In most cases, I suspect,
a community in itself so conceived has the potential of becoming a community that is also for itself, as a response to perceived threats, crises or
challenges (or opportunities) that can at any time affect the always very
real and objective common set of positioned rights or concerns and obligations or responsibilities of those appropriately positioned. In other
words there is always the potential for the positioned agency stemming
from membership of any community to morph into the *collective or corporate agency* of a community for itself, including defensive associations

and/or unions, social movements, vested interest groups and the like, strategically focused on realising and/or directing (emergent) powers to systematically engage in action to transform, retain or obtain various sets of structural features or conditions thought to be unfair or under threat or perhaps just desirable and reachable.[27]

So in summary, social reality is found to comprise a multitude of inter-relating multicomponent collective practices, processes and events that both ground and presuppose a complex system of positions, positioned rights and obligations, i.e. social relations, which are always in process and serve, amongst other things, to organise individuals as community participants and sometimes as collective or corporate agents.

3.12 Social emergence and the notion of social structure

The conception supported is clearly one of complex organisation in process. The various features discussed that result from, and serve to relationally organise, human beings and individual activities without being reducible to those individuals and their individual actions, I have previously collected under the head of *social structure*. So understood, social structure is not something additional to the phenomena so far discussed, nor is it a stuff of which they are composed. Rather, it is merely a general category that collects together the collective practices, acceptances, positions, rules, rights, obligations and such like that are emergent features of human actions and interactions and which relationally organise the individuals as communities. So the picture is one of emergent social-structural organisation-in-process.

Such social structure is (synchronically) emergent in the sense of being dependent upon, but distinct from, and ontologically and causally irreducible to, the individual activities that it serves in turn to facilitate and coordinate.

Rules in particular are, as already noted, emergent features that, although serving to guide individual action, can be broken or ignored or misinterpreted in individual acts as well as remain unacknowledged or never codified. Rights allow ways of proceeding but without determining specific actions. And even with obligations, there are many ways of acting in accordance with the rules; there are many conceivable ways, for example, of fulfilling one's duty to give a lecture, bring up children, drive within the rules of the road, etc. Moreover, there are occasions when *formal* rules at least are *systematically* broken, such as maximum speed limits on UK motorways (and yet still influence actual speeds in that drivers typically do not exceed the formal limits 'excessively').

3.13 Process once more

Clearly social structure, so conceived, is continually undergoing transformation, whether intended or unintended, understood or hardly recognised.

I have already noted how power relations can be affected by the intentional establishment of novel legal entities. In addition, and again as already observed, once numerous individuals have been allocated to (or have had allocated to them) a given position, and no matter what the basis for being so allocated, they frequently seek, as collective or corporate agents, to transform the accepted sets of rights and obligations (to challenge the power structure) associated with their position (and conceivably thereby transform the nature of that position in some more or less fundamental manner). In the past, individuals allocated (typically, but not necessarily, at birth) to the gender category 'women' have campaigned for the right (where it was denied) of women to vote, and still seek everywhere to transform structures of discrimination and/or oppression; frequently, specific categories of employees agitate for better work conditions and (other) rights in the workplace, etc.

But at least as (ontologically) significant, even where position occupants do not intentionally seek so to transform their positional rights and obligations, these powers are nevertheless continually being transformed through practice (whether inadvertently or otherwise). And indeed this applies to the content of all forms of collective acceptances. All social phenomena depend on us, and so their continuing existence depends on their being reproduced through our individual practices in total. This is their mode of being. But we can systematically change how we behave, whether through learning, technological advances, accidents or whatever. When we come to act, the contents of previous acceptances, whether embedded in agreements, precedents or whatever, are given to us; and through our acting we both draw on them (whether or not we are explicitly aware of this) and also (if typically unintentionally) contribute not just to the reproduction of social structures but also to their transformation. Notice that even where reproduction of aspects is the outcome, this is a contingent achievement, warranting as much explanation as does change. Social reality is everywhere intrinsically dynamic in nature.

But so, too, the human individual exists as a process of transformation. The structural context facing the individual makes a difference not just through enabling and constraining and facilitating certain causal powers amongst others, it also affects the very nature of human individuals. It makes a difference to the path and form of development of the capabilities, motivations and acquired needs, etc. (in short, to the formation and evolution of the nature), of a particular human being whether 'he' or 'she' is situated, say, as a slave or slave-owner in a slave-owning society; as a serf (freeman, villain or cottager) in European Manorialism (or Seigneurialism); as a worker or employer of modern capitalism; or indeed as a gendered man or woman at almost any time and place.

We develop psychological tendencies and social capabilities according to how and where in space–time we are situated and as a result of our experiences through life. Like social systems, human beings are organisations in process; and we have here a clear process of co-development of human individuals and society as each are continuously reproduced and transformed through the sum total of individual practice.

Parenthetically, it is notable that this vision is very different from that conveyed by (or most easily read into) the theory of society developed by Searle (despite the significant similarities that I believe exist between Searle's basic account and that maintained here), just because of Searle's lack of attention to emergent organisation-in-process. According to the conception I defend, human beings and their personal identities, activities and opportunities, are organised through emergent social structure that is itself reproduced and transformed through the sum total of the individual practices that this structure in turn facilitates. Searle's focus is on the effects of individuals on social structure to the seeming exclusion, certainly a relative neglect, of the effects of the latter on the former. A significant result is the repeated use of the category of *creation* in Searle's writing and the almost total absence of categories of 'reproduction' or 'transformation' or 'process'.

Notice, finally, that there is nothing that is non-naturalistic about the account of social reality that I am maintaining. Some aspects are structural patterns or structural features of accepted forms of collective practices. Others are ideational, including varying representations or interpretations of aspects of collective practices, other features of social structure, as well as of social totalities, along with the content of all community acceptances, including the outcomes of past decision-making processes or official declarations bearing on matters such as collective practices or the distribution of rights of access to community positions (and so to accompanying positional rights and obligations), etc. And social entities or wholes will include the human individuals or material objects that the noted features of social structure serve to relationally organise. But there is nothing mysterious or non-naturalistic in any of this.

3.14 Human intentionality

If in being consistent with naturalism the focus is upon intentional states and practices of individuals, a seemingly inevitable and indeed fundamental part of the concern must also be with the capacity for human beings to cooperate. Indeed the concern is with how individuals are able to cooperate in a manner such that each is doing something as a part of numerous others doing either that same thing or something that is in some constitutively way related. This will most obviously be so in the case of a collective event. An individual playing football will be doing so as part of a team activity or an individual may be playing the violin as part of an orchestra, etc.

This form of cooperative behaviour can be described as, or as involving, the sharing of intentional states, whether beliefs, goals, desires, intentions, etc. For completeness, then, I should, in concluding the current section, briefly consider the remaining rather fundamental question of how shared intentions and individual intentions are related.

One line of reasoning, prominent at least in contemporary economics, which at first sight may seem to address this issue in a satisfactory way (but ultimately does not), is that formulated under the head of *common knowledge*. According to this conception, an event or state of affairs is said to be the object of common knowledge among a group of individuals if each one knows it, and if each one knows that the others know it, and if each one knows that each one knows that the others know it, etc. Common knowledge is thus the limit of a potentially infinite chain of reasoning about the event in question.

Common knowledge, moreover, is assumed to be achievable. So if there is to be a coordinated action, then the notion that say two of us intend to do something together amounts to the idea that I intend to do it in the belief that you also intend to do it; and you intend to do it in the belief that I also intend to do it. Each of us believes the other has beliefs about our own such beliefs, and beliefs too about those, and so on *ad infinitum*.

As well as the sheer implausibility of this theory of intentionality, in the end it does not provide a conception of a collective or shared intention anyway. It does not deliver an account whereby the individual intentions of each participant in an activity derive from shared intentions. At no point do we have 'we intentionality', only 'I intentionality' (perhaps plus something else). Yet in reality, if to repeat, a musician in a band, or a sportsperson participating in a team game, has the intention to play but only as *part of* the wider intentional activity.

An alternative conception, one seemingly derivative of contributions of Wilfred Sellars (e.g., 1965, 1974), but in fact significantly advanced, much elaborated and made influential by Searle himself (e.g., Searle, 1995), holds that the capacity for collective intentionality is a biological primitive. On this view collective intentions cannot be reduced to or eliminated in favour of something else; specifically, 'we intentionality' cannot be reduced to 'I intentionality', which is essentially the strategy of the previous conception with its notion of common knowledge.

On Searle's conception it can be maintained that all mental life of a given individual remains inside her or his own brain (or anyway body) without necessitating that an individual's mental life be expressed only in the form of a singular noun phrase referring to her/himself. An *individual* can have a collective intentionality taking the form of 'we intend', etc., allowing that, in the case of cooperative behaviour of the sort under discussion, the individual intends only as part of a group intending.

Even this idea seems to require the further human capacity of being able to connect in a deep way with others. And indeed the latter appears to happen continuously, as a condition even of following an argument in a research paper, or a play or programme on TV. Where such identification is contingently achieved by one or more individuals and a third party speaks or otherwise intervenes, the connection can easily be lost or broken.

If the notion of collective intentionality as developed by Searle is the more viable of the contending alternatives and, indeed, collective intentionality, or something like it, seems to be an essential condition for the emergence of a social reality of the sort maintained here, it remains the case that, in any context of collective cooperative activity, each individual needs to know both what to do and how to do it. And this of course is where (the contents of) collectively accepted ways of doing things *or collective practices* and/or of the distribution of positional power enter the picture, and return us to the social ontology laid out.

To summarise, the foregoing is an outline of the ontological conception I have previously defended, interpreted more explicitly and systematically from the perspective of social reality as an emergent human-agent-dependent (set of) social organisation(s)-in-process. It is a conception in which the causal powers of human beings *qua* social beings are the positional powers and properties of emergent social systems or set of organisations-in-process, organisations in which the human individuals are socially situated, and through which they are themselves continually formed and transformed.

Needless to say, I have provided here only a sketch (if a longish one) of a conception of social ontology. But I hope I have elaborated certain key features sufficiently to convince that it is possible to sustain an account of emergence of the sort I have previously advanced, one that abstractly applies to social and non-social realms alike, without the result seeming to be overly mysterious or compromising the thesis of (ontological) naturalism.

4. Social objects including human artefacts and other inanimate objects

Let me lastly return briefly to the earlier-noted observation that it is not just human beings that are attributed social identities through their being socially positioned; inanimate objects are so as well, including artefacts.[28] Think of large sea pebbles, say, being positioned as paperweights; or pieces of paper or bits of metal positioned as cash; bits of plastic positioned as passports or credit cards, etc. Some constructions in the UK as elsewhere that were originally designed as churches or schools or barns are now positioned as homes, etc.

Social reality comprises in some part a multitude of inanimate objects, mostly humanly constructed as artefacts, that obtain social identities through being socially positioned in various ways. Seemingly, all constructions and uses of artefacts or inanimate devices are intended to expand the range of human capabilities, and the positioning of inanimate objects serves the same end.

This positioning of objects (as with the positioning of humans) is always as components in the formation of an emergent organisation or system, however rudimentary. A result is that in describing the properties of any particular object the primary focus is very often on that subset of its causal powers that contribute to the overall workings or maintenance of the system. Indeed these causal powers tend, thereby, to be referred to as the positioned object's *functions*; they are looked upon according to how they function as a component of the system.

Thus objects become positioned as, say, tables, seats, eating and drinking and serving utensils, etc. Over different times, places and cultures, the objects so positioned will vary in shape, size, form and material content (just as, at any point in time and space, there are very often entirely different inanimate objects that could have been successfully positioned in the place of each). But in all cases, positioned objects of the sort listed facilitate the needs of a system of human beings participating in collective practices bound up with sharing food together. And the (set of) power(s) of each of the objects that contributes to this end is seen as its (set of) function(s). (In turn, of course, the meal itself may be a component of a wider system, functioning perhaps to facilitate regular family or tribal gatherings, or in specific cases perhaps to celebrate a family member's birthday or mark another occasion.)

Very often it is the case that certain items can be (and are) positioned in two (or more) different systems simultaneously and so possess two (or more) sets of functions, one for each system (just as a human individual can simultaneously serve as, say, a parent and a grocer). Thus an item of clothing may serve both as part of a system providing protection from the elements for a particular human being in winter, say, and also by identifying the wearer of the clothing as a police person, member of a specific football team, or a bride or a priest, as part of an additional (more collective) system. A house or painting or ornament may function according to the specific uses made of it in servicing, say, a family home, but share in common a power to retain, and so function as a store of, value in another system.

Similarly, of course, those powers or properties interpreted as functions can change as objects are repositioned. An item for sale in a shop is identified as a commodity and has the function of being tradable (for credit) at a given price. But from the perspective of a different system (and once purchased it can be inserted into a system where) its function is in line with its more specific uses (as a hammer, screwdriver, etc.).

Notice that the object(s) positioned in any social system may be, and typically will be, modifications of antecedent or precursor objects as, say, when a block of wood is resized and reshaped to function as a door in a building, or a piece of card is engraved or marked in order to serve as a ticket to a concert or for a train journey, or bits of metal are stamped, etc., in order to serve as coins. Thus although certain capacities or powers that are treated by us as functions may in some cases (as with the sea-pebble paperweight) be possessed before the object is incorporated into the social system, typically they will be acquired/achieved through the process of modification and/or positioning.

I noted earlier that legal entities like companies and the like are typically created derivatively of the desire on the part of some to acquire positional power. It should be clear that similar objectives govern the production and positioning of many concrete artefacts, not least buildings positioned/identified as offices, factories, stadia, university departments, etc. The latter, as with the legal entities with which they may be associated, are not prime determinants, but the ever dependent, always potentially transformable, products of practices oriented to accumulating positioned powers for specific individuals.

There are numerous issues of significance that arise from this brief account that I cannot explore here. I am certainly not seeking to advance a comprehensive theory of artefacts. However, there is one matter that I do want to address just because of its relevance to all that has gone before. I have argued that where positions are immediately occupied by human individuals, the associated positional powers (over others) of which positioned individuals are the agents take the form of (system) rights and obligations. However, for the agent or bearer of any such powers to be able to exercise these powers effectively, the individuals concerned have to be identifiable as their bearers. In consequence very many inanimate objects are positioned in just such a manner that (relative to a particular system) their function is precisely to identify an individual as an occupant of a specific position, and so the bearer of the set of associated positional rights and obligations. This is the case of objects positioned as, say, uniforms, deeds of property rights, certificates of all forms, wedding rings, identity cards, passports, tickets, licences, etc.

In such cases as those just listed, I suspect it is not overly contentious to claim that, in each case, a capacity that is singled out as the positional function in at least one system is that of serving as a symbolic identifier (of the position or status of the possessor of the object). I want briefly to suggest that the capacity of symbolic identification underpins the function even of forms (at least) of monetary items, not least those objects that are positioned as cash or currency (banknotes and coins).

4.1 The nature of cash

This is no more the place to advance a general theory of money than it is to develop a comprehensive account of artefacts, but I do want to expand this latter claim about the function of cash a little, for two reasons. The first is that this role of cash (along with all other identifiers) is so important to the functioning of the above-elaborated social system based on positional power that the claim warrants some emphasis and elaboration. The second is to attempt to shed some clarity on the claims of those money theorists who advance a credit interpretation of the nature of money. I want to suggest that, strictly speaking, items positioned as cash function (via collective acceptance within a relevant community of course) to identify individuals who are the positioned holders, bearers or agents of particular credit-rights or debt-obligations; as such it is not clear that cash is the credit itself.

Imagine a situation in which I shop at my local grocers but forget my wallet and the owner of the shop, recognising me, and believing me to be both trustworthy and having access to an income (literally that I am credit-worthy), allows me to take my 'purchases' on credit (this is an event that has actually happened on more than one occasion). I could sign a piece of paper, and so create an IOU, recording my debt; the IOU would serve both to identify myself as the debtor (the person with the obligation) by my signature (say), as well as the creditor (the person with the right to expect payment), namely the grocer, through possession of the IOU. I am taking for granted here that a monetary/accounting system is accepted throughout the community involving an accepted unit of account, in terms of which debts are conventionally recorded (as of course is the case in the early twenty-first-century UK). If the baker next door to the grocer shares the same opinion of my trustworthiness and creditworthiness, the grocer could in principle use this credit with me to 'purchase' bread or whatever, transferring that credit (with me) to the baker to cancel the debt incurred by this purchase of bread, etc., *and in addition* passing on the IOU (perhaps endorsed by the grocer) to the baker so that the latter can be identified as the person now holding the credit.

It is important to recognise that it is the credit relation that has value and can be used to cancel other debts. It exists whether or not an IOU is created. If an IOU is created then it acts merely as an identifier; it is not *per se* the credit–debt (right–obligation) relationship itself. If the grocer or baker were to misplace the IOU I could still seek to fulfil my obligations if I remembered them; indeed there is a good chance we would all remember the nature of the credit–debt or right–obligation relation involved (and if the grocer, baker and I knew each other very well it is conceivable that the credit relation could even be repeatedly transferred between the three of us, with or without written IOUs, as often effectively happens within some families or between some friends).

Up to a point, paper or metal serving as cash in a modern economy such as the UK work in much the same way as the IOU. Specifically, for an object positioned as cash, the primary causal power or function is precisely to identify an underlying specific credit–debt (right–obligation) relationship, between the current possessor of the cash (the creditor) and whoever issued it (the debtor).[29]

A significant difference in the case of cash (an additional one to the obvious contrasts like the sheer quantity of credit usually in circulation in the wider society, the sorts of guarantees and requirements or fiats that come with state backing [usually entailing, in fact, that all participants in the monetary system are potentially debtors], or the contribution of other significant institutions, etc.) is the impersonal nature of it all. At any moment in time the current creditors are unknown to the actual debtor(s) or issuers of the cash and identifiable only through their possession of the cash.

Thus, because a £20 note will be a unique identifier/record of a particular credit–debt relationship, if it is accidentally destroyed it appears that value is destroyed. However, I suggest that technically it is not, and the underlying credit–debt relationship still remains; what disappears is any means of proving the identity of the parties involved and, in particular, the creditor. Indeed, if instead of being accidentally destroyed the bank note is merely severely damaged or contaminated, it is often the case that it will be replaced by the issuer, even when the latter is a central bank.[30] But the credit relation itself is not thereby replaced; indeed it is the latter's continuing existence that explains the issuer's willingness to replace the damaged note.[31] Notice, too, that when on 'decimal day' (15 February 1971) UK and Irish citizens exchanged 'old' notes and coins denominated in imperial units for 'new' ones denominated in metric ones, the credits (and value of credits) possessed on the issuing bank remained intact throughout.[32] The notes and coins *per se* are not the credit relations, but merely symbolic markers or identifiers of those currently standing in them (and of the values of the obligations involved). It is the distinction between the two, the cash and credit, that makes the events of 'decimal day' intelligible.

It follows, then, that objects positioned as cash do not store (or are not a store of) value, strictly, but rather are primarily devices that facilitate the storing of value by providing a means by which a possessor of accumulated credit can be recognised. Similarly, objects positioned as cash do not themselves possess (and are not) exchange value, but merely facilitate exchange or trade between the possessors of credit and those possessing specific commodities or services, etc. They achieve the latter through providing a means whereby emergent debts (that accompany purchases) are repeatedly cancelled as the underlying credit on the issuer of the cash is transferred across different parties.

It also follows that if we insist that money is always a social relation (as for example does Geoffrey Ingham, 2004, in an account that in many ways is similar to the above), then cash is not strictly money; it is *not* the social relation *per se* (the right–obligation or credit–debt relation) but a symbolic identifier of a particular social relation or of those standing in such a relationship. Alternatively, if we prefer to designate cash as a form of money, then either it alone is the money component in the current example, in which case money here is not the social relation *per se* but a positioned device for keeping track of it, or the cash and the underlying credit relation are both money, or perhaps *together* constitute a form of money.

In any case it is clear that cash along with other monetary mechanisms (such as credit cards, cheques and electronic banking devices, etc.) facilitate the transmitting/transferring of debt/credit by way of allowing the bearers of debt and credit to be identified. As such, whatever we choose to designate with the category money, it is the case that cash and the related devices are (currently) essential components of modern accounting/monetary systems that go hand in hand with forms of credit, and indeed allow the expansion and speedy transference of the latter.

In short, the functioning of a system where positioned rights and obligations are essential features will be dependent on devices that allow the agents or bearers of specific powers to be readily and accurately identified. And under capitalism any devices that function to identify the agents of credit rights (and debt obligations) are fundamental indeed, whatever forms those devices take (and whatever aspects of the overall accounting system to which we may choose to attach the term money).

There is certainly more to be said about systems of symbolic identifiers or markers in general. But for current purposes I merely emphasise two features. The first is that the functionality of the objects so positioned as cash, deeds of ownership, passports, etc., i.e. their capacity to serve as identifiers, rests on their incorporation/positioning within a wider system via collective acceptance. The second is that once so incorporated, these identifiers can often be made to work to allow systems in which they are components to expand way beyond small communities with personal ties (wherein acquired powers can rest on memory) and sometimes, as in the case of forms of money, to cover the totality of communities on the planet, and in ways that allow, for example, an unceasing accumulation of power (always over others) in the hands of a relative few, and in ways that affect us all.

There is, as I say, much more to be said on all this and indeed on the subject matter of social artefacts in general.[33] But the foregoing must suffice here. Even before I considered the social positioning of inanimate objects, the case for the relative autonomy of social science was found to be established. However, because the system of positional powers (of individuals and groups over each other) in the form of rights and obligations is found to be so fundamental to human society, and because the positioning of inanimate objects and in particular those serving as identifiers is essential to the functioning of this power system, the latter must equally be recognised as of fundamental interest to social science. It is often no trivial matter to understand the way in which objects positioned as identifiers facilitate, maintain and extend the powers (rights and obligations) that appropriately positioned groups and individuals can wield. And such matters are of consequence. Amongst other things, indeed, they are fundamental to understanding the very stability (and crises, not least financial crises – see Lawson, 2009) of the worldwide social system as a whole, a system in which the accumulation and distribution of power, as theorised here, are all-pervading determining features.

4.2 Similar conceptions, quasi-abstract entities and objects of knowledge

Let me close this section by briefly drawing out some important features of the position I have been advancing through examining its bearing on certain related assessments proposed by others. Specifically, in debate with Searle, Barry Smith writes:

> More precisely, property relations belong to the realm of the quasi-abstract and they are in this respect comparable to symphonies, laws and other quasi-abstract denizens of the social world. That they exist on the side of the objects and not on the side of the concepts in people's heads can be seen from the fact that concepts can exist even where there are no corresponding objects.
>
> (Smith, 2008, p. 47)

He adds:

> When we buy and sell, however, we are interested not in concepts but in the objects themselves: in equity and capital, and in all that goes together therewith – starting with the simple trading, offering, and splitting of stock and moving on to the unimaginably complex edifices of contemporary derivatives markets.
>
> (Smith, 2008, pp. 47–8)

In response, Searle writes of Smith that:

> I think that he is being needlessly paradoxical when he suggests that there is some challenge to naturalism here; that somehow or other, in addition to physical particles and fields of force, there are all these abstract entities running around between the molecules. That's a misleading picture, which comes from treating the object as the unit of analysis. We're not interested in the object, we're interested in the processes or, as I like to put it, we're interested in the facts. It isn't the obligation as an object that is the topic of our investigation, rather it is our undertaking an obligation, our recognizing a pre-existing obligation, our fulfilling an obligation. And when you realize this the threat to naturalism disappears.
>
> (Searle, 2008, p. 48)

From the vantage point of the conception I have been developing, I am not convinced there is any real opposition here and nor is there a threat to naturalism. Social relations, whether property, credit or whatever, are indeed objects of knowledge and not reducible to our concepts of them. But there is no need to locate them in some mysterious 'quasi-abstract' realm, whatever that might mean. They take the form of the content of previous collective practices, the outcomes of past interactive processes within some social organisation, indicating the collectively accepted rights and obligations. As such they are no challenge to naturalism. Although Searle's response is consistent with this, I see no reason to conclude, as Searle seems to imply, that the obligation, as a form of positional negative power or requirement accepted within the community, is something in which we are not interested as an object *per se* or a property of a social object/system.

Indeed, I suspect that a rather high proportion of disputes that come before the law courts, or which take place in the workplace, or industrial relations tribunals, or even family homes, are disputes regarding the nature or content of existing rights and obligations. The resolving of such disputes may require the scouring of relevant documents, the rehearsing of earlier conversations, a tracing out of past patterns of practice to uncover implicit acceptances, including the content of agreed or tacitly accepted collective practices or norms, etc. But all such matters constitute a legitimate subject matter for social science. The latter is concerned with all aspects of the emergence, nature, (re)production and transformation of the positional power structure that organises human social being.

This is not a topic I take further here. For now it is enough to suggest that by accepting the framework of rights and obligations as one comprising real irreducible system features, as objects of knowledge sometimes to be understood only through lengthy investigation, we can reconcile the likes of both Smith and Searle. We also achieve a social realism of the sort that accommodates the version of emergence advanced, without in any way compromising a commitment to naturalism.

5. Final comments

In the light of the particular account of social reality defended above it *could* simply be argued that social science obviously exists, and does so as a legitimate practice, just because, like every other extant form of cooperative interactive human activity, it is a collective practice named and sponsored, and so accepted, within various communities and carried on by a group of people, appropriately positioned (i.e. in conformity with accepted collective practice) as agents of associated (again communally accepted) rights and obligations, and thereby identified as social scientists.

Of course the contention really objected to by the earlier-noted detractors of social science is that this particular community of would-be social scientists, however we name their practices, can in principle make the same sort of contribution to understanding our world as does the community of (non-social) natural scientists. The presumption here is that the material conditions for supporting a social science that could be scientific in the sense of natural science are absent.

However I have argued that this latter presumption is incorrect. All forms of established science have objects of study that are effectively (synchronically irreducible) emergent forms of organisations-in-process, and in this respect social science is no different. And just as with other sciences, social science is especially concerned with the (irreducible) causal properties of its domain of study.

Of particular interest are social causal powers that exist at the level of structure. Here social causal properties are those of the collective practices, positions and associated rights and obligations and so forth that serve to organise us all. So social science is found to be, amongst other things, a discipline significantly concerned with the production, reproduction, distribution and redistribution of positioned powers in all their numerous (monetary, industrial/corporate, financial, educational, legal, gendered, age, inter-regional, communicative, familial, religious, tribal, cultural, ethnic, etc.) forms.

Of course I have only briefly touched upon many of the various issues mentioned above, achieving little more at the level of social theory than outlining a possible *agenda* for social science. But that is essentially the point: to establish that a meaningful agenda for (a sustainable) social science is entirely feasible.

I might stress, finally, that because social reality is found *everywhere* to be constituted through social relations or positioned powers, dependent upon and reproduced and transformed through human practice, it follows that all the various traditional branches of social science are ultimately dealing with the same basic subject matter and are thus best conceived not as separate disciplines but as divisions of labour in a single (if as yet insufficiently integrated) social science (as I have often argued – see, e.g., Lawson, 2003, 2006). Accepting or acknowledging this situation, I suggest, does not constitute a diminution of the various existing strands of social science but rather amounts to recognition of the basis on which the relative autonomy of each is legitimately founded.

Notes

1 The basic arguments and positions defended in this paper were worked out over many years and usually presented, if not determined, at meetings of the Cambridge Social Ontology Group (CSOG), and I am very grateful to members of CSOG in more ways than I can acknowledge. I have been convinced of the usefulness of revisiting the topic and belatedly 'putting out' the paper at this time, and in its current form, both by the re-emergent topicality of the subject matter, as well as what I believe to be common misapprehensions over what can be, or is, defended concerning the matters discussed. Additional presentations of the content of the paper include talks given when, in 2008, I spent a period of time visiting the Berkeley Social Ontology Group (BSOG). I am especially grateful to John Searle and other members of BSOG for their feedback. I am also indebted to referees and the assessors of the *Cambridge Journal of Economics*, and numerous others for additional helpful comments

along the way. For financial support with finishing off this paper I am grateful, too, to the Independent Social Research Foundation. First published in *Cambridge Journal of Economics*, 2011, Vol 36, No 2, 345–385.

2 The same reception, needless to say, greets would-be specialist (branches of) social science, such as a putative economic science (for recent dismissals see, e.g., John Kay, 2010; Rupert Read, 2007) or a political science. Some commentators of course reject the idea of science altogether. None of these positions, it will be seen, coincide with my own.

3 See Andy McSmith (2010).

4 Thus the philosopher of science Brian Ellis (2002) has concluded that

> however successful the sciences of ecology, economics, sociology and the like might be in achieving their aims, we have no good reason to be realistic about the theoretical entities they employ, for these theoretical entities are invariably just the elements of model theories.

He dismisses the theoretical entities and claims of modern economics in particular as 'just economic fantasy' (Ellis, 2002, p. 32).

5 By 'objective' I mean existing independently of or at least prior to their being studied. Of course I do not suppose that social reality (or indeed any other form of reality ultimately) remains totally unaffected by its being studied or indeed by any other form of interaction with it.

6 By designating a science as relatively autonomous here I mean simply that it is a form of study whose results are indispensable to understanding and not merely temporary stand-ins for (awaiting redescription in terms of) the results of some more fundamental reducing science(s), such as psychology and/or (other aspects of) biology.

7 Prior to studying the nature of society as such, Searle had already developed a theory of speech acts to explain the move from physical utterances to meaningful speech acts; as well as a theory of the mind to explain how a world of consciousness, intentionality and other mental phenomena 'fit into a world consisting entirely of physical particles in fields of force' (Searle, 1995, p. xi).

8 These are questions of morphogenesis (see Lawson, 2012).

9 Of course, quite different accounts of the interconnectedness (or otherwise) of reality prevail, far more certainly than I can seriously consider here. Some are very different indeed. For example, the vision of the Amerindians is that originally there was no differentiation between humans and (other) animals, and separation occurred *not* as humans evolved from animals but as animals lost qualities retained by humans. Animals are ex-humans. In some accounts, indeed, humankind is the original form of everything and not just of animals. It is also held that many animal species, as well as certain other types of non-human beings, retain a spiritual component that qualifies them as 'people'. In certain versions, moreover, the manifest bodily forms of various non-human species conceal internal humanoid forms visible to shamans and certain other privileged beings. From this perspective the task that I have set myself above of explaining the emergence of social relations and such like is a non-issue: all relations (between all phenomena in the world) are social relations and were so from the start. See, e.g., Claude Lévi-Strauss (1964–71), Gerald Weiss (1972) or Eduardo Batalha Viveiros de Castro (1998, 2004).

10 It is a confusing of the two that encourages some contributors to advance the confused notion of 'downward causation' according to which a whole can somehow have a causal impact on its own components/parts (see Lawson, 2012).

11 When such modification occurs it is even clearer that emergent properties are irreducible to the original items, where the latter must now be seen as antecedents to or precursors of (as opposed to) constituents of the emergent organisation or whole.

12 Of course there are notable exceptions. Amongst those contributors who at some point connect causal powers to organisation, some (but not all) of whom adopt roughly similar positions to my own, see Conwy Lloyd Morgan (1923), Ludwig von Bertalanffy (1971), Margaret Archer (1982), Roger Sperry (1986), Donald Campbell (1990), Thomas Smith (1997), Walter Buckley (1998), Paul Cilliers (1998), Mark Bickhard (2000), Bryon Cunningham (2001), Keith Sawyer (2001) and David Elder-Vass (2007).

13 For example, any such emergent-order-as-remainder may take the form of simple configurations left in place following processes of lower-level mutual cancelling; or the cumulative multiplication of initial 'constraints' of lower-level elements that are contingently amplified during any such process; or, at higher levels of complexity, of features that become fortuitously reinforced and amplified through processes of reciprocal selection, as or where processes such as those discussed become recursively embedded (see Lawson, 2012).

14 Previously, the hadrons (mesons and baryons such as the proton and neutron) and even (whole) atoms have been regarded as elementary particles.

15 I do not wish to suggest that this is the only interpretation of quantum field theory or that this interpretation is devoid of problems. Some do still hold to a particle interpretation of quantum field theory (see Nicolaas Landsman, 1996; Paul Teller, 1990, 1995) and others hold different ontologies still, including event ontologies (see, e.g., Sunny Auyang, 1995; Dennis Dieks, 2002). However, it is the field process interpretation that seems the more explanatorily successful (see Harvey Brown and Rom Harré, 1988; Bickhard, 2000). For an accessible general discussion and overview see Meinhard Kuhlmann (2009), and for related discussions on all aspects of the issues touched upon, see, e.g., Tian Yu Cao (1997, 1999), Elena Castellani (2002), Paul Davies (1989), Jan Faye *et al.* (2000), Kuhlmann (2000), Kuhlmann *et al.* (2002), Michael Redhead (1980, 1983, 1988) and Johanna Seibt (2002).

16 Moreover, it is held that quantum field processes themselves, being processes, have no existence independent of how they are organised and that these processes can only exist in organised patterns (see Alfred North Whitehead, 1967 [1925]; Brown and Harré, 1988; Bickhard, 2000). I might acknowledge, though, that many interpreters of quantum theory maintain, along with Niels Bohr who first introduced the quantum into the atom, that quantum theory actually refutes the doctrine of realism itself. For a good discussion of the realism issue in the history of quantum theory, particularly focusing on the main early protagonists for realism (Albert Einstein) and against it (Niels Bohr), see Manjit Kumar (2009). Perhaps the most recent experimental input widely interpreted as supporting the antirealist viewpoint has come from a group of physicists in Austria whose findings seem to rule out a broad class of hidden-variables theories (for an explanation and particular defence of hidden-variables theories see Christopher Norris, 2000) that focus on realism and, in reporting to find 'local realistic theories untenable', have encouraged an interpretation of their results that implies that reality does not exist when we are not observing it (see Simon Gröblacher *et al.*, 2007). Others claim on separate grounds that quantum theory implies that reality is only our creation. Each such antirealist interpretation has its specific limitations. But as a general response, I think it is sufficient to recognise that the numerous surprising, and, for many, often shocking, quantum experimental findings are themselves indicative of an objective reality existing independently of us; these experiments repeatedly give rise to the same often difficult to interpret, and equally often actually undesired, outcomes, not because of us, but despite us. In other words, the history of quantum theory indicates very well that the aspects of reality studied act reliably according to their *own* natures, affecting how we

can interact with them, including observing or measuring them, whatever the (often intellectually opposed) experimenters differentially expected, wished for or feared in their (repeated) findings. In other words, even, and seemingly especially, at the atomic level, nature does not allow us to find of it anything we prefer or choose.

17 For good discussions of the category 'convention' see especially John Latsis (2005, 2006, 2009) and Latsis *et al.* (2010).

18 Many years ago, on a Monday evening, in the bar in King's College Cambridge, I happened to bump into a student of whom I was a supervisor. We discussed philosophical ideas germane to the student's research. The student thought it would be helpful to meet again and about a week seemed to be the required time to prepare. So we arranged to meet the following Monday, in the same place. Other students that I supervised, who were also interested in philosophy, asked if they could come along too. They did, the meeting was successful and we agreed to meet once more on the following Monday evening. Twenty-two years on, the meetings are still occurring on Monday evenings. They are now known as the Cambridge Realist Workshop and visitors often structure visits to Cambridge to ensure an overlap with Mondays within the Cambridge University term in order to come along. Other events in Cambridge are structured to coordinate with the Realist Workshop. For many of us the Workshop signals ways for going on that have become the accepted ones for achieving various wanted outcomes, even though this was never an original plan or expectation.

19 It is this belief that in some part underpins Searle's conclusion that society is essentially linguistic, that there are no social objects but merely different (social and 'institutional') facts about naturalistic objects and how we treat them.

20 Of course the category of social rule is also highly contested. For a useful overview see Ismael Al-Amoudi (2010).

21 A further distinction that is usefully drawn is between rules that are implicit within a collective practice but perhaps not articulated or acknowledged by a relevant body, and those that are explicitly acknowledged and stipulated by a relevant community authority. Though in many workplaces various perks are widely treated as norms and so rule-governed, these are often never explicitly acknowledged as such by those with the power to formulate rules of employment (and in consequence are often the first to be disputed when changes are deemed necessary). In contrast, matters concerning wages, normal working hours, lengths of holidays and various other terms of employment are often formalised and explicitly stated in a contract. In the UK, the maximum speed limit for motorway driving laid down by the relevant authorities is 70 miles per hour, though the operative rule, nowhere explicitly acknowledged, seems to be that driving at 80 miles per hour is everywhere allowed. I adopt the practice of referring to the rules that are operative but not explicitly acknowledged by a relevant body as 'informal rules' and to those that are explicitly recognised as 'formal rules'. The latter are usually codified, but the former could be as well. So the formal/non-formal distinction is not identical to the codified/non-codified differentiation.

22 An interesting question is whether a specific collective practice can be participated in by a single individual. I see no paradox in answering in the affirmative. At a moment in time there may be only a single prime minister in the UK, or president in the USA, but over time different individuals may undertake similar practices. Perhaps someone who has served an institution in a fundamental way is given an honorary post carrying various rights and so allowed to follow certain practices, and this turns out to be a unique situation/creation. Even so, I think there is an implication that had someone else been in a position to make the same contribution they, too, would have been granted the same sort of

status. The ways of proceeding so facilitated remain accepted as ways of going on by a relevant community (for a relevant [set of] individual(s)) and participation always requires the participation of others in interaction.

23 An alternative terminological strategy would be to refer to all such allowed social practices as rights, with the subset of required practices being obligations. Instead I have chosen to refer to all positionally allowed practices as powers, reserving the term 'rights' for those allowances that are not also required. As such, rights and obligations might be thought of, respectively, as positive and negative powers.

24 Of course, the establishment of formal organisations can facilitate positions of power over others in ways that are not, or not primarily, centred on the production of profits. The establishment of media outlets is an obvious example. In the UK many tabloids are currently run at a loss, but allow their owners and/or editors to influence public opinion in ways they could not without the device of newspaper proprietorship or the legitimating status of editorship, etc. Somewhat related, within the academy an increasingly common development is for specific individuals (or small groups) to set up new journals and to announce themselves as the editors. In a context where publications and citations, etc., make a significant difference to academic careers, the ease with which specific individuals can, and do, establish for themselves positions in which they immediately acquire the right/authority to arbitrate on these matters is perhaps a matter of interest (or concern). Self-appointed editors immediately assume for themselves the right to determine, for their journal, which would-be contributors are to be published, the content encouraged of authors, which additional authors and/or contributions should be (and sometimes even which should not be) cited and discussed, and so on. To achieve this end a foundation or charitable trust or some other formal organisational entity may also be set up, or an alignment with an existing one established, or both, but the procuring of the relevant novel powers is seemingly typically the motivating factor.

25 Despite elaborating a conceptual framework on social reality that in many ways (not explored here) is different from that which I defend, this is a conclusion that, at least with respect to corporations, Searle also reaches in his recent book (Searle, 2010, p. 98). Thus he writes of the act of creating a corporation 'that the whole point of doing this is to create a rather elaborate set of power relationships between actual people; indeed, the corporation consists of such relationships'. Searle's treatment of the corporation here departs from his earlier conception (Searle, 1995) and is seemingly presented as a somewhat exceptional feature of social reality. However, working within Searle's framework, Alexandra Arapinis (2011) suggests instead that the structure involved is likely the generic case, concluding that 'institutional entities are, above all, "placeholders for a set of actual power relationships among actual people"'.

26 Actually it is not so easy to identify position occupants where subgroups at least *never* come together as communities, as I have discovered through using Google. If we consider position occupants such as academics, British citizens, wives or refugees, the former two are clearly familiar enough as groups who self-consciously come together in promotion of shared concerns – under the categories of the academic community or, say, the British community in Spain or Hong Kong. But actually although categories of wife or refugee might seem less promising (or did so to me), a quick search on Google reveals tens of thousands of examples of communities of each.

27 An alternative categorical strategy is to restrict the term 'community' just to members of any position where there is indeed a 'coming together' over shared concerns. I go with the strategy laid out in the main text (that each position

grounds a community in itself, a potential community for itself), but either way the important point is that the category 'community' rests on the central one of social position and either way the usage seems satisfactory if consistently applied. Indeed, either way the association of the category 'community' with that of 'social position' has analytical advantages. In social theory there seemingly is no term in ready use for the collection of individuals that share any given position. At the same time the category 'community' is often contested, usually left unsystematised and sometimes even abandoned as without referent. Understood here as occupants of a given position, even if restricted to cases where there is a coming together based on shared concerns, the category community thus unusually performs an unambiguous, systematic and fundamental role. Other advantages include allowing the familial use of the term 'community' to alert us to the existence of (positioned) rights and obligations that have in no way been formally or perhaps even knowingly instituted. A local village may have evolved certain 'community' practices regarding transport, tidiness, noise, dress or whatever, and newcomers and visitors can be reprimanded if they seek to participate in (the rights of) village life without conforming to what are effectively the obligations of the community.

28 The analysis which follows can be extended to various animate 'objects' as well, e.g., all those positioned as pets or livestock.

29 And of course the pieces of paper or bits of metal positioned as cash possess all the additional causal powers associated with paper and the metal concerned, and numerous substitute items or devices are imaginable that could serve uniquely to identify those standing in the underlying credit/debt relations, including increasingly electronic forms.

30 For example, on a section of the Bank of England's current (November 2011) web site entitled 'Damaged and Mutilated Banknotes', the public are informed that:

> The Bank will give reasonable consideration to claims made in respect of banknotes which have been damaged accidentally. In making our assessment we take into account a number of factors. A key consideration for the Bank is that we should not knowingly pay out twice on the same banknote. Therefore, as a general rule, there should be physical evidence of at least half a banknote before payment can be made although an explanation of how damage has occurred to the banknote will be taken into account. If the Bank receives an application where less than half a banknote has been submitted and the Bank is unable to reasonably ascertain whether a larger portion of the banknote still exists, it is unlikely that payment will be made … The Bank currently receives around 30,000 individual applications per year, totalling around £18 million. Despite the high volumes the majority of claims are assessed within a few days. The list of ways in which banknotes become damaged is almost endless – from those accidentally put through a washing machine to those chewed by the family pet. Banknotes hidden for safe keeping can often be overlooked. Those concealed in places such as ovens or microwaves run the risk of burning whilst banknotes hidden under floorboards or in gardens become damp and eventually decay.

See www.bankofengland.co.uk/banknotes/damaged_banknotes.htm.

31 Also notice that when, in comparison, a signed cheque (say also to the value of £20) is lost or damaged the result need not be that the underlying credit relation, and in particular the identity of the creditor (as well as the payer), cannot be established. Lost or damaged cheques are often replaced by the payer of the cheque because the latter possesses an alternative record of the credit relation (including a record both of the credit that had been issued and of what had, and had not, been 'cashed in'). Of course this is a case of personal credit; though that should not detract from the point.

32 Actually the switch over was not quite a one-day event; in fact the transition process started several years before the arrival of decimal day, with numerous items priced in both currencies for some time both before and after decimal day. The 5p and 10p coins appeared indeed in April 1968, taking the same size and composition as the shillings and florins that remained in circulation with them. The 50p coin appeared in October 1969, with the old ten-shilling note being withdrawn in November 1970. The old halfpenny was withdrawn from circulation on 31 July 1969 and the old half-crown (2s 6d) followed on 31 December. The new ½p, 1p and 2p were introduced on 15 February 1971, and on 31 August 1971 the penny and threepenny were officially withdrawn from circulation, ending the transition period.

33 Further, related discussions of such matters can be found in Clive Lawson (2008; Lawson *et al.*, 2007).

References

Al-Amoudi I. 2010. Immanent non-algorithmic rules: an ontological study of social rules. *Journal for the Theory of Social Behaviour*, vol. 4 (3): 289–313.

Arapinis A. 2011. Anchoring the Institutional in the Material: Searle's Constitutive Rule Revisited, paper presented at the Making the Social World Conference, Milan, June, mimeograph, IHPST.

Archer M. 1982. Morphogenesis versus structuration: on combining structure and action. *British Journal of Sociology*, vol. 33: 455–83.

Auyang S.Y. 1995. *How is Quantum Field Theory Possible?* Oxford and New York: Oxford University Press.

Bertalanffy L. von. 1971. *General Systems Theory*. London: Allen Lane.

Bickhard M.H. 2000. Emergence, pp. 322–48. In: Andersen P.B., Emmeche C., Finnermann N.O., Christiansen P., editors. *Downward Causation*. Aarhus. University of Aarhus Press.

Brown H.R., Harré R., editors. 1988. *Philosophical Foundations of Quantum Field Theory*. Oxford: Clarendon Press.

Buckley W.F. 1998. *Society – A Complex Adaptive System: Essays in Social Theory*. Amsterdam: Gordon and Breach.

Campbell D.T. 1990. Levels of organisation, downward causation, and the selection-theory approach to evolutionary epistemology, pp. 1–17. In: Greenberg G., Tobach E., editors. *Theories of the Evolution of Knowing*. Hillsdale: Erlbaum.

Cao T.Y. 1997. *Conceptual Developments of 20th Century Field Theories*. Cambridge, UK: Cambridge University Press.

Cao T.Y., editor. 1999. *Conceptual Foundations of Quantum Field Theories*. Cambridge, UK: Cambridge University Press.

Castellani E. 2002. Reductionism, emergence, and effective field theories. *Studies in History and Philosophy of Modern Physics*, vol. 33: 251–67.

Cilliers P. 1998. *Complexity and Postmodernism: Understanding Complex Systems*. London and New York: Routledge.

Cunningham B. 2001. The reemergence of 'emergence'. *Philosophy of Science*, vol. 68: S62–S75.

Davies P., editor. 1989. *The New Physics*. Cambridge, UK: Cambridge University Press.

Dieks D. 2002. Events and covariance in the interpretation of quantum field theory, pp. 215–34. In: Kuhlmann M., Lyre H., Wayne A., editors. *Ontological*

Aspects of Quantum Field Theory. Singapore, London and Hackensack: World Scientific Publishing.

Elder-Vass D. 2007. For emergence: refining Archer's account of social structure. *Journal for the Theory of Social Behaviour*, vol. 37 (1): 25–44.

Ellis B. 2002. *The Philosophy of Nature: A Guide to the New Essentialism*. Chesham: Acumen Publishing Limited.

Faye J., Scheffler U., Urchs M., editors. 2000. *Events, Facts, and Things*. Vol. 72. *Poznań Studies in the Philosophy of the Sciences and Humanities*. Amsterdam: Rodopi.

Fullbrook E. 2009. *Ontology and Economics: Tony Lawson and His Critics*. London: Routledge.

Gröblacher S., Paterek T., Kaltenbaek R., Brukner Č., Żukowski M., Aspelmeyer M., Zeilinger A. 2007. An experimental test of non-local realism. *Nature*, vol. 446: 871–5.

Ingham G. 2004. *The Nature of Money*. Cambridge, UK: Polity Press.

Kay J. 2010. Economics may be dismal, but it is not a science. *Financial Times*, 13 April.

Kim J. 1993A. *Supervenience and the Mind*. Cambridge, UK: Cambridge University Press.

Kim J. 1993B. The non-reductivist's troubles with mental causation, pp. 189–210. In: Heil J., Mele A., editors. *Mental Causation*. Oxford: Oxford University Press.

Kuhlmann M. 2000. Processes as objects of quantum field theory, pp. 365–88. In: Faye J., Scheffler U., Urchs M., editors. *Events, Facts, and Things*. Vol. 72. *Poznań Studies in the Philosophy of the Sciences and Humanities*. Amsterdam: Rodopi.

Kuhlmann M. 2009. Quantum field theory. In: Zalta E.N., editor. *The Stanford Encyclopedia of Philosophy*, Spring edn., http://plato.stanford.edu/archives/spr2009/entries/quantum-field-theory/ (date last accessed 8 February 2012).

Kuhlmann M., Lyre H., Wayne A., editors. 2002. *Ontological Aspects of Quantum Field Theory*. Singapore, London and Hackensack: World Scientific Publishing.

Kumar M. 2009. *Quantum: Einstein, Bohr and the Great Debate about the Nature of Reality*. London: Icon Books.

Landsman N.P. 1996. Local quantum physics. *Studies in History and Philosophy of Modern Physics*, vol. 27: 511–25.

Latsis J. 2005. Is there redemption for conventions? *Cambridge Journal of Economics*, vol. 29 (5): 707–27.

Latsis J. 2006. Convention and intersubjectivity: new developments in French economics. *Journal for the Theory of Social Behaviour*, vol. 36 (3): 255–77.

Latsis J. 2009. Hume and the concept of convention. *Recherches sur la Philosophie et le Language*, vol. 26: 217–34.

Latsis J., de Larquier G., Bessis F. 2010. Are conventions solutions to uncertainty? Contrasting visions of social coordination. *Journal of Post Keynesian Economics*, vol. 32 (4): 535–58.

Lawson C. 2008. An ontology of technology: artefacts, relations and functions. *Techné: Research in Philosophy and Technology*, vol. 12 (1) 48–64.

Lawson C., Latsis J., Martins N., editors. 2007. *Contributions to Social Ontology*. London and New York: Routledge.

Lawson T. 1994. A realist theory for economics, pp. 257–85. In: Backhouse R., editor. *New Directions in Economic Methodology*. London: Routledge.

Lawson T. 1997. *Economics and Reality*. London: Routledge.

Lawson T. 2003. *Reorienting Economics*. London: Routledge.

Lawson T. 2006. The nature of heterodox economics. *Cambridge Journal of Economics*, vol. 30 (2): 483–507.

Lawson T. 2009. The current economic crisis: its nature and the course of academic economics. *Cambridge Journal of Economics*, vol. 33 (4): 759–88.

Lawson T. 2012. Emergence, Morphogenesis, Causal Reduction and Downward Causation, mimeo, Cambridge.

Lévi-Strauss C. 1964–71. *Mytholiques*; vols. 1–4. Paris: Plon.

Lloyd Morgan C. 1923. *Emergent Evolution*. Gifford Lecture delivered in 1922 at the University of St Andrews. London: Williams and Norgate.

McSmith A. 2010. *No Such Thing as Society: A History of Britain in the 1980s*. London: Constable and Robinson.

Norris C. 2000. *Quantum Theory and the Flight from Realism*. London and New York: Routledge.

Read R. 2007. Economics is philosophy, economics is not science. *International Journal of Green Economics*, vol. 1 (3/4): 307–25.

Redhead M.L.G. 1980. Some philosophical aspects of particle physics. *Studies in History and Philosophy of Science*, vol. 11: 279–304.

Redhead M.L.G. 1983. Quantum field theory for philosophers, pp. 57–99. In: Asquith P.D., Nickles T., editors. *Proceedings of the Biennial Meeting of the Philosophy of Science Association: PSA 1982*. Vol. 2. East Lansing: Philosophy of Science Association.

Redhead M.L.G. 1988. A philosopher looks at quantum field theory, pp. 9–23. In: Brown H.R., Harré R., editors. *Philosophical Foundations of Quantum Field Theory*. Oxford: Clarendon Press.

Sawyer R.K. 2001. Emergence in sociology: contemporary philosophy of mind and some implications for sociological theory. *American Journal of Sociology*, vol. 107: 551–85.

Searle J.R. 1992. *The Rediscovery of the Mind*. Cambridge, MA: MIT Press.

Searle J.R. 1995. *The Construction of Social Reality*. London: Penguin Books.

Searle J.R. 1999. *Mind, Language and Society: Philosophy in the Real World*. London: Weidenfeld and Nicolson.

Searle J.R. 2008. Coda: Searle versus Smith (replying to Barry Smith 2008), pp. 48–51. In: Smith B., Mark D.M., Ehrlich I., editors. *The Mystery of Capital and the Construction of Social Reality*. Chicago and La Salle: Open Court.

Searle J.R. 2010. *Making the Social World: The Structure of Human Civilisation*. Oxford: Oxford University Press.

Seibt J. 2002. The matrix of ontological thinking: heuristic preliminaries for an ontology of QFT, pp. 53–97. In: Kuhlmann M., Lyre H., Wayne A., editors. *Ontological Aspects of Quantum Field Theory*. Singapore, London and Hackensack: World Scientific Publishing.

Sellars W. 1965. Imperatives, intentions, and the logic of 'ought', pp. 159–218. In: Castaneda H.N., Nakhnikian G., editors. *Morality and the Language of Conduct*. Detroit: Wayne State University Press.

Sellars W. 1974. *Essays in Philosophy and its History*. Dordrecht: Reidel Publishing.

Smith B. 2008. Searle and De Soto: the new ontology of the social world, pp. 35–48. In: Smith B., Mark D.M., Ehrlich I., editors. *The Mystery of Capital and the Construction of Social Reality*. Chicago and La Salle: Open Court.

Smith T.S. 1997. Nonlinear dynamics and the micro–macro bridge, pp. 52–63. In: Eve R.A., Horsfall S., Lee M.E., editors. *Chaos, Complexity, and Sociology.* Thousand Oaks: Sage.

Sperry R.W. 1986. Macro- versus micro-determinism. *Philosophy of Science*, vol. 53: 265–70.

Teller P. 1990. What the quantum field is not. *Philosophical Topics*, vol. 18: 175–86.

Teller P. 1995. *An Interpretive Introduction to Quantum Field Theory.* Princeton: Princeton University Press.

Viveiros de Castro E.B. 1998. Cosmological deixis and Amerindian perspectivism. *Journal of the Royal Anthropological Institute*, vol. 4 (3): 468–88.

Viveiros de Castro E.B. 2004. Exchanging perspectives: the transformation of objects into subjects in Amerindian ontologies. *Common Knowledge*, vol. 10 (3): 463–84.

Weiss G. 1972. Campa cosmology. *Ethnology*, vol. 11 (2): 169–70.

Whitehead A.N. 1967 [1925]. *Science and the Modern World.* New York: Free Press.

16 Open and closed systems and the Cambridge school[1]

Vinca Bigo

Introduction

Economics has recently taken something of an 'ontological turn', at least amongst its heterodox traditions.[2] Much of the credit for this can be given to a group of researchers referred to by Andrew Mearman (2006) as the 'Cambridge school'. And indeed such labelling is not inappropriate: very recently those within reach of Cambridge (UK) have instituted an ontologically oriented project around the research to which Mearman refers, under the auspices of the *Cambridge Social Ontology Group* (or CSOG).

Like most other commentators on this ontological project, Mearman singles out two books by Tony Lawson (1997, 2003a)[3] for close attention. This is not unreasonable as the Cambridge group is closely associated with Lawson, and his are the first two full-length monographs on the Cambridge approach. A strength of these two books is their comprehensive coverage. A disadvantage, perhaps, is that the many issues they cover are treated as more or less on par, without consideration as to which ones will seem the most difficult, important or contentious to the reader. With the benefit of hindsight, however, it is possible to see which have caught the attention of those wishing to engage with the project.

One such feature is the Cambridge conception and analysis of open and closed systems. Indeed, Mearman's paper is one of several to focus on this topic.[4] Mearman in fact advances three criticisms of the Cambridge position on these matters. Criticism of course is vital to enable us all to move forward. However, in advancing his criticisms of the Cambridge position, I think that Mearman misinterprets the latter on various key issues. And this matters. For it can be reasonably held that the Cambridge group has contributed as much as any in recent years to understanding and transcending the problems of the contemporary discipline of economics. And the manner in which the Cambridge group employs its categories of open and closed systems figures centrally in this endeavour.

My limited intention in the current essay is thus to address the three basic criticisms made of the Cambridge approach by Mearman. Specifically, by seeking to clarify the Cambridge position on relevant points, I shall show that each of Mearman's criticisms fail.

According to Mearman the Cambridge approach is at fault for:

1   tying the idea of closure too closely to events;
2   defining open systems in a negative (and apparently often dualistic) fashion as 'not closed'; and
3   polarising conceptions of open and closed systems, and in turn methodological debate in economics, thereby encouraging heterodox economists sympathetic to the Cambridge position to be overly dismissive of certain methodological approaches.

The remainder of the paper is a response to Mearman, considering each of these points in turn.

Closed systems and event patterns

Mearman starts that section of his paper which criticises the Cambridge association of closures with event patterns by acknowledging that in fact there is a 'small range' of definitions of closed systems in the wider project of critical realism. Specifically: 'Closed systems are variously defined as being "cut off" from external influences [...]; "isolated" [...]; where outside factors are "neutralise[d]" [...]; and in which all disturbances are anticipated and "held at bay"' (Mearman 2006: 49).

Noting this apparent variety Mearman complains that 'the Cambridge school definition of open and closed systems has been, and is being increasingly, restricted to one' (ibid.: 50). Specifically, 'closed (and hence open) systems are defined in terms of events and their regularity' (ibid.: 50). What is more, this 'event-level definition' is 'beginning to be the dominant definition' in social theorising more widely, but particularly in economics (ibid.: 51).

Why is this a problem? First, according to Mearman, 'to define closures as regularities is inconsistent with the definitions of closed and open systems' supposedly advanced elsewhere in critical realism that 'stress the nature of the object, conditions placed on it, its location, its being cut off' and so forth (ibid.: 53).

More importantly, in Mearman's view, when properly interpreted, 'closure occurs beneath the level of events: the nature of the objects and their relation to other objects are the defining factors in creating a closed system' (ibid.: 53). It is Mearman's view that the Cambridge approach, by focusing on events, fails to appreciate this.

And there is no doubt, in Mearman's mind, that the Cambridge group's event-level conception of closure leads to further problems:

This confusion of closure and its evidence is potentially serious: The claim conflates the empirical with the real; this is known as *empirical realism*, a flattening of ontology. It also suggests that the *epistemic fallacy* has been committed: what exists is reduced to what is known. It also suggests *actualism*, defined as the denial of the existence of underlying mechanisms and acknowledges only actual events or experiences [...]. Empirical realism, the epistemic fallacy and actualism are all explicitly denied and rejected by [the Cambridge group and other critical realists]. These contradictions arise here because of the event-level definition of closed systems.

(Ibid.: 53)

This, then, is the nub of Mearman's first, seemingly potentially serious, criticism of the Cambridge approach. Mearman considers various implications. He also suggests some possible (mainly strategic) lines of defence of the position he attributes to the Cambridge school, but finds none to hold their own. Let me respond to Mearman's first line of critique by way of seeking to clarify the Cambridge conception of a closed system.

Closed systems: a response

If we examine the way in which Lawson, in particular, *introduces* the category of closure in his two books, we find that closed systems are indeed conceptualised *in terms of* events and their regularities. On this point Mearman is correct. However, closures are interpreted *not* as events or their regularities *per se*, but as *systems* in which event regularities occur. In fact, closures are formulated as an essential component of the explanatory approach that Lawson terms deductivism. Thus in *Reorienting Economics*, closures are introduced as follows:

> By deductivism I mean a type of explanation in which regularities of the form 'whenever event x then event y' (or stochastic near equivalents) are a necessary condition. Such regularities are held to persist, and are often treated, in effect, as laws, allowing the deductive generation of consequences, or predictions, when accompanied with the specification of initial conditions. *Systems in which such regularities occur are said to be closed.*
>
> (Lawson 2003a: 5, my emphasis)

As the sentence to which I have added emphasis states quite clearly, closed systems are conceptualised not as event regularities *per se*, but systems *in which* event regularities occur.[5]

In a similar fashion, in his earlier *Economics and Reality*, Lawson introduces the idea of closure as follows:

It is clear, in fact, that if the theory of explanation and science in question turns upon identifying or positing regularities of the form 'whenever event x then event y' – let us refer to systems in which such constant conjunctions of events arise as *closed* – then a precondition of the universality, or wide applicability, of deductivism is simply that reality is characterised by a ubiquity of such closures.

(Lawson 1997: 19)

Lawson, then, is quite consistent in maintaining that there is a difference between an event regularity and a system in which it occurs; in particular, that the latter is irreducible to the former.[6]

The term system here, it should be clear, is serving as a placeholder, specifically as one for the structural arrangement in which the event regularity occurs. The standard meaning of a system is something like a group of interrelated elements comprising a unified whole. In science it is an object of study composed of interrelated parts. From the Latin and Greek, the term system means to combine, to set up, to place together. Very often a system is conceived as a collection of components so organised (whether intentionally or not) that a specific function or outcome is the result. This is the meaning employed by the Cambridge group. And a closed system specifically is simply one in which the outcome is an event regularity.

Now to identify any thing, including a system, according to one of its features, is not *per se* to reduce that thing to its features. A female of a species may well be identified or distinguished by the possession of reproductive capabilities, but this is not to reduce the former to the latter. Similarly a sports team may be identified according to some kind of colour scheme on its team kit, but again that is not to reduce the team to its colour scheme. Likewise, to identify closed systems according to event regularities occurring within them is in no way to necessitate any reduction of either to the other, and certainly the Cambridge group keeps the distinction clear. For the Cambridge group specifically, the association of an event regularity with a system has served to set a marker for investigating the sort of thing or assemblage, i.e. system, in which an event regularity is (or would be) produced.

It is worth emphasising, in fact, that when the Cambridge group has examined the conditions or type of system in which strict event regularities occur they have focused not on necessary conditions (as Mearman suggests when he does acknowledge the Cambridge concern with closure conditions[7]) but on *sufficiency* conditions. Why is this? In part it is just because, no matter how unlikely it is that such a scenario will emerge, it seems impossible to rule out the theoretical possibility of an event regularity of the sort with which economists are concerned,[8] coming about under varying conditions. That is, although extremely implausible, it is logically conceivable that a regularity at the level of events could be the outcome of sets of interacting causes that are different on each occasion. As such, necessary conditions may not exist. By focusing on (sets of) sufficiency conditions it is at least possible to indicate that, should they be satisfied, an event regularity is guaranteed.

But even more to the point, to the extent that economists seek general (and typically parsimonious) theories of behaviour, they tend to suppose that any specific event regularity, if and where it should occur, would have a fixed explanation: that the reason x is followed by y today is the reason x was followed by y yesterday and will be so tomorrow. So the ontological identification of (sets of) sufficiency conditions for closure should help us to understand the sorts of (typically fictitious) assumptions entertained within modern mainstream theorising, given its overriding commitment to mathematical–deductivist modelling.

This certainly has been the Cambridge group's line of thinking. In particular, it has underpinned the identification of the intrinsic and extrinsic closure conditions. The former stipulates that individuals or mechanisms posited have fixed internal structure constraining them to act in identical ways in repeated conditions. The latter stipulates that such individuals or mechanisms posited in any theory act in conditions of relative insulation from, or are orthogonal to, other causal factors in play. Such conditions do seem to satisfy the requirement that, when such a mechanism is 'triggered' (and clearly the triggering is itself in effect part of any sufficiency conditions[9]), an event regularity is guaranteed. Moreover it is difficult to imagine a more plausible scenario under which an event regularity could be guaranteed. Thus Lawson writes:

> The desire of 'theorists' to 'explain' events in some theoretical manner, combined (if implicitly) with a belief in the universal relevance of the deductivist mode of explanation, sets them deriving theoretical constructs that have conditions to guarantee the 'whenever this event then that event' formulation built into them. Of course, logically speaking there may not be a unique set of sufficient conditions of this sort. But given the nature of social reality, the intrinsic and extrinsic conditions just outlined, by focusing directly upon both the nature of individuals and also their conditions of action, do seem to constitute obvious choices for most occasions. And the most straightforward conceptions to pursue in the endeavour to satisfy these two conditions, I have suggested, are those of atomistic individuals acting in conditions of relative isolation.
>
> (Lawson 1997: 100)

It is from the perspective of this broader understanding that we can make sense of the observations underpinning Mearman's charge, noted early on in this section, that in discussing closures (realist) contributors highlight different features. In fact, although Mearman implies that each of the varying features – e.g., isolation, disturbances being held at bay, etc. – is highlighted by a different contributor, the truth is that each contributor actually refers to most if not all of these. The reason for it is that the features described represent not competing conceptions of closure at all, but rather associated assessments of the properties, and typically sufficiency conditions, of a conception of closure held in common.

The Cambridge concern with identifying the intrinsic and extrinsic conditions that, if accompanied by a triggering of a mechanism, result in an event regularity, is at one point noted by Mearman (he refers to the conditions in question as the I.C.C. and E.C.C.). However he seems overly dismissive of the implications:

> [I]t could be argued that Lawson *et al.* are fully aware of both closure conditions, that the closure conditions occur below the level of events, and that therefore [...] the Cambridge view does not equate regularities and closures. [...] However, this paper holds that the Cambridge view mostly makes a clear distinction between closures and conditions for closures: Therefore, the I.C.C. and E.C.C. are not generally considered as closures.
>
> (Mearman 2006: 53–4)

Actually, contrary to Mearman's suggestion, there is no problem at all in distinguishing between a (closed) system as a whole and its (sufficiency) conditions; there may be, and very often will be, much going on besides the conditions that guarantee that any system is closed (that an event regularity is produced). However, the important point here is that there is a difference between the event regularity produced and the closed system in which it occurs.

Notice, too, that it is precisely in virtue of their questioning the conditions under which a closure is guaranteed that the Cambridge group can be seen to be rejecting empirical realism, and the related charges levelled by Mearman. For the empirical realist recognises only events and their patterns, and so does not have the resources to pursue the question as to *why or how* event regularities occur where or when they do; to such an individual the observation that event patterns occur systematically in some locations but not in others is necessarily an eternal mystery.

To this point I have restricted myself to demonstrating that the Cambridge school does not define closed systems as event regularities in themselves. But what, we might ask, if it did? According to Mearman, this would constitute a 'confusion of closure and its evidence', apparently justifying charges of empirical realism, the epistemic fallacy and actualism, amongst other things. But such charges would still not follow even in this hypothetical scenario. They would do so only if the Cambridge group claimed *in addition* that events and their regularities constituted all there is to (knowable) reality. Now it would be a *gross* misrepresentation to accuse the Cambridge group of this; for as far as I can see no group has contributed more in recent times to reorienting the discipline towards a greater focus on underlying structures, powers, mechanisms and the like. The central emphasis of the group has indeed been first on a recovery of ontology, and secondly, on defending an ontological conception in which depth figures large.

To take stock, the difference between the notion of closure formulated by the Cambridge school and that preferred by Mearman is *not* that the former group stick only to the level of events whilst Mearman (and others to whom he frequently refers) is prepared to go deeper. Rather the difference is that the Cambridge group, as represented by Lawson, *seeks to highlight, and to examine the nature of, that set of systems sharing the property of event regularities occurring or being produced within them,* whilst Mearman seemingly wishes to examine the nature of a set of systems delineated on some other yet to be disclosed basis.

Now it is important, finally, to question why the Cambridge group might adopt the conception of closures that it does. The group's main concern has not been with typology *per se*, but with addressing the unreasoned prevalence of deductivist methods in social theorising. That is, the motivating concern has not been to provide an account of forms of social systems in the abstract, but to critically address the widespread insistence that methods that presuppose the existence of event regularities be everywhere applied in social theory. In economics, specifically, the view that all science necessitates methods that require the uncovering of event regularities for purposes of prediction and so forth was, and remains, integral to the emphasis on mathematical-deductivist modelling. As Pratten (2005) recently documented, Lawson's opposition to this latter mainstream emphasis long predates his adoption of the terminology of closed systems.

So why adopt the terminology of closed systems for those in which event regularities occur? It is easy to suggest a reason. Notice first that Mearman asserts that there is a rich heritage of interpretations of closures that is overlooked by the Cambridge conception. This is true, but equally (as Mearman also recognises), there are very many competing conceptions, especially if we look across the disciplines. So it is not clear which is the correct or best one from a purely historical perspective. Even if it is accepted that the term closure typically captures a certain *sort* of system, namely one in which certain features of interest are effectively 'closed off' from (in the sense of being insulated from, or held in stable relation to) other features with which they might otherwise interact, or do so in unstable ways, it is not obvious how to choose within the range of possibilities if a merely historical or typological stance is adopted.

As it happens, the Cambridge project provides one answer to this 'dilemma'. For once we accept that, on the Cambridge conception, a closed system is *not* after all an event regularity but a system in which one occurs, then we can examine the properties of that system, in particular its sufficiency conditions. And doing so reveals a conception of a closure not especially out of line with the *sorts* of conceptions of a closed system to which Mearman refers, including those of General Systems Theory, etc.

Now I have acknowledged above that it is logically feasible that an event regularity could come about with the causes responsible varying all the time. However, from the ontological understanding achieved in critical realism such a scenario would appear to be a very special occurrence, and a posteriori seemingly unprecedented. It is reasonable, therefore, for it to be mostly discounted for practical purposes. I have accepted too that there may be competing sets of sufficiency conditions for the production of an event regularity. In truth, though, the seemingly only plausible scenario is the one, well illustrated by the closely controlled experiment, wherein the intrinsic and extrinsic conditions are satisfied: where an intrinsically stable mechanism is insulated from other causal factors and triggered. Thus the conditions we can reasonably expect to be associated with an event regularity are of a sort that are associated with notions of closure as defined in other disciplines.

In short, there is no problem in 1) first focusing on systems in which event regularities occur, 2) discovering a posteriori a) that we can properly talk only in terms of sufficiency conditions of such occurrences, b) that one set of sufficiency conditions is likely to characterise all actual event regularities of interest to social science, c) affinities between systems in which such conditions hold and others that have been designated in various other disciplines as 'closed', and thus 3) employing the terminology of closed systems for those scenarios in which event regularities are produced.

So in summary, the difference between the Cambridge approach and that of Mearman is not that only the latter looks at systems or depth whilst the former looks only at events. To the contrary, the Cambridge group is as interested in notions of depth, totalities, process and structure as any group of economists or social theorists of which I am aware. Rather the difference is that the Cambridge group does not use an a priori or *arbitrary* conception of closure to define a construct whose properties are then to be investigated. Instead, it adopts a largely strategic orientation in fixing the meaning of terms. As it happens, the sorts of systems it has uncovered as supporting event regularities are those that invite the designation *closed*. Of course, in labelling as closed those systems in which event regularities occur, and subjecting such systems to sustained investigation, the Cambridge group, as is widely recognised, has been able to challenge prevailing ideas in the philosophy of science and also in social theory, not least in economics, that have been detrimental to progress in understanding.

Mearman's conception of a closed system may prove to be just as legitimate as that of the Cambridge group, and perhaps even as useful in facilitating socio-theoretic understanding, though given the very brief sketch he provides of his alternative it is difficult to see precisely how. But it is certainly clear that Mearman's first criticism of the Cambridge school, that the latter confuses closed systems for event regularities (and thereby implicitly commits a host of further sins, including adhering to empirical realism, committing the epistemic fallacy and accepting actualism), is very far from being the case.

Before turning to Mearman's second criticism, I might add that coherent and justified though the Cambridge position seems to be, it continues to evolve. In recent times in particular it has distinguished *closures of causal sequence* from *closures of concomitance*, showing the former to be relatively rare in the social realm, but relevant to mainstream modelling, while the latter are fairly common, and relevant to non-mainstream alternative forms of explanation (see Lawson 2003a, especially chapters 1, 2 and 3). These are issues to which I shall return below.[10]

Open systems

I move to Mearman's second criticism, that the Cambridge group defines open systems in a negative (and seemingly dualistic) fashion as merely 'not closed'. Mearman admits that this is not always the case, but concludes that it usually is.

Supposing Mearman to be correct on this, why should it be a problem? Mearman suggests two reasons. The first follows from Mearman's (surely correct) presumption that heterodox thinkers (Mearman references Marx, Keynes and Veblen) recognise the importance of open systems. The problem here, according to Mearman, is that the practice of defining open systems 'negatively' (i.e. merely as not closed) somehow 'leads to the positive in the programme being obscured' (Mearman 2006: 61).

The 'second problem of negative definitions', according to Mearman, is that it encourages dualistic thinking, and indeed Mearman supposes the Cambridge approach to be dualistic. It is Mearman's view that a central problem here is the way in which Post Keynesianism in particular relates to the Cambridge approach. For it is often argued that Post Keynesianism is rendered coherent by recognising it as grounded in the sort of ontology the Cambridge group advances. At the same time Post Keynesianism rejects dualism. So there is a tension here at least for Post Keynesians who wish to link up with the Cambridge contributions. This then is the second strand of Mearman's critique.

Now the first point to make is that, whether or not the Cambridge group conceives of open systems in the way Mearman suggests, Mearman's worries concerning the heterodox groups show no obvious signs of materialising. Indeed, I would argue that the impact of the Cambridge contribution is precisely the opposite of that which Mearman fears.

It is true that Lawson has often (in a number of book chapters and papers) tied in his open system analysis to the heterodox projects in particular. But in doing so, as far as I can see, the primary aim has always been precisely to emphasise the positive aspects of heterodox thinkers and, if possible, actually to develop and strengthen them. Thus, we find papers with such titles as 'Institutionalism: On the Need to Firm Up Notions of Social Structure and the Human Subject' (Lawson 2003b). He has further used his analysis to point to an ontological basis for coherence in Post Keynesianism (Lawson 2003a: Chapter 7); for a constructive Veblenian project in Old Institutionalism (Lawson 2003a chapter 8); for sustaining emancipatory projects within Feminist Economics (see e.g., Lawson 1999, 2003a, 2003c, 2003d); and for a more potent heterodox economics in general (Lawson 2006). What is more, many heterodox responses to critical realism have acknowledged this (see for example the numerous heterodox responses in Lewis 2004).

On Mearman's second worry, and not unrelatedly, it seems unlikely that Post Keynesians would have been as positive as they have in their reception of the Cambridge project if the latter had been found to be dualistic. Of course, dualisms *per se* need not be problematic or inappropriate anyway. One cannot dig half a hole or be partially mortal. It all depends on what we are referring to. It is the treatment of a non-dualistic situation as though it were dualistic that is potentially problematic. Now few have criticised the latter sort of dualism more than Sheila Dow (see, for example, Dow 1990), yet Dow seems as positively disposed as any to critical realism (e.g., Dow 1999); certainly she does not seem to detect any irreconcilable tension.

Actual developments, then, do not accord with those anticipated by Mearman. Now to the extent that Mearman's expectations are logically entailed by his base assessment that the Cambridge group defines open systems 'negatively', it seems that, by this token alone, the latter assessment is seen to be faulty. As it happens, I am not sure that these 'implications' of Mearman's would follow from a negative definition, or even that a negative definition is inherently problematic. In any case, if we turn to the manner in which the Cambridge group does conceptualise open systems we can see directly that Mearman's interpretation of it is wanting anyway, that once more Mearman appears not to be looking closely enough at actual definitions. So let me briefly consider Mearman's claims on the issues in question in more detail.

According to Mearman: '[Lawson] defines open systems in terms of unpredictability (2003[a]: 100), unsusceptibility to closure (2003[a]: 62), lack of event regularities (see above), and the impossibility of experiments (2003[a]: 84)' (Mearman 2006: 60).

Now if we turn to page 100 of Lawson (2003a), as the preceding passage directs us, the only statement making any reference to 'open' reads as follows:

> In a world that is open and complex, unforeseen developments are always occurring. But by starting from a (knowledgeable) position where specific changes or developments are not foreseen, those changes such as occur provide points from which it seems feasible to

initiate an explanatory investigation, and concerning which, explanatory successes seem likely.

(Lawson 2003a: 100)

This may indeed be a reference to developments that are not predictable, but the sentence hardly amounts to a definition of an open system.

Mearman's reference to page 62 is presumably a typo; here openness is not discussed. And the only statement on page 84 making reference to open systems is the following:

> So my task, to state it now more fully, is to demonstrate that, and how, in social research [...] it is possible both to initiate and also to direct causal–explanatory endeavour, as well as to discriminate amongst any contending causal hypotheses, in an open-system context in which well controlled experimentation appears infeasible, making use only of such event patterns, and in particular demi-regularities, as are found to be available, i.e. without pretending the situation is entirely different to the way we continually find it.
>
> (Lawson 2003a: 83–4)

Once more it is surely evident that Lawson is not defining an open system, but merely pointing out that an infeasibility of controlled experimentation is a feature of the open system context of social research that he is considering.

If we turn to the start of the relevant chapter of Lawson (2003a) that contains the foregoing two passages that Mearman references, we do however find how Lawson introduces (and appears to define or anyway elaborate) the Cambridge idea of openness. Here we find openness is not at all stated in terms of non-closure. Rather Lawson writes:

> According to the conception I defend social reality is open in a significant way. Patterns in events do occur. But where the phenomena being related are highly concrete (such as movements in actual prices, quantities of materials or outputs, and most of the other typical concerns of modern economic modellers), such patterns as are found, tend to take the form of *demi-regularities* or *demi-regs*, that is, of regularities that are not only highly restricted but also somewhat partial and unstable.
>
> (Lawson 2003a: 79)

So Lawson conceives openness not negatively after all, but positively in terms of the assortment of types of patterns of phenomena that occur.

Now as noted Mearman seems to think that the risk of dualism results from a negative definition of openness. However, it is conceivable that the 'charge' of dualism could be levelled even when it is recognised that the

Cambridge group defines openness positively, so long as it is supposed that the category of open system disallows variations of form. For completeness sake I should then examine the possibility that the Cambridge group takes this latter position.

It is easy enough to see that the Cambridge group does allow for different states of openness. Just as most of us think of a window or a door as having only one state that corresponds to being closed, but infinitely many that correspond to being open (varying perhaps from slightly open, to wide open), so, for the Cambridge group, a specific domain of reality can assume any of numerous states of openness (characterised only in part by degrees of strictness of event patterns), but only one of closure (or two if we distinguish deterministic and stochastic closures – see Lawson 1997: 76). Again, as Lawson observes:

> The point that warrants emphasis is that just because universal constant conjunctions of the form 'whenever event x then event y' are unlikely to be pervasive it does not follow that the only alternative is an inchoate random flux. These two possibilities – strict event regularities or a completely non-systematic flux – merely constitute the polar extremes of a potential continuum. Although the social world is open, certain mechanisms can dominate others over restricted regions of time–space, giving rise to rough-and-ready generalities or partial regularities, holding to such a degree that *prima facie* an explanation is called for.

> (Lawson 1994: 276)

This, clearly, is not a dualistic position in the suggested sense of systems supporting only two types of event patterns. So all of Mearman's worries seem to be ill founded. Of course, it could still be the case that in recognising the above-noted spectrum of outcomes the Cambridge group focuses on only the two *extreme* possibilities, strict closure or inchoate random flux, in its assessment of the appropriateness of (chosen) methodologies. This seems to be the presumption behind Mearman's third and final criticism, the topic to which I turn next.

An overly rigid or dichotomised economics

By the time we turn to Mearman's final section we do find some acknowledgement that the Cambridge school posits a variety of feasible outcomes in terms of strictness of event patterns.[11] The issue for Mearman at this point is how these identified event-patterns bear upon the methodological approaches considered appropriate. The critique here is that Lawson and others are too dichotomous in their recommendations. In particular, according to Mearman, Lawson supposes that where a situation is regarded as open, methods that presuppose a closure are prohibited.

Thus Mearman writes: 'For, often in C.R., it seems that, if a system is not completely closed, then it is inescapably open, rendering closed-systems methods totally impotent' (Mearman 2006: 63). Developing the theme Mearman writes:

> On one hand, C.R. is developing notions of openness which transcend the strict dual of open/closed system, which had been prevalent; yet on the other, there does seem still to be evidence that the notion of perfect closure, though impossible in reality, is used as a benchmark for the assessment of reality, and as a means of criticizing various economic theories.
>
> (Mearman 2006: 67)

And Mearman adds

> [...] it is argued that the Cambridge school of C.R. in economics has tended to adopt a strategy of *rejection* of what shall be called here 'closed-systems' methods, i.e. techniques which presuppose closure [...] In contrast, this paper argues that a central tenet of an 'open-systems methodology' is that it can still employ 'closed-system methods', because the former will take seriously into account the weaknesses of the latter in open environments and employ them more cautiously and limitedly.
>
> (Mearman 2006: 67–8)

Actually it is possible that there are really two (albeit closely related) criticisms being levelled against the Cambridge group here. The first is the already noted one that they are overly (or unreasonably) dichotomous in supporting one set of methods for open systems and another for systems regarded as closed. Here the charge, in effect, is that the Cambridge group fails to examine how, or anyway fails to give due consideration to, the possibility that methods that presuppose closures can be useful in addressing open systems.

The second possible criticism, which seems to be implicit in Mearman's comments, is that, in rejecting methods that presuppose closure where the context is at odds with this presupposition, the Cambridge group adopts a rhetorical or presentational orientation that is insufficiently pluralist.

Let me address the latter possible criticism first, for it is easily dealt with. I know that the only stance the Cambridge group wishes to rule out is dogmatism, specifically a methodological form which insists, a priori, that only one sort of method be sanctioned. Indeed, the Cambridge concern is *not* to exclude a priori any method or approach. Lawson, for example, is quite clear that, although he wishes to undermine the mainstream insistence that nothing but mathematical–deductivist methods be used, he is keen that such methods be allowed in the economist's toolkit just in case contexts arise where they may prove useful.

> I am not at all suggesting that formalistic modelling methods should not exist among the battery of options available. My aim [...] is not to narrow down the range of methodological options by attempting to prohibit a particular method. Rather it is to widen the range of possibilities through criticising the fact that, and manner in which, in many quarters at least, the particular method in question is currently and unthinkingly universalised.
>
> (Lawson 2003a: 27)

Of course, none of this is to deny that Lawson is openly pessimistic about there being many occasions on which deductivist methods will prove fruitful as a tool of social analysis. But there is no contradiction in being pessimistic and yet adopting an open-minded or pluralist orientation. Whatever their expectations, Lawson and the Cambridge school as a whole are explicitly inclusive of all approaches and encouraging of experimentation (see Downward 2003).

So how about the remaining charge advanced by Mearman, that the Cambridge group is in effect too quick in its pessimistic assessment of the fruitfulness of methods that presuppose a closure in an open system context, and consequently, as Mearman views matters, overly dichotomous in its methodological recommendations or conclusions? Actually, the Cambridge position is more complicated on such matters than is typically credited, and several issues need unpacking.

The first point is that, in recent contributions especially, a role for closures has been repeatedly explicitly acknowledged. Let me briefly elaborate.

An important Cambridge contribution is the development of *contrast explanation* as a method of analysis suitable for addressing many phenomena of the open and complex social reality in which we live. Contrast explanation is concerned with asking questions of the form 'why x rather than y?' (rather than questions of the form 'why x?'). And the point is to do so in contexts where some outcomes within a certain (contrast) space have unexpectedly turned out to be different from expectations.

Thus, if some subset of outcomes in the space is found to be different from the rest – say average crop yield at one end of the field is significantly higher than the average for the (fairly uniform) rest of the field; or a certain set of cows in the UK in the 1980s (manifesting symptoms of 'mad cow disease') act differently than all other known cows – the point is to ask of the surprising subset 'why x rather than y?', why the unexpected observed behaviour rather than the expected typical behaviour? In each such scenario, prior to making the surprising observations, the observer's best understanding led her or him to conclude that the causal histories of the relevant factors in the relevant space were sufficiently similar to produce the same (or sufficiently similar) outcomes throughout. Where a subset of outcomes has unexpectedly turned out (significantly) differently there is a *prima facie* case for supposing a particular and identifiable set of causal factors at work (or that previous understandings were erroneous in some other determinable fashion).

Now the point here is that for contrast explanation, as described, to get under way, a closure of sorts is sometimes taken for granted. The crop yield is perhaps expected to be the same throughout the field; the relevant behaviour patterns of cows are expected to be the same across all cows (of the same breed and sex, etc.) in the region. Thus it is presupposed that 'whenever the average crop yield in this part of the field is P then average crop yield elsewhere is P', etc., i.e. 'whenever *x* then *y*'.

Of course this is not the sort of regularity that typically figures in economic modelling. In the sort of example just described the regularity arises not because some event *x* stands in the causal history of a subsequent event *y*. The crop yield in one side of the field is not caused by the crop yield elsewhere in the field. Rather crop yield throughout the field is the same (when it is), because it is everywhere caused by the same third set of factors. In economic modelling, by contrast, when two events are correlated it is typically supposed that one stands in the causal history of the other (rather than sharing the same causal history). Thus, for example, changes in household income are supposed to give rise to subsequent predictable changes in household consumption patterns, and so forth.

To capture these two sorts of event patterns the Cambridge group (as noted in note 10) explicitly distinguishes *closures of causal sequence* from *closures of concomitance* (see e.g., Lawson 2003a: Chapters 1, 2 and 4). Now the sorts of event patterns of relevance to modern economics, and which Mearman no doubt has in mind, are those associated with closures of the causal sequence sort, whilst it is the patterns associated with closures of concomitance that the Cambridge group assesses to be both most prevalent and also most relevant to contrast explanation.

This is not to suggest that closures of causal sequence, should they occur, would not be relevant to contrast explanation too. Examples may be geographically restricted short-term trends. Of course these trends would prove useful for contrast explanation when they break down, or change direction, when for mainstream modelling exercises they are useful only if they do not break down. Indeed, contrast explanation is an error theory of learning, and patterns of any sort are the location of discovery and increased understanding precisely when they (unexpectedly) break down. But still, the point remains that such trends and closures of causal sequence, more generally, should they occur, would be useful to contrast explanatory approaches too.

As I say, Mearman will doubtless have had closures of causal sequence in mind when making the critical comments noted above. But this does not detract from the point that, in emphasising the role of contrast explanation, closures of some kind or other are recognised as significant by the Cambridge group as well.

A second point that warrants emphasis is that it has never been the case that the Cambridge group has merely dismissed methods that presuppose closures, even closures of causal sequence, without examining the numerous potential ways in which they might prove to be (or have been held to be) illuminating. Lawson for example spends a good deal of space in *Economics and Reality* investigating different ways in which formalistic modelling methods might be useful, introducing his investigation by suggesting that 'the single most important question facing the advocate of mainstream economics' is how such models can help us understand reality despite being necessarily unrealistic in their construction (Lawson 1997: 109).

Thus Lawson examines whether closed system models can also stand as a temporary heuristic device as part of an application of the method of successive approximation. Lawson even identifies two conditions for the method to work, these being: '(1) that the factors considered in "isolation" be real causal factors, structures and/or transfactually acting mechanisms or tendencies; and (2) that the effects of the factors so considered in "isolation" combine or interact mechanically' (Lawson 1997: 129). He also considers the possibility that such models serve to provide a partial picture (or a one-sided view), to underpin the method of theoretical isolation, and much else.

I mention these issues just to counter the impression given that the Cambridge group is overly rigid in its approach. I have already acknowledged that the Cambridge group remains pessimistic in their expectations of explanatory successes or other advances in understanding, when methods are relied upon that presuppose closures of causal sequence, at least where such methods are employed in an insufficiently dialectical fashion. But this pessimism is based on analysis and not *a priori* scepticism.

Of course, the Cambridge group may be wrong in its assessments. But it is worth bearing in mind that in both his books and elsewhere Lawson's repeated starting point is the widely recognised *a posteriori* failings of deductivist methods to improve social understanding. As Lawson documents repeatedly (e.g., 2003a: Chapter 1) these failings are acknowledged by many well-respected mainstream economists themselves. It is for this reason that Lawson and others have allocated significant resources both 1) to demonstrating that methods *per se*, and formalistic–deductivist methods of the sort adopted by economists in particular, are not neutral (and in economics have been overly debilitating) and 2) to developing methods more clearly appropriate than existing ones to addressing phenomena of the open social reality in which we live.

In the end, it seems to me, it is down to Mearman and others to establish that the sorts of 'closed system methods' they wish to employ in analysing open systems are appropriate for doing so. The Cambridge group is clearly supportive of all exploratory endeavours concerned to establish the usefulness of these and any other methods. If the specific methods in question were to prove successful in some useful way, the Cambridge group would clearly be interested. And where any such successes are considered surprising I suspect that the Cambridge group's inclination would be to seek to explain them. The Cambridge stance, here, should in no way disturb Mearman and his co-researchers.

Final comments

I have attempted to clarify certain contributions of the Cambridge Social Ontology Group where the literature that has engaged with it reveals important misunderstandings. Particularly, I hope to have dispelled the idea that because the Cambridge group identifies closed systems as those in which event patterns occur it thereby reduces closures to those patterns. I have also indicated that the Cambridge group does not define open systems negatively, and certainly remains open at the level of methodology (as elsewhere).

I should, at this stage, add a small rider to the foregoing set of arguments. In my response to Mearman I have drawn attention to numerous central features of the Cambridge group's writings that go against Mearman's various criticisms. Now as it happens Mearman has noted some of these features of the Cambridge contribution himself, albeit usually in footnotes or summary asides. However, Mearman has nevertheless made the three charges noted at the outset, as well as his other related criticisms of the Cambridge project. As such I can only imagine that he has failed to recognise the significance of these noted features to the issues under discussion, or else he has failed to understand the fundamental nature of the overall Cambridge project. Either way I hope I have helped to clarify some relevant components of the latter.

Since the first draft of this response to Andrew Mearman's paper was written, I have become aware of other contributors adopting conceptions of closure that are explicitly contrasted with that of the Cambridge group. An important example is provided by Chick and Dow (2005). Like Mearman, these authors first set out their conceptions of open and closed systems without reference to event regularities; instead they treat the question of whether event regularities are confined to closed systems, as they define the latter, as a secondary issue. This is the real difference between the Cambridge or critical realist contribution and the approaches adopted by Chick and Dow, as well as Mearman.

Obviously, each of these alternative contributions must accept some basis for delimiting a conception of open and closed systems. Very many such bases are conceivable, some less arbitrary than others. In the case of Chick and Dow, a starting point, or anyway a major input, is a conception of open and closed systems found in the *Oxford English Dictionary* (see Chick and Dow 2005: 364) and (in consequence) the definition they give is that which pertains most to thermal dynamic systems.

I see nothing wrong with this latter approach. But it is clearly motivated by different concerns than the Cambridge project. Chick and Dow have noticed that open and closed systems are categories creeping into economics (mostly due to Lawson) and they wish to explore their possible meanings drawing on other literatures. In contrast, Lawson and others, though justified in using these categories, could, if necessary, abandon the terminology of open and closed systems altogether, for their primary concerns are certain critical situations and methods warranting analysis whatever terminology is used to express them.

As a parting comment, then, perhaps I might suggest that the central difference between the Cambridge approach and that of others can be summarised by noting that whilst Chick, Dow, Mearman and others are primarily analytical in their orientation the Cambridge group is more dialectical. That is, whilst the former group are primarily concerned to analyse the properties of certain systems *per se*, the Cambridge group is more concerned to identify and resolve tensions in current socio-theorising.

The starting point in the Cambridge analysis, specifically, is the unhealthy state of contemporary economics. The objective is to understand, explain and rectify this situation. Here, the categories of open and closed systems are commandeered as a means to an end, that end being a radical reorientation of the practices and procedures of the modern discipline.

Notes

1 For helpful comments on an earlier draft I am grateful to members of the Cambridge Social Ontology Group and also to three referees of the *Review of Social Economy*. First published in *Review of Social Economy*, 2006, Vol 64, No 4, 493–514.
2 See, for example, the references provided in Lawson (2003a).
3 See also the 'Symposium on Reorienting Economics' in *Post Autistic Economics Review* that began in 2004 and is ongoing at this date.
4 Prior to writing the current piece I not only read Mearman's paper but also attended his (21 February 2005) presentation of it to the Cambridge Realist Workshop (a seminar series out of which CSOG has emerged).
5 Actually the term *closed* in the emphasised sentence has attached to it a footnote that reads as follows:

> I am aware that across different literatures or disciplines (including mathematics) the category of closure is used to mean different things. Here, as I say (and state in previous contributions), I take a closed system to be one in which event regularities of the noted kind occur.

(Lawson 2003a: 284)

Here, Lawson repeats the conception of a closed system as being distinct from event regularities. We can also note from this passage that Lawson is quite aware that the conception varies across disciplines. It even varies within social theory, as Mearman notes pointing to the conceptions of Kapp (1968) and Luhmann (1995) amongst others. This is why the Cambridge school is concerned with spelling out precisely how it is using the term.
6 Perhaps Mearman can point to the odd passages in contributors other than Lawson who have sometimes been rather looser in their descriptions. But the canonical texts are clear in distinguishing closures as systems in which

event regularities occur (and not as event regularities *per se*), as have all texts I have examined. If Mearman is to mount a concerted attack on the Cambridge project it would not be very helpful to treat any stray conception seeming different from the majority of others as if it were the consensus conception.

7 See, for example, Mearman's discussion on the solar system on p. 56.

8 I add this qualification because there are different sorts of event regularities. I take economists to be interested in regularities in which one set of related events ('independent variables') stand in the causal history of others ('dependent variables'), rather than sharing the same (or a similar) causal history.

9 Though in the social realm the triggering of mechanisms or processes will typically not be optional.

10 It is insightful to note at this point that, in introducing these conceptions into the literature, Lawson remains clear in 1) indicating that event regularities and closures are not identical; and 2) applying the term closure because the term captures the nature of each system as a whole. Thus Lawson writes:

> Remember a closure just is a system in which a constant conjunction of events occurs, i.e. which supports a regularity of the sort 'whenever event *x* then event *y*'. Where the correlated events are held to stand in causal sequence, a guaranteeing of an event regularity requires the insulating of a (stable) mechanism from all others, as we saw in Chapter 1. In this case, the term closure is appropriate in that it captures the idea of a specific mechanism being 'closed off' from the influence of others. However, where *x* and *y* are correlated because they share similar causal histories, the term closure better captures the idea of 'closing over'. The reference is to a similar set of causal forces covering a particular region. If the former captures the idea of isolation, the latter captures the idea of continuity or connection.
>
> Thus, if considered under the aspect of causal forces in play, a closed system of the former type might be distinguished as a *closure of isolation* (or insulation) whilst one of the latter sort might appropriately be designated a *closure of continuity*. Alternatively, if considered under the aspect of events (being connected), a closed system of the former sort might be termed a *closure of causal sequence*, whilst an example of the latter type might be labelled a *closure of concomitance*.
>
> (Lawson 2003a: 41–2, my emphasis)

11 In fact (slightly mis-)quoting Lawson, Mearman observes that:

> Lawson (1994b: 276) suggests 'two extremes – strict event regularities or a completely non-systematic flux – merely constitut[ing] the polar extremes of a potential continuum'. Later (277) he proposes 'a continuum of outcomes … ranging from closed systems of constant conjunctions of events to an inchoate random flux'.
>
> (Mearman 2006: 63–4)

References

Chick, Victoria and Sheila Dow 2005. 'The Meaning of Open Systems', *Journal of Economic Methodology*, 12(3), September: 361–381.

Dow, S.C. 1990. 'Beyond Dualism', *Cambridge Journal of Economics*, 14: 143–157.

Dow, S.C. 1999. 'Post Keynesianism and Critical Realism: What is the Connection?', *Journal of Post Keynesian Economics*, 22: 15–33.

Downward, P.M. (ed.) 2003. *Applied Economics and the Critical Realist Critique.* London: Routledge.

Kapp, W. 1968. 'In Defense of Institutionalist Economics', *Swedish Journal of Economics*, 70: 1–18.

Lawson, Tony 1994. 'A Realist Theory for Economics.' In R. Backhouse (ed.) *New Directions in Economic Methodology*. London: Routledge.

Lawson, Tony 1997. *Economics and Reality*. London and New York: Routledge.

Lawson, Tony 1999. 'Feminism, Realism and Universalism', *Feminist Economics*, 5(2): 25–59.

Lawson, Tony 2003a. *Reorienting Economics*. London and New York: Routledge.

Lawson, Tony 2003b. 'Institutionalism: On the Need to Firm Up Notions of Social Structure and the Human Subject', *Journal of Economic Issues*, 37(1): 175–201.

Lawson, Tony 2003c. 'Ontology and Feminist Theorising', *Feminist Economics*, 9(1), March: 119–150. Reprinted in John B. Davis (ed.) *Recent Developments in Economic Methodology*. Cheltenham: Edward Elgar.

Lawson, Tony 2003d. 'Theorising Ontology', *Feminist Economics*, 9(1), March: 161–169.

Lawson, Tony 2006. 'The Nature of Heterodox Economics', *Cambridge Journal of Economics*, 30(2), July: 483–507.

Lewis, Paul (ed.) 2004. *Transforming Economics: Perspectives on the Critical Realist Project*. London and New York: Routledge.

Luhmann, Niklas 1995. *Social Systems*. Stanford, CA: Stanford University Press. (Translated by J. Bednarz, Jr. from N. Luhmann, *Soziale Systeme: GrundriBeiner allgemeinen Theorie*. Frankfurt am Main: Suhrkamp. 1984.)

Mearman, Andrew 2006. 'Critical Realism in Economics and Open-Systems Ontology: A Critique', *Review of Social Economy*, 64(1), March: 47–75. Mimeograph. Version presented at the Cambridge Realist Workshop, February 2005.

Pratten, S, 2005. 'Economics as Progress: The LSE Approach to Econometric Modelling and Critical Realism as Programmes for Research', *Cambridge Journal of Economics*, Vol 29, No 2, 179–205.

'Symposium on Reorienting Economics.' 2004. *Post Autistic Economics Review*. www.paecon.net. No. 28 onwards.

17 The nature of gender[1]

Tony Lawson

How in the context of the currently developing global order (and consequent ever-changing local political frameworks) might feminists most sensibly seek to transform the gendered features of society in such a manner as to facilitate a less discriminating scenario than is currently in evidence? This is a question that motivates much of the thinking behind this book. (The book to which Lawson refers is Jude Browne (ed.) (2007) in which the current chapter first appeared – S.P). But posing it carries certain presuppositions. In particular it takes for granted the notion that gender is a meaningful as well as useful category of analysis. And it presumes, too, that, whatever the socio-political context, it is always feasible to identify some forms of emancipatory practice, at least with respect to gender discrimination. Or at least there is an assumption that such emancipatory practice is not ruled out in principle. Both sets of presuppositions have been found to be problematic. Specifically, various feminist theorists hold that there are conceptual and political difficulties to making use of the category of gender in social theorising (see, e.g., Bordo 1993; Spelman 1990). And the reasoning behind such assessments tends in its turn to be destabilising of the goal of emancipatory practice.

In this chapter I focus on these latter concerns rather than the more specific question posed at the outset. For unless the noted difficulties can somehow be resolved any further questioning of appropriate local and global strategies appears to beg too many issues.

I shall suggest that the difficulties in question can indeed be resolved, but that this necessitates a turn to explicit and systematic ontological elaboration, a practice that feminists have tended to avoid (see Lawson 2003), but which, I want to suggest, needs now to be (re)introduced to the study and politics of gender inequality.

By ontology I mean the study of the nature and structure of (a domain of) reality, including the identification of its most fundamental components; and here my concern is primarily with social ontology, the study of social being. I must acknowledge at the outset that philosophy in the guise of ontology can never be a substitute for substantive theory. However, it can serve a ground-clearing role, facilitating substantive theoretical and political advance and/or clarification. Here, I shall be using ontology to under-labour for substantive socio-political analyses concerned with addressing the question posed at the outset.

Specifically, after suggesting that ontological theorising, as here conceived, can render the category of gender meaningful – and given the relative neglect of ontology in feminist theorising I shall set out in some depth the ontological conception I believe to be the most sustainable – I draw out various optimistic implications of the analysis regarding the possibility of emancipatory change, including change concerned with undermining gender-based hierarchies and forms of discrimination.

Some problems of gender

I start, though, by rehearsing some of the problems often associated with the study of gender. A first difficulty, one frequently raised, is that it is not at all clear what sort of thing the category signifies. Within modern feminist thought the standard definition of gender is something like 'the social meaning given to biological differences between the sexes' (Ferber and Nelson 1993: 9–10; Kuiper and Sap 1995: 2–3).[2] Though this is widely accepted, a problem with this sort of formulation is that it allows of various interpretations (for example, gender as a subjective experience, a psychological orientation, a set of attributes possessed, a normative image or ideal, and so forth), whilst a satisfactory elaboration has proven elusive.

Further, whatever the precise interpretation of the category, and despite the significant use made of the sex/gender distinction by early (second-wave) feminists, numerous theorists now appear sceptical about its analytical usefulness. Let me briefly recap.

In the late 1970s and early 1980s feminists began increasingly to emphasise the partiality of all knowledge, and to criticise the tendency of (typically white and male) scientists to presume their views to be uninfluenced by local biases, and personal histories and values. The dominant message of these feminists was that a fuller vision of reality could be uncovered by drawing attention to gendered locations, that a theorising of gender was a useful way of uncovering previously hidden aspects of the social process (see, for example, Chodorow 1978 and Keller 1985). These gender theorists argued that concepts commonly used to evaluate behaviour (such as calculative rationality in economics) do not express universal values or ideals but male ones.

Although insightful, by the late 1980s this early feminist contribution was being challenged by other feminists for making the same sorts of ('essentialist') mistakes that it itself criticised. Specifically, the earlier (typically white, middle-class) feminists were charged with treating their own particular experience of gender differences as universal; they were criticised for taking 'the experience of white middle-class women to be representative of, indeed normative for, the experience of all women' (Spelman 1990: ix). In so doing, these early feminists were accused of marginalising differences of race, ethnocentricity, culture, age and so forth;

women of colour, lesbians and others found their history and culture ignored in the ongoing discussions relating to gender.

As a result of this criticism there emerged an epistemological position often referred to as gender scepticism, characterised precisely by its 'scepticism about the use of gender as an analytic category' (Bordo 1993: 135). Gender sceptics argue that an individual's gender experience is so affected by that individual's experience of class, race or culture, etc., that it is meaningless to consider gender at all as a useful category. For once we are attentive to differences of class, ethnic origin, sexual orientation, and so on, the notion of gender disintegrates into fragments unusable for systematic theory. According to this assessment it is impossible to separate facts about gender from those about race, class, ethnic origin, and so on. Spelman writes:

> If it were possible to isolate a woman's 'womanness' from her racial identity, then we should have no trouble imagining that had I been Black I could have had just the same understanding of myself as a woman as I in fact do ... It is thus evident that thinking about a person's identity as made up of neatly distinguishable 'parts' may be very misleading.
>
> (Spelman 1990: 135–6)

In short, early feminist (and other) gender theorists were criticised for assuming cross-cultural stability of facts about gender, and a separability of the parts of a person's achieved identity.

If the intent of this criticism was to be corrective, it was soon to be pushed to destructive extremes. Specifically, some 'post-modernists' came to argue that, because of differences of ethnic origin, sexual orientation, culture and so forth, not only is each individual's experience unique but no category can legitimately be treated as stable or separable. The fact of differential historical experiences means that each 'woman' differs from every other and it is impossible or meaningless to talk of the 'authentic woman' and so to unify different individuals under the signifier 'woman'. There is no woman's (or of course man's) experience, situation or point of view. As a result, it is difficult to make sense of feminist projects of collective emancipation. For who is to be emancipated, and from whom? The sort of perspective in question leads to a view of a world only of differences, an individualist perspective in which it is impossible to make much sense of any system or collectivity, whether oppressive or otherwise.

This post-modernist critique of (interpretations of) early gender theorising contains much insight and can indeed be read in part as a corrective of the excesses or errors of naive essentialist positions. However, the critique itself is ultimately not satisfactory, in that it loses the central insight of the earlier feminist contribution entirely. For according to the logic of this critique there is no basis for systematic forces of societal discrimination.[3] Yet it cannot really be denied that there are systematic forms of domination in society as we experience it, and in particular that biological females are very often dominated or oppressed by males, and in ways that have little if anything to do with sexual as opposed to social differences[4] (see Bryson, 2007).

Put differently, the post-modernist critique, in highlighting the problems of essentialism, loses the insight for which gender analysis was originally formulated, namely the discrimination of individuals classified as 'women' in ways that have little directly to do with the quality of being female.[5] If it is widely recognised that there are many types of differences between members of society, specifically between those classified as men and women, we need to attend to ways of disentangling rather than neglecting the types that there are.[6]

Such considerations suggest that what is needed is a conception of gender that can sustain both (1) the insights underpinning the noted criticisms of early gender theorising, specifically the fragmented experiences of us all and the difficulties of partialling out the gendered aspects of our experiences, as well as (2) the (widely recognised) feature of our world that gender is an objective category that (currently) marks the site of the domination of one (gendered) group by another.

We need a conception that can sustain the insight that we all are different, that our experiences and identities are historically, culturally and socially, etc., variable and indeed unique, as well as the deep intuition that there is a need for, and legitimacy to, collective organisation and struggle.

We need, in short, a conception that transcends the opposition of difference and unity with a clear basis for achieving both, a conception precisely of unity in difference. I now want to indicate that ontological elaboration can facilitate a conception of the sort required.

Ontology

By social ontology, let me recall, I mean the study (or a theory) of the basic nature and structure of social being.[7] And by the social, I just mean the domain of those phenomena whose existence, at least in part, depends on us. Thus the domain includes artefacts, technology, wars, pollutions, social relations, institutions, and so forth.

Now a first fundamental feature of the social realm, one of significance to the issues being addressed here, is that it is structured in the sense of comprising more than one ontological level. Specifically, it consists in far more than actualities such as (actual) human behaviour including its observable patterns. It also comprises features such as social rules, relations, positions, processes, systems, values, meaning and the like that do not reduce to human behaviour. Nor do features such as these exist just in their instantiation or manifestation in behaviour. Rather they are mostly ontologically distinct from behaviour. Such features that do not reduce to behaviour can be termed social structures, constituting, in their entirety, social structure. How do I defend the claim that social reality includes structure that is ontologically irreducible to human agency or behaviour? I go into this at length elsewhere (e.g., Lawson 1997, 2003). Basically the argument is that a conception of social reality as structured is required if we are to explain numerous widespread features of everyday life. Most clearly the distinction is required if we are to make sense of the widespread observation of a gap between cultural norms or stipulations and patterns of individual behaviour. More precisely, the distinction is necessitated if we are to explain the fact of practices in which rules affect action, but are systematically contravened in it. For example, workers in conflict with their employers or management could not threaten to 'work-to-rule', as they do in the UK, if any rule (or set of rules) in question just reduces to the norm or average form of the work activities that are already being undertaken. Nor could the workforce sensibly make such 'threats' if they did not have the power or agency to do so, a power that is not reducible to what in the event happens (whatever the outcome).

Also in the UK, not all, but some, motorway drivers regularly exceed the legal speed limit. In some cities of the world (for example, Naples) most drivers pass some (but rarely all) red lights, and so on. In short, rules and the practices upon which they bear are sometimes aligned but at other times are systematically out of phase. This is a feature of reality we can render intelligible only by recognising that social structures and the practices they condition, though presupposing of each other, are irreducible each to the other. For it is only because they are ontologically distinct and irreducible that they can be aligned on occasion, or that any 'threat' (promise or request) to align them makes sense.

Human beings too are structured. Individual agents have capacities and dispositions, for example, which are irreducible to the behaviour patterns we produce. Each of us has capacities that may never be exercised. And, individually, we are continually reflexive, even having ('inner') conversations with ourselves as well as other first-person experiences that are not open to inspection by others. These clearly have their conditions of possibility, presumably including processes in the brain. But the subjective aspects appear irreducible to any neurobiological activity. Most clearly, what we can do does not reduce to the patterns of behaviour that others can observe; and nor even does all of what we actually do.

Notice that this irreducibility of social structure and human subjectivity can be rendered intelligible only if we further recognise the reality of processes of emergence, underpinning emergent social and psychological realms in particular (see, e.g., Lawson 1997, especially chapters 6 and 13, and Lawson 2003). Let me briefly elaborate.

A stratum of reality can be said to be emergent, or as possessing emergent powers, if there is a sense in which it (1) has arisen out of a lower stratum, being formed by principles operative at the lower level; (2) remains dependent on the lower stratum for its existence; but (3) contains causal powers of its own which are both irreducible to those operating at the lower level and (perhaps) capable of acting back on the lower level. Thus organic material emerged from inorganic material. And, according to the conception I am defending, the social realm is emergent from human interaction, though with properties irreducible to, yet capable of causally affecting, the latter. For example, language systems have emerged from human interactions, and bear powers that act back upon, but remain irreducible to, the speech acts which they facilitate.

So interpreted, the theory of emergence commits us to a form of materialism which ultimately entails the unilateral ontological dependence of social upon biological upon physical forms coupled with the taxonomic and causal irreducibility of each to any other. Thus, although, for example, the geo-historical emergence of organic from inorganic matter and of human beings from hominids can be acknowledged, when we come to explain those physical and biological states that are due, in part, to intentional human agency it is necessary to reference properties, including powers, not designated by physical or biological science (again see Lawson 1997).

So the social realm consists, in part, of (emergent) social structures and human subjects that are reducible neither to each other nor to human practices. It may already be clear how I am going to argue that the category gender can be retained as a meaningful object of reality with a degree of stability. For I will argue that gender is in large part a feature of (emergent) social structure, i.e. something that is irreducible to human practices or experiences. First, though, let me say something more about the forms of social structure as well as its (processual) mode of being.

Social positions and relations

In emphasising the structured nature of social life I have so far focused upon social rules. But this is not all there is to social being. For society is also constituted in a fundamental way by both social relations and positions. These features are essential to understanding the precise manner in which human agency and structure come together.

The significance and fact of social relations and positions are easily recognised once we take note (and inquire into the conditions) of that general feature of experience that there is a systematic disparity across individuals regarding the practices that are, and apparently can be, followed. Although most rules can be utilised by a wide group of people, it by no means follows that all rules are available, or apply equally, to everyone, even within a given culture. To the contrary, any (segment of) society is highly differentiated in terms of the obligations and prerogatives that are on offer. Teachers, for example, are allowed and expected to follow different practices from students, government ministers to follow different ones from lay-people, employers from employees, landladies/lords from tenants, and so on. Rules as resources are not equally available, or do not apply equally, to each member of the population at large.

What then explains the differentiated ascription of obligations, prerogatives, privileges and responsibilities? This question directs attention to the wider one of how human beings and elements of social structure such as rules come together in the first place. If these elements such as rules are a different sort of thing from human beings, human agency and even action, what is the point of contact between human agency and structure? How do they interconnect? In particular, how do they come together in such a manner that different individuals achieve responsibilities and obligations available to some but not all others, and thereby call on, or come to be conditioned in their actions by, different social rules and so structures of power?

If it is clearly the case that teachers have different responsibilities, obligations and prerogatives from students, and government ministers face different ones from the rest of us, then it is equally apparent that these obligations and prerogatives exist independently of the particular individuals who happen, currently, to be teachers, students or ministers. If I, as a university teacher, were to move on tomorrow, someone else would take over my teaching responsibilities and enjoy the same obligations and prerogatives as I currently do. Indeed, those who occupy the positions of students are different every year. In short, society is constituted in large part by a set of positions, each associated with numerous obligations, rights and duties, and into which agents, as it were, slot.

Internal relations

Something more about this system of societal positions can be expressed if we take note of the additional observation that practices routinely followed by an occupant of any position tend to be orientated towards some other group(s). The rights, tasks and obligations of teachers, for example, are orientated towards their interactions with students (and vice versa), towards research funding bodies or governing institutions, and so forth. Similarly the rights and obligations of landladies/lords are orientated towards their interactions with tenants, and so on.

Such considerations indicate a causal role for certain forms of relation. Two types of relation can be distinguished: external and internal. Two objects or aspects are externally related if neither is constituted by the relationship in which it stands to the other. Bread and butter, coffee and milk, and barking dog and mail carrier provide examples. In contrast, two objects are internally related if they are what they are, or can do the sort of thing they do, by virtue of the relationship in which they stand to one another. Landlady/lord and tenant, employer and employee, teacher and student, and magnet and its field are examples that spring easily to mind. In each case it is not possible to have the one without the other; each, in part, is what it is, and does the sort of thing it does, by virtue of the relation in which it stands to the other.

Now the intelligibility of the rule-governed and rule-differentiated social situation noted above requires that we recognise first the internal relationality of social life, and second that the internal relationality in question is primarily not of individuals per se but of social positions; it is the positions (say of teachers and students) that are relationally defined.

The picture that emerges, then, is of a set, or network, of positions characterised by the rules and so practices associated with them, where the latter are determined in relation to other positions and their associated rules and practices. On this conception the basic building blocks of society are positions, involving, depending upon or constituted according to social rules and associated tasks, obligations and prerogatives, along with the practices they govern, where such positions are both defined in relation to other positions and are immediately occupied by individuals.

Systems and collectivities

Notice further that notions of social systems or collectivities can be straightforwardly developed using the conceptions of social structure as rules, practices, relationships and positions now elaborated. Most generally, social systems and collectivities can be viewed as ensembles of networked, internally related positions with their associated rules and practices. All the familiar social systems, collectivities and organisations – the economy, the state, international and national companies, trade unions, households, schools and hospitals – can be recognised as depending upon, presupposing or consisting in internally related position-rule systems of this form.

Sub-distinctions can be drawn. If a social system is best conceived as a structured process of interaction, a social group or collectivity can be understood as consisting in, or depending upon, or as a set of people distinguishable by, their current occupancy of a specific set of social positions. Notice that, at any one time, a particular individual will occupy any number of positions. That is, the same person may be a parent and a child, a worker and a boss, a teacher and a student, immigrant and native, old and young, a member of religious or political or community organisations and so on. The resulting conception then is one that (1) renders intelligible the often noted, but reputedly difficult to sustain, sense of a group or collective interest and thus the basis for a theory of collective action; and yet (2) allows the possibility of a conflict of interest at the level of individuals.

Put differently, on this relational conception any specific collectivity can be understood in terms both of its relations to other groups, especially those against which it is defined and/or is opposed, and of the complex of internal relationships within the collectivity itself. Amongst the many advantages of this conception is the feature that it allows a meaningful focus not only upon production and exchange activities but also upon a range of distributional issues as well, such as resources to groups as well as people to positions (or positions to people).

To anticipate the discussion of gender that follows shortly, my contention will be that gender is usefully viewed as intimately bound up with nexuses of internally related positions to which perceived-to-be biological females and males are (differentially) assigned in any context (or which are assigned (differentially) to individuals identified as biological females or males), along with the associated rules, rights and obligations and so forth. This enables us to locate the site of domination (and recognise that feminist distributional studies ought indeed to be concerned with the allocation of positions) whilst allowing that every individual's path is unique, just as her or his occupancy of positions is variable and complex and again unique. This conception thus allows uniqueness at the level of the actual, including experience, the focus of post-modernists, whilst maintaining the ability to locate the forces of discrimination so many also regularly experience.

Social being as process

If the above account is to prove sustainable, it clearly follows that the societal positions that individuals occupy and the rules associated with them be (or can be) relatively enduring. Yet the whole question of the fixity or otherwise of social structure, as well as of the human individual, is a topic that has yet to be broached. These are issues that must be addressed, especially if we are ultimately concerned with questions of emancipatory change.

It is instructive at this point to consider the mode of being of social structure. To focus the discussion, let me again consider the example of a system of language. Clearly we are all born into language systems; none of us creates them. At the same time, being social phenomena, language systems depend on us, and specifically on transformative human agency. So they do not determine what we do, and do not create our speech acts; they merely facilitate them. So in theorising the relationship of agency and structure, the categories of creation and determinism are out of place here. Rather we must view matters in terms of the categories of transformation and reproduction. For any given language system, its structure of rules, etc., is given to the individual when he or she comes to speak, and it is reproduced and/or transformed through the sum total of individuals engaging in speech acts. The social structure in question, then, is the (typically unacknowledged) condition of a set of practices; just as its reproduction and/or transformation is the (typically unintended) result of these practices.

Now what is true of the mode of being of a language system holds for all social structure; social structures exist as processes of reproduction and transformation. A market or a university or a language system does not exist in a primarily static form, subject at most to moments of change (owing to new technology or whatever). Rather, change is essential to the mode of being of such structures; they exist as continuous processes of transformation and/

or reproduction. Even where aspects of certain social structures appear a posteriori to remain intact, this is only and always because they have been actively (if mostly unintentionally) reproduced. On this conception, which has elsewhere in economics been systematised as the transformational model of social activity, no aspects are fixed and out of time. All are subject to processes of transformation. So there is no ontological prioritisation of continuity over change (or vice versa); continuity and change are ontologically equivalent. And each, when it occurs, is open to, and for understanding necessitates, (a causal) explanation (see, e.g., Lawson 1997, 2003).

Social structure, then, is reproduced and transformed through human practice. But so is each individual human agent. For, as we have seen, the human individual too is structured. To speak a language such as English presupposes the capacity to do so. To possess the capacity to speak English presupposes the more basic capacity for language acquisition, and so on. Human individuals are far more than their behaviours. And the ways in which capacities and dispositions are developed and maintained or transformed depends on individual practices. The same applies, of course, to tastes or preferences, long-term and short-term plans, other features, psychological make-up, and so forth. So the individual agent, just like social structure, is continually reproduced and transformed through practice.

The social world, including both structure and human agency, then, turns on human practice. Social structure and human agency each condition the other, although neither can be reduced to the other, nor to the practices through which both are reproduced and/or transformed.[8]

The foregoing is a brief overview of aspects of a transformational model of social activity. It is a model that is seen to be appropriate once social reality is conceptualised as being structured. And a conception of social reality as structured is found to be a requirement of explaining familiar aspects of everyday experience. The overall transformational conception is a thoroughly non-reductionist account of linked (or co-) development. Neither structure nor agency has analytical priority, for each depends irreducibly on the other. And although each develops at its own ontological level, it does so only in conditions set by the other. Thus each is significantly dependent on, though not created or determined by, the other. Social life, then, is intrinsically dynamic, and interdependent.

Theorising gender

So how does all this help with theorising the category of gender? Let me stress once more that ontology cannot do the work of substantive social theorising. Although I now want to suggest an interpretation of gender consistent with the ontological framework elaborated, it will not be the only possibility. Even so, in that the interpretation provided evades the charges levelled by gender sceptics whilst retaining the ability to explain domination and discrimination, it is one that does seem worth considering seriously.

The key to combining the insights both of gender theorists and of gender sceptics lies in recognising ontological distinctions between social structure, human agency and practice. These distinctions allow that individuals can indeed have unique, including fragmented, experiences and social identities, and yet be conditioned (and facilitated) by relatively enduring, if always space–time-specific, social structures, including internally related positions, and associated rights and practices that allow the systematic subjugation or oppression of some by others.

For if the continually reproduced and transformed social structures, comprising networks of internally related positions and associated rights and obligations, provide the sites, the objective bases, for forms of discrimination, it warrants emphasis that there is no one-to-one mapping from social structure to individual pathways, experience or personal identities.

Furthermore, each individual occupies many positions simultaneously, and life is a unique path of entering and exiting. So the perspective sustained is quite consistent with the insight of multiple or fragmented experiences.

Of course, the fact of systematic discrimination presupposes there is nevertheless a way or sense in which some individuals, whatever their experiences, are nevertheless marked as similar (and different from some others). The markers can be age, skin colour, language, accent and a host of other (actual or perceived) human qualities. Gender, I suggest, is bound up with one such system of identification and differentiation, one that (as it happens in seemingly all societies so far) serves to privilege some over others.

Essential to such a system are the following two components:

1 a distinction repeatedly drawn between individuals who are regularly/mostly observed or imagined to have certain bodily features presumed to be evidence of a female's biological role in reproduction and others who are regularly/mostly observed or imagined to have certain bodily features presumed to be evidence of a male's biological role in reproduction;

2 a set of mechanisms or processes which work in any given society or locality to legitimise/motivate the notion that individuals regarded as female and those regarded as male ought to be allocated to, or to have allocated to them, systematically differentiated kinds of social positions, where the nature of the allocations encouraged need not, and typically does not, reflect any commonalities or differences located at the biological level.[9]

Currently, as I say, in seemingly all societies, the positions characterised as being for women are in fact mostly subordinate along some prominent set of axes, whilst those for men are typically privileged.

What precisely is gender on this conception? I would define it neither as a substance, nor simply a category of analysis, but rather as a social totality, a social system. It is a system of processes and products (of processes in product and products in process). The processes in question (which are always context specific) are precisely those that work to legitimise/motivate the notion that individuals regarded as female and those regarded as male ought to be allocated to, or to have allocated to them, systematically differentiated kinds of (relationally defined) social positions. The products are the (equally transitory and spatially/culturally limited) outcomes of these processes. If the processes serve to gender, i.e. are gendering processes (or processes of genderation), the products (aspects of social relations, positions (with associated rights and norms), practices, identities) must be regarded as gendered.

Where precisely is the gender system? So conceived, I do not think the gender system can be isolated from the rest of social reality; rather it is the whole of social reality considered under a particular (albeit only one[10]) aspect. That is, the gender system comprises all social processes/products viewed under the aspects of gendering/being rendered gendered. In all our practices we draw upon the structures of society as we (momentarily) find them, including their gendered aspects. And through our acting, these structures – whether bearing on issues of material distribution, status, power or whatever[11] – are, wittingly or not, continually reproduced and/or transformed. This transformational activity is the mode of being of all social processes. And all structures and their processes of reproduction seemingly have gendered aspects.

Often processes of gendering are intended/fully conscious. Such processes will include not only overtly sexist practices of some adults but also perhaps the differentiating practices of rival siblings responding to the 'trauma' of discovering differences.[12]

But mostly, I suspect, gendering processes are implicit and unnoticed; with specific gendered structures or features being the typically unacknowledged conditions as well as the usually unintended outcomes of our practices[13] (where gendering processes of this sort will include, significantly, those in which already prevalent gendered categories – e.g., leadership (male), dexterous (female) – are reinforced through being used in turn to signify relationships of power – e.g., through being used to signify typical characteristics of, respectively, employers and employees).[14]

If gender is an (intrinsically dynamic and open) system comprising processes of gendering and the (again always open and dynamic) products of such processes, it is the forces for continuity and change, along with the changing nature of gender, that are analytically interesting.

Personal identities

Parenthetically, I might note that nothing in this analysis undermines the possibility of our establishing personal identities, albeit identities which are always unique, changing and relational.

Such identities, if and where established, will be conditioned by our experiences, fallible knowledge of situations, perceived possibilities, normative ideals, plans and constraints. As such they are open to evaluation. Indeed, in that we continually reproduce and transform our identities, they are something of an (ongoing) achievement.

An individual's experiences will of course vary according to social positions entered and retained and others previously exited. But there is no strict correspondence between the structures experienced and identities formed. Like everything else, experiencing is fallible. Moreover we mostly recognise this. Just as we each regularly find we experience a given situation differently from others, we can also come to reinterpret our experiences over time.

But, if the reduction of identities to conditions experienced is a theoretical error, it remains the case that the conditions we experience do nevertheless make a difference. If we ultimately make our own identities, we do so only with the resources available, and in conditions not all of our own choosing. In particular the nature of gender positions we occupy or have occupied, along with all other features of our specific social situations, many of which have been allocated to us, causally impinges on our experiences and so constitutes conditioning factors of our identities.[15] Our identities are themselves a form of emergent, relationally conditioned, social structure in process.

Overview

My overall contention, then, is that the conception defended here retains the insights both of the early gender theorists and of their post-modernist critics. It retains the latter's emphasis on multiple or fragmented experiences, whilst also sustaining the wider feminist insight that our societies provide an objective basis for the discriminating tendencies already noted.

The central idea underpinning my arguments is that there is an ontological distinction between (emergent) social structure and human agency, whereby neither can be reduced to the other, though each is continually transformed through practice in a process of linked (or co-) development.

In the light of the perspective defended, we find that gender sceptics portray early (supposedly essentialist) feminists as, in effect, reducing agency to specific (gender) structures, or at least to specific aspects regarded as fixed, whilst gender sceptics themselves have responded by more or less cutting the individual free of structural forces of determination entirely. However, we can now recognise the initial (essentialist) form of gender theorising as well as the out-and-out deconstructive response to be polar degenerate cases of the range of real possibilities, with the deconstructive response in particular achieving its credibility only by situating essentialism as the only alternative. There are additional possibilities. And once the conception elaborated above is accepted we have a basis for sustaining the insights of both essentialist and post-modernist perspectives, whilst avoiding the limit weaknesses of each.

The broad implications for theorising are clear: the study of gender requires attention not just to individuals and their experiences but equally to explaining specific networks of internally related position–practice systems, including their conditions and how they are reproduced and/or transformed over time and space. The focus is precisely on specific examples of social reproduction and social transformation (methodological aspects of this are discussed elsewhere; see Lawson 2003, especially chapter 4).

The possibility of emancipatory practice

Of central interest here is that implications also follow at the level of emancipatory practice. Specifically, the ontological conception sustained allows us to acknowledge the relativity of knowledge as well as the uniqueness of experiences and yet still entertain the possibility of progressive, including emancipatory, projects. For it is now clear that there is no contradiction in both recognising each of us as a unique identity or individuality, resulting (in part) from our own unique paths through life, and also accepting that we can nevertheless stand in the same or similar positions and relations of domination to those of others around us, including gender relations. From this perspective there is no contradiction in recognising our different individualities and experiences as well as the possibility of common interests in transforming certain forms of social relationships and other aspects of social structure. Fundamental here once more is the fact that human subjectivities, human experiences and social structure cannot be reduced one to another; they are each ontologically distinct, albeit highly interdependent, modes of being.

I re-emphasise that I make no presumption that any aspects of social structure, including its gendered features, are other than intrinsically dynamic, or are everywhere the same. It is evident that gender relations in most places (still) serve to facilitate (localised) practices in which men can dominate/oppress women, or appear in some way advantaged. But the extent of commonality/difference across time and space is something to be determined a posteriori.

This conception also allows that although the individualities/personalities of people from quite diverse backgrounds may be quite different, when they arrive in the same location they are likely to be subject to, or forced to stand within, similar, i.e. local, gender (and other) relations, whether or not they are aware of this, and whether or not they learn to become locally skilful. For example, it seems that currently in parts of the UK any (person identified as a) woman going alone to a pub in the evening is likely to meet with harassment by some 'men' whatever the former's previous experiences, realised capacities, acknowledged needs, expectations, self-perceptions or understandings of the local gender relations, and so on.

Gender relations with a degree of space–time extension along with practices they facilitate can be transfactually operative irrespective of the knowledges or understandings and wishes of those affected. The existences of multiple differences in manifest identities and individual experiences is not inconsistent with this insight – any more than the unique path of each autumn leaf undermines the hypothesis that all leaves are similarly subject to the transfactual 'pull' of gravity.

In short, once a structured ontology is recognised, multiplicity in the course of actuality is found to remain coherent with a degree of uniformity at the level of underlying causes or structure. The conception defended thus secures the basis for an emancipatory politics rooted in real needs and interests. In so doing it provides grounds, in particular, for feminist projects of transforming gender relations, in an awareness that the existence of multiculturalism or of differences in general need not in any way undermine or contradict such emancipatory practice. It also preserves, without strain, the possibility of strategies of solidarity or meaningful affiliated action between groups. In short, it transcends the sorts of tensions that currently seem to pervade much of feminist epistemology and political theory.

Social transformation and the good society

A more specific implication of the framework is that emancipatory social change is found to be a matter not only just of ameliorating events but also, and especially, of social transformation. Now given that social structures depend on our practices, then, whatever the appropriate feminist orientation to the state, we can recognise that social change may be brought about not just through central state action, but equally through each of us changing the conceptions which guide our practices. Radicals of all sorts have always understood this, that we can transform social reality by increasing our awareness and understanding of it, and in turn change the practices via which existing structures are reproduced.

What more can be said? I think the framework defended here bears implications, albeit still at a very abstract level, about the (conception of the) sort of society that might reasonably inform our emancipatory structural transformations. I think it is an inescapable conclusion that the ultimate goal of emancipatory practice is a form of society. Moreover, given the interconnectedness of social life, entailing that all actions are affecting of others, the basic unit of emancipatory analysis is presumably (at least) the whole of humanity. However, emancipatory practice must equally recognise our differences. My suggestion here is just that (given both our (structured) interrelatedness as well as differences at the level of each individual) the concern of emancipatory action must be with the possibility of a society so constituted as to allow that the flourishing of each is a condition of the flourishing of all and vice versa; or, as Marx put it, 'an association in which the free development of each is a condition of the free development of all' (Marx and Engels 1952 [1848]: 76).

I emphasise that in proposing this formulation of the 'good society' I do not presuppose any fixity; the formulation allows for the openness of everything to the future, including human 'nature', society, knowledge, technology, science, and all else. But anything short of this formulation, as a goal, it seems to me, is likely to beg the questions of the sort as to whose interests are to be met.

Is the above conception of the good society consistent with one constituted in large part by social positions? Now in the light of the analysis sustained it appears feasible that society will for a long time, if not always, be in large part constituted by networks of internally related social positions, marking divisions of labour, or of age or of political, religious or other attachments. But there is no obvious reason to suppose that a structuring of society cannot be achieved that, though in some part constituted by objective (though always transient) positions, nevertheless avoids being hierarchically organised. That is, (always transient) positions can conceivably be facilitating without providing the basis for the unreasonable privileging of some over subjugated others. Also, social positions can be rotated amongst the population. Perhaps participating first as a speaker, then as a member of the audience, and later perhaps as a chair, at a feminist meeting is a relevant illustrative model; objective positions all, but surely non-discriminatory in any necessarily excluding fashion and acceptable.[16]

A sustainable conclusion, then, is that the theorising of strategy for a developing global order, including the adoption of an appropriate orientation to the state, is reasonably informed by such an (open) conception of the good society. Specifically, in proposing measures to transform social reality, it seems that a criterion of relevance is whether such measures appear capable of moving us in the direction of a society in which the flourishing of each is consistent with, and a condition of, the flourishing of all others, and vice versa.

From this perspective the strategy adopted by some post-modernists of emphasising an ontology of mere difference – on the reasoning that if no objective basis is admitted for including only some individuals, there is equally no basis admitted for excluding any[17] – can be seen not only as based on an unrealistic assessment of the nature of social reality, but also as marking a scenario that is but a degenerate special case of the above conception of the good society, one in which all positions, all divisions of labour and of other practices, have all but disappeared.

Even where the latter scenario is believed to constitute a real possibility, there is, to put it differently, little reason to suppose it is the only feasible structure of an emancipated society, and even less reason to suppose that we have reached it already, or can achieve it just by denying the objective structures including positions of gender system in which we currently live. Though we can change the world by becoming more aware of the way it is constituted, and thereby adjust our practices, it does not follow that we can achieve a particular social structure merely by wishing that the (thought-to-be) desirable features are already in place (or undesirable ones absent). More to the point, by focusing on only one version of the good society, we unnecessarily constrain our options for bringing an emancipated society about.

Conclusions

I have defended a conception that preserves and endorses, indeed itself incorporates, the impulse behind the 'deconstructive' turn in recent feminist theory, but which simultaneously, through its emphasis on ontology, avoids complete self-subversion, maintaining, amongst other things, the basis for an intelligible account of gender as well as the possibility of emancipatory action.

The particular theory of reality defended is of a structured and open world. It is a conception which recognises that in our everyday practices we, all of us, as complexly structured, socially and culturally situated, purposeful and needy individuals, knowledgeably and capably negotiate complex, shifting, only partially grasped and contested structures of power, rules, relations and other possibly relatively enduring but nevertheless transient and action-dependent social resources at our disposal. Ontological analysis provides an insight into this reality.

My primary focus here has been gender and the possibility of transforming gender aspects of society that are found to be discriminatory. In the light of the framework sustained, gender can be understood as turning on a positioned feature of human life, specifically a network of internally related positions with associated rule-governed rights and practices. In fact, according to the conception defended, gender is very likely a feature of everything social. It is nothing less than the social system as a whole viewed under a particular aspect, that whereby social discriminations are made between individuals solely on their being identified or perceived as being of different biological sexes, discriminations that mostly have nothing to do with any differences that may be found at the biological level. Transforming the undesirable gender features of society, then, amounts to a generalised project of social transformation.

In discussing the specific implications of the analysis for projects of social emancipation, I have argued that whatever the orientation of feminists and others to the state, the goal of a society in which the flourishing of each is a condition of the flourishing of all is appropriately brought to bear in formulating substantive measures or political strategies. It is the task of formulating the latter measures or strategies that now requires our attention.

I re-emphasise, finally, that the orientation of the chapter has been ontological. It is noticeable that the study of gender, and indeed feminist theorising quite widely, has tended to neglect ontology in favour of epistemology. My own view is that this is an error, and that the two activities, along with all other forms of theorising – ontology, epistemology and substantive analysis – need to be co-developed. Indeed, it seems quite possible that if feminists allow explicit ontological analysis more fully out of the margin the opportunities for advance thereby opened up will prove to be quite significant.

Notes

1 This chapter first appeared as Chapter 7 'Gender and Social Change' in Browne, J, ed, 2007, *The Future of Gender*, Cambridge University Press.
2 The distinction between sex and gender on which this conception builds derives from the work of the psychologist Robert Stoller (1968) who first formulated it to differentiate the socio-cultural meanings ('masculinity' and 'femininity') from those of biological sex differences ('male' and 'female') on which they were erected (see Oakley 1972).
3 As Kate Soper complains:

> ... the logic which challenged certain kinds of identity thinking and deconstructed certain notions of truth, progress, humanism and the like, has pushed on to question the possibility of any holistic and objective analysis of societies of a kind which allows to define them as 'capitalist' or 'patriarchal' or indeed totalitarian, together with the transformative projects such analyses advocate. It gives us not new identities, not a better understanding of the plural and complex nature of society, but tends rather to collapse into an out and out individualism.
>
> (Soper 1991: 45)

4 This is indeed manifest in the orientations, language, values and priorities of academic disciplines, as economics, my discipline, illustrates as well as anything else (see, e.g., the contributions in Ferber and Nelson 1993).
5 As Susan Bordo summarises the situation:

> Assessing where we are now, it seems to me that feminism stands less in danger of the totalizing tendencies of feminists than of an increasingly paralysing anxiety over falling (from what grace?) into ethnocentrism or 'essentialism' ... Do we want to delegitimate a priori the exploration of experimental continuity and structural common ground among women? ... If we wish to empower diverse voices, we would do better, I believe, to shift strategy from the methodological dictum that we foreswear talk of 'male' and 'female' realities ... to the messier, more slippery, practical struggle to create institutions and communities that will not permit some groups of people to make determinations about reality for all.
>
> (Bordo 1993: 465)

6 As Anne Phillips has observed: 'Notwithstanding the conceptual difficulties feminists have raised around the distinction between sex and gender, we will continue to need some way of disentangling the differences that are inevitable from those that are chosen, and from those that are imposed' (Phillip 1992: 23).
7 It is no secret (though somewhat puzzling) that feminist theorists have tended to fight shy of ontology/metaphysics. Sally Haslanger's recounting of her own experience captures this situation:

> Metaphysics has never been without critics. Plato's efforts have repeatedly been a target of attack; Hume ranted against the metaphysicians of his day; and one of the founding missions of logical positivism was to show that metaphysical claims are meaningless. More recently, feminist theorists have

joined the chorus. To reveal among academic feminists that one's specialization in philosophy is metaphysics is to invite responses of shock, confusion and sometimes dismissal. Once after I gave a presentation at an American Philosophical Association meeting on social construction, a noted senior feminist philosopher approached me and said, 'you are clearly very smart, and very feminist, so why are you wasting your time on this stuff?' Academic feminists, for the most part, view metaphysics as a dubious intellectual project, certainly irrelevant and probably worse; and often the further charge is levelled that it has pernicious political implications as well.

(Haslanger 2000: 107)

Why should ontology be so treated? Some seem to suppose ontology must be foundationalist. But ontology is just an epistemological project, and like any other must be recognised as situated, practically conditioned, partial and in parts at least probably transient. Sandra Harding (1999: 132) suggests that existing ontological/realist presuppositions of science can be entrenched, and that epistemic standards are an easier target for criticism. But surely the insights of recent feminist theorising have stemmed from the fact that almost all claims and suppositions, no matter how entrenched, have been regarded as legitimate targets of deconstruction or other forms of criticism. Harding (1999: 132) also gives a Kuhnian argument as to why implicit and naive ontological presuppositions may be worth persevering with anyway. Whether or not this can be shown to be provisionally the case with regard to some branches of natural science, it is certainly not so with regard to studies of the social realm, as I have shown at length elsewhere (Lawson 2003). A final explanation is that ontology may reveal objective grounds for identifying groups, and so group-memberships, whereas such a finding does not help the overriding cause of being non-exclusive (see Fricker 2000 or Haslanger 2000). As Donna Haraway (1985: 372) puts it, 'Consciousness of exclusion through naming is acute.' This is a line of reasoning I briefly address in the main text below.

8 One further component of this transformational conception is that there are both synchronic and diachronic aspects to agency–structure interaction. It is, of course, human beings that make things happen. And it is only through the mediation of human agency that structures have a causal impact. Now if a person who speaks only English makes a short (possibly unplanned) visit to a region where English is not spoken, the inability to speak the local language (or the existence only of languages other than English) will be experienced by the traveller as a constraint. It forces her or him to seek a translator or whatever. If, however, English is spoken as a second language, this will be experienced by the traveller as an enabling (as well as constraining) feature of the local social structure. Here, with the momentarily enabling and/or constraining aspects of social structure, we have the synchronic aspect of agency–structure interaction. However, if the individual who speaks only English decides to settle in a non-English-speaking region, then, if he or she is to become competent, it will be necessary to acquire the local language (and indeed become competent in numerous aspects of the local culture). The process through which this happens is the diachronic aspect of agency–structure interaction. If at a point in time structure serves to constrain and enable, over time it serves more to shape and mould. As new practices are repeatedly carried out they become habitual as dispositions are moulded in response. This, of course, cannot happen without the collusion of the individual in question (and the mediation of his or her practices). If the individual remains for a long time in the new language or culture zone, he or she may even lose the capacity to speak English, or at least to do so competently. Just as human capabilities, etc., can be transformed via the relocation, so the maintenance of those previously held may require active reproduction. Experience suggests that

individuals can lose a significant degree of competence in languages with which they once were fluent (also, of course, what is true of capabilities and dispositions applies equally to tastes, preferences, and the like).

9   I hope it is clear that in advancing this conception I neither assume fixity, nor deny variability (if within limits), at the biological level, and nor do I suppose that any biological sex form, or for that matter form of sexuality, is more natural than any other (nor, of course, do I endorse any such differences as there are, or perceptions of them, being used to legitimate social inequalities). I do hold that if biological differences/commonalities, as they are perceived, affect emergent social structure, then equally the (emergent) social structure can act back on the biological. However, the two domains, the biological and the socio-structural, remain ontologically distinct, though causally interacting; neither is reducible to, or explicable completely in terms of, the other. It will be clear, then, that however I suggest we conceptualise gender as an aspect of social structure (see below), I am accepting the reality (and the explanatory significance) of maintaining the sex/gender distinction.

10 In viewing gender as everything considered under only one aspect (but without wishing to detract from the emphasis on everything) I concur with Fraser (2007) in viewing 'gender struggles as one strand among others in a broader political project aimed at institutionalizing democratic justice across multiple axes of social differentiation'.

11 See Fraser (2007) on the need to hold distributional and status issues together in considering matters of gender inequality.

12 This view is advanced by Juliet Mitchell who argues that 'sibling trauma instigates the construction of gender difference. Gender is engendered in the sibling (or sibling equivalent) relationship' (2003: 216). When 'the child is overwhelmed by the trauma of one who, in the mind, was supposed to be the same as itself inevitably turning out to be different, it finds ways to mark this difference – age is one, gender another' (ibid.: 216). This trauma ensures that violence is latent and always possible between either the actual siblings or their replacements in the wider world. 'The cradle of gender difference is both narcissistic love and violence at the traumatic moment of displacement in the world. Gender difference comes into being when physical strength and malevolence are used to mark the sister as lesser' (ibid.: 219–20).

13 And more subtly gendering will probably be implicated even within discussions of gender discrimination, such as this chapter, so that the successful eradication of gender inequalities will require that, amongst other things, we continually challenge the frameworks within which equality is debated (see Bryson 2007).

14 As such the conception advanced here encompasses the distinction between sexual difference and gender advanced by Juliet Mitchell (2007). However, in emphasising how siblings reveal how crucial a force is sexuality in psychosocial dynamics, Mitchell is wary of any conception of gender that does not place sex or sexuality at the centre.

15 Although the conception here is derived by way of first elaborating the ontological conception discussed above and defended more fully elsewhere, others have reached a similar position on certain aspects via alternative routes. See, for example, Mohanty (2000) and Moya (2000).

16 This seems consistent too with Nancy Fraser's 'status model' which encourages a politics aimed at overcoming subordination by recognising all individuals as full members of society whatever their socio-cultural positions, or perceived identities, etc. (see Fraser 2000). This conception of justice is advanced in Fraser's formulation of 'the principle of parity of participation' according to which 'justice requires social arrangements that permit all (adult) members of society to interact with one another as peers'. See Fraser (2007) for a discussion of the preconditions for such 'participatory parity'.

17 Miranda Fricker (2000: 148) captures the motivation of the latter well:

> Postmodernists typically advocate a social ontology of fragmentation not on grounds of social accuracy, but on the political ground that any other ontology would be exclusionary ... In feminist postmodernism ... to recognise difference is to meet an obligation to political inclusiveness rather than empirical adequacy.

Sally Haslanger (2000: 122) summarises how this works in the arguments of Judith Butler in particular:

> Remember how the move to nominalism functions in the structure of Butler's strategy: if there is no objective basis for distinguishing one group from another, then no political regime – especially the dominant one – can claim authority by grounding itself in 'the way the world is'; instead ... the choice will have to be made on normative argument. The worry seems to be that if we allow objective types, then we are politically constrained to design our social institutions to honour and sustain them.

References

Bordo, S. (1993) 'Feminism, Post Modernism and Gender Scepticism', in *Unbearable Weight: Feminism, Western Culture, and the Body*, The Regents of the University of California; reprinted in Anne C. Herrmann and Abigail Stewart (eds), *Theorizing Feminism: Parallel Trends in the Humanities and Social Sciences* (Boulder, San Francisco and Oxford: Westview Press, 1994) (page references to the latter).

Browne, J. (ed.) (2007) *The Future of Gender* (Cambridge: Cambridge University Press).

Bryson, V. (2007) 'Perspectives on Gender Equality: Challenging the Terms of Debate', in Jude Browne (ed.), *The Future of Gender* (Cambridge: Cambridge University Press), 35–53.

Chodorow, N. (1978) *The Reproduction of Mothering: Psychoanalysis and the Sociology of Gender* (Berkeley: University of California Press).

Ferber, M. and Nelson, J. (eds) (1993) *Beyond Economic Man: Feminist Theory and Economics* (Chicago: University of Chicago Press).

Fraser, N. (2000) 'Rethinking Recognition', *New Left Review* 3, May–June: 1–10.

Fraser, N. (2007) 'Mapping the Feminist Imagination: From Redistribution to Recognition to Representation', in Jude Browne (ed.), *The Future of Gender* (Cambridge: Cambridge University Press), 15–34.

Fricker, M. (2000) 'Feminism in Epistemology: Pluralism without Post Modernism', in M. Fricker and J. Hornsby (eds), *The Cambridge Companion to Feminism in Philosophy* (Cambridge: Cambridge University Press), 146–65.

Haraway, D. (1985) 'A Manifesto for Cyborgs: Science, Technology, and Socialist Feminism in the 1980s', *Socialist Review* 80: 65–108.

Harding, S. (1999) 'The Case for Strategic Realism: Response to Lawson', *Feminist Economics*, Vol 5, No 3, 127–33.

Haslanger, S. (2000) 'Feminism in Metaphysics: Negotiating the Natural', in M. Fricker and J. Hornsby (eds), *The Cambridge Companion to Feminism in Philosophy* (Cambridge: Cambridge University Press), 107–26.

Keller, E. (1985) *Reflections on Gender and Science* (New Haven: Yale University Press).

Kuiper, Edith and Sap, Jolande (eds) (1995) *Out of the Margin: Feminist Perspectives on Economics* (London and New York: Routledge).

Lawson, T. (1997) *Economics and Reality* (London and New York: Routledge).

Lawson, T. (2003) *Reorienting Economics* (London and New York: Routledge.

Marx, K. and Engels, F. (1952 [1848]) *Manifesto of the Communist Party* (Moscow: Progress Publishers).

Mitchell, J. (2003) *Siblings: Sex and Violence* (Cambridge: Polity Press).

Mitchell, J. (2007) 'Procreative Mothers (Sexual Difference) and Child-Free Sisters (Gender)', in Jude Browne (ed.), *The Future of Gender* (Cambridge: Cambridge University Press), 163–88.

Mohanty, Chandra Talpade (2000) 'Under Western Eyes: Feminist Scholarship and Colonial Discourses', in *Feminism without Borders: Decolonizing Theory, Practicing Solidarity* (Durham, NC: Duke University Press), 333–58.

Moya, P. (2000) 'Postmodernism, "Realism", and the Politics of Identity: Cherrie Moraga and Chicana Feminism', in P. Moya and M. Hames-Garcia (eds), *Reclaiming Identity: Realist Theory and the Predicament of Postmodernism* (Berkeley: University of California Press), 67–101.

Oakley, A. (1972) *Sex, Gender and Society* (London: Temple-Smith).

Phillips, A. (1992) 'Universal Pretensions in Political Thought', in M. Barrett and A. Phillips (eds), *Destabilizing Theory: Contemporary Feminist Debates* (Cambridge: Polity Press), 10–30.

Soper, Kate (1991) 'Postmodernism, Critical Theory and Critical Realism', in Roy Bhaskar (ed.), *A Meeting of Minds* (London: The Socialist Society), 42–9.

Spelman, Elizabeth V. (1990) *Inessential Woman: Problems of Exclusion in Feminist Thought* (London: The Women's Press).

Stoller, Robert (1968) *Sex and Gender* (London: Hogarth Press).

18 Technological objects, social positions, and the Transformational Model of Social Activity[1]

Philip Faulkner and Jochen Runde

Introduction

Critical Realism has developed significantly over the years since the publication of Bhaskar's (1975, 1979, 1986, 1989) seminal books, so much so that there will inevitably be differences between authors about what its defining features are. But there are at least two things that most people familiar with Critical Realism would accept. The first is that it is primarily ontological in orientation, and concerned with investigating the nature of social reality in particular. The second is that it is committed to a particular representation of social reality called the Transformational Model of Social Activity. While we accept that it is good practice to avoid acronyms, the term Transformational Model of Social Activity is such a mouthful and will recur so often in what follows, that we will henceforth refer to it as the TMSA.

The TMSA offers a highly generalised but in our view descriptively accurate image of how society is organised, reproduced and transformed. Its focus, however, has tended to be on the relationship between social structure and human agency, and it remains underdeveloped on how the non-human world, and the world of technological objects in particular, may be implicated in this relationship. Of course this has not prevented the TMSA and Critical Realism more widely from being used to inform some very good work about social phenomena in which technology plays a role (Bygstad 2010; de Vaujany 2008; Dobson 2002; Dobson *et al.* 2007; Mingers 2004a, 2004b; Morton 2006; Mutch 2002, 2012; Smith 2006; Volkoff *et al.* 2007). Nevertheless, it seems to us that this stream of the literature still lacks an explicit theory of the nature, position and identity of technological objects within the social world. Our aim in this chapter is to fill this gap by proposing a general theory of technological objects and showing how this might be incorporated within the TMSA.[2] A theory on these lines would be of considerable value, in our view, in providing an explicit conceptual basis for further theoretical work on technological objects, in helping guide empirical work in this area, and in surfacing hidden assumptions about how technology is implicated in human doings.

Our argument begins with a brief overview of the TMSA, focusing on its rendition of how human activity draws on social structure that is then reproduced and/or transformed through such activity. As we are interested in the general features of this model that most proponents of Critical Realism would accept, we focus on its original formulation as it appears in Bhaskar (1989; first published in 1978), supplemented by some material on specific forms of social structure drawn from Lawson (1997, 2003). This is followed by a discussion of technological objecthood and a summary of the theory of the nature and identity of technological objects that we have developed in earlier work (Faulkner and Runde 2009, 2011, 2012; Runde *et al.* 2009). We then move on to what we regard as the main contribution of the present chapter, which is to integrate this theory within the TMSA. A good bit of the ensuing discussion is given to bitstrings, the sequences of 1s and 0s used in computing to represent information in binary form and an important instance of what we call non-material technological objects of particular relevance to information systems (IS) research. We close with some implications and a brief conclusion.

The Transformational Model of Social Activity

The TMSA consists of a stripped-down representation of three aspects of the social domain: human agency, social structure and the relationship between the two.

Human agency, in Bhaskar's scheme, refers to the activities of people who in normal circumstances are self-reflexive and have the capacity of conscious choice. While Bhaskar places considerable emphasis on the intentional, goal-oriented nature of human action – the 'genesis of human actions, lying in the reasons, intentions and plans of human beings' (Bhaskar 1989: 79) – he also alludes to unconscious or subconscious drivers of human behaviour (Bhaskar 1989: 97). That is to say, he allows that even consciously intended human activities involve dispositions of which the actors concerned may be unaware and capacities they are able to exercise without attending to them. Dispositions are propensities to act in certain ways, such as an inclination to tell the truth, work hard or avoid conflict. Capacities are abilities such as being able to ride a bicycle, play chess or converse in a foreign language. As we will explain below, many human dispositions (capacities) involve the propensity (ability) to respond appropriately to pre-existing rule structures.

Given the importance of social structure in Bhaskar's thought, it is curious that his account of the TMSA contains neither a definition of the term nor much in the way of concrete examples. Nevertheless, it is clear enough what he has in mind: the emergent realm of social rules, social positions and social relations that condition and provide order to human affairs. The guiding idea in his work and Critical Realism more generally is that while social structure underpins and shapes the activities of human actors, it is nevertheless distinct from those activities and cannot be reduced to them. If what human actors do is analogous to natural events, as Bhaskar (1989: 78) puts it, then social structure is analogous to the natural-science mechanisms that produce those events. Further, he argues that social structure is usually already in existence prior to the activities of those it conditions, and is accordingly better conceived as something reproduced and transformed through human activity rather than created by it.

The distinctive feature of the TMSA is how it pictures the coming together of human agency and social structure, specifically that they are recursively organised and that the reproduction and transformation of social structure is a generally unintended consequence of human action. The first idea corresponds to what Giddens (1984) calls the duality of structure, that social structure is constantly reproduced as an ongoing consequence of human activities, where those same activities presuppose, and are conditioned by, the very structures that are being reproduced. The second corresponds to what Bhaskar (1989: 92–93) calls the duality of praxis, that while human doings are generally consciously directed at intended ends, their contribution to structural reproduction is for the most part unconscious and unintended. These ideas are captured in the familiar diagram depicted below (Figure 18.1; reproduced from Bhaskar 1989: 77).

Referring to the left-hand side of the diagram, human actors always operate within a pre-existing social system (social structure), which provides a framework that both enables and constrains their activities (socialisation). The total of these activities then lead to the unconscious and unintended reproduction of the social system to be drawn on in future rounds of activity. It is always possible that there may be variations in human practices, whether these arise spontaneously or from perturbations to the social or natural environment. If these variations 'take' and catch on more widely, they can themselves lead to variations in social structure, which may themselves be reproduced over time in subsequent rounds of human activity. These possibilities are represented on the right-hand side of the diagram where the activities of individual actors lead to the reproduction and/or transformation of structure. Finally, note that the influence of social structure is felt even when the activity it conditions appears to run in a contrary

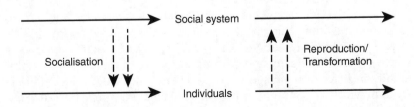

Figure 18.1 The Transformational Model of Social Activity

direction. For example, while the act of rebelling against a social rule presupposes the existence of that rule, this is clearly something different from instantiating or 'performing' that rule in a direct way (see Lawson 2003: 37). To use a phrase favored by Lawson, human practices may be 'out of phase' with the social structure that conditions them.

This concludes our overview of the TMSA. But before we move on it will be useful to say a little more about the three particular types of social structure we mentioned above – social rules, social positions and social relations – since these play a significant role in what follows. By *social rules* we mean generalised procedures of action expressible as injunctions of the form 'if X in situation C, do Y', and where 'do' should be read as a placeholder for phrases such as 'this counts as', 'take this to mean', 'refrain from' and so on (Lawson 2003: 36–37). Social rules have normative force, namely that in the community in which a rule has currency, if it is the case that X in situation C then one ought to do Y. The sanctions felt by those who fail to conform vary greatly depending on the rule and community in question, and may range from mild disapproval or ridicule to something much more serious.

Social positions are the 'slots' or 'roles' that individuals occupy within communities, and include positions associated with such things as occupation, gender, family and so on (Lawson 2003: 38–39). Every social position is defined by a complex of social rules consisting of various rights and responsibilities, the enjoyment and performance of which is generally associated with and expected of the people who occupy them. Thus, the position of CEO within a corporation, for example, typically encompasses various rights (e.g., to make executive decisions over some domain; to have access to particular kinds of information; to receive compensation in accordance with their contract of employment; and so on), as well as responsibilities (e.g., to shape, communicate and implement the corporation's vision, mission and strategy; to lead, direct and evaluate the work of other executives; to maintain awareness of the competitive and regulatory landscape, and so on). While these rights and responsibilities are vested in whoever is occupying the position of CEO for as long as he or she is doing so, they are associated with the position rather than any particular individual. When a CEO is replaced, he or she typically loses the rights and responsibilities associated with being CEO, which then transfer to the new occupant of that position.

Finally, *social relations* refer to the 'other-relatedness' of many items in the social realm, including humans and their activities, as well as social positions and other kinds of entities (Lawson 2003: 39). There are many ways in which different things may be related in the social realm, including by proximity in space or time, age, size and so on. A subset of these relations are ones in which one or more of the relata are what they are in virtue of the relationship in which they stand to one another. Social relations of this kind are called internal social relations, as distinct from external social relations in which the relata are not so constituted. Internal social relations are an important constituent of social structure and include human position to human position relations (husband to wife), and, as we will see, human position to non-human position (computer programmer to computer) and non-human to non-human position (computer to computer code) relations.

An important question that arises here is how social structure impresses itself on human actors so that it is felt in their practices. Take the case of social rules, for example, which might be learned in a conscious, discursive fashion, even if they subsequently slip from conscious view with practice and become tacit knowledge. This is one possibility. A more interesting possibility, however, albeit one not mentioned by Bhaskar (1989) himself, is the case of what Searle (1995: 127–147) calls 'background causation'. Background causation occurs where people's activities reflect their capacities to behave in ways appropriate to particular rule structures, but where those capacities might never have involved their internalising or 'knowing' those rules consciously or even subconsciously. The rules in question nevertheless have a causal role, insofar as they have to have been *in situ* in order for people to develop the capacities to behave in ways that are appropriate to them. Rules of grammar are a good example here, which many people are able to conform to without being able to articulate them or indeed without their ever having learned and internalised them in a conscious way. This is so not least because much of people's ability to use language grammatically is developed before their language skills have become sophisticated enough to learn rules of grammar in a discursive way.

Objecthood and technological objects

While contributors to Critical Realism have had a good deal to say about subjectivity and the nature of the human subject (e.g., Archer 2000, 2003; Collier 1994: 151–156; Lawson 2003: 944–53), they have had rather less to say in theoretical terms about the nature of the contents of the non-human world including technological objects. As a first step towards filling this gap we will begin by specifying what we mean by objects and technological objects in particular (Faulkner and Runde 2011). Starting at the most abstract level we consider objects to be one of the basic kinds of entity or existent found in reality, alongside other basic kinds of entity such as events and properties. The defining characteristic of objects is that they are structured continuants. By something being structured we mean that it is composed of distinct parts – objects in their own right – that are organised in some way. Thus, an inkjet printer comprises belts and rollers, paper tray and feeder assemblies, imaging units and so on, arranged in a particular way. By something being a continuant we mean that it is fully present at each and every point in time at which it exists. Objects are therefore distinct from other kinds of entities, such as events, that are occurrents and whose different parts occur at different points in time.[3]

The universe is filled with all manner of objects, only a subset of which are technological objects. We define a technological object as any object that has one or more uses assigned to it by the members of some human community.[4] Most technological objects are human artefacts, such as printers, phones and e-readers. But there are also cases in which they are naturally occurring objects that have been appropriated and put to some use without being modified by human intervention, such as when a stone is used as a paperweight, a tree as a parasol, or a stray reed as a drinking straw.

Technological objects fall into two broad categories. The first is the class of what we will call material technological objects, namely those that possess a physical mode of being, with the attendant properties of location, mass, shape and volume. Examples include paper clips, office chairs and flipchart stands. The second is the class of what we will call non-material technological objects, namely those that possess a non-physical mode of being and are thus 'aspatial', lacking the aforementioned properties (Faulkner and Runde 2011). Many of the most common examples of non-material technological objects are what we will call syntactic entities, namely objects composed of symbols phrased into well-formed expressions, where 'well-formed' means that these expressions adhere to the syntactical and semantic rules of the language in which they are couched. Examples include research articles, sales reports, employment contracts, product designs, musical compositions, and bitstrings such as computer files.[5]

We return to the distinction between material and non-material technological objects later in the chapter. An interesting point to note before moving on, however, is that according to the definition of technological objecthood we have given, humans and human collectivities may be technological objects too. Thus, private investigators, air traffic controllers and armies are all structured continuants that have uses assigned to them by the agencies that deploy them. In what follows, however, we will focus on *non-human* technological objects, since our principal goal is to locate non-humans within the TMSA. From this point on, then, and unless we indicate otherwise, when we talk about technological objects we refer exclusively to non-human technological objects.

Technical identity

With our conception of what it is for something to be a technological object in place, we now attempt to situate technological objects within social reality more widely. We proceed in two stages. In the first we briefly review some of our earlier work on what we term the 'technical identity' of an object (Faulkner and Runde 2009, 2011). In the second we expand on this idea by showing how it fits into the framework of the TMSA.

Our theory of the technical identity of technological objects is a version of what in the philosophy of technology is sometimes called the 'dual-nature' conception of technology (Kroes 2010; Kroes and Meijers 2006; Meijers

2000). This theory is based on the simple idea that the technical identity of an object, namely the kind of thing that object is within some community, flows from two considerations: its 'function' and its 'form'. The function of a technological object is the use that members of some community impose on that object in pursuit of their practical interests (Searle 1995, 1999, 2001). Examples of functions include those of a flip chart to facilitate brainstorming, a desktop scanner to digitise documents or images, and a network-monitoring app to provide information on the status of devices located on a local area network. As functions are collectively assigned by members of social groups they are never intrinsic to the objects concerned and so are always necessarily community-relative (Searle 1995: 13–19; Feenberg 2000: 305). As the technical identities of objects depend on those functions, it then follows that technical identities are necessarily community-relative too.

With regard to the form of a technological object, in order for the function assigned to it to be sustained that object must generally possess the characteristics and capabilities required to perform that function. The qualifier 'must generally possess' is to allow for cases in which technological objects malfunction and can no longer perform the function assigned to them. A digital camera with a defective power supply can no longer be used to capture images, but is no less a digital camera for that.

According to the dual-nature conception, the function and form of an object are together constitutive of its technical identity within some community. One problem with this, however, is that it is common to think of the form of an object as being restricted to its physical or material properties. In this case the theory would have little to say about non-material technological objects. This shortcoming can however be overcome by substituting the notion of an object's form with the more general notion of an object's structure (Faulkner and Runde 2011). Recall that objects are structured in the sense of being composed of constituent parts that are organised in some way. For material objects such as an office chair, structure is equivalent to its physical form, namely its material components and how these are arranged and interact. For non-material objects, structure again refers to its components, their arrangement and interactions, but in this case these are not physical attributes. In the case of syntactic entities, for example, comprising well-formed expressions in an appropriate language, the components are symbols and their arrangement is a logical one – requiring conformity with the rules of the language in which the object is expressed – rather than a spatial one.

Our generalised theory of the technical identity of an object can be stated as follows: an object possesses a particular technical identity within the community in which it is used and/or appropriately referenced if:

1 it has assigned to it the function associated with that technical identity; and
2 its structure is such that it is generally able to perform that function.

It is easy to see that this theory applies to non-material as well as material technological objects. Take a particular bitstring such as the iPhone app 'Net Status'. This bitstring is a network monitoring app within the community in which it is used and/or appropriately referenced if:

1   it has assigned to it the function of enabling people to monitor the status of routers, hosts and other devices located on a local area network; and

2   the structure of that bitstring is such that when it is executed on the appropriate hardware and attendant operating system, it can generally be used to monitor the status of routers, hosts and other devices located on a local area network.

A network monitoring app such as 'Net Status' thus derives its identity, not only from the structure of the bitstring comprising it, but also from the function assigned to that bitstring – in this case, to facilitate the monitoring of devices connected to a local area network.

Technological objects of a given technical identity often vary in the details of their structure. This raises the question of how, in the face of such diversity, people are able to identify different objects as tokens of the same type of technological device. In response to this question, we adopt a 'family resemblance' (Wittgenstein 1953: §65–71) view of technological objects, the idea that particular objects often share enough in the way of their structural features and capabilities to be grouped as tokens of the same type, even if the set of features common to all of them is quite small or even empty. Thus, while the Archos 70, the Kindle and the Sony PRS-T1 and their various competitors all vary somewhat in their structure, they share sufficient commonalities to be grouped together as e-readers.

It is also possible that similar or even identical objects may have different functions assigned to them, perhaps so much so that the same object may have radically different technical identities in different communities (e.g., the case of the gramophone turntable becoming a musical instrument in certain communities (Faulkner and Runde 2009)). This is probably not a particularly common case, although it is something that is more likely to be found in the case of intermediate products further upstream in the manufacturing process. Finally, it should be clear that technical identities might reside at different levels of abstraction. What we have in mind here is the idea of nested technical identities. For example, the class of objects that are network-monitoring iPhone apps are members of a wider class of objects that are iPhone apps, which are themselves members of an even wider class of objects that are application software, and so on. Which of these is the appropriate technical identity to invoke or act upon will depend on the context in which that object is being used or referenced.

Importing technology into the TMSA

We are now in a position to integrate the preceding theory of technological objects with the TMSA. The guiding idea is that technological objects occupy positions in the social world analogous to the positions occupied by humans, and in virtue of which they acquire a technical identity. We begin, therefore, by looking more closely at the notion of a social position. Proponents of Critical Realism often base their arguments for the existence of social positions on the observation that human practices appear to be systematically differentiated, with people often being differently empowered to do, or have access to, certain things (Lawson 2003: 38–39). For example, the practices of mothers, as well as their rights, responsibilities and so on, are distinct in many ways from those of members of parliament and medical practitioners. This observation suggests that there are differentiated and relatively stable complexes of rules in play in each case, which condition the practices and delimit the rights and responsibilities of those who fall within their ambit. These rule complexes define the social positions we described at the beginning of the chapter, which are themselves reproduced in the usual way in, and through, the actions of those who occupy and/or reference them.

The notion of identity can be introduced into the TMSA by noting that a person acquires a particular identity in virtue of occupying the social position associated with that identity. The idea, then, is that someone acquires the identity of mother, member of parliament or medical practitioner by moving into the pre-existing social position of mother, member of parliament or medical practitioner. Of course it is possible for people to occupy multiple positions and thus bear multiple identities at the same time. No doubt there are even a few people who are at once mothers, members of parliament and medical practitioners.[6]

Analogous arguments apply in the case of technological objects. Again, it is a common feature of everyday life that human practices associated with different kinds of object tend to be systematically differentiated. Thus, the ways in which we interact with an e-reader are systematically different from the ways that we interact with flash drives, fingerprint scanners and other kinds of devices. As before, this observation suggests that there are relatively stable complexes of rules that condition people's interactions with technological objects, and that these complexes define the social positions of the objects concerned in the same way they do the social positions occupied by humans. Further, and as is the case with social positions occupied by humans, the social positions occupied by technological objects tend to endure largely independently of their particular occupants. This means, for example, that manufacturers might discontinue old models of objects such as computer screens, inkjet printers and iPhone apps, and introduce new models, without affecting – indeed often relying on – the social positions concerned to persist in largely unchanged form.

That is to say, such positions are important constituents of what is often referred to in talk about there being a 'market' for some or other product, namely a place for that product in people's lives that is significant enough for them to be prepared to purchase it.

According to the view we wish to advance, then, just as there exist social positions that may be occupied by humans, so too there exist social positions that may be occupied by objects. And just as humans acquire identities in virtue of being positioned, the same also goes for technological objects. That an object is a printer, phone or e-reader, therefore, arises in virtue of being put in the position of printer, phone or e-reader and thereby acquiring the identity associated with that position. These identities, together with the social positions that support them, are elements of social structure on our account. And it is their continued reproduction that accounts in no small way to the relative stability of the contents of our artefactual worlds.

So much for the similarities between the positioning of humans and the positioning of technological objects. We will now highlight two important differences. The first is that although they occupy social positions, technological objects do not have practices in the way that human actors do. They are not agents, if by agents we mean beings that are self-reflexive and have the capacity to exercise conscious choice (Bhaskar 1989: 79). This means that the reproduction of the social structures associated with the positioning of technological objects comes not from their intrinsic affordances and capacities in the first instance – although these will certainly have to be salient and relatively stable in order for these positions to be sustained – but from their being implicated in structured human activities in ways that are relatively stable over time. So there are position-practices involved here too, but where the practices are not those of the occupants of the social positions (one or other technological object) but those of human actors who use or reference the object in question.

Similarly, and this is the second difference we want to highlight, non-human technological objects do not have rights and responsibilities in virtue of the positions they occupy in the way that human occupants of social positions do. There are of course often rights, responsibilities and so on involved in the use of technological objects, such as who in an organisation may use a particular device, or ensuring that safety procedures are followed when using a mechanical device that could cause injury. But again, while these rights and responsibilities emanate from the social position occupied by the object concerned, it is incumbent on the human actors that are using or otherwise implicated in the use of the objects concerned to behave in accordance with them. This is not something that the objects themselves can do.

We now turn to the question of how the structure and function of a technological object fit into this conception, given that our earlier discussion of the dual nature of technological objects – in which structure and function were crucial – made no reference to the idea of social positions. Let us start with function. Recall that we defined technological objects as objects that have one or more agentive function assigned to them by the members of some community. This assignment of function, as we see it, is partly constitutive of the social position of the object concerned and is something that object acquires as a consequence of being positioned. So in virtue of being slotted into the position of computer keyboard, for example, the object concerned assumes the function associated with that position – of being for manually inputting information into a computer – and the attendant technical identity. Further, such assignments of function are a form of social rule. Recall that we defined social rules as generalised procedures expressible by suitable transformations of the formula 'if X in situation C, do Y', where these rules are sustained in virtue of being accepted by, and implicated in the activities of, the members of a social group. Collective assignments of agentive function to certain types of object are no more than one such procedure, expressible as an injunction of the form 'objects that occupy such-and-such social position are for this purpose in such-and-such a situation'.

With respect to the structure of an object, in our account of the dual-nature perspective we said that for the assignment of function to an object to be sustained that object must generally possess the characteristics and capabilities required to perform that function. While we maintain this view, the idea that technological objects occupy social positions allows us to provide a more detailed account of the relationship between an object's structure, its function and its identity. As we see it, when an object is positioned it has a function assigned to it and acquires a technical identity as a result. Now in principle any object may be put in any position, but an object is only likely to remain in some position, and thereby maintain its function and identity over time, if it has an appropriate structure, namely one compatible with its performing the function assigned to it. Where an object is inappropriately positioned, lacking the characteristics required to perform the function assigned to it, that object is unlikely to remain in that position, and so retain its function and its technical identity, for long.

In practice, of course, technological objects are usually designed with their intended position in mind. Consequently, and provided the design process is successful, most technological objects possess structures that are well suited to the function subsequently assigned to them. In such cases ongoing use of an object helps to sustain its position and thereby the function assigned to it and its associated technical identity. Where the design process fails in some way, yielding an object that either lacks the capabilities required to perform its intended function or to do so in a way that is safe, reliable, useable, economical and so on, that object is likely to be discarded and replaced in its position by some more appropriate object. Of course even an object whose structure is initially well suited to the position it occupies may find itself replaced. Typically this would be because a superior design emerges, resulting in an object that is able to perform that function better than its predecessor.

The main elements of our account of how technological objects may be brought into the TMSA are now in place. The picture that emerges is of objects occupying social positions broadly analogous to the positions occupied by human actors, and in virtue of which they have an agentive function assigned to them and, flowing from this, acquire a distinct technical identity. Further, these positions are drawn on in human action and reproduced and/or transformed in much the standard way described by the TMSA, albeit with the caveats we raised about non-human technological objects not having practices or intrinsic rights and responsibilities.

We close this section with four further aspects of the account we have been developing. The first concerns some further attributes of social positions occupied by technological objects, the second the subject of relationality, the third the position-independent existence of technological objects once they have been brought into being, and the fourth, the idea of human technological objects.

First, we have focused so far on only a limited, albeit extremely important, aspect of the social positions occupied by technological objects, that having to do with agentive functions and technical identities. This aspect corresponds to the realm of what Feenberg (2000) calls 'primary instrumentalisation', which has to do with basic technical relations and the 'functional constitution' of technical objects. But there is also the realm of what Feenberg calls 'secondary instrumentalisation', which has to do with the realisation of technological objects in larger technical devices, networks and social contexts. The associations that arise here are far wider than structure, function and technical identity, and range from the economic and political on the one hand to the cultural and the aesthetic on the other. In our view, the social positions occupied by technological objects are also the loci of these secondary associations. That is to say, technological objects from collars to cufflinks and watches to websites have all manner of historical, cultural, economic and even political connotations in virtue of their social positions, all of which are reproduced and/or transformed by the activities of those who use or reference those objects, no less than are their functions and associated technical identities.

Second, our picture of the social world becomes considerably more complex with the inclusion of technological objects, due in part to the variety of internal relations this adds to it. Perhaps most obvious here are the cases in which social positions occupied by humans are internally related to social positions occupied by non-humans. For example, the various practices and attendant identity associated with the social position of computer programmer help sustain the social position and attendant technical identity of what we call computer programs (and vice versa), such that neither position would exist without the other. Internal relationality also arises in other ways, such as where different social positions occupied by humans are internally related, but where this relation is in turn dependent on the existence of a particular kind of technological object. An example of this would be the social position of computer programmer being internally related with the social position of computer manufacturer. Again, the two are mutually dependent, and where this dependency is itself dependent on the social position of the objects we call computers. Finally, there is the possibility of the social positions occupied by non-humans being internally related. For example, the social position of the kind of object we know as a computer program is internally related to the social position of the kind of object we know as a computer. In each of these cases the relata are what they are in virtue of the relation in which they stand to each other, and it is not possible to have one without the other.

Third, in distinguishing between technological objects and the positions they occupy, our account attributes an existence to objects that is independent of their social positioning. We recognise of course that the structure of just about every material or non-material technological object is 'socially shaped' insofar as it is the product of progressive human design, manufacture and modification. What we are claiming however is that, *once they have been brought into being*, that is, have been built, manufactured, written down and so on, both material and non-material technological objects have an intrinsic structure that is independent of the interpretations of their designers, builders, users and so on. Thus, the structure of an object such as a mug or a motorcar, for example, may remain in existence for many years to come, possibly even for generations after having been superseded and fallen into disuse.

This point is sometimes overshadowed in constructivist accounts of technology, where the emphasis tends to be on how the nature and what is sometimes called the 'meaning' of technological objects is dependent on the attitudes and attributions of the communities in which they arise (Bijker 1995, 2010; Bijker, Hughes and Pinch 1987; Bijker and Law 1992; Pinch 2010; Pinch and Bijker 1987; Pinch and Trocco 2002) or the networks in which they are located (Latour 1987, 1999, 2005). The advantage of recognising the independent existence of technological objects, once they have been brought into being in the sense mentioned above, is that it makes it possible to explore some of the implications of the fact that social positions themselves are different from, and so may be more or less enduring than, the particular objects that occupy, or go on to occupy, them. We explore some of these implications below.

Our final point concerns the possibility that humans may be technological objects too, something we noted earlier as being compatible with our general conception of technological objecthood. The central idea here is that many of the social positions humans occupy involve the occupant(s) being assigned an agentive function and thus acquiring a technical identity within that community. Consider the position of software tester, for example, constitutive of which is that the function of the person who fills that role is to identify defects within a given piece of software. Positions such as personnel manager, private investigator and policeman similarly involve individuals being assigned agentive functions.

While the idea that humans (and human collectivities) may be technological objects will likely jar with many, and is indeed something we ourselves took time to get used to, it does seem to us both a consistent and useful way of characterising technology. It allows us to make sense, for example, of cases in which new discoveries or innovations have led to humans being replaced in their roles by non-humans, such as switchboard operators being replaced by automatic exchanges, navigators by GPS systems, or cashiers by self-checkout stands. While clearly disruptive to the occupants of each role, such changes also involve considerable stability, at least initially, at the level of the social positions and their attendant assignments of function. Over time, of course, these too are likely to evolve, with the assignment of function, as well as other rules associated with each position, adapting to the different affordances and capabilities of the new occupants.

Non-material technological objects

The IS literature, and the organisational literature generally, are currently seeing rising interest in materiality and the materiality of technology in particular (Leonardi, Nardi and Kallinikos, 2012), the most prominent single example of which is probably the 'sociomateriality' perspective championed by Orlikowski (2007, 2010) and Orlikowski and Scott (2008). We welcome this development, which resonates in many ways with the themes we have been developing in this chapter. One of the consequences of the emphasis on materiality in this literature, however, and with the exception of the work of a few more or less closely related fellow travellers (Kallinikos 2002, 2011; Kallinikos, Aaltonen and Marton 2010; Leonardi 2010; Volkoff, Strong and Elmes 2007), is that it has led to what we call non-material technological objects slipping off the radar. This is unfortunate, because it seems to us that it is precisely the non-material nature of many artefacts, particularly those associated with ICT, that have contributed so much to their impact on organisations and larger social systems.

The importance of the distinction between material and non-material technological objects is particularly evident in the realm of computing, where all manner of tangible technological objects such as desktop computers, tablets, smartphones, servers, routers, switches and the like operate alongside intangible entities such as application programs, databases, webpages, emails, digitised images and so on. Although the two types of entity are closely related and indeed presuppose each other, they are nevertheless distinct. The difference between them lies in that while the former have a physical mode of being and so possess properties such as mass, volume, location and so on, the latter have a non-physical mode of being and so lack properties of this sort. We touch on some of the organisational implications of this difference, and of the non-physical mode of being of non-material technological objects, in the final part of the chapter.

The digital revolution, and especially the rapid development and widespread adoption of digital computing and ICT over the last thirty years, has led to a particular type of non-material technological object becoming ubiquitous in modern society. This is of course the bitstring, the sequences of 1s and 0s (or 'bits') used by silicon-based von Neumann computers, such as traditional transistor-based devices, to encode information in machine-readable form. Bitstrings range from software applications such as web browsers, word processors and ERP packages, where the encoded information consists of sets of logical instructions, to data files, where the encoded information consists of text, images, audio recordings and so on. In view of their ubiquity, not to mention their importance within IS research, we will use the example of bitstrings in what follows to expand on the distinction between material and non-material technological objects, and to develop the notion of a non-material technological object in particular.

We regard bitstrings as non-material technological objects because they fulfil the three criteria for non-material technological objecthood raised earlier. First, they are objects in virtue of being both continuants and structured; continuants because, once created or otherwise brought into being, they endure as a coherent whole over time, and structured because they comprise a number of distinct parts, in this case 1s and 0s, that are arranged in some way. Second, they are technological objects in virtue of having agentive functions imposed on them by human communities, where these functions relate to their use as a means of encoding information in machine-readable form. Third, they are non-material technological objects in virtue of having a non-physical mode of being. That is to say, no matter how much their use may rely on material technological objects, bitstrings themselves are no more than a collection of 1s and 0s and as such have none of the spatial attributes associated with material technological objects.

An important implication of the preceding point, and a distinguishing feature of our account of bitstrings and other non-material technological objects, is that bitstrings are distinct from what we call their material 'bearers', things like CD-ROMs, flash drives or pieces of paper, on which they may be said to reside or be inscribed. Material bearers are a necessary part of any account of the ontology of bitstrings, for a bitstring has to be borne on an appropriate physical medium if it is to be read, stored, transported and so on. Again, however, bitstrings are distinct from any and all such bearers in virtue of possessing distinct and separate properties, not least of which is that while the latter have a physical mode of being and the attendant properties, the former do not.

In addition to the material bearers just described there are also non-material bearers of non-material objects, a possibility that has particular significance in the context of modern digital computing. Consider a non-material technological object such as a design for a new product. This object might be borne by a variety of material objects such as a blueprint, computer printout, microfilm aperture card or Photostat. But it might also be borne in the form of a computer file, perhaps as a CAD drawing, in a PPT file or, if a printout of it has been photographed, in a JPEG file. These last cases are all examples of non-material, in this case bitstring, bearers of the design. Of course these bitstring bearers might themselves be borne by other bitstrings, although eventually all such bitstring bearers will have to be borne by a material bearer, such as a hard-drive or CD-ROM.

Note in conclusion that bitstrings, and indeed non-material technological objects in general, can be incorporated into our account of the social positioning of technological objects in exactly the same way as their material counterparts. Take the example we used earlier to illustrate our notion of technical identity in the case of a non-material object: a bitstring that acquires the identity of an iPhone network-monitoring app in virtue of its structure and function. On our more detailed account we would say that this bitstring is put in the position of network-monitoring app, on the basis of which it acquires the associated assignment of function and technical identity. Provided the bitstring is well suited to serving the function assigned to it – of enabling people to monitor devices connected to a local area network – its continued use for this purpose will sustain its position, and so its function and attendant technical identity.

Implications and avenues for future research

Our aim in this chapter was to develop an ontology of technological objects within the context of the TMSA, and thereby to contribute to the foundations of work in the Critical Realist tradition in the IS literature as well as the wider organisational literature in which technology comes to the fore. There are numerous ways in which our extension of the TMSA might itself be extended and/or inform work on more concrete issues. We propose three broad directions for future research in this regard, focusing on: (1) some ways that our theory might be developed further; (2) some implications of our account for how we think about technological change; and (3) some organisational implications of particular characteristics of non-material technological objects.

1. Developing the theory: extensions and transpositions

There are many ways in which our generalisation of the TMSA might be developed. High on the agenda, in our view, would be the construction of a more detailed ontology of technological objects than we have attempted so far. Particularly relevant to IS research in this regard would be a theory of hybrid technological objects, where such hybridity might lie either in the multifunctionality of devices, such as printers that also serve as scanners, photocopiers and fax machines, or in the constitution of devices that comprise both material and non-material elements, such as tablets, PCs and smartphones. Another avenue would be to develop more detailed ontologies of specific kinds of non-material technological objects, a project already under way under the banner of Critical Realism in Mutch (2010) and Bygstad's (2010) work on the organisational implications of different kinds of data structures (see also Bowker 2000). And yet another would be to develop the ontology of different kinds of technical systems, technical integration issues, and platform strategies (and the standardisation of interfaces and boundaries these involve).

Looking beyond immanent extensions of our theory, there is also scope for further elaboration of our account drawing on alternative approaches within Critical Realism. The most obvious source here is Archer (1988, 1995, 2000, 2003, 2007), whose contributions on agency, identity and culture we have already noted. However, the part of her work most directly relevant to our concerns in the present chapter is the 'morphogenetic approach' outlined in Archer (1979, 1988, 1995, 1998). Although the TMSA and the morphogenetic approach have different origins, it is clear that they share many of the same features and are generally complementary in their portrayal of the connections between social structure and human agency (Archer 1998: 372–379). In fact, an early and very partial version of the ideas developed in the present chapter was originally put forward using Archer's morphogenetic model (Runde *et al.* 2009).

An advantage of Archer's approach, one exploited in the paper just mentioned, lies in its emphasis on temporality and, specifically, on the pre-existence and autonomy of social structure in the sense of pre-dating action that subsequently reproduces or transforms it. This feature of the morphogenetic approach is especially useful in the context of conceptualising technological change, where for example innovation frequently involves changes in the features of objects that occupy pre-existing social positions, and which may then lead to subsequent mutations in the positions themselves when those innovations take hold. Thus, the digital camera was originally introduced as a new form of device to capture still images, with the manufacturers making concerted efforts to present digital cameras and their use as being as close as possible to what had been the case with analogue photography. But once they took hold, the social position of the camera changed significantly (Runde *et al.* 2009). We say more about the conceptualisation of technological change in the following subsection.

Yet another direction in which our framework may usefully be developed lies in exploring its fit with, and possible transposition to, alternative theoretical frameworks, particularly those that already have currency within the IS community. Perhaps the most obvious candidate here is Giddens' (1984) structuration theory, which has been highly influential in the IS literature (Orlikowski 1992, 2000, 2007; Orlikowski and Gash 1994;

Orlikowski and Iaconno 2001; Orlikowski and Yates 1994; Walsham 1993, 1997, 2001; Yates and Orlikowski 1992). Our suggestion that this link be explored may come as a surprise to proponents of Critical Realism, who often seek to distance themselves from Giddens rather than the reverse. Archer (1995, 1998) in particular is highly critical of what she calls his 'central conflationism', that is, of conflating agency and structure and so eliding important temporal features of the structuring and restructuring of society. Nevertheless, there are significant parallels between the TMSA and structuration theory, which are both founded on the idea that social structure and human agency are recursively organised. Even Bhaskar (1983: 85) himself, at least in earlier work, allows that structuration is 'very close' to his own conception of the reproduction and transformation of social structure.

As will have become apparent from our own argument, we would side with Archer on the need to avoid conflating agency and structure. However, this shouldn't be allowed to obscure the rich conceptual resources that Giddens provides for thinking about different aspects of social structure (Giddens 1984: 1–40), or the sophisticated theory he provides of social positions as identity-conferring intersections of signification, domination and legitimation (Giddens 1984: 83–92). It would therefore be interesting to see what might emerge if his own concepts and theory of the social positioning of human actors were generalised to technological objects on the lines we have attempted for the TMSA.

Finally, the idea that technological objects might be treated symmetrically with human actors, with respect to being socially positioned, invites comparison with Actor Network Theory (Latour 1987, 1999, 2005), which is well known for treating 'non-humans' symmetrically with 'humans'. There are various connections to be made here, not least with respect to Latour's (1986, 1987, 1999) notion of 'immutable mobiles' which are similar in many ways to what we call non-material technological objects (the similarities and differences are considered in more detail in Faulkner and Runde 2011). But the differences between our generalisation of the TMSA and Actor Network Theory are rather greater than is the case with structuration theory. This is not the place for detailed comparisons, but the most fundamental difference is that we embrace rather than reject the idea of social structure. In particular, we favour a 'depth' or stratified ontology, in which relatively enduring social structure underpins and conditions the practices of human actors, over the 'flat' ontology of Actor Network Theory, in which humans and non-humans are seen as mere nodes in networks and where it is assumed that there is nothing outside those networks (see Mutch 2002).

2. Applications: conceptualising technological change

Our generalisation of the TMSA to technological objects led to a number of key distinctions. Some of these may be relatively familiar, such as the distinction between material and non-material technological objects, and, possibly, that between non-material technological objects and their non-material or material bearers. But others may be less so, especially the distinction between material or non-material technological objects on the one hand, and the social positions they occupy, the function assigned to them and the technical identity they enjoy, on the other. This second set of distinctions is important and invites exploration of the relationship between technological objects *qua* objects and the social positions they occupy. There are many directions in which such exploration might go, but we will restrict ourselves here to a few thoughts on the conceptualisation of technological change.

Viewed from the perspective developed earlier in the chapter, three broad forms of technological change stand out:

1 where a new type of technological object replaces the current occupant of an already existing social position;
2 where an already existing social position occupied by a certain kind of technological object is transformed; or
3 where a new social position for a technological object emerges.

The first kind of change occurs when new types of material or non-material object replace the current occupants of an existing social position within some community. There are two main possibilities here. The first is where the new occupants of the position are the latest generation of an essentially unchanged object, as when manufacturers release updated versions of objects such as graphics cards, Blu-ray drives or device drivers. The second case is where a significantly different type of object replaces the previous incumbent of a position. The most familiar variant of this case is where the new occupant is a new type of object designed with that position in mind, such as LCD monitors replacing their CRT predecessors in the position of computer monitor. A less familiar variant is where the object that comes to newly occupy the position already occupies some other social position (which it may or may not retain). Examples include the Bankside power station building in Central London that became the art museum we now know as Tate Modern, or the gramophone turntable originally designed and used as a playback device but now deployed as a musical instrument within hip-hop music (Newman 2003; Webber 2000). The same kind of thing arises in relation to software, where re-use and repurposing of existing objects is common.

The second of our three broad forms of technical change has to do with changes to social positions. Cases of this sort arise when an existing social position is transformed, which is to say that either the assignment of function associated with that position within some community is modified in some way, and/or the community within which that position has currency changes. A striking example of the former case concerns the position of mobile phone, where the assignment of function has changed in recent years from that of making and receiving telephone calls over a radio link, to something much more wide ranging that also includes sending and receiving email, accessing the web, text messaging and so on. A prominent example of the latter case is the tablet PC, which initially served a small community of users limited to particular industries such as health care and logistics, but which in large part due to the success of the Apple iPad is now used and/or referenced by a far larger community.

The third of our three forms of technical change consists of the emergence of new social positions, where the function or functions associated with these positions are novel within the community concerned. There are two distinct cases here. The first involves the emergence of more specialised forms, or sub-types, of existing positions, where the functions associated with these new positions are narrower, more specific, versions of the function associated with the more general position. Thus, the positions of desktop replacement, netbook and tablet have emerged as sub-types within the more general position of laptop computer. The second case involves the emergence of positions associated with new, rather than more specialised, assignments of function. A good example here is the introduction of new types of software application such as email clients and web browsers, where these positions arose as a result of new affordances associated with technologies such as the internet.

We hope these brief observations are sufficient to demonstrate the value of thinking about technological change in the way we have suggested. There are many issues that might be explored further from this perspective and we will close by mentioning three. The first concerns the relationship between the three cases we have highlighted. Positions and the objects that occupy them generally co-evolve. Thus, changes to the type of objects that occupy a given position (case 1) often prompt (more or less subtle) changes to the social position concerned (case 2), particularly where the initial changes to the objects are substantial. Witness our earlier example of the mobile phone, where technological developments in relation to handsets contributed to the subsequent changes in the position of mobile phone that we have described. Similarly the emergence of new positions (case 3) may either precede, or be preceded by, the creation of the objects that subsequently occupy those positions. Thus, the first prototype of the Space Shuttle *Enterprise* (OV-101) was only completed towards the end of 1976, despite the project being commissioned by President Nixon at the beginning of 1972. In this case there was therefore a large community of people, both those at NASA working on the project and others following and talking about it, that contributed to the reproduction of the position of Space Shuttle well before the physical construction of its first occupant.

The second issue relates to the degree of disruption associated with different forms of technological change. Consider for example the case where a new type of object occupies an existing position (case 1). Where this involves a new generation of object replacing earlier generations of that same object the potential for disruption is low, since the new objects are designed with the existing position in mind and the minor, incremental, changes in form tend not to upset the existing practices of users, retailers and so forth. In contrast, where change involves a significantly different kind of object, the scope for disruption is greater, whether this be at the level of manufacturers and retailers and/or at the level of users. Our final point concerns the idea of obsolescence. The most familiar case here is that in which particular types of object become obsolete and their technical identity is then no longer sustained through their being used in the appropriate way in the relevant community. The identity of such objects becomes in a sense dormant, and is sustained only to the extent that it remains in the collective memory, in historical records and so on. Cases in point include the abacus and the slide rule, which have been supplanted by electronic calculators and computers. A more extreme case is that in which the position and identity of particular objects have disappeared completely, as illustrated by the mysterious devices sometimes found in anthropological museums that were clearly fashioned with some function in mind, but whose position and associated identity have been lost in the mists of time.

3. Applications: non-material technological objects as analogues to public goods

It is often observed that non-material technological objects such as computer programs and media files are analogous to public goods in that they possess to a high degree the properties of non-rivalry in use and non-excludability generally associated with such goods (Baldwin and Clark 2006; McLure Wasko *et al.* 2009; Quah 2003; Rayna 2008; von Hippel and von Krogh 2003).[7] As these properties lie at the heart of some of the most dramatic consequences of the on-going digital revolution it is important to be clear about what they entail. We close by showing how the ontology we have developed, and the distinction between non-material objects and their material and non-material bearers in particular, may help in this regard.

The property of non-rivalry in use concerns the possibility of an object being used simultaneously by a large number of parties. Thus, in contrast to most material objects where use by one party necessarily prevents use of that same object by others at the same time, the number of people who might simultaneously use the same network protocol or run the same email client is potentially unlimited. The same goes for many other kinds of non-material technological object, including languages, documents, audio and video recordings and so on, where use by one party has no impact on their possible use by others. Crucially, however, this is a property of the non-material object itself rather than of its material bearers or other complementary devices implicated in its use. Thus, while a bitstring encoding of an audio recording is perfectly non-rival, the memory card on which it is borne and the audio player on which it is played can generally only be used by one party at a time.

This last point highlights an important constraint on the extent to which the non-rival benefits of a non-material technological object can actually be utilised on a large scale, namely the ease with which necessary complementary devices can be made available to additional users. There are numerous issues here, with perhaps the most significant being the impact the growth in the downloading and streaming of computer files via the internet has had on access to the material bearers of non-material technological objects. In terms of the perspective outlined earlier, the practice of downloading, whereby a computer file is transferred from a remote system and saved to a local storage device, allows an individual to create an additional material bearer of that file on their own media almost instantaneously and at virtually zero cost. The practice of streaming, whereby a file residing on a remote system is accessed over the internet, allows an individual to make use of an existing material bearer of a file regardless of its location.

The enormous expansion in both activities over the last twenty years has greatly increased individuals' access to material bearers of computer files and thus significantly enhanced the scope for mass use of the non-rival benefits exhibited by such files. And of course these effects are not limited to computer files alone. Given that bitstrings may serve as (non-material) bearers of other non-material technological objects, the growth in the downloading and streaming of files has increased individuals' ability to benefit from the non-rivalry of any non-material technological object capable of being borne in this way.

The second property, non-excludability, concerns the difficulty that the owners of an object face in preventing others from using that thing once it has been created, particularly those who have not paid for the right to do so. That many non-material technological objects now exhibit a very high degree of non-excludability is well known and we touch on the reasons for this shortly. First, however, note that the application of non-excludability to non-material technological objects presupposes the distinction between such objects and their material bearers. The point here is that ownership of a non-material object is distinct from ownership of any and all of the material bearers of that object. While the former refers to ownership of the *intellectual* property rights pertaining to a non-material object, namely patents, copyrights and so forth, the latter refers to ownership of the property rights associated with the material object, whether this be a piece of paper, CD-ROM or whatever. Ownership of the intellectual property rights associated with a non-material object does not imply ownership of the property rights associated with the material bearers of that object, just as ownership of the latter property rights does not imply ownership of the former intellectual property rights.

Turning to the high degree of non-excludability now exhibited by many non-material technological objects, a key development here again concerns the growth in the downloading and streaming of computer files. Of particular significance is that these practices can often be undertaken without the permission of the owner of the non-material object concerned. Thus, while the legal downloading and streaming of computer files is done with the rights holder's assent, illegal forms of file sharing require only that one party is willing to make a material bearer of a computer file available while some other party is willing to download or stream that file to their local computer system.

As with non-rivalry, the effects of the growth in downloading and streaming on the excludability of non-material technological objects are not limited to computer files alone but extend to any non-material technological object that can be borne in this way. It is precisely this feature, of course, that has led file sharing to have such an impact on many of the creative industries – music, film, literature, news, software and so on – whereby providers are no longer able to control access to, and so derive revenues from, their products in the way presupposed by prior business models. In response, providers have sought either to embrace these developments by seeking out new business models more closely attuned to the digital environment (e.g., using the internet as a means of giving away free content or moving to online subscription-based models), or else attempting to shore up the excludability of their products in the face of file sharing, through the use of digital rights management technologies and demands for stronger intellectual property legislation and enforcement.

Conclusion

Despite growing interest in applying Critical Realism in IS and organisational research, the emerging literature has so far had little to say about the basic ontology of technological objects, their mode of being, their identity and, so to speak, their place in the social world. We have accordingly attempted to set out a theory of how technological objects fit into social reality within the framework of the TMSA, and then in a way that is sensitive to the distinction between what we have called material and non-material technological objects. In the process we have sought to demonstrate how technological objects acquire functions and technical identities through being positioned, the links between technological objects and the human practices in which they are implicated, and the different kinds of internal relations between the social positions occupied by humans and those occupied by non-human technological objects.

Our aim in writing this chapter was to provide a conceptual frame for thinking about these basic elements of the social world. To this extent it is very much in the spirit of Critical Realism, an exercise in Lockean pre-theoretical/philosophical ground clearing intended to provide some concepts and categories on which other researchers might build (Bhaskar 1989: 1–2). Yet the gap between the admittedly quite abstract ideas we have presented and the more practical or applied interests of many researchers is often smaller than it might first appear. As we indicated in the last section, there are many directions for research of a less abstract and more empirical nature suggested by the particular ontological orientation that we have adopted, ranging from issues in the sociology of technology regarding the relation between humans and different varieties of non-humans on the one hand, to questions about technical change, innovation and the economic and organisational consequences of bitstrings on the other.

Notes

1 We are grateful to the editor and three anonymous referees for helpful comments on earlier versions of this chapter. Many of the ideas it contains emerged and were refined in discussions at meetings of the Cambridge Social Ontology Group, which we also gratefully acknowledge. First published in *MIS Quarterly*, 2013, Vol 37, No 2, 803–818.

2 The only example of work on similar lines that we know of is Lawson (2007, 2008), who develops a 'transformational model of technical activity'. While in many ways complementary to our own approach, Lawson's perspective differs from ours in identifying a distinct realm of 'technical activity' and in focusing on issues such as the distinction between technological and other kinds of social object, and the shaping of the human agent by technology. Our own account focuses on questions pertaining to the positioning and identity of technological objects, and on the distinction between material and non-material technological objects.

3 Our use of the term 'object' therefore differs from that associated with Bhaskar and Critical Realism more widely (e.g., Bhaskar 1975). While we use the term to refer specifically to the category of structured continuants, in Critical Realism the term tends to be used to refer more broadly to anything that exists.

4 We restrict our discussion of the category of technological objects to those found in human communities, since our interest lies in incorporating technological objects into the TMSA. There is however considerable evidence of use of technological objects elsewhere in the animal kingdom, be these of the found kind such as the stones used by monkeys to crack nuts, or the built kind such as spiders' webs or beavers' dams (Aunger 2010a, 2010b).

5 Non-material technological objects are therefore instances of what Fleetwood calls 'ideationally real' entities (Fleetwood 2005), as well as being constituents of what Archer calls the Cultural System (Archer 1988).

6 Two points are worth highlighting about the notion of identity we use here. First, although our focus is on identities arising from individuals' occupation of social positions, we recognise that identities may also be acquired in virtue of individuals' membership of particular social groups as well as their own personal characteristics, attitudes and attributes. On Critical Realist approaches to identity, see Archer (2000, 2003), Birkett (2011) and O'Mahoney (2011). Second, and contrary to what might be considered orthodoxy in Critical Realism, on our account the kind of thing an object is within some community depends not only on its intrinsic structure but also on how that object is positioned within that community.

7 Gravelle and Rees (2004: Ch. 4) provide a useful overview of these two properties and the standard economic account of the difficulties they cause for the organisation and operation of private markets.

References

Archer, M. 1979. *Social Origins of Educational Systems*. London: Sage Publications.

Archer, M. 1988. *Culture and Agency*. Cambridge, UK: Cambridge University Press.

Archer, M. 1995. *Realist Social Theory: The Morphogenetic Approach*. Cambridge, UK: Cambridge University Press.

Archer, M. 1998. Realism and morphogenesis. In Archer, M., Bhaskar, R., Collier, A., Lawson, T., Norrie, A. (eds) *Critical Realism: Essential Readings*. London: Routledge.

Archer, M. 2000. *Being Human: The Problem of Agency*. Cambridge, UK: Cambridge University Press.

Archer, M. 2003. *Structure, Agency, and the Internal Conversation*. Cambridge, UK: Cambridge University Press.

Archer, M. 2007. *Making Our Way through the World*. Cambridge, UK: Cambridge University Press.

Aunger, R. 2010a. What's special about human technology? *Cambridge Journal of Economics*, 34(1): 115–123.

Aunger, R. 2010b. Types of technology. *Technological Forecasting and Social Change*, 77(5): 762–782.

Baldwin, C., Clark, K. 2006. The architecture of participation: does code architecture mitigate free riding in the open source development model? *Management Science*, 52(7): 1116–1127.

Bhaskar, R. 1975. *A Realist Theory of Science*. Leeds: Leeds Books Limited.

Bhaskar, R. 1978. On the possibility of social scientific knowledge and the limits of naturalism. *Journal for the Theory of Social Behaviour*, 8(1): 1–28.

Bhaskar, R. 1979. *The Possibility of Naturalism*. Hemel Hempstead, UK: Harvester Press.

Bhaskar, R. 1983. Beef, structure and place: notes from a critical naturalist perspective. *Journal for the Theory of Social Behaviour*, 13(1): 81–96.

Bhaskar, R. 1986. *Scientific Realism and Human Emancipation*. London: Verso.

Bhaskar, R. 1989. *Reclaiming Reality: Critical Introduction to Contemporary Philosophy*. London: Verso.

Bijker, W.E. 1995. *Of Bicycles, Bakelites, and Bulbs: Towards a Theory of Sociotechnical Change*. Cambridge, MA: MIT Press.

Bijker, W.E. 2010. How is technology made – that is the question! *Cambridge Journal of Economics*, 34(1): 63–76.

Bijker, W.E., Hughes, T.P., Pinch, T. 1987. *The Social Construction of Technological Systems*. Cambridge, MA: MIT Press.

Bijker, W.E., Law, J. (eds) 1992. *Shaping Technology/Building Society*. Cambridge, MA: MIT Press.

Birkett, H. 2011. *Identity Transitions: Towards a Critical Realist Theory of Identity*. PhD thesis, University of Warwick.

Bowker, G.C. 2000. Biodiversity datadiversity. *Social Studies of Science*, 30(5): 643–683.

Bygstad, B. 2010. Generative mechanisms for innovation in information infrastructures. *Information and Organization*, 20(3–4): 156–168.

Collier, A. 1994. *Critical Realism: An Introduction to Roy Bhaskar's Philosophy*. London: Verso.

de Vaujany, F. 2008. Capturing reflexivity modes in IS: a critical realist approach. *Information and Organization*, 18(1): 51–72.

Dobson, P. 2002. Critical realism and information systems research: why bother with philosophy? *Information Research*, 7(2).

Dobson, P., Myles, J., Jackson, P. 2007. Making the case for critical realism: examining the implementation of automated performance management systems. *Information Resources Management Journal*, 20(2): 138–153.

Faulkner, P., Runde, J. 2009. On the identity of technological objects and user innovations in function. *Academy of Management Review*, 34(3): 442–462.

Faulkner, P., Runde, J. 2011. The social, the material and the ontology of non-material technological artefacts. Unpublished.

Faulkner, P., Runde, J. 2012. On sociomateriality. In Leonardi, P.M., Nardi, B., Kallinikos, J. (eds) *Materiality and Organizing: Social Interaction in a Technological World*. Oxford: Oxford University Press.

Feenberg, A. 2000. From essentialism to constructivism: philosophy of technology at the crossroads. In Higgs, E., Strong, D., Light, A. (eds). *Technology and the Good Life*. Chicago: University of Chicago Press, 294–315. (Adapted from Feenberg, A. 1999. *Questioning Technology*. London: Routledge.)

Fleetwood, S. 2005. Ontology in organization and management studies: a critical realist perspective. *Organization*, 12(2): 197–222.

Giddens, A. 1984. *The Constitution of Society*. Cambridge, UK: Polity Press.

Gravelle, H., Rees, R. 2004. *Microeconomics*, 3rd ed. Harlow, UK: Prentice Hall.

Kallinikos, J. 2002. Reopening the black box of technology artifacts and human agency. Paper presented at the twenty-third International Conference on Information Systems.

Kallinikos, J. 2011. *Governing through Technology: Information Artefacts and Social Practice*. Hampshire: Palgrave Macmillan.

Kallinikos, J., Aaltonen, A., Marton, A. 2010. A theory of digital objects. *First Monday*, 15(6): 1–17.

Kroes, P. 2010. Engineering and the dual nature of technical artefacts. *Cambridge Journal of Economics*, 34(1): 51–62.

Kroes, P., Meijers, A. 2006. The dual nature of technical artefacts. *Studies in History and Philosophy of Science*, 37: 1–4.

Latour, B. 1986. Visualisation and cognition: drawing things together. In Kuklick, H. (ed.) *Knowledge and Society Studies in the Sociology of Culture Past and Present*, Vol. 6. Greenwich, CT: JAI Press.

Latour, B. 1987. *Science in Action*. Cambridge, MA: Harvard University Press.

Latour, B. 1999. *Pandora's Hope*. Cambridge, MA: Harvard University Press.

Latour, B. 2005. *Reassembling the Social: An Introduction to Actor-Network-Theory*. Oxford: Oxford University Press.

Lawson, C. 2007. Technology, technological determinism and the transformational model of technical activity. In Lawson, C., Latsis, J., Martins, N. (eds) *Contributions to Social Ontology*. London: Routledge.

Lawson, C. 2008. An ontology of technology: artefacts, relations and functions. *Techné: Research in Philosophy and Technology*, 12(1): 48–64.

Lawson, T. 1997. *Economics and Reality*. London: Routledge.

Lawson, T. 2003. *Reorienting Economics*. London: Routledge.

Leonardi, P.M. 2010. Digital materiality? How artefacts without matter, matter. *First Monday*, 15(6).

Leonardi, P.M., Nardi, B., Kallinikos, J. (eds) 2012. *Materiality and Organizing: Social Interaction in a Technological World*. Oxford: Oxford University Press.

McLure Wasko, M., Teigland, R., Faraj, S. 2009. The provision of online public goods: examining social structure in an electronic network of practice. *Decision Support System*, 47: 254–265.

Meijers, A. 2000. The relational ontology of technical artifacts. In Kroes, P., Meijers, A. (eds). *The Empirical Turn in the Philosophy of Technology*. Oxford: Elsevier Science.

Mingers, J. 2004a. Realizing information systems: critical realism as an underpinning philosophy for information systems. *Information and Organization*, 14(2): 87–103.

Mingers, J. 2004b. Re-establishing the real: critical realism and information systems. In Mingers, J., Willcocks, L. (eds) *Social Theory and Philosophy for Information Systems*. Chichester, UK: Wiley.

Morton, P. 2006. Using critical realism to explain strategic information systems planning. *Journal of Information Technology Theory and Application*, 8(1): 1–20.

Mutch, A. 2002. Actors and networks or agents and structures: towards a realist view of information systems. *Organization*, 9(3): 477–496.

Mutch, A. 2010. Technology, organization, and structure – a morphogenetic approach. *Organization Science*, 21(2): 507–520.

Mutch, A. 2012. Sociomateriality – taking the wrong turning? Unpublished manuscript.

Newman, M. 2003. *Pedestrian: History of Turntablism*. http://www.autistici.org/2000-maniax/texts/pedestrian%20history%20of%20turntablism.pdf

O'Mahoney, J. 2011. Critical realism and the self. *Journal of Critical Realism*, 10(1): 122–129.

Orlikowski, W. 1992. The duality of technology: rethinking the concept of technology in organizations. *Organization Science*, 3(3): 398–427.

Orlikowski, W. 2000. Using technology and constituting structures: a practice lens for studying technology in organizations. *Organization Science*, 11(4): 404–428.

Orlikowski, W. 2007. Sociomaterial practices: exploring technology at work. *Organization Studies*, 28(9): 1435–1448.

Orlikowski, W. 2010. The sociomateriality of organizational life: considering technology in management research. *Cambridge Journal of Economics*, 34(1): 125–141.

Orlikowski, W., Gash, D. 1994. Technological frames: making sense of information technology in organizations. *ACM Transactions on Information Systems*, 12(2): 174–207.

Orlikowski, W., Iaconno, S. 2001. Research commentary: desperately seeking the 'IT' in IT research – a call to theorizing the IT artifact. *Information Systems Research*, 12(2): 121–134.

Orlikowski, W., Scott, S. 2008. Sociomateriality: challenging the separation of technology, work and organization. *Acadamy of Management Annals*, 2: 433–474.

Orlikowski, W., Yates, J. 1994. Genre repertoire: the structuring of communicative practices in organizations. *Administrative Science Quarterly*, 39: 541–574.

Pinch, T. 2010. On making infrastructure visible: putting the non-humans to rights. *Cambridge Journal of Economics*, 34(1): 77–89.

Pinch, T., Bijker, W.E. 1987. The social construction of facts and artifacts: or how the sociology of science and the sociology of technology might benefit each other. In Bijker, W.E., Hughes, T.P., Pinch, T. (eds) *The Social Construction of Technological Systems*. Cambridge, MA: MIT Press.

Pinch, T., Trocco, F. 2002. *Analog Days: The Invention and Impact of the Moog Synthesizer*. Boston, MA: Harvard University Press.

Quah, D. 2003. Digital goods and the new economy. In Jones, D. (ed.) *New Economy Handbook*. San Diego, CA: Academic Press.

Rayna, T. 2008. Understanding the challenges of the digital economy: the nature of digital goods. *Communications and Strategies*, 71: 13–26.

Runde, J., Jones, M., Munir, K., Nikolychuk, L. 2009. On technological objects and the adoption of technological product innovations: rules, routines and the transition from analogue photography to digital imaging. *Cambridge Journal of Economics*, 33(1): 1–24.

Searle, J.R. 1995. *The Construction of Social Reality*. Middlesex: Allen Lane, The Penguin Press.

Searle, J.R. 1999. *Mind, Language and Society*. London: Weidenfeld & Nicolson.

Searle, J.R. 2001. *Rationality in Action*. Cambridge, MA: MIT Press.

Smith, M. 2006. Overcoming theory–practice inconsistencies: critical realism and information systems research. *Information and Organization*, 16(3): 191–211.

Volkoff, O., Strong, D., Elmes, M. 2007. Technological embeddedness and organizational change. *Organization Science*, 18(5): 832–848.

von Hippel, E., von Krogh, G. 2003. Open source software and the 'private-collective' innovation model: issues for organization science. *Organization Science*, 14(2): 209–223.

Walsham, G. 1993. *Interpreting Information Systems in Organisations*. Chichester, UK: Wiley.

Walsham, G. 1997. Actor-network theory and IS research: current status and future prospects. In Lee, A., Liebenau, J., DeGross, J. (eds) *Information Systems and Qualitative Research*. London: Chapman & Hall.

Walsham, G. 2001. *Making a World of Difference: IT in a Global Context*. Oxford: Oxford University Press.

Webber, S. 2000. *Turntable Technique: The Art of the DJ*. Boston: Berklee Press.

Wittgenstein, L. 1953. *Philosophical Investigations*. London: Blackwell Publishing.

Yates, J., Orlikowski, W. 1992. Genres of organizational communication: a structurational approach to studying communication and media. *Academy of Management Review*, 17(2): 299–326.

19 Technology and the extension of human capabilities[1]

Clive Lawson

1. Introduction

There is a tension in many discussions of technology concerning the distinction between technical objects and other artefacts. On the one hand, a variety of artefacts, such as paintings, sculptures, jewellery, food, toys, passports, etc., tend not to be considered as technical objects. Such artefacts do not enter into accounts of technical change or technological trajectories and are not referred to in order to illustrate major theories of technology – for example, it is hard to imagine a theory of technological determinism having emerged from a concern with such artefacts as paintings or jewellery. On the other hand, general discussion of technology tends to shift between the word technology and undifferentiated reference to material artefacts or even simply artefacts. That is, specific talk of particular 'acceptably technical' objects, such as computers or hammers, when generalised, quickly take the form of discussions of artefacts or material things with no clearly or explicitly distinguished technical characteristics. No doubt much of this tension arises for the simple reason that it is not easy to establish what it is about certain artefacts that make them unambiguously technical in nature. Various attempts have been made to use some conception of 'function' or 'means' to mark the difference. But such attempts quickly unravel. Is art or food without function? Are not most actions or productions a means to some other action or production?

The main argument of this paper is that a defining aspect of technology is the role that it plays in extending human capabilities. Moreover, drawing attention to this aspect of technology, I suggest, serves not only to help distinguish technology from other material artefacts but also goes some way to explaining the peculiar position technology occupies in modern societies, or at the very least provides a useful framework for posing important questions about technology.

These arguments, however, require a fair amount of elaboration. First, a variety of definitional issues are raised. For example, can a role be a defining aspect of a 'thing'? Can a thing be defined in terms of the position it occupies or the role it serves in some larger system – i.e. by something that is extrinsic to it? Second, the sense in which I understand technology to extend human capabilities can usefully be conveyed by distinguishing it from similar ideas in the philosophy of technology literature. The ideas I have in mind here are those in which technology is conceived of as the more or less direct extension of human faculties. It proves useful to begin by introducing some of the main ideas from this literature. It is beyond the scope of the present paper, however, to provide any kind of review of the extension literature. My intention in referring to these authors' work is simply to clarify the sense of 'extension' I have in mind by both drawing upon the wealth of examples and illustrations of the basic extension idea and also by drawing out some of the differences between these ideas and the particular sense of extension I have in mind. Briefly touching upon this literature, however, also serves to introduce some ideas that are returned to in the concluding section. In the second section, I shall try to integrate the conception of 'extension' I wish to defend within a general conception of technology that addresses more general definitional issues along the way, before finally drawing out some implications of the account I am suggesting. To repeat, the main task is to indicate how the idea of extension acts to mark off, at least partially, technical from other artefacts, along with suggesting some of the benefits that follow from such an understanding.

2. Extension theories of technology

By extension theory, I mean any theory in which technical objects are conceived of as some kind of extension of the human organism by way of replicating, amplifying or supplementing bodily or mental faculties or capabilities. This basic idea of extension recurs throughout the study of technology, and is found in discussions of technology that go back at least as far as Aristotle. The more systematic treatments tend to emphasise one or more of three features: a focus upon the direct, often very mechanical, extension of human physical faculties; a focus upon the extension of cognitive (especially information processing) capabilities; the extension of human agents' 'will' or intentions. I shall illustrate each feature by briefly referring to the work of Ernst Kapp, Marshall McLuhan and David Rothenberg.

The first occurrence of a detailed and sustained example of an extension theory is that provided by Ernst Kapp (1877). For Kapp, technical objects are quite simply projections of human organs:

> the intrinsic relationship that arises between tools and organs ... is that in the tool the human continually produces itself. Since the organ whose utility and power is to be increased is the controlling factor, the appropriate form of a tool can be derived only from that organ.
>
> (Kapp. 1877, pp. 44–5)

All technology is, quite literally, a direct projection or morphological extension of human organs. Throughout his book, Kapp is at pains to note how a wealth of different devices originate from such projections: ... 'the bent finger becomes a hook, the hollow of the hand a bowl; in the sword spear, oar, shovel, rake, plow and spade one observes sundry positions of arm, hand and fingers' (ibid.).[2] The strength of Kapp's account is his tirelessly enthusiastic and detailed use of one example after another to support the claim that technical objects are little more than organ projections. Whole chapters of his book are given over to the more important developments of the time (e.g., chapter 7 is given over to the idea that the railroad is the externalisation of the circulatory system, and chapter 8 to the telegraph, which is an externalisation of the nervous system).[3]

A variety of later works drew upon and developed Kapp's basic ideas. For example, Marshall McLuhan similarly conceived of technology as some form of extension, and shared many of the specific interests of Kapp, e.g. the railroad and telegraph, adding to it more recent interests in electronic media:

> During the mechanical ages we had extended our bodies in space. Today, after more than a century of electronic technology, we have extended our central nervous system itself in a global embrace, abolishing time and space as far as our planet is concerned.
>
> (McLuhan, 1964, p. 19)

The crucial difference between Kapp and McLuhan's work is that the latter distinguishes two broad classes of extensions: of the body and of cognitive functions. Extensions of the body refer for the most part to those mechanical extensions that form the basis of Kapp's earlier work. McLuhan's emphasis is however slightly different, focusing more upon the isolation of particular properties and amplifying or augmenting these:

> What makes a mechanism is the separation and extension of separate parts of our body as hand, arm, foot, in pen, hammer, wheel. And the mechanization of a task is done by segmentation of each part of an action in a series of uniform, repeatable and moveable parts.
>
> (Ibid.)

The senses, the central nervous system, and higher cognitive functions are not, however, defined as part of the body. It is in terms of these that McLuhan analyses his central concern – the media – especially sight and sound, e.g., the radio is long-distance ears. Electronic media are understood as extensions of the information processing functions of the central nervous system. Consequently, a human being in the electronic age is quite literally, for McLuhan, 'an organism that now wears its brain outside its skull and its nerves outside its hide' (ibid.).

This difference in emphasis (and concern with electronic media) leads McLuhan away from Kapp's insistence that the form of technological arte-facts imitates the form of human organs. Instead, McLuhan argues that it is only functional properties of humans that are translated (in amplified form) to artefacts; thus the focus is away from the role played by the pro-jection of organs and functions onto artefacts. McLuhan's main concern is to understand the implications that follow for personal autonomy as bod-ily functions are taken over by machines, a point that is returned to below.

The work of David Rothenberg provides an example of the emphasis upon the extension of intentions. More specifically, technology is under-stood to be a process whereby intentions are realised via the extension of human 'aspects' that we understand the workings of:

> A part of the human essence is evident in the things which we build, create, and design to make the Earth into *our* place. Techniques can extend all those human aspects for which we possess a mechanical understanding. Telescopes and microscopes can extend the acuity of our vision, because we know something about how our eyes perceive the world optically. But we cannot technically extend our sense of what is right, because we do not understand how this judgment operates
>
> (Rothenberg, 1993, p.16)

Rothenberg considers both thought and action as faculties that become extended in technical objects. The extension of action is, like McLuhan's bodily extensions, close to the work of Kapp, and similarly Rothenberg's extensions of thought equate roughly to McLuhan's extensions of the senses, the nervous system and consciousness. These include artefacts that improve the senses (telescopes, radios, etc.); tools of abstraction that extend abstract thought and language functions (computers, calculators, etc.); and material extensions of memory (photographs, video, etc.). Rothenberg, like McLuhan, does not restrict his ideas of extension to morphological projec-tions of human organs. However, the crucial point is that for Rothenberg, technical objects are not *primarily* extensions of human capabilities either; rather they extend human intentions. To talk of technology as 'an extension means that when we make something, we thrust our intentions upon the world' (ibid.). Intentions or desires are normally contained within our own organism, but as we create technologies, these technologies become carriers of our intentions, and hence extensions of them.[4]

There are few attempts to systematically compare different extension theories. One useful source of comparison, however, which also attempts a useful development of its own, is provided by Philip Brey (2000). Brey is concerned with the possibility of generalising the concept of extension developed by various extension theorists. Specifically, he is concerned that none provide a sufficiently restrictive sense of 'extension' according to which *all* technical artefacts can be claimed to be extensions of human faculties (i.e. without counterexample). For example, whilst impressive, Kapp's accounts of artefact–organ pairings are ultimately unsatisfactory because many artefacts, have no obvious origin in human organs: '... books, cigarette lighters, telephones, and airplanes, for example, do not have clear morphological similarities to human organs' (Brey, 2000, p. 66). Brey criticises others, such as Rothenberg, for being ambiguous. Sometimes Rothenberg claims, along with McLuhan, that artefacts functionally correspond to some human organ (which appears to be unsustainable), and at other times it is only human intentions that are extended, in which case it is not a theory of the extension of human capabilities at all.

It is Rothenberg's ideas, however, that Brey most closely builds upon in his own formulation of an extension theory; the idea that human intentions are extended in some way is central to Brey's reformulation. For Brey, however, the emphasis is upon the way that technology extends the *means* by which human intentions are realised. Thus it is not human intentions that are being extended, but in trying to realise intentions human beings develop technical objects that extend the arsenal of means by which such intentions can be realised. Initially intentions are realised through what Brey terms 'the inventory of original means' – in order to change the world so that it conforms to our intentions, we have only our bodily and mental faculties available. Technical artefacts extend or add to these means.

Brey's account clearly highlights some of the ambiguities in the ideas of extension theories, and undermines the idea that, by itself, the extension idea can generate a definition of technology, given the existence of important counterexamples. But this ambiguity is not really avoided in Brey's own account. Specifically, it is left unclear exactly what is meant by the key term extension and what exactly it is that is being extended. If it is *means* that Brey has in mind, does it not make more sense to talk of simply *adding to* the arsenal of means? If extension is to connote the extension of the human agent, what exactly is it about the *agent* that is being extended? On Brey's conception, technology appears to be simply a distant 'means' to be utilised in some instrumental manner. In which case it is unclear how it is an extension in any obvious sense.

It is, however, also unclear that such a sharp differentiation between intentions and means is helpful. If, rather, human agents are conceived of as ensembles of powers, or more specifically as centres of powers (Bhaskar, 1978), then intentions and means are simply part of the structural requirement for the possession of capabilities in any real sense. All that is needed here is some commitment to the broad idea that agents possess powers in virtue of the way they are structured, which seems hardly implausible.[5] This point is familiar to those drawing upon a distributed cognition perspective (Hutchins, 1995). Here, although the focus is more narrowly on *cognitive* capabilities, the point is the same; the very capabilities that people have depend upon the relations in which people stand both to other people and to things. Of course, the manner of this dependence will change; it may involve important iteration changing the nature of the agent or simply be some kind of off-loading of capabilities (Salomon, 1993). Capabilities of the human agent become augmented and extended across time and space.

There is, however, a limitation to the above extension ideas which is worth focusing upon. This is that the ideas of extension tend to end in the acquired capability or the effects of the acquisition of that capability. But for the extension in capabilities to be realised, I want to argue, the artefacts or devices which are used to extend the capability must be enrolled in both technical and social networks[6] of interdependencies. To pursue this idea it is helpful to turn to a set of ideas that are not normally considered in this context, i.e. of those of Actor Network Theory, and argue that it too is a form of extension theory, one with some important advantages.

Extension as enrolment

Perhaps the central proposition of Actor Network Theory (ANT) is that technical objects cannot be understood in isolation. Rather, technical objects take on their properties, characteristics, powers or whatever only in relation to the networks of relations in which they stand. This idea is often presented by arguing that artefacts *are* important social ties. For example, Latour even likens technical artefacts to the mass that physicists cannot find in the universe but which it needs to hold together (Latour, 1996). In sociology, Latour argues, there has been a similar problem, i.e. of finding the social ties that constitute or reproduce human societies. These missing ties are, he argues, technical artefacts and they can only be understood in terms of the linking or relational properties they have, or the actual position they occupy.

Latour tends to present his ideas with the aid of a series of 'mundane' examples (for example, see Latour, 1994). At one point Latour talks of his frustration at trying to persuade his son (being too old for a child seat but too young for a seat belt) not to sit in the, more dangerous, middle of the back seat – dangerous that is if braking were to occur too quickly. After failing with commands and the use of his arm to restrain his son, Latour finally purchases a padded bar to hold him in place – thus the work done previously by his voice and arm are 'delegated' to a technical object (the padded bar). Such stories, and Latour gives many, are examples of a form of extension, in this case of the extension of the power of a parent–driver over his son.

Elsewhere, Latour introduces his now famous mechanical door-closer (or groom). Here, sparked off by a sign pleading that in the absence of a working groom could people please shut the door, Latour gives an account of the networks of use in which the door-closer exists and operates. The account is wide-ranging, moving from a discussion of what it would be like not to have gaps in walls at all, to the benefits of doors and hinges, through to the multiple kinds of problems that arise in attempting to discipline the users of the door to keep it shut after they have walked through it (thus ensuring a good warm temperature inside the building). Multiple 'delegations' are considered, in which people could stand by the door to make sure it is shut (thing to human), through to the deskilling and displacement issues of introducing a mechanism which despite its imperfections (overly tight spring, hard-to-push hydraulics, etc.) in some sense gets the work done (human back to thing).

Throughout, Latour is drawing out implications or lessons from his examples. Centrally, they are intended to show how morality or ethics are imposed on the user or 'prescribed' through use. Foucault's influence is of course noticeable here. But the process of enrolling things into networks is not always something to do with disciplining. Rather, I want to suggest, what such examples show is that such delegations involve extensions of capabilities. But, more importantly, they involve extensions of capabilities by the *enrolment* of artefacts in particular networks, these networks consisting in relations of interdependencies with their own built-in politics, asymmetries, etc. More specifically these examples illustrate the use made of the intrinsic properties of material artefacts to extend the extrinsic properties or powers of people[7] (to discipline the son or to enforce door-closing, etc.). But this is always done via enrolment. The bar used to prevent the child moving is inserted not only into the technical relations of the car (the physical layout of the interior, the connections to the frame of the car, etc.), but within the social relations between father and son, the etiquette of 'good parenting', etc. A new phone must be inserted within technical networks where it has access to the right kind of telephone signal or the correct voltage of electricity, etc., but to be useable it must also be inserted within particular relations, which might mean being left outside the house for Amish communities or it might assume the status of a best friend for a chatty teenager. Such enrolment typically involves investing the device with meaning and aesthetics as well as politics and power. It is this conception of extension, as enrolment within existing networks of interdependencies, that I wish to develop and utilise in the remainder of this paper. It both draws on the intuitions that technical artefacts extend ourselves in some way, but combines this with the insight that such extensions are always dependent on the context of interdependencies that artefacts must be inserted into in order to function.[8]

3. Technology and the extension of human capabilities

At the outset I suggested that a major reason for considering extension ideas is that they help us demarcate technical from other artefacts. As has become clear in the discussion above, however, the notion of extension, even after modification, certainly cannot provide a definition of technology by itself. Rather, I want to suggest that extension ideas provide an element of a conception of technology, and take on this role in relation to a more encompassing conception of technology and technical objects. In order to pursue this I begin by giving an account of technical activity and the dual nature of artefacts within which extension ideas can be located. In so doing I am summarising and drawing upon an account of technical activity developed elsewhere (Lawson, 2007, 2008, 2009). This starting point is adopted because it proves impossible to provide a conception of technology that is independent of human activity.

The Transformational Model of Social Activity (or TMSA), as developed within critical realism, is best viewed as a very general sketch of a conception of human action.[9] But the main concern of those developing the TMSA has been that of locating or emphasising the nature of social structure, which is done in relation to human activity. This activity, on this account, reproduces or transforms particular social structures, and in so doing conditions of action become the results of action in a complex and recursive manner. Such recursivity takes the form of two dualities: from Giddens the duality of structure emphasises that structure is both condition and consequence of human activity (Giddens, 1984); from Bhaskar the duality of praxis emphasises the fact that some structures are reproduced without being the intention of any particular action (Bhaskar, 1989). Social structure, in that it exists prior to a particular activity, is clearly not reducible to that activity, but, in that it only exists as (is an emergent feature of) social activity, it is neither external to nor outside of human activity. Such emergent features exist as sets of social relations, rules, etc., that are reproduced and transformed through action. Individuals typically 'slot' into such structures by occupying positions, which are best understood in terms of mediating concepts (where both dualities come together), that Bhasker has termed positioned-practices (ibid.). Whilst human action is best understood as transformational, social conditions and consequences of human action, social structure, are best understood relationally.

These ideas are relevant to a conception of technology in various ways. First, human activity can be viewed as a process of interaction not only with social structures but with human artefacts, i.e. as also technical activity.[10] Such activity still takes place within certain limits, using materials to hand, recursively creating the conditions for future action, etc. Indeed, some aspects of the technical object can be treated in exactly the same way as social structure within the TMSA for the simple reason that the social relations, in which artefacts stand, are constitutive of the artefact. In other words, the relationality of objects is exactly what the TMSA is concerned with. When a tree stump in the forest becomes a table it is because of the relationships in which it stands, relationships that have the same mode of existence that is the focus of the TMSA.

Perhaps more important, however, are the differences with the TMSA; essentially, the conditions and consequences of human (technical) activity are not *simply* transformed or reproduced through that activity. For example, the act of making a hammer serves to give our ideas a material form; unlike speaking a language (and so reproducing or transforming it), it serves to make our idea of a hammer durable. If human society disappears over night, hammers, in an important sense not shared by the highway code, language, etc., do not. To be clear, what persists is the physical presence of the hammer, not its *being* a hammer, which of course is a construction that would indeed disappear along with human societies. But this physical presence comes about through a process of human interventions in the world, continually moulding and physically transforming the materials to hand. Thus, the very structure of the material artefact (e.g., the hammer) is the result of social activity and in a sense concretises not only our ideas, but knowledge, values, intentions, purposes, etc., of its designers and makers. Recent constructivist accounts have ably demonstrated the contingency of different design processes, and that 'final' design reflects far more than some impartial process of efficiency (Bijker, 1995). But such ideas are hardly new and were clearly well known to those such as Marx, who emphasised that the machine process came to concretise the class differences in the technology of the production line (see for example Kirkpatrick, 2008; MacKenzie, 1984).

Moreover, in making and using a hammer much is simply not transformable. We have no control over gravity or the rate at which water boils; we must simply work around and respect the operation of such mechanisms. In other words, we must position ourselves with respect to the operation of such mechanisms. Such comments as Bacon's 'nature to be controlled must be obeyed' clearly arise from this feature. Thus, technical activity involves more than transformation and reproduction. Specifically, in addition to maintaining a conception (from the TMSA) of relationality, we also require elements of materialisation and positioning with respect to material artefacts.

Given these modifications, how best might human interaction with material artefacts best be understood or conceptualised? I have argued that technical objects can be understood as 'slotting' into positions in much the way that individuals do, but that the positions they occupy are not reproduced through their own practices as in the TMSA, but by the technical activity of human agents. To capture these features of technical activity I have used the term *harnessing* (Lawson, 2008).[11] The important point is that it is activity concerned with artefacts of a dual nature, natures that have different modes of existence. And whilst the mode of existence of material objects is not simply human activity (it is not human activity that makes a stone hard or heavy, but it is human activity that makes a rule strict or lasting), the positions into which technical objects 'slot' are reproduced and transformed as human agents attempt to *harness* the causal powers of such objects.

Although it is not possible to develop this idea here, the term 'harness-ing' is significant in other senses too.[12] Specifically, I have argued that technical activity, understood as some kind of harnessing, contains two, at least analytically distinct, moments, i.e. of isolation and reconnection. These moments are more or less in line with Andrew Feenberg's system-atisation of primary and secondary instrumentalisations (see especially Feenberg, 2000, 2002). The former relates to the process whereby the affordances or properties of particular objects are focused upon. At this stage various properties of existing things (artefacts or naturally occurring objects or mechanisms) are isolated and refined. The second stage focuses upon the way that such isolated properties or objects are recombined or assembled into objects with particular capacities or powers. Here the con-cern is not isolating or identifying objects with particular capacities and powers but inserting them into particular networks of social and technical interdependencies. In order for an object to be open to technical control, it must first be split off from its original environment and then simplified so that certain aspects (that can be functionalised in terms of some goal) can shine through. But, as noted in the discussion of enrolment above, for a device to actually function some degree of re-contextualisation then needs to be undertaken. This involves insertion within a system of work-ing devices, and within particular social networks of use, as well as some measure of compensation for the simplifications undertaken, that embed the device ethically and aesthetically in particular contexts of use. Both moments must be involved for the act of harnessing to be realised.[13]

To take stock, I am suggesting that technical activity can usefully be understood as activity aimed at harnessing (in the special sense outlined above) the causal powers of material artefacts. But a moment's reflection reveals that even with such a specialised understanding of the term har-nessing, such a conception still does not provide a means for distinguishing between different artefacts. That is, this kind of harnessing seems as much a part of eating food, playing with toys, producing works of art and using a passport to get through customs as it is with using or inventing different technologies. In order for such distinctions to be possible, I want to argue, two further additions to this account must be made.

The first concerns the kinds of causal powers of an artefact that are drawn upon in some activity. Technical objects, I want to suggest, are those objects whose primary causal powers are intrinsic to them, as opposed to objects whose causal powers are relational. In other words, the powers of technical objects are not primarily deontic.[14] For exam-ple, consider a £5 note. When I use such a note to purchase something in a shop I am harnessing the causal powers of that note. But the physi-cal or intrinsic properties of the piece of paper in question are actually a very small component of the causal mechanisms I draw upon to make the purchase. Rather, I am drawing upon all manner of social relations, promises, financial institutions, etc. Similarly, when I use a passport, I am also drawing upon a range of different relations (between the owner and his or her country of origin, between the two nations the owner is travelling between, etc.). Such objects as passports, money, identity cards, etc., have powers that do not simply depend on their own physical structuring. Elsewhere I have termed these powers extrinsic causal powers.[15] Technical objects, in contrast, may well be relational in some sense, but when they are used it is not crucially the extrinsic relations that are being harnessed, rather it is the intrinsic powers and properties of that material artefact. To mend my shutter with a hammer, I am not denying the importance of social relations that constitute it as being a hammer and are important for identifying it as a certain kind of thing. But such relations are not constitutive of the causal powers that my (technical) act of hammering is attempting to harness.[16]

If technical activity can be understood as harnessing the intrinsic properties of material artefacts, then it is possible to distinguish technical artefacts from such social objects as passports, money, etc. But we still are not able to distinguish technical artefacts from food, toys or art. The category that usually comes in to play at this point is *use*: technical objects are used *for* something; they are a means to a particular end or have some kind of function. But still this does not quite make the distinction. Political drama or art serve the purpose, sometimes, of sensitising the population to all manner of 'issues', toys serve the purpose of play, food serves the purpose of sustenance, etc.

It is here, I want to argue, that the idea of extending human capabilities, developed in the first section above, becomes useful, i.e. in making this last step in the definition. Specifically I want to suggest a conception of technical activity as that activity that harnesses the intrinsic causal powers of material artefacts *in order to extend human capabilities*.

It is helpful to consider some specific examples in order to clarify how this conception of extension is intended to operate here. For example, could eating food be a technical activity? On the basis of this definition, it would not. Many technical processes are involved in farming and processing food. Food may also be eaten in order to generate certain activity – sugar or coffee to help remain awake, carbohydrates to give lasting energy, protein to build muscles and so increase strength capabilities, etc. There is also a thin line between eating food and taking medicines, vitamins, etc. But still *eating* food is not itself a technical activity. Any item of food is a one-off act of consumption that has an effect (which may simply be pleasure or self-reproduction). But there is no sense in which it is an extension via some kind of enrolment in existing networks of interdependencies. This latter component becomes important as a common intuition about technical devices concerns their (perhaps inevitable) proliferation and recombination into technical networks and/or machines. The ways in which we either design or incorporate technical devices into our lifeworlds, by enrolling them in technical and social networks of interdependencies, does not much resemble our digestion of foodstuffs.

Similarly, playing with toys, on this account, is not a form of technical activity. Clearly children use toys to *develop* their capabilities; hand-to-eye co-ordination may improve with play along with an understanding of how objects function, break, etc. But the point is that such toys might be taken away and the capability remains. This is not the case with technical objects. Capabilities are extended only as long as artefacts are enrolled in their networks of interdependencies; once removed, capabilities disappear. Indeed, as noted above in the extension theory literature, the main worry is that capabilities are effectively off-loaded, creating a dependency upon machines and a lack of autonomy.

Similarly much art is, of course, concerned with harnessing the intrinsic properties of material artefacts. Sculpture, painting, jewellery, etc., are certainly concerned with the intrinsic properties of their materials. But such concern is not for the sake of extending capabilities. The object is typically intended for some (aesthetic) form of consumption, play, fun or whatever. It is intended to bring pleasure. Alternatively put, once some 'thing' becomes simply an artefact for the sake of instrumentally extending our capabilities, it is not clear that it is art in any sense.

In short, I am suggesting that technical activity be understood as that activity which harnesses the intrinsic capabilities of material artefacts in order to extend human capabilities and that technical artefacts are those artefacts that are harnessed in such activity. This definition does appear to provide a sustainable basis for distinguishing different kinds of artefacts and suggests a range of advantages. Before indicating some of these benefits it is useful to briefly focus on several qualifications and comments upon the kind of definition being advanced.

First, the definition of technical artefacts is derived from a conception of technical activity. This, I would suggest, is most in keeping with our intuitions and highlights the complex manner in which technical objects depend upon human activities and the dual nature of artefacts appealed to at the outset. Secondly, it is worth underlining that there is more than one kind of definition being combined here. Specifically, it is possible to distinguish causal–explanatory definitions and taxonomic definitions. The former hopes to identify something in terms of what it does, in terms of its essential features or causal powers. A taxonomic definition is very much relative to the class of possible things it needs to be distinguished from in some particular context. The idea that technical objects can be distinguished from other kinds of material artefact in terms of the kinds of causal powers that are being harnessed and, in particular, the reasons for harnessing them (i.e. in order to extend human capabilities) are closer to taxonomic than causal explanatory definitions.

Thirdly, there will of course be borderline cases and counterexamples (the border between food and chemicals/medicines may be difficult to maintain, toys that are very close to artefacts (plastic drills, saws, etc.), or that involve a large technical component, such as computer games, protective clothing, art used in advertising, etc). The boundaries of any categories, especially where the social world is so firmly implicated, are always open to such grey areas. Many artefacts have technical aspects; technical objects have aesthetics and other properties that will be more or less important in different contexts. The point is that there still remains a great many artefacts that clearly fall into the technical fold. That these have sufficient 'characteristic' properties and that the account being suggested here captures these is as much as can be asked of such a definitional exercise.

4. Concluding remarks

To sum up, then, I am suggesting that it is possible to distinguish technical artefacts as those whose intrinsic causal powers are harnessed in order to extend human capabilities. Of course, how we use categories, such as technology, money, passports, social relations, water, etc., is always conventional in the sense that settling disputes about the use of such categories is always a matter of persuasion, not of discovery. In this regard, I have so far attempted to provide an ontologically grounded account that is in line with both our intuitions and many prominent accounts of technology. By way of concluding remarks, I also want to suggest, somewhat more speculatively, certain lines of inquiry that are opened up by a focus on extending human capabilities.[17] To this end, I wish to return briefly to some of the central themes of the extension theories referred to above and in particular to some of the questions that arise from an extension perspective, amending these in the light of the enrolment conception of extension I have argued for. In particular I wish to focus upon some lines of development that are opened up by an extension perspective, principally on the ability to recast arguments, concerns and themes of the philosophy of technology (which often appear, to those outside the philosophy of technology at least, as esoteric and obscure) as well as upon the conceptualisation of technical change.

One ever-present concern in discussions of technology, from Heidegger to the Amish, is how we are ourselves transformed by using some particular technology; what does using some particular technology make us become? This issue arises in the extension literature in a variety of different forms. For example, Rothenberg and McLuhan ask what we are extending ourselves for and which artefacts extend us in ways that are desirable or compatible with that which we most desire (or with the kinds of us that we wish to be). More generally perhaps, given the particular focus suggested here, we might ask what kinds of things we wish to be capable of and, of course, are we happy with what others are capable of. But, perhaps more importantly, we can distinguish a general need for increasing capabilities or realising potential capabilities and the effects that such capabilities might have. That is, whereas technical advance may appear inevitable, out of control, etc., it makes more sense to think of the real driver of such processes as our need to extend our capabilities. Which capabilities, and which effects, are choices that (whilst circumscribed) remain ours.

In this light, if we take Rothenberg's ideas seriously, a related issue is whether we re-create ourselves in our technology, if only partially. If technology provides a mirror to view ourselves, then does our conception of our self become one-sided or mechanical, implicitly devaluing all of the human faculties that cannot be so extended in technical objects? However, it is not simply that we extend those aspects of ourselves that we understand, as Rothenberg and others claim. Rather, extension, on the account provided here, involves (as technical activity) moments of isolation and reconnection. Thus, our extensions are concerned with functional properties that may indeed be isolatable at least momentarily. The result, however, is similar – a tendency for the *life-world*, if only influenced by matters of technical expediency or efficiency, to become mechanistic and a source of an impoverished conception of ourselves pretty much, of course, as those such as Heidegger and his followers suggest. However, an immediate corrective can be found in the secondary moment of technical activity – i.e. that of reconnection. The need to make technologies 'work' always involves some enrolment and reconnection to existing networks of interdependencies. The implication of this is that it is not simply the case that using technology encourages mechanistic conceptualisations of ourselves, but that such a process will be most accentuated where the secondary moment is constrained from operating. This is a useful way of interpreting criticisms that critical theorists of technology, such as Feenberg, make of modernity in general and capitalism in particular (Feenberg, 2002, 2009). The institutional separation between these primary and secondary moments results in relatively sheltered environments, in which a preoccupation with the isolative moment can dominate.[18]

A related idea is that the extension of capabilities also involves some degree of off-loading of certain functions and abilities to machines. Such a process has caused concern from a variety of quarters as one in which human beings are reduced to a state of greater passivity (see for example Borgmann, 1984; Illych, 1973; Marcuse, 1964). Translated to an extension perspective, the worry, for McLuhan at least, is a lack of personal autonomy and concern about how the intentions of different members of society are likely to be represented. The extension–enrolment perspective suggested here would amend the general thrust of this concern in that this process be understood at least in part by the way that extending our capabilities commits us to, or encourages us to invest in, particular networks of interdependencies. Whilst absolute isolation or passivity will not generally be the results of such enrolments, such features as the distancing of ourselves from the effects of our actions and the disruption of existing networks of interdependencies, etc., will involve moments of disconnection and a general tendency towards isolation and passivity under certain circumstances. For example, if new technical objects emerge at a rate that is too fast for the secondary moment of reconnection to compensate – that is, it becomes difficult to develop very healthy or meaningful 're-connections' (that incorporate lessons we learn about the 'good life' on a daily basis) – then a degree of dislocation or disconnection would seem to follow. Moreover, such dislocation would tend to be accompanied by the experience of 'out-of-control-ness' that has been the focus of so many authors often termed technological determinists (Lawson, 2007).

A last line of development I wish to consider briefly is that of conceptualising the relationship between technology and social or institutional change. Technology has always been considered to play a central role in such change, even though the character of its influence has varied from author to author. Whether new technology is understood, as for example it is by institutionalist economists such as Ayres (1978), to be *good* in that it tends to undermine vested interests and outmoded 'ceremonial' institutions, or whether technology is viewed as essentially *bad* in that it undermines the basis of community and the *good-life* as for example in the work of Borgmann (1984), the point is that the introduction of technology tends to disrupt and undermine current ways of doing things. But rarely is it explained why technology might have such a disruptive influence or whether there are commonalities about the processes by which such disruption takes place. The focus upon extension leads us to understand such disruption in terms of disruption of existing networks of interdependencies as some capabilities are extended. The introduction of a particular technology involves the extension of the capabilities of some, empowering them while making others disempowered or even redundant. Thus, a central task will be to question whose capabilities (to control, to defend, to manipulate, etc.) are being extended, and what the implications of this might be. Technical advance is often portrayed as inevitable, unambiguously progressive and potentially good for all (Smith and Marx, 1994). But an emphasis on extension as enrolment, thus on the disruptive extensions of the power of some, is a useful corrective to such thinking and at least part of the story that various social critics of technology, such as Marx, have attempted to draw attention to.[19] Technical change is far from neutral and deciding whether or not we should embrace or welcome a particular technology should not simply reduce to a decision about how efficiently some technology performs a particular task. An extensions conception provides a fresh perspective on such issues as well as, of course, helping us identify what technology might be in the first place.

Notes

1 First published in *Journal for the Theory of Social Behaviour*, 2010, Vol 40, No 2, 207–223.
2 Cited in Mitcham (1994).
3 It is worth noting that Kapp is careful to argue that this extension is rarely conscious, and that it is only after some time that a particular development

can be understood as an extension of any kind. Kapp's motivation in all this is the idea that, in the course of history, humanity would grow towards greater self-consciousness, and that humanity could learn much from the organic projections from the unconscious that technical objects represented.

4   The main purpose of conceiving of technology as an extension in this way is to make it possible to question our relation to the world we inhabit and construct. Rothenberg asks what we are extending ourselves for and whether we might be better served by different kinds of extensions. But like McLuhan, a crucial factor in assessing different artefacts seems to become the degree of autonomy they encourage or facilitate. A use of some simple hand-held device is a straightforward task, the consequences of which are relatively transparent; our intentions are easily realised in an effortless and mostly predictable way. In contrast, buildings and road systems create their own world of order and may take away much of our autonomy. A crucial point is that in extending our intentions, artefacts also serve to modify those intentions and generate new ones, thus serving to change our experience of ourselves.

5   In this case, the question becomes where does the internal structuring of the human agent end, given that many of a human being's capabilities are dependent upon the relations in which he or she stands, to other people as well as particular artefacts? Such attempts to demarcate need not detain us here; the point is that such boundaries are likely to be fluid and important for understanding what any human agent is able to do.

6   The use of the term network requires a little qualification here. As will become clear, I use it in order to draw upon much of the work in Actor Network Theory, as well as Feenberg's secondary instrumentalisation ideas. But enrolment takes place within all manner of rules, relations, positions, etc., as well as technical interdependencies. This issue is addressed in the discussion of technical activity in the following section.

7   For more on this use of intrinsic and extrinsic properties, see below.

8   This point will be returned to below, especially in relation to what Andrew Feenberg has termed secondary instrumentalisation.

9   The basic features of the TMSA have been presented in different ways, notably as a corrective to existing voluntaristic or reificatory accounts of social structure or as a transcendental argument from the existence of generalised features of experience of the social world, such as routinised practices. For a statement of the former see Bhaskar (1989) and Archer *et al.* (1998); and for a statement of the latter see Lawson (1997, 2003).

10   The term 'artefactual' activity might appear more correct here. But apart from being a very 'ugly' term, I do intend to fill in enough further details to provide an account of technical activity, so will suggest this term from the start.

11   See also the work of Pickering (1995). Although in Pickering's account, such differences between the social and material become effectively indistinguishable in the 'mangle' of practice.

12   Although see Lawson (2008).

13   Although this is not an issue that can be pursued here, the relative importance and the character of each of these moments must of course depend upon the *isolatability* of the functional properties in question. For some development of this issue see Lawson (2009).

14   I use the word deontic here for the benefit of those readers familiar with the work of Searle (see especially Searle, 1995).

15   See Lawson (2009).

16   It is beyond the scope of this paper to pursue this component of the technology definition here (although see Lawson, 2009). But a useful thought experiment

might be to consider what other kind of thing might substitute for the artefact in question. As is obvious, many very different kinds of things substitute for money (a promise to pay, a credit card, a blip on a computer screen, etc.). The variety will depend upon institutional conventions, etc. Whereas a working substitute for the hammer might be a spanner or stone, objects which greatly resemble the physical constitution of the hammer.

17 For some discussion of other advantages of the general account being defended here see Lawson (2008).
18 For further discussion of this point see Lawson (2008).
19 For a good recent account of this, see Kirkpatrick (2008).

References

Archer, M., Bhaskar, R., Collier, A., Lawson, T. and Norrie, A. (1998). *Critical Realism: Essential Readings*. London: Routledge.

Ayres, C. E. (1978). *The Theory of Economic Progress*. Kalamzoo, Mich.: New Issues Press.

Bhaskar, R. (1978). *A Realist Theory of Science*. Brighton: Harvester.

— (1989). *The Possibility of Naturalism*. Brighton: Harvester.

Bijker, W. E. (1995). *Of Bicycles, Bakelites, and Bulbs: Toward a Theory of Sociotechnical Change*. Cambridge, Mass: MIT Press.

Borgmann, A. (1984). *Technology and the Character of Comtemporary Life*. Chicago: University of Chicago Press.

Brey, P. (2000). 'Theories of technology as extension of the human body', in C. Mitcham (ed.), *Research in Philosophy and Technology, Volume 19* (pp. 59–78). New York: JAI Press.

Feenberg, A. (2000). *Questioning Technology*. New York: Routledge.

— (2002). *Transforming Technology: A Critical Theory Revisited*. New York: Oxford University Press.

— (2009). *Between Reason and Experience: Essays in Technology and Modernity*. Cambridge, Mass: MIT Press.

Giddens, A. (1984). *The Constitution of Society: Outline of the Theory of Structuration*. Cambridge: Polity Press.

Hutchins, E. (1995). *Cognition in the Wild*. Cambridge, Mass: MIT Press.

Illych, I. (1973). *Tools for Conviviality*. New York: Harper and Row.

Kapp, E. (1877). *Grundlinien einer Philosophie der Tecknik*. Braunschweig, Germany: Westermann.

Kirkpatrick, G. (2008). *Technology and Social Power*. New York: Palgrave Macmillan.

Latour, B. (1994). 'Where are the missing masses? The sociology of a few mundane artifacts', in W. E. Bijker and J. Law (eds), *Shaping Technology/Building Society: Studies in Sociotechnical Change* (pp. 225–58). Cambridge, Mass: MIT Press.

— (1996). 'On actor-network theory: a few clarifications', *Soziale Welt*, 47(4), 369–81.

Lawson, C. (2007). 'Technology, technological determinism and the transformational model of technical activity', in C. Lawson, J. Latsis and N. Martins (eds), *Contributions to Social Ontology* (pp. 32–49). London: Routledge.

— (2008). 'An ontology of technology: artefacts, relations and functions', *Techné: Research in Philosophy and Technology*, 12(1), 48–64.

— (2009). 'Ayres, technology and technical objects', *Journal of Economic Issues*, September, 43(3), 641–660.

Lawson, T. (1997). *Economics and Reality*. London: Routledge.

— (2003). *Reorienting Economics*. London: Routledge.

MacKenzie, D. (1984). 'Marx and the machine', *Technology and Culture, 25,* 473–502.

Marcuse, H. (1964). *One-Dimensional Man*. Boston: Beacon Press.

McLuhan, M. (1964). *Understanding Media: The Extensions of Man*. New York: McGraw-Hill.

Mitcham, C. (1994). *Thinking through Technology: The Path between Engineering and Philosophy*. Chicago and London: University of Chicago Press.

Pickering, A. (1995). *The Mangle of Practice: Time Agency and Science*. Chicago: University of Chicago Press.

Rothenberg, D. (1993). *Hand's End: Technology and the Limits of Nature*. Berkeley: University of California Press.

Salomon, G. (1993). *Distributed Cognitions: Psychological and Educational Considerations*. Cambridge [England]; New York: Cambridge University Press.

Searle, J. R. (1995). *The Construction of Social Reality*. London: Penguin Books.

Smith, M. R. and Marx, L. (1994). *Does Technology Drive History?: The Dilemma of Technological Determinism*. Cambridge, Mass: MIT Press.

20 What is an institution?[1]

Tony Lawson

What is an institution? One thing is clear is that it is a category that figures throughout social theory including economics. Equally clearly, though, it is a term that is rarely elaborated in detail. In some ways this is surprising, at least in economics, particularly in regard to the heterodox traditions. This is just because one of the central alternatives to the hugely dominant mainstream approach in economics, namely the (old) institutionalist tradition, makes the institution a central category.

A close examination of modern usages of the category within this institutionalist tradition, however, reveals that there is significant variation in the way the category is interpreted, not least because even here the category is rarely elaborated. It is easy to be persuaded of the idea that one reason this tradition is not more successful, and has to a significant extent lost its way since the heady days of its inter-war popularity, is that it no longer has a coherent account of its central category.

Other heterodox economic groups, especially post-Keynesians, equally make frequent reference to institutions without indicating clearly what they mean. Like old institutionalists, post-Keynesians view their heavy reliance on this category as a feature that differentiates them from the mainstream (see Davidson, 1980). But without their elaborating how they understand the category we have no automatic reason to suppose the mainstream should not also make use of it. Indeed, in recent years one branch of mainstream economics has actually identified itself explicitly as 'new *institutional* economics'. For various reasons, then, the explicit investigation of the category institution seems overdue.

This paper aims to make a start with this. There is, though, an immediate problem in deciding how to proceed, and I think it is important that I delineate the criteria I shall draw upon in defending the conception of an institution given below.

The central problem here is the unreliable and contested nature of much social theorising, particularly in economics. If there were modern theories widely accepted as sufficiently reliable that employed the category of an institution it would make sense to tease out and elaborate the conception implied along with its presuppositions, etc. But such is not the case.

In the absence of such resources we have to fall back on others that are available. With this in mind I am proposing that the criteria developed below are appropriate to fashioning a sustainable conception of an institution.

The first suggested criterion is that our conception of an institution (or indeed of any other social entity) be coherent with our best account of social (philosophical) ontology.

By social (philosophical) ontology I mean study into the basic nature and structure of social being, the theorisation of those constitutive features of social reality (if any) that underpin all other aspects. By social reality I mean that domain of phenomena whose existence depends (non-contingently) at least in part on us.

Of course, it could be that we are just as badly off in terms of ontological theories of the noted sort as we are with social–substantive theories. Actually, though, I believe recent years have witnessed substantial advances in social ontology. Clearly if we possess a sustainable ontological theory of the relevant sort, i.e. an explanatorily powerful conception of the fundamental constituents of social reality, it would be unreasonable to advance a conception of institutions that was *in*consistent with it. To the contrary it makes sense to use any such ontological theory to direct our endeavour to elaborate a conception of any important social category, such as the institution.

My second suggested criterion is that there should be a degree of continuity or conformity with past usages of the term institution. It would be unhelpful, not to mention confusing, to seek to interpret the term otherwise, say to define it as a central category of nuclear physics or ornithology.

The specific strategy I adopt here will be to examine the way the term has been used in the project of old institutionalism. Of course I have already noted that the term is variously interpreted in that tradition, at least in modern contributions. If we could read the meaning of the term straight off from these there would be little need for the current paper. What I do contend is that the project of (old) institutionalism has had a historical mission, and that it would be surprising if a project so named did not make the category of institution central to that mission. Thus my strategy here will involve a degree of historical reconstruction.

It may be the case too that a (dialectical) synthesis is required of any historical interpretation uncovered with the insights of recent ontological theorising.

Notice that in seeking conformity with the most significant historical precedent, my strategy departs from that of others, like John Searle, who is not much interested in the etymology of the term. Although Searle's conception of social ontology and my own may not actually be that different,[2] Searle is explicit that he is not much interested in how others have used the category. Rather, he is primarily concerned to set out an account of how social reality fits together, and the category institution (or of an institutional fact) is one he has happened to seize upon to express certain features of his conception (see below) regardless of how the term is, or has been, used by others.

A third criterion that I think is essential is that the conception has utility in its context of usage. Here the relevant context is social theorising. Of course, operational usefulness will be achieved just if the category picks out a definite feature of reality, if it has a definite reference. This is also a criterion that will need to be met.

But there will be gains, too, to avoiding unnecessary repetition. Of course, all progressive projects transform understandings, and it is often necessary that meanings of categories be adapted in line with new understandings. But there seems to be little point in transforming the meaning of a category if it ends up signifying what other terms already signify. Thus in the case of institution, specifically, there seems little point arguing for conceptions that, say, use the term as an additional way to name little more than a rule, or set of rules, a social system, or a patterning of behaviour, and so on. Something more distinctive seems required.

I do not pretend that these criteria will always, or perhaps even normally, be sufficient to tie down the meaning of a social category, or even convince that a proposed interpretation is sufficiently coherent or complete. But they do seem necessary. To formally complete the picture I can add, as a yet further criterion, that the conception defended be shown to fit with, or be coherent in the face of, context- (including analysis-) dependent features of the situation. In particular, any tensions or loose ends generated by the analysis ought reasonably to be at least highlighted, and, to an extent, addressed, if not actually fully resolved (all analyses remain partial at some level). And where there remain competing conceptions, the version to accept is perhaps that which fits best with any other relevant context-dependent features of the situation, where terms like 'relevant' and 'best' must also be determined from context.

These criteria, if rarely spelt out, seem, for the reasons given, sufficiently compelling that I will not discuss them further. Rather, I will now develop a conception of institutions that is coherent with them.

A conception of social ontology

So what theory of social (philosophical) ontology can inform our conception of an institution? I have elsewhere (Lawson, 1997, 2003a) elaborated at length the theory of the fundamental categories of the social realm that I find to be the most sustainable, so here I merely elaborate its main features.

According to it, social reality is, amongst other things, *structured*, that is, it is irreducible to any one ontological realm, such as that of actualised practices.

In particular it is constituted in part by *social rules*. By a social rule I understand a generalised procedure of action or way of doing things that, under a suitable transformation at least, can (whether or not it ever is) be expressed as an injunction of the form: 'if x do y under conditions z'. For example, 'if driving, keep to the left-hand side of the road, when in twentieth-century Britain'. The stipulation 'under conditions z' will often be dropped in any explicit formulation but will always be implicated, albeit unacknowledged. All action, for example, takes place over limited regions of time and space and in some community or other.

This formulation is quite general and intended to apply equally to semantic, moral, constitutive, regulative, etc., forms, or aspects, of rules alike. The 'do y' in other words is to be interpreted widely and to include such injunctions as 'interpret … as', 'count … as' 'take … to mean', and so on.

It is just because social rules can be out of phase with the practices they govern (workers, in the UK at least, can meaningfully threaten to work to rule, meaning that the latter is contravened by current practices; motorists break the speed limits on motorways) that we can recognise them as ontologically irreducible to those practices.

A second widespread feature of society is that it is highly *interconnected*, with aspects constituted through their relations to other aspects, resulting in totalities.

Significant here is the prevalence of *internal social relations* in addition to *external* ones. Two objects or aspects are said to be *externally related* if neither is constituted by the relationship in which it stands to the other. If there are externally related features in reality, promising examples include bread and butter, coffee and milk, barking dog and post-person, or two passing strangers. In contrast, two objects are said to be *internally related* if they are what they are by virtue of the relationship in which they stand to one another. Landlord and tenant, employer and employee, and teacher and student are examples that spring easily to mind. In each case it is not possible to have the one without the other; each, in part, is what it is, and does what it does, by virtue of the relation in which it stands to the other.

A form of social structure, forming a significant component of the interconnectivity of society, is the category of *positions* into which people slot. It is the positions in particular, via community-accepted rules delineating sets of associated specific rights and obligations, that are internally related to each other, say those of teachers to students. This position–rules–relations conception allows us to understand how different people can (and often must) follow different rules, governing practices that are often oriented to others, and how practices can persist even as the practitioners change. Thus the practices of teaching and studying are regularly reproduced in my university even though the people occupying the positions of students regularly change, as often do those that adopt the roles of teachers.

In short, if the ontological picture I am setting out includes the category of interconnectivity, this takes the form of a structured social network. Specifically it is manifest as a network of positions characterised by the rules (and thereby tasks, rights, obligations, perks and prerogatives) and so practices associated with them, where each set of positions, rules and practices is determined in relation to other positions and their associated rules and practices, and wherein these positions are immediately occupied by individuals.

With the features of social ontological conception so far laid out the more complex categories of *social systems* or *collectivities* can also be elaborated quite straightforwardly. For the conception of social systems and collectivities that is supported in this framework is precisely of an ensemble of networked, internally related, positions with their associated rules and practices.

All the familiar social systems and collectivities – the economy, the state, international and national companies, trade unions, households, schools and hospitals – can be recognised as depending upon, presupposing or consisting in internally related position-rule systems of this form.

Sub-distinctions can be drawn. While a *social system* is best conceived of as a structured process of interaction, a *social group* or *collectivity* can be understood as consisting in, or depending upon, or as a set of people distinguishable by, their current occupancy of a specific set of social positions (see Lawson, 1997).

Notice that at any one time a particular individual will occupy any number of positions. That is, the same person may be a parent, child, worker/boss, teacher/student, immigrant/native, male/female, old/young, member of religious or political or community organisations and so on. The resulting conception then is one that: (1) renders intelligible the often noted, but reputedly difficult to sustain, sense of a group or collective interest and thus the basis for a theory of collective action, and yet (2) allows the possibility of a conflict of interest at the level of the individual.

Put differently, on this relational conception any specific collectivity can be understood in terms both of its relations to other groups, especially those against which it is defined and/or is opposed, as well as of the complex of internal relationships within the collectivity itself. Amongst the many advantages of this conception is the feature that, in stark contrast to mainstream economics, it allows a meaningful focus not only upon production and exchange activities but also upon a range of distributional issues, such as the allocation of resources to groups as well as of people to positions.

A further fundamental feature of this theory of social ontology that I have yet to emphasise is that all of social life is *intrinsically dynamic*. Social life is inherently processual.

These social dynamics take the form of processes of transformation, with all social structures being reproduced or transformed through human agency. The upshot is a *transformational conception of social being*. Let me briefly elaborate.

Consider a social structure such as a system of language. Clearly we are all born into language systems. None of us create them. At the same time, being social phenomena, language systems depend on us and specifically on transformative human agency. So they do not determine what we do, and they do not create our speech acts; they merely facilitate them. Thus the categories of creation and determinism are out of place here. Rather, we must view matters in terms of the categories of transformation and reproduction.

For any given language system, its structure of rules, and so on, is given to the individual when he or she comes to speak, and it is reproduced and/or transformed through the sum total of individuals engaging in speech acts. The social structure in question is the (typically unacknowledged) condition of a set of practices, just as its reproduction and/or transformation is the (typically unintended) result of these practices.

In short, social structures exist as processes of reproduction and transformation. This is their mode of being. A market or a university or a language system does not exist in a primarily static form subject at most to moments of change (due to new technology or whatever). Rather, change is essential to their modes of being; they exist as continuous processes of transformation and/or reproduction. Even where aspects of certain social structures appear a posteriori to remain intact, this is only and always because they have been actively (if mostly unintentionally) reproduced. On this conception, no aspects are fixed and out of time; all are subject to processes of transformation. So there is no ontological prioritisation of continuity over change (or vice versa); continuity and change are ontologically equivalent. And each, when it occurs, is open to, and for understanding necessitates, (a causal) explanation (see, e.g., Lawson, 1994, 1997, 2003a).

A final fundamental category of the ontological conception I am laying out is that of *emergence*. A stratum of reality can be said to be emergent, or as possessing emergent powers, if there is a sense in which it:

1   has arisen out of a lower stratum, being formed by principles operative at the lower level; and
2   remains dependent on the lower strata for its existence; but
3   contains causal powers of its own which are both irreducible to those operating at the lower level and (perhaps) capable of acting back on the lower level.

Thus, organic material emerged from inorganic material. And, according to the conception I am defending, the social realm is emergent from human (inter-) action, though with properties irreducible to, yet capable of causally affecting, the latter.

On this conception, institutions, whatever else they are, will be an emergent social phenomenon. Indeed, I think we can conclude from ontological considerations laid out that if institutions are more than social practices, they will take the form of specific emergent, dynamic, holistic social structures. The question is: of what sort?

Notice that if all that is being suggested is that institutions signify social systems (including systems of rules) or collectivities, etc., we can easily do without the category, and perhaps we should. If, in contrast, and as seems plausible, the institution is a form of social structure, possibly a social system, *viewed under but just one (set) of its aspects*, the task is to determine which one.

Historical lineage

As already indicated, in seeking an interpretation of an institution consistent with some prominent historical usage of the term, I intend to focus on the tradition of old institutionalism. And I also repeat that my strategy is to unearth the nature of the project of old institutionalism. For, as I say, once this is discerned it ought to be easy to see how the central concept of institution fits into (and presumably serves to underpin) that paradigm; it ought to be possible to determine the traditional meaning of the term by examining the nature and purpose of the tradition that has grown up around it.

So how should we distinguish the project of old institutionalism? Because there is often thought to be a good deal of overlap between the various heterodox traditions, I need to distinguish institutionalism both from other heterodox traditions as well as from the dominant modern mainstream project. So let me first indicate how I think all the heterodox traditions part company with the mainstream, and then indicate how I believe the various heterodox groupings are to be differentiated from each other. These are matters I have sought to address elsewhere (Lawson, 2003a). My assessment, in brief, is that:

1　A distinction between the modern heterodox traditions in economics and the mainstream approach can be coherently sustained only on ontological, rather than substantive or policy, grounds.
2　The various heterodox traditions can be coherently distinguished from each other not on ontological, substantive or policy grounds, but according to their individual concerns or questions of interest.

Let me briefly elaborate. The modern mainstream tradition, as I have elsewhere demonstrated (Lawson, 1997, 2003a), must be characterised itself not in terms of substantive theories or policy stances but in terms of its method: the one enduring and distinguishing feature of the project is its insistence that all economic explanation be couched in terms of mathematical–deductivist methods.

These methods can be shown to presuppose an implicit ontology of closed systems, resting on atomism and isolationism. And in opposing the mainstream orientation, as I have elsewhere argued, heterodox economists have (implicitly at least) recognised that social reality is not closed and atomistic, but rather is open, structured, intrinsically dynamic or processual, and highly internally related, or mutually constitutive, amongst other things. In other words the heterodox traditions implicitly presuppose the ontological framework elaborated above. This has led to their alternative approaches.

However, ontological criteria do not divide the heterodox projects from each other, just because each seems implicitly to presuppose the same ontological conception (of openness, structure, process, internal-relationality, and so forth). Rather, as I have also argued elsewhere, each heterodox position is best conceived as a division of labour within a relatively coherent overall economics project (Lawson, 2003a, chapter 7).

Notice that in advancing this contention, I am suggesting that the heterodox traditions within economics relate to each other in much the way that economics relates to other social-scientific sub-disciplines. Because all the branches of social science deal with similar material, specifically with processes of social transformation, rules, relations and positions, etc., then (as with natural sciences dealing with their own common material) it is reasonable to interpret each sub-discipline (including economics) as a division of labour within one overall social-scientific endeavour.[3] I am adding to this that the separate heterodox traditions are best conceived as divisions of labour within economics.

The reason I reject the view that any heterodox tradition be identified according to substantive theories, methodological principles, policy stances and so forth is just because there is much disagreement on such matters within any given heterodox tradition as well as development of them over time. Rather, as I have shown elsewhere (Lawson, 2003a), the feature that has continually united each heterodox tradition is a continuing interest with a particular set of questions or interests.[4] My task here, then, is to indicate the set of questions and concerns that most characterise the history of the institutionalist tradition.

In my view the concern that has traditionally and uniquely most taxed (and continues to tax) the old institutionalist tradition is how to deal with continuity and change, or reproduction and transformation, in social life. In particular, that tradition has pursued an interest in this as it relates to open systems (albeit not using this terminology) where continuity and change are ontologically on par, with each in need of explanation (albeit perhaps with some contributors seeing the explanation of continuity/stability the more challenging and others the explanation of change).

It is in the context of this concern that the institution has been focused upon. Specifically, in a world of flux and uncertainty, the institution has been regularly identified as a relied-upon source of endurability, of continuity and stability, and indeed as the most significant such source.

If this interpretation is correct then formulating it in a manner consistent with the conception of ontology outlined gives rise to a conception of institutions that I have briefly given elsewhere, namely as *particular social phenomena, mostly social systems, or structured processes of interaction, that are relatively enduring and recognised as such* (see Lawson, 1997, pp. 317–18; Lawson, 2003a, pp. 43, 332).

Actually I need to modify this conception to capture the insight that some structures are actually set up as institutions, that is are formally *instituted*, but turn out to be short lived. Such occurrences need to be acknowledged alongside the typically (though not necessarily) non-planned 'spontaneously' emergent forms that with time are *found* to be relatively enduring. So my modified conception of an institution runs as follows:

> *Institutions are particular forms of emergent social phenomena, mostly social systems, or structured processes of interaction, that are either intended to be (whether or not they are), or are discovered a posteriori to be and are recognised as, relatively enduring.*

The contribution of Veblen

To defend my conception of old institutionalism and the category of institution that best fits with this tradition, let me briefly consider both the central contribution of Veblen, surely the figurehead of the old institutionalist tradition, and also the way Veblen's message was taken up by post-Veblenian institutionalists, specifically through their wielding of the 'Veblenian dichotomy' as a major tool of the institutionalist tradition.

Veblen's central concern is summed up in his formulating one of the most famous questions of economics: 'Why is economics not an evolutionary science?' As I have argued elsewhere (Lawson, 2002, 2003a) Veblen clearly thought economics should become an evolutionary science (even though he believed, wrongly, that it was evolving into one anyway, and not necessarily for laudable reasons, i.e. without his providing a teleological account). By an evolutionary science, Veblen understood the concern with, and study of, (non-teleological) processes of cumulative change and causation. In the context of economics specifically, Veblen opens his discussion, writing:

> There is the economic life process still in great measure awaiting formulation. The active material in which the economic process goes on is the human material of the industrial community. For the purpose of [an evolutionary] economic science the process of cumulative change that is to be accounted for is the sequence of change in the methods of doing things – the methods of dealing with the material means of life.
>
> (Veblen, 1898, pp. 70–1)

And he closes it, writing:

> ... an evolutionary economics must be the theory of a process of cultural growth as determined by the economic interest, a theory of a cumulative sequence of economic institutions stated in terms of the process itself ... It is necessarily the aim of such an economics to trace the cumulative working out of the economic interest in the cultural sequence. It must be a theory of the economic life process of the race or the community.
>
> (Veblen, 1898, pp. 77–8)

Various aspects of these passages are worth emphasising. Observe, first of all, that Veblen makes reference from the outset to the economic *life process*. By this expression I take Veblen to be concerned with the way human society and culture, and human beings in society and in culture, develop or change over time. Just as Darwin was interested in the history of all life regulated by 'descent with modification', so I think Veblen takes the goal of evolutionary social theory to be human socio-cultural history regulated through descent with modification. The second passage seems to confirm this interpretation.

Of course, Veblen is focusing on economics. So his primary concern is with one aspect of this life process, namely the economic aspect. By *economic* Veblen means methods for dealing with (or actions concerned with, or interests in) the 'material means of life'. So Veblen is concerned with socio-cultural evolution primarily as it connects to changes in the methods of dealing with the material means of life, basically technology.

The point I really want to draw out, though, is that Veblen is dealing with process, with change over time. And as the second passage reveals, an evolutionary theory must be 'a theory of a cumulative sequence of economic institutions stated in terms of the process itself'. I want to suggest that institutions are mentioned here just because they are being interpreted as a relatively enduring feature of social life, albeit a feature that is subject to evolutionary change and development. Unfortunately, before I can establish this contention, I must first deal with a prominent misreading within (old) institutionalism concerning Veblen's notion of an institution.

There is a passage in *The Limitations of Marginal Utility*, much quoted by (old) institutionalists, and widely interpreted as in effect Veblen's definition of an institution. According to this interpretation Veblen conceives institutions to be 'settled habits of thought common to the generality of men'.

But now consider a rather more extended version of the passage from which the above 'definition' is extracted. The context is Veblen's discussion of the 'premises of marginal-utility economics'. At the relevant point of the discussion, in a passage that includes the suggested definition of an institution, Veblen is arguing that

> [these premises of marginal-utility economics] ... are principles of action which underlie the current, business-like scheme of economic life, and as such, as practical grounds of conduct, they are not to be called in question without questioning the existence of law and order. As a matter of course, men order their lives by these principles and, practically, entertain no question of their stability and finality. That is what is meant by calling them institutions; they are settled habits of thought common to the generality of men.
>
> (Veblen, 1909, p. 239)

Veblen immediately continues, however:

> But it would be mere absentmindedness in any student of civilisation therefore to admit that these or any other human institutions have this stability which is currently imputed to them or that they are in this way intrinsic to the nature of things. The acceptance by the economists of these or other institutional elements as given and immutable limits their inquiry in a particular and decisive way. It shuts off the inquiry at a point where the modern scientific interest sets in.
>
> (Veblen, 1909, pp. 239–40)

It is clear from the wider passage that Veblen is not here offering a definition of an institution in terms of habits of thought at all. Rather, in the often-quoted passage, the subject of the sentence is not even institutions but (certain) principles of action. By calling them institutions Veblen is drawing attention to their perceived 'stability and finality', on their being 'settled' and 'common to the generality of men'. Veblen is not offering a strict definition here, but implying they share the characteristics of institutions, that in effect they are relatively enduring and widely recognised as such.

Consider, too, that part of the extract that immediately follows the familiar short excerpt. From Veblen's suggesting it would be absentmindedness to 'admit that these or any other human institutions have [the noted] stability', it is apparent that he has been referring not to institutions *per se*, but rather to particular examples of social phenomena that might be called institutions.

What is more significant here is that Veblen is noting the degree to which stability is imputed to institutions. Veblen is acknowledging that their stability is but relative (to most other social phenomena); indeed he is explicitly emphasising that no social phenomenon can be treated as given or fixed. His more specific contention though is that if institutions are relatively enduring compared to other social phenomena, it is precisely in the nature of institutions to be subject to processes of evolutionary change or adaptation over time.

The Veblenian dichotomy

Unfortunately, those institutionalists who took up this theme of theorising change and continuity did not always follow Veblen in insisting that institutions are, whilst relatively stable, also continually subject to change. Rather the analysis of continuity and change became somewhat dichotomised, even being referred to as the Veblenian dichotomy. This, however, does not matter for my immediate concern, which is to establish the traditional institutionalist focus on questions of process, of reproduction and transformation. But let me go through some of it anyway, to indicate that the dichotomy in question is indeed as I have portrayed it.

Precisely put, the Veblenian dichotomy is the idea that social life, or more specifically culture, is essentially decomposable into two components: technology and institutions. Or rather that it is the idea that culture is decomposable into technology and the ceremonial features of life, where prominent amongst the latter are institutions. And these two components are interpreted as very different. The former serves as a continuous internal impulse to change; the latter acts merely to constrain, to render everything static: without technology there would be no change.

Consider, for example, the writings of David Hamilton, in a book whose publication 50 years ago was recently marked by a special symposium in the institutionalist *Journal of Economic Issues*. Hamilton raises the 'enigma' that social life, including especially culture, reveals both continuity and change, and wonders how this is possible. His explanation is simply that technology provides the latter while institutions impose the former, that once the distinction between technology and institutions is recognised the enigma to which he refers is clear:

> Once this distinction is clearly seen, the seeming enigma of the dynamic and static aspects of culture becomes clear. Culture is made up of dynamic and static elements that appear 'in some sort of symbiosis'. Veblen and other institutional economists call the static element institutions; the dynamic element is called technology.
>
> (Hamilton, 1991, p. 84)

As is well known, institutionalists who take the view described draw significantly on the (early) writings of Clarence Ayres in particular, for whom the following summary statement is perhaps characteristic:

> The history of the human race is that of a perpetual opposition between ... the dynamic force of technology continually making for change, and the static force of ceremony – status, mores, and legendary belief – opposing change.
>
> (Ayres, 1944, p. 176)

Now, whatever we may think of the 'dichotomy' as portrayed by Hamilton, Ayres and others, I think it is clear that the notion of an institution embedded in their analyses conforms to the conception of it I am defending: as expressing those features of social life that are relatively enduring and recognised as such. It is clear that Hamilton and Ayres, etc., go overboard with this notion and regard institutions not merely as relatively enduring, but as more or less fixed over a significant period of time, after which they still do not change but wither away (see Lawson, 2003b, p. 179). As Veblen recognised, in reality institutions undergo continuous processes of change, and are essential components of an impetus to change elsewhere. But this discussion should be sufficient to drive home my central claim that, for the institutionalist tradition, the concern has long been to develop an understanding of the social process, in terms of relative continuity as well as change. And the notion of the institution has figured in this just because it has been thought to provide a major element of continuity or durability that arises in social life.

The usefulness of the category

If within the context of economics as social theorising the conception of an institution I defend has been found to be coherent with our best account of social ontology and receives historical support, does it remain useful as a modern analytical category? I think the answer is yes. This is so just because:

1   there indeed exist *relatively enduring* emergent structures of social interaction (satisfying the condition of realism);
2   there is no other term that captures the *relatively enduring* (and recognised as enduring) structures of society;
3   these sorts of structure are sufficiently analytically important to warrant identifying in social theory.

In reference to (1), we need only think of language systems, money, property, organisations including Cambridge University, or even the (British) tea break.

In reference to (2), we might notice that whilst the interpretation advanced here identifies a feature of social reality expressed by no other category (in English), other interpretations are not so indispensable. Indeed, and as I have already stressed, if the category of institution is reinterpreted as yet another term for (sets of) social rules (customs, norms, conventions), or patterns of behaviour, or a social system or collectivity, it is difficult to see the point.

In reference to (3), it warrants emphasis that the issue I really need to address is whether relatively enduring emergent social structures, including social systems, are analytically important *in lieu of the characteristic of their being relatively enduring and being recognised as being so.*

The generalised structuring of society is a feature that is everywhere enabling (as well as, or better through being, constraining). This is so not least through the production and reproduction of forms of deontic powers attached to particular positions and taking the forms of rights, obligations, duties, perks, authorisations, legitimisations and so on.[5] Society, in short, can be recognised as a system of (enabling and constraining) power relations.

But although deontic powers and other enabling features of social structures may be found to be components of, or even on occasion to constitute, institutions, certain instances may not be institutional at all; a one-off seminar, for example, can be so structured that specific deontic powers can be momentarily brought into being, and then abolished. So the analytical value of the category of an institution cannot reside in the constitution of such powers *per se* or indeed in any enabling features that are common to all social structures.

This, then, is where my conception differs from that of John Searle, who does suggest that the creation of deontic powers is defining of institutions. In fact, as I have already noted, Searle is not really interested in the meaning of the category *per se*, but with social ontology more broadly conceived, and in particular with identifying 'the glue that holds society together' (2004, p. 11). An institution is just the term he adopts to label important features of human society.[6]

My own orientation here is somewhat different. Not only am I interested in understanding society's glue, but I also seek to delineate one of society's basic, if integrated or stuck-in, components. Here it matters that I do not just assimilate more or less everything socially significant under the head of institution, but distinguish the latter category according to historical understanding and particular analytical insight.

Thus, to recall, on the basis of historical analysis and other considerations, the particular conception of institutions I have elaborated is as particular forms of emergent social phenomena, mostly social systems, or structured processes of interaction, that are either intended to be (whether or not they are), or are discovered a posteriori to be and are recognised as, relatively enduring. Clearly I now need to consider what it is that renders these specific social forms analytically important, that is as important under their aspect of being relatively enduring.

My contention is that the reason the institution, so conceived, is analytically important is just because in an uncertain and often perilous, largely open, social (and natural) reality it alone facilitates opportunities for planning that would otherwise not be possible.[7] Let me examine this claim in detail.

As I have argued elsewhere (Lawson, 2003a), human beings are forward looking; we are not just passive reactors, but fundamentally initiators of action. However, this realisation has also to be balanced with the recognition that (*pace* many formulations of mainstream economists, for example) human beings have somewhat limited cognitive and computational capacities.

In addition, social reality is found to be fundamentally open. Social event regularities of the causal sequence sort (such as pursued by modern economic modellers) are neither universal nor ubiquitous. Indeed they are rather rare in the social realm, and those that are found are very often not only severely restricted but highly partial.

There are thus limits to anticipating future outcomes. Yet despite this I think it can be accepted that human beings not only make plans but also, and in many ways, are often rather successful in their forward-looking undertakings. This can be so even with regard to objectives that individuals set themselves knowing that their realisation may take a matter of days, months or even years.

The reason this is possible is that some (knowable) features of social life – namely institutions – do possess a significant degree of endurability.

It seems to follow then, given that successful forward-oriented behaviour is in evidence, that individuals must form their longer-term goals mostly in terms of those mostly highly abstract features of society that are found to be the more enduring, i.e. in terms of institutions. However, these aspects, being mostly highly abstract, rarely facilitate knowledge of concrete details. So it seems that to make sense of the behaviour in question it must be the case that individuals: (i) form broad, somewhat abstract, *plans* (Lachmann, 1971, 1991), *projects* or *schemes* on the basis of a knowledge of such structures, (ii) with the intention of filling in details, or adapting these plans to specific conditions and contexts, as the individuals move through life. People likely form long-term plans in terms of broad goals or purposes which (from the individual's [always situated] perspective) are currently viewed as possible and desirable, leaving the details open to determination at a later date.

At a very high level of abstraction, individuals may, for example, decide to seek positions of power whatever the form of society in which they find themselves may take. Or, somewhat less abstractly, they may suppose (with reason) that the society in which they are situated will continue and seek goals compatible with its most fundamental or otherwise enduring aspects.

Thus, an individual situated in early twenty-first-century western society may form plans to pursue a certain type of career, to become a political or religious activist, to get married and/or have a family, to travel, to go to university, to teach, to care for others, to help preserve the environment, and so forth.

It seems entirely possible that our only feasible option, if we are to succeed in future-oriented behaviour in an open world, is to formulate abstract plans such as these. The task is then, as I say, to fill in the concrete details as we go along, depending on the nature of the contexts of action; to adapt plans formed to other plans (of one's own and/or of others) or to changed understandings or situations, etc.

In any case, it is surely clear that institutions so understood are a very fundamental feature of human societies.[8]

Remaining issues of relevance

Finally, there is the question as to whether there remain any tensions or loose ends, etc., thrown up by the analysis, that warrant addressing. I think there is at least one. I suggested earlier that social reality is inherently open and processual. I have also defended a conception of an institution that turns on its (actual or intended) relatively enduring nature. It is the latter feature (endurability) in the former conditions (openness and change), indeed, that, I have suggested, renders the institution such an important analytical category.

But it can fairly be asked how it is that, in an open and dynamic social world, such endurability as we find in institutions is possible. Alternatively put, if we do have before us an acceptable and sustainable conception of an institution (as an actually acknowledged, or intended to be, *relatively enduring* emergent social structure), a task that remains is to elucidate something of an institution's causal conditions. In virtue of what are institutions possible?

Like all social structures, institutions are reproduced (or not) through human practice. More specifically, the mode of being of the institution (again as with any social structure) will be in conformity with the transformational model of social activity described earlier. According to this formulation, structure is given to human beings who draw on it in their practices. And it is through being drawn on in human practices that all social structure in turn is reproduced and/or transformed. This is the transformational conception. Specific social structures, including institutions, are the conditions, as well as reproduced outcomes, of human practices.

The endurability of institutions, then, will be related to the sorts of practices through which they are reproduced. And the practices that presumably contribute most to the reproduction of social structures are those of a routinised sort, including any that have become habitual. This seems to be what Veblen was getting at:

> The growth and mutations of the institutional fabric are an outcome of the conduct of the individual members of the group, since it is out of the experience of the individuals, through the habituation of individuals, that institutions arise; and it is in this same experience that these institutions act to direct and define the aims and end of conduct. It is, of course, on individuals that the system of institutions imposes those conventional standards, ideals, and canons of conduct that make up the community's scheme of life.
>
> (Veblen, 1909, p. 243)

The task before us, then, is to determine how routinised forms of behaviour arise. And an obvious first issue to take up, given this discussion, is to determine whether the explanation must be completely circular. Specifically, do we have a (possibly, but not necessarily, fragile) 'equilibrium' type situation, a spontaneous, quite arbitrary, form of order, in which, perhaps as a result of (Darwinian) evolutionary forces, institutions are there solely because of the routines through which they are reproduced, *and* routines are there solely because this is the sort of practice that institutional structures encourage; or is there more to the story? I suspect the latter is the case.

First of all, of course, many institutions are in fact instituted; they are designed to be enduring structures. This is especially true of that subcategory of institutions that have 'constitutions' laying down rules governing issues of responsibility, sovereignty, boundaries and indeed continuity. These types of institutions (whether planned or not) can be delineated under the head of *organisations* (though taking care always to distinguish the organisation *qua* totality from the latter's organising structure).

Other institutions, though not planned as such, will confer sufficient advantages to some that their continued reproduction will be accepted as a specific goal of the advantaged group, and sometimes by many others as well.

Of course, all social structures are facilitative of (some) increased human capability; they confer power in allowing practices to be possible that would likely not have been in their absence. But organisations, whether planned or spontaneous, typically have hierarchically structured positions of power built into them, providing incentives to their occupiers to generate rules and routines that increase the likelihood that these organisations will indeed endure.

Nor are such incentives to reproduce hierarchical structures confined to those holding formal positions in organisations. Wherever authority or power over others or over significant resources exists, whether this is the authority of patronage, magic, religion, spiritual leadership, myth or whatever, there is an incentive for some practitioners to see the supporting practices and structural framework reproduced.

Of course, these are hardly novel insights. In particular, the picture conveyed was always the emphasis of the old institutionalist tradition. If we ignore his contention (already criticised above) that institutions are static (as opposed to being merely relatively enduring), we find that Hamilton expresses this understanding very well:

> What makes institutions static is the fact that the ultimate test of authenticity for any institutional pattern rests on authority – the authority of magic, religion, habit, and custom reinforced by a mythical efficacy. The institutional pattern is tied closely to the system of status of the community to which is attributed great significance. All groups have been graded into positions of higher and lower status in accordance with an imputed efficacy to perform feats of prowess, whether religious, military, pecuniary, or scientific.
>
> (Hamilton, 1991, p. 84)

Thus, it comes about that there are various roles in society which give to those fulfilling them a particular status within the institutional framework. These status positions are defined by mores which prescribe what is construed to be appropriate behaviour within any given role. Such mores define status-relationships within the institutional fabric. The whole process is justified by myth and has the authentication of the ancestors. As such it is not subject to empirical verification and is believed to be true beyond the necessity of further inquiry. In fact inquiry would be impertinent. This supposition gives to the ceremonial behaviour pattern its peculiar rigidity. Hence it is the rigid aspect of culture.

(Hamilton, 1991, p. 85)

Routinised practice

So far I have emphasised the incentives for particular structures to be instituted and for existing institutions to be further reproduced. These will in turn encourage the take-up of routinised forms of behaviour, often via the instigation of formal rules. But I think that relatively autonomous forces work the other way too; that we have direct incentives, and indeed exhibit tendencies, to engage in routinised, including habitual, practices *per se*, i.e. for reasons apart from any desire to contribute to the continued reproduction of structures as institutions that this may facilitate.

In particular, the more that we do habitually the more that can be carried out tacitly, that is without conscious reflection, so that, in short, the more we can each achieve. This applies to ways of talking, working, making music and so on. So it is not surprising that we frequently enter into routinised forms of conduct, allowing forms of behaviour to become habitual.

Equally clearly, we could not act in such ways, i.e. follow habits, without possessing the capacity so to do. In other words, a condition of possibility of any habit is a *disposition* to act in the said manner, where a disposition just is a capacity so structured, that it is perpetually oriented or directed to generating some form of behaviour (habit) in the appropriate conditions.

Now it seems to be the case that we regularly act in many habitual ways simultaneously. It thus seems to follow that an individual, in part, comprises a complex structure of (durable if also transformable) dispositions. This structure is one which, following Bourdieu (e.g., 1990, chapter 3), we might refer to as the *habitus*. It is a structure that enables us to negotiate a number of obstacles in a manner that would be impossible if we had to reflect upon them all. Thus the habitus seems to be an essential ingredient in an understanding of routinised behaviour.

But the point of these few remarks is just that human beings seem to have the (highly useful) capacity to act on many levels simultaneously if they allow the performance of such activities to become tacit, particularly habitual, and this is most easily facilitated if practices become repeated or routine. This will tend to mean that where structures are chosen (for whatever reason) as the grounds of forms of practice they will tend to be reproduced to the extent that the practices they ground become routinised. In short, the ability to engage in routine actions, and the advantages of so doing, will tend to facilitate institutions, as the structures drawn upon are in their turn reproduced.

Unconscious motivations

However, there seems to be more still to the following of routines and the forming of habits. For individuals are observed to engage in such practices even when there is no straightforwardly apparent benefit. And it is often observed that when most individuals find themselves, even temporarily, constrained from engaging in routine patterns, stress and tension sets in (Lawson, 1997).

Human beings, in short, appear to engage in routinised forms of behaviour whether or not there is any *direct* motivation rooted in the pragmatic, historically specific, goals of daily life, and seem to need to do so.

To account for this situation it is necessary to acknowledge a role for something like unconscious motives that indirectly dispose human agents to engage in institutionalised or routinised forms of conduct.

The most obvious explanation of the noted phenomenon is a human need for, or one that is (or appears to be) satisfied by, a significant degree of continuity, stability and sameness in daily affairs, the avoidance of radical disruption. At the level of the unconscious is a basic need for inner security grounding a generalised disposition towards the maintenance of trust in the world and the avoidance of anxiety, a disposition that is in practice fulfilled (or anyway met) through, if amongst other things, the doing of familiar things routinely.

It can be argued (Lawson, 1997) that the psychological origins of ontological security (to adopt, but modify the meaning of, Laing's expression[9]) are to be found in basic anxiety-controlling mechanisms, hierarchically ordered as components of personality. The generation of feelings of trust in others, as the deepest element of the basic security system, depends substantially upon predictable and caring routines established by parental figures. The infant is very early on both a giver as well as a receiver of trust. As he or she becomes more autonomous, however, the child learns the importance of protective devices, which sustain the mutuality implied via tact and other formulae that preserve the face of others. Ontological security is protected by such devices but maintained in a more fundamental way by the very predictability of routine, something that is disrupted in circumstances of radical disjuncture (Lawson, 1997).

According to this interpretation, because an orientation to the avoidance of anxiety occurs early on between the infant, through her or his interaction with the closest guardian, typically the mother, and because it occurs before any significant acquisition of language, the mechanisms developed to counteract the development of anxiety are, in part at least, unconscious ones.

As the infant grows into an adult, the controlling of anxiety remains a basic need or disposition, one that is largely unconscious. But whereas in infancy the experience of trust, stability, sameness and continuity is achieved through the parental maintenance of predictable caring routines, in adult life it is obtained in the routine modes of conduct that facilitate going on generally. The performance of routines, in other words, is not only essential to the reproduction of social structure but is equally fundamental to the production and reproduction of each individual personality.[10] Here though I focus on the endurability of social structures and in particular of those that are repeatedly reproduced, namely institutions.

Notice that in this brief outline I have allowed (in parentheses) for the *possibility* that the need for inner security, for control of anxiety, only 'appears to be' satisfied by a significant degree of continuity, stability and sameness in daily affairs, by the avoidance of radical disruption. That is, I have not excluded the possibility that (over)reliance on routines in an open world is ultimately as much a cause as a consequence of anxiety.

We need look only to modern economics to recognise that many do choose to treat the open world as closed in conditions where it is quite inappropriate to do so. Yet most of us can easily refuse to rely on practices that (mis)treat open systems as closed. Indeed, acknowledging the openness of our world can be not only conducive to gaining awareness but also liberating and somewhat invigorating. For those modern economists for whom this is not so, it seems that a previous immersion in closed systems thinking has been so prolonged that the thought of letting go is met mostly by overwhelming anxiety.

In a similar fashion, it is quite conceivable that in the social world more widely the (relatively) ontologically secure person will often participate in the following of routines without becoming anxious when routines are disrupted. It is equally conceivable that those who most experience the disruption of routines as a direct threat to the self tend to be those that have previously immersed themselves most (and overly so) in routinised forms of conduct.

Fundamental here are questions concerning the nature of human development. It is widely accepted in modern psychology that the infant starts out in life with a form of non-dualistic being and awareness, and that this comes to be replaced by a more dualistic mode of being and awareness following subject–object differentiation. More specifically it is accepted that:

1   non-dualistic awareness is in a sense primary, and dualistic awareness is an alienated expression of non-dualistic awareness, serving to displace and partly to conceal it; and
2   the 'normal' progression from non-dualistic to dualistic awareness is not irreversible; and
3   threats to dualistic awareness are continually posed by the fact of the openness of human existence.

If these propositions hold, then it can be argued (against Freud and other dualistic thinkers) that the reliance upon routine and other features that serve to maintain a sense of solidity and security of (unified) self apart from others is ultimately illusory and 'dehumanising'.

From this latter perspective, adopted notably by Willmott (1986), 'the primacy of non-dualistic awareness is always present in the gaps between the screen of solidifying thought and feelings' (Willmott, 1986, p. 116). However, the situation tends to be misdiagnosed as one in which the problem is not the pursuit of solidity but of challenges to it, so that 'paradoxically, it is this ever-present challenge to solidity and security that stimulates, and seems to justify, efforts to gain reassurance about the security of being – for example, through immersion in routine' (Willmott, 1986, p. 116).

It follows, according to this perspective, that immersion in routine is ultimately a condition of anxiety rather than of its control, so that 'seeking to contain anxiety through immersion in routine can offer only a fitful and ultimately illusory resolution of the existential contradictions of human life' (Willmott, 1986, p. 115).

This is not the place to develop or assess contending positions. I only note that there are competing conceptions of why unconscious motivations dispose us to engage in institutionalised or routinised forms of conduct. All I need note here is that they do. And to the extent that these routines become shared and overlap, they can lead to the instigation, and certainly serve the reproduction, of social structures as institutions.

Of course, if theorists like Willmott are correct it is interesting to question the sorts of institutionalised structures that are most conducive to human flourishing on this particular conception. Clearly, institutions, i.e. recognisably enduring structured processes of interaction, allow possibilities for human action that would otherwise not occur. But to the extent they serve to regiment and atomise rather than to facilitate and connect with others, then presumably there is a case for transforming them into something more in line with our needs. Still, these, too, are issues that are largely tangential to the topic of the current paper.

The point, here, is that there are various reasons why certain practices, once enacted, will be followed routinely. And where specific structures, or sets of structures, are drawn upon in the undertaking of these practices, they can, with the production of routinisation, clearly become institutionalised, i.e. are transformed into institutions.

Conclusion

I have suggested an interpretation of an institution consistent with both our best account of social ontology and the mission of the old institutionalist tradition, and which has clear analytic usefulness. Modern economics is unfortunately replete with ill-defined terms, even including those such as markets, money, choice, institutions, wealth and firms that many regard as central categories of the economics discipline. It has been the aim of this paper to contribute to a sustainable interpretation of at least one of these categories, one that is intended to be of particular value to those interested in modern heterodox thinking.

Notes

1 A talk based on this paper was originally presented at the 6th international workshop on institutional economics held at the University of Hertfordshire from 30 June to 2 July, 2004. I am grateful to the participants for helpful comments. I am also grateful to Stephen Pratten for reminding me of the paper's existence and providing an outlet for it in the current volume.

2 Though we do have different terms for our fundamental categories, with Searle's consisting in collective intentionality, assignment of function, status function, and the background. See, e.g., Searle (1995, 1999, 2004).

3 And I have argued in particular that economics is best conceived as the identification and study of the factors, and in particular social relations, governing those aspects of human action most closely connected to the production, distribution and use of the material conditions of well-being, along with the assessment of alternative really possible scenarios (see Lawson, 2003a, chapter 6).

4 Thus, for example, Post Keynesians can be identified according to their concern with the fact of fundamental uncertainty stemming from the openness of social reality. Such a focus could take in the implications of uncertainty or openness for the development of certain sorts of institutions including money, for processes of decision-making, and so forth. At the level of policy the concern may well include the analysis of contingencies that recognise the fact of pervasive uncertainty, given the openness of the social reality in the present and to the future, etc. For those influenced by Keynes especially, a likely focus is how these matters give rise to collective or macro outcomes, and how the latter in turn impact back on individual acts and pressures for structural transformation, etc.

   By similar reasoning Austrians may perhaps be best identified according to their emphasis on studying the market process and entrepreneurship in particular, or perhaps in line with the attention given by this project to the role of intersubjective meaning in social life, and so on.

   Feminist economists already tend to identify their own project, namely as one that (in addition to proceeding very differently to the mainstream) concerns itself with women as subjects (which may include, for example, giving attention to differences amongst women, as well as between genders), and takes a particular orientation or focus, namely on the position of women (and other marginalised groups) within society and economy. The latter focus includes an attention to the social causes at work in the oppression of, or in discrimination against, women (and others), the opportunities for progressive transformation or emancipation, questions of power and strategy, and so forth. This orientation has inevitably meant a significant attention, within feminist economics, to issues which historically have been gender-related, such as caring, especially for children, and indeed the nature of family structures in specific locations. But in principle there is no area of social life that is excluded. It is the sorts of questions pursued that seems most to distinguish an approach *within* the heterodox traditions as feminist, not specific substantive claims or methodological principles.

5 Notice that the power relations involved provide system-specific reasons for acting, reasons that would not exist in the absence of the system. Thus we seek certification (perhaps through higher education) in order to gain access to employment just because the systems of certification exist and are widely recognised.

6 Indeed, when suggesting that it is the creation of these power relations that 'distinguishes human from other animal societies' (2004, p. 12), Searle recently acknowledges that by his definition even a relationship between two friends qualifies as an institution to the extent it carries obligations, rights and responsibilities (whereas the practices of religion, education and science are considered

not to just because they are considered not to involve the creation of deontic powers – 2004, p. 24). In fact, Searle eventually admits:

> I do not much care whether or not we want to use the word 'institution' for both those practices whose names specify a deontology and those that do not, but it is crucial to emphasise the important underlying idea: we need to mark those facts that carry a deontology because they are the glue that holds society.
>
> (Searle, 2004, p. 23)

7 The uncertainty and precariousness of social life was recognised by early institutionalists, of course, albeit perhaps best expressed by John Dewey. John Dewey was never an institutionalist. But he was an influence and fellow traveller. Certainly, many seem to share Ayres' assessment that 'an institutionalist has quite as much to learn from John Dewey ... as from Veblen and his interpreters' (Ayres, 1951, p. 47).

Dewey's emphasis is on the precariousness, uncertainty and instability of all, especially social, existence. He describes his starting point as the recognition that

> the things of ordinary experience contain within themselves a mixture of the perilous and uncertain with the settled and uniform. The need for security compels men to fasten upon the regular in order to minimise and to control the precarious and fluctuating.
>
> (Dewey, 1925, p. xi)

He eventually writes:

> A feature of experience which is emphasised by cultural phenomena is the precarious and the perilous ... Man finds himself living in a perilous world; his existence involves, to put it baldly, a gamble. The world is a scene of risk; it is uncertain unstable, uncannily unstable. Its dangers are irregular, inconstant, not to be counted upon as to their times and seasons. Although persistent, they are sporadic, episodic. It is darkest just before dawn; pride goes before a fall; the movement of the greatest prosperity is the moment most charged with ill-omen, most opportune for the evil eye.
>
> (Dewey, 1925, p. 41)

Adding:

> If unknown forces that decide future destiny can be placated, the man who will not study the methods of securing their favour is incredibly flippant. In enjoyment of present food and companionship, nature, tradition and social organisation have co-operated, thereby supplementing their own endeavours so petty and so feeble without this extraneous reinforcement. Goods are by grace not of ourselves. He is a dangerous churl who will not gratefully acknowledge by means of free-will offerings the help that sustains him.
>
> These things are as true today as they were in the days of early culture. It is not the facts which have changed, but the methods of insurance, regulation and acknowledgement.
>
> (Dewey, 1925, p. 43)

Dewey is critical of philosophy for treating the stable as more real and focusing more on the former. But he is not critical of the human disposition to seek or hope for stability, only of the presumption of its ubiquity. For Dewey,

> the significant problems and issues of life and philosophy concern the rate and mode of the conjunction of the precarious and the assured, the incomplete and the finished, the repetitious and the varying, the safe and sane and the hazardous ... Structure and process, substance and accident, matter and energy, permanence and flux, one and the many, continuity and discreteness, order and progress, law and liberty, uniformity and growth, tradition

and innovation, rational will and impelling desires, proof and discovery, the actual and the possible, are names given to various phases of this conjunction, and the issue of living depends on the art with which these things are adjusted to each other.

(Dewey, 1925, pp. 75–6)

It is these oppositional couples connected with endurability/reproduction and change/transformation that, I am suggesting, provide the abiding concerns of institutionalists.

8 This is surely Common's understanding when he suggests that an 'institution is defined as collective action in control, liberation and expansion of individual action' (Commons, 1931, p. 648).

9 Laing advanced the notion of ontological security originally as a contrast to a very insecure state in which the person is preoccupied with 'contriving ways of trying to be real … of preserving his identity, in efforts, as he will often put it, to prevent himself from losing himself' (Laing, 1965, p. 39).

10 Supportive evidence for such a conception of a system of inner security, one grounding various needs and motivations originating at the level of the unconscious, is provided through examining human responses to situations in which continuity, sameness and trust are undermined, through observing human responses to situations wherein habitual modes of activity are swamped by anxiety which cannot be adequately contained by the basic security system. For example, Bettleheim (see Lawson, 1997) provides a first-hand account of the profound effects of enforced de-routinisation on the experiences of inmates in a Nazi concentration camp. As individuals lose any certitude from the reproduction of rules and predictable routines, they lose any sense of autonomy in action. At the limit they lose their most basic sense of control over their own physical doings.

References

Ayres, C.E. (1944) *The Theory of Economic Progress*, 1st ed. Chapel Hill, NC: University of North Carolina Press.

Ayres, C.E. (1951) 'The Co-ordinates of Institutionalism', *American Economic Review* 41 (May): 47–55.

Bourdieu, P. (1990) *The Logic of Practice*, Translated by Richard Nice, Cambridge: Polity Press.

Commons, J.R. (1931) 'Institutional Economics', *American Economic Review* 21 (December): 648–57.

Davidson, P. (1980) 'Post Keynesian Economics', *The Public Interest, Special Edition*, pp. 151–73, reprinted in *The Crisis in Economic Theory*, edited by D. Bell and I. Kristol, New York: Basic Books.

Dewey, J. (1925) *Experience and Nature*, London: Allen and Unwin.

Hamilton, D. (1991) *Evolutionary Economics: A Study of Change in Economic Thought*, reprint, New Brunswick, NJ: Transaction Publishers.

Lachmann, L. (1971) *The Legacy of Max Weber*, Berkeley: The Glendessery Press.

Lachmann, L. (1991) 'Austrian Economics: A Hermeneutic Approach', in *Expectations and the Meaning of Institutions: Essays in Economics by Ludwig Lachmann*, edited by Don Lavoie, London and New York: Routledge.

Laing, R.D. (1965) *The Divided Self*, Harmondsworth: Penguin.

Lawson, T. (1994) 'Philosophical Realism', in *The Elgar Companion to Institutional and Evolutionary Economics*, edited by Geoff Hodgson, Marc Tool and Warren J. Samuels, Cheltenham: Edward Elgar.

Lawson, T. (1997) *Economics and Reality*, London and New York: Routledge.

Lawson, T. (2002) *'Should* Economics Be an Evolutionary Science? Veblen's Concern and Philosophical Legacy', *Journal of Economic Issues* 36, 2: 279–92.

Lawson, T. (2003a) *Reorienting Economics*, London and New York: Routledge.

Lawson, T. (2003b) 'Institutionalism: On the Need to Firm Up Notions of Social Structure and the Human Subject', *Journal of Economic Issues* 37, 1: 175–206.

Searle, J.R. (1995) *The Construction of Social Reality*, London: Penguin.

Searle, J.R. (1999) *Mind, Language and Society: Doing Philosophy in the Real World*, London: Weidenfeld and Nicolson.

Searle, J.R. (2004) 'What is an Institution?', unpublished mimeograph.

Veblen, T.B. (1898) 'Why is Economics Not an Evolutionary Science?', *The Quarterly Journal of Economics*, vol. XII, July. Reprinted in *The Place of Science in Modern Civilization and Other Essays*, 1919, Viking Press. Republished (with a New Introduction by Warren J. Samuels) in 1990 by Transaction Publishers, New Jersey (page references to the latter).

Veblen, T.B. (1909) 'The Limitations of Marginal Utility', *The Journal of Political Economy*, vol. XVII, no. 9, November. Reprinted in *The Place of Science in Modern Civilization and Other Essays*, 1919, Viking Press. Republished (with a New Introduction by Warren J. Samuels) in 1990 by Transaction Publishers, New Jersey (page references to the latter).

Willmott, H.C. (1986) 'Unconscious Sources of Motivation in the Theory of the Subject: An Exploration and Critique of Giddens' Dualistic Models of Action and Personality', *Journal for the Theory of Social Behaviour* 16, 1: 105–22.

Index

9780415858298